# Understanding Minority-Dominant Relations

## Sociological Contributions

# Understanding Minority-Dominant Relations

## Sociological Contributions

EDITED BY

# F. JAMES DAVIS

*Illinois State University*

*AHM Publishing Corporation*
*Arlington Heights, Illinois 60004*

ISBN:0-88295-210-2, paper

Library of Congress Card Number: 77-90671

Printed in the United States of America

719

**To Lucy**
**for daily support**

# Contents

## ONE

## THEORETICAL APPROACHES

# TWO
## CONFORMING PREJUDICE

# THREE
## PATTERNS OF DISCRIMINATION: RACIAL AND CULTURAL GROUPS

# FOUR
## PATTERNS OF DISCRIMINATION AGAINST WOMEN

# FIVE

## ETHNICITY, PLURALISM, AND ASSIMILATION

# SIX

## MINORITY PROTEST AND CHANGE

x    Contents

# Preface

In this book a sociological framework is used to organize significant research findings, key concepts, and major issues in the study of minority-dominant relations. The book may thus be used as a supplement to one of the current textbooks on minorities, including my own, or it may stand on its own for classroom use. The quality of the articles will make it a useful reference work as well. Materials have been selected that undergraduates and general readers ought to find readable and illuminating, but that also have met the rigorous standards of referees for sociology journals in recent years. The selections, all from journals and most of them published after 1972, are presented here in their entirety.

The space devoted to particular topics has been influenced both by the relative amounts of emphasis in the journals and my own theoretical biases. Interaction between minority and dominant groups is the central focus, and unequal power relations, conflict, institutional discrimination, ideological justifications, pluralism versus assimilation, and strategies and processes of change are emphasized. The selections on prejudice stress the most common kind—conforming prejudice—and its connections with patterned discrimination. Historical and comparative materials are included for perspective on the studies of recent developments in the United States.

Women receive major emphasis, and the selections document the importance of including sex discrimination in the study of minority-dominant relations. Blacks understandably receive the heaviest coverage. Other racial minorities, and many national and religious groups, are also included. Although five of the selections on women are grouped together in one section, the objective throughout the book is to aid understanding of the processes of minority-dominant interaction, rather than to consider one group at a time descriptively.

Acknowledgment of the source of the selection appears at the beginning of each one, but I wish to express my gratitude to all the authors, the nine different journals and their referees, and to all who encouraged or helped to shape these contributions. Building sound knowledge about anything as complex as minority-dominant relations requires the time, labor, and critical faculties of many people. I am grateful to my family and to colleagues and friends who have encouraged my own efforts, and I wish to thank Hamid Taheri for his careful attention to the tedious, mechanical tasks involved in preparing the manuscript.

*F.J.D.*

# Introduction

Minorities are groups that are discriminated against by groups that have the power to subject them to unequal treatment. All groups involved in a pattern of discrimination against a given minority constitute the dominant community. Whether a minority is small or large in numbers—and it may even be larger than the dominant community—it is relatively powerless to control its own status and life chances in the society. Whether the visibility of the minority is based on physical or cultural traits, it is more than a category. It is a social group with a sense of identity that is based at least partly on shared experiences with discrimination.

Until recent years the study of minorities was confined almost entirely to racial, national, and religious groups. Races are overlapping biological categories (subspecies), based on certain physical traits. Racially mixed people also may occupy minority status, depending on the dominant social and legal definitions of race. In the United States, for example, anyone with any amount of known black ancestry is defined, and socially and officially treated, as a black. No other racial minority is defined in this extremely racist manner in this country. Sex, age, and physical handicaps are physical traits that also may become the basis for categorical discrimination, and for a sense of identity as a minority group. Women have been brought into discussions of minorities only in recent years, as a result of the women's movement. The aging and the handicapped have not yet been studied much as minorities.

National and religious minorities are cultural groups, visibly distinguishable from the dominant community by differences in language, dress, customs, and religious symbols and practices. Some religious groups have a total cultural blueprint for community life, but most have a subculture—that is, a set of beliefs and practices distinctive in some respects, but congruent with the larger cultural pattern. An ethnic group, whether or not it has common ancestry, is a group with a sense of identity based on loyalty to a highly distinctive cultural pattern. Deviant behavioral groups are minorities to the extent that they share a common subculture and have a sense of identity based on common experiences with illegitimate treatment, as opposed to legitimate efforts to control deviance. Harassment and exploitation of homosexuals, prostitutes, ex-prisoners, alcoholics, or other deviant groups are examples of categorical discrimination.

The major emphasis in this book is on racial and cultural groups, but considerable attention is also given to women. Despite the differences, there are many similarities in the patterns and ideologies of discrimination against women and racial and cultural minorities. Blacks receive the heaviest attention, partly due to their numbers and important place in American history, but also because of the influence their protests and movements for change have had on other minorities. Other racial groups, and national and religious minorities, also are included.

The most drastic outcomes of group contact and interaction are the voluntary emigration of a group, expulsion, and genocide (extermination). Intergroup contact is ended by all three of these outcomes, except for the expulsion of a group from one area and relocation of it in another part of the same society, as illustrated by the removal of Japanese Americans during World War II. The main concern of students of minorities, as reflected by the selections in this book, is with the continuing interaction between groups that remain in the same society. Typically this means some pattern of stratified accommodation —unequal status relationships—and usually it involves some form and degree of involuntary segregation. The Swiss experience is a rare example of the stabilization of a pattern of equal-status relationships—equalitarian pluralism. The ultimate outcome of continued interaction in some cases is complete assimilation of the minority, so that it loses its separate identity, as well as its own culture and social patterns. However, assimilation is not at all inevitable for cultural groups, and certainly not for racial, or other physically different, groups.

Institutional discrimination refers to the way unequal treatment of groups becomes embedded in social structures, and the way the practices in different institutions reinforce each other. One need not intend to discriminate, or even be aware of discriminatory effects, in order to participate in such patterns. As the student will discover in some of the selections in this book, the term racism is often used to cover all practices that operate to the disadvantage of a racial minority—i.e., to all institutional discrimination. The more limited meaning of racism—that institutional discrimination for which racist beliefs are offered in justification—seems preferable. (Racist beliefs include the convictions that races are physically and mentally unequal, that race determines cultural development and individual temperament, and that racial mixing causes biological degeneration. There are parallels between racism and some of the sexist beliefs used to justify institutional discrimination against women.) Other ideologies (belief systems) may be used to support institutional discrimination besides racism. The meanings attached to systematic discrimination are important in weighing the probabilities of change, and also the strategies to be used.

Understanding of minority-dominant relations requires observation of both minority and dominant communities, but the focus of attention is on the interaction between them. Much of this interaction involves some type and degree of conflict, which is latent even during relatively stable periods of accommodation to patterns of inequality. It is the institutional patterning of discriminatory practices that denies equality to entire groups. Attitudes of group prejudice are normally learned as part of the process of socialization to patterns of institutional discrimination, and to the ideologies used to justify them.

There are wide variations in the patterning and the degree of discrimination. Not only are some groups discriminated against more than others, but also there frequently are ups and downs in the status of a group. Minority responses to unequal treatment also vary, and they influence both the pattern of accommodation and the processes of change. The responses range from total acceptance through resignation, covert aggression, protest and reform movements to either separatism or total rebellion. They also range from nonavoidance to marked avoidance of contacts, and from a desire for assimilation to pluralistic equality. To help provide perspective on the wide range of minority-dominant phenomena, and to help prevent overgeneralizing, selections are included in this book on other historical periods and other societies. The majority of the selections are reports of research in the United States in recent years, and some are discussions of key issues in the study of minority-dominant relations.

Minority-dominant interaction is an important interest for social scientists because of its effects on human societies, but only under certain conditions does it become a major public issue. Extremely oppressive intergroup relations have typically been less controversial within a society than have considerably less unequal patterns. Groups that feel totally powerless do not initiate public debate and try to bring about change. Also, minorities lack access to channels of communication to the general public, so only when a considerable segment of the dominant community becomes upset about discrimination does it tend to become a major issue. Discrimination against groups has become a central national and international issue in recent decades because it conflicts with values that have been widely endorsed as basic human rights. The issues persist because of continuing conflicts of values, and conflicts of beliefs about reality, and also because of the extent to which discrimination is embedded in institutional structures.

Part One of the book provides commentary on a number of key concepts, general hypotheses, and theoretical models, acquaintance with some major issues in the study of minority-dominant relations, and some cross-cultural perspective. The selections in Part Two are concerned with the nature and role of attitudes of prejudice in systematic discrimination. Parts Three and Four deal with institutional patterns of discrimination, first those concerned with racial and cultural minorities, and then with women. In Part Five the concern is with ethnic identity, pluralism, and the process of assimilation. The last part of the book emphasizes minority protest, and the strategies and processes of change, as groups strive for equal treatment.

# ONE

## THEORETICAL APPROACHES

*The term* minority peoples *was used by a sociologist in 1932 in a book on both racial and cultural minorities (Young, 1932). Nevertheless, attention continued to be concentrated on race groups, mainly American blacks. One of the most widely used textbooks until after World War II, for instance, dealt almost exclusively with the black "race problem" (Reuter, 1927, revised in 1938). Soon after the war a text appeared that treated all American racial, national, and religious minorities (Rose and Rose, 1948), and several other new texts with a similar scope followed in the 1950s and 1960s. In recent years increasing mention has been made of the minority status of some other groups, including women, the aging, and a variety of deviant behavioral groups (Sagarin, 1971). The sociological study of minorities continues to stress racial and cultural groups, but the amount and quality of relevant published material on women clearly warrants their inclusion in general treatments.*

*The article by Lavender and Forsyth demonstrates that the three top general journals in sociology have published far more articles on blacks than on all the other racial and cultural minorities combined, throughout the century. The ratios would probably be about the same for other sociology journals, both general and specialized. Some journals publish more material on minorities than others do, but there is no reason to postulate a selective bias for or against particular groups. The most plausible interpretation is that most of the material on minorities submitted to these journals has dealt with blacks. Studies of blacks appear to be just as predominant in the research monographs, many of which are cited in the selection by Vander Zanden.*

*Those who have written texts or theoretical treatises on minorities as a whole, or who have edited collected works of the same scope, have been able to draw on a vast literature on blacks in sociology and outside of it. As for other racial and cultural minorities, it has been necessary to borrow large amounts of material from history, anthropology, and other fields, as well as from books on particular groups intended for the general reader. The relevant data for analyzing minority-dominant relations continue to come from many disciplines and interest groups. Sociologists, along with other social scientists and historians, have apparently been devoting more attention to ethnic groups in recent years, although Lavender and Forsyth see a need for much more.*

*Probably a major reason why sociologists emphasized blacks so heavily between the two world wars is that a large portion of the research on minorities was guided or inspired by Robert E. Park of the University of Chicago, where the graduate department of sociology was so dominant during that time. Park and others considered his conceptual framework helpful for the study of national and religious minorities, but much more often it was used for research on blacks (Park, 1950). Apparently it was because of his own strong interest in that group, and his extended association with Booker T. Washington and Tuskegee Institute, that Park strongly encouraged the study of blacks. Ironically, his theoretical approach suggests that the ultimate outcome of racial and cultural contact is assimilation, yet the barriers to assimilating the group in which he was most interested have been very great. Nevertheless, Park helped forward understanding of the processes of intergroup competition, conflict, and accommodation, and of ethnic assimilation. His concepts are still useful, although assimilation is not inevitable, especially not for racial groups.*

*Vander Zanden's summary of theoretical approaches to the study of blacks emphasizes developments from the 1950s to the early 1970s. He notes a number of key concepts, hypotheses, and issues, and offers theoretical suggestions. It should be clear from his discussion that the black protest of the 1950s and 1960s, especially the latter decade, stimulated a great deal of sociological thought and research.*

*In the history of the United States there has been heavy pressure on minorities to become assimilated in Anglo-American society. There have also been barriers to assimilation, especially for race groups, and notably for blacks. Ethnic group models for analyzing race relations, depicting racial minorities on the path up the class ladder toward assmiliation that was followed earlier by European immigrant groups, do not fit the data at all well. Moore's discussion of the use of two third-world models for analyzing American race relations introduces the colonial model, according to which the dominant community controls and exploits the racial minorities in urban ghettos in a colonial manner. The argument is then made that the dual economy model fits the facts of American race relations better, especially for Mexican Americans. In this latter model, the minority is seen as a low-paid, unskilled group that does service work and is separate from the dominant economic system.*

*Moore does not discuss a related but more Marxist model, that of the marginal underclass, conceived of as a group that is exploited both by capitalist owners and the more "aristocratic" laborers (Tabb, 1971). Still another model inspired by Marx is that of the split labor market, in which the exploitation of groups with high rates of unemployment and underemployment is stressed (Bonacich, 1976). None of these models fits American race relations very closely, but each at least has suggestive value for analysis.*

*Race groups being small in Canada, English-French relations and the statuses of groups of immigrants from Europe have been paramount in the national outlook on minorities. Like other Canadians, sociologists there have generally conceptualized intergroup relations as a mosaic of coexisting groups with separate identities, according to the selection by Clairmont and Wien. This is the position these authors define as descriptive pluralism, an approach new to American society and sociology in recent years. Clairmont and Wien reject the applicability to Canada of either the model of internal colonialism or evolutionary universalism, an American ethnic group model. They concentrate on race relations; in Section Five there is an article on relations among Canada's ethnic groups.*

*Building general theories of minority-dominant relations is a very demanding task, and not often attempted. There are valuable summaries and discussions of general hypotheses or propositions (Williams, 1947; Blalock, 1967), and some monographs that combine critiques with tentative efforts toward building theory (Schermerhorn, 1970; Newman, 1973; Kinloch, 1974; Frances, 1976). There are also some theoretical statements in journals (Lieberson, 1961; Noel, 1968; Bonacich, 1971).*

*The Labovitz-Hagedorn selection is a modest effort to construct a theory of antagonism between groups, with emphasis on the effects of group power, contact, competition, and the structure of the labor force. Since the authors define antagonism as including both discriminatory behavior and attitudes of prejudice, it appears to be an attempt to explain variations in intergroup conflict as well as prejudice. It is not clear whether "greater prejudice" refers to wider prevalence or stronger intensity, or both. This effort is notable for its clarity, simplicity, apparent testability, and inclusion of variables emphasized in current thinking about minority-dominant relations.*

## REFERENCES

*Blalock, Hubert M., Jr.*
1967    Toward a Theory of Minority-Group Relations. New York: Capricorn Books.
*Bonacich, Edna*
1971    "A Theory of Ethnic Antagonism: The Split Labor Market." American Sociological Review 37 (October): 547–59.
1976    "Advanced Capitalism and Black/White Relations in the United States: A Split Labor Market Interpretation." American Sociological Review 41 (February): 34–51.
*Frances, E. K.*
1976    Interethnic Relations: An Essay in Sociological Theory. New York: Elsevier.
*Kinloch, Graham C.*
1974    The Dynamics of Race Relations: A Sociological Analysis. New York: McGraw-Hill.
*Lieberson, Stanley*
1961    "A Societal Theory of Race Relations." American Sociological Review 26 (December): 902–10.
*Newman, William M.*
1973    American Pluralism: A Study of Minority Groups and Social Theory. New York: Harper and Row.
*Noel, Donald L.*
1973    "A Theory of the Origin of Ethnic Stratification." Social Problems 16 (Fall): 157–72.
*Park, Robert E.*
1950    Race and Culture. New York: The Free Press.
*Reuter, Edward Byron*
1927    The American Race Problem. New York: Thomas Y. Crowell.
*Rose, Arnold, and Caroline Rose*
1948    America Divided: Minority Group Relations in the United States. New York: Alfred A. Knopf.
*Sagarin, Edward*
1971    The Other Minorities. Waltham, Massachusetts: Xerox College Publishing.
*Schermerhorn, Richard A.*
1970    Comparative Ethnic Relations: A Framework for Theory and Research. New York: Random House.
*Tabb, William K.*
1971    "Race Relations Models and Social Change. Social Problems 18 (Spring): 431–44.
*Williams, Robin M., Jr.*
1947    The Reduction of Intergroup Tensions: A Survey of Research on Problems of Ethnic, Racial, and Religious Relations. New York: Social Science Research Council.
*Young, Donald*
1932    American Minority Peoples: A Study in Racial and Cultural Contacts in the United States. New York: Harper and Brothers.

# The Sociological Study of Minority Groups as Reflected by Leading Sociological Journals: Who Gets Studied and Who Gets Neglected?[1]

## Abraham D. Lavender

## John M. Forsyth

*University of Maryland*

*American sociology has made intergroup relations synonymous with race relations. A result is that there has been little study of nonblack ethnic minority groups in the United States. This paper documents that imbalance by surveying 482 articles in the* American Journal of Sociology, *the* American Sociological Review, *and* Social Forces. *Over 70% of the articles dealt with blacks, while no more than 6% of the articles dealt with any other group. In*

*Source:* Abraham D. Lavender and John M. Forsyth, "The Sociological Study of Minority Groups as Reflected by Leading Sociological Journals," Ethnicity 3, 4 (December 1976): 388–98. Copyright © 1976 by Academic Press, Inc., Publishers. Reprinted by permission.

*view of the small amount of attention given to nonblack ethnic groups in the sociological literature, this paper suggests that it is no wonder that so little is known about ethnic-ethnic, ethnic-black, and ethnic-dominant society relations. This paper concludes with seven reasons why this imbalance should be corrected.*

In a 1973 article, Vander Zanden reviewed the sociological literature dealing with American blacks in the last five decades. He distinguished five underlying and recurring themes and suggested that the sociological literature has reflected the condition for blacks in the United States. Gordon in 1963, and Yinger in 1968, have similarly summarized the literature in minority groups and race relations in the United States. In actuality, however, both Gordon and Yinger also primarily reviewed the sociological literature dealing with American blacks. Gordon devoted 7 pages of his 9-page article to blacks and 2 pages to "other minorities" (Jews, Catholics, Italian-Americans, Puerto Ricans, and Chinese). Yinger actually devoted only a few passing comments to "other minorities." Other articles could be mentioned,[2] but the point is that these three articles, rather than necessarily reflecting priorities of these three sociologists, accurately reflect the actual condition concerning the study of minority groups in American sociology. As Deloria (1970, p. 87) has concluded in his book on American Indians, " 'Intergroup Relations' has become synonymous with race relations, which means whites and blacks."

The result of intergroup relations becoming synonymous with race relations is that there has been little study of nonblack ethnic minority groups. Despite the consequences, the reasons for this synonymy are not clear. It is possibly due to the assimilationist bias in American sociology, a bias (at least partly Marxist in origin) which has in general discouraged the study of any societal divisions other than class-related divisions (Metzger, 1971, p. 627). Hence, ethnic groups are often the object of sociological concern and support as long as they are economically oppressed, but lose not only support but also concern the moment they are no longer economically oppressed (Rubin, 1973, p. 12).

Under the assimilationist bias, blacks have received a large amount of analytical attention not because of their racial status, but because of their economic oppression. This does not explain why other groups, for example, American Indians, who are equally oppressed have received almost no sociological attention. Possibly it is due to the fact that blacks are more visible because of both physical characteristics and numbers. Possibly it is due to a belief that blacks are unassimilable anyway and, therefore, can be treated as an "exception" to the assimilationist bias. It may also be due to the fact that most of the nonblack ethnics in the United States are either Catholic or Jewish, and that an extensive anti-Catholic (Abramson, 1973, p. 9) and anti-Jewish bias exists in American society. While the liberalism of American sociologists has sometimes been sufficient to overcome prejudices against blacks because of the obviousness of their oppression, it may not be sufficiently broad to overcome prejudices against Catholics and Jews, who, from the perspective of assimilationist-oriented individuals (including scholars and laypersons) are still "foreigners."

The attitude toward studies of ethnic diversity has sometimes been indifference, as described above. Other times there has been concern, but a failure to understand the depth of feeling of many ethnics, and at still other times there has been actual hostility toward the study of ethnic diversity. Stein's (1974, p. 96) review of Novak's book (1972), for example, illustrates at least the second, and perhaps to some degree also the third, of these possibilities in concluding that ethnicity "marks the retreat into parochial separation." That retreat is a danger and must be guarded against, but it does not necessarily follow. As Rubin (1973, p. 20), among others, has stated, ethnicism is not the same as—and should not be equated with—ethnocentrism. Stein's review is mild, however, when compared to a recent article by Cox (1974).[3]

Despite the intensity of these attitudes, however, in recent years a small number of sociologists have begun to question the lack of concern with non-black ethnic groups. This sociological questioning (see, for example, Lavender, 1976), combined with protests by spokesmen of various ethnic groups because of a neglect of concern with their ethnic groups (for example, *Newsweek*, 1970), has led to a reappraisal of the situation. And yet, while any cursory examination of the sociological literature indicates the validity of the basis of this questioning, no study has empirically verified just how much American sociology has been selective in its study of ethnic groups. This paper attempts to document this situation and to suggest reasons why the situation should be corrected.

## METHODOLOGY

This paper takes the three journals—the *American Journal of Sociology,* the *American Sociological Review,* and *Social Forces*—which are generally recognized as the leading journals in American sociology (see, for example, Knudsen & Vaughan, 1969) and surveys the attention which they have given to ethnic groups as reflective of the position of American sociology.[4] This paper begins with the January 1900 (Vol. 5, No. 4) issue of the *American Journal of Sociology* (it had been founded in July 1895) and with the beginning issues of the *American Sociological Review* (February 1936) and *Social Forces* (November 1922). All journals were checked through December 1974. All issues were checked for primary concern with ethnic groups in the United States. If the concern was with the ethnic group, either by itself or in interaction with any other group or with the larger society, the article was counted. If the subjects happened to be of a particular ethnic group, but the concern of the article was not with a study of that group as an ethnic group, the article was not counted. The number of articles obtained by this method was less than the number obtained by checking the subject indexes of the journals,[5] but these articles obtained were more specifically focused on particular ethnic groups. In a few cases a particular article was specifically concerned with two or more ethnic groups, and in these cases the article was counted two or more times as appropriate. If, however, the article dealt with such a large number of groups that the concern was with ethnicity in general rather than with specific ethnic groups, it was not counted. Letters to the Editor were not counted, but rejoinders, research notes, and commentaries on ethnic groups were counted as separate articles.

This is not meant to imply that all the articles on ethnic groups reflect concern for the group or, more specifically, concern for the survival of the group. Not all articles study the same issues that the group itself would view as important. Some articles are concerned with principles which help the ethnic group assimilate into the dominant society rather than with principles which help the ethnic group survive. Other articles obtain information which may help perpetuate the *status quo,* to the detriment of the ethnic group, and other articles are "blame the victim" articles in which the concern is with how the ethnic group can "correct" its shortcomings. Sometimes, of course, the literature can raise valid negative points about the ethnic group which the group would prefer not be raised. Certainly the point that quantity of treatment is not necessarily related to favorableness of treatment as viewed by the ethnic group is illustrated by Vander Zanden's discussion of blacks (1973, p. 32).

Nevertheless, the point is that at least knowledge is being gained about the group or about perceptions of the group. As Campbell (1969, p. 264) has stated, "there is no special virtue in the minority, the reformer," but neither is there necessarily virtue to the dominant society. All the proponents of the study of ethnic diversity ask is that ethnic groups receive objective, unbiased sociological analysis.

## FINDINGS

Table 1 shows the total number of articles which have appeared on various ethnic groups throughout the time periods surveyed. As indicated, of 482 articles, 344 (71%) dealt with blacks. For *AJS,* the percentage was 58; for *ASR,* 64; and for *SF,* 81. The percentage for *SF* is undoubtedly explained at least partly by the fact that it is a southern-based journal. Together, these three journals represent over 165 years of publication. And yet, while 344 articles (71%) dealt with blacks, only five other groups were the attention of as many as 10 or more articles in all these years of publication. American Jews actually were in second place, but with only 28 (6%) articles. American Indians were next with 22 articles, Japanese-Americans followed with 18. Chinese-Americans with 14, and Mexican-Americans with 10. However, while these numbers are all small, the selectivity is even more glaring when other groups are noted. *AJS,* for example, in the 74 years surveyed, has never had an article on Irish-Americans. *ASR* has never had an article on Irish-Americans in 39 years of publication, and *SF* has had one article on Irish-Americans in 52 years of publication. The neglect of other ethnic groups is almost as glaring. For example, in the entire publishing years of these three journals, only four articles have dealt with Italian-Americans, only three articles have dealt with Polish-Americans, and only five articles have dealt with Scandinavian-Americans.

It must also be remembered that there are a number of ethnic groups which are not listed in Table 1 because they were not studied even one time. Figure 1 shows the results graphically, with the 28 groups collapsed into eight

**TABLE 1**

**Number of Articles on Ethnic Minority Groups Appearing
in Three Surveyed Journals**

| ETHNIC MINORITY GROUP | AJS | ASR | SF | TOTAL |
|---|---|---|---|---|
| Arab (Syrian) | 0 | 1 | 1 | 2 |
| Armenian | 0 | 1 | 0 | 1 |
| Chinese | 9 | 1 | 4 | 14 |
| Cuban | 0 | 1 | 0 | 1 |
| Czechoslovakian | 1 | 0 | 0 | 1 |
| Finnic | 1 | 0 | 0 | 1 |
| French | 0 | 0 | 2 | 2 |
| German | 3 | 0 | 0 | 3 |
| Greek | 1 | 1 | 0 | 2 |
| Hungarian | 2 | 0 | 0 | 2 |
| Indian (American) | 9 | 4 | 9 | 22 |
| Icelandic | 0 | 0 | 1 | 1 |
| Irish | 0 | 0 | 1 | 1 |
| Italian | 2 | 0 | 2[a] | 4 |
| Japanese | 7 | 7 | 4 | 18 |
| Jewish | 8 | 8 | 12 | 28 |
| Lithuanian | 2 | 0 | 0 | 2 |
| Mexican | 7 | 1 | 2 | 10 |
| Mestizo | 1 | 0 | 0 | 1 |
| Norwegian | 1 | 2 | 1 | 4 |
| Negro | 85 | 53 | 206 | 344 |
| Polish | 1 | 0 | 2[a] | 3 |
| Puerto Rican | 2 | 2 | 0 | 4 |
| Russian | 2 | 0 | 1 | 3 |
| Serbian | 0 | 0 | 1 | 1 |
| Slovak | 1 | 0 | 0 | 1 |
| Spanish-speaking | 0 | 1 | 4 | 5 |
| Yugoslavian | 1 | 0 | 0 | 1 |
| Total | 147 | 83 | 252 | 482 |

[a]*Indicates an article on Polish-Italian intermarriage counted for each group.*

larger categories. The results in Table 2 show the numbers of articles found by decade (remembering, of course, that not all three journals were published in all decades). Some overall trends are noticeable, however, particularly the large decrease in the number of articles in the 1950s as compared to the 1940s, followed by only a partial increase back to the previous level in the 1960s. For blacks, however, it is noted that the increase in the 1960s equalled the level of the 1940s, indicating the possible consequences of the civil rights movement of the 1960s. Of particular interest is the decade pattern for Oriental-Americans. There was an increase in the 1940s (followed by a sharp decrease in the 1950s), particularly due to emphasis on analyzing the effects of detention-camp life on Japanese-Americans. It is noted, however, that only *ASR* reflected this emphasis. It is noted that the percentage of articles devoted to Indian and Spanish-speaking Americans, for instance, has not increased thus far in the 1970s despite the governmental attention which has been given to the deprived condition of these groups. It is also noted that there continues to be virtually no attention

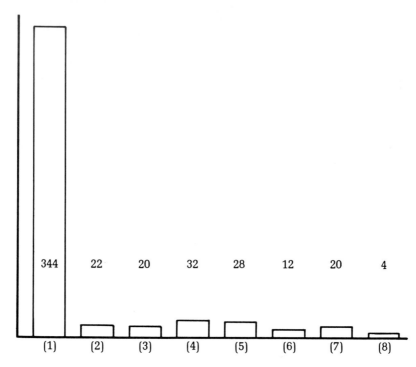

Fig. 1   Total number of articles (*N* = 482) for 28 groups in Table 1, collapsed into eight larger categories. (1) Blacks. (2) American Indians. (3) Spanish-Americans: Cuban, Mexican, Puerto Rican, Spanish-speaking. (4) Orientals: Chinese, Japanese. (5) Jews. (6) Western and northern Europeans: Finnic, French, German, Icelandic, Irish, Norwegian. (7) Eastern and southern Europeans: Czechoslovakian, Greek, Hungarian, Italian, Luthuanian, Polish, Russian, Slovak, Serbian, Yugoslavian. (8) Others: Arab, Armenian, Mestizo.

given by these journals to the European Catholic and Jewish minorities despite the plea of these groups for more attention.

In view of the small number of articles concerned with these ethnic groups, it is no wonder that so little is known about ethnic-ethnic, ethnic-black, and ethnic-dominant society relations.

## CONCLUSIONS AND SUGGESTIONS

Having documented the neglect of ethnic groups by American sociology, this paper concludes by suggesting a number of reasons why more information is needed about ethnic groups, particularly about those groups which have been most neglected thus far.

First is the simple fact that ethnic minorities account for a sizeable proportion of the American population. Estimates are that there are at least 50 million nonblacks in the United States who might be considered "ethnics" (Lahart,

**TABLE 2**

**Number of Articles for Eight Categories,
by Journal and by Decade**

| CATEGORY AND JOURNALS | DECADE | | | | | | | | |
|---|---|---|---|---|---|---|---|---|---|
| | 1900s | 1910s | 1920s | 1930s | 1940s | 1950s | 1960s | 1970s | TOTAL |
| Blacks | 7 | 6 | 35 | 58 | 72 | 51 | 72 | 43 | 344 |
| AJS | 7 | 6 | 1 | 22 | 14 | 7 | 11 | 17 | 85 |
| ASR | — | — | — | 2 | 16 | 19 | 5 | 11 | 53 |
| SF | — | — | 34 | 34 | 42 | 25 | 56 | 15 | 206 |
| American Indians | 0 | 3 | 3 | 3 | 6 | 2 | 4 | 1 | 22 |
| AJS | 0 | 3 | 1 | 0 | 3 | 1 | 1 | 0 | 9 |
| ASR | — | — | — | 1 | 2 | 1 | 0 | 0 | 4 |
| SF | — | — | 2 | 2 | 1 | 0 | 3 | 1 | 9 |
| Spanish-Americans | 0 | 0 | 1 | 3 | 6 | 1 | 7 | 2 | 20 |
| AJS | 0 | 0 | 1 | 3 | 1 | 0 | 3 | 1 | 9 |
| ASR | — | — | — | 0 | 2 | 0 | 2 | 1 | 5 |
| SF | — | — | 0 | 0 | 3 | 1 | 2 | 0 | 6 |
| Orientals | 0 | 0 | 1 | 6 | 18 | 3 | 4 | 0 | 32 |
| AJS | 0 | 0 | 0 | 5 | 7 | 1 | 3 | 0 | 16 |
| ASR | — | — | — | 1 | 7 | 0 | 0 | 0 | 8 |
| SF | — | — | 1 | 0 | 4 | 2 | 1 | 0 | 8 |
| Jews | 0 | 0 | 3 | 4 | 9 | 7 | 3 | 2 | 28 |
| AJS | 0 | 0 | 1 | 1 | 2 | 3 | 0 | 1 | 8 |
| ASR | — | — | — | 0 | 4 | 1 | 2 | 1 | 8 |
| SF | — | — | 2 | 3 | 3 | 3 | 1 | 0 | 12 |
| Western and northern Europeans | 0 | 0 | 2 | 3 | 5 | 1 | 1 | 0 | 12 |
| AJS | 0 | 0 | 1 | 1 | 2 | 1 | 0 | 0 | 5 |
| ASR | — | — | — | 0 | 2 | 0 | 0 | 0 | 2 |
| SF | — | — | 1 | 2 | 1 | 0 | 1 | 0 | 5 |
| Eastern and southern Europeans | 1 | 2 | 2 | 5 | 4 | 2 | 3 | 1 | 20 |
| AJS | 1 | 2 | 1 | 5 | 2 | 1 | 1 | 0 | 13 |
| ASR | — | — | — | 0 | 1 | 0 | 0 | 0 | 1 |
| SF | — | — | 1 | 0 | 1 | 1 | 2[a] | 1 | 6 |
| Others | 0 | 0 | 0 | 0 | 3 | 1 | 0 | 0 | 4 |
| AJS | 0 | 0 | 0 | 0 | 1 | 0 | 0 | 0 | 1 |
| ASR | — | — | — | 0 | 2 | 0 | 0 | 0 | 2 |
| SF | — | — | 0 | 0 | 0 | 1 | 0 | 0 | 1 |
| Total | 8 | 11 | 47 | 82 | 123 | 68 | 94 | 49 | 482 |
| AJS | 8 | 11 | 6 | 37 | 32 | 14 | 19 | 19 | 146 |
| ASR | — | — | — | 4 | 36 | 21 | 9 | 13 | 83 |
| SF | — | — | 41 | 41 | 55 | 33 | 66 | 17 | 253 |

[a]Indicates an article on Polish-Italian intermarriage counted for each group.

1971, p. 4). These individuals should also be studied if for no other reason than that they are also part of the society.

Second, much of the black-white interaction in the United States is actually black-ethnic white interaction. The characteristics, attitudes, and priorities that apply to "whites" (i.e., white Anglo-Saxon Protestants who comprise the oldest, largest, and most powerful group in [the] United States, and who are often synonymous with "white" as well as with "American") may not apply to ethnic whites. Some ethnic whites may have values unique to—or at least emphasized differently by—themselves because of their own histories, migration patterns, religions, and positions in the society (Hamill, 1969; Levine & Herman, 1972b). Increasingly, the black-white conflicts in the United States are not between blacks and WASPs in the southern United States, but between blacks and ethnic whites in urban areas primarily in the north (Levine & Herman, 1972b, p. 4); for example, busing in Irish areas of Boston, school hirings in Jewish areas of New York, and union hirings in Italian areas of Philadelphia. Problems are not solved, however, by having knowledge of only one of the combatants. The desires, hopes, etc., of both sides of a conflict, however trivial and "wrong" to the social scientist, must be known if intergroup relations are to be improved. One cannot always assume racism or prejudice on either side, but one must examine the underlying reasons for the conflict (Lerner, 1969).

Third, much of the conflict in the United States has historically been between different ethnic groups. In some cases conflicts from the old country were brought to the United States, and in other cases the conflicts arose after the groups came into contact in the United States (Kolodny, 1969, p. 20; Abramson, 1973, p. 9; Glazer & Moynihan, 1970). Even such "historical allies" as blacks and Jews have not been without conflict (Glazer, 1964; Podhoretz, 1963; Weisbord & Stein, 1970). As Levine has accurately stated, blacks are America's first priority, but also "the lower-middle-class whites are the second agenda and we're going to have to deal with both agendas at the same time to get the black priority adopted" (quoted in Scott, 1971).

Fourth, there has also been dominant society-ethnic group conflict, and the principles which apply to dominant society-black relations do not always apply to dominant society-ethnic group relations. Deloria (1970, p. 88) illustrates this point when he states that "The whole of American society has been brainwashed into believing that if it understood blacks it could automatically understand every other group simply because blacks were the most prominent minority group with which society had to deal."

Fifth, to the extent that the purpose of sociology is to focus attention on problems in the society, it must be recognized that some nonblack ethnic groups are also oppressed in the United States.[6] American Indians have about equalled blacks in the amount of oppression. Japanese-Americans, although generally middle class, suffered greatly as a result of being forcefully detained for years during World War II. Other groups, for example, Jewish-Americans and Japanese-Americans, while not economically oppressed as a group, still suffer from sporadic acts of discrimination as well as pervasive feelings of marginality (see, for example, Lavender, 1975; Gross, 1975). And other groups, for example Italian-Americans, while not economically oppressed, have large numbers of individuals who have not "made it." A number of groups, for example, Jewish-Americans, Italian-Americans, and Polish-Americans, often suffer from "cultural discrimination" (Greeley, 1972).

Sixth, ethnicity can be stressed as a constructive force and has potentials for principles of intergroup relations which can be applied to other groups as well as to the larger society. Greeley (see Lahart, 1971, p. 4), for example, states that "the extended family relationships and sense of identity found in 'ethnic' neighborhood communities may well be a solution to much of what's ailing America." Levine and Herman (1972a, p. 3) note that ethnic factors have been stressed as tools for building unity in unions, and Pettigrew (1971) suggests that a sense of ethnicity can counteract some of the sense of insecurity felt by many members of the working class.

Finally, as noted by Yinger (1968, p. 132), most of the scholarly work on minority groups has been descriptive, and yet we need more information about ethnic groups if we are to develop a more formal and more accurate theory of intergroup relations. Some theories have been inaccurate because of a limited base of knowledge. The assimilationist-oriented theories of dominant society-minority group relations, for example, possibly have been accepted to a large degree because data were lacking on a large number of ethnic groups.

It has been assumed that ethnic groups wanted to assimilate in the past and that there is a current "revival" of ethnic interest in the United States. And yet, Greeley (1974, p. 207) suggests that the interest has been there all along among the ethnics, it is simply that "the elites in American society have rediscovered ethnicity—hesitantly, fearfully, ambivalently." Regardless of whether there is a birth or a revival of ethnicity in America, the imbalanced situation described in this paper must be corrected if progress toward understanding is to be made.

## NOTES

1 Appreciation is expressed to Hari Ruiz and to John Blanchfield for their extended assistance.

2 The most formal and official review of similar articles was the American Sociological Association–sponsored reader by van den Berghe in 1972. While van den Berghe was concerned with intergroup relations per se and put together a reader which included a number of ethnic groups, he had a focus different from this paper. In addition to a deeper concern with specific topical areas of intergroup relations, he was also more concerned about the provincialism of American sociology [he noted that "81.3 per cent of the articles deal exclusively or predominantly with the continental United States" (p. 5)] and the resulting tendency to reify "race" as an inherent difference. Undoubtedly, the assimilationist bias of American sociology is also at least in part a result of its provincialism, of its failure to recognize the historic importance of ethnic diversity in many parts of the world. This paper is concerned only with American ethnic groups, not because it disagrees with van den Berghe, but because its aim is to focus on another aspect of the situation regarding the study of intergroup relations. Hopefully, this paper illustrates how points made in van den Berghe's reader and points made in this paper are interrelated. It should also be noted that van den Berghe (p. 10), like Vander Zanden, Gordon, and Yinger, discussed the chronological changes in the study of race and ethnic relations in the United States.

3 The article by Cox is probably the most hostile (and potentially dangerous) of any recent articles which have appeared in a respectable sociological journal. His comments concerning Jews are similar in negativism to comments concerning blacks which appeared in a number of the earlier articles surveyed in this paper. He comes close to accusing United States Jews of secretiveness (for example, p. 192: "the Jewish promoters [of national celebrations] are largely hidden"), selfishness, insincerity, and a lack of a sense of justice in concluding that Jewish self-concern with pluralism "frequently" is so overriding that "the valid Negro's cause and even the nation's welfare may be overlooked" (p. 188). He goes on to say, for example, that no matter "how specious or inapplicable such a program of ethnic pluralism might be for Negroes, it still will be advocated for them [by Jews] if it seems to serve the purpose

of Jews" (p. 190). He brings back Hertzler's 30-year-old idea that it is a "privilege" —which "a large number of Jews want"—to be both an American and Jewish. And in an interesting twist for a "liberal sociologist" of "blaming the victim," Cox concludes without any apparent sense of either professional or personal hesitation or shame that Jews have divided loyalties and that this "trait" has "been a factor in universal anti-Semitism." Cox is not content to fill his paper with such statements, but even uses the suggestive phrase of "Jewish Self-Interest" in his article title. He goes even further to make a specific opening notation (p. 183) that "We use the term Jewish here advisedly since we do not intend to say 'the interest of Jews.'" Cox's article not only illustrates the extremely hostile attitude of some American sociologists to ethnic diversity, but also raises the disturbing question, in regard to Jews, of why his comments have met with virtually no rebuttal from "liberal" sociologists.

4  It is true, of course, that ethnic groups have also received attention from other discipline-wide journals. Because of their prestige, however, these three are selected as representative of the "official" position of the discipline. This basic assumption was also made by van den Berghe (1972). In putting together a collection of articles from *ASR* on "intergroup relations," he states that "the collection represents, in a sense, the voice of American sociology" (p. 3). There are also journals which deal with a specific ethnic group or exclusively with ethnic groups in general. *Phylon,* for example, is concerned with blacks, and *Jewish Social Studies* is concerned with American Jews, although both are oriented to other disciplines in addition to sociology. *Ethnicity* and the *Journal of Ethnic Studies,* for example, are concerned exclusively with minority groups in general. To some extent these journals also reflect the interests of the discipline. On the other hand, these journals may be in existence at least partly because of neglect of their topics by the discipline-wide journals. Some books have also appeared, of course, but again it is assumed that the journals surveyed in this paper are a more accurate reflection of the discipline of sociology.

5  The coverage was not as broad as that used by van den Berghe (1972). For instance, he included articles that mentioned "race" as one of the variables studied, even if it was not the focus of the study.

6  This is one point made repeatedly by proponents of ethnic studies but which is often not recognized by critics of ethnic studies. That is, most proponents of ethnic studies will agree that blacks are understandably America's first priority because of degree of oppression and because of numbers, but that other groups should also be studied more (see, for example, Lavender, 1975). A beginning toward this goal, a "National Project" on ethnicity, is discussed by Levine and Herman (1972b, p. 4).

## REFERENCES

*Abramson, H. J.*
1973   *Ethnic Diversity in Catholic America.* New York, Wiley-Interscience.
*American Journal of Sociology*
1900   vol. 5, no. 4, January.
1974   vol. 80, no. 3, November.
*American Sociological Review*
1936   vol. 1, no. 1, February.
1974   vol. 39, no. 6, December.
*Campbell, E. Q.*
1969   Negroes, education, and the southern states. *Social Forces* 47, 253–265.
*Cox, O. C.*
1974   Jewish self-interest in 'black pluralism.' *The Sociological Quarterly* 15, 183–198.

*Deloria, V., Jr.*
1970    *We Talk, You Listen.* New York, Macmillan.
*Glazer, N.*
1964    Negroes and Jews: The new challenge to pluralism. *Commentary* 38, 29–34.
*Glazer, N., and D. P. Moynihan*
1970    *Beyond the Melting Pot.* Cambridge, Mass., M.I.T. Press.
*Gordon, M. M.*
1963    Recent trends in the study of minority and race relations. *The Annals of the American Academy of Political and Social Science* 350, 148–156.
*Greeley, A.*
1972    Letters from readers: Ethnicity. *Commentary* 54, 16–22.
1974    Editorial: Ethnicity and Politics. *Ethnicity* 1, 207–208.
*Gross, B.*
1974    What shylock forgot, or making it and losing it in America. *The Journal of Ethnic Studies* 2, 50–57.
*Hamill, P.*
1969    The Revolt of the white lower middle class. *New York* (April 14), 24–29.
*Knudsen, D. D., and T. R. Vaughan*
1969    Quality in graduate education: A re-evaluation of the rankings of sociology departments in the Cartter Report. *The American Sociologist* 4, 12–19.
*Kolodny, R. L.*
1969    Ethnic cleavages in the United States. *Social Work* 14, 13–23.
*Lahart, K.*
1971    What happens when the melting-pot fire goes out. *Newsday* (June 5).
*Lavender, A. D.*
1975    Disadvantages of minority group membership: The perspective of a "nondeprived" minority group. *Ethnicity* 2, 99–119.
*Lavender, A. D.*
1976    Studies of Jewish college students: A review and a replication. *Jewish Social Studies* (forthcoming).
*Lerner, M.*
1969    Respectable bigotry. *The American Scholar* 38, 606–617.
*Levine, I. M., and J. Herman*
1972a    The life of white ethnics. *Dissent* 19, 286–294.
1972b    Search for identity in blue-collar America. *Civil Rights Digest.*
*Metzger, L. P.*
American sociology and black assimilation: Conflicting perspectives. *American Journal of Sociology* 76, 627–647.
*Newsweek*
1970    A rising cry: 'Ethnic power.' *Newsweek* 76(5), 32–36.
*Pettigrew, T.*
1975    Ethnicity in American life: A social psychological perspective, in *Ethnicity in American Life.* New York, Anti-Defamation League of B'nai B'rith.
*Podhoretz, N.*
1963    My negro problem—And ours. *Commentary* 35, 93–101.
*Rubin, R. I.*
1973    Where have all the liberals gone? *Jewish Life* 41, 9–21.
*Scott, G.*
1971    Ethnics: A positive approach. *The Christian Science Monitor.*
*Social Forces*
1922    vol. 1, no. 1, November.
1974    vol. 53, no. 2, December.
*Stein, H. F.*
1974    The rise of the unmeltable ethnics: A review. *Society* 11, 94–96.

*Vander Zanden, J. W.*
1973    Sociological studies of American blacks. *The Sociological Quarterly* 14, 32–52.
*Van den Berghe, P., (Ed.)*
1972    *Intergroup Relations: Sociological Perspectives.* New York, Basic Books.
*Yinger, M.*
1968    Recent developments in minority and race relations. *The Annals of the American Academy of Political and Social Science* 378, 130–145.

# Sociological Studies of American Blacks*

## James W. Vander Zanden
### Ohio State University

*The paper reviews sociological work dealing with American Blacks. In the past five decades three themes have largely dominated the work: (1) a description and documentation of Black disadvantage within American life; (2) an attack upon racist notions of Black biological inferiority; and (3) an interpretation of Black disadvantages as derived from White prejudice and discrimination. The work has been largely static and non-processual in character, derived largely from the structure-function model of society. The paper calls for the employment of multiple models and for emphasis upon a dynamic, processual model of social life. The concepts of network and field appear to offer much promise.*

Scientific knowledge cannot be divorced from its social milieu. No clearer demonstration of this fact can be found than the field of race relations. During the Great Depression years of the 1930s—with concern revolving about unemployment, poverty, immigrant assimilation, and the plight of Blacks (all closely tied to the issue of social and economic equality)—the field was perhaps the

*Source:* James W. Vander Zanden, "Sociological Studies of American Blacks," Sociological Quarterly 14 (Winter 1973): 32–52. Copyright © 1973 by the Midwest Sociological Society. Reprinted by permission of the Society, the editors of Sociological Quarterly, and the author.
*This article was prepared with the assistance of the State of the Field Editor, Irwin Rinder.

most productive of any within American sociology, associated with such names as St. Clair Drake and Horace R. Cayton (1945), W. E. B. DuBois (1935; 1939; 1940); Charles S. Johnson (1934; 1941; 1943; 1946), E. Franklin Frazier (1932; 1939; 1940), Hortense Powdermaker (1939), John Dollard (1937), W. Lloyd Warner (1936; Warner and Srole, 1945; Davis et al., 1941), and Gunnar Mydral (1944), although some of the work was not published until the 1940s. This interest continued into the 1940s, associated with the war against fascism and the hopes it engendered for Democracy and One World. Probably the last great and commanding work of this era was *The Authoritarian Personality* (Adorno et al., 1950). A good deal of the research of these two decades was financed either by universities or foundations, although in some cases it was undertaken on shoe-string budgets by individual sociologists.

The McCarthy years of the early half of the 1950s and the sharp Southern White reaction against desegregation brought with it a hiatus that lasted until 1964, during which time no major works in race relations appeared. The work of the Cornell Studies in Intergroup Relations (financed by the Rockefeller Foundation), begun in 1948, continued through 1956, but other than for an occasional paper, the results of this research were not published until 1964 (Williams, 1964). Research funds were no longer available, as foundations became timid under attack from rightist and segregationist sources (recall the congressional inquiry into the affairs of the Ford Foundation).

Since 1964, the picture has again changed. Four of the major works of the period—on the Black family (Moynihan, 1965), Black isolation (U.S. Commission on Civil Rights, 1967), Black education (Coleman et al, 1966), and Black riots (National Advisory Commission on Civil Disorders, 1968, and Campbell and Schuman, 1968)—have been sponsored, paid for, and published by government agencies: the Department of Labor, the Civil Rights Commission, the Office of Education, and the National Advisory Commission on Civil Disorders. As Tumin (1968:118) notes, these documents were generated within government bureaus as direct and surprisingly rapid responses by government to the tensions and pressures generated by social action in the Black community. This work has been paralleled by privately published studies, including that by Gary T. Marx (1967), Elliot Liebow (1966), and Lee Rainwater (1970)—although it should be noted that the Liebow and Rainwater studies were financed by government agencies.

Accompanying this recent awakened interest in race relations research have been a number of "state of the field" type reviews (Westie, 1964; Hyman, 1969; Yinger, 1968). Further, there have been any number of efforts to summarize the literature on Black Americans (Pettigrew, 1964; Pinkney, 1969; Broom and Glenn, 1965; Parsons and Clark, 1966). Indeed, in comparison with a good many other fields in sociology, race relations can hardly be cited as lacking in summaries or appraisals.

As we survey the work of the past five decades, we find a number of recurrent and underlying themes: (1) a description and documentation of Black disadvantage within American life; (2) an attack upon racist notions of Black biological inferiority; and (3) an interpretation of Black disadvantage as derived from White prejudice and discrimination which in turn has been largely treated in psychological and social psychological terms. And associated with this latter perspective there has emerged a literature dealing with the combating of prejudice and discrimination (see Vander Zanden, 1972: Chapter 15; Simpson and Yinger, 1965; Chapters 23 and 24).

The work and activity of sociologists and other social scientists in these three areas has had a continuous and enduring impact upon the American scene and upon the civil rights movement for whom social scientists functioned as ideological protagonists. In large measure sociologists have been committed to an image of American society that is set forth by American liberalism: the "minority problem" is narrowly defined as requiring the provision of adequate opportunity for members of minority groups to ascend as *individuals* into the mainstream culture. This liberalistic approach differs from that of American conservatism largely on the matter of whether the opportunities already present are adequate and takes its reformist cast from its recognition that they are not. Hence, there has been a striking convergence of liberal and sociological thought in the area of race relations, raising questions about the "value-free" character of sociological inquiry in this area (Metzger, 1971:628–629). In any event, as Tumin observes, social scientists within the field of race relations can hardly be accused of ivory-tower escapism (Tumin, 1968:117). Let us briefly appraise the situation with regard to these three broad themes of race relations research.

## DEPICTING BLACK DISADVANTAGE

The task of describing and documenting Black disadvantage has proved to be one that is unending. The racial picture has hardly been static, and on-going research depicting the situation has been and continues to be an important requirement for formulating social action and policy. Indeed, abundant evidence suggests that even were the United States to eliminate discrimination tomorrow, the heritage of Jim Crow would nonetheless live on (Broom and Glenn, 1965; Lieberson and Fuguitt, 1967). The handicaps and disadvantages sown by racism cannot be overcome immediately by simply opening the gates of opportunity; low status tends to be self-perpetuating.

Yet one danger seems to lurk in this area, namely that an ideological commitment be made to "finding" Black disadvantage at all times and circumstances as a reaction to America's long tradition of racism. Sociologists and civil rights activists have for decades confronted the fact that White America has tended either to deny the Black's right to participate in the society—on grounds that he is a biological inferior—or to ignore his existence through making him an "invisible" man (the South traditionally followed the first path; the North, the second). As a consequence, much research was designed to awaken White America, making Black disadvantage visible and highlighting the contradiction between the Creed of Democracy and America's racial practice.

In the process, however, sociologists often find themselves slipping into an "Isn't it awful. . . ." orientation, and possibly becoming entrapped by it. Lest pressure for social change be slackened in the wake of accomplishment, we often feel it incumbent upon us to "find" new counter-balancing evidence of intensified racism. But change does occur; disadvantage may be lessened—

Palmore and Whittington (1970), for instance, found that during the 1960s non-Whites made substantial gains in income, occupation, and education (Palmore and Whittington developed and employed an equality index designed to reflect the overlap in the distributions of two populations). We need, then, to remind ourselves that science requires us rigorously to cultivate a disciplined approach to the phenomena that we study so that we might determine facts as they are and not in conformity with our ideological or emotional commitments.

We need also to remind ourselves that description and documentation—the mere compiling of statistical data detailing Black disadvantage and documenting the "tangle of pathology" within Black ghettos—is not enough. As undertaken within the field, such an approach has tended to be static and to overlook the dynamic, processual nature of human behavior. Thus Black disadvantage existed for decades and yet the "Black Revolt" is a relatively recent phenomenon, a development which incidentally was not anticipated by sociologists (Coleman, 1960). Nor does a reporting of attitudes at a given point in time suffice. A good illustration of this is Gary T. Marx's study (1967) of the basic orientations of Blacks toward themselves and toward Whites, based on interviews conducted by NORC in late 1964. The study is a good one and employs sophisticated methodology. Yet, we are unable to find in the data a foundation for predicting what actually occurred within months of the study. This certainly brings into question the value of this sort of survey for a sociology seeking to explain and predict social behavior.

In considering these matters it is worth noting that a good many interpretations of the Black Revolt and ghetto rioting have appeared, but such hypotheses need to be tested. Among them are the following:

## 1. The Relative Deprivation Thesis

Relative deprivation refers to the gap between what people actually have and what they have come to expect and feel to be their just due. It suggests that the Black Revolt was bred by the discrepancy between the rapid escalation of Black expectations and what in fact Blacks have been able to attain. There are any number of variants of the theory (see: Geschwender, 1964), most of which are derived from reference group theory.

## 2. Social Disorganization Thesis

Black rioting and militancy have also been attributed to a breakdown of consensual norms within society, and to the inability or unwillingness of the agencies of social control to effect their restoration (Bowen and Masotti, 1968; Downes, 1968). Such circumstances derive from massive social change—from such trends as industrialization, urbanization, and modernization that give birth to new classes and groups with new social perceptions and life styles. Accompanying these changes go anomie and alienation, conditions in which individuals no longer feel attached to or a part of the existing social and political order. As the Black population migrated to urban centers, the traditional structure of race relations, characterized by Black subordination and adapted to a feudal, rural environment, was no longer appropriate. The Black

Revolt, then, is interpreted as an attack upon an earlier arrangement of race relations.

### 3. Group Conflict Thesis

The Black Revolt also has been viewed as incubated by a struggle for power, wealth, status, and territory among various groups within American society. A number of sociologists, for instance, have suggested that the looting accompanying racial outbreaks has constituted a bid for a redistribution of property: "It is a message that certain deprived sectors of the population want what they consider their fair share—and that they will resort to violence to get it" (Dynes and Quarantelli, 1968:14). Such sociologists note that in Watts, Newark, and Detroit, the main businesses affected were groceries, supermarkets, pawn shops, and furniture and liquor stores: while banks, utility stations, industrial plants, schools, hospitals, and private residences were usually ignored. Further, the looters generally received support from many people in their community and often worked together in small groups. Indeed, looting became the socially *expected* thing to do. Ghetto riots, then, are seen as a kind of mass protest against Establishment conceptions of property.

### 4. Psychology of Violence Thesis

"At the level of individuals, violence is a cleansing force. It frees the native from his inferiority complex and from his despair and inaction; it makes him fearless and restores his self-respect." This approach is outlined by Frantz Fanon (1966:73) in *The Wretched of the Earth.* He argues that violence is not only a political necessity for colonial peoples seeking their independence, but a personal necessity for "colored natives" striving to be men. Because the systematic violence of colonialism deadened and degraded the natives, Fanon insisted, they could achieve psychic wholeness only by committing acts of violence against the White rulers and masters whom they wished to supplant. Kenneth B. Clark (1967) and Robert W. Friedrichs (1968) have advanced somewhat similar interpretations, namely that the Black Protest and ghetto rioting constitute a search for self-esteem and a positive group identity.

### 5. Riot Ideology Thesis

T. M. Tomlinson (1968) suggests that a "riot ideology" has become fashionable in Black communities and that a significant minority of Blacks have come to view civil violence as a legitimate and productive mode of protest. It is of interest to note in this regard that the idea that ghetto "riots" are "weapons" and "rebellions" only began to be publicized and to gain popular acceptance during the spring of 1966. The kind of behavior manifested in these later "riots," including those following Dr. Martin Luther King's assassination in the spring of 1968, were practically indistinguishable from that typical of the 1964 "riots" or the 1965 Watts "riot." What changed were the accompanying attitudes and interpretations. Hence, the McCone Commission report was probably correct in denying a political or revolutionary basis to the Watts disturbance. Further support of this verdict is reflected in the post-riot lead article, "Watts, L.A.: A First Hand Report, Rebellion Without Ideology," which appeared in the September, 1965, *Liberator*, and which explicitly stated that the riots lacked purpose, ideology, and organization. It took roughly a year and a half after the 1964 "riots" for militant Black intellectuals, for instance, Stokely Carmichael and Rap Brown, to formulate the interpretation that the "riots" had a revolutionary message—that they were conscious political acts. It took another two years for this conclusion to be ratified by a significant number of rank-and-file Blacks (Hubbard, 1968; Spilerman, 1970).

We have outlined five hypotheses concerning the sources of Black militancy. Sociologists are not in agreement on this matter, and clearly empirical research is called for. Moreover, these approaches are not necessarily mutually exclusive. Perhaps the most satisfactory approach would be one that would view the various interpretations as complementary rather than as contradictory.

## COMBATING IDEOLOGICAL RACISM

The second concern, that of racist notions of Black biological inferiority, seemingly was scientifically laid to rest (see Klineberg, 1935; Lee, 1951), only to be resurrected again in the past decade. Recently a group of "new hereditarians" have appeared, such men as Dwight J. Ingle (1964, 1968), professor of physiology at the University of Chicago; William Shockley (1966, 1968), a Nobel Prize–winning physicist at Stanford University; and Arthur R. Jensen (1969), University of California (Berkeley) educational psychologist, who argue that hereditary factors have a major influence on "racial" differences in intelligence. Jensen's work in particular has commanded considerable interest and generated considerable controversy, in part because his paper appeared in the prestigious *Harvard Educational Review*. Jensen argues that hereditary factors are primarily responsible for the fact that Blacks average 15 points below Whites on I.Q. tests. Blacks, he indicates, are disadvantaged when it comes to "cognitive" or "conceptual" learning—the capacity for abstract reasoning and problem-solving—while tending to do well in tasks involving rote learning. He views the influence of environment as limited by the "threshold" effect—that is, below a certain threshold of environmental adequacy, deprivation does have a marked depressing effect on intelligence, but above that threshold, remedial action does little to raise intelligence. Hence, "compensatory" education is doomed to failure for Black children so long as the stress falls upon "cognitive" learning.

Of interest is the fact that the new hereditarians employ a social definition of race and rely primarily upon sociological data, rather than biological or genetic data, to support their arguments. The distinctive genetic background of the individuals under review is generally assumed rather than demonstrated; in a scientific sense, it is uncontrolled. Curiously, "racial" studies of intelligence revert to lay conceptions of race; most commonly, the racial sorting is done on the basis of the subject's self-classification or on the opinion of the researcher. The sole or dominant criterion is usually skin color. Moreover, it is baffling as to why genes influencing skin color or hair texture should be assumed to be concordant with those influencing intelligence, especially in light of contemporary knowledge—Scott and Fuller (1965), for example, in their dog experiments, found no support for the idea that differences in hair color or hair length are associated with genetically determined differences in behavior.

Further, the issue posed by the new hereditarians—the relationship between "racial" hereditary factors and intelligence—has its roots in the old nature-nurture controversy. The kinds of questions they ask reveal a preoccupation with "either/or" and "how much of which" strategies; they give either no or insufficient attention to development and process—to the fact that the human organism modifies itself by responding. Hence, it is not sufficient to divide the variance with respect to a behavioral trait into genetic and environmental variance, for this way we lose what in many cases is the most important part of the variance, the *interaction* between genotype and environment (Caspari, 1968).

In truth, the issue raised by the new hereditarians cannot be separated from still another controversy that has raged within scientific circles within recent years, namely whether there are valid races among man—that is, whether human interpopulation variability is such that the process of clustering people or populations into races can be done on an objective basis. In the early 1960s the debate was carried on in the pages of *Current Anthropology* (3: 1962; 4: 1963; 5: 1964); in 1964, Ashley Montagu brought together the contributions of a number of physical anthropologists and biologists in a volume appropriately entitled *The Concept of Race;* and, at the December, 1966, meetings of the American Association for the Advancement of Science, a symposium was held on science and the concept of race (Mead et al., 1968).

Of growing influence in this controversy has been the no-race school (Hogben, 1931; Huxley and Haddon, 1936; Livingstone, 1962, 1963, 1964; Montagu, 1964). It does not deny that biological variability exists between human populations, but only that the variability is in the form of discrete biological entities which exist "out there" in nature (and it further denies that races constitute units of evolution). The no-race school notes the absence of boundaries between populations (there are not races, only clines—traits that reveal a gradual geographical transition from a higher to a lower incidence) and the fact that trait distributions tend to be discordant (maps showing the patterns of distribution of various blood group systems, for instance, reveal at best only a partial coincidence). The no-race school has taken strong exception to the work of Carleton S. Coon (1962; 1965), especially its racist overtones.

Actually, much of the difficulty revolving about the concept of race derives from the "thing-concept" confusion. When we begin with a concept, we tend to see and order the world about us in terms of the requirements of the concept. We fit the facts to conform with our theoretical definitions and become insensitive to the facts as they are. In short, many biologists and anthropologists have found "races" because they were looking for them (Montagu, 1964). Races exist, not as biologically discrete entities, but as *social categories.*

W. I. Thomas (1931:189) once observed, "If men define situations as real, they are real in their consequences." What people believe, then, affects their behavior, whether the beliefs are true or not, or whether the proponents of the beliefs call themselves scientists or not. Unhappily the new hereditarians have taken a social category and treated it as a discrete biological category, feeding racist mythology.

## INTERPRETING WHITE PREJUDICE AND DISCRIMINATION

The third concern, that of interpreting Black disadvantage as derived from White prejudice and discrimination, has had a psychological and social psychological emphasis. Much of this work has been built around the concepts of prejudice and discrimination, with greater emphasis on the former than the latter (Westie, 1964:581). Blumer (1958:420) refers to this orientation as the "prejudice-discrimination axis" which he characterizes in these terms:

*It rests on a belief that the nature of relations between racial groups results from the feelings and attitudes which these groups have toward each other. . . . It follows that in order to comprehend and solve problems of race relations it is necessary to study and ascertain the nature of prejudice.*

In truth, the picture that has emerged is that of prejudice as some sort of little demon which comes to characterize people because they are depraved, and suffering from some psychological "hang-up" (the frustration-aggression and projection theories) or a sick personality structure (an "authoritarian personality"). Attention, then, has been focused upon the deep-seated anxieties, insecurities, and fears that often underlie and accompany "prejudiced personalities," and as a consequence such specialists take a rather dim view of efforts to combat racism that do not come to grips with an individual's basic personality structure.

The authors of *The Authoritarian Personality* are representative of this orientation. They argue that educational approaches which employ rational arguments cannot be expected to have deep or lasting effects upon a phenomenon that is as intrinsically irrational in nature as is prejudice. Similarly, appeals to sympathy may backfire when they are directed toward individuals, one of whose deepest fears is that they might be identified with weakness or suffering. Nor can closer contact with members of a minority help when an individual's basic personality organization impairs or even precludes him from establishing a deep or meaningful relationship with anybody, regardless of racial or ethnic membership. What then is the answer? Adorno and his associates (1950:973–974) indicate that, ideally, psychological techniques need to be employed to change personality.

This type of approach is "safe"; it does not rock any boats in the sense that fundamental institutional arrangements are jeopardized. Yet simultaneously one can still be on the side of the angels—indeed, lacking prejudice, one can be counted among the angels. It probably is not accidental that the heyday of this approach was the McCarthy and post-McCarthy years. And it was in keeping with sociology's tradition of political liberalism which viewed America as a Melting Pot in which members of minority groups ascended as *individuals* into the mainstream—in brief, the issue was one of individual acceptance and acceptability. Further, the approach fitted neatly with the methodological bias within sociology, emphasizing as it did the sample survey of attitudes. Thus the focus was upon people's states of mind, rather than upon action. And when attention was given to action, it fell upon relations between prejudiced *individuals* and victimized *individuals.* In brief, with the notable exception of a few studies employing a reference group approach (e.g., Killian, 1952; 1953; and Biesanz and Smith, 1951), prejudice and discrimination were treated largely within a social vacuum.

A concern with prejudice and discrimination is of course useful, but it leaves much to be desired in studying the ways in which people of one racial or ethnic group are systematically oppressed and/or exploited by the institutions of a society controlled by another racial or ethnic group. Carmichael and Hamilton make the point in these terms (1967:4):

*When white terrorists bomb a black church and kill five black children, that is an act of individual racism, widely deplored by most segments of the society. But when in the same city—Birmingham, Alabama—five hundred black babies die each year because of the lack of proper food, shelter and medical facilities, and thousands more are destroyed and maimed physically, emotionally and intellectually because of conditions of poverty and discrimination in the black community, that is a function of institutional racism. When a black family moves into a home in a white neighborhood and is stoned, burned or routed out, they are victims of an overt act of individual racism which many people will condemn—at least in words. But it is institutional racism that keeps black people locked in dilapidated slum tenements, subject to the daily prey of exploitative slumlords, merchants, loan sharks and discriminatory real estate agents.*

The concept of institutional or structural racism has been introduced within recent years to refer to the type of phenomenon described by Carmichael and Hamilton. It calls our attention to the fact that one or more of the institutions of a society function to impose more burdens and give less benefits on an ongoing basis to the members of one racial or ethnic group than to another. According to Friedman (1969:19):

*This means (in the American context) that decisions are made, agendas structured, issues defined, beliefs, values, and attitudes promulgated and enshrined, commitments entered into, and/or resources allocated, in such a way that non-whites are systematically deprived or exploited. It should be emphasized that ... that intentions of the actors, or the formal statements of the relevant norms, laws, and values, are irrelevant to the question of whether an institution is acting in a structurally racist manner. What counts is whether its actions in fact distribute burdens and rewards in a racially biased fashion or defends or supports other actors who are making biased distributions.*

Viewed from this perspective, then, prejudice is not a little demon that emerges in people simply because they are depraved, but because society itself is structured in a racist fashion. Institutions structure, shape, and restrict the experiences that people will have. Prejudices, accordingly, are acquired from concrete social experiences in a racist social order. And it follows that discrimination is not primarily an expression of prejudice but rather a byproduct of purposive striving to attain or hold social, economic, and political advantages and privileges. We need, then, to recognize that minority-dominant relations are *group* relations; a study of prejudice does not suffice.

## THE LEGACY OF STRUCTURE-FUNCTION SOCIOLOGY

As we review the field we find that the study of race relations constitutes in a very real sense a microcosm of sociology. For one thing, to examine race relations, and more particularly Black America—to do justice to a description and analysis of the behavior involved—is to examine the totality of behavior encompassed by sociology, be it, for instance, the study of religion, the family, or some other institutional arrangement, power, small group interaction, socialization, deviance, ecology, demography, or collective behavior. For still another, the study of race relations tends to reflect the weaknesses of the larger discipline. Throughout this review, attention has been called to the static, non-processual character of much of the work: the concern with compiling statistical data detailing Black disadvantage and documenting the "tangle of pathlogy" within Black ghettos; the adherence to old typological notions of human biological variation; and the preoccupation with a "prejudice-discrimination" axis. As a consequence, American sociology was caught flat-footed in anticipating the Black Revolt (Coleman, 1960) and is being compelled to evolve new tools for interpreting the phenomenon. Much of this difficulty has stemmed from sociology's structural-functional emphasis with its curiously synchronic, ahistorical orientation.

Central to the structure-function model of society is the concept of system, a structured arrangement made up of interdependent and semi-autonomous parts. One of the features of a system stressed by structural-functionalists is its tendency toward equilibrium; although the opposing forces are never perfect, final, or permanent, there is a tendency for the system to realize some sort of balance between contending forces. Although time can be introduced as a factor within the model, American structure-function sociologists have stressed static over dynamic properties. Dahrendorf (1968:117) has aptly characterized the matter in these terms:

*... the structural-functionalist insists that his equilibrium is not static but moving. But what does he mean by a moving equilibrium? He means, in the last analysis, that the system is a structure not of the building type but of the organism type. Homeostasis is maintained by the regular occurrence of certain patterned processes which, far from disturbing the tranquillity of the village pond, in fact are the village pond. Heraclitus's saying, "We enter the same*

*river, and it is not the same," does not hold here. The system is the same however often we look at it. Children are born, and the same happens all over again. What a peaceful, what an idyllic, world the system is! Of course, it is not static in the sense of being dead; things happen all the time; but happily they are under control, and they all help to maintain that precious equilibrium of the whole. Things not only happen, they function, and so long as they do, all is well.*

Yet the problem which Dahrendorf identifies can be met by broadening the concept of equilibrium, as some sociologists have done in recent years, so as to include morphogenic (developing) properties in addition to those that are homeostatic (self-maintaining) (Buckley, 1967; Olsen, 1968; Parsons, 1966; von Bertalanffy, 1956).

The problem with structure-function analysis, however, is more fundamental than merely noting that in practice it has yielded an undynamic picture of social life. By its inherent nature it has difficulty handling process. Yet the real world is process (Olsen, 1968:1–2; Sheldon, 1954:542; Whitehead, 1929:33, 42, 317); there are no fixed "entities" or "things," only transition and flux. Although the real world constitutes process, our thinking apparatus demands that we be furnished with discrete and identifiable "things." Our scientific procedures have not escaped this requirement, for they have involved conceptualizing perceptual data and treating them *as if* they are real and exact entities. This procedure is fictitious although we commonly justify it if it contributes to an understanding of behavior (Rice, 1928:22–25). The ever-present danger, perhaps even an inevitable one, is that by virtue of the procedure we come to reify our constructs.

As we inquire more carefully into nature we find, then, that solidity and "thinghood" is more often than not the substance of our perceptual limitations. In physics, for instance, conceptions of "stuff," mass in the old sense of quantity of matter, have largely been displaced by more dynamic, processual conceptions; the old atoms, supposedly fixed and solid, have broken down into protons, neutrons, electrons, etc., and these in turn have been broken down into radiant energy, motion, etc. (Sheldon, 1954:542–547). Zoology found itself confronted with the vexing, unsolved (insoluble!) problem of delimiting the boundaries of "species" so long as it persisted in its dogged commitment to an entity model, since such a model cannot handle borderline and intermediate evolutionary forms—organisms that defy the docketing and pigeonholing of the museum taxonomist (Mayr, 1954; 1965;24ff; Wilson and Brown, 1953).

Similarly treating social life in entity terms—partitioning it into discrete structures—divests life of its essential quality, its processual, diachronic nature. Indeed, by dichotomizing between structure and process we give birth to problems which are unnecessary and which by their nature are insoluble. Parsons asserts, for instance: "Structural analysis must take a certain priority over the analysis of process and change" (Parsons, 1966:111). It is little wonder then that he finds that "a general theory of the processes of change of social systems is not possible in the present state of knowledge," because there is insufficient knowledge "of process of the system" (Parsons, 1951:486). In truth, by giving "priority" to structure, Parsons has destroyed the heart of social life —its process—and it seems to me that this, not the reason he cites, is why he has difficulty handling change. Moreover, the word "change" itself is saturated with certain non-processual connotations; it implies a shift from one static, equilibrated "state" to another in contrast to a dynamic picture of processual flow. Admittedly, the English language does not help us in formulating these matters since the nouns that provide the subjects of most of our sentences largely refer to static objects, not to ongoing process (Olsen, 1968:44).

I recognize the response of critics to this position (Gross, 1967:64):

*The scientific enterprise seems impossible without some minimum distinction between things and their doings, or less crudely speaking, between behavior which is relatively constant and behavior which is relatively changeable. If all aspects of phenomena were changing at unknown rates and no aspect could be regarded as more stable than any other it would be impossible to discover or invent parameters which could serve as reference points for concept formation, generalization, and prediction. These key objectives depend upon some degree of constancy or recurrence within phenomena. How else would it be possible to derive knowledge from one space-time framework and apply it to another except for the presence of interchangeable similarities? If all were change with no differentiation in process or activity, human learning would be impossible. . . .*

I would respond to this argument as follows. The nature of reality is one matter. Our ability to provide adequate models or representations of it for scientific purposes is still another. That we are continuously confronted with a variety of conceptual and perceptual limitations posed by our human existence is no excuse for us to commit ourselves fatalistically, eternally, or dogmatically to one tool, in this case, a system's model, or to equate it with science. I do not agree with Parsons, therefore, that ". . . the concept of system is so fundamental to science that, at levels of high theoretical generality, there can be no science without it" (1961:337), and "System . . . is therefore the concept around which all sophisticated theory in the conceptually generalizing disciplines is and *must* be organized" (1968:458; italics added). What Parsons takes for granted is precisely what needs first to be demonstrated, namely that a system's model has a meaningful correspondence with an objectively verifiable reality. For once having a priori accepted the model, we have already implicitly answered the question, "How does it work?" In other words we should not take it as axiomatic that populations behave as systems (Campbell, 1958).

The study of race relations—and sociology in general—requires multiple models. For some purposes it may be useful to focus upon "being," that is, upon an "instantaneous" status or cross-section of a phenomenon in time (organization). A structure-function model is well suited to this purpose. For other purposes, it may be useful to focus upon "behaving," that is, upon those transient and reversible—often repetitive—aspects of nature (stability, order). A system's model appears well suited to this purpose. For still other purposes, it may be useful to focus upon "becoming," that is, upon the irreversible, developing aspects of nature (history) (cf. Gerard, 1957). For this purpose a process model seems to be a useful tool. Each model calls our attention to problems and data that might be overlooked by the other models.

## SOCIAL ACTION

The task of evolving tools for describing and analyzing Black America cannot be separated from the broader task of evolving tools for dealing with race relations in general. Indeed, as we have observed, the work that has treated Black America has suffered from parochialism in terms of problems and focus. That the sociological literature on ethnic and race relations is primarily American, with a heavy emphasis upon Black-White relations, is partly attributable to the fact that empirical sociology is so largely an American product (Dotson and Dotson, 1968:1). Yet this very fact has been at the bottom of many of our difficulties, including the structural-functional preoccupation. What, we might profitably ask, would the field of race relations look like had it not derived from the Old South and the Chicago of Robert E. Park but from Africa, Southeast Asia, or Eastern Europe? If we are not to stagnate, simply doing more of the same old things in the same old ways, we need to broaden our horizons cross-culturally and explore new approaches.

We have already noted that the study of race relations requires, in addition to other models, a dynamic, processual model of social life. In brief, we need models in which the emphasis falls upon action, or more particularly interaction, rather than upon groups or other social entities (structures)—upon process rather than "things." It might be argued that Talcott Parsons has already provided us with a theory of action. Yet as several critics have noted, it is curious how little action, in any ordinary sense of the term, actually gets discussed by Parsons (Black, 1961; Swanson, 1953).

The classical sociological and anthropological approach is of little help to us in treating process. This approach entails taking a unit—a "tribe," "society," or "community"—and presenting the behavior of its members in terms of a series of interlocking institutions, positions, statuses, or cultural patterns (norms and values). While this type of model has provided a useful tool in the description and analysis of "societies" that are relatively small, homogeneous, and static, it is faced with decided limitations in the study of large, complex, dynamic "societies," variously labeled "dual," "composite," "multiple," and "plural societies." Much of Africa (Dotson and Dotson, 1968; Epstein, 1958; 1961; Mayer, 1961; 1962; 1964; Mitchell, 1956; van den Berghe, 1965a; 1965b), the Caribbean (Benedict, 1962; Despres, 1964; Smith 1965), Central America (Gillin, 1945; 1948; Nash, 1957; Tax, 1941; Tumin, 1952; Wagley and Harris, 1955), and Southeast Asia (Bruner, 1961; Freedman, 1960; Furnivall, 1944; 1948; Hunter, 1966; Kunstadter, 1967; Lehman, 1967; Skinner, 1959) present a picture of "societies" that are structurally segmented and culturally diverse—matrices or networks of relationships characterized by such features as a relative absence of value consensus; multiple, deep-seated ethnic identities; stressful intergroup relationships; and considerable institutional duplication between the various segments (van den Berghe, 1964:12).

Subsaharan Africa, for instance, confronts us with the clear challenge of devising new models to describe the conditions of the towns and cities where people of vastly different ethnic backgrounds are thrown together (Mayer, 1964; Mitchell, 1966; Plotnicov, 1967:8). We cannot handle rural migrancy to urban centers in terms of any of the integrated systems or wholes which have until recently been the object of most sociological and anthropological analysis. Viewed in terms of the conventional model, the migrant appears as an interchangeable component who takes his place alternatively in different structures —the tribal and the urban—now here and then there.

To approach the matter in the traditional fashion makes it impossible to bring the migrant into focus as a single person; we disintegrate him into two unrelated halves (Mayer, 1964:22). Now in some circumstances it may be useful to portray an individual situationally in these terms, that is, individuals may act in the context of given roles (cognitive models of expected behaviors)—we encounter them not as total "individuals" but as "segments." Yet such clearcut role compartmentalization is not always possible. The African migrant in town is often not simply holding his rural roles in obeyance; he is discharging them in absentia, for instance, although one might claim that his rural economic roles are "latent" so long as he remains working in an industrial setting, he nonetheless is still a family member earning "for" his family in the country (Mayer, 1964:22–23). Hence, as Mayer (1964:23) observes:

*No one structure or culture, no one community, no one society, will contain or exemplify the phenonemon of African labour migrancy, not even any one State, for migrancy commonly flows back and forth across State boundaries. The study of migrancy has to encompass two fields which appear to be structurally unrelated as "wholes", i.e., the town and the home rural community; it also has to take into account policies and administrative measures, race relations and historical developments, which can only be understood by reference to facts outside both fields. Moreover it is largely concerned with individual decisions, choices and alternatives, and these as such have been difficult to accommodate in most of the classic anthropological [and sociological] models.*

Nor does the classical "acculturation" or "detribalization" model help matters. McFee (1968) shows, for instance, that among the Blackfeet such a conceptual framework distorts reality; it views an individual in terms of a continuum of change wherein a given amount of "tribal loss" is replaced by a comparable amount of "Westernized gain." In reality we often find a "150% man," one who learns new ways without abandoning the old, who activates given roles in terms of the situational context.

The classical model—essentially one of a socially and culturally homogeneous national state—similarly has limited applicability to the United States; when confronted with the reality of American ethnic and racial heterogeneity, the model looks to a movement toward homogeneity via assimilation, a questionable analytical tool for understanding current episodes of Black-White confrontation. Indeed, once we grasp the idea of overlapping and sometimes conflicting and contradictory intergroup relationships, it soon becomes clear that the commonly used vocabulary of race relations, such words as "assimilation," "integration," and "accommodation," is inadequate. Such vocabularies assume a "host-immigrant" framework in which the culture and values of the "host society" are seen as essentially non-contradictory and static and in which immigrants are viewed as altering their patterns of behavior until they finally conform to the "host society" (Rex and Moore, 1967:13–14; Metzger, 1971), a framework with an obvious ideological preference for an assimilationist "Anglo-Saxonizing (Americanization) solution," Such a model overlooks the fact that cultural differences are not simply innocent or neutral variations in customs but an integral part of a broader picture of group differentials in power, wealth, and status. And it overlooks the phenomenon of ethnogenesis, the process whereby a new ethnic group comes into being (Singer, 1962).

In light of the deficiencies of the traditional approach, it is encouraging to note some recent work that has moved in new directions and that has concerned itself with process. Lieberson (1961), for instance, shows that the type of contact which occurs between groups assumes critical importance: migrant superordination leads to conflict; indigenous superordination to assimilation. Noel (1968) formulates a theory that ethnic stratification emerges when distinct ethnic groups are brought into sustained contact *only* if the groups are characterized by a high degree of ethnocentrism, competition, and differential power. Van den Berghe (1967) comes up with a series of generalizations based upon a cross-cultural examination of race relations in Mexico, Brazil, the United States, and South Africa. And Schermerhorn (1967; 1970) provides us with a consideration of polar forces in intergroup relations, an approach that emphasizes the interplay of forces advancing, retreating, converging, or diverging in patterns of greater or lesser stability. Also of noteworthy interest are Killian's (1968) *The Impossible Revolution,* Clark's (1965) *Dark Ghetto,* and Michael Banton's (1967) *Race Relations.*

In dealing with the matter of process I find the work of Barnes (1954; 1968), Bott (1957), Epstein (1961), Adrian C. Mayer (1966), Philip Mayer (1961; 1962; 1964), Srinivas (1964), and Turner (1968) to be most suggestive, particularly in their employment of the concepts "network" and "field." Barnes (1954), for instance, utilized these concepts in describing the relationships of people in a Norwegian island parish, collecting these relationships into what he calls "social fields" of three different kinds. First, there was the "territorially-based social field, with a large number of administrative units, arranged hierarchically, one within the other"—hamlets or neighborhoods, wards, the parish itself, and several larger ascending series of units with administrative, judicial, or ecclesiastical functions that included other parishes of Norway. Second, there was the industrial social field that revolved about fishing vessels, marketing cooperatives, and herring-oil factories—a set of activities, attitudes, and relationships centering upon industrialized fishing. Third, there was a social field that Barnes calls a "network." A network consisted of relationships between friends, neighbors, and kinsmen that did not make up a larger whole in the sense that the relationships were encompassed by a common boundary, that is, each person was in touch with a number of people, some of whom were directly in touch with each other and some of whom were not. X, for example, may have had a relationship with A, and beyond that A may have related to B, but X may not have had a relationship with B. B in turn may have had ties with C and D, so that the interaction patterns went on indefinitely in many directions. Every individual in the parish participated in slightly different aspects of each of these three fields.

Although various writers have employed the concepts network and field somewhat differently (Barnes, himself, revised his formulation to some extent in his 1968 paper), I find the overall approach to offer a good deal of promise for rich, productive exploration. For my purposes here I find it useful to conceive of networks as interactive webs—flows of action—among people; in other words, they are activated relationships between people. Fields are spheres of social living—situational contexts in which given flows of action tend to converge in the pursuit of some goal or goals. Fields, then, may be thought of as a series of interconnected, activated (energized) relationships that are set off from other flows of social action, not by sharp boundaries, but by a zone of lowered, cross-circuited permeability. Hence, there is some degree of continuation between the interpenetration (or overlap) among fields.

Returning to my earlier illustration of Subsaharan Africa, I find the concepts of field and network to be useful tools for dealing with what, for want of a better term, have been called "plural societies." In the multitribal mining towns of the Rhodesian Copperbelt, for instance, we find different social identities being activated in different fields: in the work setting, tribal interests are transcended by common ("class") interests so that in recent years mineworkers have come to favor union to "tribal" representation vis-à-vis the White management; in other fields, those generally defined as revolving about an individual's "private life," tribal identifications play a dominant part (Epstein, 1958; Mitchell, 1956). And in East London, South Africa, Mayer (1961; 1962; 1964) found that certain types of urban migrants (Red Xhosa) "encapsulate" themselves in a tight-knit network, and that this network, which extends into the rural area, serves at once to protect its members from being drawn into town-based relationships and to reinforce their rural orientations. Other migrants (School Xhosa) have loose-knit networks that enable them to participate in town-based activities without thereby impairing their relationships with their rural associates and kinsmen; the School Xhosa "shuttle" or "commute" between fields, activating rural or urban identities as the case may be. Bruner (1961) describes somewhat similar patterns as those existing among the School Xhosa for the urban Toba Batak of North Sumatra, Indonesia. And Killian (1953) noted a not dissimilar picture among southern White migrants to Chicago; they maintained segregated racial patterns in their interaction within the field of a White migrant tavern while adjusting to integrated patterns in the field of the nonsegregated restaurant next door.

## CONCLUSION

In considering these matters it is useful to recall the perceptive discussion by John Dewey (1909) on ideas contained in his paper on Darwinism:

*Old ideas give way slowly; for they are more than abstract logical forms and categories. They are habits, predispositions, deeply engrained attitudes of aversion and preference. Moreover, the conviction persists—though history shows it to be a hallucination—that all the questions that the human mind has asked are questions that can be answered in terms of the alternatives that the questions themselves present. But in fact intellectual progress usually occurs through sheer abandonment of questions together with both the alternatives they assume—an abandonment that results from their decreasing vitality and a change of urgent interest. We do not solve them: we get over them. Old questions are solved by disappearing, evaporating, while new questions corresponding to the changed attitude of endeavor and preference take their place.*

We appear to be in much the situation that Dewey describes with regard to Black America in particular and race relations in general. We observed, for instance, when considering ideological racism, that old questions rooted in the nature-nurture controversy, in mistaken notions about intelligence, and in a typological approach to human biological variation persist. The same has held true for the issues dealt with by the static, synchronic sociology derived from the structure-function tradition. These old matters obstruct use in getting on with the task of understanding the dynamic, processual nature of ethnic and race relations.

## REFERENCES

Adorno, T. W., Else Frenkel-Brunswik, Daniel J. Levinson, and R. Nevitt Sanford.
1950   The Authoritarian Personality. New York: Harper & Row.
Banton, Michael
1967   Race Relations. London: Tavistock Publications.
Barnes, John A.
1968   "Networks and political process." Pp. 107–130 in Marc J. Swarz (ed.), Local-Level Politics. Chicago: Aldine.
1954   "Class and committees in a Norwegian island parish." Human Relations 7:39–58.
Benedict, B.
1962   "Stratification in plural societies." American Anthropologist 64 (December): 1235–1246.
Biesanz, J. and L. M. Smith
1951   "Race relations in Panama and the Canal Zone." American Journal of Sociology 57 (July): 7–14.
Black, Max
1961   "Some questions about Parsons' theories." Pp. 268–288 in Max Black (ed.), The Social Theories of Talcott Parsons: A Critical Examination. Englewood Cliffs, N.J.: Prentice-Hall.
Blumer, H.
1958   "Research on racial relations: the United States of America." International Social Science Bulletin 10 (1): 403–447.
Bott, Elizabeth Jane
1957   Family and Social Network. London: Tavistock Publications.
Bowen, Don and Louis Masotti
1968   Riots and Rebellions. Beverly Hills: Sage Publications.
Broom, Leonard and Norval D. Glenn
1965   Transformation of the Negro American. New York: Harper & Row.
Bruner, E. M.
1961   "Urbanization and ethnic identity in North Sumatra." American Anthropologist 63 (June): 508–521.
Buckley, Walter
1967   Sociology and Modern Systems Theory. Englewood Cliffs, N.J.: Prentice-Hall.
Campbell, Angus and Howard Schuman
1968   Racial Attitudes in Fifteen American Cities. Washington, D.C.: U.S. Government Printing Office.
Campbell, D. T.
1958   "Common fate similarity, and other indices of the status of aggregates of persons as social entities." Behavioral Science 3:14–25.

*Carmichael, Stokely and Charles V. Hamilton*
1967    Black Power. New York: Random House.
*Caspari, E.*
1968    "Genetic endowment and environment in the determination of human behavior."
        American Educational Research Journal 5 (January): 43–55.
1967    "The search for identity." Ebony 22 (August): 42
*Clark, Kenneth B.*
1965    Dark Ghetto. New York: Harper & Row.
*Coleman, A. L.*
1960    "Social scientists' predictions about desegregation, 1950–1955." Social Forces 38
        (March): 258–262.
*Coleman, James S., Ernest Q. Campbell, Carol J. Hobson, James McPartland, Alexander
M. Mood, Frederic D. Winfeld, and Robert L. York.*
1966    Equality of Educational Opportunity. Office of Education, U.S. Department of
        Health, Education, and Welfare. Washington, D.C.: U.S. Government Printing
        Office.
*Coon, Carleton S.*
1965    The Living Races of Man. New York: Alfred A. Knopf.
1962    The Origin of Races. New York: Alfred A. Knopf.
*Dahrendorf, Ralf*
1968    Essays in the Theory of Society. Stanford, Calif.: Stanford University Press.
*Davis, Allison, Burleigh B. Gardner, and Mary R. Gardner*
1941    Deep South. Chicago: University of Chicago Press.
*Despres, L. A.*
1964    "The implications of nationalist politics in British Guiana for the development of
        cultural theory." American Anthropologist 66 (October): 1051–1078.
*Dewey, John*
1909    "The influence of Darwinism on philosophy." Popular Science 1909. Reprinted in
        John Dewey, The Influence of Darwin on Philosophy. Bloomington: Indiana Uni-
        versity Press.
*Dollard, John*
1937    Caste and Class in a Southern Town. New York: Harper & Row.
*Dotson, Floyd and Lillian O. Dotson*
1968    The Indian Minority of Zambia, Rhodesia and Malawi. New Haven: Yale Univer-
        sity Press.
*Downes, B. T.*
1968    "Social and political characteristics of riot cities: a comparative study." Social
        Science Quarterly 49 (December): 504–520.
*Drake, St. Clair and Horace R. Cayton*
1945    Black Metropolis: A Study of Negro Life in a Northern City. New York: Harcourt,
        Brace and Company.
*DuBois, W. E. Burghardt*
1940    Dusk of Dawn. New York: Harcourt, Brace and Company.
1939    Black Folk, Then and Now. New York: Henry Hold and Company.
1935    Black Reconstruction. New York: Harcourt, Brace and Company.
*Dynes, R. and E. L. Quarantelli*
1968    "Looting in American cities: a new explanation." Trans-action 5 (May): 9–15
*Epstein, A. L.*
1961    "The network and urban social organization." The Rhodes-Livingston Journal
        29:29–62
1958    Politics in an Urban Community. Manchester: Manchester University Press.
*Fanon, Frantz*
1960    The Wretched of the Earth. New York: Grove Press.
*Frazier, E. Franklin*
1940    Negro Youth at the Crossways. Washington, D.C.: American Council on Education.

1939  The Negro Family in the United States. Chicago: University of Chicago Press.

1932  The Negro Family in Chicago. Chicago: University of Chicago Press.

*Freedman, M.*

1960  "The growth of a plural society in Malaya." Pacific Affairs 33 (June): 158–168.

*Friedman, S.*

1969  "How is racism maintained?" Et Al 2 (Fall): 18–21.

*Friedrichs, R. W.*

1968  "Interpretations of Black aggression." The Yale Review 19 (Spring): 358–374.

*Furnivall, J. S.*

1948  Colonial Policy and Practice. Cambridge: Cambridge University Press.

1944  Netherlands India: A Study of Plural Economy. Cambridge: Cambridge University Press.

*Gerard, R. W.*

1957  "Units and concepts of biology." Science: 125 (March 8): 429–433.

*Geschwender, J. A.*

1964  "Social structure and the Negro revolt." Social Forces 43 (December): 248–256.

*Gillin, J.*

1948  " 'Race' relations without conflict: a Guatemalan town." American Journal of Sociology 53 (March): 337–343.

1945  "Parallel cultures and the inhibitions to acculturation in a Guatemalan community." Social Forces 24 (May): 1–14.

*Hogben, Lancelot*

1931  Genetic Principles in Medicine and Social Science. London: Williams and Morgate Ltd.

*Hubbard, H.*

1968  "Five long hot summers and how they grew." The Public Interest 12 (Summer): 3–24.

*Hunter, Guy*

1966  Southeast Asia: Race, Culture, and Nation. New York: Oxford University Press.

*Huxley, Julian S. and A. C. Haddon*

1936  We Europeans. New York: Harper & Row.

*Hyman, Herbert H.*

1969  "Social psychology and race relations." Pp. 3–41 in Irwin Katz and Patricia Gurin (eds.), Race and the Social Sciences. New York: Basic Books.

*Ingle, Dwight J.*

1968  "The need to investigate average biological differences among racial groups." Pp. 113–121 in Margaret Mead, Theodosius Dobzhansky, Ethel Tobach, and Robert E. Light (eds.), Science and the Concept of Race. New York: Columbia University Press.

1964  "Racial differences and the future." Science 114 (16 October): 375–379.

*Jensen, A. R.*

1969  "How much can we boost IQ and scholastic achievement?" Harvard Educational Review 39:1–123.

*Johnson, Charles S.*

1946  Into the Mainstream. Chapel Hill: University of North Carolina Press.

1943  Patterns of Negro Segregation. New York: Harper & Row.

1941  Growing Up in the Black Belt. Washington, D.C.:   American Council on Education

1934  Shadow of the Plantation. Chicago: University of Chicago Press.

*Killian, Lewis M.*

1968  The Impossible Revolution? New York: Random House.

1953  "The adjustment of southern White migrants to northern urban norms." Social Forces 33 (October): 66–69.

1952  "The effects of southern White workers on race relations in northern plants." American Sociological Review 17 (June): 327–331.

*Klineberg, Otto*
1935    Negro Intelligence and Selective Migration. New York: Columbia University Press.
*Kunstadter, Peter*
1967    "Introduction." Pp. 3–72 in Peter Kunstadter (ed.), Southeast Asian Tribes, Minorities, and Nations. Vol. 1. Princeton, N.J.: Princeton University Press
*Lee, E. S.*
1951    "Negro intelligence and selective migration: a Philadelphia test of the Klineberg Hypothesis." American Sociological Review 16 (April): 227–233.
*Lehman, F. K.*
1967    "Ethnic categories in Burma and the theory of social systems." Pp. 93–124 in Peter Kunstadter (ed.), Southeast Asian Tribes, Minorities, and Nations. Vol. 1. Princeton, N.J.: Princeton University Press.
*Lieberson, S.*
1961    "A societal theory of race and ethnic relations." American Sociological Review 29 (December): 902–910.
*Lieberson, S. and G. V. Fuguitt*
1967    "Negro-White occupational differences in the absence of discrimination." American Journal of Sociology 73 (September): 188–200.
*Liebow, Elliot*
1966    Tally's Corner. Boston: Little, Brown and Company.
*Livingstone, Frank B.*
1964    "On the non-existence of human races." Pp. 46–60 in Ashley Montagu (ed.), The Concept of Race. New York: The Free Press.
1963    "Comment." Current Anthropology 4 (April): 199–200.
1962    "On the non-existence of human races." Current Anthropology 3 (June): 279–281.
*McFee, M.*
1967    "The 150% man, a product of Blackfeet acculturation." American Anthropologist 70:1096–1107.
*Marx, Gary T.*
1967    Protest and Prejudice. New York: Harper & Row.
*Mayer, Adrian C.*
1966    "The significance of quasi-groups in the study of complex societies." Pp. 97–122 in Michael Banton (ed.), The Social Anthropology of Complex Societies. New York: Frederick A. Praeger.
*Mayer, Philip*
1964    "Labour migrancy and the social network." Pp. 21–34 in J. F. Hollman (ed.), Problems of Transition. Durban: Natal University Press.
1962    "Migrancy and the study of Africans in towns." American Anthropologist 64 (June): 576–591.
1961    Townsmen or Tribesmen. Cape Town: Oxford University Press.
*Mayr, Ernst*
1965    Animal Species and Evolution. Cambridge, Mass.: The Belknap Press of Harvard University Press.
1954    "Note on nomenclature and classification." Systematic Zoology 3:86–89.
*Mead, Margaret, Theodosius Dobzhansky, Ethel Tobach, and Robert E. Light*
1968    Science and the Concept of Race. New York: Columbia University Press.
*Metzger, L. P.*
1971    "American sociology and Black assimilation: conflicting perspectives." American Journal of Sociology 76 (January): 627–647.
*Mitchell, J. Clyde*
1966    "Theoretical orientations in African urban studies." Pp. 37–68 in Michael Banton (ed.), The Social Anthropology of Complex Societies. New York: Frederick A. Praeger.
1956    The Kalela Dance. Manchester: Manchester University Press.

*Montagu, Ashley*
1964    The Concept of Race. New York: The Free Press.
*Moynihan, Daniel P.*
1965    The Negro Family: The Case for National Action. Office of Policy Planning and Research, Department of Labor. Washington, D.C.: U.S. Government Printing Office.
*Myrdal, Gunnar*
1944    An American Dilemma. New York: Harper & Row.
*Nash, M.*
1957    "The multiple society in economic development: Mexico and Guatemala." American Anthropologist 59 (October): 825–833.
*National Advisory Commission on Civil Disorders.*
1968    Report of the National Advisory Commission on Civil Disorders. Washington, D.C.: U.S. Government Printing Office.
*Noel, D. L.*
1968    "A theory of the origin of ethnic stratification." Social Problems 16 (Fall): 157–171.
*Olsen, Marvin E.*
1968
The Process of Social Organization. New York: Holt, Rinehart and Winston.
*Palmore, E. and F. J. Whittington*
1970    "Differential trends toward equality between Whites and Nonwhites." Social Forces 49 (September): 108–116.
*Parsons, Talcott*
1968    "Social systems." Pp. 458–473 in David Sills (ed.), International Encyclopedia of the Social Sciences. New York: The Macmillan Company and the Free Press.
1966    Societies: Evolutionary and Comparative Perspectives. Englewood Cliffs, N.J.: Prentice-Hall.
1961    "The point of view of the author." Pp. 311–363 in Max Black (ed.), The Social Theories of Talcott Parsons. Englewood Cliffs, N.J.: Prentice-Hall.
1951    The Social System. New York: The Free Press.
*Parsons, Talcott and Kenneth B. Clark*
1966    The Negro American. Boston: Houghton Mifflin.
*Pettigrew, Thomas F.*
1964    A Profile of the Negro American. Princeton, N.J.: D. Van Nostrand
*Pinkney, Alphonso*
1969    Black Americans. Englewood Cliffs, N.J.: Prentice-Hall.
*Plotnicov, Leonard*
1967    Strangers to the City. Pittsburgh: University of Pittsburgh Press.
*Powdermaker, Hortense*
1939    After Freedom. New York: The Viking Press.
*Rainwater, Lee*
1970    Behind Ghetto Walls. Chicago: Aldine.
*Rex, John and Robert Moore*
1967    Race, Community, and Conflict. London: Oxford University Press.
*Rice, Stuart A.*
1928    Quantitative Methods in Politics. New York: Alfred A. Knopf.
*Schermerhorn, Richard A.*
1970    Comparative Ethnic Relations. New York: Random House.
1967    "Polarity in the approach to comparative research in ethnic relations." Sociology and Social Research 51 (January): 235–240.
*Scott, John P. and John L. Fuller*
1965    Genetics and the Social Behavior of the Dog. Chicago: University of Chicago Press.
*Sheldon, Wilmon Henry*
1954    God and Polarity. New Haven: Yale University Press.

*Shockley, William*
1968  "Proposed research to reduce racial aspects of the environment-heredity uncertainty." Science 111 (26 April): 433.
1966  "Possible transfer of metallurgical and astronomical approaches to the problem of environment versus ethnic heredity." Unpublished presentation at the Regional Meeting of the National Academy of Science.
*Simpson, George E. and J. Milton Yinger*
1965  Racial and Cultural Minorities. 3rd ed. New York: Harper & Row.
1959  "The sociology of race and ethnic relations." pp. 376–399 in Robert K. Merton (ed.), Sociology Today. New York: Basic Books.
*Singer, L.*
1962  "Ethnogenesis and Negro Americans today." Social Research 29 (Winter): 419–432.
*Skinner, G. William*
1959  Local, Ethnic, and National Loyalties in Village Indonesia: A Symposium. New Haven: Yale University Southeast Asia Studies.
*Smith, M. G.*
1965  The Plural Society in the British West Indies. Berkeley: University of California Press.
*Spilerman. S.*
1970  "The causes of racial disturbances: a comparison of alternative explanations." American Sociological Review 35 (August): 627–649.
Srinivas, M. N.
1964  "Networks in Indian social structure." Man 64 (November–December): 165–168.
*Swanson, G. E.*
1953  "The approach to a general theory of action by Parsons and Shils." American Sociological Review 18 (April): 125–134.
*Tax, S.*
1941  "World view and social relations in Guatemala." American Anthropologist 43:27–42.
*Thomas, W. I.*
1931  "The relation of research to the social process." In Essays on Research in the Social Sciences. Washington, D.C.: The Brookings Institution.
*Thomlinson, T. M.*
1968  "The development of a riot ideology." American Behavioral Scientist 2 (March): 27–31.
*Tumin, Melvin M.*
1968  "Some social consequences of research on racial relations." American Sociologist 3 (May): 117–124.
1952  Caste in a Peasant Society. N.J.: Princeton University Press
*Turner, Victor*
1968  "Mukanda: the politics of a non-political ritual." Pp. 135–150 in Marc J. Swartz (ed.), Local-Level Politics. Chicago: Aldine.
*U.S. Commission on Civil Rights*
1967  Racial Isolation in the Public Schools. Washington D.C.: U.S. Government Printing Office.
*van den Berghe, Pierre L.*
1967  Race and Racism. New York: Wiley.
1965a  Africa: Social Problems of Change and Conflict. San Francisco: Chandler.
1965b  South Africa: A Study in Conflict. Middletown, Conn.: Wesleyan University Press.
1964  "Toward a sociology of Africa." Social Forces 43 (September): 11–18.
*Vander Zanden, James W.*
1972  American Minority Relations. 3rd ed. New York: Ronald Press.

*von Bertalanffy, L.*
1956   "General systems theory." General Systems 1:1–10.

*Wagley, C. and M. Harris*
1955   "A typology of Latin American subcultures." American Anthropologist 57 (June): 428–451.

*Warner, W. L.*
1936   "American caste and class." American Journal of Sociology 32 (September): 234–237.

*Warner, W. Lloyd and Leo Srole*
1945   The Social System of American Ethnic Groups. New Haven: Yale University Press.

*Westie, Frank R.*
1964   "Race and ethnic relations." Pp. 576–618 in R. E. L. Faris (ed.), Handbook of Modern Sociology. Chicago: Rand McNally.

*Whitehead, Alfred North*
1929   Process and Reality. New York: Macmillan.

*Williams, Robin M., Jr.*
1964   Strangers Next Door. Englewood Cliffs, N.J.: Prentice-Hall.

*Wilson, E. O. and W. L. Brown, Jr.*
1953   "The subspecies concept and its taxonomic application." Systematic Zoology 2:97– 111.

*Yinger, J. M.*
1968   "Recent developments in minority and race relations." The Annals of the American Academy of Political and Social Science 378 (July): 130–145.

# American Minorities and "New Nation" Perspectives

## Joan W. Moore

*University of Wisconsin, Milwaukee*

Almost fifteen years ago Lipset (1963) anticipated the bicentennial analysis of American society in his book *The First New Nation.* Largely a cultural analysis, the work is concerned with explaining continuities in American cultural patterns and their initial and continuing contribution to the maintenance of this nation's dynamic equilibrium in the polity, religion, character structure, and other latency institutions. The comparative focus—and the source of the title—was primarily with African nations newly freed from colonial domination, and was largely confined to the issues of stabilization of a democratic polity.

Since then, the experience of new nations of the Third World has begun to impinge seriously on our rather ethnocentric social science. To relate conventional sociology of American minorities to that experience, we must start (turning Lipset on his head) by acknowledging that first, the United States has acted as a colonial power within its current continental limits as well as its overseas territories. Second, we must realize that the dominance structures developed during that period of expansion have their own continuities and greatly affect the racial groups involved both with political expansion and in the economic development of the American nation. Third, the primary sources of contemporary international migration to the United States are Third World

*Source:* Joan W. Moore, "American Minorities and 'New Nation' Perspectives," Pacific Sociological Review 19, 4 (October 1976): 447–67. Copyright © 1976 by the Publisher, Sage Publications, Inc. Reprinted by permission.

nations with salient postcolonial dominance structures (including dominance by the United States). Fourth, the primary sources of internal migration of racial minority groups to American cities are sectors of our own society with salient postcolonial dominance structures. Fifth, there may be some true analogues to the Third World postcolonial situation now existing among American minorities.[1]

## COMPETING MODELS OF RACE RELATIONS

It is not possible to "demystify" the analysis of race relations as easily as Marx promised by standing Hegel on his head. It is particularly difficult with the so-called "Third World perspective" because of its volatile and emotional roots. The important sources include the writings of African and Latin American intellectuals, many of them involved in political revolutions and/or subsequent nation-building (Fanon, 1968; Gonzalez-Casanova, 1969; Memmi, 1967; Nkrumah, 1966; Emmanuel, 1972; Amin, 1974; Stavenhagen, 1968). In the United States, the earliest contributions came from black activists and intellectuals (Carmichael and Hamilton, 1967; Clark, 1967; Cleaver, 1968). Most of these writings either overtly appeal to the emotions of their readers and/or outline explicit action together with their analyses.

Even beyond emotional roots, Blauner (1972) notes that the Third World concepts entered universities in an atmosphere of protest rather than scholarly "objectivity." They challenged the university as an institution and directly confronted traditional paradigms as an ideology of racial oppression. Many of these challenges were related to the academic resurrection of Marx and his descendants: the challenge to conventional sociology went far beyond the relatively depreciated study of race and ethnicity. Some of the early work by minority sociologists reflected a Third World perspective and was focused and analytical (e.g., Thomas, 1966–1967), but many simply reflected enthusiastic revisionism. They were permeated with the rhetoric of ethnic action—and even ethnic mystique. Often they were published in outlets with a very limited circulation among traditional sociologists and were relatively uncritical applications of the colonial analogy.

The reaction among conventional sociologists was predictable. It is well indicated by the findings of Record (1973) on the reactions of white sociologists to the related phenomenon of black studies—that is, some have been antagonistic, some related to it, and a significant portion in essence withdrew their interest.

The "Third World models" discussed here are, specifically, the concept of "internal colonialism" and the related idea of a "dual economy/society" that is especially prominent in the literature on urbanization in African and Latin American nations. These concepts are valuable as heuristics, as analogies and sensitizing concepts. They call attention to sets of variables that are often overlooked. In this respect the Third World models are similar to more conventional models in minority studies. Generally even conventional models do not specify variables to be selected for analysis but rather tend to provide a context for explanation of specific types of behavior ranging, e.g., from school performance through family behavior. The "race" variable is too often left *not* conceptualized. Furthermore conventional sociology has drawn heavily on analogy, a good example being the Hindu caste system (Davis and Gardner, 1941; Dollard, 1957). The underlying assumption in most sociology of race has been that of a reasonably integrated social system with varying degrees of internal consistency. The state of the field of minority studies does not provide a disciplinary base for rejecting sensitizing concepts that are fruitful. Blumer (1954) argues, in fact, that most of our disciplinary apparatus consists precisely of such sensitizing concepts. The sociologist would be well advised to judge a competitive conceptual framework, such as the Third World models, more in terms of fruitfulness than in terms of specificity. This is especially true in a context for the interpretation of urban minorities.

## THE CONCEPT OF INTERNAL COLONIALISM

The concept of "internal colonialism" has acquired a bewildering variety of meanings in the recent literature. The core of the concept seems to be clearest in the case of neocolonialism. Let us imagine a Third World nation, newly freed from directly exploitative colonial dominance. In short order, if the new nation has resources that are useful for more advanced or "late monopoly" industrialized nations (oil, minerals, cheap labor) neocolonial mechanisms will develop for the direct or indirect foreign exploitation of those resources. This is done in a number of ways, including a continued dependency on consumer goods and machinery. It is done through education and the provision of foreign "experts," controls and constraints over money, and through the direct or indirect manipulation of internal politics. But it is important to realize that none of these mechanisms will work without the existence of an appropriate ideology and the existence of elite groups within the new nation who actively cooperate with the neocolonialist powers in the exploitation of their own people.[2] At later stages, the function played by the intermediary elites can "pass" or "diffuse" to a bourgeois stratum, to a racial caste, or even to a more highly developed region or sector of the new nation.

The immediate appeal of this internal colonialist model in conceptualizing analogous situations in the United States should be obvious. Here seems to be a new way of conceptualizing the traditional "Uncle Tom," the paralegal power of powerful bureaucracies in East Los Angeles *barrios,* and the massive flows of cheap labor into the industrialized farms of the American Southwest. But beyond the immediate (and often superficial) analogy the question of "How well does the colonial model fit?" is critical. (The analogy of caste was fruitful in analyzing black and white relationships in the Deep South. It is far less useful in understanding Mexican and Anglo relations in the rural Southwest.)

### Indians and Internal Colonialism

Particularly during the first century of Indian and settler contact, the colonial concept fits Indians astonishingly well. (This period is generally described by historians as the Colonial epoch.) But we note almost at once that the particular form of colonial exploitation of Indians varies greatly over time and between tribes. This is evident whether we draw on the Marxist-derived analysis of colonialism based on issues of gain for the advanced capitalist nations or whether we use the more sociologically complex paradigms posed in the British tradition, e.g., Furnivall (1948) and Kuper and Smith (1969). The great variety of forms of exploitation included (1) trading exploitation, (2) the use of Indian military manpower for political control, (3) the settlement of land, (4) plantation-type exploitation through the Spanish mission system, and (5) cultural aggrandizement through missionaries and detribalization. By the turn of the twentieth century most of these colonial objectives were either obsolete goals or fully accomplished.

After the age of direct colonial exploitation, we have a chance to test the utility of the concept of internal colonialism. To reiterate, the critical features of the model are: an external dependency on a power that gains an exploitative advantage, and a specific and clearly defined subordinate group or territory which itself is internally stratified. It is clear that in the postcolonial era of the twentieth century the notion of "internal colonialism" is hard to apply to all American Indians. In fact, the idea best fits a situation that concerns the smallest number of Indians—that is, those Indian groups which show a direct structural continuity with the structures that were developed for direct colonial exploitation. These are the Indians on reservations administered by the Bureau of Indian Affairs (BIA). Less than half of the Indians in the United States were ever confined to reservations. Perhaps only a third were in the "restricted" status that made them utterly dependent on the Bureau (Spicer, 1969). It would seem that there would be no exploitative advantage accruing to the colonial power, since decade after decade, the BIA and the reservation system are defined as an excessive financial burden. Accordingly, federal policy since the 1930s has been dominated by considerations of cost. The varying strategies for reducing costs have been uniformly salted with a rhetoric of expiation, a set of official "regrets" for the past exploitation. This rhetoric seems to serve an ideological function for maintenance of the national self-concept. But the dominant consideration is always cost. In 1934, the policy of reservation development was cheaper. In 1954, the termination of tribal dependencies was cheaper. In 1963, the policy of urban relocation was cheaper. The Indians were seen always as dependents and the primary argument was always the cost of their dependency. It will also be interesting to follow the expiatory rhetoric as Indians become more visible as an urban minority and their problems more closely resemble the problems of other urban minorities.

The analogy of "internal colonialism" is also useful in directing attention to some factors in the change of tribal cultures.[3] This is well illustrated in the analysis by Thomas (1966–1967) of the contrast between the strategies followed in the "hidden colonialist" administration of the Pine Ridge Sioux with the revitalizing consequences of a self-help project among the Tama Fox, in which indigenous social control mechanisms were mobilized for tribal self-development. At the very least, the concept of internal colonialism (a) reorders the traditional variables or factors, emphasizing the actions of intermediary elites, (b) focuses attention on specific mechanisms of social control rather than on broad, predisposing cultural factors, and (c) emphasizes those aspects of sociocultural change that seem to presage self-determination.

It is probable that the full theory of "internal colonialism" is vitiated in application to the Indian reservation because of the missing element of exploitative gain.[4] (A parallel situation in the Mexican struggle in Crystal City, Texas, is quite different.)[5] When the concept is applied to older Latin American nations, the "intermediary elite" that gains can be a class, an economic sector, a region, or a racial group. In economic terms, the reasoning assumes there is always something to be gained—that is, underdeveloped regions add to the capital growth of more highly developed regions. It is doubtful that a psychic contribution to the national ideology is truly an exploitative gain (which appears to be the only significant gain in BIA policy), especially when there is so much complaint at the high cost of a colonialist structure. The British tradition of colonial analysis mentioned earlier tends to emphasize the variations in colonial structures and their postcolonial consequences. This may very well be the best possible approach in understanding the consequences of Indian policy.

### Urban Ghettoes and Internal Colonies

If among American minority situations the reservation best fits the "internal colonialism" model, the urban ghetto probably represents the worst fit. It is also the situation that generates the most political rhetoric. Some of the early work on internal colonialism associated almost every grievance against superordinate systems with "exploitation," which as part of the internal colonialist model should have a much more precise definition.[6]

The internal colonialist model is weak when applied to the urban minority ghetto in at least the following respects: (a) the ambiguity of territorial boundaries, (b) the ambiguity of definition of intermediary elite or bourgeois stratum as vehicle of exploitation, and (c) the ambiguity of what is meant by exploitation.

With respect to exploitation it is true that ghetto residents depend on consumer goods and there are yet other forms of economic dependency (cf. Tabb, 1970), but many analysts feel that the analogy is stretched much too far. The question of labor exploitation is particularly salient. Ironically, we may draw on Wilhelm (1971) to set the frame of the controversy in his argument that there has been a shift for blacks from "the economics of exploitation to the economics of uselessness." Many observers note that current racial minorities in the city face a very different situation from that of earlier European immigrants because the changed structure of large-scale corporate enterprise has reduced the importance of interworker competition in lowering wage levels. Corporate enterprise no longer "needs" a large labor pool. Piven and Cloward (1971) point out that technical and market management gains mean there is less incentive for large corporations to depress wages and inhibit unionization in the core industries. The incentive is rather to hire, train, retain, and promote stable workers (Gordon, 1972).

But large-scale corporate enterprise (the "core industries") are far from all employment sources in this nation. There is beginning to be a significant literature from the "dual labor market" school of labor economists. These economists argue that the labor market is stratified in a manner that matches the industrial structure of the United States. In addition to the core industries, there are "peripheral" industries. Piore, in particular, argues that core industries have the incentives and the ability to pay the price for a stable worker. But the very existence of a pool of workers motivated by lifetime job experience and age-graded expectations to have little hope of mobility permits a wide range of "secondary" or "peripheral" industries to flourish—or at least to survive. The size of the secondary labor market and its precise delineation are matters of controversy. Yet the endless and astonishing employability of Mexican nationals without significant work experience in urban settings indicates the significance of such a pool.

The economic function of this "useless" minority labor pool suggests that perhaps socialization for dropping out of the schools and the disarranged teenage job market are not just mechanisms for exclusion from the traditional ladders of social mobility but are socialization for yet another role which is significant in the economy. If we assume that *everyone* can be successfully qualified for employment in the core industries, what then about the labor needs of the restaurant and hotel industry, the garment industry, and the many other enterprises that rely on "unmotivated" as well as "unqualified" workers? Increasingly analysts of urban minority problems are beginning to realize that society does indeed have a dual labor market, that the urban minority ghettoes contribute disproportionately to the secondary labor market and are actually its principal source of workers. This idea is enormously important, yet for the moment we must be content to note that the identification of the beneficiaries of minority labor exploitation has not yet been integrated into the literature on internal colonialism.

## THE CONCEPT OF DUAL ECONOMY/SOCIETY

There is yet another concept borrowed from the literature on classic colonialism and this is the "dual economy." This analytic model was perhaps clearest in Africa where the "modern" sector of the economy coexists with a tribal sector. Economic distinctions and sociocultural distinctions are sharpened.[7] Berg (1966) notes that this distinction was made very early and was used in colonial policy. He notes particularly that the concept of the "target worker" linked to the "backward sloping" labor function (that the supply of labor is inversely related to the rate of wages) has been applied with great profit despite its dubious validity. This argument is twofold: (a) that raising wages will not increase the productivity of the tribal worker, but will just make him quit his job earlier because he can attain his target earlier; and (b) lowering wages will increase the labor supply because more people will be forced to enter the labor market in order to meet a family or subgroup target. There is an interesting echo of this formulation with regard to the "urban lower class" in Banfield's (1970) suggestions for eliminating regulations over school-leaving age and wages, and thereby regenerating a work-orientation in the urban lower class.

A useful conceptualization of the dual economy/dual society model for American minorities departs sharply from the internal colonial theorists. They tend to reject the "dual society" idea precisely because it draws attention from the interpenetrations between the two sectors. It especially draws attention from the dependency of the "modern" sector upon the "archaic" sector. The concept of a "dual society" serves as a valuable heuristic corrective to American analysts of urban minority life precisely because it does draw attention away from the historical institutional arrangements that work toward societal articulation and toward those arrangements which tend to promote dualism.

In the case of the urban ghetto the dual economy/dual society model has a major analytic advantage over the idea of internal colonialism. It is less necessary that there be a specific territory and population and a resident intermediary elite or bourgeois stratum (cf. Cervantes, 1976; Mindiola, 1975). It is in these latter respects that the internal colonialist model is most unsatisfactory and the analogy most strained when applied to the urban ghetto. The living situations of the urban ghettoes lack the structures and the boundaries of such places as Crystal City or the Pine Ridge reservation of the Sioux.

### Ecology of Urban Minority Communities

In order to define the populations that may be either "peripheral" or core, we will begin with the ecological level of analysis. Patterns of urbanization in the Third World will be most useful because they are frequently conceptualized in terms of the dual economy/society model. No matter where they may occur, such patterns tend to include the squatter settlement, the shantytown, or other economically, politically, and socially peripheral settlement, often supplementing a more conventional "inner city" slum. In the United States we are so accustomed to the "inner city" slum that we fail to see other kinds of ecological locations for minorities that encourage different kinds of social processes. As Ward (1971) indicates, the pattern of central settlement of urban immigrants was confined in time very largely to the late nineteenth century and the early twentieth century. Before that time, Irish and Germans settled in shantytowns as well as central business districts with employment opportunities. And after that time the ecological circumstances that created inner city settlement changed. During the past 50 years, most of the migration of racial minorities to the cities of the North, Middlewest, and West occurred. Thus the ecology of Mexican settlement in the Los Angeles area during the 1920s is more like the peripheral settlements of Third World cities than the inner city patterns of Chicago stamped on the sociological collective unconscious. The new Mexican immigrants in California built self-help housing, often with neither water nor sewer lines, on cheap land close to agricultural work or other employment, largely nonmanufacturing. The current heavy migration of Mexicans to the Lake Michigan industrial areas similarly appears to be settling much less in the inner city areas than on the urban fringe so the immigrants may be close to decentralized manufacturing and service industries.

The dual economy/dual society concept can greatly help us toward a typology of urban poverty minority communities in terms of their ecological origin and their degree of peripherality. It is plain to any student of society that Saginaw is not Detroit and the two Chicano communities in the two cities will vary greatly. Even within Los Angeles county we found that the historical origin of the *barrio* as a shacktown or as a portion of the inner city gave more insight into (to name one social structure) the structure and values of youth gangs than did (to name a favorite measure) their members' parental social or marital status.

### The Economic Base

Another concept that becomes sharper under conceptualization of the dual economy is what Bullock (1973) calls the "subeconomy." This "subeconomy" is the combination of hustling, traffic in illegal goods and services, barter and exhange in a *gemeinschaft* network as well as a criminal network. It is also found in peripheral settlements in Third World nations. This subeconomy is by no means confined to the peripheral sector of our society; in fact, it is probably more significant financially in nonpoor nonminority settings than with minorities. But in the urban minority ghetto it is as closely related to the peripherality of the ghetto labor as it is in Third World shacktowns. For both it serves more of a survival function and less of a lifestyle function than for the middleclass subeconomy. (To make a bizarre case: a middle-class family really does not need the illegal venison sausage but during the rapid inflation of two years ago the *barrio* Mexican family may have survived through the sale of stolen beef.) It is just as difficult for academic people to visualize and acknowledge a widespread subeconomy as it is for a Third World government to acknowledge the subeconomy of their urban shacktowns. The study by Bullock is one of the few which attempts to place youthful Chicano and black involvement in the subeconomy in the context of "normal" economic activities, most particularly job search in the secondary labor market. Yet the widespread failure of hundreds of millions of dollars of minority training programs remains unexplained, persumably on the grounds of maladministration and lack of motivation.

### The Motivational Structure and Social Mobility

Another issue that becomes more interesting in the dual economy framework is the fate of the concept of alienation, as viewed in its social psychological rather than Marxist tradition, especially when it is applied to values and the attendant behavior, rather than identity. Morse (1971) argues cogently that this concept as developed in American sociology assumes alienation *from* a particular form of advanced societal social relations, and in the particular case of Merton's anomie, from a gap between lower-class means and middle-class success goals in such a society. Morse suggests that it "assumes societies in which life chances depend on the efficacy of internal police mechanisms, euphemistically called 'personality organization.' (The hallmarks of good self-policing and therefore success, are the sociologist's familiar indices of education, occupation, and income.) Such a society is thought of as the sum of its members, *not as something 'external'* to large numbers of them."[8] Thus the fruitfulness of the alienation/anomie concept is open to question in the case of Latin American dualism precisely because of its assumption of successful latency institutions and the consequent internalization of success values among *all* members of the society. Piven and Cloward (1971) comment on the "loss of legitimacy" or minority trust in the system—a parallel, it appears, of the concept of alienation with all of its weaknesses.

The dual society/economy concept permits us to question the appropriateness of concepts emphasizing withdrawal from the system *if* an attachment to the system is problematic. Morse emphasizes that the problem in Latin American squatments is survival—not making good. He suggests that access to the means of power, or control over one's destiny, is a more useful basis for a typology than is the issue of anomie opposed to integration.

It is useful to remember that at present there are at least several million "illegal" Latin American residents of the United States, most of them living in urban areas. With them it is in most cases a travesty to talk about alienation, legitimacy, or any of the usual terms used to describe "urban lower class" subcultures in the Banfield sense. Samora (1971) is one of the few students to study the "illegal" Mexicans and he speaks, as an example, of the "half life" of the illegal alien, a man who is quite unable to share in any of the customary benefits of American citizenship and who, in fact, does not even exist because he is not noted by any public agency, not even the Bureau of the Census. It appears therefore that this presence in the United States is better conceptualized in terms of an impact in the already peripheral minority communities whose labor serves an economic function as the pool for peripheral industries. The communities are permeated by the ancillary subeconomy, in which survival and "making out" values prevail over mobility and positive values, in the conventional sense. The metabolism of the ghetto (a continuous process of moving and replacement of the movers) excludes those who "make good" from the community. It seems that the mobile residents leave relatively little trace. Most particularly, they leave no trace that might possibly ameliorate the de facto socialization to low expectations from the world of work. This is the motivational set of the secondary labor market pool.

In an earlier work (Grebler et al., 1970) . . . the importance to a community of its modal pattern of distribution of income by age [was noted]. In the middle-class community, age is positively correlated with income but in the poverty community there is no such correlation. All local institutions are affected by this fact. The departure from the urban ghetto of the occupationally mobile and the continued influx of the survival-oriented continued (and this is a critical point) over many generations. It reinforces many of the features that are so reminiscent of the Third World squatments.

But one major area in which the Third World squatment differs significantly is, of course, the pervasive effect of the "welfare state." Welfare institutions have been viewed in turn as a mechanism of internal colonialist control —and this was especially well done in the analysis offered by Piven and Cloward (1971) who emphasize the function of welfare money used to control urban disorders. This immediately brings up the issue of cost to the dominant society. If exploitative gains accrue to the private sector of the economy, it is the public sector that bears (and complains about) the cost. And further, the welfare agencies are seen as the natural habitat of the intermediary elites who include the tiny but variable amount of political leadership elected at the local level (cf. de la Garza et al., 1976). But when Cervantes (1976) comments on Almaguer's definition of the welfare system as an institutionalization of internal colonialism, he argues that the exclusion of minorities from the benefits of the welfare state is equally seen as a measure of oppression. "To be sure, a welfare bureaucracy creates dependence. But it is odd to consider welfarism colonialist activity when so much energy in the Chicano movement has been spent to make governmental agencies more responsive to the welfare of Chicanos."

## Welfare Agencies and the Dual Economy

Welfarism and politics are intertwined. There has been lively controversy, especially among minority political scientists, about the fruitfulness of the internal colonial model in identifying and interpreting various forms of political inclusion and exclusion. There is yet another and more subtle effect. Welfare institutions range from those which overtly control minority behavior to the more "ameliorative." In the dual economy/dual society model, the welfare institutions articulate the two sectors. Articulating institutions can also be socializing institutions, tending to work from the core sector to the peripheral sector. This is much discussed from opposing points of view; it is said, for example, that this is a socialization to dependency. It is also described (cf. Valle, 1974) as a ghetto infrastructure that permits the survival-oriented ghetto resident to utilize the ameliorative agencies in his repertory of survival techniques. It is unfortunate that most of this material is interpreted more often in the social-work framework of informal mechanisms that facilitate or inhibit service delivery rather than in the dual society conceptualization. In the latter, it would be possible to emphasize the full range of survival mechanisms and structures.

Recent research in Los Angeles on resource utilization by Chicano ex-convicts brings up a somewhat different set of considerations.[9] These are concerned with the depth and pervasiveness of socialization to norms of interaction with the formal organizations of the welfare state. Most of our sample and their families rely on such organizations for a very wide range of services: medical, mental health, financial. Most saw very little difference in the processes of interaction within these agencies and those concerned with overt police control—that is, the criminal justice system. The juvenile court system and the county hospital are, in effect, very much alike. There are long lines, long waits, there is very little information exchanged between the professional and his client, and the agency itself appears to be much more concerned with bureaucratic efficiency (a matter of the bureaucrats' personal convenience) than effective administration of justice or effective medical treatment. There are virtually no alternative organizational models.

This condition becomes extremely obvious when convict-staffed agencies are studied. These are part of the resources available to a Chicano ex-convict as part of his postprison survival repertory. There are two kinds. There are formal agencies which in Los Angeles were originally supported by funds from the OEO and model cities. And there are self-help groups, street groups that tend to replicate the convicts' identity-sustaining structures developed in prison. (In turn these structures replicate life-long patterns of informal organization.) The formal agencies are, of course, subject to the normal organizational controls through short and unpredictable funding and through formal evaluation by criteria that may have very little grounding in any understanding of the Mexican-American convict and his problems. In addition they are staffed by men and women whose intense and uniform socialization to welfare organizations seems to limit their organizational creativity very effectively. In fact, it often seems to limit even the consideration of options. In some cases these organizations reproduce prison-like methods of control over both "unruly" staff members and "unresponsive" clients.

Dos Santos (1969) comments about the effect of economic dependency in new nations. He notes that "dependence is not an 'external factor' . . . national economies limit their possibilities of expansion, or rather, they redefine them at the level of their concrete functioning." Following dos Santos it is almost surely true that welfarism plays a similar role in urban minority ghettoes in ways which have yet to be explored systematically. Third World squatments tend to be organized and therefore there is much written about the continuities of such organization with tribe, village, and other forms of social grouping. There is some parallel concern in the fairly thin literature on organization within the urban minority ghetto. But the dual society/dual economy model inside the welfare state also points to the need for consideration of the effective socialization to what are very real constraints on organizational development.

But when we turn to subjective aspects of the analysis of *barrio* residents the dual economy/dual society model begins to raise all of those familiar "identity" issues that plague academic and minority intellectuals—at least since the work of DuBois (1961) with his concept of "twoness" and the "Veil of Color." Cruse (1968) discussing blacks and de la Garza et al. (1976) on the subject of Chicanos remind us that large numbers of each group do, in fact, consider themselves as "hyphenated Americans." Recent census surveys among Mexican-Americans confirm the increasing Chicano self-selection of a hyphenated self-designation ("Mexican-American") in preference to "Chicano" that emphasizes a greater degree of separateness. One may take this as a permanent fact of minority life or as a transitory choice but it certainly serves to remind the Anglo observer of the diversity within "the" urban minority ghettoes.

## FINAL NOTE

In this paper it is only suggested that some consideration be given to diversity. With Chicanos particularly, the author's own research has shown the serious inadequacy of the conventional models. It is unfortunate that the most theoretically complete and popular "alternative" conceptualization of "internal colonialism" does not help very much. But the related model of the "dual economy" considers both the literature on Third World urban squatments and the extreme sectionization and segmentation of modern urban minority communities. It is therefore proving to be a rich source of interpretive insight into the growth of Thomas Jefferson's nightmare—an urban proletariat, and a racial proletariat, at that.

## NOTES

1   The first two points are reasonably acceptable to most social scientists. I am suggesting that we add the impact of the large-scale immigration from Latin America and

that we begin to think about American urban structures in terms of the in-migrants who served as a labor force in a primarily rural economy still permeated by the remnants of structures used to "open up" a new area. These plantations, factory farms, and extractive industries (lumber, mining) no longer need their labor pools.

2  Petras (1975) argues that these elites vary in their strategy toward foreign dominance and toward their own people.

3  Cf. Spicer, 1961. This research group identified four critical factors: (1) the nature of Indian resources, (2) the extent of BIA interference and paralysis of local initiative, (3) demographic characteristics of the tribe, and (4) the special history and religious and social organization of the tribe.

4  It may be argued that the end goal of the federal Indian policies is an echo of the detribalization efforts of the late nineteenth century. This goal was to bring the reservation Indian into the unskilled labor pool of the cities. This might appear to be true of contemporary policy if one takes at face value the Indian Relocation Service Program of the BIA, established in 1952, just two years before the termination policy. This began as an economy move (Neils, 1971) but its history is one of bureaucratic overdevelopment (an almost fivefold increase in cost per client between 1955 and 1970), inadequate performance (no training of migrants began until six years after program started), and trivial accomplishment. Neils estimates that three-quarters of the migrants from reservation to city leave the reservation without government assistance of any kind.

5  The events in Crystal City and Zavala county are illuminated and made coherent in terms of "internal colonialism." "Liberation," in terms of a political change from Anglo to Chicano control, was followed by a turnover in the intermediary elites from the 1960s to the present, and consequent changes in strategies of development (cf. Shockley, 1974). From the Chicano point of view, the current crisis in Zavala county is the dilemma posed for the Chicano political leaders by continued economic dependence although they hold almost complete political control. At the present various strategies for gaining control over the major resources (land) are being developed (Mindiola, 1975).

6  The point is raised by Walton (1975) and most explicitly by Cervantes (1976) who writes, "Why the legacy of this important colonial experience which today manifests itself in the racism and oppression many Chicanos have learned to expect, and in the proletarianization of Chicano workers, should be called 'internal colonialism' is unclear to me."

7  Even for Africa the distinction is most useful in analytical terms because tribal economies are affected by the market economy (Berg, 1966).

8  Parentheses and emphases added.

9  Grants from NIDA (1-R01-DA0–1053–01) and NSF (ERP 14–15580) funded this research. The funding sources, of course, bear no responsibility for statements in this paper.

# REFERENCES

*Almaguer, Tomas*
1974  "Historical notes on Chicano oppression." Aztlan 5 (Spring/Fall): 27–56.
*Amin, Samir*
1974  Accumulation on a World Scale: A Critique of the Theory of Underdevelopment. New York: Monthly Review.

*Banfield, Edward C.*
1970    The Unheavenly City. Boston: Little, Brown.
*Berg, E. J.*
1966    "Backward sloping labor supply functions in dual economies—the Africa case," in Immanuel Wallerstein (ed.), Social Change: The Colonial Situation. New York: John Wiley.
*Blauner, Robert*
1972    Racial Oppression in America. New York: Harper & Row.
*Blumer, Herbert*
1954    "What is wrong with social theory?" Amer. Soc. Rev. 19 (February): 3–10.
*Bullock, Paul*
1973    Aspiration vs. Opportunity: "Careers" in the Inner City. Ann Arbor: Institute of Labor and Industrial Relations of the University of Michigan and Wayne State University.
*Carmichael, Stokely and Charles Hamilton*
1967    Black Power. New York: Vintage.
*Cervantes, Frederick H.*
1976    "Chicano politics as internal colonialism and American pluralism: a conceptual paradox." Presented at the meeting of the International Studies Association, March.
*Clark, Kenneth*
1967    Dark Ghetto. New York: Harper & Row.
*Cleaver, Eldridge*
1968    Soul on Ice. New York: Dell, Delta.
*Cruse, Harold*
1968    Rebellion or Revolution. New York: William Morrow.
*Davis, Allison, Gardner, Burleigh B., and Mary R. Gardner*
1941    Deep South. Chicago: Univ. of Chicago Press.
*de la Garza, Rudolph O., Charles Cottrell, and George Korbel*
1976    "Internal colonialism and Chicanos: a reconceptualization." Presented at the meeting of International Studies Association, March.
*Dollard, John*
1957    Caste and Class in a Southern Town. Garden City, N.Y.: Doubleday.
*dos Santos, Theotonio*
1969    "La crise de la théorie du développement et les relations de dépendence en Amerique Latine." L'Homme et la Société 12. [Cited in Walton, 1975.]
*Du Bois, W. E. B.*
1961    The Souls of Black Folk. Greenwich, Conn.: Fawcett.
*Emmanuel, Arghiri*
1972    Unequal Exchange: A Study of the Imperialism of Free Trade. New York: Monthly Review.
*Fanon, Frantz*
1968    The Wretched of the Earth. New York: Grove.
*Furnivall, J. S.*
1948    Colonial Policy and Practice. Cambridge: Cambridge Univ. Press.
*Gonzolez-Casanova, Pablo*
1969    "Internal colonialism and national development," in Irving L. Horowitz et al. (ed.), Latin American Radicalism. New York: Random House.
*Gordon, David M.*
1972    Theories of Poverty and Underemployment. Lexington, Mass: Heath.
*Grebler, Leo, Joan Moore, Ralph Guzman, et al.*
1970    The Mexican American People. New York: Free Press.
*Kuper, Leo, and M. G. Smith*
1959    Pluralism in Africa. Berkeley and Los Angeles: Univ. of California Press.

*Lipset, S. M.*
1963   The First New Nation: The United States in Historical and Comparative Perspective. New York: Basic Books.

*Memmi, Albert*
1967   The Colonizer and the Colonized. Boston: Beacon.

*Mindiola, Tatcho*
1975   "Marxism and the Chicano movement." Presented at the meeting of the Chicano Social Science Association, March.

*Morse, Richard*
1971   "Trends and issues in urban research." Latin American Research Rev. 6: 3–52.

*Neils, Elaine M.*
1971   Reservation to City. Univ. of Chicago: Department of Geography, Research Paper No. 131.

*Nkrumah, Kwame*
1966   Neo-Colonialism. New York: International Publishers.

*Petras, James F.*
1975   "Sociology of development or sociology of exploitation?" Presented at the meeting of the American Sociological Association, August.

*Piven, Frances F. and Richard A. Cloward*
1971   Regulating the Poor. New York: Pantheon.

*Record, Wilson*
1973   "Can sociology and black studies find a common ground?" Presented at Black Cultural Forum, Portland, Oregon.

*Samora, Julian*
1971   Los Mojados: The Wetback Story. Notre Dame: Univ. of Notre Dame Press.

*Shockley, John*
1974   Chicano Revolt in a Texas Town. Notre Dame: Univ. of Notre Dame Press.

*Spicer, Edward H.*
1969   A Short History of the Indians of the United States. New York: Van Nostrand Reinhold.
1962   Cycles of Conquest. Tucson: Univ. of Arizona Press.
1961   Perspectives in Indian Culture Change. Chicago: Univ. of Chicago Press.

*Stavenhagen, Rudolfo*
1968   "Seven falacies about Latin America," in James Petras and Maurice Zeitlin (eds.), Latin America: Reform or Revolution? New York: Fawcett.

*Tabb, William*
1970   The Political Economy of the Black Ghetto. New York: Norton.

*Thomas, Robert K.*
1966–1967   "Colonialism: classic and internal." New Univ. Thought 4 (Winter): 36–44.

*Valle, Juan Ramon*
1974   "Armistad-compadrazgo as an indigenous webwork compared to the urban mental health network." Ph.D. dissertation, University of Southern California.

*Wallerstein, Immanuel*
1966   Social Change: The Colonial Situation. New York: John Wiley.

*Walton, John*
1975   "Internal colonialism: problems of definition and measurement," in Wayne A Cornelius and Felicity Trueblood (eds.), Latin American Urban Research, Vol. 5. Beverly Hills: Sage.

*Ward, David*
1971   Cities and Immigrants: A Geography of Change in Nineteenth Century America. New York: Oxford Univ. Press.

*Wilhelm, Sidney*
1971   Who Needs the Negro? New York: Anchor.

# Race Relations in Canada

## D. H. Clairmont

## F. C. Wien

*Dalhousie University*

On a numerical basis, racial minorities have not been a significant portion of the Canadian population since the early years of European settlement. It is not surprising, therefore, that Canadian writings and public concern on the subject of race have been dominated by attention to what we would call ethnic relations (i.e., relations among cultural sub-groups within a common racial category—particularly French-English relations and European immigration). The Canadian mosaic image has largely been constructed out of this reality; in much of the literature, racial groups are included in the picture primarily to illustrate the vertical nature of the mosaic.

In the United States, the reverse appears to be the case. A large oppressed racial minority has dominated public and academic attention and from time to time there are protests by or on behalf of the forgotten ethnics (Novak, 1972). Given this situation and the pervasive influence of American events in Canada, it is understandable that the way in which race relations are perceived in Canada and, to some extent, actual behaviour, are significantly affected by American patterns.

It is worthwhile for a number of reasons to look specifically at race relations in Canada. Because of demographic and other changes, the subject is of

*Source:* D. H. Clairmont and F. C. Wien, "Race Relations in Canada," Sociological Focus 9, 2 (April 1976): 185–97. Copyright © 1976 by the North Central Sociological Association. Reprinted by permission of the Association, the editors of Sociological Focus, and the authors.

increasing importance in the country while at the same time the significance of some ethnic differences appears to be declining. In addition, racial minorities have long roots in Canada. Their relation with the larger society has been marked by subordination, control, and, in some instances, by sustained efforts at assimilation. Their history, therefore, presents a different side to the popular image of the mosaic. There are also sufficient differences with the American experiences that an attempt to sort out the unique features of the Canadian situation is warranted.

## AMERICAN INFLUENCES

There appear to be at least three distinct American sociological approaches to race relations, each of which has been applied in Canada: evolutionary universalism, internal colonialism, and descriptive pluralism. The perspective identified as evolutionary universalism essentially posits that American society is proceeding by an evolutionary route to resolve its racial antagonisms in that citizenship is being expanded and ascription and particularism are giving way to achievement and universalism as variables patterning the bulk of social relationships (Parsons, 1971). From this vantage point, cultural and structural supports for racial antagonism and communal boundaries, while perhaps subject to some erratic shifts, will progressively diminish. This perspective is the chief basis for the celebration of the "melting pot" ideology and also provides the underpinning for the liberal social problems approach that is so common in American (and Canadian) writings on race relations. The central thrust of this literature has been on the gap between standards and actuality in socioeconomic status, and on individual prejudice and discrimination as explanatory variables. Emphasizing consensus and desiring integration, these social scientists have tended to see racial groups as aggregations rather than as organic entities; they have underestimated the staying-power of racial categorization as a basis for organization and mobilization, and have exhibited little awareness of alternative directions which diverse racial groups might pursue. The particular theoretical perspective with which evolutionary universalism is most closely associated is structural functionalism.

In Canada, this approach has been particularly common in studies of the small, scattered black population (Potter, 1961; Henry, 1975). Although the associated melting-pot ideology has not been dominant in Canada (for reasons to be discussed below), it has nevertheless been quite pervasive in white attitudes towards certain racial minorities and in policies of assimilation and relocation directed at the native Indian, Inuit and black populations (Clairmont and Magill, 1974; Chamberlin, 1975).

The internal colonialism approach to race relations has deep historical roots in American thinking, but in this century it has become widespread only in the past decade. Emphasizing the economic system and racial antagonism, it sees race relations as complicating the inevitable class struggle of capitalism, with blacks and Indians bearing a disproportionate share of the exploitative burden that keeps the system going. In this perspective race relations assume considerable importance since the oppressed non-whites, concentrated in the urban ghetto and patrolled by an occupying army of police, are often identified as the core of the vanguard who will force widespread qualitative societal change (Blauner, 1972). There is also the premise that capitalism is the principal barrier to racial harmony and equality. Marxist and neo-marxist theory is most often associated with the internal colonialism perspective. In the Canadian context, the expansion of white European settlers across North America at the expense of the aboriginal population, plus the establishment of reserves and the rigid control of the native population through the Indian Act by the federal government, has made the internal colonialism perspective the dominant one in describing Indian-white relations (Carstens, 1971; Patterson, 1972; Frideres, 1975). Some native spokesmen have, however, resisted complete identification with this model by articulating the differences between the Third World and the aboriginal or Fourth World (Manuel and Posluns, 1974). The metropolitan-hinterland variation of the internal colonialism model is also frequently seen in Canadian writings (Cohen, 1970; Davis, 1971).

Recently a third general perspective, descriptive pluralism, has emerged among American students of race relations. It has developed largely in response to the resurgence of sub-group loyalties and identification and the advocacy, especially by native Indians and blacks, of collective rights and group autonomy. Numerous social scientists have written to challenge the melting-pot model in terms of both empirical support and social policy, and they have stressed the importance of intermediate, ascriptive groupings between the level of the family and mass society (Fein, 1970; Novak, 1972; Greeley, 1973).

Although there is no particular theoretical system which unifies the descriptive studies, the theoretical and comparative work of scholars such as van den Berghe (1967) and Schermerhorn (1970) is compatible with this approach. The descriptive pluralism framework is the most congruent with past and present Canadian social science studies of race relations. In fact, until the recent popularity of this approach in the United States, it was a distinguishing characteristic of Canadian studies which usually featured descriptions of the settlement patterns and communal organization of racial minorities (Clark, 1974).

Turning to interaction between racial minorities across the border, the close ties of blacks and Native peoples are particularly striking. Until the significant West Indian immigration of the past fifteen years, virtually all blacks in Canada had come here from the United States. Loyalist blacks, some free, some slave, came to Nova Scotia during the American revolution. Refugee blacks, all free, settled in Nova Scotia as a consequence of the War of 1812 while many others, escaping the oppression of slavery via the "Underground Railroad," settled in southern Ontario and the West during the pre-Emancipation nineteenth century. The bulk of the latter returned to the U.S. after the Civil War, however, and many Nova Scotia blacks, like white Maritimers, emigrated to the New England states in the last half of the nineteenth century and first years of the twentieth (Winks, 1971). The small Canadian black community has drawn heavily upon the larger American Black population for its heroes (e.g., Martin Luther King), policies (e.g., affirmative action), organizational models (e.g., Nova Scotia Association for the Advancement of Coloured People) and even its leaders (e.g., recruitment of Baptist pastors in the United States) (Clairmont and Magill, 1970).

With respect to the aboriginal population, the border between Canada and the United States was established in relatively recent times and in some instances through the middle of Indian cultural groupings. Consequently the border has much less meaning for native people, either symbolically and/or legally through the provisions of the Jay Treaty; in fact there is extensive mobility among Indians between the two countries. Organizations such as the American Indian Movement have chapters in Canada, and at a recent conference in Canada the World Council of Indigenous Peoples was established.[1]

The Canadian population generally has been fascinated with and well informed about American developments in race relations. The initial response of many young Canadians to the U.S. civil rights movement of the early 1960s was to volunteer for projects in the U.S. South, and some support organizations such as SNCC chapters were established at Canadian universities for fundraising purposes. The Ku Klux Klan also moved across the border in certain periods, becoming established in Ontario and Alberta; and American immigrants to Canada, ranging from Loyalists with their slaves to war resisters and liberal professors, have brought their perspectives on race relations to this country. Canadians have often copied U.S. policy initiatives, sometimes profiting from the trial run experienced in the U.S., but also adopting policies at the point when, with good reason, they were falling out of favour south of the border, as in the case of the residential boarding school concept for "educating" native people and the disastrous U.S. Indian termination policy of the 1950s.

The above is not to suggest that America is responsible for the bigotry and racial discrimination that occurs in Canada; in some respects the American record in race relations has been much better than the Canadian. It does suggest, however, that the race situation in the United States is an important contextual variable for developments in Canada and for Canadian interpretation of these developments and that this will continue to be so. At the same time, however, there have historically been significant differences in the nature of race relations between the two countries and in the dominant ideology that characterizes them. Recently there has also been a substantial increase in non-white immigration to Canada via the Commonwealth connection, for which American precedents are not entirely appropriate.

## THE CANADIAN WAY

In contrast to the United States, Canada has often been characterized as a mosaic rather than a melting-pot in terms of race and ethnic relations. The implication is that Canada is composed of a multiplicity of collectivities or sub-groups, each with its own cultural, racial, or historical identity, who co-exist in an atmosphere of mutual toleration within a liberal democratic form of political economy. Such a system, sometimes labelled organic liberalism, stands in contrast to the conception of a new cultural and biological blend being created in America "in which the stocks and folkways of Europe, figuratively speaking, were indiscriminately mixed in the political pot of the emerging nation and fused by the fires of American influence and interaction into a distinctly new type" (Gordon, 1961).

Much scholarly effort has been expended concerning both the empirical and normative supports of the so-called Canadian Way. It is obviously an ideal construct which has been of some value in the attempt to grasp the uniqueness of Canadian reality and it remains an important consideration in a Canada still being shaped by immigration. In examining the roots of Canadian pluralism, most scholars point to the founding of Canada by the English and French and the basic conception and constitutionally enshrined principle of duality. This historical situation is congruent with an organic liberalism model and has been seen as the context within which other ethnic and even racial groups can establish claims and maintain some autonomy. While native people ironically have not been included among the charter groups, their special status has been recognized in treaties, the British North America Act, and subsequent legislation.

Patterns of immigration and settlement have also contributed to the mosaic. European immigrants, for example, came in much larger numbers in relation to the domestic population in certain decades such as in the early 1900s than was the case in the U.S. and settled in self-contained communities. Non-white minorities have also either chosen or been restricted to their own communities—rural and isolated in the case of blacks and Indians, urban and ghettoized in the case of the Chinese.

Another set of factors often presumed to be at the root of Canada's essential difference regarding race and ethnic relations is the conservative philosophy of the Loyalists fleeing the American revolution and the particular brand of liberalism brought by immigrants to Canada from Europe after the mid-nineteenth century. Some writers also point to the threat of American expansion into Canadian territory as the West was being settled as leading to a development pattern that was more orderly and controlled by the central government than was the case on the American frontier, and consequently less destructive of native and immigrant communities (Clark, 1968; Chamberlin, 1975). In comparison with the American treatment of the Indian population, for example, reserves in Canada were set up close to traditional hunting grounds rather than relocating native communities further west; the boundaries of reserves have not been redefined or violated as much, and both Canadian treaties and Indian policy via the Indian Act have had a more stable, more legally enshrined character (Lurie, 1968).

In a structural sense, then, considering the identifiable communities and the distinctive cultures or life styles of racial minorities, it can be argued that they contribute to the image of a mosaic in Canada. In other respects, particularly in their relationship with the larger society, the experience of the racial minorities parts company with that of the ethnic groups. Porter (1965) and Hughes and Kallen (1974), among others, have documented the vertical nature of the mosaic, with white Anglo-Saxons at the top of the socio-economic pecking order, and the non-white groups at the bottom. The relationship with the larger society is better characterized by terms such as dependence, control, and domination-subordination than it is by the rhetoric associated with equal participation in the mosaic. Segregated black schools; the relocation of the Japanese on the West Coast during World War II; the detailed controls spelled out in the Indian Act including, in the past, limitations on the right to vote, to organize, and to carry out traditional cultural ceremonies; the racial limitations included in a series of Immigration Acts of which the Chinese Immigration Act of 1923 is but one example[2]—these are instances of the kind of relation that has existed between the racial minorities and the dominant white society. Sustained attempts at cultural assimilation have in particular been directed at the Indian and Inuit population through the efforts of missionaries to "civilize" the natives and by secular educational authorities in more recent times (Cardinal, 1969; Hobart and Brant, 1969; Manuel and Posluns, 1974).

Pierre van den Berghe (1967) has used the term *"Herrenvolk* Democracies" to describe the situation in the United States and South Africa where liberal democracy has existed only for the white population. Similarly in Canada, while the institutionalization of race relations is significantly less, non-whites have more often been the unwilling subjects of policies formulated and administered by the white population than active participants in shaping their own future (Hughes and Kallen, 1974; Thompson, 1974). Moreover, the Canadian Way, while legitimizing ethnic differences and emphasizing liberal democratic means of interest resolution, also has a practical corollary: a high degree of sensitivity among Canadians to the size and concentration of ascriptive groupings and to the expectations of differential advantage. In other words, it was not left to the mosaic ideology alone to guarantee collective rights effectively, as exemplified by English manipulation of immigration policy to limit French immigrants in the hundred years after the conquest, and by the French Canadian "strategy" of *"la revanche des berceaux."* Immigration policy and the size of the ascriptive groupings have always been contentious issues in Canada. This fact, when reinforced by racist attitudes and ideologies, has caused Canadians to be especially sensitive to non-white demographics and to take appropriate action to keep their numbers small and ensure that they pose no threat (e.g., by blocking Chinese immigration and by discouraging blacks from settling in the West). Despite an apparent decline of racist stereotypes and ideologies, it is not surprising that fear and distrust would begin to grow as this immigrant-dependent society began to find that in recent years non-whites have made up an increasing proportion of total immigration and many more are eager to come.

## RECENT TRENDS IN RACE RELATIONS

Since the Second World War, and particularly in the 1960s, substantial changes in the significance and nature of race relations have taken place in Canada. In particular, race relations have become much more important than they have traditionally been in the society, due to such factors as the receding importance of ethnic differences among the English-speaking white population; changes in the number, distribution, and composition of the racial minorities; and the increasing organization and extension of citizenship rights among the latter.

While the English-French duality and problems in ethnic relations remain very important, there is considerable evidence that ethnic differences among the English-speaking European population are becoming less significant, the multiculturalism policy notwithstanding. Reitz (1974) has shown, for example, the high rates of language loss among Germans, Poles, Ukrainians, and Italians in urban areas across Canada, and it is expected that cultural and structural assimilation will continue among groups such as these, particularly when sources of renewal are diminished by the changing composition of immigrants to Canada (Breton, 1968). Noting this trend, some social scientists argue that the celebration of multiculturalism serves only to enhance the status of "ethnic" leaders and keeps the English-speaking Canadian population from mobilizing itself adequately to deal with the important problems of American domination and social justice (Horowitz, 1972).

Demographic changes have also elevated the relative importance of race relations. Prior to the immigration of the post–World War II period, blacks constituted about 0.3% of the Canadian population and were concentrated chiefly in Nova Scotia, Montreal, and Southwestern Ontario. The Inuit, strung out along the Arctic coast, accounted for approximately 0.1%, while estimates of the native Indian population (excluding non-status Indians and métis) are slightly higher than 1%. The Asian population, chiefly Chinese and Japanese, were concentrated in the urban areas of Vancouver, Toronto, and Montreal and contributed about 0.5%. In total, the non-white population prior to the war was about 2% of the Canadian population. The Asian group was declining—virtually all were the products of immigration between 1870 and the early 1920s and, with the government-imposed immigration restrictions of the 1920s, the disproportionately male population was not reproducing itself (Kalbach and McVey, 1971). The black population was growing but not significantly since the small trickle of immigrants from the United States and the West Indies was offset by a probably larger movement to the United States. Recently, the native Indian and Inuit population has been increasing dramatically. Almost faced with extinction as a result of the European invasion, these groups had recovered their pre-European population by the end of World War II, and they have been the fastest-growing groups in Canada in the last two decades (Kalbach and McVey, 1971). In 1968, the rate of natural increase of Indians peaked at 3.4%, declining in 1970 to 2.9%, to be compared with a 1.5% rate of increase in the Canadian population (Frideres, 1974).

Post–World War II immigration has boosted the percentage of non-whites in Canada, although their numbers are still small.[3] About 160,000 blacks, overwhelmingly from the West Indies, have immigrated to Canada since 1946, according to government statistics. This figure is probably a significant understatement; newspaper accounts indicate that in recent years there has been a flourishing business in "illegals" who are exploited in low-wage industries. It appears that in 1976 there may be about a quarter of a million blacks in Canada, or about 1% of the total population. Asian immigration during the same period has been about 290,000 and the Asian sub-group now accounts for approximately 2% of Canada's population. Of these, 120,000 immigrants have been from China, making them the largest Asian sub-group. Japanese immigration totalled about 10,000, while those identified with the Indian sub-continent have been counted at 125,000 persons. As a result of the post–World War II immigration and the large natural increase among Native peoples, the proportion of non-whites has more than doubled and is now approximately 5% of the Canadian population. The addition of the métis and non-status Indian population would further increase that proportion by one or more percentage points, depending on the criteria and population estimates used.

The significant non-white immigration in recent decades reflects a liberalization of Canadian immigration policy, with the major change occurring in 1962.[4] While the degree of opening up is controversial—it is one thing to have a non-discriminatory policy and quite another to facilitate, in an equitable manner, immigration among all foreigners—there is no doubt that it has led to sharp increases in the number of non-white immigrants arriving in Canada from Commonwealth countries. The estimated proportion of blacks and Asians to total immigration has risen from 2% in 1946–61 to approximately 37% in 1973 and 1974 (Richmond, 1975). Overall, the non-white proportion of total post-war immigration has been slightly better than 15%. Most of these new immigrants have settled in the major metropolitan areas, with blacks chiefly in the Toronto area and Asians in Vancouver and Toronto. The urbanization of the long-standing racial minorities has also proceeded apace; for example, in 1961, 87% of Canadian Indians lived in rural areas, whereas in 1971 the figure had dropped to 69.3% (Statistics Canada, 1974). Again, the larger urban areas have drawn the bulk of the urban migrants.

The greater visibility of non-whites and tensions in race relations are also related to the changing composition of post-war immigrants, as well as their numbers. In contrast with previous immigrants, they are much more urbanized, more highly educated, better placed occupationally, and more actively involved in the host society. This trend was evident even before the 1962 Immigration Act which based selection on a points system emphasizing educational and occupational qualifications. For example, among foreign-born Asiatics, 14.3% of the post-war immigrants had "some university or degree" compared with only 2.2% of the pre-war Asiatic immigrants (Kalbach and McVey, 1971). In sharp contrast to the 1931 data, by 1961 almost 50% of the Asians in the labour force were classified as managerial, professional and technical, and craftsmen and production workers (Vallee, 1975). A 1974 study in Toronto dealing with an indicative though not representative sample of black adults (largely immigrant) revealed that 60% had achieved at least "grade 13 or community college" and that about one-third were in the occupational categories professional, managerial, and technical, and another 15% were in skilled crafts. Only 2% were in unskilled labour and 11% in service-recreation (Head, 1975). Another study reveals that the total family income of immigrants from the West Indies in 1972 surpassed that of immigrants from Greece and Italy, although it is still well below the figures for the British, French, Americans, and other groups (Manpower and Immigration, 1974).

While these and other figures reveal the improved educational and occupational levels of non-white post-war immigrants, the social costs and disadvantages of being non-white still persist. There is evidence of economic exploitation of non-white immigrants, especially the illegals; they still suffer significantly from employment and other forms of discrimination (Head, 1975). In relation to their position back home, many non-white immigrants have probably experienced a drop in occupational status.

Social and economic disadvantage is particularly acute for the long-standing racial minorities in Canada, particularly blacks and Native people (Institute of Public Affairs, 1969; Adams et al., 1971). The most promising developments in recent years have been the institutionalization of legal rights and citizenship privileges of non-whites and the development of new organizations to protect and enhance their interests and to effect greater correspondence between their official citizenship and their everyday treatment by the majority. Beginning in the mid-1940s, human rights legislation and commissions were established in most Canadian provinces and at the federal level. Canadian Indians have organizations in each of the provinces, and at the national level the National Indian Brotherhood and the Native Council of Canada represent status and non-status/métis concerns respectively. The Inuit Tapirisat was established in 1971. Among Nova Scotia blacks, the N.S.A.A.C.P. was formed in 1945 and the Black United Front in 1969; blacks throughout Canada have formed a National Black Coalition. Such organizations, along with government departments, have spawned a host of social and cultural programmes. There have also been developments linking various non-white groupings. This is particularly the case among Native Indians and Inuit who have come together in organizations such as the Committee for Original Peoples' Entitlement and the Federation of Natives North of Sixty. Non-whites also often find themselves grouped together with respect to governmental institutions (e.g., human rights commissions) and policy issues (e.g., multiculturalism, immigration). Not much is known about their attitudes and behaviours vis-à-vis one another. The sparse data suggest that a positive empathy exists (Clairmont, 1963; Head, 1975). These organizational developments also reflect the "shrinkage" of society due to mass media, urbanization, transportation developments, the expansion of government, and the thirst for resources to exploit. Native-born blacks living on the outskirts of cities have increasingly found their land and homes threatened by urban developments. Native people, whether in the Arctic, northern Manitoba, or James Bay, find their life-styles and land rights threatened by hydro-electric, oil, and gas explorations.

To some degree, the white reaction to these organizational and demographic changes outlined above has been one of fear and hostility. Native people have experienced substantial racial antipathy in communities such as Kenora (Stymeist, 1975), Regina, Inuvik, and Frobisher Bay, and the pressing of aboriginal title and land claims promises to lead to more conflict in most areas of the country. In the case of non-white immigrants who have migrated heavily to urban areas such as Toronto and Vancouver, numerous racial incidents have occurred. In Vancouver, for example, members of the Indo-Pakistani community talk of establishing vigilante groups to prevent harassment. They are most likely to be singled out by Canadians as non-desirable immigrants (Richmond, 1975) and are the subject of vicious widely circulating "paky jokes." In Toronto the blantantly white racist Western Guard movement promotes its anti-immigrant, save-Western-civilization campaign (Head, 1975). Frideres (1975) compares survey data collected in Calgary in 1965 and 1975, and finds a lesser degree of acceptance of non-white immigrants by white respondents. Race relations have, in short, become a significant issue in Canadian society.

## IMPLICATIONS FOR POLICY AND THEORY

Since World War II and particularly since the early 1960s some progress has been made—racial minorities are more active and, in some respects, more equal participants in the Canadian mosaic. There are also indications that they find the mosaic concept quite attractive insofar as they desire to retain the integrity of their cultures and communities. A recent study of the Chinese has revealed that the majority of Chinese post-war immigrants live in the traditionally Chinese areas and over 90% wish to retain their language and thus maintain their cultural heritage (Lai, 1971). Black immigrants are seeking to define their place in the Canadian mosaic and those with longer roots in the society are attempting to revitalize their culture. Similar attempts at cultural revitalization are evident among native people along with the continuing struggle to preserve and develop the reserve communities. It is claimed that it is not only a matter of self-protection and enhancement of interest groups but also a question of pride in their own heritage and confidence that Canada will be richer if the diverse groups are allowed to maintain and develop their own identity.

This raises the question, then, whether a harmonious multi-racial society can be created in a country that has both a tradition of racism and an ideology potentially congruent with racial and cultural diversity. Are there some strategies that might be employed to achieve such a goal? This is not idle speculation; Canada has a falling birth rate, as do most of the countries from which it has historically drawn immigrants. Recently the Economic Council of Canada has noted that if Canada is to attain in the near future the kind of economic growth characteristic of the post-war era, it will have to maintain—if not increase—current immigration levels and that, under the present universalistic immigration policy, would imply more non-whites.

The government's response to these challenges has not been clearly articulated. With respect to immigration, it appears that at least the level, if not the composition, of immigration will be cutback in response, in part at least, to the tensions we have noted above. At the same time the priorities of the multiculturalism policy are being changed to give greater attention to the socio-economic problems of the "visible minorities." This rearrangement suggests that the race question does not quite fit into the mosaic concept as it has been traditionally understood and that the ethnic mosaic as perceived by the politicians may be passé, less in many respects resembles the American termination policy of the 1950s. It recommended that on another front, the Department of Indian Affairs in 1969 proclaimed a new Indian policy that in many respects resembles the American termination policy of the 1950s. It recommended that other government departments and the provincial governments take increasing responsibility for Indian affairs as part of a gradual process of eliminating the special status and protected lands of Indian people. In the face of vociferous protest by native organizations, the Government publicly withdrew its policy, but there is considerable evidence that in practice it is being implemented, perhaps over a longer time period than originally envisaged. An economic development plan is to facilitate the transition. Although theoretically the extensive control exercised by the Department of Indian Affairs will be eliminated, native spokesmen fear that the reserve communities will be lost, as they were for some tribes in the U.S., and that the historical obligations incurred by the Europeans will be unilaterally dismissed. They argue for the recognition of and compensation for aboriginal title and land claims which will provide the basis for economic development based around the reserve communities.

The trend of government policy, then, appears to be in the direction of continuing efforts to reduce the vertical nature of the mosaic for non-whites, but in doing so it also appears to be moving away from the realization of a multiracial and multicultural organic liberalism. Cynics might well contend that the government is responding to white fears and distrust concerning the growing number of non-whites while simultaneously attempting to salvage its official morality by treating the small proportion of non-whites in the country more equitably. It could also be argued that current policy proposals might produce greater acceptance of non-whites by the majority and thus lay the basis for their more harmonious immigration in the future.

The intellectual community has also not fully come to grips with the potential inherent in the situation. There does not appear to be a profound appreciation for the cultural contribution of non-white groups, for example, nor a willingness to see them develop their own institutions to any significant degree (Wien et al., 1976). Nor have Canadian social scientists developed adequate theoretical models to interpret race relations in modern societies such as Canada. None of the three theoretical approaches referred to earlier are rich enough in concepts and propositions to enable us to account for and attempt to predict race relations in Canada. Evolutionary universalism has merit at the individual level but it does not get at the extra-individual reality—the continuing significance of collectivities based on ascriptive criteria and the fact that people remain extremely sensitive regarding developments at that level while behaving more universalistically at the individual level. The internal colonialism approach applies less as the races approximate each other more in terms of income and occupation and as their interaction becomes more diversified. Descriptive pluralism is useful insofar as it suggests the importance of intermediate groupings between the individual family and the state and the insufficiency of other bases of social identification, such as occupation. The theoretical elaboration of these insights, connecting them with the structural aspects of society and their historical development, has not been achieved, however.

The continuing significance of communal boundaries based on race under conditions of increasing modernization and in the face of (hopefully) receding racist ideology and stereotyping poses a theoretical enigma to students of race relations. To some extent the Canadian Way model described earlier provides some insights. Insofar as its organic liberalism component is concerned, it has stressed the political and social significance of corporate affiliation beyond the family and apart from the state. This resonates well with some current conceptions of modern North American society which see society structured such that one's relative advantage is tied to one's corporate attachments (e.g., companies, unions, etc.). Corporate attachments provide that "extra edge" which is so important to relative advantage in a society where there is an increasingly high level of education, expanding bureaucracy, a high degree of organization, and an apparent inability to provide all with satisfactory employment. Affiliation with racial groups may be seen in this context of competitive advantage, providing a basis for mobilization and advancement on the one hand or denigration and limitation on the other. Racial ascription is clearly a relevant variable, given the relative ease with which one can assign or be assigned to racial collectivities and the empirical evidence of racial strife and inequality throughout the world.

If the above is indicative then a theory of race relations in modern western societies such as Canada must be *holistic,* connecting structural aspects of society with the way interest groups are organized bureaucratically and symbolically (Cohen, 1974); *comparative,* examining societies with different racial mixes and with different ideologies; and *contextual,* taking into account the shrinking world and the fact that individuals and groups are sensitive to occurrences and race relations elsewhere. Current racial tension in Canada has as much to do with anticipated numerical growth of non-whites as with the present numbers, and is rooted as much in white fear and guilt concerning their privileged position as it is with racial bigotry in the conventional sense.

## NOTES

1  Inuit in the MacKenzie Delta Region have always had close ties with their Alaskan counterparts and have been significantly influenced by them with respect to nativistic pentecostalism and land claims (Clairmont, 1963).
2  The 1923 act almost completely closed the door to Chinese immigrants; only forty-four were allowed to enter between 1923 and 1947 (Lai, 1971).
3  The numbers are also very difficult to estimate and the figures given should be treated with caution. Our estimate of the Black population is slightly higher than usually reported but it appears to be consistent with Richmond (1975).
4  The liberalization of immigration policy has its roots in the World War II experience; the Canadian government relaxed its restrictions on Chinese immigration at that time since China was an ally.

## REFERENCES

*Adams, Ian, William Cameron, Brian Hill, and Peter Penz*
1971   The Real Poverty Report. Edmonton: Hurtig.
*Blauner, Robert*
1972   Racial Oppression in America. New York: Harper and Row.
*Breton, Raymond.*
1968   "Institutional completeness of ethnic communities and the personal relations of immigrants." Pp. 77–94 in Bernard R. Blishen et al. (eds.), Canadian Society: Sociological Perspectives. Toronto: Macmillan (3rd edition).
*Cardinal, Harold*
1969   The Unjust Society. Edmonton: Hurtig.
*Carstens, Peter*
1971   "Coercion and change." Pp. 126–145 in R. J. Ossenberg (ed.), Canadian Society: Pluralism, Change and Conflict. Scarborough: Prentice-Hall.
*Chamberlin, J. E.*
1975   The Harrowing of Eden: White Attitudes Toward North American Natives. Toronto: Fitzhenry and Whiteside.
*Clairmont, D. H.*
1963   Deviance Among Indians and Eskimos in Aklavik, N.W.T. Ottawa: Northern Coordination and Research Centre, Canada Department of Northern Affairs and National Resources.
*Clairmont, D. H. and Dennis W. Magill*
1970   Nova Scotia Blacks: An Historical and Structural Overview. Halifax: The Institute of Public Affairs.

1974    Africville: The Life and Death of a Canadian Black Community. Toronto: McClelland and Stewart.

*Clark, S. D.*

1968    The Developing Canadian Community. Toronto: University of Toronto Press (2nd edition).

1974    "Sociology in Canada: An historical overview." Paper presented at a joint session of the International Sociological Association and the Canadian Association of Sociology and Anthropology, Toronto.

*Cohen, Abner*

1974    Two Dimensional Man: An Essay on the Anthropology of Power and Symbolism in Complex Society. Berkeley: University of California Press.

*Cohen, Ronald*

1970    "Modernism and the hinterland: The Canadian example." Pp. 4–27 in W. E. Mann (ed.), Social and Cultural Change in Canada, Vol. I. Toronto: Copp-Clark.

*Davis, Arthur K.*

1971    "Canadian society and history as hinterland versus metropolis." Pp. 6–23 in R. J. Ossenberg (ed.), Canadian Society: Pluralism, Change and Conflict. Scarborough: Prentice-Hall.

*Fein, Lawrence*

1970    "The limits of liberalism." Saturday Review of Books. June: 83–96.

*Frideres, James S.*

1974    Canada's Indians: Contemporary Conflicts. Scarborough: Prentice-Hall.

1975    "Prejudice and discrimination in western Canada: First and third world immigrants." Paper prepared for Conference on Multiculturalism and Third World Immigrants in Canada. Edmonton: University of Alberta.

*Gordon, Milton M.*

1961    "Assimilation in America: Theory and reality." Daedalus 90:263–85.

*Greeley, Andrew M.*

1973    "Making it in America: Ethnic groups and social status." Social Policy 4:21–29.

*Head, Wilson A.*

1975    The Black Presence in the Canadian Mosaic: A Study of Perception and the Practice of Discrimination Against Blacks in Metropolitan Toronto. Toronto: Ontario Human Rights Commission.

*Henry, Frances*

1973    Forgotten Canadians: The Blacks of Nova Scotia. Don Mills: Longman.

*Hobart, C. W. and C. S. Brant*

1969    "Eskimo education, Danish and Canadian: A comparison." Pp. 68–87 in Anand Malik (ed.), Social Foundations of Canadian Education. Scarborough: Prentice-Hall.

*Horowitz, Gad*

1972    "Mosaic and identity." Pp. 465–73 in Bryan Finnigan and Cy Gonick (eds.), Making It: The Canadian Dream. Toronto: McClelland and Stewart.

*Hughes, David R. and Evelyn Kallen*

1974    The Anatomy of Racism: Canadian Dimensions. Montreal: Harvest House.

*Institute of Public Affairs*

1969    Poverty in Nova Scotia. Halifax: Dalhousie University.

*Kalbach, Warren and Wayne W. McVey*

1971    The Demographic Bases of Canadian Society. Toronto: McGraw-Hill.

*Lai, Vivien*

1971    "The new Chinese immigrants in Toronto." Pp. 120–140 in Jean Leonard Elliott (ed.), Minority Canadians: Immigrant Groups. Scarborough: Prentice-Hall.

*Lurie, Nancy O.*

1968    "Historical background." Pp. 49–81 in Stuart Levine and Nancy O. Lurie (eds.), The American Indian Today. Baltimore: Penguin.

*Manpower and Immigration*

1974    Three Years in Canada. Ottawa: Department of Manpower and Immigration.

*Manuel, George and Michael Posluns*
1974   The Fourth World: An Indian Reality. Don Mills: Collier-Macmillan.
*Novak, Michael*
1972   The Rise of the Unmeltable Ethnics. New York: Macmillan.
*Parsons, Talcott*
1971   The System of Modern Societies. Englewood Cliffs: Prentice-Hall.
*Patterson, E. Palmer*
1972   The Canadian Indian: A History Since 1500. Don Mills: Collier-Macmillan.
*Porter, John*
1965   The Vertical Mosaic. Toronto: University of Toronto Press.
*Potter, Harold H.*
1961   "Negroes in Canada." Race 3:39–56.
*Reitz, Jeffrey G.*
1974   "Language and ethnic community survival." Canadian Review of Sociology and
        Anthropology, Special Edition on the occasion of the 8th World Congress of Sociol-
        ogy, Toronto: 104–122.
*Richmond, Anthony H.*
1975   "Black and Asian immigrants in Britain and Canada: Experiences of prejudice and
        discrimination." Paper presented at Conference on Multiculturalism and Third
        World Immigrants in Canada. Edmonton: University of Alberta.
*Schermerhorn, R. A.*
1970   Comparative Ethnic Relations: A Framework for Theory and Research. New York:
        Random House.
*Statistics Canada*
1974   Perspective Canada: A Compendium of Social Statistics. Ottawa: Information Can-
        ada.
*Stymeist, David H.*
1975   Ethnics and Indians: Social Relations in a Northwestern Ontario Town. Toronto:
        Peter Martin Associates.
*Thompson, Colin A.*
1974   "The ultimate Canadian and the blacks: 1860–1920." A paper presented to the
        Canadian Association of African Studies Conference, Halifax.
*Vallee, Frank G.*
1975   "Multi-ethnic Societies: The issues of identity and inequality." Pp. 162–202 in
        Dennis Forcese and Stephen Richer (eds.), Issues in Canadian Society: An Introduc-
        tion to Sociology. Scarborough: Prentice-Hall.
*van den Berghe, Pierre L.*
1967   Race and Racism. New York: John Wiley.
*Wien, F., P. Buckley, H. Desmond, and K. Marshall.*
1976   Opinions from the Centre: The Position of Racial Minorities in the University.
        Halifax: The Institute of Public Affairs.
*Winks, Robin W.*
1971   The Blacks in Canada: A History. Montreal: McGill-Queen's University Press.

# A Structural-Behavioral Theory of Intergroup Antagonism

## Sanford Labovitz

*University of Calgary*

## Robert Hagedorn

*University of Victoria*

*Based on structural and behavioral orientations, a theory of intergroup antago-
nism (subsuming ethnic prejudice, racism, and sexism) is developed interlink-
ing social power, competition, labor force structure, and contact. The
behavioral orientation is invoked chiefly on matters of interpersonal contact,
and the development of individual attitudes and behavioral patterns toward
others. Employing a structural orientation, social power, competition, and the
labor force structure are assumed to affect intergroup relations directly. Given
the learning of prejudicial attitudes and discriminatory behavioral patterns,
differences in power, competition, and the structure of the labor force lead to
five hypotheses on intergroup antagonism.*

The aim of this paper is to develop a theory of intergroup antagonism, interlink-
ing the variables of social power, competition, labor force structure, and con-

*Source:* Reprinted from Social Forces 53, 3 (March 1975): 444–48. "A Structural-Behavioral
Theory of Intergroup Antagonism," by Sanford Labovitz and Robert Hagedorn. Copyright © 1975 The University of North Carolina Press.

tact.[1] Intergroup antagonism subsumes both attitudes and behavior,[2] and refers to a variety of forms of prejudice, discrimination, racism, and sexism.[3]

## GENERAL THEORETICAL POSITION

The theoretical position is derived from a combination of both structural and behavioral orientations. The critical variables explored under the structural orientation are the differential distribution of power resources, the nature of the labor market, and competition. Under the behavioral orientation, the critical variable is the degree of interpersonal contact.[4]

In the behavioristic tradition, it is assumed that members of a group become antagonistic toward outsiders as learned responses to certain kinds of situations. When an individual interacts with those of his own social group, he learns (among other things) who are members and nonmembers and codes of conduct appropriate in each. When he interacts with outsiders, he also learns codes of conduct in treating them; these codes may or may not be supported by his contacts within his own group.

Patterns of responses are assumed to occur in the same way that a child learns to love or hate bugs. If, to illustrate, the parents despise bugs, they will display and communicate certain negative ideas and behavior patterns to the child. Upon seeing a bee, the child will respond adversely and feel negatively toward it. If parents respond positively about bees, if they explain their usefulness and life patterns, and if they literally smile when teaching a child about bees, then the child is likely to learn positive responses. Applied to antagonism, an individual learns to respond in racist or sexist ways depending on what he or she has learned from others. These others may be members of his social group or of an outside group. It is assumed that the person learns most behavioral responses from those closest to him or her—parents, friends, co-workers, and playmates.

The behavioral approach does not depend on any kind of need or personality theory of intergroup antagonism.[5] There is no required "intervening mechanism" generating an aberrant self-image, an authoritarian personality, displaced aggression, or frustration that characterizes the racist or sexist. Such postulated explanatory concepts as scapegoating, fear, competition, or a balance principle[6] are not necessary within this framework. If there are intervening mechanisms between the stimuli and the response of antagonism, they are included in the process of learning: and they occur under specific situations.

The structural orientation assumes that there are factors independent of individuals that impinge upon them and shape the way in which they think and behave. This approach is consistent with behaviorism, because the others with whom an individual interacts are part of the structure, and the learning process is tied to the characteristics of the structures. For example, learning may be enhanced or hindered by the amount and kinds of stimuli in the environment, by the openness of communication and degree of feedback, and by the nature of interpersonal control. The social structure, in addition, includes an authority and communication system, an interdependent network of statuses and roles, and a complex of social norms (among other characteristics) that are assumed to govern the activities of members. Members are socialized within the sometimes conflicting dictates of a particular social structure, and at times they are confronted with two or more structures or with diverse substructures.

A preeminently pertinent aspect of the social structure is the nature and distribution of power resources among identifiable social groups.[7] Such resources include social status, occupational prestige, wealth, education, membership in voluntary organizations, expertise, and the ability to apply social norms or sanctions to situations.[8] Social power is defined as a capacity to affect the outcomes of social relations. The control of scarce resources is the basis for social power. Power is assumed to be unequally distributed in a society; and this differential distribution along with the degree of competition and labor force relations affects intergroup antagonism.

Competition occurs when two or more persons or groups attempt to obtain the same scarce resources. The closer two groups are in social power, or as two groups become closer in social power over time, whether (and how much) they compete for scarce resources (jobs, money, education, political favors) becomes a critical variable. If they do *not* compete, then as they become more equal in power, antagonism is expected to decrease between them. Consistent with this notion, the less they compete, the greater the relation between differences in power resources and antagonism. It is assumed that power equality between groups results in few relevant distinctions between them. Therefore, individuals in each group are treated favorably by those in other groups.

The critical nature of labor force relations, a particularly difficult case for the theory, is the manner in which subordinate groups are treated by those superordinate. If a subordinate population is used as an economic resource, for example slave labor, and the group is extremely important to the economic structure of the area, then antagonism should develop between the groups. This is not a competitive situation as defined above, but it is clearly different from noncompetitive groups in a situation where one group is not used as a resource in production. As characterized by blacks in the United States before the Civil War, the white slave owners and the black slave workers were not competing for the same jobs, but they were dependent on one another in the plantation system in the South. The very fact of dependency probably led to some antagonism of the dominant white group toward the subordinate black group. Members of the black group appeared to be angered by the inequity of the system, by their subordinate status, and by being used as a resource in production. The antagonism between labor and management may be viewed in these terms, since labor is being used as a resource and the two are seldom competing for the same jobs. If so, and if these two broad groupings become more equal in power, the degree to which labor is used as a resource should decrease—the net result predicted by the theory is less antagonism.

These ideas on competition and labor force structure can be stated formally as Hypothesis 1: *for noncompetitive groups where no group is treated as a resource in production, differences in social power are directly related to antagonism (that is, the greater the power differential, the greater the antagonism).* It should be noted that if a subordinate group is treated as a resource in production, then by definition the differences in power resources are large, and the degree of antagonism is predicted to be high.

As two groups become more equal in social power, one quite likely will infringe upon the resources of the other. Members of one group may enter the job market of the other; they may increasingly leave low paying jobs and enter the more highly evaluated and prestigious jobs formerly dominated by the other group. They may enter into the neighborhoods and their children may go to the schools of the other group. Once competition in any sphere takes hold (as in the job market), it probably will extend to education, voluntary associations (churches and clubs), recreation facilities, and the like. Subordinate group members, furthermore, may increasingly enter the political arena for direct power confrontations with the previously dominating groups. Under such conditions of competition, intergroup antagonism should increase. The key to the predicted increase is competition, which may result from a gain in social power by a previously subordinate group. Subordinate group members in a split labor market (Bonacich, 1972) work for comparatively lower wages than do members of superordinate groups, and thereby effectively compete for jobs. This type of competitive situation seems particularly conducive to antagonistic relations. Consistent with these ideas, Hypothesis 2 asserts that *for competitive groups, differences in social power are inversely related to antagonism (that is, the less the power differential, the greater the racism, sexism, and ethnic prejudice).*

Schematically, the two hypotheses can be represented as follows:

### HYPOTHESIS 1

**Noncompetitive Situation and Groups Are Not Treated as a Resource in Production**

| DIFFERENCES IN SOCIAL POWER | DEGREE OF ANTAGONISM | |
|---|---|---|
| | HIGH | LOW |
| Large | 10 | 0 |
| Small | 0 | 10 |

### HYPOTHESIS 2

**Competitive Situation**

| DIFFERENCES IN SOCIAL POWER | DEGREE OF ANTAGONISM | |
|---|---|---|
| | HIGH | LOW |
| Large | 0 | 10 |
| Small | 10 | 0 |

These propositions relating power differentials, competition, and the labor force structure to antagonism take on additional importance when tied to the behavioral aspect of the degree of contact between social groups. It is theoretically possible for groups to compete but have minimal contact with one another. The competition could flare up episodically or intermittently, but be extremely intense when it occurs. Some of the Indian tribes in the Southwest of the United States had infrequent but fierce contact with white settlers in the seventeenth and eighteenth centuries. Relatively noncompetitive groups may range anywhere on the spectrum from high to low intergroup contact. What effect does increasing contact have on antagonism under the varying conditions of differences in social power (large to small) and differences in the degree of competition (high to low)?

Under the noncompetitive conditions of Hypothesis 1, where no group is used as a resource in production, the degree of contact between social groups is expected to have an independent and additional effect on antagonism. Noncompetitive contacts are assumed to reflect a generally rewarding situation for all groups in question, resulting in mutual and positive social reinforcement. Of course, it will become increasingly difficult to maintain a noncompetitive situation if the power differences between groups are leveling and contact is increasing. Nonetheless, under the condition of noncompetitiveness, Hypothesis 3 asserts that *the degree of intergroup contact is inversely related to intergroup antagonism (the greater the contact, the less the antagonism).*[9] In the slave situation, where a subordinate group is treated as a resource in production, a direct relation is predicted.

In a fourfold table, Hypothesis 3 is indicated as follows:

**HYPOTHESIS 3**

**Noncompetitive Situation and Groups Are Not Treated as a Resource in Production**

| *DEGREE OF CONTACT* | *DEGREE OF ANTAGONISM* | |
|---|---|---|
| | *HIGH* | *LOW* |
| High | 0 | 10 |
| Low | 10 | 0 |

The competitive condition is somewhat complex when treated in conjunction with power differences, degree of contact, and antagonism. When groups are competing for the same resources, the degree of contact is expected to *interact* with the extent of power differences in producing certain affects. Accordingly, Hypothesis 4 states that *in a competitive situation where differences in power are small, the degree of intergroup contact varies directly with antagonism (the greater the competitive contact between equally powerful groups, the greater the antagonism).* The hypothesis is derived from the assumption that groups equal or nearly equal in power who are competing for the same resources will develop antagonistic feelings toward one another. Hypothesis 4 has two conditional properties:

**HYPOTHESIS 4**

**Competitive Situation with Small Power Differences**

| *DEGREE OF CONTACT* | *DEGREE OF ANTAGONISM* | |
|---|---|---|
| | *HIGH* | *LOW* |
| High | 10 | 0 |
| Low | 0 | 10 |

Under the competitive condition, where the power differential is large the nature of the relation between contact and antagonism is complex. As long as there is competition, greater contact should lead to greater intergroup antagonism. But if the power-holding groups can effectively block others from the scarce power resources (adequate medical facilities, good universities, country clubs) then a large part of the intergroup contact would be in relatively "safe" areas (sharing nonpersonal recreational areas or shopping centers). By keeping subordinate groups "in their place," competition is confined to the job market, and antagonism may be kept to a fairly low level. This situation may be somewhat descriptive of Jewish merchants in some of the European countries in the nineteenth century, and it may also describe some of the black-white relations in demographically integrated sections of U.S. cities. Despite the complexity of the relation indicated by these examples, under the dominant impact of competition, Hypothesis 5 stipulates that *where differences in power are large, the degree of intergroup contact varies directly but is not substantially related to antagonism (a positive but comparatively low relation is predicted between contact and racism, sexism, and ethnic prejudice)*. Hypothesis 5 is schematically presented as follows:

**HYPOTHESIS 5**
**Competitive Situation with Large Power Differences**

| DEGREE OF CONTACT | DEGREE OF ANTAGONISM | |
|---|---|---|
| | HIGH | LOW |
| High | 7 | 3 |
| Low | 3 | 7 |

A variable not considered in the rationale but perhaps of some importance is group size. The antagonism toward blacks by whites in U.S. northern and western cities may have increased as a result of increasing numbers (which occurred by migration as well as by natural increase). Group size appears to be related to some extent to power or power potential (Bierstedt, 1950). If so, as a subordinate group increases in numbers, it may increasingly threaten other societal groups. The group, if organized, becomes a social power that can actively compete for scarce resources formerly controlled by others. Group size has not been singled out as a separate independent variable in the hypothesis because it is assumed that the degree of contact and social power differences adequately account for its effects on antagonism. It is possible, however, that size may interact with competition, contact, and power to increase the magnitude of the relations predicted in the hypotheses.

A basic assumption of the structural-behavioral rationale is that social groups are "visible." To some extent, at least, group members must be readily identifiable. Any perceivable characteristic may be used. Obvious characteristics are race and sex, but social or cultural characteristics also may be used, for example, language, manners, dress, residence, religion, or knowledge. If the groups in question are not identifiable, assimilation is likely and antagonism cannot be maintained or is shifted to an identifiable group. In this regard, the arm bands and stigmata required of Jews in Nazi Germany may have added to the antagonism against them.

## CONCLUDING COMMENTS

This structural-behavioral theory of intergroup antagonism links social power, competition, labor force structure, and contact. The theory's five hypotheses can be subjected to empirical testing. Although each concept has a variety of possible empirical measures or indicators, it is possible to make the necessary observations. For example, group power may be indicated by income level or educational level or even by the percentage of members in prestigious political and organizational positions. In the labor force structure, the treatment of subordinate groups may be observed by the ease with which their members are upwardly mobile. The degree of occupational and even residential mobility could serve as useful indicators. Competition is a difficult concept to translate into direct observations. But it might be indicated by such factors as the percentage of members of different groups in the same occupational categories, or in the same formal organizations, or living in the same areas. Finally, one indicator of interpersonal contact is intermarriage rates. Membership in the same community associations also may be a fairly adequate indicator. Research and testing are clearly warranted, and should be carried out on different races and ethnic groups, and on a variety of different populations.

## NOTES

1  For two other "social" theories of race and ethnic relations see Bonacich (1972) and Lieberson (1961).
2  It is recognized that the theory may explain or predict behavior to a greater degree than attitudes (or vice versa). At this rather modest stage in theory construction, it was assumed to be a better strategy to keep the theory broad in scope and to revise it later as empirical evidence may dictate.
3  Antagonism, prejudice, racism, sexism, discrimination, race, and ethnicity are defined and used in the following way. The more general and neutral (Bonacich, 1972) term of antagonism is used to refer to all types of discriminatory behavior or prejudicial attitudes from one group to another. Discrimination is overt antagonism and refers to behavior of members of a group in preventing or restricting access to scarce resources to members of other groups. Prejudice is covert antagonism and refers to negative evaluations of members of a group, because they belong to that group (Allport, 1958). Racism is antagonistic behavior or attitudes of members of one group toward members of another on the basis of certain physical characteristics. Sexism is subsumed under racism and refers specifically to the differences between males and females. Ethnicity is used as the most encompassing category referring to any social, cultural or physical differences between groups.
4  For a very different orientation to interpersonal contact with regard to discrimination, see Molotch (1969).
5  For a summary of such ideas, see Allport (1958) and Wrightsman (1972).
6  On this issue, see Rokeach (1970).
7  The concept of "social group" is used throughout the manuscript. The concept is not used to refer necessarily to interacting individuals characterized by certain social norms (like religious ceremonies) or by some explicit identification or name (like the KKK, the Republican party, or a nuclear family). The concept of "social category" and even "aggregate" could be substituted in the place of social groups. Females, blacks,

Chicanos, French Canadians, and Russian Jews are heterogeneous on several dimensions and should not be viewed as comprised of completely interacting members with a united formal structure. Social group, consequently, is used in a very broad sense referring to any mutually identifiable individuals.

8   Power resources may be classified as utilitarian, coercive, and normative. On classifications of power resources, see Lehman (1969), French and Raven (1959), Gamson (1968), Secord and Bachman (1964:273–93), and Clark (1968).

9   An equal-status contact hypothesis, which is somewhat similar to this one, received support in studies by Hamblin (1962) and Ford (1973).

## REFERENCES

*Allport, Gordon W.*
1958    *The Nature of Prejudice.* New York: Doubleday Anchor.
*Bierstedt, R.*
1950    "An Analysis of Social Power." *American Sociological Review* 15 (December): 730–38.
*Bonacich, E. E.*
1972    "A Theory of Ethnic Antagonism: The Split Labor Market." *American Sociological Review* 37 (October): 547–59.
*Clark, Terry N.*
1968    *Community Structure and Decision-Making: Comparative Analysis.* San Francisco: Chandler.
*French, J. R. P., and B. Raven*
1959    "The Bases of Social Power." In Dorwin Cartwright (ed.), *Studies in Social Power.* Ann Arbor: Institute for Social Research, University of Michigan.
*Ford, W. S.*
1973    "Interracial Public Housing in a Border City: Another Look at the Contact Hypothesis." *American Journal of Sociology* 78 (May): 1426–47.
*Gamson, William A.*
1968    *Power and Discontent.* Homewood, Ill.: Dorsey.
*Hamblin, R. L.*
1962    "The Dynamics of Racial Discrimination." *Social Problems* 10 (Fall): 103–21.
*Lehman, E. W.*
1969    "Toward a Macrosociology of Power." *American Sociological Review* 34 (August): 453–65.
*Lieberson, S.*
1961    "A Societal Theory of Race and Ethnic Relations." *American Sociological Review* 26 (December): 902–10.
*Molotch, H.*
1969    "Racial Integration in a Transition Community." *American Sociological Review* 34 (December): 878–94.
*Rokeach, Milton*
1970    *Beliefs, Attitudes, and Values.* San Francisco: Jossey-Bass.
*Secord, Paul F., and Carl W. Bachman*
1964    *Social Psychology.* New York: McGraw-Hill.
*Wrightsman, Lawrence S.*
1972    *Social Psychology in the Seventies.* Belmont, Calif.: Brooks/Cole.

# TWO

## CONFORMING PREJUDICE

*Evidently most attitudes of prejudice against out-groups are learned, in order to conform to patterns of prejudice and discrimination. Some persons apparently have deep-seated emotional needs for negative attitudes toward other groups, whether because they are highly authoritarian (Adorno et al., 1950), have a need to displace repressed feelings of aggression to out-groups that make safe targets (Dollard, 1939; Allport, 1954:351–52), or a need to attribute (project) to other groups the traits they fear in themselves or in the in-group (Bettelheim and Janowitz, 1950:43; Ackerman and Jahoda, 1943:57–59). Emotional disturbance can perhaps help explain why prejudice is sometimes so strong, and how it is maintained, but most people who learn attitudes of prejudice do not have abnormal personalities (Blalock, 1967:42–54; Ehrlich, 1973:143–51). Most attitudes toward other groups appear to be learned from parents and others in the in-group, and they help persons adjust to social role expectations (Pettigrew, 1976:487; Ehrlich, 1973, Ch. 5).*

*Negative response tendencies (prejudices) toward other groups are based on stereotyped beliefs about what the group is like and ethnocentric value judgments of the image. A stereotype is a conception of a group consisting of distorted, overgeneralized beliefs, usually learned from others as part of a pattern of conforming prejudice. Maykovich's study of racial stereotypes in California shows that under certain conditions there is mutual influence of the images race groups hold of each other. Her comparisons with earlier studies indicate that racial stereotypes reflect group statuses in given times and places, and that stereotypes change to conform to changes in patterns of intergroup relations. It is interesting to relate these changes to van den Berghe's thesis about change from the stereotype of a minority as happy children to that of aggressive and violent people, as paternalistic systems of domination change to more competitive ones (1967:29–30).*

*Muir's longitudinal study shows great changes in attitudes toward blacks held by whites at the University of Alabama from 1963 to 1972. These changes include large declines in the acceptance of beliefs comprising traditional racist stereotypes of blacks, in the amount of opposition to the integration of public schools, and in social distance. Apparently there was rather rapid unlearning of older attitudes, and the learning of newer ones more appropriate to the changing patterns of racial interaction on campus and in the region. Stereotypes of race groups are often held very rigidly, but both this study and the one by Maykovich indicate that they change as patterns of intergroup behavior change.*

*The WASP concept has become a stereotype, according to the selection by Allen, with consequences both in racial and cultural relations and in the sociological study of them. Minorities understandably hold stereotypes of the dominant community, but such images are not satisfactory analytical concepts any more than stereotypes of minority groups are. The nationality and religious composition of the dominant community in the United States has varied considerably over time, from place to place, and for different minority groups. There are also stereotypes of anglos and whites, but social scientists are not so likely to accept these as accurate characterizations.*

*The feminine stereotype is central to the ideology (system of beliefs) used to justify continuing the status of women as housewives and mothers, and as subordinate to men. Sexist beliefs supporting the stereotype often include the convictions that, because of their biological nature, all females have a feminine temperament; feminine interests, attitudes, and aptitudes; and that they are physically and mentally inferior to males. The selection by Albrecht, Bahr, and Chadwick reports a study of the stereotyping of both female traits and occupations in Utah, including the finding that males and females largely held the same beliefs. Is this an instance of the acceptance by the minority of the stereotypes of them held by the dominant group, or what? Attitudes are presumably changing as women enter new occupations, and other changes take place in the complex pattern of social relations between the sexes, but the feminine stereotype does not change readily or all at once.*

*Ever since Allport stated the hypothesis that equal-status contacts reduce prejudice, studies have been made to test and refine it. He qualified his thesis by saying that prejudice is reduced especially when the two groups work toward common goals, cooperate rather than compete, and when the community and its legal officers actively oppose prejudice and discrimination (Allport, 1954: Ch. 16). The hypothesis has been supported or partly supported in many studies, but not all. In the article by Robinson and Preston, it is reported that prejudice was reduced for white teachers but not for black ones. One interpretation suggested by the researchers is that the whites apparently perceived the situation as one of equal-status contact, but the blacks did not. The reduction of discrimination evidently reduces prejudice in the dominant group, at least in time, but the specific conditions under which the attitudes change are not yet clear.*

## REFERENCES

*Ackerman, Nathan W., and Marie Jahoda*
1950    Anti-Semitism and Emotional Disorder. New York: Harper and Row.
*Adorno, T. W., Else Frenkel-Brunswik, Daniel J. Levinson, and R. Nevitt Sanford*
1950    The Authoritarian Personality. New York: Harper and Row.
*Allport, Gordon*
1954    The Nature of Prejudice. Boston: Beacon Press.
*Bettelheim, Bruno, and Morris Janowitz*
1950    Dynamics of Prejudice. New York: Harper and Row.
*Blalock, Hubert M., Jr.*
1967    Toward a Theory of Intergroup Relations. New York: Capricorn Books.
*Dollard, John, et al.*
1939    Frustration and Aggression. New Haven: Yale University Press.
*Ehrlich, Howard J.*
1973    The Social Psychology of Prejudice. New York: Wiley Interscience.
*Pettigrew, Thomas Fraser*
1976    "Race and Intergroup Relations," Chapter 10 in, Robert K. Merton and Robert *Nisbet*, Contemporary Social Problems, 4th ed. New York: Harcourt Brace Jovanovich.
*van den Berghe, Pierre L.*
1967    Race and Racism. New York: John Wiley and Sons.

# Reciprocity in Racial Stereotypes: White, Black, and Yellow [1]

## Minako Kurokawa Maykovich

*University of Hawaii*

*Mutual and self-perceptions of racial images of white, black, and Japanese Americans are studied among adult, college student, and schoolchild age groups in California. For adults and college students, Katz and Braly's adjective list was used, in which subjects were asked to choose five traits out of 84 to describe each racial group. Children were instructed to describe racial images in their own words.*

*The hypothesis that dominant whites are endowed with positive traits and minority groups with negative traits was only partially supported. Another hypothesis concerning minority acceptance of a negative image ascribed by the dominant group, which was true in the 1930s, was invalid in this study. The whites were stereotyped as materialistic and pleasure loving; the blacks, as musical, aggressive, and straightforward; and the Japaneses, as industrious, ambitious, loyal to family, and quiet.*

A stereotype is a standardized concept or image invested with special meaning and held in common by members of a group (Allport 1958; Rose 1964; Palmore

*Source:* Minako Kurokawa Maykovich, "Reciprocity in Racial Stereotypes: White, Black, and Yellow," American Journal of Sociology 77, 5 (March 1972): 876–97. Copyright © 1972 by The University of Chicago. Reprinted by permission.

1962). Defined in this way, stereotypes are essentially social norms for describing recognized groups, reflecting the power relations of dominant versus minority groups in a given social structure. A dominant group usually establishes social norms to which the rest of society is to conform. The Negro, for instance, as a member of American society, tends to adopt the norms of that society, including its prejudice and negative stereotypes assigned to him (Rose 1949). This paper deals with reciprocity in perceptions of racial stereotypes among white, black, and Japanese Americans. The issue is whether contemporary blacks and yellows (the Japanese Americans) conform to the expectation that minorities will absorb negative stereotypes regarding themselves held by the majority.

Previous literature indicates two opposing tendencies in the minority response to stereotyping. On the one hand, there is the "mirror-image" phenomenon (Bronfenbrenner 1961; Marx 1967; Noel and Pinkney 1964; Seeman 1966; Simmons 1961), which implies that minority members accept the dominant image of the minority and reinforce it. For instance, light-skinned Negro children are more acceptable to other Negroes as friends than darker ones (Clark and Clark 1958; Goodman 1954). Some Negroes accuse other Negroes of having precisely the qualities that anti-Negro whites say they have. Here, the process of the self-fulfilling prophecy (Merton 1948) is in operation. On the other hand, instead of confirming the expectation by the dominant group, the minority may form reciprocal prejudice and attribute negative stereotypes to the dominant group (Adelson 1958; Dworkin 1965).

## BACKGROUND

Using the small number of systematic longitudinal studies of persistence and change of sterotypes, I have attempted to determine whether there has been any trend in changes occurring in relation to social changes.

### In the Thirties

During several decades after the end of slavery, profound changes occurred in the society, but the status of the blacks remained relatively fixed (Aptheker 1951; Frazier 1957; Pinkney 1969). U.S. participation in World War I did little to improve the status of blacks except to expand their geographical distribution. Nor did widespread economic prosperity of the 1920s have much effect on the status of the blacks. In the depression of the 1930s the hard-hit blacks again felt discrimination in obtaining public assistance. Where segregation and discrimination were not lawful, they were deeply ingrained in the mores.

Berelson and Salter's (1946) systematic study of popular fiction characters (1937 and 1943) indicated that major roles were played by white Anglo-Saxon Protestants depicted as tall, handsome, wealthy, and intelligent. In the 1932 study by Katz and Braly (1933),[2] white Americans were described as industrious, intelligent, ambitious, and materialistic. Even the blacks in 1935 (Meenes 1943), 1938 (Bayton 1941), and 1942 (Meenes 1943) characterized whites as intelligent, progressive, ambitious, and materialistic, as well as pleasure loving and conceited.

In 1932 (Katz and Braly 1933), the blacks were overwhelmingly described as superstitious (84%), lazy (75%), and happy-go-lucky (38%). Blacks (Bayton 1941; Meenes 1943) themselves acknowledged that they were superstitious (46%), although they also assigned to themselves such neutral traits as being very religious and musical. Thus, the mirror-image hypothesis that whites' positive image of whites and negative image of blacks are reflected in blacks' views of whites and blacks is attested to in the 1930s.

By 1924 agitation against Asiatic immigration culminated in the passage of a law that prohibited Japanese immigration (Kitano 1969). The attack against the Japanese was based on race (unassimilable), nationality (landhungry, imperialistic, warlike), styles of life (mysterious, un-American), personal habits (sly, greedy, dishonest), economic competition (undercutting labor standards), and sexual conduct (breeding like rabbits) (Hyde 1955; Keim 1941; Mackie 1857; Prosser 1908). The Japanese, on arrival in California, inherited the Chinese legacy of the Yellow Peril and were labeled as coolies, Asiatics, and yellow. The contraction "Jap," later accentuated during World War II, first appeared consistently in the columns of the *Coast Seamen's Journal* during the 1890s (Matthews 1964).

In the thirties, as Katz and Braly (1933) observed, people on the East Coast knew little about Asians except through the California anti-Asian propaganda but seemed to be aware of the rapid industrialization and modernization of Japan and viewed the Japanese as industrious and intelligent. Southern blacks (Bayton and Byoune 1947; Meenes 1943) shared the whites' view of the Japanese.

### World War II

Studies (Gundlach 1944; Seago 1947; tenBroek 1968) of stereotypes before and after Pearl Harbor indicated changes in the Japanese image perceived by white and black Americans. Japanese were typified by whites as sly, treacherous, cruel, and warlike during the war and even five years after (Gilbert 1951). Blacks shared the white view, understandable in view of the widespread participation of blacks in World War II.

### Around 1950

During the war, blacks made significant entries into the white social structure. In the army they fought beside white soldiers (Stouffer et al. 1949) and played an important part in the war industry. After World War II, New York enacted the first state Fair Employment Practices Law. The Supreme Court began in 1946 to issue a series of decisions outlawing segregation in various aspects of American life, culminating in the 1954 decision calling for desegregation in education. Along with the legal changes of black status, change was also taking place in the cultural area. The entertainment and communication media were curtailing and discouraging traditional patterns of stereotyping. Comparing Princeton students of 1932 in the Katz and Braly sample and those of 1951,[3] Gilbert (1951) found uniformity in verbal stereotyping considerably reduced.

Between 1932 and 1951 the self-image of whites changed considerably from one of industriousness and intelligence to one of materialism and pleasure loving. The degree of absorption of the earlier positive white image by the blacks decreased by the late forties. The blacks in a 1946 study (Bayton and Byoune 1947) still assigned such positive characteristics to whites as intelligence, progressiveness, and ambition but did not hesitate to assign such negative traits as graspingness, deceit, conceit, and cruelty. The blacks were portrayed by whites as superstitious, musical, lazy, ignorant, and very religious. Blacks, however, assigned some positive traits to themselves such as progressiveness and intelligence.

### In the Sixties

The 1954 Supreme Court decision for educational desegregation became the turning point in the history of black-white relations. Until 1954, a few civil rights professionals, religious leaders, and white liberals were leading the desegregation movements, and the change was slow and piecemeal. In 1955, in their first major act of resistance, the blacks used Gandhi's technique of nonviolent direct action, and the civil rights movement spread rapidly (Laue 1965; Pettigrew 1969). Blacks won important victories such as the Civil Rights Act of 1964 and the Voting Rights Act of 1965. Despite these sizeable gains, or perhaps because of them, there was conflict and confusion within the movement. Leaders stated that mere desegregation was not enough: new images of identity and autonomy would be required for true integration. "Black is Beautiful" emerged as the slogan to cultivate racial pride (Abrahams 1970).

Meanwhile, Japanese Americans were making a fast recovery from such damages inflicted by the war as loss of property through wartime relocation and hostility directed at them as enemies. By 1960 Japanese Americans had attained middle-class educational and occupational levels (Caudill 1952). Toward the end of the sixties, younger Japanese Americans, influenced by the blacks, began to raise questions about the efforts of their parents toward assimilation through hard work and quiet conformity to white cultural values (Hosokawa 1969; Peterson 1966). The advocates of Yellow Power began to develop a new image as Asian Americans in lieu of the previous Quiet American stereotype (Uyematsu 1969).

The 1967 study of Princeton students (Karlins et al. 1969)[4] reflected the changing racial relations in American society. In comparison with the previous studies of 1932 (Katz and Braly 1933) and 1951 (Gilbert 1951) at Princeton, the white subjects' characterization of themselves in 1967 was less flattering. The terms "intelligent," "industrious," and "alert" had declined in frequency and the majority described themselves as materialistic. In contrast, the characterization of the blacks by the whites was more favorable than before. In place of the traditional stereotype of the blacks as superstitious and lazy, the new image of the blacks focused on the terms "musical," "happy-go-lucky," and "pleasure loving." This image would appear to be a more innocuous modern counterpart of the minstrel figure, probably reflecting the success of the blacks in the popular entertainment world supported by teenage and collegiate audiences. The civil rights movement of the past decade has strongly influenced the present generation of college students, and the appearance of "sensitive" in the top six traits might well indicate a projection of some of the white subjects' own heightened awareness onto the decidedly neutralized stereotype. The Japanese stereotype produced by the war was short-lived. By 1967 (Karlins et al. 1969) the Japanese were described as industrious, ambitious, efficient, and intelligent.

No study is available at present to indicate the contemporary black views to be compared with the white perceptions of racial images. Thus, the present paper is focused on the mutual characterizations of racial images among whites, blacks, and Japanese.

## HYPOTHESES

To the extent that racial stereotypes are social norms, they are likely to reflect existing social structures. The position of minority groups in American society has been changing since 1932 when the original stereotype study was conducted. Blacks and Japanese Americans have gained significant power, which affects their self-images as well as their views of dominant whites. In addition to the historical facts, previous research on stereotypes suggests that the amount of minority members' absorption of negative images held by the dominant group has been reduced. Thus, the major hypothesis is offered that contemporary blacks and Japanese Americans fail to conform to the expectation that minorities will mirror the dominant views.

More specifically, the following hypotheses will be examined:

$H_1$   Whites are likely to attribute positive traits to themselves.

$H_2$   Blacks and Japanese Americans of 1970 are unlikely to absorb the white view and tend to characterize whites with neutral or negative terms.

$H_3$   Whites are unlikely to portray blacks with the traditional stereotype of superstitious and lazy Negro but tend to use the contemporary version of negative portrayal.

$H_4$   Blacks and Japanese Americans are more likely than whites to describe blacks in favorable terms.

$H_5$   Japanese Americans are likely to be viewed in a favorable light by whites and blacks.

$H_6$   Japanese Americans are likely to be critical in describing themselves and to reject the traditional stereotype of themselves as industrious and reserved.

The above hypotheses concern the college student population, which often plays the role of an opinion leader in social change. Perception of stereotypes by college students will be compared with those other age groups, namely, adults and schoolchildren. Age-differentiated hypotheses are developed as follows:

$H_7$   Middle-aged adults are more likely than college students to adhere to the traditional stereotypes. Blacks and Japanese are likely to absorb the racial stereotypes held by whites, which consist of a positive white image and a negative minority image.

$H_8$   The prejudice of children is likely to be inconsistent, since the hierarchy of attitudes has not become well established (Horowitz 1939). They are likely to be pressured by the norms of their immediate social group. Thus, children in white-dominant schools are likely to accept stereotyped images of racial groups produced by the dominant whites, while children in racially mixed schools are likely to have nonstereotypical ideas of different races (Goodman 1954; Zeligs 1941).

## METHOD

The Katz and Braly (1933) inventory was adopted as the research instrument. A list of 84 adjectives was shown to the subjects, who were instructed to choose five each to describe whites, blacks, and Japanese Americans. When Katz and Braly were developing the inventory, they originally asked 25 students to list as many specific characteristics as were thought typical of 10 racial and national groups; the researchers then asked 100 students to select from and add to the list as many traits as they needed to characterize the same 10 groups. Thus, the inventory was exhaustive in listing traits and was standardized for the population they were studying at that time, namely, Princeton students in 1932. However, an application of this inventory to a different population in a different time produces difficulties in interpretation, which will be discussed later.

Racial images held by children were determined by asking them to describe whites, blacks, and Japanese Americans freely in their own words rather than restricting them to the use of a difficult word list such as the Katz and Braly inventory (Zeligs 1941).

The sample of college students consists of 100 white, 100 black, and 100 Japanese American students at Sacramento State College. The test was given to several classes in order to select as a sample white and black students with equal numbers of both sexes and similar major-subject composition for each group. Because the number of Japanese Americans in these classes was too small, the sample for this group was selected from the registration cards with the ratios of sex and the major subject in mind. In addition to Sacramento students, who are considered to be relatively conservative, 50 Japanese American students were chosen from the Berkeley and Los Angeles campuses of the University of California who were enrolled in the Asian American Study Programs and who were considered to be active in the civil rights movement. Here the sample was not intended to be random but was chosen to obtain a profile of politically active Japanese American students. They were predominantly social science majors with a working-class origin.

One hundred whites, 100 blacks, and 100 Japanese American adults were selected by the quota sample method. This sample had (1) equal numbers of males and females; (2) adults in their forties exclusively; (3) a middle-class versus working-class ratio of three to two for whites and two to three for blacks and for Japanese Americans, according to Hollingshead's (1957) two-factor determinants of social class; and (4) residents of Sacramento exclusively.

For children, two white-dominant schools and two racially mixed schools in Sacramento were selected, and the test was given to all the fourth and fifth graders in the classrooms. Later, 100 whites, 100 blacks, and 100 Japanese Americans were selected for analysis. Two-thirds of the whites were from the white-dominant schools, while two-thirds of the blacks and the Japanese Americans were from the mixed schools.

## FINDINGS AND DISCUSSION

### College Students' Perception

IMAGE OF THE WHITES    The hypothesis *(H₁)* that whites characterize themselves with positive traits is supported to the extent that they do not explicitly refer to negative traits. Two-thirds of the whites describe themselves as materialistic; one-half, as aggressive; and one-third, as pleasure loving. According to the Karlins et al. (1969) scale of favorableness, "materialistic" ranks forty-ninth; "aggressive," fortieth; and "pleasure loving," twenty-ninth from the top out of 84 traits. In other words, the whites are predominantly described in neutral terms. However, as Vinacke's (1956) examination of autostereotypes suggests, whites may rate self-traits such as materialism and pleasurism more highly than nonwhites. With pride rather than with shame, whites may recognize conspicuous consumption (Veblen 1934) as a result of their instrumental activism (Merton 1957; Parsons 1937) by being ambitious (30%) and industrious (30%) (see Table 1).

Apparently the contemporary white stereotype is that of being materialistic and pleasure loving, and this sterotype is recognized by others as well. The second hypothesis *(H₂)*, that blacks tend to describe whites in negative terms, is attested to. In addition to materialism (43%) and pleasurism (41%), blacks refer to traits such as deceit (37%) and conceit (35%) significantly[5] more frequently than whites. "Deceitful" ranks the second lowest and "conceited," eighth lowest on the 84-point rank order scale of favorableness (Karlins et al. 1969).

The minority responses of the Sacramento Japanese Americans to the dominant whites does not support the hypothesis *(H₂)* concerning their negative characterization of the latter. Their image of whites is almost a reflection of the white self-image described as materialistic (50%), pleasure loving (42%), aggressive (27%), and ambitious (23%).

Politically active Japanese American students in Berkeley and Los Angeles portray whites in quite a different manner. They are much more critical of whites than are other groups in this study *(H₂)*. More than two-thirds of the activist Japanese Americans describe whites as materialistic and pleasure loving, do not hesitate to list negative traits such as deceit (41%) and conceit (34%), and outspokenly assert that whites are talkative (25%) and straightforward (25%). These traits, except materialism, are significantly less frequently mentioned by whites themselves. In fact, the radicals are quite rigid in describing whites. The degree of rigidity against dispersion is measured by the number of traits which have received 50% of the votes. Had there been no patterning in the respondents' picture of the whites, 42 (half of 84 characteristics listed) of the traits would have received 50% of the votes. The uniformity of rigidity in attitudes among radical Japanese Americans is shown by the fact that half of all selections referring to whites are subsumed under only 5.5 traits, while

# TABLE 1
## Students' Image of Racial Groups (in Percentage)

### IMAGE OF THE WHITES

| | $W^a$ | $B^b$ | $JA^c$ | $JA^d$ |
|---|---|---|---|---|
| Materialistic | 67 | 43 | 50 | 70 |
| Aggressive | 46 | 34 | 27 | 34 |
| Pleasure loving | 32 | 41 | 42 | 68 |
| Ambitious | 30 | 21 | 23 | ... |
| Industrious | 30 | ... | ... | ... |
| Impulsive | 22 | ... | 23 | 20 |
| Stubborn | 16 | ... | ... | 18 |
| Conservative | ... | ... | 23 | 18 |

### IMAGE OF THE BLACKS

| | $W^a$ | $B^b$ | $JA^c$ | $JA^d$ |
|---|---|---|---|---|
| Musical | 38 | 61 | 50 | 40 |
| Aggressive | 32 | 45 | 23 | 50 |
| Impulsive | 32 | 21 | 15 | 20 |
| Persistent | 24 | ... | ... | 36 |
| Pleasure loving | 22 | 15 | ... | ... |
| Straightforward | 19 | 34 | 19 | 54 |
| Grasping | 19 | ... | ... | ... |
| Revengeful | 16 | ... | ... | 38 |

### IMAGE OF THE JAPANESE

| | $W^a$ | $B^b$ | $JA^c$ | $JA^d$ |
|---|---|---|---|---|
| Loyal to family | 67 | 51 | 31 | 40 |
| Ambitious | 51 | 42 | 31 | 21 |
| Intelligent | 38 | 33 | ... | 20 |
| Industrious | 35 | 32 | 35 | 20 |
| Courteous | 27 | 23 | 23 | 16 |
| Conventional | 24 | ... | ... | 22 |
| Efficient | 19 | ... | 15 | ... |
| Neat | 16 | ... | 15 | ... |

(continued)

87

**TABLE 1** (*Continued*)

### IMAGE OF THE WHITES

| | $W^a$ | $B^b$ | $JA^c$ | $JA^d$ |
|---|---|---|---|---|
| Talkative | ... | ... | 23 | 26 |
| Straightforward | ... | ... | 15 | 26 |
| Conceited | ... | 35 | ... | 34 |
| Deceitful | ... | 37 | ... | 40 |
| ... | ... | ... | ... | ... |
| Traits (N) on which 50% of the sample is dispersed | (7.8) | (10.3) | (10.3) | (5.5) |

### IMAGE OF THE BLACKS

| | $W^a$ | $B^b$ | $JA^c$ | $JA^d$ |
|---|---|---|---|---|
| Quick-tempered | ... | 25 | 31 | 26 |
| Jovial | ... | 25 | 23 | 20 |
| Materialistic | ... | 21 | 19 | ... |
| ... | ... | ... | ... | ... |
| ... | ... | ... | ... | ... |
| Traits (N) on which 50% of the sample is dispersed | (11.0) | (14.0) | (8.0) | (6.6) |

### IMAGE OF THE JAPANESE

| | $W^a$ | $B^b$ | $JA^c$ | $JA^d$ |
|---|---|---|---|---|
| Tradition loving | ... | ... | 38 | 30 |
| Reserved | ... | 25 | 31 | 38 |
| Conservative | ... | ... | 21 | 54 |
| Artistic | ... | ... | 23 | 20 |
| Quiet | ... | 23 \*\* | 19 \*\* | 60 |
| Traits (N) on which 50% of the sample is dispersed | (7.5) | (9.1) | (9.0) | (6.1) |

[a] 100 white students at Sacramento State College.
[b] 100 black students at Sacramento State College.
[c] 100 Japanese American students at Sacramento State College.
[d] 50 Japanese American students at University of California.

* $p < .05$ ($\chi^2$ test).
** $p < .01$.

Sacramento students used 10.3 traits. The difference is significant by the Kolmogorov-Smirnov test.[6] The targets of the attacks against "white racism" by the radicals (Uyematsu 1969) are, in their own words, the materialism and pleasurism of capitalism under a pretense of democracy.

IMAGE OF THE BLACKS    The hypothesis *(H₃)* that contemporary whites do not characterize blacks by the traditional stereotype but have developed a new stereotype is attested to. Instead of being viewed as superstitious and lazy, blacks are now described as musical (38%), impulsive (32%), and aggressive (32%). On the 84-point scale of favorableness (Karlins et al. 1969), "musical" ranks twenty-first and impulsive ranks forty-sixth from the top, which indicates neutrality of these traits. The white view of blacks as aggressive, persistent (24%), straightforward (19%), grasping (19%), and revengeful (16%) appears to reflect the former's apprehensiveness about increasing black militancy.

The hypothesis *(H₄)* that blacks are more likely than are whites to describe blacks in favorable terms is supported only to the extent that the former do not use obviously negative expressions such as "grasping" and "revengeful." Otherwise, black and white characterizations of blacks are quite similar, producing a new stereotype as musical and aggressive. The 1970 black-white consensus differs from that of 1932, which implied the minority absorption of the dominant groups' negative image of blacks. It appears that in 1970 blacks are creating a new image for themselves, which whites reflect.

Blacks' self-image and their image perceived by Sacramento Japanese Americans coincide fairly well, although blacks accentuate certain traits more than the Japanese do.

The politically active Japanese American students emphasize different characteristics of the blacks from those selected by the Sacramento students. Although musicality, joviality, and impulsiveness are mentioned, a large percentage assign such traits as straightforwardness (53%), aggressiveness (51%), revengefulness (39%), and persistence (35%). An interpretation of this result from the present study alone is impossible. However, research on the identity crisis of radical Japanese American students, reported elsewhere (Minako Kurokawa, *Japanese American Identity Dilemma,*) sheds some light. Rebelling against the image of the Quiet Americans, younger Japanese Americans are inclined to adopt as a model the tactics of confrontation used by the blacks (Bell and Kristol 1968). As a likely result, they would tend to view the blacks in the framework of militancy and aggression.

IMAGE OF THE JAPANESE    The hypotheses *(H₅)* that the Japanese are likely to be viewed in a favorable light by whites is supported. The Japanese are characterized by instrumental activism and traditional Oriental culture. They are seen as ambitious (51%), intelligent (38%), industrious (35%), and efficient (19%), and also loyal to family (67%), conventional (24%), and courteous (27%). Measured on the scale of favorableness (Karlins et al. 1969), a cluster of these traits scores higher than the traits attributed by whites to themselves. For instance, on the 84-point rank order "intelligent" ranks second; "industrious," seventh; "efficient," eleventh; "courteous," twelfth; "ambitious," fourteenth; and "loyal to family ties," twenty-eighth from the top, in comparison with the whites' predominant traits of "materialistic," ranking forty-ninth, and "pleasure loving," twenty-ninth. However, a favorable view of the other group does not necessarily mean closeness in social distance. As pointed out by Karlins and others (Karlins et al. 1969; Marx 1967; Noel and Pinkney 1964), a person's social stereotypes do not always favor his own group. The character of stereotyping may follow an ethnocentric pattern or may not, depending upon the perceivers, but ethnocentrism is evidently not inherent in the stereotyping itself.

As hypothesized $(H_5)$, blacks assign favorable traits to the Japanese. The major difference between black and white views is that the former characterize the Japanese as reserved (25%) and quiet (23%) significantly more frequently than do the latter.

The sixth hypothesis $(H_6)$ states that Japanese Americans are critical of their traditional stereotype as industrious and quiet. From our data alone it is difficult to test this hypothesis, since a mere mention of such traits does not mean approval nor disapproval. However, a comparison of Sacramento and Berkeley–Los Angeles students gives some clues. While some Sacramento students describe the Japanese as reserved (31%), and quiet (19%), radical Japanese Americans in Berkeley and Los Angeles overwhelmingly characterize the Japanese as quiet (61%), conservative (54%), and reserved (39%). Since radical students are far more outspoken and "nonquiet" than the Sacramento Japanese Americans, it appears that the former's reference to quietness does not imply their self-portrayal but rather their self-criticism. At least they are much more concerned with such traits as quietness or reserve than with industriousness and intelligence. Although "quiet" (thirty-ninth) and "aggressive" (fortieth) both occupy middle ranks on Karlins's (Karlins et al. 1969) scale of favorableness, studies (Uyematsu 1969) of radical Asian American students indicate that quietness ranks very low in their own estimate.

In the student population, the hypothesis of the lessening of minority absorption of dominant views is supported. In the 1930s the dominant whites set the social norms of a positive image of whites and negative images of minorities to which the minority members were expected to conform. In the 1970 study, minority groups are failing to conform to this expectation and are obviously attempting to create new images for themselves.

**Adult Perception**

In comparison with college students, it is expected $(H_7)$ that adults are likely to be more conservative and to have more traditional stereotypes of racial groups.

In the 1970 sample even white adults do not describe themselves exclusively as industrious, intelligent, and ambitious but are self-critical enough to mention traits like being materialistic and pleasure loving. In fact, the order of selection of traits by adults is similar to that of the students. However, as hypothesized $(H_7)$, students are significantly less stereotypical than the adults. The responses of the former are dispersed over a wide range of characteristics rather than clustered about a few traits. The degree of uniformity in attitudes among the white adults is shown by the fact that half of all selections referring to the whites are subsumed under 3.9 traits, compared with 7.8 traits in the case of white students (see Table 2).

The same thing can be said about black and Japanese American views of whites; that is, adults are significantly more stereotypical than students, as

## TABLE 2
### Adults' Image of Racial Groups (in Percentage)

#### IMAGE OF THE WHITES

| | W[a] | B[b] | JA[c] |
|---|---|---|---|
| Pleasure loving | 83 | 71 | 75 |
| Materialistic | 63 ** | 45 | 50 |
| Aggressive | 50 | 40 ** | 62 |
| Ambitious | 50 | 42 | 50 |
| Progressive | 42 ** | 20 * | 25 |
| Industrious | 29 | ... | ... |
| Intelligent | 29 | 23 | 21 |
| Individualistic | 29 | ... | 21 |
| Conventional | 25 | ... | ... |
| Scientifically minded | 25 | ... | 25 |

#### IMAGE OF THE BLACKS

| | W[a] | B[b] | JA[c] |
|---|---|---|---|
| Musical | 69 * | 81 | 87 |
| Pleasure loving | 42 | 54 | 50 |
| Loud | 38 * | 21 ** | 40 |
| Lazy | 35 | ... | 35 |
| Happy-go-lucky | 31 | 32 | ... |
| Sensitive | 31 | ... | ... |
| Aggressive | 19 | 23 | 19 |
| Jovial | 19 * | 35 * | 33 |
| Materialistic | 19 | 21 | ... |
| Very religious | 19 * | 33 | ... |

#### IMAGE OF THE JAPANESE

| | W[a] | B[b] | JA[c] |
|---|---|---|---|
| Loyal to family | 77 * | 60 ** | 50 |
| Ambitious | 50 | 52 * | 33 |
| Courteous | 50 * | 62 ** | 32 |
| Industrious | 50 | 41 ** | 62 |
| Efficient | 42 ** | ... | 21 |
| Intelligent | 42 ** | 21 | ... |
| Artistic | 31 | 20 | ... |
| Tradition loving | 31 | ... | ... |
| Conservative | 27 ** | ... | 48 |
| Neat | 27 ** | 23 ** | 50 |

(continued)

**TABLE 2** (*Continued*)

| | IMAGE OF THE WHITES | | | | IMAGE OF THE BLACKS | | | | IMAGE OF THE JAPANESE | | |
|---|---|---|---|---|---|---|---|---|---|---|---|
| | $W^a$ | $B^b$ | $JA^c$ | | $W^a$ | $B^b$ | $JA^c$ | | $W^a$ | $B^b$ | $JA^c$ |
| Alert | 21 | ... | 23 | Quick-tempered | 27 | 23 | 22 | Alert | 23 | ... | ... |
| Imaginative | 21 | ... | ... | Quarrelsome | 23 | ... | 17 | Quiet | 23 | 35 | 23 |
| Practical | 21 | 25 | 23 | Revengeful | 23 | ... | ... | Reserved | 23 | 23 | 52 |
| Talkative | ... | ... | 48 | Talkative | ... | ... | 38 | Practical | ... | ... | 32 |
| Gregarious | ... | ... | 21 | Unreliable | ... | ... | 27 | Conventional | ... | ... | 25 |
| Argumentative | ... | ... | 21 | Ignorant | ... | ... | 25 | Honest | ... | ... | 23 |
| ... | ... | ... | ... | Impulsive | ... | 24 | 27 | Faithful | ... | ... | 19 |
| ... | ... | ... | ... | Frivolous | ... | ... | 25 | Imitative | ... | ... | 19 |
| Traits (N) on which 50% of the sample is dispersed | 3.9 | 6.6 | 4.4 | | 6.1 | 6.5 | 5.0 | | 4.8 | 5.0 | 5.1 |

(In the IMAGE OF THE JAPANESE section, ** brackets connect the *Reserved* values of $W^a$–$B^b$ and $B^b$–$JA^c$.)

[a] 100 white adults in Sacramento.
[b] 100 black adults in Sacramento.
[c] 100 Japanese American adults in Sacramento.

\* $p < .05$.
\*\* $p < .01$.

hypothesized *(H₇)*. Also, among adults there is a greater degree of minority absorption of white values, since black and Japanese American adults rarely use explicitly negative epithets. On the contrary, they are adding positive adjectives, such as "progressive," "individualistic," and "scientifically minded," to the list of traits selected by students.

As hypothesized *(H₇)*, there is a significantly greater uniformity of black stereotypy among the adults than among the students of each racial group. White and black adult characterizations of blacks assume levels of consensus twice as high as those found in student descriptions. Not only are the adults more stereotypical than college students in portraying blacks, but the former tend to add traditionally negative traits such as laziness and ignorance. Japanese Americans are particularly critical about blacks, stating that the latter are lazy, unreliable, ignorant, and frivolous. All of these traits rank low on the scale of favorableness. This may be explained by the fact that current Japanese American adults (Nisei), children of Japanese immigrants, have tended to conform strongly to white values (Hosokawa 1969). They tend to reflect and magnify the latter's prejudice against blacks. In general, however, the trend toward neutralization of the black image in recent years is recognizable even among adults. They no longer describe blacks as superstitious and ignorant but rather as musical, pleasure loving, and aggressive.

As hypothesized *(H₇)*, adults are more stereotypical than students in describing the Japanese, although the traits chosen are basically similar, namely, a combination of traditionalism and instrumental activism. They are depicted as loyal to family, courteous, reserved, and quiet, and at the same time ambitious, industrious, efficient, and intelligent.

In general, the differences in uniformity between adults and students are mostly significant. Adults are slightly more inclined toward the traditional stereotype, and the degree of minority absorption of the dominant stereotypes is slightly greater among them than among students, especially radical students.

## Child Perception

IMAGE OF THE WHITES    The eighth hypothesis *(H₈)* states that the degree of minority absorption of the dominant image is greater in white-dominant schools than in racially mixed schools. In other words, whites are more likely to be described in positive terms by children of all races in white-dominant schools than by those in mixed schools.

The data (see Table 3) reject the hypothesis and indicate an opposite tendency. In white-dominant schools, black and Japanese American children are significantly more likely than are white children to describe whites in such negative terms as "aggressive," "mean," and "cheating," while in mixed schools there is no significant difference among the children of the three racial groups. In fact, black and Japanese American children in mixed schools are significantly less inclined to describe whites negatively and more inclined to use friendly terms. In white-dominant schools, while white children describe themselves as popular and attractive and as leaders, minority children fail to absorb this image. In short, minority children in white-dominant schools are more likely to view whites negatively than are nonwhite children in mixed schools.

## TABLE 3
### Children's Image of Racial Groups (in Percentage)

| IMAGE OF THE WHITES | $W^a$ | $B^b$ | $JA^c$ | IMAGE OF THE BLACKS | $W^a$ | $B^b$ | $JA^c$ | IMAGE OF THE JAPANESE | $W^a$ | $B^b$ | $JA^c$ |
|---|---|---|---|---|---|---|---|---|---|---|---|
| Economic features: high living level, materialistic, snobbish | 55 | 61 | 52 | Positive traits: good in sports, in music, in dancing | 31 | 40 | 32 | Quietness: shy, not speaking in classes | ** [78 ** 80 * 68 | | |
| | (64) | (50) | (50) | | (50) | (57) | (46) | | (38) | (39) | (40) |
| Protestant ethics: ambitious, industrious, practical, individualistic | 48 | ... | ... | Friendliness: sensitive, jovial, happy, nice, outgoing | * [25 48 18 | | | Tolerance: "OK," nice, good | ** [20 ** 15 ** 26 | | |
| | (45) | ... | ... | | (30) * (65) * (30) | | | | (50) | (45) | (68) |
| Religiosity: faithful, honest, kind, religious | (28) | ... | ... | Neutrality: larger family, poor, different language | * [34 * 60 18 ** | | | Intelligence: smart, good grades | 65 * [60 82 | | |
| | | | | | (40) (30) * (20) | | | | (46) * (50) | (70) | |
| Popularity, leadership: center of attraction, tall, handsome * | ** [65 ** 32 28 | | | Negative traits: lazy, not smart, mean, fighting ** | ** [82 ** 20 36 | | | Traditionalism: loyal to family | 36 | 45 | 56 |
| | (41) | (40) | (30) | | (28) | (15) | (30) | | (38) | (49) | (58) |

(continued)

**TABLE 3** (*Continued*)

| | IMAGE OF THE WHITES | | | IMAGE OF THE BLACKS | | | IMAGE OF THE JAPANESE | | |
|---|---|---|---|---|---|---|---|---|---|
| | $W^a$ | $B^b$ | $JA^c$ | $W^a$ | $B^b$ | $JA^c$ | $W^a$ | $B^b$ | $JA^c$ |
| Friendliness: outgoing, friendly | 27 | 21 * | 28 | Physical difference ... | ... | 56 ** | 26 | Negative traits 17 | 19 | 28 |
| | (26) | (40) | (62) | | ... | (25) | (20) | | | |
| Negative traits: aggressive, mean, cheating | 22 * | 60 ** | 74 | ... | ... | ... | ... | Physical difference 11 | 71 ** | 18 |
| | (20) | (33) | (30) | | | | | ... | (20) | ... |
| Physical difference ... | ... | 50 | 30 | ... | ... | ... | ... | ... | ... | ... |
| | ... | (30) | (16) | | | | | | | |

*Note:* Figures within parentheses indicate percentages for racially mixed school, while figures without parentheses refer to white-dominant schools.

a 100 white children in Sacramento.

b 100 black children in Sacramento.

c 100 Japanese American children in Sacramento.

* $p < .05$.

** $g < .01$.

The difference in characterization of whites appears between the whites and nonwhites rather than between white-dominant and mixed school populations. Nonwhite children are significantly more concerned than are white children with such physical characteristics as skin color. White children are significantly more likely to give themselves an idealistic image derived from Protestant ethics such as faithful, honest, kind, religious, ambitious, industrious, practical, and individualistic.

As in the case of adults, children of all racial groups in both school contexts delineate the white image repeatedly in economic terms. Whites have higher living standards, are rich, have big houses, and so on. White children describe whites as materialistic and pleasure loving, while nonwhites describe them as snobbish and conceited.

IMAGE OF THE BLACKS    The hypothesis $(H_8)$ that the minority children in white-dominant schools tend to absorb a negative image of blacks is not supported. White children in white-dominant schools describe blacks in negative terms—lazy, not smart, mean, or fighting (82%)—but whites in mixed schools and nonwhites tend to be much less negative in their characterization of blacks. Black children in white-dominant schools are significantly more concerned with physical differences, such as curly hair, big noses, big lips, than those in mixed schools. It is interesting that white children are least concerned with physical differences in describing either themselves or other racial groups.

Seemingly factual descriptions of blacks are given most frequently by black children in white-dominant schools: blacks are poor, have large families, speak a different language, or go to different schools. Although apparently factual in nature, the content of these descriptions is not complimentary. It may be that black children in white-dominant schools are more concerned with their self-image both in terms of their physical appearance and their social and economic conditions than black children in mixed schools.

Black children are significantly more likely than whites or Japanese Americans to describe blacks as friendly, sensitive, jovial, happy, nice, or outgoing. Positive traits ascribed to blacks by children of all racial groups consist of their being good in sports, in music, or in dancing. In short, they are "fun to be with."

IMAGE OF THE JAPANESE    As hypothesized $(H_8)$, children in white-dominant schools are significantly more likely than those of mixed schools to accept the stereotypical image of the Japanese as quiet. However, reports by the children that the Japanese are shy and do not speak in classes indicate that the image of the Japanese may be based on observation rather than on acceptance of a stereotype. Also, it is significant that Japanese children in white-dominant schools are described as "shy, bashful, dainty, humorless, and square and do not speak up" and seem to be intimidated by the dominant and popular white children. Negative traits such as cowardess, sneaking, imitativeness, and deceit and physical differences such as having black hair and almond eyes are significantly more frequently mentioned by children of white-dominant schools than those of mixed schools. In mixed schools, Japanese children are characterized as friendly, kind, or nice, whereas in white-dominant schools they are tolerated as "OK" by others.

The Japanese are overwhelmingly described as intelligent, smart, industrious, or getting good grades by children of all racial groups in this study.

Another outstanding feature of the Japanese image is traditionalism. They are considered to be loyal to their family ties, religious, courteous, neat, honest, artistic, and good at handwork.

## CONCLUSION

In this study, racial stereotypes are viewed as social norms that reflect the dominance of whites over the minorities. So heavy is the prevailing social pressure exerted by the dominant group, as Allport (1958) says, that members of minority groups tend to look at themselves as well as others through the same lens as the dominant group. This mirror-image effect or minority absorption of dominant views was found in the 1930s study in which whites were characterized by positive traits and blacks were stereotyped negatively by both whites and blacks. According to the traditional stereotype, whites are intelligent, ambitious, and industrious, while blacks are superstitious, ignorant, and lazy.

The social structure has changed. Through the civil rights movement, minority groups have gradually improved their position in society. This improvement should be reflected in their images of themselves and others. There is some evidence in the studies made around 1950 that minority absorption of images created by the dominant group considerably decreased. Derived from these facts is the major hypothesis of this paper, that the amount of minority absorption of negative images is considerably less in 1970.

Comparisons of white, black, and Japanese American self-images and images of others were made among college students, adults, and schoolchildren. The fading of the mirror image is seen in the discrepancy between white and black as well as radical Japanese American students' views of whites. While whites are inclined to characterize themselves by neutral traits such as materialism and love of pleasure, blacks and radical Japanese Americans resist absorbing this white image and attribute to whites such negative traits as deceitfulness and conceit.

There is a fair amount of consensus among racial groups in describing blacks. The mirror image still exists, but the direction of the reflection is changing. In the past it was the minority group that reflected the dominant views. The recent emergence of Black Power, however, seems to have changed the direction of influence in disseminating the stereotype. Since 1965 blacks have shifted their tactics from integration toward racial autonomy and identity, and from peaceful accommodation to militant confrontation. They are trying to create a new image, with the slogan "Black is Beautiful." In the present study, blacks are described as aggressive and straightforward by blacks as well as by others. It appears that the blacks' attempt to create a new image for themselves is reflected in white perceptions.

Influenced by the Black Power movement, the Japanese Americans have become critical of their traditional stereotype as industrious and reserved. Radical Japanese Americans in this study show a great dislike for their image as Quiet Americans.

Although still existing to some extent, the minority absorption of racial images created by the dominant group has declined considerably since 1932 among college students. As expected, this is less true among adults, who are more inclined toward the traditional stereotyping. Among schoolchildren, racial composition of the school has some bearing on their perception of stereotypes.

Finally, reliability and validity of the research instrument should be considered. The Katz and Braly inventory has its advantage in its quantitative comparability of various study groups. However, its simplicity in processing produces difficulties in interpretation. First of all, respondents are constrained to the selection of only five adjectives to describe a given group, which causes their resistance and may affect individual respondents differently in making generalizations. Second, the implication of positive versus negative, or favorable versus unfavorable, qualities derived from an adjective trait is not reliable, since the basis for evaluation varies from time to time and from social group to social group (materialism and pleasure loving, the main elements of the prevailing stereotype of whites found in this study, may be highly negative, rather than neutral as in the 1930s). Third, uniformity or great consensus in verbal stereotyping does not necessarily mean the existence of prejudice and ethnocentrism. It may indicate consensus due to widespread knowledge about a given group. Finally, stereotype affirmation, whether positive or negative, may be verbal artifacts of a situation rather than a true self-estimate or estimate of others.

## NOTES

1   This study was supported by the U.S. Public Health grant no. 1 R03 MH 18751-01. The author wishes to thank Ms. Florence Levinsohn for her editorial assistance.
2   Although not specifically stated, the sample is assumed to consist predominantly of whites. Before 1940, fewer than 25% of the Princeton student body came from public schools.
3   Although not specifically mentioned, the sample is assumed to consist predominantly of white students. The ratio of public high school graduates to private high school graduates was 45:55.
4   The sample consists of white students only. The ratio of public high school graduates to private high school graduates in the sample was 90:60.
5   Chi-square test of significance at the .05 level.
6   Significant at the .05 level by the Kolmogorov-Smirnov test of dispersion. The differences in dispersions of distributions are tested by this test throughout the paper.

## REFERENCES

*Abrahams, Rodger D.*
1970   Positively Black. Englewood Cliffs, N.J.: Prentice-Hall.
*Adelson, Joseph.*
1958   "A Study of Minority Group Authoritarianism." In The Jews, Social Patterns of an American Group, edited by Marshall Sklare. New York: Free Press.

*Allport, Gordon W.*
1958   The Nature of Prejudice. New York: Doubleday.
*Aptheker, Herbert.*
1951   A Documentary History of the Negro People in the United States. New York: Citadel.
*Bayton, James A.*
1941   "The Radical Stereotypes of Negro College Students." Journal of Abnormal and Social Psychology 36:97–102.
*Bayton, James A., and E. F. Byoune.*
1947   "Racio-National Stereotypes Held by Negroes." Journal of Negro Education 16:49–56.
*Bell, Daniel, and I. Kristol, eds.*
1968   Confrontation. New York: Basic Books.
*Berelson, Bernard, and P. J. Salter.*
1946   "Majority and Minority Americans: An Analysis of Magazine Fiction." Public Opinion Quarterly 19 (Summer): 168–90.
*Bronfenbrenner, Urie.*
1961   "The Mirror Image in Soviet-American Relations." Journal of Social Issues 17:45–56.
*Carmichael, Stokely, and C. Hamilton.*
1967   Black Power: The Politics of Liberation in America. New York: Random House.
*Caudill, William.*
1952   "Japanese-American Personality and Acculturation." Genetic Psychology Monographs 15:3–102.
*Clark, Kenneth B., and M. P. Clark.*
1958   "Racial Identification and Reference in Negro Children." In Readings in Social Psychology, edited by Eleanor E. Maccoby et al. New York: Holt.
*Dworkin, Anthony G.*
1965   "Stereotypes and Self-Images Held by Native-born and Foreign-born Mexican Americans." Sociology and Social Research, vol. 49 (January).
*Frazier, E. Franklin.*
1957   The Negro in the United States. New York: Macmillan.
*Gilbert, G. M.*
1951   "Stereotype Persistence and Change among College Students." Journal of Abnormal and Social Psychology 46 (April): 245–54.
*Goodman, Mary E.*
1954   Race Awareness in Young Children. New York: Macmillan.
*Gundlach, Ralph H.*
1944   "The Attitudes of Enemy, Allied, and Domestic Nationality Groups as Seen by College Students of Different Regions." Journal of Social Psychology 19:249–58.
*Hollingshead, August B.*
1957   "Two Factor Index of Social Position." Yale Station, New Haven, Conn.: privately printed.
*Horowitz, Ruth.*
1939   "Racial Aspects of Self-Identification in Nursery School Children." Journal of Psychology (January), pp. 91–99.
*Hosokawa, Bill.*
1969   Nisei: The Quiet American. New York: William Morrow.
*Hyde, Stuart W.*
1955   "The Chinese Stereotype in American Melodrama." California Historical Society Quarterly (December), pp. 357–67.
*Karlins, Marvin, et al.*
1969   "On the Fading of Social Stereotypes: Studies in Three Generations of College Students." Journal of Personality and Social Psychology 13:1–16.

*Katz, Daniel, and K. W. Braly.*
1933    "Racial Stereotypes of 100 College Students." Journal of Abnormal and Social Psychology 28:280–90.
*Keim, Margaret L.*
1941    "The Chinese as Portrayed in the Works of Bret Harte." Sociology and Social Research (May), pp. 441–50.
*Kitano, Harry H. L.*
1969    Japanese Americans. Englewood Cliffs, N.J.: Prentice-Hall.
*Laue, James H.*
1965    "Changing Character of the Negro Protest." American Academy of Political and Social Science, Annals 352 (January): 119–26.
*Mackie, J. Milton.*
1857    "The Chinaman." Putman's Monthly (April), Pp. 337–50.
*Marx, Gary T.*
1967    Protest and Prejudice. New York: Harper & Row.
*Matthews, Fred H.*
1964    "White Community and 'Yellow Peril.'" Mississippi Valley Historical Review (March), pp. 612–33.
*Maykovich, Minako Kurokawa.*
1972    Japanese American Identity Dilemma, Tokyo, Japan: Waseda University Press.
*Meenes, Max.*
1943    "A Comparison of Racial Stereotypes of 1935 and 1942." Journal of Social Psychology 17:327–36.
*Merton, Robert K.*
1948    "The Self-Fulfilling Prophecy." Antioch Review 8:193–210.
1957    Social Theory and Social Structure. New York: Free Press.
*Noel, D. L., and A. Pinkney.*
1964    "Correlates of Prejudice: Some Racial Differences and Similarities." American Journal of Sociology 59:609–22.
*Palmore, Erdman B.*
1962    "Ethnophaulisms and Ethnocentrism." American Journal of Sociology 67 (January): 442–45.
*Parsons, Talcott.*
1937    The Structure of Social Action. New York: Free Press.
*Peterson, William.*
1966    "Success Story: Japanese American Style." New York Times, January 9, pp. 19–43.
*Pettigrew, Thomas F.*
1969    "Racially Separate or Together?" Journal of Social Issues 25:43–69.
*Pinkney, Alphonso.*
1969    Black Americans. Englewood Cliffs, N.J.: Prentice-Hall.
*Prosser, W. Thornton.*
1908    "The Western View of the Japanese." World's Work (December), pp. 10989–91.
*Rose, Arnold M.*
1949    The Negro's Morale. Minneapolis: University of Minnesota Press.
*Rose, Peter I.*
1964    They and We. New York: Random House.
*Seago, Dorothy W.*
1947    "Stereotypes: Before Pearl Harbor and After." Journal of Psychology 23:55–63.
*Seeman, Melvin.*
1966    "Status and Identity: The Problem of Inauthenticity." Pacific Sociological Review. 9:67–73.
*Simmons, Ozzie G.*
1961    "The Mutual Images and Expectations of Anglo-Americans and Mexican-Americans." Daedalus (Spring), pp. 286–99.

*Stouffer, Samuel A., et al.*
1949   The American Soldier. Vol. 1. Princeton, N.J.: Princeton University Press.
*tenBrock, Jacobus, et al.*
1968   Prejudice, War and the Constitution. Berkeley: University of California Press.
*Uyematsu, Amy.*
1969   "The Emergence of Yellow Power in America." Gidra (October).
*Veblen, Thorstein.*
1934   The Theory of the Leisure Class. New York: Modern Library.
*Vinacke, W. E.*
1956   "Explorations in the Dynamic Processes of Stereotyping." Journal of Social Psychology 43:105–32.
*Zeligs, Rose.*
1941   "Influencing Children's Attitudes toward the Chinese." Sociology and Social Research 26:126–38.

# Through the School-House Door: Trends in Integration Attitudes on a Deep-South Campus During the First Decade of Desegregation*

## Donal E. Muir

*University of Alabama*

*Four surveys of the attitudes of the white students on the main campus of the University of Alabama begun in 1963 and continued at three-year intervals consistently indicate increasing acceptance of blacks. Most of these students now approve of desegregation in all major areas, have rejected the classic Southern stereotype of blacks and uphold ideals of political and economic equality. Blacks are strongly accepted on campus as students, but still tend to be rejected as roommates, social intimates, or dates. The data indicate, however*

*Source:* Donal E. Muir, "Through the School-House Door: Trends in Integration Attitudes on a Deep-South Campus During the First Decade of Desegregation," Sociology and Social Research 58, 2 (January 1974): 113–21. Copyright © 1974 Sociology and Social Research. Reprinted by permission.

*that social distance is rapidly decreasing. It would appear that the desegrega-*
*tion of any social system, including educational systems tends to result in rapid*
*rejection of "racial" roles for interaction assuming that the setting has been*
*politically neutralized.*

The University of Alabama, typical of state universities in the deep South
in many respects, has served as a national symbol of Southern white resistance
to school desegregation on two occasions. In February 1956, the first black
student, Autherine Lucy, was admitted to the university by federal court order.
Riots occurred on campus and at one point Ms. Lucy was rescued from a
classroom building by state troopers. Her accusation that the university was
involved in the demonstrations against her presence, not sustained in court,
served as the formal basis for her being expelled by the trustees (see Egerton,
1969: 39).

In June 1963, a second attempt to desegregate the university was made by
Vivian Malone and James A. Hood, again admitted by federal court order. It
was on this occasion that then-Governor George C. Wallace made his highly
publicized but ineffectual "stand in the school-house door." Ms. Malone remained at the university (during that summer, on a visit to the campus the
author asked one of the well-advanced hostesses of the guest residence how
integration was going and was told, "Oh, she's very nice!") becoming, in May
1965 the first black student to graduate.

In the decade following the university's effective desegregation in 1963, the
university maintained a formal posture of nondiscrimination, allowing it to
receive both state and federal financial support. Small, but increasing, numbers
of black students were admitted (Figure 1), but the athletic teams, fraternities,
and sororities remained "lily white." In 1968 black students filed suit against
the university noting that there were still no black athletes on the teams. In
1969 the university signed a black as a basketball player and, in 1970, two blacks
were signed to play football (Crimson-White January 18, 1973). By the Fall of
1973 blacks not only had starting positions on most teams but, most significantly, played starring roles on the Crimson Tide, which in recent years has
served as almost the sole symbol of national recognition (e.g., countless signs
proclaiming "We're no. 1") in a region noted for its ethnocentrism.

As Emory Bogardus (1933) noted in his pioneering work with social distance, resistance to interaction with members of an outgroup increases with
social intimacy. No blacks have been invited to join the existing fraternities or
sororities, a fact that the president of the Interfraternity Council explained by
lack of interest ("none have gone through our rush for the last three years").
The contention of black students that they are unwelcome would seem, however, to be validated by this same president who notes that "the Interfraternity
Council has been trying for several years to get a *black* (italics mine) fraternity
on campus" (Crimson-White March 12, 1973). In August, 1973, a black fraternity
was formed and it formally affiliated with the Interfraternity Council. Plans are
now being formulated for a black sorority because as one black coed put it. "The
University of Alabama . . . disappointed me extremely in the fact that there was
no leeway for a good social life along with no sororities I could join" (Black
Community Newsletter, October 18, 1973).

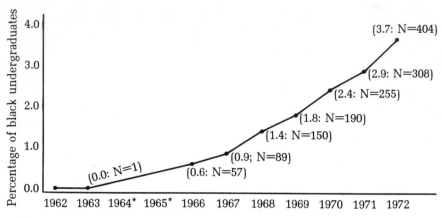

**Fig. 1   Percentage of black undergraduates, University of Alabama Main Campus.**

Recognition of this formal atmosphere of official nondiscrimination/non-support, with still-active forces tending to maintain social segregation, is necessary to fully evaluate the changes in attitude which have occurred on this campus, as measured by the four surveys taken over a ten-year period and reported below.

## METHOD

During this first decade of the University of Alabama's desegregation experience, four surveys concerning integration attitudes were administered to approximately 10 percent of the white undergraduates using quotas based on academic year, sex, and college. The first was completed in April 1963, two months before the enrollments of Hood and Malone, with the other surveys following at three-year intervals during November of 1966 (Muir and McGlamery 1968), 1969 (Muir 1971a and 1971b), and 1972. The twenty-seven items examined below were included, in identical form in the anonymous questionnaires used in all four of these surveys. Likert-type response sets ("strongly disagree, disagree, undecided, agree, strongly agree") were employed with all items.

## FINDINGS

### Attitudes Regarding Major Areas of Desegregation

Responses to items dealing with marriage, religion, sociable interaction, and education are presented in Table 1. Even before the effective desegregation of the university in 1963, the majority of students viewed both marriage and religion as private matters. Less than a majority, however, indicated approval of social mixing or the desegregation of the university. In each of the later surveys, the proportion of students approving all items increased, strongly indicating a unidirectional shift in general cultural values toward increasing favorableness to integration (the probability that all twelve of the twelve possible increases would occur by chance is .0002).

Since "100 percent approval" is the upper limit for such measurements, the level of approval necessarily increases less as this maximum is approached. This "ceiling effect" is clearly evidenced by these data with the items which had more initial agreement (marriage, worship) noticeably tapering off in the 80–90 percent region while the items which started lower (social mixing, university desegregation) continue their rapid climb to comparable levels. As a social system moves from one cultural orientation to another, an S-shaped curve can be expected to describe the level of acceptance of new attitudes overtime, and it is just this function which seems indicated by these data (see Coleman 1964: 192–514).

## Social Distance on Campus

The seven items concerning social distance are shown in Table 2. In 1963, a majority of the white students had no objection only to attending classes with

### TABLE 1
#### Attitudes Regarding Major Areas of Desegregation

|  | PER CENT "AGREE" OR "STRONGLY AGREE" | | | |
|---|---|---|---|---|
| *ITEM* | *1963 (N = 676)* | *1966 (N = 871)* | *1969 (N = 1039)* | *1972 (N = 1020)* |
| 1. The choice of a marriage partner is a private affair and no legal restrictions should be placed on the choice in terms of race, religion, or creed. | 61.8 | 62.6 | 81.0 | 81.7 |
| 2. Freedom of worship means that all individuals without regard to race, should be able to attend any service they choose. | 54.4 | 62.1 | 80.6 | 85.1 |
| 3. *There should not be legal restrictions to keep Negroes from mixing with whites. | 44.5 | 57.8 | 74.2 | 83.1 |
| 4. Desegregation of the University of Alabama is a step in the right direction to improve the quality of citizenship in the state. | 30.0 | 45.7 | 59.3 | 71.5 |

*The "Not" has been inserted in item no. 3 so that it has the same direction as the other items for clarity (i.e., the responses to this item are the combined percentages "disagree" and "strongly disagree" to the original item, without the "not").*

blacks. By 1966, a majority were also willing to sit next to black students in class. By 1969, interaction had taken on a sociable dimension, with a majority willing to walk on campus and eat with blacks. Even by 1972, however, a majority still had reservations concerning the close personal involvement associated with rooming with, double dating with, and dating black students. Nevertheless, these data indicate that there are increasingly strong cross-pressures developing, illustated by a recent case coming to my attention where a white girl, with a very conservative background, was assigned a black roommate in the dorm. She insisted that she be immediately reassigned to a room with a white roommate. Although this request was carried out, the girl has begun to make frequent, and increasingly friendly, visits to see her ex-roommate.

Since blacks still constitute less than 4 percent of the undergraduate student body, such personal contact is, of course, somewhat limited. Even limited interaction with blacks, such as in the classrooms, tends, however, to call into question the traditional stereotypes upon which high levels of prejudice are based (as shown in Table 4, to be discussed later). While thus leading to an immediate, if perhaps small, lowering of the level of prejudice, such initial superficial contact appears to be an important factor in preparing the individual for the later, more dramatic, reductions in prejudice which tend to follow more intimate interaction. As Berelson and Steiner (1964: 510–512) put it, "Personal contact with members of ethnic minorities does not automatically increase or reduce tensions: it can do either or neither" but "*in situations of not very high prejudice* [italics mine], the introduction of personal contacts between members of different ethnic groups tends to lead to a lessening of prejudice, and even of discrimination." If this two-step model of prejudice reduction is valid, it follows that the effect of the mere presence of limited numbers of black students on this campus, in producing readiness for further integration favorableness, far exceeds their proportionate representation. Further, since it can be reasonably assumed that the proportion of black students will continue to increase, the probability that a prejudiced student will not only come to question his stereotypes, but will experience the more intimate forms of social

TABLE 2

Social Distance on Campus

| "IF QUALIFIED NEGROES ARE ADMITTED TO THE UNIVERSITY OF ALABAMA, I HAVE NO OBJECTION TO . . ." | PER CENT "AGREE" OR "STRONGLY AGREE" | | | |
|---|---|---|---|---|
| | 1963 (N = 676) | 1966 (N = 871) | 1969 (N = 1039) | 1972 (N = 1020) |
| 1. attending classes with them. | 56.4 | 76.6 | 92.2 | 92.5 |
| 2. sitting next to them in class. | 39.1 | 55.3 | 80.0 | 88.3 |
| 3. walking on campus with them. | 27.7 | 35.8 | 61.6 | 81.7 |
| 4. eating in the cafeteria at the same table with them. | 18.2 | 30.0 | 53.9 | 73.4 |
| 5. having them room with me. | 5.8 | 17.6 | 23.0 | 39.8 |
| 6. double dating with them. | 2.5 | 12.3 | 20.9 | 36.7 |
| 7. having a date with them. | .9 | 11.0 | 11.9 | 23.1 |

interaction which produce substantial reductions in prejudice, can also be expected to increase. Interestingly, such changes can be expected to occur disproportionately rapidly to the extent that resistance to change is directly related to the relative size of supporting groups (see Coleman 1964: 479–491). Such factors as well as general societal changes (see Muir, 1971b), appear to have effected dramatic changes in peer group positions, according to these data: in 1963, "most students" objected to being with blacks in almost all situations by 1972, "most students" accepted blacks as fellow students with "many" indicating a readiness to interact socially.

These social distance data disclose the expected trend toward increasing favorableness in all cases (the probability that all twenty-one instances of possible change were in this direction by chance being less than .0000005). The magnitude of change in a single decade is, moreover, quite remarkable, the proportion of students accepting the items increasing by factors ranging from 1.6 to 25.7. The ceiling effect, leading to the S-shaped cultural transition curve discussed earlier, is noticeably operating in connection with the two items with most approval (attending classes with, sitting next to), but the other attitudes continue to change rapidly.

Controlled comparisons indicate little difference by sex, not surprising in a cultural area in which blacks tend to be defined as an outgroup for both sexes. Controlled comparisons by college, however, produce striking differences (see Table 3). As traditionally expected, Arts & Sciences students reported the highest level of acceptance on all four surveys (not including the new program in social work). In the breakdown of the 1972 data, as shown, the highest proportion of social work students accepted every item, the next highest proportion of acceptance of every item being by A&S students compared to the remaining colleges (the probability of this occurring by chance being less than .00002 in both instances. The reader is cautioned that these differences between colleges have been shown to be largely, if not wholly, due to the tendency for liberal applicants to choose traditionally liberal programs, rather than to any differentially liberalizing effects of the programs themselves (see Muir, 1971b).

### Perception of Negro Characteristics

Many of the attitudes held by whites concerning blacks are based upon a stereotype developed in past centuries, when blacks were in formal servitude. The continued relative exclusion of blacks from economic and educational opportunity, especially those most frequently encountered by whites (e.g., maids, cooks, yard workers), tends to provide apparent validation for those whites who seek it. In Table 4, items related to such stereotyping are reported. In 1963, a majority of students regarded Negroes as relatively superstitious and incapable, while roughly half of them also thought Negroes were generally shiftless, lazy, unambitious, and relatively untrustworthy. In each succeeding survey, such negative views were increasingly rejected (of the twenty-seven opportunities for indicated change, twenty-four are in the direction of increasing favorableness, the probability of such an extreme result occurring by chance being less than .000005). By 1972, less than 30 percent of the students still regarded blacks as relatively superstitious, only about 24 percent thought of them as relatively incapable, unintelligent, and unworthy of opportunity,

## TABLE 3
### Social Distance on Campus in 1972, by College

| "IF QUALIFIED NEGROES ARE ADMITTED TO THE UNIVERSITY OF ALABAMA, I HAVE NO OBJECTION TO ..." | PER CENT "AGREE" OR "STRONGLY AGREE" | | | | | | |
|---|---|---|---|---|---|---|---|
| | SOCIAL WORK (N = 19) | ARTS & SCIENCES (N = 439) | EDUCATION (N = 199) | ENGINEERING (N = 52) | COMMERCE (N = 244) | HOME EC. (N = 54) | ADJUSTED UNIVERSITY TOTAL (N = 1020) |
| 1. attending classes with them. | 100.0 | 94.3 | 92.5 | 86.5 | 89.3 | 92.6 | 92.5 |
| 2. sitting next to them in class. | 100.0 | 92.3 | 89.5 | 78.9 | 81.1 | 88.9 | 88.3 |
| 3. walking on campus with them. | 100.0 | 86.1 | 79.9 | 75.0 | 75.4 | 79.6 | 81.7 |
| 4. eating in the cafeteria at the same table with them. | 94.7 | 78.4 | 71.4 | 63.5 | 66.4 | 72.2 | 73.4 |
| 5. having them room with me. | 63.2 | 47.4 | 32.7 | 36.5 | 34.4 | 20.4 | 39.8 |
| 6. double dating with them. | 68.4 | 44.0 | 30.2 | 32.7 | 29.1 | 27.8 | 36.7 |
| 7. having a date with them. | 42.1 | 30.5 | 17.6 | 23.1 | 16.8 | 9.3 | 23.1 |

## TABLE 4
### Perception of Negro Characteristics

| ITEM | PER CENT "AGREE OR "STRONGLY AGREE" | | | |
|---|---|---|---|---|
| | 1963 (N = 676) | 1966 (N = 871) | 1969 (N = 1039) | 1972 (N = 1020) |
| 1. Most Negroes are more super-stitious than any white persons I have ever met. | 61.4 | 54.0 | 43.3 | 29.8 |
| 2. Some Negroes may be just as capable, intelligent, and worthy of opportunity as the white man but this is the exception rather than the rule. | 60.8 | 54.4 | 38.0 | 24.2 |
| 3. The Negro is generally shiftless, lazy, and lacks ambition. | 49.7 | 50.5 | 26.4 | 16.1 |
| 4. *Most Negroes are not just as trustworthy as most white peo-ple I know. | 47.6 | 45.8 | 32.2 | 21.3 |
| 5. The moral standards of the South will drop if the Negro is given the same opportunities to use public facilities as the white people. | 42.4 | 30.4 | 18.3 | 9.7 |
| 6. American Negroes do not have the capacity to compete with white students at white univer-sities. | 38.2 | 20.3 | 10.6 | 7.2 |
| 7. Negroes will probably take re-venge on the whites in the South if their economic posi-tion is raised to that of the average white person. | 24.7 | 24.7 | 18.4 | 10.3 |
| 8. If given an equal chance to ob-tain a college education at a white institution, most Negroes would become officious, over-bearing, and disagreeable. | 23.5 | 14.9 | 15.2 | 7.9 |
| 9. I have never met a Negro who is my equal in intelligence. | 23.5 | 22.2 | 9.5 | 7.7 |

*The "Not" has been inserted in item no. 4 so that it has the same direction as the other items, for clarity (i.e., the responses to this item are the combined percentages "disagree" and "strongly disagree" to the original item, without the "not").

**TABLE 5**

Attitudes Regarding Political and Economic Equality

| ITEM | PER CENT "AGREE" OR "STRONGLY AGREE" | | | |
|---|---|---|---|---|
| | 1963 (N = 676) | 1966 (N = 871) | 1969 (N = 1039) | 1972 (N = 1020) |
| 1. Negroes should be treated exactly like white people by the police and courts. | 90.8 | 88.8 | 92.7 | 90.1 |
| 2. Negroes have as much right to any job for which they are trained as a white man. | 85.2 | 82.7 | 88.7 | 89.6 |
| 3. *Negroes should be given the same voting privileges as white people. | 72.9 | 76.5 | 88.4 | 88.7 |
| 4. *There should be no legal restrictions against Negroes running for public office. | 69.8 | 81.1 | 89.8 | 92.6 |
| 5. Negroes should be chosen for jury duty on the same basis as white people. | 67.6 | 77.6 | 86.2 | 85.5 |
| 6. All citizens, regardless of race, religion, or creed, should have equal right to stage a protest march or picket against something they dislike. | 55.0 | 55.2 | 62.4 | 74.3 |
| 7. *Segregation of the races conflicts more with the ideals of freedom in a democracy than does desegregation. | 37.7 | 41.3 | 49.4 | 58.9 |

*Items 3, 4, and 7 were modified (by removing a "not", inserting "no", and removing "does not", respectively) so that they have the same direction as the other items, for clarity (i.e., the responses to these items are the combined percentages "disagree" and "strongly disagree" to the original items).

while only 16 percent held to the notion of blacks as generally shiftless, lazy, and unambitious. Clearly, the classic stereotype of blacks has now been rejected by most of these students.

## Attitudes Regarding Political and Economic Equality

If, as is usually argued in commencement addresses, these students constitute the future leadership of the state, the future of the black citizenry depends greatly upon their attitudes, especially in the strategic areas of political and economic equality. These attitudes are explored in Table 5, where it is seen that political and economic equality were upheld by a majority of the students even in 1963. The response to item no. 7 indicates, however, that such equality was then generally defined within the context of segregation. Although increasing integration favorableness is clearly indicated by these data (the probability that as many as seventeen of the twenty-one instances of possible change were in this direction by chance being less than .004), the high level of acceptance of the top five items has resulted in ceiling-effect attenuation of absolute changes. The bottom two items, concerning the right to public dissent and inconsistency between segregation and democracy, beginning lower, continue to win rapidly increasing approval.

## SUMMARY AND CONCLUSIONS

Four surveys of the attitudes of the white students on the main campus of the University of Alabama, begun in 1963 and continued at three-year intervals, consistently indicate increasing acceptance of blacks. Most of these students now approve of desegregation in all major areas, have rejected the classic Southern stereotype of blacks, and uphold ideals of political and economic equality. Blacks are strongly accepted on campus as students, but still tend to be rejected as roommates, social intimates, or dates. The data indicate, however, that social distance is rapidly decreasing.

Since these attitudes, as well as belief in and identification with "races," are learned (see Clark and Clark, 1958), it is not surprising that they can be unlearned. It is more than a little ironic, however, that the University of Alabama, once used as a national symbol of "segregation forever," provides the politically neutralized setting for demonstrating how quickly such attitudes change in desegregated social systems.

POSTSCRIPT    "Hundreds of Crimson Tide supporters looked on Friday night as Terry Points, a black coed from Birmingham, was named University of Alabama Homecoming Queen at the annual pep rally and bonfire. The first black ever to be selected for the honor, she was presented her trophy by Alabama Governor George C. Wallace . . ." (Tuscaloosa News, November 17, 1973).

## REFERENCES

*Berelson, Bernard and Gary A. Steiner*
1964    Human Behavior: An Inventory of Scientific Findings. New York: Harcourt, Brace & World.
*Bogardus, Emory S.*
1933    "A social distance scale." Sociology and Social Research 17 (January–February): 265–271.
Clark, Kenneth B., and Mamie Clark
1958    "Racial identification and preference in Negro children," in E. E. Maccoby, T. M. Newcomb, and E. L. Hartley (eds.), Readings in Social Psychology. New York: Holt, Rinehart, and Winston.

*Coleman, James S.*
1964   Introduction to Mathematical Sociology. New York: Free Press.
*Egerton, John*
1969   State Universities and Black Americans: An Inquiry into Desegregation and Equity for Negroes in 100 Public Universities. Atlanta: Southern Education Foundation.
*Muir, Donal E.*
1971a   "Six-year trends in integration attitudes of deep-south university students." Integrated Education 9 (January–February): 21–27.
1971b   "The first years of desegregation: patterns of acceptance of black students on a deep-south campus. 1963–69." Social Forces 49 (March): 371–378.
*Muir, Donal E., and C. Donald McGlamery*
1968   "The evolution of desegregation attitudes of southern university students." Phylon 29 (Summer): 105–117.

# WASP–The Emergence of an Ethnic Epithet [1]

## Irving Lewis Allen

*University of Connecticut*

*WASP (WOSP)* n. *1. A member of the Women's Airforce Service Pilots, an organization disbanded in 1944. 2.* Often Disparaging. *A white Anglo-Saxon Protestant (as considered by minority groups to be a dominant type in American society that maintains an inflexibly clannish solidarity).* The Random House Dictionary of the English Language, *1966.*

*WASP*—White Anglo-Saxon Protestant—is one of those pronounceable and irresistable acronyms that is finding a firm niche in the American language. *WASP* has appeared in the mass media with rising frequency in the discussion about ethnic identity of the last few years. Many sociologists and other academics matter of factly use WASP as jargon in their writing and speech and have been doing so for perhaps 15 years. A reification of the WASP concept, as it is coming to be used, defines little or no sociological reality. The connotations, if not also the denotations, of the acronym have become, at worst, epithetical and, at best, questionable sociology.

Taken at face value, WASP would seem simply to designate white Protestants of Anglo-Saxon or perhaps more generally British background, especially descendants of the early immigrants. The term, however, has much wider connotations to include any and all white Americans of Protestant orientation

*Source:* Irving Lewis Allen, "WASP—From Sociological Concept to Epithet," Ethnicity 2, 3 (June 1975): 153–62. Copyright © 1975 by Academic Press, Inc., Publishers. Reprinted by permission.

or background. The new (1970) *American Heritage Dictionary of the English Language* confirms this usage in noting that the term broadly refers to white Protestants of North European extraction. A "WASP" then is almost any white English-speaking American who is not Catholic, Orthodox or Jewish, or of African or Asian descent.

E. Digby Baltzell (1964) in his book, *The Protestant Establishment,* used the acronym to refer to the elite segment or caste of white Protestants who dominated American power and culture well into the Twentieth Century. Baltzell used the acronym solely as an adjective to modify "upper class" and "establishment." It is clear from current usuage, however, that *WASP* refers to all white Protestants, most of whom are not and never were of an elite.

An observation of past sociological usage, moreover, bears out that the Anglo-Saxon referent in *WASP* refers not to a stock of Americans, it is clear, but to the historically dominant culture, language and custom in this country, especially perhaps that brand that emanated from New England. *WASP* could convey a useful concept denoting historically and culturally dominant elements in American society, namely whiteness, a doctrine or an assumption of the "superiority" of Anglo-Saxon culture and traditions, and Protestantism. At first glance, *WASP* would appear to be a useful, even an essential, concept for the discussion of ethnicity in American life. *WASP* does denote an important residual category of multiethnic reality in American life having a common denominator of Protestant orientations, however diverse. The appearance of some kind of term was probably inevitable, and *WASP* was a reasonable one. It is unfortunate that the concept was cast as such a catchy acronym.

As originally used by sociologists, the term indicated a useful abstraction. The abstract noun, however, has emerged as a concrete one. Some sociologists, moreover, following recent popular usage, have fallen into an error of reification and are using the term to denote a material category of persons, assign stereotypical traits, and suggest that such persons constitute an ethnic monolith. In addition, *WASP,* in this reification, has taken on the connotations of an epithet and that particular term should have lost its utility to sociological language.

## AS IDEOLOGICAL RHETORIC

Neither the second edition (1953) nor the third edition (1961) of *Webster's International Dictionary* lists *WASP* as meaning white Anglo-Saxon Protestant, only *wasp* as a metaphor for an irrascible, unpleasant person. The 1963 Funk and Wagnalls unabridged *New Standard Dictionary of the English Language* does not list the Anglo-Saxon referent either. *WASP* with this meaning apparently came into currency sometime before 1966 when the *Random House Dictionary* noted it. As nearly as I can determine short of a content analysis of sociological and journalistic sources, *WASP* with the Anglo-Saxon referent was being used by some sociologists as early as the late fifties, and it is my impression that it was used rather neutrally as an acronym and abstraction. It is not clear to me whether sociologists borrowed the acronym from common parlance and journalism or vice versa. It is more certain that it was not until the mid or late sixties that *WASP* was bandied about in common parlance, in journalism and by some sociologists, *as a word* with its present connotations.

It is interesting to note, parenthetically, that some writers, especially those in the mass media, seem to have recently wearied of the pretense that it is merely an acronym and increasingly use it in upper and lower case—*Wasp.* The new (1970) *American Heritage Dictionary* lists the upper and lower case as the *preferred* form, followed by an all upper case and an all lower case form, in that order. The *American Heritage Dictionary* does *not* note that the term is often disparaging, and gives the definition a literary context with a quotation from Norman Mailer, "The Wasps have taken power." So it is not really an acronoym anymore, but perhaps it never entirely was.

It is my contention that *WASP* began to become objectified and to emerge as an epithet in the mid to late sixties, and even more sharply in the early seventies. During the Civil Rights Movement the term was used by white liberals and blacks to denote the white Protestant Establishment in this country, and I suspect that *WASP* began to take on its present connotations about that time. But it was not until the early seventies that it emerged as a studied epithet and I believe this was associated with the new white ethnic identity movement, the rise of the unmeltable "ethnics."[2] Today, the *WASP* invective seems to be used principally by the "ethnics"—or rather their intellectual or academic spokesman and others who identify with non-Protestant ethnic groups—to perceive and perhaps reprove white Protestants as a category.

Sociological linguistics and symbolic interaction theory hold that new words appear in a language or in argot or take on new meanings when they usefully denote some "new" entity or category of social reality that was previously of less or no use to define or identify. (cf. Strauss, 1959, 15–25). This theory views language as a dynamic process of categorizing and codifying consensually defined social objects. Most social movements, and ethnic identity movements are no exception, develop an ideology in an attempt to explain the social reality that the movement is oriented towards or is rejecting, to explain social injustices of the past and present, to identify devils and scapegoats, and to generate in-group solidarity by defining a hostile, monolithic out-group. For some of the ideological spokesmen for the white "ethnics," the outgroup is the "WASPs." Two recent trade books, Peter Schrag's (1971) *The Decline of the WASP* and Michael Novak's (1972) *The Rise of the Unmeltable Ethnics,* represent a systematization of the rhetoric.[3]

## ANATOMY OF AN EPITHET

Lewis M. Killian (1970, 1) in *White Southerners,* writes that

*the epithet "WASP"... could easily appear to have been coined to describe the white Southerner... The term WASP is not merely a label for a dominant but residual ethnic category in a nation of minorities. It also connotes unseemly ethnic pride and prejudice toward other groups. Because a common stereotype of the white Southerner makes him the epitome of WASP bigotry, there may be an emotional opposition to treating him as a member of a minority. To ascribe to the traditional symbol of racial oppression any of the liabilities of minority status may seem somehow to make less distinctive and exquisite the sufferings of "real" minorities.*

Many of the academics who still use the acronym intend no sly disparagement, but merely use it unmindfully as fashionable jargon. *WASP,* nevertheless, is coming to serve along with that score or so of ethnic epithets coined by early immigrant groups to disparage more recent immigrants to these shores. The white Protestants are getting their epithetical comeuppance. Paradoxically, it cannot be strictly an ethnic epithet because the "WASPs" are not an ethnic group, but are a diverse array of ethnic groups. But the "ethnics" and others seem to think they are some kind of ethnic monolith and have proceeded to deal with them as such in the ideological rhetoric of the new ethnicity. It is exactly as such a monolith that the Yankees at the turn of the century saw the hordes of the new immigration.

*WASP* is rich in innuendo, which is part of the reason for its attractiveness as an epithet. The connotations of *WASP* are clearly disparaging, even if the ostensible denotations are not. *WASP,* in connotation, has all the earmarks of an epithet—it disparages, it ridicules, and it stereotypes.

As Disparagement    The users of *WASP* seem to be quite comfortable, even satisfied, with the redundancy of white *and* Anglo-Saxon when referring to white Protestants. It would seem bizarre to speak of white Slavs, for example. Actually, it would make more sense for "Anglo-Saxon" to modify "white" (ASWP) than vice versa, but that would not spell anything. Wags sometimes suggest that the acronym ought to be shortened to merely *ASP,* which is equally pronounceable and connotes an equally irrascible creature. But this would ruin the point of the redundancy and lose the innuendo. *White* Anglo-Saxon has just the connotation intended. The reiteration recalls and is intended to remind of the present and historical *whiteness* of a "group" that is perceived by minorities to have long dominated power and culture in American society. And the reiteration of whiteness in combination with Anglo-Saxon*ism* also associates this "group," quite accurately, with slavery, racism, theories of Anglo-Saxon superiority, and attempts to foist Anglo-Saxon culture and values onto more recent white immigrant groups.[4]

It is revealing that when white Protestants speak of themselves as "WASPs" it is often in a context of expressing collective guilt for racism. Lois Mark Stalvey (1970, 1) who describes herself as a "German-American WASP" in her book *The Education of a WASP,* says, "We are WASPs, my husband and I, lifelong members of the white Anglo-Saxon Protestant majority group, and some people say that it is primarily our group who created and continue 'white racism' in America." I have seen a few guilt-ridden intellectual whites of Protestant background turn the WASP invective on themselves in a genuine spirit of self-hatred, as though seeking atonement through self-flagellation. I am also reminded of John Canaday's (1972) quaint confession of racial and ethnic naivete in the *New York Times Magazine,* "A Wasp's Progress." The distinguished art critic is perplexed that he is suddenly a member of an "unpopular minority group." "I am a Wasp, just the way other people who now outnumber me used to be niggers and kikes and wops and dagos." He feels put upon and says, "This is unfair, because although I am a Wasp, I am a nice Wasp."

He documents this with childhood memories and anecdotes of his encounters with Catholics, Jews, and blacks in Fort Scott, Kansas, and pleads that he is personally not guilty.

As RIDICULE    In addition to disparaging the outgroup, most ethnic epithets ridicule, usually by cartooning customs, mannerisms, and attitudes. Ridicule serves to diminish further the influence of and respect for the outgroup —a further rejection of its cultural authority. And *WASP* has clearly intended connotations of, largely, good-natured ridicule. Entirely expectedly, adjectival forms have appeared—"Wasp-ish" and "Wasp-y," which brings the word into line with the derivatives from the name of the irascible insect. The new *American Heritage dictionary* (1970) has also legitimized these adjectives. Did the coinage (or borrowing) of *WASP* have anything to do with a delightfully and identically spelled *wasp*—the insect? If it was coincidence, then it was a happy and most useful one. Wilfred Sheed (1972) reviewing Peter Schrag's *The Decline of the WASP* and Michael Novak's *The Rise of the Unmeltable Ethnics* in the *New York Times Book Review,* remarks that both authors "suggest that white Protestants are so stiff with inner-discipline ('robots,' says Novak) that it's a wonder they still croak out their dismal hymns of a Sunday." "Waspy" seems to connote a rather humorless, driven disposition or manner.

In the last few years writers for some of the mass media, especially in the *New York Times* and the national news magazines, have had a heyday with the "WASP" handle.[5] "WASPs" are fair game and WASP-baiting has become a sport. A few "WASP" jokes are being heard to match, tit for tat, the Italian and Polish jokes, which seem unsinkable. Now the chickens have come home to roost. An article by Mel Watkins (1971) in the *New York Times Book Review* is an example of systematic WASP-baiting. Mr. Watkins has a bit of satirical fun imagining what book titles may appear to accompany a "WASP" ethnic identity movement, which is fantasy at best. The whole stereotype is there, including three or four allusions to "WASP" racism and bigotry, and among the punning book titles—"Wasp Nests: Enclaves in the Urban Ghetto." Those white Protestants who do have a prideful identity of being white *and* Protestant and, perhaps, also Anglo-Saxon, and there are many of them, are probably too arrogant or oblivious of the sniping to mind much. *WASP* is really an inside joke.

As A STEREOTYPE    The most significant abuse of the reified concept is that it has lead to a gross stereotype. My observation of the contexts in which WASP is used leads me to suspect that it deliberately connotes more than just white Protestants as just white and Protestant, but rather whites who are more specifically non-Catholic and perhaps non-Jewish, which is to suggest that the "WASPs" are not real "ethnics." In this sense, then, WASP is a residual category. If white Protestants can be identified as a kind of ethnic group, a relative monolith of religion, ideology, custom, association, and common interest then they can be identified, labeled, and generalized about. The WASP concept represents to the "real ethnics" a kind of negative reference group, a value system to become disaffiliated from. But this monolithic perception is at variance with cognition and objective reality. A variegated, originally polyglot, regionally diverse category of white Americans who have some kind of connection, often nominal, with several score of Protestant denominations and sects is not a very clear target, much less a scapegoat.

An ethnic epithet is an in-group's stereotype of an out-group, and *WASP* is an exceeding crude stereotype. The stereotype *WASP* takes no account of national and linguistic white Protestant origins or of distinctive regional cultures that have developed over many generations, and this has become the greatest sociological sin of the reified concept. The stereotype lumps New England "Yankees," Appalachian white, Scots Presbyterians, Mormons, Swedish Lutherans, the Amish, Tennessee Scotch-Irish, Missouri Synod Lutherans, the Pennsylvania Dutch, white Southern Baptists and a variety of distinct regional and national groups under the single rubric—*WASP.* Much of the ethnic differentiation among white Protestants, of course, is among the rural and low-income segments, but not all of it. This relative invisibility of the poor and the more differentiated white Protestants may account for some of the tendency of the "ethnics" to see the middle-class white Protestants in the cities and suburbs of the Northeast and Midwest as a relative ethnic monolith.

Careful attention to how *WASP* is emerging in the American language reveals that it is used to connote mannerisms that are expressions of an uptight life style. *WASP* often alludes to another but now bygone figment of the sociological imagination—the supposedly homogeneous middle-class life styles of suburbia, especially when contrasted to the working-class white ethnic "urban villages" of the central cities.[6] The suburbanization of the American metropolis has been a panethnic phenomenon, at least for whites since World War II or before. The suburban stereotype has all the "WASPs" in affluence, working at bland corporation jobs, soullessly attending interdenominational suburban churches, rearing 2.0 children in isolated nuclear families. "WASPs," then, are uptight, arrogant, steady, compulsively hardworking, acquisitive automatons. Non-WASPs—the "real ethnics"—are effusive, impulsive, outgoing, warm, and kin oriented. The opposite of "WASP" style conjures up the crude but popular southern and eastern European stereotypes. Wilfred Sheed (1972) in his review of the Schrag and Novak books correctly observes that in trying to stereotype the "WASP," the "real ethnics" are stereotyping themselves.

One can find, however, some authorative support from sociologists of ethnicity that white Protestants are a relative ethnic monolith. For example, Milton M. Gordon (1964, 220–224) in his book, *Assimilation in American Life,* describes white Protestants (he does not use *WASP*) as an "ethnic group" differentiated mainly by social class and denominationalism, which are closely associated. He discounts the role of regional difference as "a distinctively minor one." He says "it is the intersection of Protestant ethnicity with social class that forms the boundaries of the communal system within which Protestant primary group relations tend to be confined." Gordon (126) says that those white Protestants whose forebears immigrated in colonial times and the first three-quarters of the nineteenth century have "now been absorbed into the general white 'sociological Protestant' sector of American life." "... And as far as they understand it, they are simply 'Americans'...."

Charles H. Anderson (1970, xii–xiv) in his book *White Protestant Americans* also regards white Protestants as largely assimilated into the core society, with only vestigal traces of their origins. He points out that white Protestants (he does not call them "WASPs") have by and large never regarded themselves as an ethnic group. "But white Protestants, like other Americans, are as much an ethnic group as anyone else, however privileged the majority of them might be. . . . As Catholics, Jews, and blacks press in around them, and as internal differences decline, white Protestants increasingly perceive that they, too, constitute a definable group with distinctive social and familial networks, and psychological and cultural moorings."

Gordon and Anderson, I think, are in many ways correct and many sociologists would agree. It is a question, rather, whether one wants to emphasize the homogeneity or the heterogeneity of white Protestants. White Protestants have been in this country longer as a large group and, thus, many have assimilated moreso into a nondescript amalgam than have other groups. It may not be entirely accurate to say, as some pluralists want, that everyone is a member of an ethnic group. Many whites with remote Protestant orientations, many of whom have mixed religious and national backgrounds, are in fact absorbed into a nondescript amalgam of "rootless cosmopolitans." They may belong to an ethnic group in the usual, traditional sense only by attribution. Or perhaps it is time that sociologists recognize a new emergent rootless "ethnic" group, but not suggest that it contains all white Protestants. Many, if not most, white Protestants, especially the distinctive regional and denominational groupings, are as "ethnic" as anyone else.

The social class of white Protestants may have a greater variance, in the statistical sense, than other groups. There may be greater extremes of wealth and poverty—a flatter, possibly bimodal, but less skewed income distribution. They are greatly varied by denominationalism, and Protestantism is not a church. Moreover, I suspect that regional-cultural differences, while they developed, not abroad, but in this country during the last two centuries, are more important as an ethnic differentiation than many believe to be the case.

## CONCLUSIONS

I think that some of the "ethnics" and perhaps a few sociologists are too eager to view white Protestants as a single ethnic group with a cultural homogeneity and an emergent homogeneity similar to that of the large European ethnic groups. The urge to stereotype and, thus, simplify complex reality is sometimes hard to resist. The professional ideologies of sociologists have led them into myopic perceptions of social reality before, and this may be but the latest instance.

Catholics, Jews, and increasingly, blacks, are concentrated in metropolitan areas, especially the older industrial cities in the North and Midwest. White Protestants, especially the segments with the greatest cultural variety, are distributed more in small towns and rural areas. The frequent characterization and identification of white Protestants with an affluent, middle-class, suburban Establishment and the cartooning of suburban life styles may have some credibility in the eyes of the recently mobile and often frustrated immobile "ethnics" in the central cities and newer suburbs. Stereotypes sometimes have a grain of truth in them, and some of the white Protestants in the white enclaves of the central cities and those ensconced in the affluent suburbs may indeed suggest the stereotype.

The main traffickers of the *WASP* cliche in journalism and sociology are not the "ethnics" themselves but usually are their intellectual spokesmen and other sympathizers with the ethnic underdogs in the American class system. And they have correctly perceived the real resentment of the "ethnics," the blacks and others, toward the privileged and affluent in the highly visible neighborhoods of the metropolis. Nonetheless, I think the WASP cliche is counterproductive to promotion of the value of ethnic pluralism and to serious analysis of ethnicity in American life. Sociologists, moreover, have an obligation to acknowledge and allow for the real ethnic and quasi-ethnic diversity among white Protestants, and certainly the *WASP* label should be avoided.

## NOTES

1    I am indebted to Harold J. Abramson and Jane Riblett Wilkie for invaluable suggestions. I take full responsibility for my conjecture and contrariety. The University of Connecticut Research Foundation is supporting Abramson's and my study of the ethnic mosaic in Connecticut cities, which prompted these thoughts. An earlier version was presented at the annual meeting of the Eastern Sociological Society, Philadelphia, April 6, 1974.

2    The adjective *ethnic* is emerging in common parlance as a noun, mainly as a plural. *Ethnics* is not in the dictionary yet but it likely will be soon. The common denominator among the "ethnics" seems to be that most are Catholics. The "ethnics" are mainly the sons and daughters of relatively recent immigrant groups, especially those from southern and eastern Europe, who are questioning the melting-pot ideology and experiencing a resurgence of ethnic identity and pride. While it makes little sociological sense to restrict the idea of ethnicity or even being an "ethnic" to Catholics, more particularly those of southern and eastern European national origins, the concept and the noun is poking into the language and is being used by some sociologists.

3    Novak introduces a note of the bizarre into the discussion by using yet another acronym, PIGS (Poles, Italians, Greeks, and Slavs), which he uses interchangeably with "ethnics."

4    The tortured redundancy of *WASP* makes me suspicious of the origins of the acronym. Did it just appear as a "natural" acronym for "white Anglo-Saxon Protestant," or did it, like a hermit crab, inhabit someone else's acronym? Gale's (1970) *Acronyms and Initialisms Dictionary,* in addition to the Anglo-Saxon designation, shows *WASPs* to stand for "white *Appalachian Southern* Protestants," and notes that it is "Chicago slang." I heard the acronym in this usage in the fifties among Appalachian social workers who used it as a kind of form-filling shorthand to designate the whites of Appalachia, but especially the migrant poor whites in the ghettoes that began to appear after World War II in the large industrial cities of the Midwest. I am uncertain whether the two acronyms were coined independently, or whether *WASP* for white southerners from Appalachia came first and the now current *WASP* was an irresistible corruption. It is speculative at best.

5    *New York* magazine is the latest to jump on this pop-sociology bandwagon with a cover illustrated with a "conformist organization man" image replete with wasp wings and a tailstinger. In the cover story, "The New York Wasp is Not an Endangered Species," Owen Edwards (1974) word-plays and puns on the acronym to what must be the last word. But at least he confines his lampoon to a small economic and social elite. The current wave of anti-Wasp chic in the magazines moved Robert

Claiborne (1974) in a *Newsweek* essay, "A Wasp Stings Back," to deny the stereotype and defend "wasp values."

6  Bennett M. Berger (1961) noted that the "myth of suburbia" in the 1950s had functions for intellectuals, and they clung to the myth in the face of all evidence. The myth was invented by intellectuals so they could hate it and "suburbia" was a codeword for "bourgeoisie," I think the culture critics' new anti-hero, the "WASP," and the linking of it to stereotypical suburban life styles represents a survival of the "myth of suburbia" and that it serves a similar set of needs for some intellectuals involved in the ethnic-revival discussion.

## REFERENCES

*Anderson, C. H.*
1970  *White Protestant Americans,* Englewood Cliffs, N.J., Prentice-Hall.
*Baltzell, E. D.*
1964  *The Protestant Establishment,* New York, Random House.
*Berger, B. M.*
1961  The myth of suburbia. *Journal of Social Issues* Vol. 17, No. 1.
*Canaday, J.*
1972  A Wasp's progress. *The New York Times Magazine* (March 19).
*Claiborne, R.*
1974  A Wasp stings back. *Newsweek* (September 30).
*Edwards, O.*
1974  The New York Wasp is not an endangered species. *New York* (August 12).
*Gale Research Company*
1970  *Acronyms and Initialisms Dictionary,* Third edition, Detroit, Gale Research Company.
*Gordon, M. M.*
1964  *Assimilation in American Life,* New York, Oxford University Press.
*Killian, L. M.*
1970  *White Southerners,* New York, Random House.
*Novak, M.*
1972  *The Rise of the Unmeltable Ethnics,* New York, Macmillan Company.
*Schrag, P.*
1971  *The Decline of the WASP,* New York, Simon and Schuster.
*Sheed, W.*
1971  Wasp wasting and ethnic upping. *New York Times Book Review* (June 4).
*Stalvey, L. M.*
1970  *The Education of a WASP.* New York, A Bantam Book, the William Morrow Company.
*Strauss, A. L.*
1959  *Mirrors and Masks,* New York, The Free Press.
*Watkins, M.*
1971  Finally the Wasp. *The New York Times Book Review* (November 28).

# Public Stereotyping of Sex Roles, Personality Characteristics, and Occupations*

## Stan L. Albrecht

## Howard M. Bahr

## Bruce A. Chadwick
*Brigham Young University*

*The incidence and correlates of sex-roles stereotyping of selected personality traits and occupations are assessed for a random sample of Utah residents. Results show moderate sex typing of personality traits and very pronounced stereotyping of occupations among Utah adults. Respondents of both sexes tend to sex type personality characteristics and occupations along the same lines. Observed age differences in sex stereotyping are consistent with the presumed*

*Source:* Stanley L. Albrecht, Howard M. Bahr, and Bruce A. Chadwick, "Public Stereotyping of Sex Roles, Personality Characteristics, and Occupations," Sociology and Social Research 61, 2 (January 1977): 223–40. Copyright © 1977 Sociology and Social Research. Reprinted by permission.
*Research reported in this paper was supported by a grant from the Research Division: Brigham Young University.

*national trend toward the greater equality of the sexes; both for occupations
and personality characteristics the young are less apt to sex stereotype in the
traditional manner than are the older respondents. Most of the explained variance in traditional sex-stereotyping of personality traits was accounted for by
the variable age. Attitudes toward the feminist movement explained more of
the variation in sex-typing of occupations. Other variables (religious affiliation,
sex, education, income) identified by previous researchers were not particularly useful predictors of the dependent variables. Additional exploratory work
is needed to identify and verify the correlates and antecedents of sex stereotyping.*

Four decades ago Ralph Linton (1936) observed that divisions of labor and
assignment of statuses on the basis of sex seemed to be basic in all societies. The
universality of that generalization seems much less certain now than in recent
years. Traditional definitions of masculine and feminine sex roles are under
attack, and even appeals to biological imperatives are refuted. "Freud's dictum
that 'anatomy is destiny' is regarded by many women as a 'male chauvinist'
premise, to be categorically rejected" (Block, Von der Lippe, and Block,
1973:321). The effort to de-emphasize longstanding sex role definitions and
divisions of labor has been led by an increasingly powerful and activist feminist movement, and the goals of the feminists are now buttressed by new
state and federal laws which seek to guarantee "equal opportunity regardless
of sex."

However, public attitudinal change frequently lags well behind the vanguard of important legal and institutional changes. Thus, although important
advances have been made by the feminist movement, there have also been
some setbacks. Notable among these has been the failure of the states to ratify
the 27th Amendment. In 1975, approval of only five states was needed, but the
Amendment was ratified by only one additional state. Legislatures in Louisiana, Oklahoma, Virginia, Arizona, Georgia, Utah, and Nevada all rejected
the Equal Rights Amendment. To further complicate matters, two state
legislatures that had previously ratified the Amendment (Nebraska and
Tennessee) voted to rescind the ratification, though the legality of such
action is still a matter of question and the ability to rescind has now gone
before the courts. More recently, voters in both New York and New Jersey
have rejected state constitutional amendments patterned after the 27th
Amendment.

Resistance has been experienced in other areas as well. For example, recent
court actions have been filed arguing that certain hiring practices constitute, in effect, reverse discrimination putting the so-called WASP male at
a disadvantage in competition with females and other minority persons.
Apparently traditional attitudes about masculine and feminine roles still
prevail, and, though they are changing, the change is a long and slow
process.[1]

The present paper is an analysis of prevalence and change in public sex-role
stereotypes.[2] Specifically, it is an assessment of adults' attitudes about the desirability of certain occupational roles and personality characteristics for males
and for females. A careful analysis of existing stereotypes about sex differences
in occupational desirability and personality characteristics seems a useful pre-

liminary step in charting the kinds of change we may anticipate. To the degree that there are important socio-demographic correlates of sex-role stereotyping, it will be useful to identify these. In this regard, three primary research questions are asked: (1) To what extent are occupations and personality characteristics sex-typed by a large sample of adults? (2) Are the age differences in the designation of certain characteristics and occupations as more appropriate for one sex than the other consistent with the presumed trend toward greater equality? And (3) what are the other social and demographic correlates of sex-role attitudes? Data on these questions should better allow us to understand the dynamics of the public response to the Equal Rights Amendment as well as to other efforts to eliminate discrimination on the basis of sex. If, for example, sex-role stereotyping is still widely evident in a large sample of adult respondents, this should provide some clues to the action of legislators in states that have defeated the ERA as well as other examples of resistance.

Our effort is an attempt to illuminate an area recently identified by Block, Von der Lippe, and Block (1973: 321), Hochschild (1973: 1023), and others as a "blind spot," an area where there has been little systematic empirical work. We begin with a discussion of the importance of the socialization process in the development of attitudes, including sex-role stereotypes, and then review briefly the literature on the sex-typing of occupations and personality traits.

## SOCIALIZATION, PERSONALITY TRAITS, AND OCCUPATIONAL PREFERENCES

Sex role definitions are generally seen as products of the socialization process. In the numerous attempts to explain the development of sex-role characteristics in males and females (see Bronfenbrenner, 1960; Heilbrun, 1965; Kohlberg, 1966; Mischel, 1966), the most popular approach has been to treat the learning of sex roles as part of the same process as the learning of other roles. That is, sex roles are learned as part of the basic attitudes and patterns of behavior which are transmitted during the socialization process.

The basic social-psychological theory accounting for sex differences in occupational achievement and preferences is based on the work of McClelland (1953), Sears *et al.* (1957), Kagan and Moss (1962), and others who have argued that girls and boys are socialized differently. Girls are taught to be more tractable, obedient, suggestible, dependent, and to follow "feminine" interests (Josselyn, 1967), and both sexes seem to acquire a sense that girls are less worthwhile than boys. Sanctions are imposed when behavior and attitudes contrary to the culturally prescribed patterns are exhibited, and activities that are defined as inappropriate for one's sex come to be avoided because they bring rejection rather than approval.

The development of individual personality traits and of preferences for occupation and life goals are among the important outcomes of this sex role socialization. Kagan (1964:138) suggests that learning a "sex role standard" involves learning an "association between certain attributes, behaviors, and attitudes, on the one hand, and the concepts male and female, on the other." Thus, intellectual achievement and assertiveness often come to be defined as unfeminine, and some talented females develop a "fear of success" as a defensive mechanism to protect their femininity.[3] However, this "fear of success" is incongruent with their urges for achievement, mastery, and independence, and the conflict between the two may produce psychological strains (Breedlove and Cicirelli, 1974:183–186).

Turning to the question of occupational *selection,* Siegel (1973) has noted that interest in possible future occupations is sex-typed as early as the second grade. Several other studies (Brim, 1958; Knudsen, 1969) have shown that women anticipate and prepare for occupations that are consistent with the traditional sexual division of labor. Thus, women have been more likely to choose roles that Klemmack and Edwards (1973) call "primarily social-emotional, nuturant, and person-centered."

An increase in the number or proportion of working women provides no grounds for asserting changes in occupational sex roles unless it can be shown that women are making inroads into areas which formerly were defined as male. Most women aspire to and pursue occupations congruent with traditional adult female roles (Klemmack and Edwards, 1973:511) although there is some evidence, at least in the expectations of college women, that this preference for traditional feminine occupations is on the decline.[4]

In sum, while the campaign for greater equality of opportunity without regard to gender gains momentum, there is evidence that there are important attitudinal barriers that will impede equal treatment of the sexes. Moreover, general stereotypes are apt to have a pervasive and continuing influence because sex roles usually are learned at home and parental attitudes tend to be transmitted to their offspring.

Many of those who seek change have recognized the importance of culturally prescribed attitudes and values in perpetuating traditional definitions. For example, Block, Von der Lippe, and Block (1973:321) have noted:

*In the view of those seeking redefinition of traditional sex roles, the extant cultural forces powerfully shaping sex-role socialization in the developing child attenuate the human possibilities residing in the individual, whether male or female. Concern with this issue is intense; the implications. . . . are profound.*

Similarly, Webster (1975: 113) has argued that until very recently in our culture,

*. . . sex roles were the most encompassing and most strongly sanctioned of all roles. There were more norms prescribing how one should act as a male or as a female, and the social penalties for violation were stronger, than for any other identifiable role. Knowing the sex of the person with whom you were interacting gave an enormous amount of information about how he or she was likely to think, to act, and to react.*

The extent to which this description is still appropriate may be gauged, in part, from people's sex-role stereotypes. If, in fact, sex roles are learned largely through the socialization process, then significant change will be, at least in part, a function of change in attitudes and behavior patterns transferred from parents to their children. It seems important that the parental attitudes be identified, and their diversity or homogeneity documented.

## HYPOTHESIZED CORRELATES OF SEX-ROLE STEREOTYPING

The review of the developing literature on sex-role stereotypes suggests several important variables that may be related to preferences about personality traits and the division of labor by sex. One variable that has received relatively little research attention but which is of primary concern here is that of age. Because of the *contemporary* significance of the move for greater equality among the sexes, we would anticipate some important generational differences to exist. For one thing, exposure to the ideology of the feminist movement has probably been greater among the young than the old. And even if such exposure were not age-specific, receptivity to pressures for attitudinal and behavioral change is probably lower when the patterns to be changed are more established and longstanding. Thus, we would predict that *the older the respondent, the greater the likelihood of preference for more traditional sex-role definitions.*

Several other variables appear in the literature as potentially important influences on the degree of sex-role stereotyping. For example, there is some evidence that fathers are more likely than mothers to sex-type behavior. Block (1973:517) has noted that "Although maternal child-rearing orientations do differ depending on the sex of the child, the attitudes of the father appear to be even more strongly determined by the child's sex." Cross-national data reported by Brun-Gulbrandsen (1958) using Norwegian data and Holstrom (1973) using data from Turkey indicate similar differences in these countries. On the basis of this literature, our second general hypothesis is that *males will exhibit greater sex-role stereotyping (preference for traditional sex-role definitions) than females.*

Most of the sex-role research has focused on the middle class and few good comparisons between classes have been made (Hochschild, 1973). The available work suggests that lower class parents are more likely than others to stress sex-role typing (Kohn, 1959), and that lower class children are more likely than middle class children to avoid sexually ambiguous roles and to prefer what are generally defined as "masculine" (for boys) and "feminine" (for girls) sex roles (Hall and Keith, 1964; Rabban, 1950). Our third hypothesis, therefore, is that *social class will be inversely related to degree of sex-role sterotyping.*

In view of evidence that Catholics are more apt than Protestants to favor traditional roles for women (Stolka and Barnett, 1969; Campbell, 1966; Christopherson and Walters, 1958), we anticipated that *persons who belong to churches that are generally classified as conservative and which have gener-*

*ally supported traditional male-female role assignments would be more likely to exhibit strong sex-role stereotypes.*

Finally, many other attitudes should also be correlated with sex-role stereotyping. In this study we anticipated that attitudes toward the feminist movement and its goals would be one of the attitude sets most clearly associated with sex-role stereotyping. Thus, we predicted that *the more favorably inclined one was toward the feminist movement, the less likely one would be to exhibit traditional sex-role stereotyping.*[5]

## RESEARCH PROCEDURES

Data for the project were collected by mail questionnaire from a random sample of adult residents of the State of Utah. The cultural and religious peculiarities of Utah would, of course, lead us to expect a strong expression of support for more traditional sex stereotypes and divisions of labor. However, we would not expect Utah to differ significantly from many other areas of the country, particularly those areas where the Equal Rights Amendment has failed passage or where once passed, strong legislative efforts have been made to rescind passage.

Telephone directories serving all of the State of Utah were compiled as a sampling frame.[6] The total number of names, excluding businesses, contained in the books was calculated and a systematic random sample was selected. This procedure resulted in a sample of 2,227 households.

Two copies of the questionnaire, two return envelopes, and a cover letter were sent by first-class mail to each household in the sample. The cover letter asked that both the husband and wife fill out a questionnaire. Two weeks later a postcard encouraging the respondents to return the questionnaires was sent out by first-class mail to those households that had not responded.

Four weeks after the postcard was sent, a complete new packet including a different cover letter, two questionnaires, and two return envelopes were mailed first class to those households from which there had been no response. Four weeks after this second packet, a third was sent by certified mail. In this final mailing, two questionnaires were sent to those households who had not responded, while a single questionnaire and an appropriate cover letter were sent to those households from which one questionnaire had been received. Six weeks were allowed after the certified mailing for return of the questionnaires.

Of the 2,227 names initially selected, 148 had moved leaving no forwarding address and another 25 questionnaires were returned with the notation that the respondent whose name had been in the telephone directory was deceased. These 173 households were removed from the sample leaving a sample size of 2,054. A grand total of 2,005 useable questionnaires were eventually returned. In 771 cases, questionnaires were received from both husband and wife. The remaining were received from persons who were unmarried, divorced, or separated or from one spouse in a married household.[7]

## MEASUREMENT OF VARIABLES

### Dependent Variables

The primary dependent variables were the degree of adult sex-stereotyping of personality traits and occupational types. The questionnaire included a series of items developed from extensive reviews of the sex role literature in which respondents were asked the desirability of a number of personality traits and the suitability of a number of occupations for males and females. The first question read as follows: "People often differ about the personality characteristics desirable for men and women. If you were a parent, what would be your opinion on the desirability of boys or girls having each of the following characteristics?" The list of characteristics included timid, brave, good looking, sensitive, affectionate, independent, intelligent, cooperative, virtuous, understanding, sympathetic, aggressive, generous, daring, responsible, rebellious, creative, obedient, and submissive. Alternative choices presented to the respondent included: (1) desirable for boys only; (2) more desirable for boys than girls; (3) equally desirable for boys and girls; (4) more desirable for girls than boys; (5) desirable for girls only; and (6) undesirable for either boys or girls.

The second question stated that "There is much discussion about whether women and men should work at the same kinds of jobs or whether some should be for men only and others for women only. Please give us your own opinion about each of the following occupations." The list of occupations included detective, school teacher, congressman,[8] actor, auto mechanic, doctor, secretary, scientist, social worker, business executive, lawyer, airline pilot, truck driver, nurse, and housekeeper in one's own home. Alternative responses were the same as for the previous question with the exceptions that the terms "men" and "women" were substituted for "boys" and "girls," and that the category "undesirable for either" was dropped.

### Independent Variables

The independent variables employed in the present analysis were identified earlier. Two indicators of social class are used. Each respondent indicated his or her formal education by selecting one of the following categories: (1) grade school only, (2) some high school, (3) high school graduate, (4) some college, (5) college graduate, and (6) graduate degree. In addition, annual income was reported in eleven categories ranging from "none" to $30,000 plus.

Respondents' age was ascertained by a direct question asking this information. Religious preference was reported in the following categories: (1) Catholic, (2) Protestant, (3) Jewish, (4) Mormon, (5) other, and (6) no preference. Protestants were asked to specify denomination.

Finally, attitude toward the feminist movement was operationalized by asking the following question: "Leaving the question of tactics aside, what is your attitude toward the women's liberation movement?" Responses included "entirely favorable," "most favorable," "undecided," "most unfavorable," and "entirely unfavorable."[9]

## FINDINGS

### The Incidence of Sex-Stereotyping

Tables 1 and 2 show the responses of males and females in the sample to the question of the desirability of the personality traits for boys and girls and of the suitability of the occupations for men and women. Perhaps the most striking finding is the extent of inter-sex agreement on the items listed in the two tables. In no instance did a substantial number of respondents of one sex indicate that a characteristic was more desirable for one sex than the other, while respondents of the other sex took the opposite position.

Where there are sex differences in responses, males are somewhat more likely than females to sex-type both the personality traits and the occupations. Thus, while both sexes agreed that girls should be more timid, good looking, sensitive, affectionate, virtuous, sympathetic, and submissive than boys, males were more likely than females to identify each of these characteristics as feminine. Similarly, while both male and female respondents tended to identify the characteristics of bravery, independence, aggressiveness, and daring as only or more desirable for boys, in all four cases male respondents are more likely than females to sex-type these characteristics. These findings are highly consistent with the results reported by Kagan (1964), Josselyn (1967), and others discussed above.

Despite the general tendency noted in Table 1 for respondents to identify some characteristics as female and others as male, it should also be noted that over 80 percent of both male and female respondents said that being affectionate, intelligent, cooperative, virtuous, understanding, sympathetic, generous, responsible, creative, and obedient were *equally* desirable for both boys and girls. Similarly, over half of both male and female respondents agreed that being timid, rebellious, and submissive were characteristics desirable for *neither* boys or girls. These observations indicate that the differences between male and female respondents are overshadowed by their similarities. Males and females tend to sex-type personality characteristics along the same lines.

Turning to the list of occupations (Table 2), extensive male-female attitude congruence is again apparent. Both sexes agree that the occupations of detective, congressman, auto mechanic, doctor, scientist, business executive, lawyer, airline pilot, and truck driver are only or more suitable for men than for women. Three other occupations—secretary, nurse, and housekeeper—are viewed as more suitable or only suitable for women. Both males and females tended to define the occupation of social worker as slightly more suitable for women, though almost 80 per cent of both sexes said that it was an occupation equally suitable for both men and women. Again, while some of the traditional stereotypes come through clearly as indicated by the consistency of inter-sex response to items such as business executive and secretary, over half of all

**TABLE 1**

Desirability of Personality Characteristics for Boys and Girls, Controlling for Sex of Respondent

| | PERCENT SAYING CHARACTERISTIC IS: | | | | | | | |
| PERSONALITY CHARACTERISTIC | ONLY OR MORE DESIRABLE FOR BOYS | | EQUALLY DESIRABLE FOR BOYS AND GIRLS | | ONLY OR MORE DESIRABLE FOR GIRLS | | UNDESIRABLE FOR EITHER BOYS OR GIRLS | |
| | MALES | FEMALES | MALES | FEMALES | MALES | FEMALES | MALES | FEMALES |
|---|---|---|---|---|---|---|---|---|
| Timid | 2 | 1 | 13 | 14 | 24 | 22 | 61 | 64 |
| Brave | 36 | 26 | 63 | 73 | 1 | 1 | 1 | 0 |
| Good looking | 1 | 1 | 79 | 86 | 19 | 12 | 1 | 1 |
| Sensitive | 0 | 1 | 79 | 83 | 16 | 12 | 5 | 4 |
| Affectionate | 1 | 1 | 85 | 94 | 14 | 5 | 0 | 0 |
| Independent | 31 | 19 | 67 | 79 | 1 | 1 | 1 | 0 |
| Intelligent | 4 | 2 | 95 | 97 | 1 | 1 | 0 | 0 |
| Cooperative | 2 | 1 | 97 | 98 | 2 | 1 | 0 | 0 |
| Virtuous | 2 | 1 | 89 | 92 | 9 | 7 | 0 | 0 |
| Understanding | 1 | 1 | 96 | 97 | 2 | 2 | 0 | 0 |
| Sympathetic | 2 | 1 | 90 | 92 | 8 | 7 | 0 | 0 |
| Aggressive | 55 | 50 | 37 | 39 | 1 | 1 | 7 | 11 |
| Generous | 3 | 2 | 93 | 96 | 3 | 2 | 1 | 0 |
| Responsible | 6 | 3 | 92 | 95 | 1 | 1 | 1 | 1 |
| Rebellious | 5 | 3 | 14 | 14 | 1 | 0 | 80 | 83 |
| Creative | 2 | 1 | 93 | 94 | 5 | 6 | 0 | 0 |
| Obedient | 1 | 1 | 96 | 97 | 2 | 2 | 1 | 1 |
| Submissive | 1 | 1 | 32 | 30 | 11 | 9 | 56 | 59 |

N = 2005.

**TABLE 2**

**Desirability of Occupation for Men and Women, Controlling for Sex of Respondent**

*PERCENT SAYING CHARACTERISTIC IS:*

| OCCUPATION | ONLY SUITABLE OR MORE SUITABLE FOR MEN | | EQUALLY SUITABLE FOR BOTH MEN AND WOMEN | | ONLY SUITABLE OR MORE SUITABLE FOR WOMEN | |
|---|---|---|---|---|---|---|
| | MALES | FEMALES | MALES | FEMALES | MALES | FEMALES |
| Detective | 73 | 71 | 24 | 27 | 1 | 0 |
| School teacher | 3 | 1 | 87 | 95 | 10 | 4 |
| Congressman | 53 | 47 | 47 | 52 | 1 | 0 |
| Actor | 5 | 5 | 93 | 95 | 2 | 0 |
| Auto mechanic | 89 | 85 | 11 | 15 | 1 | 0 |
| Doctor | 36 | 29 | 62 | 70 | 2 | 1 |
| Secretary | 2 | 2 | 26 | 37 | 72 | 61 |
| Scientist | 20 | 19 | 79 | 80 | 1 | 1 |
| Social worker | 3 | 2 | 82 | 87 | 15 | 11 |
| Business executive | 56 | 47 | 43 | 52 | 1 | 0 |
| Lawyer | 52 | 44 | 48 | 56 | 1 | 0 |
| Airline pilot | 80 | 75 | 19 | 25 | 1 | 0 |
| Truck driver | 87 | 85 | 12 | 15 | 1 | 0 |
| Nurse | 2 | 1 | 28 | 43 | 71 | 56 |
| Housekeeper—own home | 1 | 1 | 17 | 18 | 82 | 81 |

N = 2005.

respondents agreed that occupations such as doctor and scientist were equally suitable for men and women.

### Correlates of Traditional Sex-Stereotyping

Table 3 presents bivariate correlations between the independent variables and traditional sex-stereotyping of personality traits and occupations. In this case, a single measure of degree of "traditional" sex-stereotyping of personality and of occupational roles was used. This score was computed by combining the preference scores for those personality characteristics defined by the sample as most sex-linked, including four defined as masculine (brave, independent, aggressive, and daring) and five designated as feminine (timid, good looking, sensitive, affectionate, and submissive). Possible scores on each item ranged from 1 ("desirable for boys only") to 5 ("desirable for girls only"). In totaling scores, responses on the "feminine" items were reversed to create a single index of sex-stereotyping of the personality characteristics. This reversal means that the range on each item was interpretable as going from 1 (desirable only for the sex traditionally assigned this characteristic) to 5 (desirable only for the sex *not* traditionally assigned this characteristic). The possible range on the cumulative score is from 9 (for characteristics totally sex-stereotyped in the traditional direction) to 45 (the characteristics are totally sex-stereotyped but in the non-traditional direction).

A similar procedure was used with the occupational choices. Those occupations that were most strongly identified as only or more suitable for men (detective, congressman, auto mechanic, airline pilot, business executive, and truck driver) were combined with a reversal of the scores on those items identified as only or more suitable for women (secretary, nurse, and housekeeper) to create a single index of degree of traditional occupational sex-stereotyping. These scores for traditional sex-stereotyping were then correlated with each of the independent variables. The resulting coefficients are presented in Table 3.[10]

TABLE 3

Bivariate Correlations Between Selected Independent Variables and
Traditional Sex-Stereotyping of Personality Traits and Occupations

| INDEPENDENT VARIABLE | CORRELATION WITH TRADITIONAL SEX-STEREOTYPING FOR: | |
| --- | --- | --- |
| | PERSONALITY TRAITS | OCCUPATIONS |
| Age | −.25** | −.21** |
| Education | .22** | .19** |
| Income | .19** | .11** |
| Sex | .08* | .10** |
| Religion | .02 | .18** |
| Attitude toward feminist movement | −.01 | −.25** |

*N = 2005.*
*Statistically significant at the .05 level.*
**Statistically significant at the .001 level.*

The highest bivariate correlation between traditional sex-stereotyping of personality characteristics and the independent variables occurs with respondent's age. As expected, older respondents were more likely than younger respondents to sex-type the various personality characteristics in the traditional manner. The next strongest predictors of stereotyping are education ($r = .22$) and income ($r = .19$). Thus, as anticipated, better educated and higher income respondents are less likely than others to sex-stereotype personality traits.

Age also turns out to be a strong correlate of occupational sex-stereotyping ($r3/4 - .21$), ranking just behind respondents' attitudes toward women's liberation and just ahead of education ($r$'s $- .25$ and $.19$ respectively.) The older the respondent, the more likely he or she is to sex-type the various occupations. Similarly, the more educated are less likely than the others to sex-type, and family income operates in the same direction. The strongest correlate of occupational sex-stereotyping, however, is attitude toward the women's liberation movement. Persons most in favor of the movement are least likely to sex-stereotype occupations in the traditional manner. The central position of equality in employment as part of the popular support for women's liberation is apparent in the contrast between the position of attitudes about women's liberation as a predictor of occupational sex-stereotyping and personality trait stereotyping. Apparently the concerns which motivate respondents in the present study to support women's liberation have much more to do with occupational equality than sexual uniformity of personality characteristics.

To isolate the effects of each of the independent variables operating independently, a stepwise multivariate regression analysis was run.[11] Table 4 summarizes the stepwise regression for both dependent variables.

The results of this analysis do not reveal much that is not apparent in the bivariate correlations reported in Table 3. For the stereotyping of personality characteristics, respondent's age and education combine to account for just nine percent of the variance and the other four variables only add an additional two percent. For occupational sex-stereotyping, attitude toward women's liberation accounts for six percent explained variance, adding age and education increases the explained variance to 13 percent and the remaining variables only add an additional three percent.

## DISCUSSION AND CONCLUSIONS

Let us return now to the three major questions introduced in the "research objectives" section of this paper. Concerning the extent of sex-typing of occupations and personality characteristics by adults, the data show that for the 19 personality characteristics considered, most were identified by very high proportions of both males and females as *equally* desirable for both boys and girls. Only two of the 19 characteristics were identified by as many as half the respondents as more desirable for boys than girls, and even if we lower the threshold of recognition of a sex-linked characteristic to 10 percent or more, only four of the characteristics (bravery, independence, aggressiveness, and

TABLE 4

Stepwise Multiple Regression Between Selected Independent Variables and
Traditional Sex-Stereotyping of Personality Traits and Occupations

| VARIABLE | MULTIPLE R | $MR^2$ | BETA | F |
|---|---|---|---|---|
| CORRELATIONS WITH TRADITIONAL SEX-STEREOTYPING OF PERSONALITY TRAITS | | | | |
| Age | .25 | .06 | −.19 | 73.2** |
| Education | .29 | .09 | .14 | 38.4** |
| Income | .32 | .10 | .14 | 40.1** |
| Sex | .33 | .11 | .11 | 24.1** |
| Attitude toward feminist movement | .33 | .11 | −.04 | 2.8* |
| Religion | .34 | .11 | .01 | .1 |
| CORRELATIONS WITH TRADITIONAL SEX-STEREOTYPING OF OCCUPATIONS | | | | |
| Attitude toward feminist movement | .25 | .06 | −.24 | 126.1** |
| Age | .32 | .11 | −.15 | 45.7** |
| Education | .36 | .13 | .15 | 43.2** |
| Sex | .38 | .14 | .13 | 39.0** |
| Religion | .40 | .16 | .12 | 29.3** |
| Income | .40 | .16 | .08 | 15.1** |

*N = 2005.*
*Statistically significant at the .05 level.*
**Statistically significant at the .001 level.*

daring) are typified as male and five (timidity, being good looking, sensitivity, being affectionate, submissiveness) as female.

Of course estimations of "high" or "low" rates of anything necessarily require a standard of comparison. Indeed, one of the chief objectives of the present study is to provide baseline data, though limited to a fairly specific geographic base, for future studies of sex-stereotyping. But the ten percent standard does not seem excessively high, and if that is applied, it is appropriate to conclude that while a minority of respondents sex-stereotype certain personality characteristics in the traditional direction, the degree of personality sex-stereotyping observed in these data is far less than might be anticipated from accounts in the media or from unsystematic observation.

This finding contrasts markedly with that for occupational sex-stereotyping. Most of the occupations studied were highly sex-stereotyped: in fact, only five of the fifteen listed were described by over half of the male respondents as equally suitable for both men and women, and female respondents were only slightly more generous to themselves, with eight occupations identified by at least half of them as equally suitable for both sexes.

The costs of sex-stereotyping in reducing the alternatives available to women seeking employment is particularly apparent in the designation of jobs as "more suitable" for women than men. Only three occupations—secretary, nurse, and housekeeper—were identified by more than half of either male or female respondents as primarily feminine pursuits. On balance, then, there is evidence of some, but not extensive sex-stereotyping of personality traits among Utah adults. Much more pronounced is the degree of occupational sex-stereotyping.

The second major research question was whether age differences in sex-stereotyping were consistent with the presumed national trend toward greater equality of the sexes, i.e., was there a positive relationship between age and degree of traditional sex-stereotyping. Here the answer was clearly positive. Both for occupations and personality characteristics, the younger respondents were less apt to sex-stereotype in the traditional manner than were the older respondents. This finding needs to be corroborated by other cross-sectional studies, but it does make sense in the present historical perspective and is congruent with observations by journalists and less systematic personal experience.

The final research objective was to assess the degree of association with traditional sex-stereotyping of a number of characteristics identified by previous researchers as correlates of sex-stereotyping. Most of these proved rather disappointing in their predictive power. Age by itself explained most of the variation in sex-typing of personality traits (the six independent variables accounted for a total of only 11 per cent of the variation in sex-stereotyping of personality traits, and more than half of this was accounted for by age alone), and age in combination with attitude toward women's liberation accounted for over three-fifths of the variance explained in traditional sex-stereotyping of occupations.

In view of the low level of variance in sex-stereotyping explained by the six independent variables it is apparent that a great deal of work remains to be done in identifying and verifying the correlates and antecedents of sex-stereotyping. Two of the variables identified in previous work, religious affiliation and sex proved particularly disappointing, and social class as measured by income and education was not as strongly correlated with traditional sex stereotyping as the literature had led us to expect.

In conclusion, while the amount of explained variation in the present study is relatively low and points to a need for additional work to identify the major correlates of sex-role stereotyping, perhaps our major "finding is further confirmation of the prevalence of stereotyping of occupational roles by sex. We began by noting that despite important legal and institutional changes in this area, public attitudes often change much more slowly. One important implication of our confirmation of this lag is that the socialization experience of a good many young people will continue to strongly sex-type occupational choices. Because of the pervasive nature of the socialization process, this can continue to act to effectively circumscribe the range of acceptable occupational choices long after other constraints have been removed. In addition, it can slow the removal of these other constraints as evidenced by such things as the continuing failure to ratify the 27th Amendment.

## NOTES

1   Even among professionals, change appears to be occurring only slowly. In research with a group of clinical psychologists, Broverman *et al.*, (1970) found that a list of traits selected by the respondents to describe a healthy adult was almost identical with a list developed to describe a healthy male and very divergent from a list developed to describe a female. Moreover the attitudes of professional

counselors and counselor educators support traditional sex stereotypes (Naffziger and Naffziger, 1971) and there is evidence that vocational counselors are more biased against women entering nontraditional occupations than are the women they counsel (Medvene and Collins, 1973).

2   While longitudinal data are not available for our analysis some attempt will be made to assess the question of changing sex-role stereotypes by looking at different age cohorts in the larger sample.

3   The concept "fear of success" defined as "anxiety about competitiveness and its aggressive overtones" was greatly popularized following the work of Horner (1968). In Horner's study a majority of coeds responded with negative imagery to a hypothetical case depicting a female finishing at the head of her medical school class. More recent research findings in this area however indicate that "fear of success" among women is not at all universal. For example, Tomlinson-Keasley (1974) found that the elicitation of negative imagery in response to "female-inappropriate" role cues varied significantly in the two colleges she studied as well as by age and marital status. Tomlinson-Keasley concludes that the fear-of-success data must be viewed with caution since it focuses on an extreme group, the unmarried college coed.

4   A demographic analysis by Edward Gross (1968) shows that there was as much sexual segregation of occupation in 1960 as in 1900 and suggests that while there has been a marked increase in the number of women entering into the labor force, that increase has not been accompanied by a disappearance in sex typing of occupations. Instead, it has occurred through the expansion of occupations that were already heavily female in 1900, combined with the creation of new occupations defined as female from the start, rather than by females taking over occupations formerly occupied by males. In fact, where there are sexually integrated occupations, they tend to be occupations once dominated by females where males are also now accepted. Gross reports that "male occupations have become rather more segregative or resistant to female entry, whereas female occupations have become less segregated, or more permissive if one likes, about including males" (Gross, 1968:202–208).

5   In addition to these independent variables which are suggested by the literature, several other control variables were included in the analysis including such things as rural vs. urban background of the respondent. None of these significantly increased the amount of explained variation.

6   Almost all of the state is serviced by one telephone company (Mountain Bell) and even in those cases where small private companies are operative, their telephone listings are included in the larger Mountain Bell directory for that geographical area. As has been noted by Dillman, et al., (1974), phone directories have the advantage of being readily available, at least fairly up-to-date in their listings, and free from legal entanglements. The primary source of bias associated with using directories as a sampling frame results from the fact that not all households have telephones and that those which do not tend to have lower incomes. Utah counties generally have a high percentage of households having listed telephones (over 90 percent). When such is the case, the bias associated with using directories as a sampling frame is probably not particularly different from that associated with the use of other sources.

7   Because of the potential bias associated with lack of independence for those cases in which both husband and wife completed questionnaires, the 771 married pairs were initially analyzed independently. However, no significant differences were found between the married pairs and the remainder of the sample on variables relevant to this paper. Accordingly, the analysis which follows will deal with the complete sample.

8   As pointed out to us by several reviewers, we should have said "congressperson."

9   Marginal frequencies on the independent variables were as follows: (1) Age: 0–29

(N = 547); 30–44 (N = 588); 45–64 (N = 642); 65 and over (N = 195). (2) Education: Grade School only (N = 63); Some High School (N = 230); High School Graduate (N = 579); Some College (N = 626); College Graduate (N = 337); Graduate Degree (N = 128). (3) Sex: Male (N = 927); Female (N = 1,071). (4) Religion: Mormon (N = 1,464); Catholic (N = 121); Protestant (N = 200); Other, no preference (N = 220). (5) Income: None (N = 22); 1–1,999 (N = 42); 2,000–3,999 (N = 92); 4,000–5,999 (N = 108); 6,000–7,999 (N = 173); 8,000–9,999 (N = 206); 10,000–11,999 (N = 328); 12,000–14,999 (N = 266); 15,000–19,999 (N = 199); 20,000–29,999 (N = 110); over 30,000 (N = 67). (6) Attitudes Toward Feminist Movement: Entirely Favorable (N = 43); Mostly Favorable (N = 475); Undecided (N = 374); Mostly Unfavorable (N = 778); Entirely Unfavorable (N = 239). Total marginal frequencies vary somewhat because of incomplete responses.

10    In analyzing the data on religion, two different procedures were tried. First, religion was treated as a series of dummy variables that were run against the dependent variables. For example, in the dummy variable analysis, a respondent would be given a score of 0 if he or she was a Catholic and a 1 otherwise. Then the respondent would be given a score of 0 if he or she was a Mormon and a 1 otherwise, and so on. For the present paper, religion was treated as a measure of denominational conservatism with Mormonism and Catholicism treated as the most conservative, followed by Protestants, Jews, other, and no preference responses. Both the dummy analysis and present procedure were consistent in indicating that religious identification in the Utah sample had little effect on degree of sex-role stereotyping.

11    In effect, multiple stepwise regression analysis permits the independent variables to compete with each other in explaining variation in a dependent variable. Each variable's independent contribution is determined by a statistical partialling out of the effects of the variables already entered in the regression equation. In addition, such analysis provides a cumulative measure of the variation accounted for by different combinations of independent variables.

# REFERENCES

*Block, J. H.*
1973    "Conceptions of Sex Role: Some Cross-Cultural and Longitudinal Perspectives," American Psychologist 28 (June): 512–526.
*Block, J., A. Von der Lippe and J. H. Block*
1973    "Sex Role and Socialization Patterns: Some Personality Concomitants and Environmental Antecedents," Journal of Consulting and Clinical Psychology 41 (December): 321–341.
*Breedlove, C. J., and V. G. Cicirelli*
1974    Women's Fear of Success in Relation to Personal Characteristics and Type of Occupation," Journal of Psychology 86 (March): 181–190.
*Brim, O. G., Jr.*
1958    "Family Structure and Sex-Role Learning by Children: A Further Analysis of Helen Koch's Data." Sociometry 21: 1–6.
*Bronfenbrenner, U.*
1960    "Freudian Theories of Indentification and Their Derivatives," Child Development 31: 15–40.
*Broverman, I. K., D. M. Broverman, F. E. Clarkson, P. S. Rosenkrantz and S. R. Vogel*
1970    "Sex-Role Stereotypes and Clinical Judgments of Mental Health," Journal of Consulting and Clinical Psychology 34 (February): 1–7.

*Brun-Gulbrandsen, S.*
1958   Kjonnsrolle Og Ungdomskriminalitet. Oslo: Institute of Social Research.
*Campbell, D. F.*
1966   "Religion and Values Among Nova Scotian College Students," Sociological Analysis 27 (Summer): 80–93.
*Christopherson, V. A., and J. Walters*
1958   "Responses of Protestants, Catholics, and Jews Concerning Marriage and Family Life," Sociology and Social Research 43 (September–October): 16–22.
*Dillman, D. A., E. H. Carpenter, J. A. Christenson and R. M. Brooks*
1974   "Increasing Mail Questionnaire Response: A Four State Comparison," American Sociological Review 39 (October): 744–756.
*Gross, E.*
1968   "Plus Ca Change ...? The Sexual Structure of Occupations Over Time." Social Problems 16 (Fall): 198–208.
*Hall, M., and R. A. Keith*
1964   "Sex-Role Preference Among Children of Upper and Lower Social Class," Journal of Social Psychology 62:101–110.
*Heilbrun, A. B.*
1965   "Sex Differences in Identification Learning," Journal of Genetic Psychology 106 (June): 185–193.
*Hochschild, A. R.*
1973   "A Review of Sex Role Research," American Journal of Sociology 78 (January): 1011–1029.
*Holmstrom, E. I.*
1973   "Changing Sex Roles in a Developing Country," Journal of Marriage and the Family 35 (August): 546–553.
*Horner, M. S.*
1968   Sex Differences in Achievement Motivation and Performances in Competitive and Noncompetitive Situations. Unpublished Doctoral Dissertation. University of Michigan.
*Josselyn, I. M.*
1967   "Sources of Sexual Identity," Child and Family 6 (Spring): 38–45.
*Kagan, J.*
1964   "Acquisition and Significance of Sex Typing and Sex Role Identity," in M. L. Hoffman and L. W. Hoffman, Review Child Development Research. New York: Russell Sage Foundation.
*Kagan, J., and H. A. Moss*
1962   Birth to Maturity. New York: John Wiley and Sons.
*Klemmack, D. L., and J. N. Edwards*
1973   "Women's Acquistion of Stereotyped Occupational Aspirations." Sociology and Social Research 57 (July): 510–525.
*Knudsen, D. D.*
1969   "The Declining Status of Women: Popular Myths and the Failure of Functionalist Thought," Social Forces 48 (December): 183–193.
*Kohlberg, I.*
1966   "A Cognitive-Developmental Analysis of Children's Sex-Role Concepts and Attitudes," in E. E. Maccoby (ed.). The Development of Sex Differences. Stanford California: Stanford University Press.
*Kohn, M. L.*
1959   "Social Class and Parental Values," American Journal of Sociology 64 (January): 337–351.
*Linton, R.*
1936   The Study of Man. New York: Appleton-Century.

*McClelland, D. J., Atkinson, R. Clark and E. Lowell*
1953    The Achievement Motive. New York: Appleton-Century-Crofts.

*Medvene, A., and A. Collins*
1973    "Occupational Prestige and its Relationship to Traditional and Non-traditional Views of Women's Roles." Research Report: Counseling Center, University of Maryland.

*Mischel, W.*
1966    "A Social Learning View of Sex Differences," in E. E. Maccoby (ed.). The Development of Sex Differences. Stanford California: Stanford University Press, pp. 56–81.

*Naffziger, C. D., and K. Naffziger*
1974    "Development of Sex Role Stereotypes," Family Coordinator 23: 251–258.

*Rabban, M.*
1950    "Sex-Role Identification in Young Children in Two Diverse Social Groups," Genetic Psychology Monographs 42:81–158.

*Sears, R. R., E. E. Maccoby and H. Levin*
1957    Patterns of Child-Rearing. New York: Row, Peterson & Co.

*Siegel, C. L. F.*
1973    "Sex Differences in the Occupational Choices of Second Graders," Journal of Vocational Behavior 3 (January): 15–19.

*Stolka, S. M., and I. D. Barnett*
1969    "Education and Religion as Factors in Women's Attitudes Motivating Childbearing," Journal of Marriage and the Family 31 (November): 740–750.

*Tomlinson-Keasley, C.*
1974    "Role Variables: Their Influence on Female Motivational Constructs," Journal of Counseling Psychology 21:232–237.

*Webster, M., Jr.*
1975    Actions and Actors: Principles of Social Psychology. Cambridge, Massachusetts: Winthrop Publishers.

# Equal-Status Contact and Modification of Racial Prejudice: A Reexamination of the Contact Hypothesis*

## Jerry W. Robinson, Jr.

*University of Illinois*

## James D. Preston

*Memphis State University*

*Recent research on equal-status interracial contact suggests that such contact lessens prejudice. The present study extends research on equal-status contact into a situation designed to elicit favorable contact, namely faculty desegregation in public schools. Black and white teachers were interviewed with regard to their levels of prejudice both before and after participating in an in-service*

*Source*: Reprinted from Social Forces 54, 4 (June 1976): 911–24. "Equal-Status Contact and Modification of Racial Prejudice: A Reexamination of the Contact Hypothesis," by Jerry W. Robinson, Jr., and James D. Preston. Copyright © 1976 The University of North Carolina Press.

*This research was conducted under grant no. MH-14622 from the National Institute of Mental Health. The authors are indebted to Lynn Weber Cannon for her helpful critique and suggestions for revision.

*training institute on problems of school desegregation in Houston, Texas. In addition, a follow-up survey was administered sixteen months after the conclusion of institute training. The conclusions were: (1) after completion of institute training white respondents scored significantly lower on all measures of prejudice while black scores remained relatively stable; (2) teachers who participated in institute training were significantly less prejudiced than were a random sample of non-institute participants selected from the same schools; and (3) institute training was more effective in lessening white prejudice toward blacks than in reducing black prejudice toward whites. In relating these findings to recent research by Cohen and Roper and W. Scott Ford, we conclude that many interracial contact situations that are perceived as being of equal status by whites are not perceived in the same manner by blacks, a conclusion which suggests a modification of the traditional equal-status contact hypothesis as well as having direct implications for policy-making in the area of school desegregation.*

Studies of the effects of equal-status interracial contact on attitudes and behavior of majority and minority group members have generally yielded consistent results. Most such research has concluded that social contact between participants of equal status reduces prejudice (Amir; Brophy; Gundlach; Mann; Meer and Friedman; Yarrow et al.). Research has also found reduction of prejudice in situations where contact is between majority group members and high-status representatives of the minority group (Amir; Irish; Mannheimer and Williams; Watson).

The concept "contact" has been applied to a wide spectrum of situations with a variety of subjects. Contact situations studied include the armed services, residential areas, recreational activities, occupational endeavors, and various types of classroom situations. Subjects include children and various categories of adults, frequently segregated by sex. Activities studied as examples of contact can be viewed as existing on a continuum ranging from extreme forms of cooperation (e.g., white and black groups in combat together) to competitive and conflict situations (e.g., invasion of a white residential area by blacks). The most appropriate generalization is that the nature and type of contact is just as important as the contact itself. The effects of contact may be either negative or positive, depending on the nature of the contact situation, the characteristics of the participants, and the types of activity which occur. Thus we need to specify further the dimensions of contact and to indicate which of the dimensions will lead to favorable and which to unfavorable results.

From findings in the various studies on interracial contact (Allport; Amir), the following generalizations emerge.[1]

First, interracial contact is most likely to yield favorable results (i.e., reduce prejudice) when participants are: (a) of equal statuses; (b) majority group members interacting with high-status representatives of the minority groups; (c) in a voluntary contact situation; and (d) engaged in intimate interaction, pursuing common goals in a cooperative relationship with institutional supports.

Second, interracial contact is most likely to yield unfavorable results (i.e., intensify prejudices and sterotypes) when participants are: (a) of unequal statuses; (b) majority group members interacting with low-status representatives of the minority group; (c) in involuntary contact situations; (d) engaged in casual interaction, competing; and (e) in conflict for goals which cannot be shared.

In brief, when there is equal-status contact between members of diverse ethnic groups, the chances of the contact being defined as favorable and of prejudice being reduced appear greater. The studies of the armed forces cited above (Brophy; Mannheimer and Williams) indicated that contact with members of a minority group on an equal-status basis tends to reduce prejudice toward the entire minority group. Similarly, if the contact is between members of a majority group and higher-status members of a minority group the chances for favorable contact improve (Amir). The chances of the contact situation eliciting unfavorable responses by majority group members increase as the status of the representatives of the minority group declines. Contact is also more likely to be favorable where participants come together on a voluntary basis, that is, primarily for the purpose of associating with members of the other group. Obviously some process of self-selection is present in any voluntary contact situation; those most prejudiced are perhaps most likely to avoid contact situations if at all possible (Williams). In situations where members of different ethnic groups voluntarily choose to engage in an interracial encounter, conditions are amenable to favorable interaction and to the reduction of prejudice.

If the contact has both normative support and that of legitimate authorities, it is much more likely to develop favorably. Institutional support may come from law, custom, or any authority accepted as legitimate by the interacting groups. Conversely, if the existing social climate and significant reference groups define the contact as being undesirable within the existing normative structure, then the contact and resultant attitudes of participants are likely to develop in an unfavorable direction (Amir). In a study of segregated and integrated housing, Deutsch and Collins found that many respondents in the former project would not mix with blacks because "it just isn't done," a finding which illustrates the importance of the social climate and reference groups.

The nature of the activity itself has several characteristics within any contact situation. Interaction may be casual or intimate and it may be either cooperative, competitive, or perhaps even conflicting in nature. Casual contact is not enough by itself to change attitudes and lessen prejudice. Furthermore, frequency of contact is no indicator of intimacy of contact. (A person may deal daily with a member of a minority ethnic group, yet the interaction may remain on a superficial or casual basis, thus no significant lessening of prejudice would be likely to occur.) Intimate contact is a necessary, but not sufficient, criterion for the lessening of prejudice. Intimate cooperative interaction of members of different ethnic groups in the pursuit of common goals is likely to reduce prejudice. If the participants are in conflict, as, for example, over "block busting" in residential neighborhoods or are competing for scarce resources, as in many occupational situations, contact is likely to reinforce existing stereotypes and prejudices.

In sum, equal-status contacts have been shown to reduce stereotyped images (Rose) and have been viewed as breaking the vicious circle in race relations (Myrdal).

## RESEARCH PROBLEM

This research examines equal-status contact in an institute for public school teachers, a situation designed to elicit favorable contact. There were three research objectives: (1) to examine the change in attitudes of equal-status subjects who participated in an intentional contact situation designed to reduce prejudice; (2) to ascertain if the measured reduction in prejudice would persist over an extended time period; and (3) to examine differences between the attitudes of the institute participants and a random sample of non-institute participants who were teaching in the same schools.

The research design reported herein goes beyond previous studies in overcoming several weaknesses.[2] First, the contact, public school desegregation, was not underway at the time of investigation, thus our "before" measure was not contaminated (Cook). Second, the initial attitudes of institute participants were measured directly (Preston and Robinson) prior to contact, and not recalled (Cook). Third, the contact was of equal-status individuals engaged in pursuing joint goals (Amir). Fourth, general measures of attitudes were used instead of specific measures (e.g., attitude measures were not limited to one contact situation, such as on the job or in a residential area). Since non-prejudice can be specific, as, for example, in the educational setting, general measures of prejudice are needed to investigate whether contact lessens general prejudice and changes general attitudes or if the nonprejudice is limited to the specific contact situation (Amir). Fifth, blacks' attitudes toward whites are studied, as well as whites' attitudes toward blacks. The emphasis in previous research has been on blacks as objects of attitudes and on treating whites as subjects having the attitudes (Amir). Finally, black males, who have been largely neglected in social science research, have adequate representation among our respondents.

## RESEARCH DESIGN

### Background of the Research

In-service training institutes for school teachers have been used all over the United States as means for promoting school desegregation, especially in the South. Such institutes are planned at least on tacit acceptance of the contact hypothesis, i.e., contact fosters positive attitude change. The researchers initially participated in twelve 8-hour training sessions on the problems of school desegregation for 180 teachers in Houston, Texas. The sessions were held on successive Saturdays at local universities. These in-service training sessions for teachers included lectures by nationally known consultants and local college professors. Seminars, films, group discussions, field observations, trips, reports, and small group sensitivity sessions were included in the institute program format. The program dealt with the social, psychological, economic, and political foundations of racial discrimination and prejudice. The role of the teacher in the desegregation process was especially emphasized. The institutes in Houston were designed to provide the opportunity for extensive communication with members of the other race. After the institute it was hypothesized that participants would appreciate the values, attitudes and life styles of persons of another race.

Training programs within the institutes were designed to promote favorable attitude change on the part of both races. Participants were of equal status (all were college graduates, school teachers, and most were from the South) in a voluntary contact situation pursuing common goals. Several common goals consisted of *interracial team* activities between training sessions. They (1) visited an agency for the disadvantaged (Goodwill, for example) and wrote a report; (2) tutored children with learning disabilities; and (3) visited the home of one black and one white and wrote a report on the visit. This biracial team activity provided the opportunity for intimate, cooperative social interaction. In addition, sensitivity sessions provided a vehicle for intimate interaction which centered around the understanding of racial prejudices by members of both races. Likewise, the fact that the school system was cooperating in sponsoring the institutes provided the participants some degree of institutional support.

A questionnaire administered to a panel of 12 faculty members of the institute inquired as to the faculty's perception of the presence of favorable or unfavorable contact conditions in institute sessions. A large majority of the panel agreed that conditions favorable to a reduction in prejudice were present in the institute (see Table 1).

TABLE 1

**Frequency Distribution of the Votes of Twelve Institute Faculty Members on the Presence of Favorable and Unfavorable Contact Conditions**

| *CONDITIONS* | *PRESENT* | *NOT PRESENT* |
|---|---|---|
| Favorable | | |
| Equal status | 12 | — |
| An "authority" and/or the social climate were in favor of promoting intergroup contact (institutional support) | 11 | 1 |
| Intimate group contact | 9 | 3 |
| Members of both groups felt their activities were important or they developed superordinate group goals more important than individual goals (common goals) | 10 | 2 |
| Unfavorable | | |
| Competition between groups | 3 | 9 |
| Contact was unpleasant, involuntary and tension laden | 1 | 11 |

## The Before-After Study

Preston and Robinson, in a before-after research design, administered a battery of five scales to all institute participants (IPS) on the first and last weeks of the twelve-week institute. The scales were taken from an earlier work by Robin Williams (396–412) and were designed to measure racial tension in the community, distastefulness, stereotyping, general prejudice, and social discrimination. White IPS revealed a statistically significant attitude change, in a favorable direction, on all scales. No statistically significant attitude change was found among the black IPS. This finding was explained by two factors: (1) most of the scales were originally designed to measure white attitudes toward blacks, and (2) black IPS reflected lower levels of prejudice at the origin of the institute, thus changes were not as great, although they were consistently in a favorable direction.

The fact that contact in the institute situation produced such a significant lowering of prejudice, particularly among white IPS, was encouraging to the researchers in its implications for promoting school desegregation. Yet, we were reluctant completely to accept these findings as indicators of genuine long-range reductions in prejudice, because the research design was simply a pretest, posttest design, with all subjects being volunteers, and including no control group. It could be argued that the measured lowering of prejudice was only temporary, in the absence of a longitudinal research design which could yield contrary data. Thus, upon receiving a grant from NIMH, the research reported herein was conducted.

## The Followup Study

In the followup study, 350 teachers of the Houston Independent School District were interviewed in small groups by the principal investigator. The samples included 152 institute participants and 198 randomly selected teachers who had not experienced in-service training on problems of school desegregation.[3] All teachers in the ramdom sample were teaching in the same schools (now desegregated) as the institute participants. Each respondent received a small stipend for his cooperation in the study. The composition of the two test groups by race and sample type is shown in Table 2.

TABLE 2
Test Group Composition by Sample Type and Race

|  | RACE | | |
| --- | --- | --- | --- |
| SAMPLE TYPE | WHITE | BLACK | TOTAL |
| Institute participants (IP) | 61 | 91 | 152 |
| Random sample of non-institute teachers (RS) | 86 | 112 | 198 |
| Total | 147 | 203 | 350 |

The investigators compared the IP and RS groups by $\chi^2$ as a measure of goodness of fit. The only two areas in which there were significant differences were sex and educational achievement. There were more black males among the institute participants, and there were more black institute participants who had their master's degrees. No statistically significant differences were found between the IP and RS on the following demographic characteristics: age, current marital status, length of in-district residence, length of in-home residence, previous residence in North or West, attendance at segregated undergraduate college, birthplace in South, home ownership, employment status (whether elementary or secondary school teacher) Democrat-Republican political party membership, number with working spouses, number whose working spouses are professional, nature of father's occupation, current family income, membership in local professional teacher's organization, evaluation of local professional teachers' organization, church membership, church attendance, and church office holder. Since there were 19 characteristics on which the participants were matched, and, as mentioned previously, all twelve institute faculty members viewed the interaction as equal-status contact, there is strong evidence that participants were of equal status. However, since significantly more blacks had master's degrees, the only evidence which seriously contradicts the equal-status assumption is in the direction of higher status to the minority group, a condition which is equally satisfactory for promoting favorable attitude change (Amir).

Different questionnaires were used for blacks and whites; for each item was written to apply to one *or* the other category. Some examples: Steckler's "Anti-Negro" scale was administered to whites and his "Anti-white" scale was administered to blacks. These scales employ different statements for each race but the content is similar.[4] The following scales were adapted for use: (1) Previous Behavior Patterns with People of the Opposite Race (R. Ford); (2) Behavior Patterns with People of the Other Race (Rosander); (3) Stereotyping (Williams); (4) Attitude Toward Integration (developed by the authors); (5) Attitude Toward Segregation (Rosenbaum and Zimmerman); (6) Anti-Negro (Steckler); and (7) Anti-White (Steckler). Space limitations preclude the presentation of all items in each scale and the statistical treatment of each.[5] Item analyses were performed on all scales using the Kelley technique (Downie and Heath) of comparing the responses of subjects who scored in the top 27 percent and the bottom 27 percent of the total scores for each scale. Item discrimination indices were computed by using Gronlund's (211) formula. Item variances were computed using grouped data techniques and identical response weights as applied to determine scale totals. Scale variances were computed similarly. Also, the Kuder-Richardson Formula 20 was used in determining coefficients of internal consistency for the various scales (Downie and Heath, 220). To test hypotheses we employed the "t" test for significant differences between scale score means.

## RESULTS

### Sample Type Differences

As indicated in Table 3, in six of the seven scales, significant differences were found between the two groups at the .001 level when sample type was used as the test variable. The institute participants were significantly less prejudiced. They were more likely to: regard previous contact with persons of another race in a favorable manner; respond with functional patterns of behavior in fictitious situations involving blacks and whites; desire to see segregation eliminated; be free from stereotypical attitudes; and participate in integrated social activities. The only scale differences which were not significant were the results on the anti-white scale, which was administered to blacks only. This finding is consistent with the before-after study (Preston and Robinson), which revealed that institute participation by blacks did not result in a statistically significant lessening of their prejudices toward whites.

TABLE 3

Test Results for Differences in Interracial Attitude Scale Score
Means by Sample Types*

| | SAMPLE TYPE | | | |
| | INSTITUTE PARTICIPANT | RANDOM SAMPLE | | |
| SCALE | MEAN | MEAN | z-VALUE | PROBABILITY |
|---|---|---|---|---|
| 1. Previous behavior patterns with people of the opposite race, range 12–60 | 46.71 | 44.94 | +3.482 | .001 |
| 2. Behavior patterns with people of the other race, range 1.2–11.5 | 85.55 | 81.85 | +5.07 | .001 |
| 3. Stereotypes, range 4–20 | 17.55 | 16.48 | +3.920 | .001 |
| 4. Attitude toward social integration, range 6–30 | 23.25 | 21.65 | +4.378 | .001 |
| 5. Attitude toward segregation, range 23–115 | 93.14 | 88.24 | +5.075 | .001 |
| 6. Anti-Negro (Whites only), range 14–60 | 56.44 | 46.32 | +5.560 | .001 |
| 7. Anti-white (Negroes only), range 14–60 | 55.09 | 54.07 | +0.934 | .20 |

*Higher scores are positive.

## Differences by Sample Type with Race Controlled

Significant differences were found between the IP and the RS whites on all scales examined in Table 4. For the anti-Negro scale, which was administered to whites only, the mean scale score difference of 10.12 was the largest variation of any test. White teachers in the random sample always scored as significantly more unfavorable on the race relations and prejudice scales.

There was not so much contrast in attitudes among blacks as among whites. Nonetheless, on all scales IP blacks had scores more favorable toward whites than did the blacks in the RS.

## Differences by Race with Sample Type Controlled

A principal aim of this research was to study the attitudes of blacks and whites within each sample type since previous research has concentrated on attitudes and prejudice of whites.

An examination of Table 5 reveals that significant differences were found for *all* tests between the blacks and whites in the random sample. Blacks tended to look with more disfavor on previous behavior patterns between the races but presently were highly disposed to interact favorably with whites; blacks were much more in favor of integration.

Differences between the black and white IP were not as consistently different. Black IP teachers' attitudes were not significantly different from the

## TABLE 4

**Test Results for Differences in Interracial Scale Score Means by Sample Type with Race Controlled***

| | BLACK | | | | WHITE | | | |
|---|---|---|---|---|---|---|---|---|
| SCALE | IP/x̄ N = 91 | RS/x̄ N = 112 | Z-VALUE | PROBA-BILITY | IP/x̄ N = 61 | RS/x̄ N = 86 | Z-VALUE | PROBA-BILITY |
| 1. Previous behavior patterns with people of the opposite race | 44.96 | 44.38 | 1.55 | 0.121 | 49.31 | 45.72 | 6.31 | .001 |
| 2. Behavior patterns with people of the other race | 85.59 | 85.46 | +0.19 | .849 | 85.48 | 77.15 | +6.81 | .001 |
| 3. Stereotype | 17.42 | 16.93 | 1.99 | 0.047 | 17.69 | 15.94 | 4.91 | .001 |
| 4. Attitudes toward social integration | 23.54 | 23.46 | 0.29 | 0.772 | 22.84 | 19.30 | 8.52 | .001 |
| 5. Attitude toward segregation | 95.20 | 94.47 | +0.73 | 0.465 | 90.10 | 80.55 | +6.96 | .001 |

*Higher scores are positive

**TABLE 5**

**Test Results for Differences in Interracial Scale Score Means
Between Black and White Teachers with Sample Type Controlled***

| SCALE | INSTITUTE PARTICIPANT | | | | RANDOM SAMPLE | | | |
|---|---|---|---|---|---|---|---|---|
| | WHITE/x N = 61 | BLACK/x N = 91 | t | p | WHITE/x N = 86 | BLACK/x N = 112 | t | p |
| 1. Previous behavior patterns with people of the opposite race | 49.31 | 44.90 | +6.13 | .001 | 45.72 | 44.38 | +1.98 | .01 |
| 2. Behavior patterns with people of the other race | 85.48 | 85.59 | −0.08 | NS | 77.15 | 85.46 | −5.85 | .001 |
| 3. Stereotype | 17.69 | 17.42 | +0.76 | NS | 15.94 | 16.93 | −2.28 | .01 |
| 4. Attitudes toward social integration | 22.84 | 23.54 | −1.44 | NS | 19.30 | 23.46 | −8.23 | .001 |
| 5. Attitude toward segregation | 90.10 | 95.20 | −3.03 | .001 | 80.55 | 94.47 | −8.20 | .001 |

*Higher scores are positive

white IP teachers on four of the tests—attitudes toward integration; stereotyping; attitudes toward people of another race in hypothetical situations; attitudes toward interracial social interaction. Other test findings were similar to those for the random sample.

### Major Findings

To summarize, there were three major findings. First, there was a statistically significant difference between the IP and the RS on all scales, with the exception of the anti-white scale which was administered only to blacks. Second, the largest statistical difference in racial attitudes and levels of prejudice was between the white IP and white RS. On every test the RS attitudes regarding stereotyping, integrated interpersonal relationships, segregation, and integration indicated significantly more prejudice. Third, in analyzing black responses only, no statistically significant differences were found between the IP and RS; however, there was a consistent tendency on all scales for black IPs to have more favorable attitudes toward whites and for blacks to reflect lower levels of prejudice than whites. Even though not significant in a statistical sense, the consistent direction of the findings represents a general trend not expected by chance alone. As Olsen (686) states:

*Even though a number of relationships may not be statistically significant by themselves, if they are consistently in the same direction, it is statistically valid to assume that the overall tendency they represent does exist in the total population. The probability of obtaining numerous consistent relationships (no matter how small) without the existence of an overall general tendency in the population is usually quite low.*

That the black IPs had a consistently more favorable attitude toward whites than the black RS is considered to be at least partially a result of the positive contact in the institute setting.

### DISCUSSION

Amir (340) summarized the findings of his exhaustive review of literature on interracial contact with the statement:

*If one wants to achieve positive results in the area of intergroup relations, it would be wise to consider carefully if prevailing conditions are suitable to bring about such a change. Experimentation prior to policy-making may eliminate illusions in this sensitive area and would enable the policy-makers to choose those programs which have the best chances of producing the hoped for results.*

Findings reaffirm the conclusion that conditions of interracial contact which encourage favorable attitude change cannot only be specified but they can also be exploited in practical situations to produce such changes. The results of the earlier study (Preston and Robinson) revealed that IPs changed their attitude in a favorable direction and lowered their levels of prejudice as a result of a favorable contact situation. Moreover, the present study shows that after a lapse of sixteen months from the conclusion of the contact situation, the IPs levels of prejudice were significantly lower than those of the RS who taught in the same schools. The findings of this research can be interpreted as tending to support the notion that equal-status interracial contact lessens prejudice, particularly for whites. The findings of the present research run remarkably parallel to those of W. Scott Ford who studied equal-status contact among housewives, both black and white, living in public housing in Lexington, Kentucky. After interracial contact occurred, Ford reported an increased racial tolerance on the part of white housewives in his sample; this was not the case for black housewives. As was the case in our research, blacks were initially less prejudiced than whites but blacks reduced their prejudice to a lesser extent than did whites after interracial contact. In his research and in ours, apparently contact has a different meaning for the black and white participants.

The apparent different meaning of equal-status contact for blacks and whites may be a result of the different types of stereotypes held by each group about the other. For example, if whites feel that blacks are dirty, loud, irresponsible, and lazy, equal-status contact as, for instance, in W. Ford's housing project could possibly prove them right or wrong. When the white housewives found themselves living similar lifestyles, they might have been prompted to change their opinions of blacks. The type of observation necessary to combat racial stereotypes of this sort is merely living in close proximity and observing whether the blacks, for example, stay clean, make noise, or attend work regularly. It is likely that in equal-status contacts black behaviors along these dimensions will not seriously differ from those of their white counterparts who are experiencing a similar life situation based on similar statuses. Thus, equal-status contact could provide the information necessary to combat whites' prejudices against blacks, and the literature has clearly supported its effectiveness (Amir).

On the other hand, black prejudice is based on an entirely different set of stereotypes which may not be as amenable to reduction through simple participation in an equal-status contact situation. Amir has stated that a number of conditions should be present in order to reduce prejudice. It is possible that equal-status contact is the more important condition for whites, but not for blacks. In W. Ford's housing project study, black women perceived condescending attitudes on the part of whites and they resented the isolation and lack of social recognition. If blacks feel that whites are untrustworthy, treat blacks as inferior, and fail to give them social recognition, it is possible that mere equal-status contact would not suffice to combat such fears and attitudes. In order for blacks to feel that whites are trustworthy and willing to treat them as social equals a very intimate type of relationship on a personal level may be necessary. Thus, black stereotypes about whites are less visible or tangible, and therefore less easily refuted in a contact situation which is less personal and durable.

Equal-status contact may have a different meaning for blacks in that it does not provide the chance to combat stereotypes unless the contact is also very intimate or personal. Amir (334) states " . . . casual intergroup contact has little or no effect on a basic attitude change. Intimate contact, on the other hand, tends to produce favorable changes." Ford reports that even though the blacks in his study were less prejudiced than the whites, black women reported fewer neighboring contacts with whites, and there were no black women who were socially intimate with more than one white housewife. If social intimacy is the more important variable in attacking black prejudice, this could provide an alternate explanation for the weakened relationships reported for blacks in Ford's study.

In the present longitudinal study blacks were also initially less prejudiced than whites. Although a certain degree of intimacy was attained in the sensitivity sessions, more frequent, intense, and intimate personal contact situations should have been arranged. For more frequent intimate contact situations might have increased the degree of change in black prejudice.

A possible explanation for both Ford's and our findings is found in the work of Cohen and Roper using the "status characteristics and expectation states" theory of Berger et al. Since whites have traditionally been the dominant group, there is a widely held belief in our culture that blacks are generally less competent than whites. There is empirical evidence that whites tend to dominate in a social situation where the two races interact or where blacks compare themselves to whites as significant others. In other words, both blacks and whites appear to have internalized the beliefs that whites are more competent. Cohen and Roper (644) called this condition "interracial interaction disability" and in a laboratory experiment with black and white junior high school boys their most important finding was the need to treat *both* black and white *expectations prior to* interracial interaction in order to attain genuine equal-status interaction. If treatment of expectations is not done prior to interaction, contact will be along the traditional dominant-minority lines. In our study of participants in an institute setting, where laboratory controls were unavailable, we matched blacks and whites along traditional social and demographic variables and demonstrated equal status on these variables. But we did not treat the expectations of either race, with the result that white prejudices and stereotypes were reduced to a significant extent and blacks' were not. A distinct possibility is that even though the contact was between equals (as to traditional social and demographic variables) it may not have been perceived as equal by black participants. This could be because (1) many situations which whites define as "equal status" are in reality laden with prejudicial and racist cues,[6] and (2) such contact, in short-run institute sessions, cannot be isolated from the total black experience with white America. For whites, however, the equal-status situation may be unique and of consequence, as it may also be the only interracial situation they have experienced.[7] As a result of such life experiences, blacks may be suspicious of any interaction with whites, even in what appear to be equal-status situations (W. Ford; Johnson). In order to reduce black prejudices and stereotypes in future institutes, expectation training, along the lines suggested by Cohen and Roper, could be incorporated into the format prior to interracial interaction and thus reduce the possibility of white dominance in actual interaction situations. From our data, "treatment" thus becomes an important variable; equal-status interracial interaction appears to be a necessary but not sufficient basis for reduction of prejudice. We do suggest that equal-status interracial interaction which is intimate, intense, of some duration, and specifically directed toward modifying attitudes of *both* black and white subjects can be highly successful in reducing prejudice.

To assess additional ramifications of the contact hypotheses, future research should go beyond simply measuring participation in a favorable contact situation to specifying the types of interaction within the overall contact situation. For example, the present research does not compare types of treatment within the overall institute situation and relate these to the conditions of the contact hypothesis. To illustrate, some sensitivity sessions within the institute undoubtedly provided negative contact between blacks and whites. Although no direct measure of this is available in the present data, a thorough analysis of these situations would be meaningful.

In conclusion, our findings, coupled with those of Ford and Cohen and Roper, suggest a modification of the equal-status contact hypothesis. Equal-status contact appears to reduce prejudices of whites toward blacks but it is clearly less effective in reducing black prejudice toward whites. Additional research is needed to focus specifically on black perceptions of and reactions to such contact situations in order to further our knowledge of interracial interaction.

## NOTES

1  These two generalizations represent ideal types, in which all the variables are interdependent, and are essentially impossible to examine empirically in the classical experimental sense. Ideally one would manipulate each of the above variables independently of the others, or find situations which differ only on the variable under examination but are similar on all other relevant variables. However, such manipulation would be exceedingly difficult, and interracial contact situations characterized by positive or negative values on only *one* of the above variables are difficult to isolate. Thus, in empirical research, the chances of evaluating the effect upon the lowering of prejudice of any of the above variables alone are minimal at best.

2  The research design was not able to overcome the possibility of the sensitizing and grapevine effects. The sensitizing effect occurs when the initial before measure influences the after measure. The grapevine effect is that information concerning the institute passes by word of mouth to non-institute participants who may have been included in the RS (random sample). However, the researchers know of no research design that would completely control for these influences.

3  No "before" measure of prejudice was deemed necessary on the random sample because the randomization procedure itself allows the researcher to assume pre-experimental equality of the stimuli under observation. In addition, a "before" measure on the random sample, or control group, could possibly contaminate the later measure. For an elaboration of these points, see Kerlinger (332–33). In any research which views reduction of prejudice as a result of interracial contact, the question arises as to what extent initially tolerant attitudes were responsible for one group entering the contact situation. Such differential selection does not offer an adequate explanation for our findings since: (1) we demonstrated that the IP and RS groupings were not significantly different along traditional sociodemographic variables, and (2) the IP grouping reflected high degrees of prejudce in our "before"

measure in the "before-after" study. Deutsch and Collins and W. Ford utilized a similar viewpoint in explaining their findings.

4 W. Ford (1434) likewise modified scale items to fit respondents of either race by alternating the object of prejudice from black to white. Some examples of our items are: (1) for blacks: (a) There is nothing lower than white trash; (b) White people are only friendly to Negroes when they want something out of them; (c) The whites have shown by their actions that they are naturally immoral, vicious, and untrustworthy; and (2) for whites: (a) One reason why racial prejudice still exists today is the fact that many Negroes are dirty, loud, and generally offensive in their ways; (b) Colored people can hardly be expected to gain social equality until many more of them exert some effort to better themselves and live more decently; (c) Negroes would solve many of their social problems if so many of them were not irresponsible, lazy, and ignorant.

5 This information can be obtained by writing to the authors.

6 The authors observed that many white institute participants pronounced Negro "nig-gra," a pronunciation which could be interpreted by blacks as indicating latent prejudice.

7 Many white subjects reported that this was their first experience in interacting with their black counterparts on an equal or professional basis.

## REFERENCES

*Allport, G. W.*
1954    *The Nature of Prejudice*. Cambridge: Addison-Wesley.
*Amir. Y.*
1969    "Contact Hypothesis in Ethnic Relations." *Psychological Bulletin* 71:319–42.
*Berger, J., B. P. Cohen, and M. Zeldith, Jr.*
1966    "Status Characteristics and Expectation States." In J. Berger, M. Zelditch, Jr., and B. Anderson (eds.), *Sociological Theories in Progress*. Boston: Houghton Mifflin.
*Brophy, I. N.*
1945    "The Luxury of Anti-Negro Prejudice." *Public Opinion Quarterly* 9:456–66.
*Cohen, E. G., and S. S. Roper*
1972    "Modification of Interracial Interaction Disability: An Application of Status Characteristic Theory." *American Sociological Review* 37:643–57.
*Cook, S. W.*
1963    "A Psychological Analysis." In W. W. Charters, Jr., and N. L. Gage (eds.), *Readings in the Social Psychology of Education*. Boston: Allyn & Bacon.
*DeFleur, M. L., and F. R. Westie*
1963    "Attitude as a Scientific Concept." *Social Forces* 42 (October): 17–31.
*Deutsch, M., and M. E. Collins*
1951    *Interracial Housing: A Psychological Evaluation of a Social Experiment*. Minneapolis: University of Minnesota Press.
*Downie, N. M., and R. W. Heath*
1965    *Basic Statistical Methods*. New York: Harper & Row.
*Ford, R. N.*
1941    "Scaling Experiences by a Multiple Response Technique: A Study of White-Negro Contacts." *American Sociological Review* 6:9–23.
*Ford, W. S.*
1973    "Interracial Public Housing in a Border City: Another Look at the Contact Hypothesis." *American Journal of Sociology* 78:1426–47.

Gronlund, N. E.
1965    *Measurement and Evaluation in Teaching.* New York: Macmillan.

Gundlach, R. H.
1950    "The Effect of On-the-Job Experience with Negroes Upon Social Attitudes of White Workers in Union Shops." *American Psychologist* 5:300.

Irish, D. P.
1952    "Reactions of Caucasian Residents to Japanese-American Neighbors." *Journal of Social Issues* 8:10–17.

Johnson, R. B.
1966    "Negro Reactions to Minority Group Status." In Bernard E. Segal (ed.), *Racial and Ethnic Relations*. New York: Crowell.

Kelman, H. C.
1962    "Changing Attitudes Through International Activities." *Journal of Social Issues* 18:68–87.

Kerlinger, Fred N.
1964    *Foundations of Behavioral Research.* New York: Holt, Rinehart & Winston.

Mann, J. H.
1959    "The Effects of Interracial Contact on Sociometric Choices and Perceptions." *Journal of Social Psychology* 50:143–152.

Mannheimer, D., and R. M. Williams, Jr.
1949    "A Note on Negro Troops in Combat." In S. A. Stouffer, E. A. Suchman, L. C. De Vinney, S. A. Starr, and R. M. Williams, Jr., *The American Soldier*. Princeton: Princeton University Press.

Meer, B., and E. Freedman
1966    "The Impact of Negro Neighbors on White House Owners." *Social Forces* 45 (September): 11–19.

Myrdal, Gunnar
1944    *An American Dilemma*. New York: Harper.

Olsen, M. E.
1970    "Social and Political Participation of Blacks." *American Sociological Review* 35 (August): 682–97.

Preston, J. D., and J. W. Robinson, Jr.
1974    "On Modification of Interracial Interaction." *American Sociological Review* 39 (April): 283–95.

Rosander, A. C.
1937    "An Attitude Scale Based Upon Behavior Situations." *Journal of Social Psychology* 8:3–16.

Rose, A. M.
1956    "Intergroup Relations vs. Prejudice." *Social Problems* (October): 173–76.

Rosenbaum, M. E., and I. A. Zimmerman
1959    "The Effect of External Commitment on Response to an Attempt to Change Opinion." *Public Opinion Quarterly* 23:247–54.

Steckler, G.
1957    "Authoritarian Ideology in Negro College Students." *Journal of Abnormal Psychology* 54:396–99.

Watson, Jr.
1950    "Some Social and Psychological Situations Related to Change in Attitude." *Human Relations* 3:15–56.

Williams, Robin M., Jr.
1964    *Strangers Next Door*. Englewood Cliffs: Prentice-Hall.

Yarrow, M. R., J. P. Campbell, and L. J. Yarrow
1957    "Acquisition of New Norms: A Study of Racial Desegregation." *Journal of Social Issues* 14:8–28.

# THREE

## PATTERNS OF DISCRIMINATION: RACIAL AND CULTURAL GROUPS

*As patterns of discrimination against groups become embedded in social orga-*
*nization, minorities and dominant groups become accommodated to unequal*
*status relations. Patterns of accommodation vary from tentative, volatile work-*
*ing relationships to those that are highly routinized. There are tensions and*
*latent conflicts in even the most stable patterns, and under appropriate condi-*
*tions overt conflict and change occur. The more the inequalities are institution-*
*alized, the greater the disruptions caused by changes and the greater the*
*opposition in the dominant community to change.*

*A major dimension of social organization is the vertical stratification of*
*populations into social classes or castes. Class systems vary in the degree of*
*upward or downward movement of persons, but neither vertical mobility nor*
*marriage outside the rank is permitted in caste systems. Social classes are large*
*segments of a society's population that are vertically stratified by differences*
*in economic status, social status (prestige), and power, and that share a style of*
*life—a subculture (Gordon, 1964:40–42). Patterns of minority-dominant rela-*
*tions involve the vertical stratification of groups, so it is important to under-*
*stand the connections between them and systems of class and caste. Both the*
*class structure of the minority community and the place and mobility of racial,*
*national, and religious groups in the class system have been studied.*

*Goyder and Pineo's concern in the first selection in this section is with the*
*way persons who are Catholics, Jews, white Protestants, or black Protestants*
*rank themselves in the American class system. The data are from national*
*public opinion survey samples. Hypotheses are tested about the relationships*
*between self-rated class status, minority identity, and objectively determined*
*economic class position of persons interviewed. Note that the term "class con-*
*sciousness" is defined as knowing accurately what economic stratum one is in,*
*and measured by agreement between self-ranked class status and objective*
*indexes of economic status (mainly occupation, but income and education are*
*also used). It will be apparent that the problems of research and interpretation*
*in this important area of overlap between minority status and social class are*
*complex (Ransford, 1977).*

*The "Moynihan Report," which attributed black poverty to the supposedly*
*disorganized ghetto family, became the chief basis for the antipoverty pro-*
*grams of the 1960s (Moynihan, Barton, et al.). Poverty was portrayed as a*
*subculture—a pattern of weak family structure due to the economic failures of*
*men, causing children to drop out of school and become unemployable and*
*deviant—a style of life passed from one generation to the next (Lewis, 1966: 19).*
*The selection by Coward, Feagin, and Williams reports one of a number of*
*studies that do not support the culture of poverty thesis (Liebow, 1967; Irelan,*
*Moles, and O'Shea, 1969; Berger and Simon, 1974). The poor and non-poor blacks*
*interviewed in a Southwestern city provided data suggesting that the poor are*
*victims of low pay, unemployment, poor housing, and other institutional con-*
*ditions beyond their control rather than of an alleged cultural pattern of their*
*own. Programs such as Head Start, Upward Bound, and other tutoring efforts*
*were intended to intervene in the transmission of the presumed culture of*
*poverty, and to encourage poor children to learn the values of individual*
*achievement. The situational explanation of poverty lends support to policies*
*aimed at creating jobs and housing for the poor, treating consumers fairly, and*
*enforcing the civil rights laws against discrimination (Rainwater and Yancey,*
*1967; Valentine, 1968; Rainwater, 1974).*

*In some theories that emphasize conflict it is assumed that power in society is monopolized by a very small group, so that vertical stratification consists of the domination of the masses by an elite. In power elite theories, including Marxist ones, racial and ethnic groups are seen as part of the exploited masses. In conflict theories based on the assumption that power is (unevenly) distributed among many different kinds of groups (power pluralism), racial and cultural groups are seen as minorities to the extent that they are discriminated against by groups with more power. In the internal colonial model, racial ghettos are depicted as being dominated by powerful, outside elites (Blauner, 1969; Kinloch, 1974; 96–97, 154–58). In applications of the Marxian concept of the underclass or marginal working class, and also in the split labor market concept, the poorest minorities are seen as low-paid, underemployed and often unemployed groups that are deliberately exploited by capitalist elites. These and other power elite perspectives compete with (power) pluralistic approaches in the study of stratification, minority-dominant relations, and social conflict in general.*

*In the selection by Szymanski, in a comparison of the 50 states based on 1970 census data, an inverse relation is reported between discrimination against women and "third world people." Using the language of the colonial model, he interprets the findings in terms that imply the underclass or marginal working class concept, saying that discrimination against race groups and against women are "functional substitutes in the labor market." That is, the capitalist system needs an oppressed group of menial workers to do its dirty work for low pay, and when one group is not prevalent in a given state (or not heavily oppressed) employers will exploit the other.*

*Wilson's article is an attempt to see how closely the history of the restoration—the rise of the Jim Crow system of segregation in the South during the latter part of the nineteenth century—fits Marxist views, especially the split labor market explanation. He emphasizes the role of Southern elites, economic and political competition and conflict, class exploitation, unequal power, institutional discrimination, and racist beliefs. He concludes that the split labor market interpretation is an oversimplification of the complex developments.*

*The selection by Johnson and Sell is one of several attempts to use 1970 census data to determine the economic status of American blacks, and the trend during the turbulent 1960s. It is reported that a large reduction in the occupational gap during the decade was not accompanied by a corresponding reduction in the income gap. Different researchers use different indexes and make different interpretations, but there is pretty good agreement that the income gap was reduced far less, if any, than was the occupational gap. Blacks made major gains on whites in educational achievement during the 1960s. A study of the first half of the 1970s found continuing gains in education, occupations, level of employment—despite the economic recession—and little change in the income gap (Farley, 1977). Large inequalities remain, one illustration of which is that whites are paid considerably more than blacks with the same amount of education for the same work (Shin, 1976; Dowdall, 1974). As black educational and occupational attainments increase, and the income gap remains about the same, the prevalence and intensity of feelings of status incongruity must be increasing.*

## REFERENCES

*Berger, Alan S., and William Simon*
1974 "Black Families and the Moynihan Report: A Research Evaluation." Social Problems 22, 2 (December): 145–61.
*Blauner, Robert*
1969 "Internal Colonization and Ghetto Revolt." Social Problems 16 (Spring): 393–408.
*Dowdall, George W.*
1974 "White Gains from Black Subordination." Social Problems 22, 2 (December): 162–83.
*Farley, Reynolds*
1977 "Trends in Racial Inequalities: Have the Gains of the 1960s Disappeared in the 1970s?" American Sociological Review 42, 2 (April): 189–208.
*Gordon, Milton M.*
1964 Assimilation in American Life. New York: Oxford University Press.
*Irelan, Lola M., Oliver C. Moles, and Robert M. O'Shea*
1969 "Ethnicity, Poverty, and Selected Attitudes: A Test of the 'Culture of Poverty' Hypothesis." Social Forces 47 (June): 405–13.
*Kinloch, Graham C.*
1974 The Dynamics of Race Relations: A Sociological Analysis. New York: McGraw-Hill Book Co.
*Lewis, Oscar*
1966 "The Culture of Poverty." Scientific American (October): 19–25.
*Liebow, Elliot*
1967 Tally's Corner. Boston: Little, Brown and Co.
*Moynihan, Daniel P., Paul Barton, et al.*
1965 The Negro Family: The Case for National Action. Washington, D.C.: United States Department of Labor.
*Rainwater, Lee*
1974 What Money Buys: Inequality and the Social Meanings of Income. New York: Basic Books.
*Rainwater, Lee, and William L. Yancey*
1967 The Moynihan Report and the Politics of Controversy. Cambridge, Mass.: The M.I.T. Press.
*Ransford, H. Edward*
1977 Race and Class in American Society: Black, Chicano, Anglo. Cambridge, Mass.: Schenkman Publishing Co.
*Shin, Eiu Hang*
1976 "Earnings Inequality Between Black and White Males by Education, Occupation, and Region." Sociology and Social Research 60, 2 (January): 161–71.
*Valentine, Charles A.*
1968 Culture and Poverty: Critique and Counter-Proposals. Chicago: The University of Chicago Press.

# Minority Group Status and Self-evaluated Class*

### John C. Goyder
*Wilfrid Laurier University*

### Peter C. Pineo
*McMaster University*

*Self-evaluated class status is shown to vary among white Protestants, Catholics, Jews, and black Protestants. Holding economic status constant, Jews are most likely to select the middle- (or upper-) class label, followed by white Protestants, white Catholics, and black Protestants. Thus, the independent effect of minority status on self-evaluated class status reinforces the ranking directly attributable to the economic levels of each of the four groups.*

*Also, the congruence between self-identified class and objective economic status is closer among Jews and white Protestants than among white Catholics or black Protestants. The hypothesis that affiliation with a minority necessarily reduces class consciousness was, therefore, not supported.*

*Source:* John C. Goyder and Peter C. Pineo, "Minority Group Status and Self-Evaluated Class," Sociological Quarterly 15, 2 (Spring 1974): 199–211. Copyright © 1974 by the Midwest Sociological Society. Reprinted by permission of the Society, the editors of Sociological Quarterly, and the authors.

*The authors gratefully acknowledge the assistance of the National Opinion Research Center Library, The Roper Public Opinion Research Center, and the University of Michigan Consortium for Political Research in making the data used here available. Our thanks also to Mrs. Marianne Bayley of the McMaster University Computer Centre for programming aid. Several helpful comments on the paper were suggested to us by Bengt Rundblad.

Stratification theorists seem to feel that minority group affiliation can be an important secondary dimension of social stratification (Barber, 1968:290–293). Some regard racial and ethnic minorities as "nonstatus groups" (Jackson and Curtis, 1968:125) but more frequently they appear to be seen as an important, independent ranking (Lieberson, 1970:172), forming an additional dimension along with socioeconomic stratification in a multi-dimensional ranking system. That such groups do fall into a consensually accepted rank order is, of course, well demonstrated (Bogardus, 1959; Warner, 1960:186–199; Skipper and Kohout, 1968).

There has been little research, however, on the relationship between minority affiliation and overall social status. In the research reported here, two questions were investigated: (1) Does minority status, holding economic status constant, influence self-evaluations of class status; and (2) does minority affiliation decrease the congruence between objective SES and self-evaluated class?

The subjective class identification question, developed by Centers (1961:76), is our measure of self-evaluated social class. Of course, this question represents a considerable abstraction from "overall status." The Centers question has received a great deal of criticism over the years, probably more than it deserves. Some problems inherent in survey research, such as the problem of never having complete certainty about the validity of survey questions, have been argued, with the Centers question as the example. Critics have noted the variations in the pattern of responses according to the wording and format of the question. An open-ended format produces a higher refusal rate and more frequent middle-class identifications than a simple check-list of class labels (Gross, 1953; Kahl and Davis, 1955). Other critics argue that such a simple opinion poll-type of question can only give a superficial view of people's identification with social classes (Gordon, 1963:197; Eysenck, 1950). Also, the literature is contradictory about the criteria for class identification. Centers (1961) conclusions about the things people state as determinants of their class identification are ambiguous. One question pointed to "beliefs and attitudes" (Centers, 1961:91) while another indicated SES characteristics (1961:98, 99). Haer (1957b:118) found "financial" criteria to be most important, although "character and attitudes" were also mentioned frequently. In terms of the main correlates of class identification, there is little doubt about the primacy of SES attributes (Centers, 1961:203; Kahl and Davis, 1955; Hodge and Treiman, 1968). Yet although SES indicators eclipse other variables as predictors of class identification, they fall, as Hodge and Treiman (1968:547) note, "far short of a full explanation of patterns of class identification."

All this, together with the generally greater predictive power of the objective status measures (Haer, 1957a), has led to the conclusion that the Centers type question is error-prone. Despite these problems with the class identification technique, we feel that it has validity as a rough self-ranking of status. In predicting phenomena such as voting it has proved to be a useful variable (Centers, 1961:130–131). Confidence in the question is raised by the fact that many of the basic patterns found by Centers were successfully replicated by him in later studies (Centers, 1949, 1950, 1956), and this stability has persisted over time (Schreiber and Nygreen, 1970). Within the context of our research it seems logical to assume that the bias or "error" in self-identified class, caused by the wording of the question, the list of class choices, or the brief time the respondent has to consider the question, should be spread randomly among the sub-groups which we examine. We have limited evidence, presented later, to support this assumption. For instance, the refusal rate on the class identification question is invariant among the four groups. To find significant minority group effects in analyzing responses to this question, despite the error, should underscore their probable level of importance.

Another limitation of this technique for our research is that we cannot be sure of the reference group toward which class identifications are directed. For total samples, evidence suggests the evaluations are made in relation to the national stratification system (Haer, 1957b:119). But the effect on class identification of internal stratification pyramids within minority groups is something we cannot examine directly.

The class identification question offers practical advantages though. It has been used in a great number of surveys and these surveys may be combined to present a sample size large enough to include groups such as blacks and Jews.

The first hypothesis we wanted to test was that ethnic standing has a direct positive effect on class identification. From the work done by Warner (1965) and by Bogardus (1959), which attributed the highest prestige to white Protestants, we expected that when economic standing was held constant white Protestants would disproportionately select the middle-class label, blacks the working class, and Jews and Catholics would fall somewhere between. This expectation is based on the assumption that there is a "minority effect" independent of the economic characteristics of minorities. Lieberson (1970: 172–173) notes "it is clear that most often ethnic groups differ in their occupational opportunities as well as their positions of power and influence, rewards and privileges, at least in part because of their ethnic group membership *per se.*"

This hypothesis was not self-evident. Minorities may perceive their group status as an alternative ranking system, relevant to some domains but not to class identification. One possibility, noted by Jackson and Curtis (1968:125), was that members of each group would inflate their class identification as a result of a self-enhancement based on minority group pride. Countering this was the hypothesis of minority self-hatred, although recent research has discounted the importance of this (Yancey et al., 1972:338–359).

Our second hypothesis was that minority identity reduces class consciousness. It frequently has been argued that the intersection of the economic stratification with minority groups reduces class consciousness (Barber, 1957: 215; Lieberson, 1970:176), although the opposite has also been suggested in reference to working-class blacks (Leggett, 1971:99; Hurst, 1972:660). Rosenberg (1953:27) argues that "the precondition for class consciousness exists when an individual possesses an internalized picture of his economic and social position which accords with his objective economic position. . . ." Thus, the strength of relationship between class identification and objective socioeconomic status is taken as an operational measure of class consciousness, and it is hypothesized that this relationship will be stronger among white Protestants than among the three minorities in our data. It need hardly be said that this is one of many possible measures of class consciousness (see Morris and Murphy, 1966, for different aspects of class consciousness). In order to emphasize its restricted meaning, we refer throughout to the relationship between class identification and objective SES as "objective economic class consciousness."

The intersection of minority affiliation with economic stratification could be expected to weaken the congruence between class identification and objective SES in at least three ways. First, if minority group membership produces less variation in class identification *within* the group, this would automatically lower the strength of the association between class identification and other variables. Secondly, ethnic affiliation could be expected to weaken the intensity of class identification because it offers an alternate identity to compete with class identity. Thirdly, there is the possibility of subcultural variations in the perceived criteria for class status. Warner (1965:285–296) ranked the minorities in the United States according to their "deviation from the dominant American culture." Those most integrated into the core culture were English-speaking white Protestants while blacks were the least integrated. Catholics and Jews were placed between these two extremes. Gordon (1964:38) notes the "unique subcultural heritage" caused by differing religious values, immigration, or the existence of enforced segregation.

## THE DATA

The data consist of several national samples merged together. The studies used to create this "combined sample" were: the Survey Research Center (SRC) Election Studies in 1956, 1960, 1964, and 1968; a NORC study in 1964; and an American Institute of Public Opinion (AIPO) study conducted in 1969.[1] Although the technical procedures employed by the different agencies vary in some details, all the studies sampled males and females (over 16 in the NORC study, over 21 in the others) without restrictions on employment or labor force status.

Recording these studies so that they could be analyzed as one large sample required considerable compromises in the detail of the categories for the variables used in the analysis. There were three different forms of the class identification question used in the studies, and in the combined sample these had to be recoded into simply "middle class" (or higher) and "working class" (or lower).[2] This simplication is not too serious since most respondents select these labels away. Occupation was coded into seven broad categories.[3] Education and income could only be coded in broad categories with some very large intervals. We relied mainly on occupation as the SES indicator, although the analysis was duplicated using education and income.

## MINORITY STATUS AND SELF-EVALUATED CLASS

Part of the stratification of minorities is due to differences in mean economic status between the groups. This has a simple, almost mathematically inevitable effect upon the class identification distributions among the minorities. Table 1 shows the proportions identifying with the middle class among white Jews, Protestants, and Catholics, and among black Protestants. The groups are arranged in order of their mean occupational status, the lower the score in Table 1 the higher the mean occupational status. (The rank order does not change when education or income is substituted.) The results show a pattern of decreasing self-evaluated class status with decreasing occupational status. The differences in the percentage identifying with the middle class are statistically significant (p < .01) between each group. Also, the mean occupational status of each group differs significantly (p < .001) from the others (Blalock, 1960:175–176).

### TABLE 1
Percentage Identifying with the Middle Class, and Mean Occupational Status
for White Jews, Protestants, and Catholics, and Black Protestants

|  | WHITE JEWISH | WHITE PROT. | WHITE R.C. | BLACK PROT. |
|---|---|---|---|---|
| Class | 74 | 47 | 43 | 23 |
|  | (265)* | (4483) | (1707) | (641) |
| Occupation | 2.65 | 3.49 | 3.67 | 4.95 |
|  | (253) | (4148) | (1591) | (577) |

*N in parentheses.*

As one would expect, the differences in occupational status between the groups are not of uniform magnitude. The two largest groups, white Protestants and white Catholics, are clustered quite close together, and this is reflected in the small difference in the proportion classifying themselves in the middle class.

Table 2 shows the percentage identified with the middle class by occupation among white Jews, Protestants, Catholics, and black Protestants. These data provide a test of our first hypothesis. According to the data in Table 2, minority status does have an independent effect upon self-evaluated class status. If the differences in mean self-evaluated class status shown previously were due solely to differences in occupational status among the four groups in the analysis, then we would expect that within each occupational category there would be no major differences in class identification among the groups. This is clearly not the case. Table 2 reveals substantial variations in the percentage identifying with the middle class among white Jews, Protestants, and Catholics, and black Protestants at each occupational level. The results, however, are not wholly as anticipated. Contrary to our expectations, there is no evidence that low minority rank is associated with downgrading of self-evaluated class status among Jews. Instead, at each occupational level Jews were the group most frequently identified with the middle class. This is not what one would expect on the basis of Warner's or Bogardus's rankings. Possibly further work is needed on the ranking of ethnic status, particularly as perceived by those within each group. If Jews do perceive themselves as a low status ethnic group, this is compartmentalized within a limited sphere and does not enter into responses to the class identification question.

In contrast, blacks do downgrade their class status.[4] Comparing Jewish and black professional workers, 94 percent of Jewish professionals in the sample identified with the middle class, while only 58 percent of black professionals did so. This pattern holds in all the occupational categories shown in Table 2.

TABLE 2

**Percentage of Respondents Identifying with the Middle Class
by Occupational Status, Religion, and Race***

| OCCUPATIONAL STATUS | WHITE JEWS | WHITE PROTS. | WHITE CATHOLIC | BLACK PROTS. |
|---|---|---|---|---|
| Major groups:† | | | | |
| Professional | 94 | 80 | 75 | 58 |
| | (47) | (608) | (179) | (48) |
| Business | 77 | 67 | 61 | 19 |
| | (73) | (718) | (256) | (21) |
| Other white collar | 74 | 54 | 48 | 21 |
| | (50) | (628) | (248) | (42) |
| Skilled labor | 74 | 33 | 34 | 29 |
| | (19) | (895) | (378) | (51) |
| Semiskilled, service | 37 | 26 | 26 | 18 |
| | (30) | (996) | (412) | (304) |
| Unskilled | ‡ | 11 | 30 | 13 |
| | (1) | (180) | (79) | (97) |
| All white collar | 81 | 67 | 60 | 37 |
| | (170) | (1954) | (683) | (111) |
| All blue collar | 50 | 28 | 30 | 18 |
| | (50) | (2071) | (869) | (452) |
| All occupations | 74 | 46 | 43 | 22 |
| | (220) | (4025) | (1552) | (563) |

*Case base for calculations of each percentage in parentheses. Refusals on class identification question excluded from calculations.*

†*Chi-squares computed for each row separately are all statistically significant and sum to 116.0 with 18 degrees of freedom (p<.001).*

‡*Less than 1 percent.*

For example, while 37 percent of the Jewish respondents in semi-skilled or service occupations categorized themselves in the middle class, this proportion fell to 18 percent among blacks in the same occupation group.

The "core society" (Gordon, 1964:72) of white Protestants falls between the two extremes represented by Jews and blacks. White Catholics adhere more closely than Jews or blacks to the pattern for white Protestants. However, there are some variations between the distributions for white Protestants and Catholics. Among Catholics there is an effect like a regression toward the mean in class identifications. Thus, while 80 percent of white Protestant professionals classified themselves as middle class, the corresponding proportion among Catholics was only 75 percent. Similarly, higher proportions of white Protestants in the business and "other white collar" occupations identified with the middle class than Catholics in the same occupational categories. In the first two blue-collar categories the white Protestants and Catholics showed little differences, but among unskilled laborers, the bottom category, 11 percent of the white Protestants, compared to 30 percent of white Catholics, categorized themselves in the middle class.

The pattern among white Catholics is clearly due to something more complex than the simple evaluation of religious prestige or the incidence of low status ethnicities in the Catholic religion. One may speculate that doctrinal differences between Protestants and Catholics are responsible. It has been suggested, for instance, that there is less shame in poverty and greater distrust of wealth in Catholicism than in Protestantism (Bakke, 1947:21, 22; Miner, 1967:96).

A weakness in our analysis of the data in Table 2 is the heterogeneity of the broad occupational categories used. This is particularly serious when comparing blacks and Jews. In any of the broad occupational groups blacks will tend to be clustered in the lower range of the category, while Jews will tend to hold positions at the upper end of the range. Some might prefer to see these results presented in a simple white collar/blue collar dichotomy so that the pretense of detailed control is dropped. These figures are shown in the bottom rows of Table 2. Although the heterogeneity of the broad occupation categories undoubtedly exaggerates the differences between the minorities in the proportions identifying with the middle class at each occupation level, we feel the basic pattern reflects reality. The patterns seen in Table 2 essentially are unchanged when education or income is substituted for occupational status. For instance, among respondents with family incomes over $10,000, 92 percent of the Jews and 53 percent of the blacks identified with the middle class, while the corresponding proportions among white Protestants and Catholics were 72 and 66 percent respectively. Similarly, among respondents having college education or more, 92 percent of the Jews and 68 percent of the blacks identified with the middle class, compared to 89 percent of the white Protestants and 86 percent of the white Catholics. We also refined the detail of the control categories by constructing an SES index, composed of the sum of the scores on occupation, education, and income. While this index is marred by the uneven intervals in the education and income codes, it does increase the number of control categories to 13. The basic patterns observed in Table 2 remained when using this SES index, bolstering our confidence in the results. Of course, the cell sizes decrease as detail is added to the stratification scale so that ultimately the problem described above is insurmountable.

The central impression from the data in Table 2 is that minority status as a determinant of class identification reinforces the ranking established already by the simple economic characteristics of the groups. After a standardization of the occupational distributions of the groups is made so that they conform to that for white Protestants, the percentage identified with the middle class becomes 65, 47, 45, and 27 for white Jews, Protestants, and Catholics, and black Protestants respectively. This is the same order as shown in Table 1 for actual economic status.

The coincidence of the rank order of the groups according to frequency of middle-class identification with their SES ranking, even when SES is controlled so far as possible, may be due to the strength of the minority subcultures, particularly in the Jewish and black cases. That is, the fact that the majority of Jews are middle class according to objective SES measures may cause the Jewish identity to be virtually synonymous with the middle-class label, so that even low SES Jews tend to perceive themselves as middle class. Conversely, the generally low economic status of blacks in the United States may be the reason that even high SES blacks tend to identify with the working class. The finding by Hodge and Treiman (1968) that the status of one's associates is an important determinant of self-identified class supports this interpretation, insofar as one can assume that the "associates" to which they refer would be largely from within the ethnic group.


## MINORITY STATUS AND OBJECTIVE
## ECONOMIC CLASS CONSCIOUSNESS

We turn now to the hypothesis that objective economic class consciousness is weaker among minorities than among white Protestants. The Pearsonian correlation of occupation with class identification for white Jews, Protestants, and Catholics, and black Protestants is shown in Table 3. The top row shows the unaltered coefficients. The coefficients in the bottom row are corrected for restriction of range in occupation (Guilford, 1956:320).[5] This correction equalizes the occupation standard deviations for the four groups. Without the correction, the hypothesis that class consciousness is lower among minorities is upheld. But the corrected coefficients reveal that the reason for the low correlation of occupation with class identification among Jews is that there is little differentiation according to occupation in this group. They are clustered in the upper categories of the occupation scale. When the correction is made to equalize the occupation standard deviations, the hypothesis is not upheld. Rather, the pattern is that the higher the mean economic status of a group, the stronger the association between the objective and subjective measure. The correction causes little alteration of the coefficients among the three other groups. Among blacks there is no change at all since the standard deviation of occupation for this group is very close to the standard deviation of occupation for the total sample and is higher than the values for the other three groups.[6]

TABLE 3

Zero-Order Correlation of Occupation with Class Identification for
White Jews, Protestants, and Catholics, and Black Protestants

|  | WHITE JEWS | WHITE PROTESTANTS | WHITE CATHOLICS | BLACK PROTESTANTS |
|---|---|---|---|---|
| Unaltered | .35 | .41 | .32 | .23 |
|  | (244) | (4025) | (1552) | (563) |
| Corrected for restricted range | .43 | .42 | .33 | .23 |

The reason for the relatively strong association between objective SES and class identification among Jews may be that there are typically middle-class and working-class ways of handling the class identification question. Much of the literature on working-class culture (Miller and Riessman, 1961:93; Gans, 1962:229–262; Cohen and Hodges, 1963:307–308) suggests the importance of particularistic values. Possibly these values lead to a seemingly idiosyncratic approach to the class identification question. It may be that the belief that self-evaluated class should be based on universalistically applied socioeconomic criteria is largely a middle-class value. Although Jews at all SES levels were more likely than blacks or Catholics to select the middle-class label, the difference between the highest and lowest SES levels in the proportion selecting the middle class was greatest among Jews. Consequently, it is not only the over-representation in the upper SES levels that accounts for the high correlation of occupation with class identification among Jews. If there is a universalistic approach to the class identification question which is characteristic of the middle-class culture, it may be that even Jews of low SES levels tend to adopt these values. Similarly, the predominately working-class economic status of blacks may cause even white collar blacks to adopt a more particularistic approach to class identification. We have no direct evidence of such an overlapping of class and minority culture, but the same theme has been noted by others (Gordon, 1964:186; Lenski, 1963:130).

While this interpretation of the pattern observed in Table 3 is highly speculative, other explanations prove to be inadequate. We expected that if minority affiliation is an alternative identity that replaces class consciousness, then the no answer rate on the class identification question would be higher among the minority groups. In fact, in the combined sample this no answer rate showed little variation among the different subgroups. It was 3 percent among both white Protestants and Catholics and 4 percent among Jews and black Protestants. Probably a more accurate test is provided by the class question used in the SRC studies. Here people were asked if they felt they belonged to either the middle or the working class (rather than being obliged to categorize themselves). The proportions answering "yes" were 63 percent of the white Protestants, 65 percent of the white Catholics, 72 percent of the black Protestants, and 74 percent of the Jews. These results help to dispel the notion that the class identification question is particularly unclear or meaningless to specific groups, such as the blacks, which could have been an explanation of the patterns observed in Table 3.[7] Instead, there is no direct relationship between the basic sense of belonging to a class and the congruence between self-rated class and objective SES.[8] The inconsistency between different measures of class consciousness has often been noted (Leggett, 1971:16; Svalastoga, 1959:191) and our results are another example of this.

Another idea which we explored was the possibility that different intergenerational mobility rates accounted for the patterns seen in Table 3. For instance, the low correlation between occupation and class identification among Catholics could be due to a large number of Catholics from working-class families entering the middle class. In fact, such considerations have little effect on the results. The correlation of occupation with class identification (corrected coefficients), partialling out father's occupation, remains higher among Jews ($r = .40$), than among white Protestants ($r = .37$), white Catholics ($r = .26$), or black Protestants ($r = .17$).

It does not seem likely that the variation in the congruence between occupation and class identification among the four groups can be explained by their simple demographic characteristics. When comparing Protestants and Catholics (the other groups were too small for detailed analysis) the correlation of occupation with class identification remained quite stable when control variables were included. For instance, the proportion of foreign-born and urban is relatively high among Catholics, and both characteristics could contribute to the weaker association between class identification and occupation among this group. Immigrants may be unsure of their new status and remain outside of the class system (Warner, 1965:68). Similarly, it may be that classes are most clearly defined in small towns (Pfautz and Duncan, 1950). Table 4 shows the correlation of occupation with class identification by religion, country of birth, and community size. As before, the coefficients were corrected for restricted range in the independent variable.

TABLE 4

Zero-Order Correlations of Occupation with Class Identification
(corrected for restricted range) for Protestants and Catholics
by Country of Birth and Community Size

| CATEGORIES | PROTESTANT* | CATHOLIC |
|---|---|---|
| Country of Birth: | | |
| United States† | .43 | .35 |
| | (4169) | (1310) |
| Foreign | .39 | .35 |
| | (126) | (143) |
| Community Size: | | |
| Over 500,000 | .46 | .38 |
| | (389) | (420) |
| 10,000–499,999† | .43 | .28 |
| | (1194) | (558) |
| Under 9,999† | .44 | .32 |
| | (1618) | (348) |

*Black and white.
†Protestant-Catholic difference in correlation significant at the .05 level.

These results show that, in each of the categories of birthplace and community size, the relationship between occupation and class identification remains higher among Protestants than among Catholics. The congruence between occupation and class identification is not greatly affected by community size or birthplace. We tried various other control variables also, including father's country of birth, region, and gender. These variables were of less theoretical interest, and space is insufficient for a report of these results. However, none of these variables "explains away" the basic Protestant-Catholic difference. These results give us some confidence that the results for Jews and blacks seen in Table 3 are not explained simply by the demographic makeup of the groups.

## CONCLUSIONS

Neither of our two initial hypotheses was supported completely. The results for Catholics and blacks conformed largely with prior expectations, but those for Jews did not. More Jews than white Protestants identified with the middle class, and objective economic class consciousness was at least as high among Jews as among white Protestants. This leads us to believe that the relationship between self-rated class status and minority status, as well as the impact of minority status on objective economic class consciousness, involves complex interaction effects.

If our results have one dominating theme, it is that in terms of the subjective aspect of stratification there is less differentiation within the Jewish, Catholic, and black groups than in the white Protestant majority. This is not merely an artifact of the objective socioeconomic composition of the groups. As noted previously, the standard deviation of occupational status is greater among blacks than among white Protestants. Low SES Jews seem to merge into the general middle-class identification of their group. Conversely, even blacks of high objective economic status tend to select a working-class label. And since many Catholics in the high and low extremes of objective SES fail to select the expected class label, they too produce less variation within the group than in the balance of the society. If further research supports this theme, minority groups may be understood to adopt the structural form of being pockets of reduced differentiation (in their own eyes) within the larger stratification system. If this were the case, partial freedom from the pressures of the stratification system could be a motivation for persisting ethnic and racial identities and for the persistence of racial and ethnic groups.

## NOTES

1  The SRC studies were all primarily concerned with presidential election compaigns: the NORC 1964 study was designed to furnish occupational prestige scores for a detailed list of occupational titles; and the Gallup 1969 study surveyed opinions on a number of national and international matters.

2  The SRC studies used the question: "There's quite a lot of talk these days about different social classes. Most people say they belong to the middle class or to the working class. Do you ever think of yourself as being in one of these classes? Which class? Would you say that you are about an average (class selected) person or that you are in the upper part of (class selected)?" The NORC 1964 study used the question: "If you had to pick one, which of the following five social classes would you say you were in—upper class, upper-middle class, middle class, working class, or lower class?" The 1969 study used the question: "If you were asked to use one of these four names for your social class, which would you say you belonged in: the middle class, lower class, working class, or upper class?"

3  The occupation code was: Professional (technical), business, white collar (clerical, sales), skilled labor, semi-skilled labor, personal service, unskilled.

4  We might infer from this that blacks evaluate their position with reference to the whole society rather than simply within their own racial group. It has often been thought that an internal stratification takes priority among blacks (Davis, 1941:10; Parsons, 1953:118).

5  The corrected correlation of occupation with class identification differs significantly (p < .05) between the following pairs of groups: Jews and blacks, white Protestants and Catholics, white Protestants and black Protestants, Catholics and black Protestants.

6   Using the 7 category occupation code, the standard deviation is 1.75 for blacks and
    1.69 for whites.
7   We also have results from the Centers study in 1945 and a NORC study from 1949
    which show little variation between Protestants and Catholics in the criteria named
    in response to the question: "In deciding whether a person belongs to your class or
    not, which of these things do you consider most important to know?" Blacks were
    actually more likely than whites to name occupation, education, or income, despite
    the weak association among blacks between these measures of SES and class identifi-
    cation.
8   These results also suggest that "false" class consciousness can be felt as strongly as
    "true" class conciousness.

## REFERENCES

*Bakke, E. Wight*
1947   Citizens Without Work. New Haven: Yale University Press.
*Barber, Bernard*
1968   "Social stratification." Pp. 288–296 in David L. Sills (ed.), International Encyclopedia
       of the Social Sciences. Vol. 15. New York: Macmillan Company and Free Press.
1957   Social Stratification. New York: Harcourt, Brace and World.
*Blalock, Hubert M.*
1960   Social Statistics. New York: McGraw-Hill.
*Bogardus, Emory S.*
1959   Social Distance. Yellow Springs, Ohio: Antioch Press.
*Centers, Richard*
1961   The Psychology of Social Classes. New York: Russell and Russell.
1956   "The intensity dimension of class identification and some social and psychological
       correlates." Journal of Social Psychology 44 (August): 101–114.
1950   "Nominal variation and class identification: the working and the laboring classes."
       Journal of Abnormal and Social Psychology 45 (April): 195–215.
1949   "Class consciousness of the American woman." International Journal of Opinion
       and Attitude Research 3 (Fall): 399–408.
*Cohen, A. K., and H. M. Hodges*
1963   "Characteristics of the lower-blue-collar-class. Social Problems 10 (Spring): 303–
       334.
*Davis, Allison, Burleigh B. Garner, and Mary Gardner*
1941   Deep South: A Social Anthropological Study of Caste and Class. Chicago: University
       of Chicago Press.
*Eysenck, J. J.*
1950   "Social attitudes and social class." British Journal of Sociology 1 (March): 50–66.
*Gans, Herbert J.*
1962   The Urban Villagers. New York: The Free Press.
*Gordon, Milton M.*
1964   Assimilation in American Life. New York: Oxford University Press.
1963   Social Class in American Sociology. New York: McGraw-Hill.
*Gross, N.*
1953   "Social class identification in an urban community." American Sociological Re-
       view 17 (August): 398–404.
*Guilford, Joy P.*
1956   Fundamental Statistics in Psychology and Education. New York: McGraw-Hill.

Haer, J. L.
1957a  "Predictive utility of five indices of social stratification." American Sociological
       Review 22 (October): 541–546.
1957b  "An empirical study of class awareness." Social Forces 36 (December): 117–121.
Hodge, R. W., and D. J. Treiman
1968  "Class identification in the United States." American Journal of Sociology 73
      (March): 535–547.
Hurst, C. E.
1972  "Race, class, and consciousness." American Sociological Review 37 (December):
      658–670.
Jackson, E. F., and R. F. Curtis
1968  "Conceptualization and measurement in the study of social stratification." Pp.
      112–149 in Hubert M. Blalock and Ann B. Blalock (eds.), Methodology in Social
      Research. New York: McGraw-Hill.
Kahl, J. A., and J. A. Davis
1955  "A comparison of indexes of socio-economic status." American Sociological Re-
      view 20 (June): 317–325.
Leggett, John
1971  Class, Race, and Labor. New York: Oxford University Press.
Lenski, Gerhard
1963  The Religious Factor. Garden City: Anchor Books, Doubleday.
Lieberson, S.
1970  "Stratification and ethnic groups." Pp. 172–181 in Edward O. Laumann (ed.), Social
      Stratification: Research and Theory for the 1970s. Indianapolis: The Bobbs-Merrill
      Company.
Miller, S. M., and F. Riessman
1961  "The working class subculture: a new view." Social Problems 9 (Summer): 86–97.
Miner, Horace
1967  St. Denis. Chicago: University of Chicago Press.
Morris, R. T., and R. J. Murphy
1966  "A paradigm for the study of class consciousness." Sociology and Social Research
      50 (April): 298–313.
Parsons, Talcott
1953  "A revised analytical approach to the theory of social stratification." Pp. 92–128 in
      Reinhard Bendix and Seymour M. Lipset (eds.) Class, Status, and Power (first
      edition). New York: The Free Press.
Pfuatz, H. W., and O. D. Duncan
1950  "A critical evaluation of Warner's work in community stratification." American
      Sociological Review 15 (April): 205–215.
Rosenberg, M.
1953  "Perceptual obstacles to class consciousness." Social Forces 32 (October): 22–27.
Schreiber, E. M., and G. T. Nygreen
1970  "Subjective social class in America 1945–68." Social Forces 48 (March): 348–356.
Skipper, J. F., and F. Kohout
1968  "Family names and social class: a teaching technique." American Sociologist 3
      (February): 37–38.
Svalastoga, Kaare
1959  Prestige, Class and Mobility. Copenhagen: Scandinavian University Books.
Warner, W. Lloyd, and Leo Srole
1965  The Social System of American Ethnic Groups. New Haven: Yale University Press.
Warner, W. Lloyd, Marchia Meeker, and Kenneth Eells
1960  Social Class in America. New York: Harper and Row.
Yancey, W. L., L. Rigsby, and J. D. McCarthy
1972  "Social position and self-evaluation: The relative importance of race." American
      Journal of Sociology 78 (September): 338–359.

# The Culture of Poverty Debate: Some Additional Data[*]

## Barbara E. Coward

*Houston Community College System*

## Joe R. Feagin

*University of Texas (Austin)*

## J. Allen Williams, Jr.

*University of Nebraska (Lincoln)*

*In this paper we briefly review relevant research on the culture of poverty and set our findings within the general context of culture of poverty arguments. Data from a community survey in a Southwestern city are analyzed using Oscar Lewis's four major culture of poverty dimensions: (1) the individual, (2) the family, (3) the slum community, and (4) the community's relation to soci-*

*Source:* Barbara E. Coward, Joe R. Feagin, and J. Allen Williams, Jr., "The Culture of Poverty Debate: Some Additional Data," Social Problems 21, 5 (June 1974): 621–34. Copyright © 1974 by The Society for the Study of Social Problems. Reprinted by permission of the Society and the authors.

*The data reported in this paper were collected as part of a larger study supported by the Department of Housing and Urban Development and prepared for the Urban Renewal Agency of the City of Austin, Texas. The authors are indebted to Louis A. Zurcher for his comments on an earlier version of this paper.

*ety. In our study a sample of 271 black respondents was divided into two groups, here termed the "poor" and the "non-poor." In noting all the broad traits studied in all dimensions taken together, some support for Lewis's culture of poverty was found in less than half of the cases: and in several cases our findings were in direct opposition to culture of poverty predictions. In addition, we have suggested that the majority of those traits that did lend support to Lewis's argument might be better classified as situational conditions of poverty rather than as a part of a bona fide "culture" of poverty. The findings of this paper may call into question the use of the "culture of poverty" perspective as a basis for policy decisions.*

The phrase "culture of poverty" and the perspective on the poor it denotes have become common in the growing literature on the poor. While criticism of this perspective, originally developed in the 1950s by Oscar Lewis, has become more frequent in recent years, surprisingly little empirical research has examined the generalizations about poverty asserted by Lewis and his followers. The purpose of this paper is (1) to review briefly the state of comparative empirical research on the culture of poverty and then (2) to examine the extent to which our findings, based on a re-analysis of a community survey, lend support to poverty culture arguments.

Let us briefly review the culture of poverty perspective. At one point Lewis (1964:149) tells us his purpose is to form a "conceptual model . . . in terms of a configuration of a large number of interrelated traits of which poverty is the crucial one." Critical to his view too is the definition of a poverty culture as a "design for living which is passed down from generation to generation" (Lewis, 1964:150). But perhaps the best explanation is this:

*. . . it has a structure, a rationale, and defense mechanisms without which the poor could hardly carry on. In short, it is a way of life, remarkably stable and persistent, passed down from generation to generation along family lines. The culture of poverty has its own modalities and distinctive social and psychological consequences for its members. It is a dynamic factor which affects participation in the large national culture and becomes a subculture of its own (Lewis, 1964:150).*

Illustrating this structure and rationale, Lewis (1965) prepared a catalogue of 70 traits which characterize a poverty culture.[1] Among these diverse traits are such things as a provincial perspective, unemployment, absence of savings, lack of privacy, gregariousness, frequent use of physical violence in child training, predisposition to authoritarianism, inability to defer gratification, fatalism, mistrust of government, and strong feelings of powerlessness, marginality, and helplessness.

Further, Lewis (1965:xiv) grouped his list of 70-odd traits into four basic categories or points of view from which one can analyze those in a poverty culture. In the order we will consider them subsequently, these categories are:

1   the attitudes, values, and character structure of the individual;
2   the nature of the family;

**3**   the nature of the slum community;
**4**   the relationship between the culture and the larger society.

That this perspective on poverty has spread rapidly among social scientists and policy makers can easily be demonstrated by reference to the burgeoning literature on poverty of the 1960s and 1970s. Indeed, examination of major government publications on poverty might lead one to the view that the federal government has played an important role in legitimizing and popularizing the culture of poverty perspective. For example, in an important summary volume for practitioners and researchers, *Growing Up Poor,* Chilman (1966) lists numerous family, life-style, and attitudinal traits of the very poor in a fashion similar to Oscar Lewis, and then links policy-oriented solutions to these traits. Considering these traits as barriers to the adaptation of the poor in American society, she (Chilman, 1966:75) concludes on a public policy note:

*From the available evidence, it seems clear that changes in subcultural patterns of a number of very poor people are probably indicated as one of a number of measures designed to facilitate upward mobility for themselves and their children. Unfortunately, planned changes in culture patterns are extremely difficult to effect.*

While Chilman's conclusions are cautiously worded, those of other writers and numerous policy makers have been less so, resulting in a heavy emphasis in some circles on remedial strategies focusing on eradicating pathological cultural traits assumed to be typical among the very poor. Such discussions indicate that the culture of poverty issue is not just an abstract theory to be analyzed in the private places of social scientists, but a critical notion with serious policy implications.

## RESEARCH AND ANALYSIS ON
## THE CULTURE OF POVERTY

While a number of critiques of the culture of poverty perspective have appeared in recent years, including those by Rodman (1964), Valentine (1971), Roach and Gursslin (1967), and Leeds (1971), few social science researchers have attempted to examine the applicability of Lewis's arguments to groups of the poor and the non-poor, for more than one aspect of one of the dimensions at a time. Indeed, in his provocative analysis Valentine has suggested that one of the most serious defects in current studies of the poor is the lack of comparative and across-the-board analysis of this type. A major task of research on the poor, he argues (1968:114–115); should be "to discern what cultural features are shared by different but related subsystems" and "what culture traits or configurations are shared by the lower class with the middle class or with the system as a whole."

As for empirical studies of poverty culture life styles, one is hard pressed to find studies which (1) explicitly attempt to test Lewis's generalizations for groups of the poor and non-poor and (2) examine traits from more than one aspect of one of Lewis's four basic dimensions of poverty culture in the same research study (an enterprise necessary, it would seem, to get at the question of an integrated *culture*). While a number of articles have dealt with one or two traits assumed to be characteristic of the poor, such as the inability to postpone gratification, we have been able to find only three studies that have made any attempt to compare two different socioeconomic groups, one poor and one not-so-poor, in regard to a *number* of different traits.

One such study was by Schneiderman (1964), who reported on a research effort that tested whether persons who were chronically impoverished did in fact have a different life style from those more affluent. He compared 35 chronic welfare assistance families with two somewhat larger samples of the non-poor. Using the five basic Kluckhohn-Strodtbeck value orientation measures, Schneiderman found that these very poor respondents differed from the more affluent comparison samples on three of the five major value orientation dimensions. The groups did not differ significantly in their values with regard to the character of human nature or with regard to the nature of man's relation to other men. They did differ significantly in regard to views of nature ("subject to" versus "mastery over"), to views on modes of human activity ("being" versus "doing"), and to views of time ("present" versus "future"). Schneiderman concludes that the impoverished man shares a common life-style or design for living that is internally consistent and distinctive from that dominant in the general community. In line with other culture of poverty theorists, he takes the position that one consequence of prolonged poverty is the production of a distinctive culture shared by the very poor and transmitted from one generation to the next through each family's socialization practices. While Schneiderman is one of the few who has examined a number of different traits, still one might question whether his sweeping generalizations are possible on the basis of a small and select group of the poor (chronic welfare recipients), particularly since these respondents cannot be considered representative of the very poor, most of whom are not on welfare.

A second study by Johnson and Sanday (1971) was focused primarily on subcultural variations among *ethnic* groups. In addition, these researchers did examine differences between socioeconomic subgroups, the poor and the non-poor, in a sample of heads of low-income and moderate-income households in three Pittsburgh neighborhoods. Their findings did not consistently support a culture of poverty interpretation. With regard to family structure (one of Lewis's family character traits), Johnson and Sanday found a statistically significant tendency for the poor to have more female-headed families than the non-poor. However, on their measure of future orientation (one of Lewis's attitudinal traits)—and in contrast to Schneiderman—they found no significant difference between the poor and the non-poor. Questions which might be considered crude indexes of two other culture of poverty traits, the achievement ethic and the trust-in-people trait, also did not reveal statistically significant differences between the poor and the non-poor.

Although the major focus was not on differences between the poor and the non-poor, but rather on ethnic variation in culture of poverty perspectives among the poor, a study by Irelan, Moles, and O'Shea (1969) does raise some serious questions about the general applicability of culture of poverty arguments across all racial and ethnic groups. Contrary to what one might predict from the Lewis perspective, Irelan, Moles, and O'Shea found that there was considerable and statistically significant variation among poor samples from three ethnic groups (Anglo, Chicano, and black) in agreement with questions which tap culture of poverty traits. Although these data could have been analyzed further, focusing on variation by socioeconomic status, no such analysis is provided. Inspection of their data on two traits, alienation and fatalism, however, does indicate weak directional support for the view that the very poor among these poor respondents were somewhat more alienated and fatalistic than the rest. Thus, our review of empirical research looking at a number of aspects of the culture of poverty did not turn up evidence of a quality or quantity to lend substantial or unequivocal support for Lewis's arguments, at least as they might be applied to the poor in the United States.

## METHOD

With this backdrop of limited empirical research in mind, we used data from a community survey that would allow us to compare groups of the poor and the non-poor within *one* specific ethnic group in the United States. Interviews were conducted with members of households in a black neighborhood designated for urban renewal in a large Southwestern city.[2] A random sample of 100 households was drawn from the entire ghetto area and no significant socioeconomic differences were found between this sample and the neighborhood sample. The total sample utilized here consists of those 271 black households on which adequate income data were available, a sample which we further divided for the purposes of this analysis into two income groups: a very low-income group (the "poor") and a moderate-income group (the "non-poor"). This procedure seemed reasonable for two reasons. First, Oscar Lewis himself has noted that very low-income black Americans are particularly likely to be characterized by the culture of poverty traits and further has suggested that those blacks somewhat better off are probably not accurately characterized in such terms. We have sorted out the very low income group in our sample to compare with those who are somewhat better off. Secondly, two research studies which we have cited previously (Irelan, Moles, and O'Shea, 1969; Johnson and Sanday, 1971) have indicated that major problems are introduced into analysis of culture of poverty hypotheses when the poor and non-poor groups analyzed are actually comprised of a number of different ethnic groups. For this reason, we would urge future analyses of poverty culture arguments to focus on differences by socioeconomic status within racial or ethnic groups, or in a larger analysis to control for race and ethnicity. Given the data available, we have chosen the former procedure—an analysis of income groups within a black sample.

The division into two groups, the "poor" and the "non-poor," was in terms of total annual income before taxes for all household members. The income figure was adjusted for size of family, roughly following the rather conservative poverty line utilized by the U.S. Census Bureau. Based on this, 132 of our respondents were classified as "poor," the rest (N = 139) as "non-poor."[3] As expected, the poor sample had a substantially lower education median. Since our total sample's overall median age was somewhat higher than that for all black adults in the city, we have controlled for age in examining the relationships between income and culture of poverty traits.

In our analysis we have grouped the relevant questions in the comprehensive survey instrument into the four basic poverty culture dimensions. Although we could not examine all 70 traits delineated by Lewis, we have been unusually fortunate in having some indicators relevant to each of the four major dimensions. Questions have been cross-tabulated by income, the independent variable, with one important category for each cross-tabulation reported in our summary tables, Chi-square statistics were calculated and tested for significance. We realize the "as if" character of reporting significance levels for a sample which is not a strictly random sample, but rather a population. We are here following the line of reasoning developed by the statisticians Hagood and Price (1952:286–294), who have suggested that in the present state of social science research statistical criteria of significance can reasonably be used as a heuristic standard for evaluating objectively relationships in observed samples.

## DIMENSION I: ATTITUDES, VALUES AND CHARACTER STRUCTURE OF THE INDIVIDUAL

Perhaps the most important, and widely discussed, poverty culture traits fall under the dimension Lewis terms the "attitudes, values and character structure of the individual." These basic attitudes and values, chief among which are such orientations as alienation and powerlessness, have become central to discussions of a culture of poverty transmitted across generations. Since these traits can easily be discussed in cultural terms, and are the least likely to be problematical—that is, the least likely to be viewed alternatively as "externally imposed conditions or unavoidable matters of situational expendiency" (Valentine, 1968:115)—demonstration of their distinctive presence among the very poor seems critical for culture of poverty theories.

What did the survey data reveal in this regard? Our data (Table 1) generally do not support arguments for the distinctiveness of the very poor with regard to the traits falling under this dimension. Included in the survey instrument were the subscales of powerlessness, normlessness, and social isolation, component parts of Dean's (1961) alienation scale. We found no statistically significant relationship between income and powerlessness, and the direction of the relationship is opposite the direction predicted by poverty culture theorists. In the case of the normlessness scale, we did find a significant relationship; but in this case too the relationship was opposite that predicted. The poor were less likely to rank high on this scale than the non-poor. However, the cross-tabulation on the social isolation scale and income shows a significant relationship in the direction predicted by poverty culture theories. Thus, the three measures of different aspects of alienation each revealed a different pattern, with support for the culture of poverty perspective in only one of the three cross-tabulations.

TABLE 1

Dimension I: Attitudes, Values, and the Character Structure of Individuals

|  | POOR | NON-POOR | CHI-SQUARE | df | P | (N) |
|---|---|---|---|---|---|---|
| Powerlessness scale (% high)* | 62 | 72 | 2.6*** | 1 | >.05 | (263)** |
| Normlessness scale (% high)* | 33 | 53 | 11.1 | 2 | <.05 | (268) |
| Social Isolation scale (% high)* | 21 | 10 | 8.1 | 2 | <.05 | (265) |
| Self-esteem scale (% high)* | 67 | 62 | .6 | 1 | >.05 | (266) |
| Psychological pathology: |  |  |  |  |  |  |
| (a) Behavior disorders among 1st children (% high) | 25 | 32 | .5 | 2 | >.05 | (62) |
| (b) Mental illness (% none) | 91 | 94 | .6 | 1 | >.05 | (271) |

*These are subscales of Dwight G. Dean's Alienation scale. The scales were kindly supplied to us by the author (see Dean, 1961).

**The actual N's vary from item to item in the tables which follow, because "no answer" and "missing data" replies have been omitted. Also, in cases of items with screening questions (mainly those about work, children, and relatives) the N's are reduced to those in the sample for whom the questions were relevant.

***Note that each line of percentages in this and subsequent summary tables is only one line, and thus one important response category from a larger cross-tabulation table. Thus the chi-square statistics reflect what is occurring in the other categories of the cross-tabulation as well as what differentials exist in the listed category.

The measure of self-esteem, drawn from Rosenberg's (1963) work, also revealed no support for the view that the poor would be more likely to rank low on self-esteem than the more affluent. While 67 percent of the poor ranked high on this scale, 62 percent of the non-poor ranked high. The association was in the direction opposite to a culture of poverty hypothesis.

The survey instrument contained two additional questions which could be used as indices of psychological pathology, a category of traits presumed to be more characteristic of the poor than the non-poor. For those families with children we found no significant association between income and a measure of behavioral disorders among first born children. The same pattern was true for second-born and third-born children, although the number of non-poor families in this latter category was small. With regard to mental illness, almost all of the respondents reported that no one in their families presently or recently had mental illness. Of course, this is based on respondent reports and not on an actual examination. Nonetheless, there was no association between reported mental illness and income.

In addition, since this southwestern sample included a somewhat higher percentage of blacks over 60 years of age than in the city's population as a whole, we controlled for age and examined the relationships between income and our six attitudinal measures. We were particularly interested in the under-60 adult respondents, those most likely to correspond to Lewis's image of poor families. In no case was a prediction in line with poverty culture theory supported for the under-60 group, when it was not for the sample as a whole (or vice versa).

Thus, only one of the six associations that we analyzed significantly supported culture of poverty hypotheses about this dimension. Indeed, with the exception of social isolation and mental illness, the associations were opposite to the direction predicted from the culture of poverty perspective.

## DIMENSION II: THE NATURE OF
## THE FAMILY

Another important dimension of the culture of poverty encompasses a variety of family variables. For the data to support Lewis's theses, the poor group should show distinctiveness in regard to consensual marriages, absence of childhood, female-centered families, authoritarianism, and verbal emphasis on family solidarity. Table 2 presents our data on the marital characteristics. Here we find little support for Lewis's argument that consensual or common-law marriages are widespread among the very poor. While the one case of a common-law marriage was to be found among the poor, this offers no support for viewing the typical married poor family in consensual terms. These data on marital status do offer support for one of Lewis's arguments, since a larger proportion of the families were "broken" in the poor group than in the non-poor group. Yet we suspect that the usual voluntary interpretation of this should be qualified, since a major reason for the high frequency of "broken" families was the death of a parent, a constraint indicating the involuntary character of much family dissolution.

**TABLE 2**
**Dimension II: Marital Status**

| MARITAL STATUS* | POOR (N = 130) | NON-POOR (N = 137) |
|---|---|---|
| Single | 8% | 12% |
| Common Law | 1 | 0 |
| Married | 31 | 53 |
| Separated | 11 | 14 |
| Divorced | 15 | 7 |
| Widowed | 35 | 14 |
| Totals | 101% | 100% |

$X^2 = 26.6$, d.f. = 5, $p = <.05$

*Respondent replies to the marital status question were carefully checked against other data available to us.*

Table 3 presents information on a number of other family traits that Lewis accentuates. The measure of female-centered families lends support to Lewis's arguments, with 55 percent of the poor families being female-headed and 28 percent of the non-poor. Lewis also argues that the poor expect their children to be more independent at earlier ages, to have a shorter childhood than more affluent children. While the available questions were not as good as we would have preferred, our findings on childhood independence indicate that neither the poor nor the non-poor group seems to be pushing its children into adulthood. In no case were the differences statistically significant. In fact, with the exception of crossing streets alone, the differences are in the direction of the non-poor expecting more independence than the poor.

The culture of poverty perspective emphasizes that the poor are distinguished by a strong disposition to "authoritarianism" in child-rearing practices. Looking at those families with children, one of our measures indicates support

TABLE 3

Dimension II: Additional Measures on Family and Child-rearing

| | POOR % | NON- POOR % | $X^2$ | df | p | (N) |
|---|---|---|---|---|---|---|
| Female-centered families: | | | | | | |
| % female household heads | 55 | 28 | 20.3 | 1 | <.05 | (271) |
| Absence of childhood: | | | | | | |
| Child should dress self by age 10 | 94 | 95 | .02 | 1 | >.05 | (89) |
| Child should help around house by age 10 | 90 | 95 | .58 | 1 | >.05 | (90) |
| Child should cross street alone by age 10 | 29 | 15 | 2.4 | 1 | >.05 | (90) |
| Child should take care of younger children by age 10 | 48 | 56 | .62 | 1 | >.05 | (91) |
| Authoritarian child-rearing: | | | | | | |
| Parents with 3 rules or more | 37 | 38 | .1 | 2 | >.05 | (87) |
| Parents using physical punishment | 77 | 43 | 10.6 | 1 | <.05 | (89) |
| Emphasis on family solidarity: | | | | | | |
| Respondents spending 6–7 evenings home | 83 | 70 | 4.1 | 2 | >.05 | (166) |
| Respondents always do things as a family | 68 | 65 | 2.3 | 2 | >.05 | (160) |

for this point of view; the other does not. First, the number of explicit behavioral rules that parents had for their children was analyzed by income; this revealed no difference between the two groups. Examination of the second measure—type of punishment for disobedience of a ten-year-old child—did show a significant difference between the two groups. Seventy-seven percent of the poor respondents said they would use some form, mild or strong, of physical punishment, compared to 43 percent of the non-poor.

In addition, according to a culture of poverty hypothesis, one should find a distinctive emphasis on family solidarity among the poor. These data revealed no statistically significant differences between the two income groups on several measures of family interaction: in regard to spending evenings at home with the family and in regard to doing things as a family. In the former case, however, the direction of the difference was in the direction Lewis would have predicted.

Examining each relationship for our sample split into a younger and an older age group revealed no change in the directions or the significance of the basic associations for the below-60 group, with regard to marital status and the two measures of family solidarity. We did not control for age with regard to the indices of absence of childhood and authoritarianism, since all but a handful of the heads of household of families with children were below the age of 60.

With regard to Lewis's predictions about family life we found limited support in these data. While the data indicate significant differences in family composition between the poor and the non-poor, the measures related to absence of childhood and family solidarity suggest no significant differences between the poor and the non-poor groups. And only one of two measures related to child rearing showed support for Lewis's generalizations.

## DIMENSION III: THE NATURE OF THE SLUM COMMUNITY

The traits Lewis itemizes under this rubric have a heterogeneous character, since Lewis includes physical housing conditions and gregariousness under the same dimension. For the data to lend strong support to the culture of poverty perspective, they should show that the poor group is in significantly worse shape than the non-poor in regard to housing conditions and social participation beyond the family, and the poor should be generally more "gregarious" with regard to primary social ties.

As can be seen in Table 4, our data indicate that the poor group is more distinctive in regard to this dimension than in regard to the two previous dimensions. Cross-classifying the housing measures with income revealed significant differences with regard to measures of housing quality and with regard to crowding (larger families, but housing units of roughly the same size). These differences are in line with what Lewis would predict.

The measure of neighborhood participation relates to respondents' perception of help patterns among neighbors, but the association was not as predicted. Our two measures of organizational (secondary) participation indicate no sig-

TABLE 4

Dimension III: Housing Conditions and Other Factors

| | POOR % | NON-POOR % | $X^2$ | df | p | (N) |
|---|---|---|---|---|---|---|
| Housing Conditions: | | | | | | |
| Deteriorating and dilapidated* houses | 58 | 46 | 8.3 | 2 | <.05 | (264) |
| Cleanliness of yards* (% cluttered) | 19 | 7 | 34.8 | 3 | <.05 | (260) |
| Partially furnished* | 61 | 48 | 4.2 | 1 | <.05 | (247) |
| Poor to very poor furnishings* | 58 | 37 | 12.0 | 1 | <.05 | (256) |
| Lighting of streets good** | 76 | 70 | 1.2 | 1 | >.05 | (269) |
| Crowding: | | | | | | |
| 1–2 bedrooms only | 74 | 75 | .1 | 2 | >.05 | (269) |
| 3 or more dependents | 42 | 33 | 2.6 | 1 | >.05 | (271) |
| Gregariousness: | | | | | | |
| Visit relatives 7/week | 34 | 42 | 2.6 | 3 | >.05 | (116) |
| Received help—housework | 10 | 7 | .8 | 1 | >.05 | (229) |
| sickness | 21 | 18 | .4 | 1 | >.05 | (229) |
| Organizational Activity Beyond Kinship Level: | | | | | | |
| People in neighborhood willing to help | 80 | 88 | 2.6 | 1 | >.05 | (242) |
| Attend church 2–4 times month | 72 | 79 | 2.9 | 2 | >.05 | (242) |
| Have contact with NAACP | 4 | 8 | 1.8 | 1 | >.05 | (270) |

*Based on interviewer assessments.
**Based on respondents' assessments.

nificant association between income and church attendance and between income and contact with the major local civil rights organization. And our measures of gregariousness other than neighboring, relating to kinship interaction, are not in line with the culture of poverty perspective. The poor and non-poor groups were not significantly different with regard to kinship interaction.

When age is controlled and the younger group examined separately, the significance of the basic associations (and the direction of the significant associations) is not affected, with two exceptions. In the case of the measures of neighborliness and number of dependents, the nonsignificant associations with income become significant when the below-60 age group is examined separately.

## DIMENSION IV: THE RELATIONSHIP BETWEEN
## THE CULTURE AND THE LARGER SOCIETY

Under this rubric culture of poverty theorists detail a lengthy list of culture traits which relate to the "integration of the poor in the major institutions of the larger society" (Lewis, 1965:xli). In Table 5 we have roughly grouped our measures into five areas that Lewis emphasized in regard to the integration of the poor into the larger society: segregation, discrimination, economic resources, political action, knowledge and use of public facilities, and attitudes toward dominant groups and institutions. Looking at specific measures relating to segregation and discrimination, we see that each of these items offers weak to strong directional support for the predictions, although only the association relating to segregated work settings attains statistical significance. The six indices of lack of economic and educational resources indicate the seriously disadvantaged pattern that the poverty culture perspective suggests. The poor were significantly more likely than the non-poor to be in unskilled jobs, to have unemployment in the family, to have serious money problems, to have second-hand furniture, and to have less in the way of education. The same was true for the one measure of political action, voting in the last presidential election, although the attitudinal item relating to Negroes organizing politically showed no differences between the two income groups.

The measures related to use of public facilities indicated that only small minorities in either group had not heard of the major public hospital. In fact, on one of the two items under this heading the directional difference is opposite to the lack of contact one might predict from a poverty culture perspective; the poor were more likely than the non-poor to have used the city hospital.

Our measures of attitudes toward dominant groups and institutions offered no significant support for Lewis's contentions about the distinctive suspicion of institutions, the fear, the apathy of those caught up in a culture of poverty. The poor were not significantly more likely than the non-poor to be critical of the jobs the schools and the police were doing, to feel public officials don't care what they think, to be critical of voting or the government, or to downgrade religion in importance, This is not to say that there was not substantial criticism of dominant groups and institutions among these black Americans. In-

TABLE 5

Dimension IV: Discrimination, Economic Resources and Other Factors

| | POOR % | NON-POOR % | CHI-SQUARE | df | p | (N) |
|---|---|---|---|---|---|---|
| Segregation and Discrimination: | | | | | | |
| Number having no white co-workers | 66 | 29 | 21.7 | 2 | <.05 | (180) |
| Harder for Negroes to get ahead due to discrimination | 45 | 38 | 1.6 | 3 | >.05 | (257) |
| Economic Resources: | | | | | | |
| Unskilled jobs | 87 | 50 | 43.7 | 2 | <.05 | (270) |
| Had someone out of work in past year | 42 | 15 | 21.9 | 1 | <.05 | (236) |
| No money left after paying bills | 61 | 34 | 54.6 | 2 | <.05 | (253) |
| Often have serious money problems | 65 | 35 | 22.1 | 2 | <.05 | (256) |
| Less than a high school education | 81 | 47 | 33.4 | 4 | <.05 | (262) |
| Poor to very poor furniture | 58 | 37 | 36.0 | 4 | <.05 | (256) |
| Political Action: | | | | | | |
| Did vote in last presidential election —Yes | 40 | 79 | 41.9 | 1 | <.05 | (269) |
| Negroes should get together politically | 87 | 87 | .9 | 3 | >.05 | (258) |
| Knowledge and Use of Public Facilities: | | | | | | |
| Had not heard of City Hospital | 5 | 2 | 5.0 | 2 | >.05 | (242) |
| Had contact with for help | 57 | 42 | 8.8 | 1 | <.05 | (265) |
| Attitudes toward Dominant Groups and Institutions: | | | | | | |
| School doing good job | 76 | 79 | .2 | 1 | >.05 | (75) |
| Impolite and inefficient police | 23 | 16 | .2 | 1 | >.05 | (67) |
| Public officials do not care | 59 | 55 | 5.2 | 2 | >.05 | (270) |
| Voting decides things | 77 | 77 | .2 | 2 | >.05 | (270) |
| I don't have a say about what the government does | 46 | 52 | .4 | 2 | >.05 | (269) |
| Government seems too complicated | 81 | 81 | 1.0 | 2 | >.05 | (270) |
| Religion is very important | 91 | 84 | 6.6 | 3 | >.05 | (249) |

deed, there was substantial criticism, but it did not vary by socioeconomic status.

When controls were applied, neither direction of differences nor statistical significance was altered for the under-60 groups, with two exceptions. Among the under-60 respondents, the poor were significantly less likely than the non-poor to have heard of the city hospital, although most had heard of it. And the poor were slightly more likely than the non-poor to feel voting decides things, but the association in the younger age group was not statistically significant.

## SUMMARY AND CONCLUSION

In this paper we have examined the four major dimensions or aspects of the culture of poverty distinguished by Oscar Lewis in *La Vida* (1965). More specifically, we have grouped indicators drawn from interviews with a large sample of black Americans in a major renewal area so that they relate to the four basic dimensions of the culture of poverty which Lewis emphasized.

Let us briefly summarize the pattern of our findings. Under the category of general attitudes, values, and the character structure of individuals, we examined five broad traits and found statistically significant support for a culture of poverty hypothesis in only one case, that of social isolation attitudes. In one other case the association was statistically significant in the direction opposite that which would be predicted by culture of poverty theory. Thus, the data relevant to this dimension provide little support for Lewis's perspective. Under the category of the nature of the family, we examined indices relevant to four basic traits and found consistent support for Lewis's perspective in only one case, that of family structure. We also found support for a culture of poverty hypothesis on one of our two measures of "authoritarian" child-rearing. Thus the data relevant to this dimension provide consistent support for only one of the four basic traits asserted to distinguish the poor from the non-poor. Under the rubric of the relationship of the subculture to the larger society, we again examined five broad traits and found some support for culture of poverty assertions in regard to segregation, political action, and lack of economic resources. However, in the first two cases not all items supported Lewis's perspective.

Taking all the broad traits in all dimensions together, we can report some support for Lewis's assertions in less than half of the cases; and in several of these instances some indices did not corroborate the predictions. With regard to about 60 percent of the fundamental poverty culture traits, we found no support for a perspective distinguishing the poor from non-poor in their way of life. Particularly striking, moreover, is the character of the majority of the traits where we did find statistically significant support for Oscar Lewis's contentions. In four of these cases the traits have to do more with what Valentine (1968:115) called the "externally imposed conditions or unavoidable matters of situational expediency, rather than cultural creations internal to the sub-society in question." These four cases are housing conditions, crowding, segregation, and the lack of economic resources. From this perspective, these seem to be alternative measures of, or indicators of, low-income status or poverty. Thus we are inclined to agree with Valentine that these can better be viewed as *conditions* of poverty than as *solutions* to poverty arising out of the cultural innovations of poor people.

Indeed, we would argue further that our findings on these four traits appear to offer more support for a "situational" interpretation of poverty than for the culture of poverty perspective. By a "situational" interpretation we mean that the poor are confronted by such situational factors as low-income, low-paying jobs, and inadequate housing in the main through no fault of their own. "That is, these conditions are phenomena of the environment in which the lower class lives, determined not so much by the behaviors and values of the poor as by the structure of the total social system" (Valentine, 1968:116). While we are inclined toward this model rather than the one outlined by Oscar Lewis, we do not here wish to contend that our evidence conclusively supports such an alternative model. However, we do wish to suggest that half of the traits for which we found strong support could as well be interpreted in situational terms rather than culture of poverty terms. At the very least, both models deserve testing in future analyses.

Thus these findings, while limited to one large black sample in a southwestern city, do not offer consistent, across-the-board support for a culture of poverty perspective, one which stresses that the very poor in all countries, and in all ethnic groups, are distinctively different in their designs for living from those who are more affluent. This point seems rather critical from the point of view of public policy, since the culture of poverty perspective now appears to be the dominant one at the level of federal government analysis and policymaking. We have already noted the great emphasis given to the attitudes and behavioral patterns of the poor in government publications such as Chilman's *Growing Up Poor* (1966). Surely it is unfortunate that theories such as that articulated by Oscar Lewis come to be accepted as fact before systematic empirical analysis of the attitudes, behaviors, and actions of the poor and non-poor has been carried out. While it has become conventional to call for additional research at the end of social science research papers, we hope that some will listen when we assert that, given the present state of social science research on the culture of poverty, no one should predicate policy decisions affecting low-income Americans, black or white, on such a theory. To do so is again to trust in unproven conventional wisdom which is increasingly becoming questionable.

## NOTES

1  A listing of these traits and a more complete analysis of the theoretical problems surrounding the culture of poverty can be found in Holland (1971).
2  The total sample consists of 321 black households in one neighborhood of this southwestern city—97 percent of all the households in the area. Attempts to assure response validity included pre-testing the schedule, intensive interviewer training (often lasting for several weeks), using only black interviewers, call-backs when information was not clear, duplicate interviews on selected households, and separate interviews with two adult members of selected households to compare responses.
3  Since the median income for the "non-poor" group is $4680 for families averaging about 2–3 persons, compared to a median of $1680 for the "poor" group, we would like to underline the fact that the term "non-poor" is here used in a relative, not an absolute, sense. Certainly, the modest per capita incomes of the "non-poor" do not qualify them for the label "affluent."

## REFERENCES

*Chilman, Catherine S.*
1966   Growing Up Poor. Washington, D.C.: U.S. Government Printing Office.
*Dean, Dwight G.*
1961   "Alienation: its meaning and measurement." American Sociological Review 26 (October): 754–758.

*Hagood, Margaret J., and Daniel O. Price*
1952   Statistics for Sociologists. New York: Holt, Rinehart and Winston.
*Holland, Barbara Coward*
1971   A study of Oscar Lewis' Culture of Poverty. Austin: University of Texas. M.A. Thesis.
*Irelan, Lola M., Oliver C. Moles, and Robert O'Shea*
1969   "Ethnicity, poverty, and selected attitudes: a test of the 'Culture of Poverty' hypothesis." Social Forces 47 (June): 405–413.
*Johnson, Norman J., and Peggy R. Sanday*
1971   "Subcultural variations in an urban poor population." American Anthropologist 73 (February): 128–143.
*Leeds, Anthony*
1971   "The concept of the 'Culture of Poverty': conceptual, logical, and empirical problems, with perspectives from Brazil and Peru." Pp. 226–284 in Eleanor B. Leacock (ed.), The Culture of Poverty: A Critique. New York: Simon and Schuster.
*Lewis, Oscar*
1964   "The culture of poverty." In John J. Tepaske and Sydney N. Fisher (eds.), Explosive Forces in Latin America. Columbus: Ohio State University Press.
1965   La Vida. New York: Random House.
*Roach, Jack L., and Orville R. Gursslin*
1967   "An evaluation of the concept 'Culture of Poverty.'" Social Forces 45 (March): 383–392.
*Rodman, Hyman*
1968   "The lower class value stretch." Pp. 270–285 in Louis A. Ferman et al. (eds.), Poverty in America. Ann Arbor: The University of Michigan Press.
*Rosenberg, Morris*
1963   "Parental self-interest and children's self-conceptions." Sociometry 26 (March): 35–49.
*Schneiderman, Leonard*
1964   "Value orientation preferences of chronic relief recipients." Social Work 9 (July): 13–18.
*Valentine, Charles A.*
1968   Culture and Poverty. Chicago: The University of Chicago Press.
1971   "The 'Culture of Poverty': its scientific significance and its implications for action." Pp. 193–223 in Eleanor B. Leacock (ed.), The Culture of Poverty: A Critique. New York: Simon and Schuster.

# Racism and Sexism as Functional Substitutes in the Labor Market

## Albert Szymanski

*University of Oregon*

*The returns from the 1970 U.S. census are used to examine whether racial and sexual discrimination tend to vary together or whether they are functional substitutes for one another in the labor market, i.e., whether they operate in the same manner to produce the same results. The impact of racial discrimination is measured by both the percentage of the population of a state that is of third world origin and the ratio of black to white male annual earnings. Sexual discrimination is measured by the ratio of white female to white male earnings and urban female to urban male earnings. The values of each of these indicators is compared for the 50 U.S. states. The effect of the percentage of the population that is urban, the percentage of the economically active population in manufacturing, the level of personal income, region, and percentage of the population that is third world is controlled for. The results show that sexual discrimination can be seen as a functional substitute for racial discrimination in the labor market. Where racial discrimination is the most significant, sexual discrimination is the least. This supports the argument that the capitalist economic system needs a specially oppressed group of menial laborers to perform its most menial and low-paying tasks. Either white women or third world people (men*

*Source:* Albert Szymanski, "Racism and Sexism as Functional Substitutes in the Labor Market," Sociological Quarterly 17, 1 (Winter 1976): 65–73. Copyright © 1976 by the Midwest Sociological Society. Reprinted by permission of the Society, the editors of Sociological Quarterly, and the author.

*and women) can fill these jobs. When third world people are available, white working women do not have to be pressed into them to the same extent. However, when third world people are not present, or are not especially discriminated against, then white working women tend more to perform the "dirty work" jobs and are consequently less likely to be found in the "better" jobs.*

It is widely accepted that third world people are concentrated in the lowest paying, most menial jobs in the American economy (Baron, 1971; Baran and Sweezy, 1966; Faltermeyer, 1974; Jacobson, 1968; O'Connor, 1973; Oppenheimer, 1974; Reich, 1971; Spero and Harris, 1968).[1] It also is widely accepted that women who work outside of the home are also concentrated in the most menial and low paying jobs (Davies and Reich, 1972; Goldberg, 1970; Kreps, 1971; Mitchell, 1966; Smuts, 1971; and U.S. Department of Labor, 1969). Further, many authors have suggested that the concentration of third world people and women in low paying and menial jobs is a manifestation of a single phenomenon. These theorists, mostly feminist, suggest that racial and sexual discrimination are really manifestations of the same thing (Cantarow et al., 1971:191–192; Firestone, 1971:Ch. 5; Millet, 1970:56–57; O'Connor, 1973:13–15, 33; Stimpson, 1971). Most of these authors argue that economic discrimination against third world people and against women serves the *same* function for the capitalist economy, namely the provision of a cheap and compliant menial labor force.[2] Stated in other terms, these authors claim that racism and sexism operate *in the labor market* in a similar way to produce the same results. For example, Stimpson (1971:623) in discussing the similarity between blacks and women argues: "In America they share the unhappy lot of being cast together as lesser beings. . . . What the economy gives both women and blacks are menial labor, low pay and few promotions. . . . The tasks of women, and blacks are usually grueling, repetitive, slogging and dirty. After all, people have servants, not simply for status, but for doing what every sensible person knows is unappetizing."[3]

If these later authors are correct in their argument that labor market discrimination against women and blacks is essentially part of the same general phenomenon, then we would expect racial and sexual discrimination in labor markets to vary *inversely* with one another. That is, since there is a more or less set proportion of "dirty work" (i.e., low paying, low status, menial) jobs in an economy, the more significant labor market discrimination is against third world people, the less it should be against white working women; and conversely, the less significant is labor market discrimination against third world people, the more intense should labor market discrimination be against white working women.[4] In other words, if the "dirty work" jobs are mostly filled by blacks, Latins, and other "people of color," then white working women do not take these jobs to the same extent; instead they tend to concentrate in the relatively less menial, higher paying jobs.

On the other hand, if few third world people are in an area, or if labor market discrimination against them is not especially intense, the authors lead us to expect that white women would be forced to take the lowest paying more menial jobs. This argument does not need to maintain that all third world people and all white women compete for all the same jobs. There are menial jobs, namely unskilled heavy labor, that are pretty much a monopoly of males. There are other menial jobs, namely lower level white-collar work, that are generally reserved for females. But there are many categories of work in which third world men, third world women, and white women compete with one another directly: namely, relatively unskilled factory labor, especially in the competitive sector, and service work of all kinds. In addition, third world women directly compete with white women for almost the full range of menial work jobs generally assigned to women. The large numbers of menial occupations where white women and third world men (and, of course, third world women) directly compete with one another is more than sufficient to be able to produce the effect that is predicted by those who argue that economic and racial discrimination are functional substitutes for one another.

## HYPOTHESES AND DESIGN

In order to test the hypothesized relationship between racial and sexual discrimination, I examined data from the 1970 census (which reports earnings data for 1969). The measure of sexual discrimination was based on both the ratio of urban female to urban male median earnings and the ratio of white female to white male median earnings; I included those who worked year-around and full time. The first of these measures was employed to control for the effect of what are probably great differences in the male-female occupational structure in rural and urban areas, while the second was used to control for factors associated with differences between racial groups in the male-female occupational structure. Thus, I separated out what may be spurious factors, in order to get to the heart of the presumed relationship between racism and sexism. If the relations turn out the same when both measures are employed, this should considerably increase our confidence in the results.

I measured the effects of racial discrimination through two different indicators. Unfortunately the data necessary to compute the median annual earnings ratio of third world male to third world female (still including only those who worked year-around full-time) was not available. This was unfortunate since the ratio would have been an important measure of the intensity of labor market discrimination against third world people. I used as a substitute the ratio of black male to white male median annual earnings for full-time, year-around workers. This approximation should be close to the ideal figure since about two-thirds of third world people in the U.S. are black, and since discrimination against blacks is a manifestation of a more general labor market discrimination against almost all third world people. No matter how great the labor market discrimination against third world people, it could have little effect on the labor market status of white women if third world people were a very small proportion of the labor force. Therefore, the second necessary measure of the potential impact of racial discrimination is the proportion of the population that is third world, i.e., black, or Spanish origin, Asian, or American Indian. Even only slight discrimination against "people of color" could exert a significant impact on the white labor force if a very large portion of the population of an area was of third world background.

For indicators of the intensity of racial discrimination I used data on men only. This controlled for complex patterns of interrelationship between racial and sexual discrimination and for the effect of differential female labor force participation rates, thereby allowing me to separate these questions from the question of the intensity of racial discrimination. Data about individual earnings was used for measures of both racial and sexual discrimination, in order to focus on point of production discrimination. This seems to get to the essence of the claims of the theorists cited.

The indicators of labor market discrimination against third world people and women could be attacked in some circles as too broad and sweeping due to the inclusion of more than just "pure economic discrimination" against persons equal in all respects except race and sex. Other circles could attack the indicators as being too narrow because they leave out social, political, interpersonal, etc., manifestations of racism and sexism as well as differential unemployment and labor force participation rates.

The indicators which I have used focus on all-around labor market discrimination, rather than on just "pure economic discrimination." This takes into account all aspects of the past and present situation of the group that explain its inferior labor market situation, e.g., inferior education, skill training, experiences, attitudes, etc. Labor market discrimination against women and people of color is not a set of discrete phenomena, but rather a unified gestalt of practices which cannot be separated. Of course, the measures of labor market discrimination do not directly measure other aspects of the oppression of women and third world people. Nevertheless, not only does labor market discrimination reach the heart of the theories of the authors cited at the beginning of the article, but it also plays a very important, if not the key role, in the all-around oppression of women and third world people.[5]

The 50 states of the U.S. served as my units of analysis. In studies of income distribution SMSAs (Standard Metropolitan Statistical Areas) sometimes are used instead of the states as units of analysis. Each unit has its advantages. The SMSAs are more or less common labor markets (which is not so much the case with the states) and are generally more economically homogeneous and compact than the states. The states, on the other hand, include all types of economic areas—small towns, small cities, and rural areas, as well as the metropolitan areas of the cities; in addition, more statistical data are available for them. In actuality both units are almost equally valid to employ in tests like this. Previous studies on income distribution using *both* units of analysis have come up with almost identical findings.[6] Although I have chosen to use the states, I welcome attempts to replicate my results using the SMSAs.

Pearsonian r correlation coefficients were computed for the relationships between each of the two indicators of labor market discrimination against women and for each of the two indicators of significance of racial discrimination. Linear regression techniques were legitimate to use because scatter diagrams of our data showed that it was not curvilinear and that there existed no extreme cases which could significantly and artificially distort the results. Statistical significance tests were not used, since the universe of the 50 states, not a sample of some larger universe, was employed. The results were thus statistically significant at any level.

After computation of the basic zero order correlations between sexual and racial discrimination, the relationships between the two variables were computed. I controlled for the factors which in previous studies of income distribution have been shown to have a significant impact: degree of urbanization, personal income per capita, percentage of third world population (where relevant), occupational and industrial composition, and region of the country.[7] These factors were controlled for both individually and simultaneously to determine whether or not the zero order correlations were real or spurious.

## THE RESULTS

The correlation between urban female/urban male median earnings and black male/white male median earnings was –.44. This shows an inverse relationship between racial and sexual discrimination as measured by the two indicators (see Table 1). The relationship was upheld with the percent third world, percent urban, personal income per capita, percent in manufacturing, and region are controlled for. When percent third world was used as the indicator of the impact of racial discrimination, the findings were similar. The zero order correlation with urban female/urban male median earnings was +.49, showing that the more third world people in a state, the less sexual discrimination there is against women. This relationship was also upheld when percent urban, personal income per capita, percentage in manufacturing, and region are controlled for.

When the indicator of sexual discrimination in the labor market was the ratio of white female to white male median earnings, the relationships observed above were even stronger. In this case the zero order correlation with black male/white male median earnings was –.50, and the correlation with percentage third world was +.67. Again, in all cases, the basic relationship held up under all the controls, although it was weakened when percent third world was controlled for in the correlation with black male/white male earnings.

The correlations were also examined for the 25 states with the highest percentage third world and the non-Southern states, each taken separately (see Table 2 and Table 3). The 25 states with the highest percentage third world (at least 12%) were examined because these states should show the greatest impact of racial discrimination on the white labor force. Also the decrease in the strength of the correlations reported when percentage third world was controlled for indicated that this factor ought to be examined in more depth. In order to be sure that the relationship remained as strong as when their (perhaps peculiar) racist conditions were included, the Southern states were removed from consideration.

When only the 25 states were examined, the correlations between urban female/urban male median earnings and the two measures of racial discrimination ran in the same direction as they did for the country as a whole; but they were weakened. The strength of the relationships was consistent regardless of the controls. When white female/white male median earnings were used as the measure of sexual discrimination, the relationship was also in the same direction as in the country as a whole. In this case, all the relations were as strong as in the whole country. Again the strength of the relationship held up with all controls.

## TABLE 1

### The Relation Between Racial and Sexual Economic Discriminations (1969, 1970)*

### (the 50 U.S. States)

| | ZERO ORDER | PERCENTAGE THIRD WORLD | CONTROLLING FOR: | | | |
| --- | --- | --- | --- | --- | --- | --- |
| | | | PERCENTAGE URBAN | PERSONAL INCOME PER CAPITA | PERCENTAGE IN MANU-FACTURING | REGION (SOUTH/NON-SOUTH) |
| *CORRELATIONS BETWEEN URBAN FEMALE/URBAN MALE MEDIAN EARNINGS AND THE INDICATORS OF RACIAL DISCRIMINATION* | | | | | | |
| Black male/White male median earnings | -.44 | -.24 | -.47 | -.57 | -.45 | -.41 |
| Percentage Third World | +.49 | — | +.48 | +.53 | +.49 | +.46 |
| *CORRELATIONS BETWEEN WHITE FEMALE/WHITE MALE MEDIAN EARNINGS AND THE INDICATORS OF RACIAL DISCRIMINATION* | | | | | | |
| Black male/White male median earnings | -.50 | -.21 | -.50 | -.54 | -.52 | -.40 |
| Percentage Third World | +.67 | — | +.68 | +.67 | +.67 | +.60 |

*Earnings data are for 1969, other data are for 1970.
Sources: U.S. Census of Population, 1970; General Population Characteristics, U.S. Summary. U.S. Census of Population, 1970; Special Reports: Persons of Spanish Origin. U.S. Census of Population, 1970; Detailed Characteristics, U.S. Summary. U.S. Census of Population, 1970; Detailed Characteristics (each of the 50 states).

## TABLE 2

### The Relation Between Racial and Sexual Economic Discrimination
in the 25 States with at Least 12 Percent of Their Population Third World (1969, 1970)*

| | ZERO ORDER | CONTROLLING FOR: | | | | |
| --- | --- | --- | --- | --- | --- | --- |
| | | PERCENTAGE THIRD WORLD | PERCENTAGE URBAN | PERSONAL INCOME PER CAPITA | PERCENTAGE IN MANU-FACTURING | REGION (SOUTH/ NON-SOUTH) |
| *CORRELATIONS BETWEEN URBAN FEMALE/URBAN MALE MEDIAN EARNINGS AND THE INDICATORS OF RACIAL DISCRIMINATION* | | | | | | |
| Black male/White male median earnings | -.37 | -.33 | -.27 | -.54 | -.33 | -.50 |
| Percentage Third World | +.16 | — | +.14 | +.25 | +.11 | +.19 |
| *CORRELATIONS BETWEEN WHITE FEMALE/WHITE MALE MEDIAN EARNINGS AND THE INDICATORS OF RACIAL DISCRIMINATION* | | | | | | |
| Black male/White male median earnings | -.58 | -.43 | -.50 | -.65 | -.57 | -.61 |
| Percentage Third World | +.52 | — | +.52 | +.55 | +.50 | +.52 |

*Earnings data are for 1969, other data are for 1970.*
*Sources: See Table 1.*

**TABLE 3**

**The Relation Between Racial and Sexual Economic Discrimination
Non-Southern States Only (1969, 1970)***

| | | | CONTROLLING FOR: | | |
| --- | --- | --- | --- | --- | --- |
| | ZERO ORDER | PERCENTAGE THIRD WORLD | PERCENTAGE URBAN | INCOME PER CAPITA | PERCENTAGE IN MANUFACTURING |
| *CORRELATIONS BETWEEN URBAN FEMALE/URBAN MALE MEDIAN EARNINGS AND THE INDICATORS OF RACIAL DISCRIMINATION* | | | | | |
| Black male/White male median earnings | -.47 | -.34 | -.49 | -.54 | -.45 |
| Percentage Third World | +.54 | — | +.48 | +.42 | +.51 |
| *CORRELATIONS BETWEEN WHITE FEMALE/WHITE MALE MEDIAN EARNINGS AND THE INDICATORS OF RACIAL DISCRIMINATION* | | | | | |
| Black male/White male median earnings | -.45 | -.28 | -.47 | -.48 | -.37 |
| Percentage Third World | +.70 | — | +.69 | +.64 | +.67 |

*Earnings data are for 1969, other data are for 1970.*
*Sources: See Table 1.*

With only the non-Southern states under examination, the relationships observed for the country as a whole were found to exist at more or less the same strength.

This was true whether urban female/urban male median earnings or white female/white male median earnings was used as the measure of sexual discrimination, and whether the ratio of black male/white male median earnings or percentage third world was used as the measure of the significance of racial discrimination. This was also the case regardless of which third variable was controlled.

## CONCLUSION

In conclusion, it is clear that sexual and racial discrimination in the labor market are functional substitutes. Regardless of how they are measured and regardless of what third variables are controlled for, there is a substantial inverse correlation between the two factors. The greater the significance of racial discrimination in an area, the less the labor market discrimination against women; and the less significant racial discrimination in the labor market, the greater the discrimination against women. Thus the suggestions offered in much of the pertinent literature are upheld. In good part, then, sexism in the labor market works in a similar manner as does racism. When sufficient numbers of third world people are available to do the low paid dirty work jobs, white women do not perform them to the same extent; instead they tend to be found in the relatively better paying jobs. On the other hand, where there are few third world people or where labor market discrimination against third world people is not so intense, white women take many of the low paying and menial jobs that in other cases are filled by third world people. Sexual and racial discrimination in the labor market thus appear to operate in a similar manner to produce similar results. It would seem that the capitalist system needs a specially oppressed group of menial laborers to perform its most menial and low paying tasks.

## NOTES

1  By "third world people," I mean blacks, persons of Spanish origin, Asians, and American Indians. The term "whites" is used to describe all others. The total number of third world people in the U.S. by this definition in 1970 was 34.5 million, of whom 22.6 million were blacks, 9.1 million were people of Spanish origin, 2.0 million were Asians, and .8 million were American Indians. (See U.S. Department of Commerce, *The Statistical Abstract of the U.S., 1973.*) The category "third world," rather than blacks, was used because of the similar economic role of most third world people. For example, in areas with few Spanish-speaking people but many blacks, blacks do pretty much of the same jobs as Spanish-speaking people do in areas where there are many of them, but few blacks.

2  The term "function" is used in the sense of a positive effect in maintaining a social institution. A given social institution is considered to need certain kinds of "inputs" in order to run smoothly. Any of a set of inputs that can satisfy such needs are considered to be "functional" for a given social institution. Functional substitutes are distinct "inputs" any of which can satisfy a given "need" of a social institution. See Bronislaw Malinowski (1960) for a good description of the concept of function as used in this article.

3  Of relevance to this study is the literature on the question of whether or not whites gain from racial discrimination. See for example: Becker (1971), Glenn (1963 and 1966), Reich (1971), Thurow (1969).

4  For discussions of the role of "dirty workers" in the U.S. economy see Faltermayer (1974) and Oppenheimer (1974).

5  Because the indicators employed only measure labor market discrimination the reader should be cautioned against interpreting the results of this analysis to mean that all white women benefit, either economically or in a total sense, from discrimination against third world people (or vice versa). Even economic discrimination is not fully measured by the indicators used since the effects of differential unemployment and labor force participation rates are not considered.

6  See, for example, Reich (1971:111).

7  See Reich (1971:111).

## REFERENCES

*Baran, Paul, and Paul Sweezy*
1966   *Monopoly Capital.* New York: Monthly Review.
*Baron, Harold*
1971   "The Demand for Black Labor." *Radical America,* 5:2 (March–April).
*Becker, Gary S.*
1971   *The Economics of Discrimination.* Chicago: University of Chicago Press.
*Cantarow, Ellen, et al.*
1971   "I Am Furious (Female)" in Michelle Hoffnung Garskof *Roles Women Play: Readings Toward Women's Liberation.* Belmont, California: Wadsworth Publishing Co.
*Davies, Margery, and Michael Reich*
1972   "On the relationship between sexism and capitalism." In Richard Edwards *et al.,* ed. *The Capitalist System.* Englewood Cliffs: Prentice-Hall.
*Faltermayer, Edmund*
1974   "Who Will do the Dirty Work Tomorrow." *Fortune,* 84:1 (January).
*Firestone, Shulamith*
1971   *The Dialectics of Sex.* New York: Bantam.
*Glenn, Norval*
1966   "White Gains from Negro Subordination." *Social Problems,* 14:2 (Fall).
1963   "Occupational Benefits to Whites from Subordination of Negroes." *American Sociological Review,* 28:3 (June).
*Goldberg, Marilyn Power*
1970   "The Economic Exploitation of Women." *Review of Radical Political Economics,* 2:1 (Spring).
*Jacobson, Julius, ed.*
1968   *The Negro and the American Labor Movement.* New York: Doubleday and Co.
*Kreps, Juanita*
1971   *Sex in the Market Place.* Baltimore: Johns Hopkins Press.

Malinowski, Bronislaw
1960    A Scientific Theory of Culture and Other Essays. New York: Oxford University Press.
Millet, Kate
1970    Sexual Politics. New York: Avon.
Mitchell, Juliet
1966    "Women: The Longest Revolution," New Left Review, No. 40 (November–December).
O'Connor, James
1973    The Fiscal Crisis of the State. New York: St. Martins Press.
Oppenheimer, Martin
1974    "The Sub-Proletariat: Dark Skins and Dirty Work." The Insurgent Sociologist, 4:2 (Winter).
Reich, Michael
1971    "The Economics of Racism," in David M. Gordon, ed. Problems in Political Economy. Lexington, Mass.: D. C. Heath and Co.
Smuts, Robert
1971    Women and Work in America. New York: Schocken.
Spero, Sterling, and Abram Harris
1968    The Black Worker and Organized Labor. New York: Atheneum.
Stimpson, Catherine
1971    "Thy Neighbor's Wife, Thy Neighbors' Servants: Women's Liberation and Black Civil Rights." In Vivian Gornick and Barbara K. Moran, Women in Sexist Society. New York: New American Library.
Thurow, Lester
1969    Poverty and Discrimination. Washington, D.C.: The Brookings Institution.
U.S. Department of Commerce
1974    The Statistical Abstract of the United States, 1973.
U.S. Department of Labor
1969    The 1969 Handbook on Women Workers. Washington, D.C.: U.S. Government Printing Office.

## NOTE

In a subsequent analysis by another researcher it was concluded that racism and sexism in the labor market are very different phenomena, not "functional substitutes" for each other, and that much greater changes in the social structure are necessary to eliminate discrimination against women than against blacks. See, Wayne J. Villemez, "The Functional Substitutability of Blacks and Females in the Labor Market: A Closer Look," The Sociological Quarterly 18 (Autumn 1977), 548–63.

# Class Conflict and Jim Crow Segregation in the Postbellum South *

## William J. Wilson

*University of Chicago*

Students of historial race relations have paid considerable attention to the
economic basis of racial antagonisms in recent years, particularly the theme
that racial problems in historical situations are related to the more general
problems of economic-class conflict. And the writings on this theme have been
influenced, in no small measure, by purported Marxian explanations of race.
Indeed, the political scientist Ira Katznelson (1973: v) maintains that "in spite
of the tendency of some Marxists to reduce issues of race to those of class—thus
not recognizing that a racial dynamic has categories of events and behavior that
must be dealt with on their own terms—Marxist theory remains the richest,
most powerful tool for understanding race and racism." Although there is some
variation in the way Marxists interpret race relations (Genovese, 1966, 1969;
Burawoy, 1974), orthodox Marxian explanations (Cox, 1948; Baran and Sweezy,
1966; Reich, 1971; Wolpe, 1970; Nikolinakos, 1973; Sivananda, 1973) continue to
be the most widely used and representative.

*Source:* William J. Wilson, "Class Conflict and Jim Crow Segregation in the Postbellum
South," Pacific Sociological Review 19, 4 (October 1976): 431–46. Copyright © 1976 by the
Publisher, Sage Publications, Inc. Reprinted by permission.
*This paper was presented at the Annual Meeting of the Pacific Sociological Association,
San Diego, California, March 25, 1976. It is part of a larger study to be published in 1977
as a volume in the Random House series on Ethnic Groups in Comparative Perspective.
Appreciation is expressed to Edna Bonacich, Michael Burawoy, Ira Katznelson, and Kath-
erine O'Sullivan. See for their helpful comments on an earlier version of this paper.

## ECONOMIC CLASS EXPLANATIONS OF RACIAL ANTAGONISMS

Orthodox Marxists generally stress that racial conflict is epiphenomenal, i.e., merely a special manifestation of class conflict. Accordingly, ideologies of racism, racial prejudices, institutionalized discrimination, segregation, and other factors that reinforce or embody racial stratification are simply part of a superstructure determined and shaped by the particular arrangement of the class structure.

Orthodox Marxists further maintain that because the ultimate goal of the capitalist class is to increase surplus value, efforts will be made to suppress workers' demands for increased wages and to weaken their bargaining power by promoting divisions within their ranks. The divisions are strengthened and institutionalized to the degree that the capitalist class is able to isolate the lower priced black force by not only supporting job, housing, and educational discrimination against blacks, but also encouraging racial prejudices and ideologies of racial subjugation such as racism. At the same time, orthodox Marxists argue, the capitalist class benefits not only because they have created a labor surplus that is not united against them, not only because the appropriation of surplus from the ethnic labor force is greater than the exploitation rate of the white labor force, but also because they can counteract ambitious claims of the white labor force for higher wages, either by threatening to increase the average wage rate of black workers, or by replacing segments of the white labor force with segments of the black labor force in special situations, such as strikes. In short, orthodox Marxists argue that racial antagonism is a function of class conflict, a "mask for privilege," designed to conceal the efforts of the ruling class to exploit subordinate racial groups and to divide the working class.

An interesting variation of the orthodox Marxist approach to historical race relations has recently appeared in the writings of Edna Bonacich (1972, 1975). The central hypothesis in Bonacich's economic based theory is that "ethnic antagonism first germinates in a labor market split along ethnic lines" (Bonacich, 1972:549). A split labor market occurs when the price of labor for the same work differs for at least two groups, or would differ if they performed the same work.

There are three distinct classes in a split labor market—(1) business or employers, (2) higher paid labor, and (3) cheaper labor. Conflict develops between these three classes because of different interests. The main goal of business or employers is to maintain as cheap a labor force as possible in order either to compete effectively with other businesses, or to maximize economic returns. As long as a labor shortage exists, higher paid labor is in a good bargaining position. Accordingly, if business is able to attract cheaper labor to the market place, the interests of higher paid labor are threatened. They may lose some of the privileges they enjoy, they may lose their bargaining power, and they may even lose their jobs. If the labor market is split along ethnic lines, e.g., if higher paid labor is white and lower paid labor is black, class antagonisms are transformed into ethnic or racial antagonisms.

However, if more expensive labor is strong enough, that is, if they possess the power resources to preserve their economic interests, they can prevent being replaced or undercut by cheaper labor. On the one hand, they can exclude lower paid labor from a given territory. "Exclusion movements clearly serve the interests of higher paid labor. Its standards are protected while the capitalist class is deprived of cheaper labor" (Bonacich, 1972:555). On the other hand, if it is not possible for higher paid labor to rely on exclusion (e.g., cheaper labor may be indigenous to the territory or may have been imported early in business labor relations, when higher paid labor could not prevent the move), then they will institutionalize a system of ethnic stratification which could (1) monopolize skilled positions, thereby ensuring the effectiveness of strike action; (2) prevent cheaper labor from developing the skills necessary to compete with higher paid labor (e.g., impose barriers to equal access to education); and (3) deny cheaper labor the political resources that would enable them to undercut higher paid labor through, say, governmental regulations. "In other words," states Bonacich, "the solution to the devastating potential of weak, cheap labor is, paradoxically, to weaken them further, until it is no longer in business' immediate interest to use them as replacements" (Bonacich, 1972:556). Thus, whereas Marxian arguments associate the development and institutionalization of racial stratification with the motivations and activities of the capitalist class. Bonacich's theory traces racial stratification directly to the powerful, higher paid working class.

As I examine the historical stages of race relations in the United States, I find that the patterns of black/white interaction do not consistently and sometimes do not conveniently conform to the propositions outlined in these respective explanations of racial antagonisms. To illustrate and amplify this point, I have chosen to examine one of the most dynamic periods of American race relations, the nineteenth century postslavery period in the South, from roughly 1865 to the turn of the century. During this period, the South progressively moved from a plantation economy to an industrializing economy and in the process, the traditional patterns of race and class relations in the South were fundamentally altered. My analysis will attempt to show that because they fail to specify the structural conditions that provide antagonistic classes with different power resources to influence racial stratification in various situations, the economic class arguments (that relate racial stratification either to the work of the capitalist class or to the victory of higher paid labor) lack sufficient scope to explain the different manifestations of racial subordination in the postbellum South. My basic thesis is that the meaningful application of the economic class arguments in any given historical period depends heavily on knowledge of the constraints imposed by the particular systems of production during that period, constraints that shape the structural relations between racial and class groups and which thereby produce different patterns of intergroup interaction.[1]

## THE PLANTER CLASS AND
## INSTITUTIONALIZED RACIAL INEQUALITY

In an argument quite similar to that advanced by Oliver C. Cox in 1948, the Marxist scholars, Baran and Sweezy (1966:247), gloss over the mass of historical data with the less than definite statement that "when Negroes tried to take advantage of their legal freedom to organize along with poor whites in the

Populist movement, the planters answered with violence and the Jim Crow system of legalized segregation."

Only if we focus on the period immediately following the Civil War can we attribute institutionalized racial inequality solely to the planter class. Initial legislation to restrict and control the black population was not generated by white workers, although they were indeed quite concerned about black competition, but by southern planters and their business and political allies.

Immediately following the Civil War, white supremacy, virtually secured by institutionalized slavery throughout the antebellum South, appeared to be in serious jeopardy. Slaves had been liberated and some were armed. Not only were fears expressed about blacks becoming full citizens and receiving equal political and civil rights, but there was even talk of blacks dividing up the plantation estates. "This was not only competition," states historian C. Vann Woodward (1971:251), "It looked to many whites like a takeover." More fundamentally, the ruling economic elite was frightened because the southern economy was on the verge of total collapse without slave labor. For the ruling elite, "black freedom" signified not only a threat to white supremacy, but also meant the loss of a guaranteed cheap and controlled labor supply for the plantations.

In 1865–1866, southern legislatures, which continued to be controlled by business and planter groups, were given freedom by Presidents Lincoln and Johnson to devise ways to resolve the problems created by an economy no longer based on slave labor. The legislatures promptly passed a series of discriminatory laws known as the Black Codes. Although the provisions of the Codes varied from state to state, one of their primary objectives was to insure an adequate and cheap labor supply for the plantations. Woodward (1971: 252) informs us that the "Black Codes of 1865–1866 were mainly concerned with forced labor and police laws to get the freedman back to the fields under control." Those blacks without a permanent residence or unemployed were classified as vagrants and could be arrested and/or fined, and if incapable of paying, were bound out to plantations under labor contracts. As a substitute for the social controls of slavery, the Codes also restricted black movement, denied blacks political and legal rights, and in some states, provided for segregation of certain public facilities.

In April 1866, the Republican-controlled Congress nullified the Black Codes by passing a Civil Rights Act which conferred citizenship on the ex-slaves and specified that discriminatory acts against them were punishable by fine and/or federal imprisonment. Black political and civil rights were further protected by the Fourteenth Amendment passed by Congress in June 1866. And, after the Republicans, dominated by the Radical wing, had gained a two-thirds majority in both houses in the November election of 1866, Congress passed two supplementary Reconstruction Acts in 1867 that divided the ten southern states into five military districts under northern supervision and granted blacks voting rights (Franklin, 1967; Bergman, 1969).

In large measure, white reaction to Reconstruction and the specter of black control of the South was shaped by social class interests. Racial tension increased significantly among lower class whites who perceived more clearly than ever the impact of large scale black competition for low status jobs. Reconstruction did not destroy the landowning white aristocracy. Both poor whites and blacks were dependent on the planter classes for their livelihood as tenants and sharecroppers at the very time when these positions were diminishing in the face of gradual industrialization. The evidence is clear that the planter class of the South effectively prevented any economic or political cooperation or class allegiance between poor blacks and poor whites (Frazier, 1957: 135).[2] As long as poor whites directed their hatred and frustration against the black competitor, the planters were relieved of class hostility directed against them. "Indeed, one motive for the Ku Klux Klan movement of these years was a desire by low class whites to remove the Negro as a competitor, especially in the renting of land" (Marshall, 1961: 66). The essential point is that during the first two decades following the Civil War, poor whites lacked the power resources needed to bring about the kind of institutional changes that would have improved their economic lives, i.e., segregationist laws that would have restricted black competition. Concentrated in positions such as tenant farmers and sharecroppers, their economic position was as precarious in the postbellum period as it was during antebellum slavery. Organized labor remained weak in the face of the overwhelming political and economic resources of the master class.

The response of the "people at the top" to the changes in race relations brought about by Reconstruction contrasted sharply with the lower class white reaction. Within a few years after Reconstruction, the ruling economic elite realized that their earlier apprehensions concerning the Negro were unwarranted. Northern Republicans gradually moved from their earlier position of radicalism and protection of black freedom to a posture of promoting eastern capitalistic expansion in the South (Woodward, 1971: 254). There was greater competition between lower class whites and blacks and therefore increased racial hostility: but the economic and political hold of the privileged classes over southern life was essentially unchallenged. The plantation elite, aligned with the growing industrial sector, was no longer fearful of a black threat or takeover. Indeed, blacks remained in a dependent economic relationship with this sector. Because of this, and because blacks were anxious about the manifestation of lower class white reaction to black competition, conservative white rulers virtually controlled the black vote prior to 1890. In this connection, Woodward states (1951:254–255):

*It was true that blacks continued to vote in large numbers and to hold minor offices and a few seats in Congress, but this could be turned to account by the conservative white rulers who had trouble with white lower-class rebellion. Black votes could be used to overcome white working-class majorities, and upper-class white protection was needed by blacks under threat of white lower-class aggression. Many reciprocal accommodations between upper-class whites and blacks were possible under the paternalistic order.*

## THE WHITE LABOR REFORM MOVEMENT AND JIM CROW SEGREGATION

Changes in the system of production exerted considerable influence on the developing patterns of class and racial tension in the New South. In the antebellum period, public power was so heavily concentrated among large planters and so clearly derived from property in slaves and land that racial stratification assumed an overwhelmingly paternalistic character—reflected in the relationships between slaveholders and slaves. This relationship persisted through the early years of the postbellum period. However, as the South experienced gradual industrialization in the late nineteenth century, as new economic institutions generated technological development, expanding modes of communications and more elaborate systems of transportation connecting cities and farms, not only was the distribution of power significantly altered in the South, but race relations became increasingly associated with class conflict (Scruggs, 1971:70–87).

After the Civil War, the planters had to share their power with a rising middle class of merchant-bankers and owners and operators of factories, mines, and railroads (Scruggs, 1971: 73). Nevertheless, they combined to form a disciplined ruling class, conscious of their overlapping economic interests. And they possesed a mutual feeling of apprehension over the gradual increase in political activity among the white working class in the 1880s and 1890s. Just as changes in the system of production modified the distribution of power among the ruling elite, so too did it place the workers of the South in greater proximity with one another and facilitated their mobilization into collective action groups.

The structural changes in the labor market accompanied severe economic dislocations for many workers of the South. During the last quarter of the nineteenth century, lower class whites found themselves in increasing contact and competition with millions of freed blacks at the very time that a labor surplus developed in the face of enormous population growth in the South (Scruggs, 1971; Woodward, 1951; Key, 1949). The problem was especially acute in the lower South. For the first time, blacks and working class whites of the lower South, historically separated in the black belt (lowlands) and the uplands respectively, were forced by economic conditions to confront one another, bump shoulders, and compete on a wide scale for the same jobs. Black youths gradually moved from the lowlands to the new mining and industrial towns of the uplands, finding dirty and low paying work in tobacco factories, mines, and turpentine camps; meanwhile, sons of white farmers, overwhelmed by debts and falling prices, sifted down from the uplands to the lowlands, settling for work in the textile mills or drifting into tenancy. A new breed of southern politician, whose style combined the evangelistic fervor of the southern preacher with the racist rhetoric of the upcountry hillbilly, emerged to articulate the feelings and represent the interests of working class whites. Their pleas for disfranchisement and legal segregation helped to set in motion a movement that produced decades of Jim Crow segregation (Scruggs, 1971:81). The signs were clear when the Farmers Alliance, a movement consisting of hundreds of thousands of lower class white farmers and tenants, was first exerting its influence in southern state legislatures, because Jim Crow segregation laws sprang up all over the South (Woodward, 1951:211–212; Scruggs, 1971:84–85). For example, in 1887 in Florida; 1888 in Mississippi; 1889 in Texas; 1890 in Louisiana; and 1891 in Alabama, Arkansas, Kentucky, and Georgia, laws requiring separate accommodations in railway stations and in streetcars were enacted. Perhaps Woodward (1951:211) comes closest to summarizing the meaning of these developments, when he states:

*It is one of the paradoxes of Southern history that political democracy for the white man and racial discrimination for the black man were often products of the same dynamics. As the Negroes invaded the new mining and industrial towns of the uplands in greater numbers, and the hill country whites were driven into more frequent and closer association with them, and as the two were brought into rivalry for subsistence wages in the cotton field, mines and wharves, the lower-class man's demand for Jim Crow laws became more insistent. . . . The Negro pretty well understood these forces and his grasp of them was one reason for this growing alliance with the most conservative and politically reactionary class of whites against the insurgent white democracy.*

Thus, the late nineteenth century, a period of economic dislocation (caused by industrial capitalism, population pressures, declining farm prices, and exploitative sharecropping) generated a labor reform movement and Jim Crow segregation which grew hand in hand.

## DISFRANCHISEMENT AND THE COLLAPSE OF THE ALLIANCE BETWEEN BLACKS AND THE WHITE BUSINESS ELITE

The real concern of the business elite in the decade or two following Reconstruction was the threat to their political and economic power by the rise of the agrarian and labor reform movements. It is ironic but not surprising that both the business elite and the black minority were fearful of the rise in white lower class power. The unholy alliance between blacks and white ruling classes prior to 1890 actually prevented the racial code from becoming more severe.

As long as the alliance between blacks and the conservative economic elite existed, the latter frequently denounced Jim Crow laws in aristocratic, paternalistic tones as "unnecessary and uncalled for" and "a needless affront to our respectable and well behaved colored people" (quoted in Woodward, 1971:257). According to Woodward (1971:257), "when the first state Jim Crow laws for trains was passed in 1887, a conservative paper rather shamefacedly admitted it was done 'to please the crackers.' "

However, at the very time that Jim Crow legislation was mushrooming throughout the South, some workers of the Populist movement recognized that as long as conservative whites were aligned with blacks, the possibility of a united working class labor movement to overcome economic exploitation would indeed be difficult. A strenuous effort by the Populists sought to create an alliance of the poor whites and poor blacks. Under the leadership of Tom Watson (Woodward, 1938), a substantial Populist appeal to the black man was generated in Georgia (Owens, 1973). Some successes also occurred in Texas and Arkansas (Bergman, 1969: 310). This was enough to alarm the conservative Democrats representing the southern business interests, and they too increased their drive to attract the support of black voters, including the stuffing of ballot boxes with fraudulent votes. After both the Populists and the Democrats sought to manipulate the black vote, they finally realized that since neither was assured of controlling the black vote, "it was much better to have clear-cut constitutional disfranchisement of the Negro and to leave the white group to fight elections out among themselves" (Franklin, 1967:337).

The conservative Democrats who had originally placed the blame for the rise of legal segregation on lower class whites when they felt secure about the black vote, joined in the movement for disfranchisement as soon as they became apprehensive about the black vote. Accompanying disfranchisement were increased Jim Crow laws of segregation in both public and private institutions and facilities, including the virtual collapse of public education and the systematic exclusion by white laborers of blacks from jobs in the skilled occupational ranks they had held since slavery, e.g., barbering and the better agricultural jobs (Young, 1932:99; Fogel and Engerman, 1974:258–264).

## WHITE ECONOMIC CLASS INTERESTS AND BLACK SUBORDINATION

Restrictive arguments that the Jim Crow system was the work of the capitalist class, or due solely to the victory of higher paid white labor, obscure the dynamics of the complex patterns of racial inequality in the postbellum South. As I have attempted to show, and historical analysis demonstrates: (1) the initial form of racial stratification in the postbellum period, formalized and sanctioned by the Black Codes, was based solely on the efforts of the plantation elite to insure an adequate and cheap labor supply for the plantations, in the aftermath of slave emancipation. Racial inequality therefore reflected the class interests of the aristocracy and entailed the exploitation of labor; (2) the emergence of initial Jim Crow segregation laws directly parallels the rise of lower class whites to political power in the labor reform movement. Racial inequality therefore reflected the class interests of white workers and was designed to eliminate black encroachment in a context of competitive race relations; (3) once the political alliance and paternalistic bond between blacks and the business classes deteriorated in the face of the Populist challenge, the struggle over the black vote resulted in a united white movement to deprive the Negroes of their political rights; and (4) the racial caste system which encompassed all aspects of black life was solidified both by the ruling class's support of disfranchisement and by the working class's drive (with tacit approval of the ruling classes) toward racial exclusiveness in occupation, education, and political power.

## THE INFLUENCE OF SYSTEMS OF PRODUCTION ON THE INTERGROUP ARENA

If the foregoing summary of the different contexts of racial antagonisms in the postbellum period raises questions about the application of economic class theories such as those advanced by the orthodox Marxists and Edna

Bonacich, they also suggest a more fundamental question, namely, what accounts for the changes in the power resources possessed by antagonistic classes that ultimately determine the direction of racial interaction? I believe that the answer to this question ultimately entails a discussion of the influence of different systems of production on the intergroup arena.

In the southern plantation economy, public power was overwhelmingly concentrated in the hands of the white aristocracy. This power was not only reflected in the control of economic resources, and in the development of a legal system that expressed the class interests of the aristocracy, but also in the way that the aristocracy was able to impose its viewpoint on the larger society (Genovese, 1974). This is not to suggest that these aspects of public power have not been disproportionately controlled by the economic elite in modern industrialized Western societies; rather it indicates that the hegemony of the southern elite had been much greater in degree, not in kind. The latter's hegemony was embodied in an economy that required little horizontal or vertical mobility. Further, because of the absence of those gradations of labor power associated with complex divisions of labor, white workers in the antebellum and early postbellum South had little opportunity to challenge the control of the aristocracy. Because white labor lacked power resources in the southern plantation economy, their influence on the form and quality of racial stratification was minimal throughout the antebellum and early postbellum periods. Racial stratification therefore reflected the relationships which were not characterized by competition for scarce resources, but by the exploitation of black labor. Social distance tended to be clearly symbolized by rituals of racial etiquette, gestures, and behavior reflecting dominance and subservience. Consequently, any effort to impose a system of public segregation was superfluous. Furthermore, ideologies of racial inferiority (i.e., racism) played less of a role in the subordination of blacks than they subsequently did in the more competitive system of race relations following the Reconstruction period (Wilson, 1973). Since the social distance gap between the aristocracy and black slaves was large and stable, racism tended to be subtle and indirect. In short, the relationship represented intergroup paternalism because it allowed for "close symbiosis and even intimacy without any threat to status inequalities" (van den Berghe, 1967: 27). This was in sharp contrast to the more competitive forms of race relations that accompanied the development of industrial capitalism in the last quarter of the nineteenth century and first half of the twentieth century, where the complex division of labor and greater mobility not only produced interaction and competition between blacks and the white working class, but also provided the latter with superior resources (relative to those they possessed in the plantation economy) to exert greater influence on the form and the content of racial stratification in the South.

In short, white working class efforts to eliminate black competition generated an elaborate system of Jim Crow segregation that was reinforced by an ideology of biological racism. The white working class was aided not only by their numerical size, but by their increasing accumulation of political resources that accompanied changes in their relations to the means of production; in other words, by their gradual transformation of increasing labor power into increasing political power.

## NOTES

1  The term "system of production" not only refers to the technological basis of economic processes of, in Karl Marx's terms, the "forces of production," but it also implies the "social relations of production," i.e., "the interaction (for example through employment and property arrangement) into which men enter at a given level of the development of the forces of production" (Smelser, 1973:xiv). According to Smelser, Marx used the notions "forces of production" and "social relations of production" as constituting the "mode of production." However, in Marx's writings the mode of production is often discussed as equivalent only to the "forces of production." To avoid confusion, I have chosen the term "system of production" which denotes the interrelation of the forces of production and the mode of production.

2  Frazier (1957:135) points out that: "The planter and propertied classes did not fail to take advantage of the traditional prejudices of the poor whites and the competition between the latter and the Negro to destroy any cooperation between the two groups. The poor whites were constantly subjected to propaganda concerning supremacy and purity of the white race."

## REFERENCES

*Baran, Paul A., and Paul M. Sweezy*
1966   Monopoly Capital: An Essay on the American Economic and Social Order. Harmondsworth: Penguin.

*Bergman, Peter M.*
1969   The Chronological History of the Negro in America. New York: Harper & Row.

*Bonacich, Edna*
1975   "Split labor markets in the United States 1830–1863." Amer. J. of Sociology 81: 601–628.

1972   "A theory of ethnic antagonism: the split labor market." Amer. Soc. Rev. 37: 547–599.

*Burawoy, Michael*
1974   "Race, class and colonialism." Social and Economic Studies 23: 521–550.

*Cox, Oliver C.*
1948   Caste, Class and Race: A Study in Social Dynamics. Garden City, N.Y.: Doubleday.

*Fogel, Robert W., and S. L. Engerman*
1974   Time on the Cross: The Economics of American Negro Slavery. Boston: Little, Brown.

*Franklin, John Hope*
1967   From Slavery to Freedom: A History of Negro Americans. New York: Knopf.

*Frazier, E. Franklin*
1957   The Negro in the United States. New York: Macmillan.

*Genovese, Eugene D.*
1974   Roll, Jordan, Roll: The World the Slaves Made. New York: Pantheon.

1969   The World the Slaveholders Made: Two Essays in Interpretation. New York: Pantheon.

1966   The Political Economy of Slavery: Studies in the Economy and Society of the Slave South. New York: Pantheon.

*Katznelson, Ira*
1973   "Introduction." Race 14: v–vi.

*Key, V. O.*
1949    Southern Politics in State and Nation. New York: Knopf.
*Marshall, Ray*
1961    "Industrialization and race relations in the southern United States," in Guy Hunter (ed.), Industrialization and Race Relations. London: Oxford Univ. Press.
*Nikolinakos, M.*
1973    "Notes on an economic theory of racism." Race 14: 365–381.
*Owens, Carmen J.*
1973    "Power, racism and coalition politics: a re-examination of the populist movement in Georgia." M.A. thesis, University of Chicago.
*Reich, Michael*
1971    "The economics of racism," in David M. Gordon (ed.), Problems in Political Economy. Lexington, Mass.: D. C. Heath.
*Scruggs, Otis M.*
1971    "The economic and racial components of Jim Crow," in Nathan I. Huggins, Martin Kilson and Daniel M. Fox (eds.), Key Issues in the Afro-American Experience. New York: Harcourt Brace Jovanovich.
*Sivananda, A.*
1973    "Race, class and power: an outline for study." Race 14: 383–391.
*Smelser, Neil J. [ed.]*
1973    Karl Marx on Society and Social Change. Chicago: Univ. of Chicago Press.
*van den Berghe, Pierre L.*
1967    Race and Racism. New York: John Wiley.
*Wilson, William J.*
1973    Power, Racism and Privilege: Race Relations in Theoretical and Socio-historical Perspectives. New York: Macmillan.
*Wolpe, Harold*
1970    "Industrialism and race in South Africa," in Sami Zubaida (ed.), Race and Racialism. London: Tavistock.
*Woodward, C. Vann*
1971    American Counterpoint: Slavery and Racism in the North-South Dialogue. Boston: Little, Brown.
1951    Origins of the New South 1877–1913. Baton Rouge: Louisiana State Univ. Press.
1938    Tom Watson: Agrarian Rebel. New York: Oxford Univ. Press.
*Young, Donald*
1932    American Minority Peoples: A Study in Racial and Cultural Conflicts in the United States. New York: Harper & Row.

# The Cost of Being Black: A 1970 Update *

## Michael P. Johnson
## Ralph R. Sell

*Pennsylvania State University*

*An analysis of U.S. census data regarding race, age, education, occupation, and income of the male experienced civilian labor force in 1960 and 1970 yields four major conclusions. (1) There were large reductions in differences between white and nonwhite occupational distributions at all ages, with the change clearest for young men. (2) The reduction of differences in these distributions is clearest at the lowest and highest educational levels. (3) The absolute gap between nonwhite and white income (in constant dollars) increased. (4) The increased income gap is due in large part to a general upward shift of the labor force into education/occupation categories with a more pronounced income differential by race. Comparisons are made with changes from 1950 to 1960 in order to evaluate recent changes in a broader context.*

In 1965 Paul Siegel reported changes in white-nonwhite occupational and income differentials from 1950 to 1960. A number of similar analyses of changes from 1960 to 1970 have appeared (e.g., Farley and Hermalin 1972: Fox and Faine

*Source:* Michael P. Johnson and Ralph R. Sell, "The Cost of Being Black: A 1970 Update," American Journal of Sociology 82, 1 (July 1976): 183–90. Copyright © 1976 by the University of Chicago. Reprinted by permission.
*This is an abridged version of a paper presented at the annual meeting of the American Sociological Association, San Francisco, August 1975. This version of the paper has benefited from many useful comments of two anonymous *AJS* referees.

1973: Hauser and Featherman 1974), but none have used the decomposition techniques utilized by Siegel to indicate the sources of income differentials and none have compared the changes from 1960 to 1970 with those from 1950 to 1960. The present paper duplicates Siegel's analysis for the 1960–70 decade and presents further evidence concerning some of the hypotheses which he presented concerning the sources of some of the patterns in the data.

## OCCUPATIONAL DISTRIBUTION

Table 1 contains indices of dissimilarity of occupation for four age cohorts by five educational levels. The index (Duncan and Duncan 1955) indicates the proportion of the nonwhite (or white) labor force which would have to change major occupational category in order to equalize the white-nonwhite occupational distribution for each particular age and educational level.

TABLE 1

Indices of Dissimilarity Between White and Nonwhite Occupational Distribution
for Males Aged 25–64 in the United States, 1950, 1960, 1970 by Age and Education

| EDUCATION (YEARS) | AGE (YEARS) | | | |
|---|---|---|---|---|
| | 25–34 | 35–44 | 45–54 | 55–64 |
| 0–7 | | | | |
| 1950 | 26.1 | 28.3 | 28.4 | 30.4 |
| 1960 | 25.1 | 25.9 | 28.8 | 30.4 |
| 1970 | 17.7 | 18.4 | 21.9 | 25.7 |
| 8–11 | | | | |
| 1950 | 29.0 | 34.2 | 36.2 | 33.3 |
| 1960 | 27.4 | 29.8 | 32.0 | 35.1 |
| 1970 | 21.7 | 26.4 | 28.8 | 31.7 |
| 4 high school | | | | |
| 1950 | 33.8 | 39.1 | 40.5 | 36.9 |
| 1960 | 33.4 | 34.1 | 35.8 | 38.7 |
| 1970 | 28.4 | 31.8 | 33.8 | 35.6 |
| 1–3 college | | | | |
| 1950 | 38.8 | 39.5 | 39.3 | 29.2 |
| 1960 | 34.4 | 38.2 | 37.6 | 34.8 |
| 1970 | 27.6 | 32.7 | 37.0 | 36.5 |
| ≥4 college | | | | |
| 1950 | 17.8 | 17.8 | 21.6 | 17.2 |
| 1960 | 18.6 | 19.1 | 18.7 | 19.0 |
| 1970 | 9.9 | 15.8 | 15.9 | 15.0 |

*Sources: U.S. Bureau of the Census 1953, table 11; 1963a, table 8; 1973a, tables 8 and 9.*
*Note: Figures for 1950 are for employed males; those for 1960 and 1970 are for experienced labor force; 1950 and 1960 figures are white-nonwhite comparisons; 1970 ones are black-nonblack.*

**Intercohort Comparisons**

Table 1 allows us to make two kinds of comparisons which can serve as indicators of change. First, intercohort comparisons indicate the extent to which the white-nonwhite occupational distributions have changed from one census year to the next. Of the 20 possible comparisons for the decade from 1950 to 1960, 12 show reductions in occupational differentiation: 19 of the 20 comparisons for the 1960–70 decade show changes in the direction of a more equal distribution. Additionally, in most cases the change from 1960 to 1970 was considerably greater than the corresponding change from 1950 to 1960, a fact that quite possibly reflects greater concern with discriminatory practices during the 1960s.

Siegel noted that in 1950 and 1960 the index of dissimilarity was generally highest for men who had completed some college and dropped fairly dramatically for those who had finished college. The same pattern is clearly present for the 1970 data. Siegel had speculated that the large index of dissimilarity for men with some college was a result of white reluctance to place nonwhites in positions of authority over whites and that nonwhite men with some college education who qualified for just those sorts of managerial positions did not get them, while their white counterparts did. Nonwhites who complete college, on the other hand, are able to move into professional positions where their clientele is more likely to be nonwhite and where they can control the nature of their own employment to a greater extent.

As Table 2 shows, this was clearly the case in 1960. The white-nonwhite difference in participation in the managerial occupations accounted for a large proportion of the differences at the level of both one to three years of college and four or more years of college. For all age categories in those educational groups, the largest difference between white and nonwhite proportions in a major occupational category was for the managerial occupations. For men who had completed only one to three years of college, the occupations in which nonwhites were most overrepresented were the service occupations, with this tendency more pronounced for older men. For men who had completed college, occupational distribution depends even more upon age. As Siegel hypothesized, young college-educated nonwhites are most overrepresented in the professional occupations. For older men the nonwhite overrepresentation seems to be spread fairly evenly among the professional, clerical, and service occupations.

For 1970 (Table 3) the pattern is similar, with greater underrepresentation of blacks in managerial positions for men with one to three years of college than for men who completed college; again blacks are most underepresented in the managerial category in all age groups. In 1970 the blacks with one to three years of college are overrepresented primarily among operatives, with a shift toward service occupations for older men. In 1970 black men who had finished college were only slightly overrepresented in the professions.

Siegel's interpretation of patterns at the upper end of the educational scale fits the data relatively well. The comparative lack of differentiation at the highest educational level is probably due to the ability of men who have finished college to control the nature of their own employment. The 1970 data, however, present us with a new phenomenon: fairly dramatic decreases in occupational differences at the very lowest educational level and only moderate to small changes among men who completed grammar school. Clearly the

## TABLE 2

### Percentage White Minus Percentage Nonwhite in Major Occupational Categories by Age and Education: 1960

| EDUCATION AND AGE (YEARS) | PROFESSIONAL | MANAGERIAL | SALES | CLERICAL | CRAFTS | OPERATIVE | LABOR | FARM | FARM LABOR | SERVICE |
|---|---|---|---|---|---|---|---|---|---|---|
| **0–7** | | | | | | | | | | |
| 25–34 | 00.3 | 01.9 | 01.3 | 00.9 | *11.5* | 09.0 | *-15.7* | -00.7 | -03.8 | -04.7 |
| 35–44 | 00.5 | 03.2 | 01.6 | 00.7 | *14.6* | 05.1 | *-16.7* | 00.3 | -04.0 | -05.1 |
| 45–54 | 00.4 | 03.8 | 01.9 | 01.0 | *15.0* | 05.0 | *-16.1* | 01.8 | -05.0 | -07.2 |
| 55–64 | 00.4 | 04.8 | 02.6 | 01.8 | *15.5* | 03.9 | *-15.9* | 01.3 | -06.7 | -07.9 |
| **8–11** | | | | | | | | | | |
| 25–34 | 01.4 | 04.3 | 03.0 | 00.1 | *15.5* | 00.7 | *-15.4* | 02.5 | -01.6 | -10.4 |
| 35–44 | 01.2 | 05.9 | 03.4 | -00.4 | *15.3* | -03.5 | *-14.8* | 04.0 | -01.1 | -10.0 |
| 45–54 | 01.0 | 08.1 | 03.8 | 00.6 | *13.8* | -03.0 | *-13.5* | 04.7 | -01.4 | -14.2 |
| 55–64 | 00.8 | 08.5 | 05.1 | 01.9 | *13.4* | -04.3 | -12.3 | 05.3 | -02.1 | *-16.5* |
| **4 high school** | | | | | | | | | | |
| 25–34 | 04.0 | 08.9 | 05.7 | -02.9 | *12.5* | -09.5 | *-11.0* | 03.9 | -00.8 | -10.9 |
| 35–44 | 03.7 | *11.1* | 06.2 | -03.7 | 10.2 | -09.0 | -10.0 | 03.0 | -00.7 | *-10.8* |
| 45–54 | 02.6 | *14.8* | 06.8 | -02.1 | 08.0 | -08.2 | -09.1 | 03.6 | -01.2 | *-15.2* |
| 55–64 | 03.6 | *16.1* | 08.4 | -00.2 | 06.9 | -07.7 | -08.5 | 03.6 | -01.0 | *-21.3* |
| **1–3 college** | | | | | | | | | | |
| 25–34 | 08.2 | *12.1* | 09.9 | -08.2 | 02.9 | -09.7 | -06.4 | 01.3 | -00.3 | *-09.9* |
| 35–44 | 07.2 | *18.1* | 10.6 | -08.6 | 00.7 | -10.7 | -06.8 | 01.6 | -00.6 | *-11.7* |
| 45–54 | 06.3 | *19.7* | 09.9 | -08.3 | 00.1 | -08.2 | -04.8 | 01.6 | -00.1 | *-16.4* |
| 55–64 | 04.8 | *21.1* | 07.5 | -04.5 | -01.1 | -06.6 | -06.8 | 01.5 | -01.0 | *-15.1* |
| **≥4 college** | | | | | | | | | | |
| 25–34 | *-08.4* | *09.2* | 07.7 | -03.9 | 01.0 | -02.0 | -01.1 | 00.6 | -00.0 | -03.0 |
| 35–44 | *-04.5* | *12.4* | 06.0 | -06.0 | 00.3 | -02.8 | -01.7 | 00.4 | -00.3 | -04.0 |
| 45–54 | *-04.2* | *13.5* | 04.7 | -05.2 | -00.7 | -02.3 | -02.2 | 00.5 | -00.1 | -04.1 |
| 55–64 | -03.4 | *14.4* | 04.3 | -03.7 | 00.4 | -02.7 | -02.6 | 00.0 | -00.1 | *-06.6* |

Source: U.S. Bureau of the Census 1963a, table 8.

Note: For example, out of a total of 815,992 white 25–34-year-old workers with 0–7 years of education, 5,960 or 0.7% are in professional occupations. For nonwhites the total is 280,542, with 989 or 0.4% similarly classified. This table and table 3 report the differences, e.g., .7−.4 = .3%. The largest positive and negative differences in each row are in italics.

## TABLE 3

### Percentage Nonblack Minus Percentage Black in Major Occupational Categories by Age and Education: 1970

| EDUCATION AND AGE (YEARS) | PROFESSIONAL | MANAGERIAL | SALES | CLERICAL | CRAFTS | OPERATIVE | LABOR | FARM | FARM LABOR | SERVICE |
|---|---|---|---|---|---|---|---|---|---|---|
| **0–7** | | | | | | | | | | |
| 25–34 | 00.6 | 02.0 | 01.1 | 00.0 | 10.6 | 03.2 | −10.8 | 00.2 | −04.1 | −02.8 |
| 35–44 | 00.6 | 02.9 | 01.4 | 00.4 | 11.7 | 00.5 | −11.6 | 01.0 | −02.7 | −04.1 |
| 45–54 | 00.7 | 03.4 | 01.5 | 00.4 | 11.8 | 02.0 | −13.1 | 02.1 | −03.1 | −05.7 |
| 55–64 | 00.6 | 03.9 | 02.2 | 01.0 | 13.2 | 01.5 | −14.4 | 03.3 | −03.4 | −07.9 |
| **8–11** | | | | | | | | | | |
| 25–34 | 00.9 | 03.7 | 02.1 | −01.3 | 13.7 | −04.1 | −08.6 | 01.3 | −01.2 | −06.4 |
| 35–44 | 01.3 | 05.8 | 02.7 | −00.8 | 13.9 | −07.9 | −08.8 | 02.7 | −00.7 | −08.2 |
| 45–54 | 01.1 | 06.5 | 03.3 | −00.6 | 13.7 | −06.6 | −10.4 | 04.1 | −00.7 | −10.5 |
| 55–64 | 01.2 | 07.0 | 04.3 | 00.0 | 13.7 | −05.7 | −10.5 | 05.5 | −00.7 | −14.8 |
| **4 high school** | | | | | | | | | | |
| 25–34 | 04.1 | 06.2 | 03.9 | −03.3 | 12.0 | −13.3 | −05.7 | 02.1 | 00.1 | −06.0 |
| 35–44 | 03.5 | 10.2 | 04.8 | −03.2 | 09.9 | −13.4 | −06.8 | 03.5 | −00.1 | −08.3 |
| 45–54 | 03.9 | 11.3 | 06.6 | −04.2 | 08.7 | −11.4 | −07.4 | 03.3 | 00.0 | −10.8 |
| 55–64 | 03.4 | 12.9 | 07.9 | −00.6 | 07.3 | −09.7 | −08.0 | 04.1 | −00.3 | −16.9 |
| **1–3 college** | | | | | | | | | | |
| 25–34 | 07.1 | 09.3 | 06.8 | −07.8 | 02.8 | −11.9 | −03.3 | 01.2 | 00.3 | −04.7 |
| 35–44 | 06.8 | 14.9 | 08.9 | −09.7 | 00.7 | −11.0 | −04.0 | 01.4 | −00.1 | −07.9 |
| 45–54 | 08.2 | 16.7 | 10.2 | −08.5 | −01.8 | −11.0 | −04.1 | 01.9 | −00.3 | −11.3 |
| 55–64 | 07.0 | 17.6 | 09.8 | −06.5 | −02.2 | −07.8 | −05.1 | 01.9 | −00.7 | −14.4 |
| **≥ 4 college** | | | | | | | | | | |
| 25–34 | −01.8 | 04.7 | 04.6 | −01.7 | −01.2 | −02.7 | −00.8 | 00.6 | 00.1 | −01.6 |
| 35–44 | −03.6 | 09.2 | 06.3 | −03.6 | −02.2 | −02.2 | −01.1 | 00.3 | 00.0 | −03.0 |
| 45–54 | 00.3 | 09.4 | 05.6 | −05.0 | −02.0 | −03.2 | −01.3 | 00.6 | 00.0 | −04.4 |
| 55–64 | 00.5 | 07.7 | 05.6 | −03.7 | −02.1 | −02.8 | −02.3 | 01.2 | −00.4 | −03.8 |

Source: U.S. Bureau of the Census 1973a, table 8.

Note: The largest positive and negative differences in each row are in italics.

problem here cannot be related to differences between employment processes for managers and professionals. The data for the two lowest educational levels (Tables 2 and 3) suggest the possibility that these differences are related to union control of craft and operative occupational categories. Proportionately more blacks entered the operative occupational category during the 1960s than during the preceding decade, but blacks continued to be excluded from the craft occupations. It would appear, then, that policies to reduce occupational discrimination among men who have not attended college will depend primarily upon the success of efforts directed at the craft occupations, while efforts to produce change within the upper educational levels must be aimed at managerial occupations.

The pattern of change by age is as one might have expected. From 1960 to 1970 the major changes at all educational levels are among the younger groups of men (Table 1), particularly those aged 25–34. This was not the case for the 1950–60 decade and seems to indicate that antidiscrimination programs are having their major impact on young men who are just entering the labor force.

### Intracohort Comparisons

A second major type of comparison which can be derived from Table 1 is comparison of occupational differences among the same group of men in each census year. Nine of the 15 possible intracohort comparisons showed improvement for the 1950–60 decade, while all 15 showed improvement for the more recent time period. Compared with the intercohort comparisons, however, these intracohort changes are relatively small. The most significant changes in occupational distributions are at young ages when men first enter the labor force.

### INCOME DISTRIBUTION

The second major section of Siegel's article dealt with income inequality within major occupational categories, educational levels, and regions of the country. Following Siegel's methodology, white-nonwhite income differentials were decomposed: results are presented in Table 4. In order to allow decade comparisons, the data analyzed by Siegel were converted to 1969 dollars and the decomposition was recomputed. A conversion ratio of 1.26 times the 1959 income was utilized, reflecting the corresponding change in the consumer price index.

Looking first at changes within educational categories, we find that (1) at all educational levels there has been a decrease in that portion of the white-nonwhite income differential which is due to differences in position in the occupational and regional structure of the nation, and (2) there has been a decrease in income differences *within* occupational and regional categories for men who have at least finished high school. Although it is somewhat discouraging to note the increased net differences at the lower educational levels, the percentage of the labor force who did not complete high school decreased

TABLE 4

Decomposition of White-Nonwhite Mean Income Differences
(in 1969 dollars)

| YEARS OF EDUCATION AND YEAR | NONWHITE WHITE | TOTAL DIFFERENCE | COMPOSITION* | NET |
|---|---|---|---|---|
| 0-8: | | | | |
| 1959 | .62 | 2,137 | 1,059 | 1,078 |
| 1969 | .70 | 2,102 | 979 | 1,123 |
| 1-3 high school: | | | | |
| 1959 | .63 | 2,557 | 952 | 1,605 |
| 1969 | .70 | 2,612 | 906 | 1,706 |
| 4 high school: | | | | |
| 1959 | .64 | 2,803 | 1,035 | 1,768 |
| 1969 | .72 | 2,618 | 880 | 1,738 |
| 1-3 college: | | | | |
| 1959 | .58 | 4,023 | 1,812 | 2,211 |
| 1969 | .69 | 3,357 | 1,233 | 2,124 |
| ≥4 college: | | | | |
| 1959 | .55 | 5,744 | 965 | 4,779 |
| 1969 | .71 | 4,459 | 761 | 3,698 |
| All educational levels: | | | | |
| 1959 | .53 | 3,587 | 2,207 | 1,380 |
| 1969 | .63 | 3,708 | 2,034 | 1,674 |

Sources: U.S. Bureau of the Census, 1963b, tables 2 and 3; 1973b, tables 3 and 4.
*Within educational levels composition is the part of the difference due to differential representation in major occupational categories and regions of the country. For "all educational levels" composition also includes the portion of the difference due to differential access to education.

for both whites and nonwhites during the 1960–70 decade, from 53% to 39% for whites and from 77% to 63% for nonwhites (see Table 5).

This shift upward in educational level for both whites and nonwhites is responsible for a phenomenon which Siegel predicted on the basis of his previous analysis. In spite of a general reduction in white-nonwhite income differences within educational levels, the overall gap between white and nonwhite income has *increased* during the 1960–70 decade. Although nonwhite income expressed as a proportion of white income has increased, suggesting improvement in the situation in one sense, the decomposition in the last row of Table 4 indicates that while the differences due to white-nonwhite social position in terms of education, occupation, and region of the country have decreased, the labor force has shifted upward to an educational level at which the gap between whites and nonwhites within educational levels, occupational categories, and regions of the country is large. The increase during the decade in the total difference between white and nonwhite income is due to the increase in what Siegel characterized as "the cost of being Negro." In 1969 dollars, the fee for being black was $1,380 in 1959 and $1,647 in 1969.

TABLE 5

Educational Attainment of White and Nonwhite Males
in Experienced Civilian Labor Force: 1960 and 1970

| YEAR AND GROUP | YEARS OF EDUCATION | | | | | |
|---|---|---|---|---|---|---|
| | 0–8 | 1–3 HS | 4 HS | 1–3 C | ≥4 C | D* |
| 1960: | | | | | | |
| White | .32 | .21 | .25 | .10 | .12 | 26.0 |
| Nonwhite | .58 | .19 | .14 | .05 | .04 | — |
| 1970: | | | | | | |
| White | .20 | .19 | .32 | .12 | .17 | 22.5 |
| Nonwhite | .37 | .25 | .24 | .08 | .07 | — |

Sources: U.S. Bureau of the Census, 1963b, table 1; 1973b, table 1.
*Duncan's index of dissimilarity.

## REFERENCES

Duncan, O. D., and B. Duncan
1955   "A Methodological Analysis of Segregation Indices." *American Sociological Review* 20 (April): 210–17.
Farley, R., and A. Hermalin
1972   "The 1960's: A Decade of Progress for Blacks?" *Demography* 9 (August): 353–70.
Fox, W. S., and J. R. Faine.
1973   "Trends in White-Nonwhite Income Equality." *Sociology and Social Research* 57 (April): 288–99.
Hauser, R. M., and D. L. Featherman.
1974   "White-Nonwhite Differentials in Occupational Mobility among Men in the United States, 1962–1972." *Demography* 11 (May): 247–65.
Siegel, P. M.
1965   "On the Cost of Being a Negro." *Sociological Inquiry* 35 (Winter): 41–57.
U.S. Bureau of the Census.
1953   *U.S. Census of Population: 1950. Education.* Vol. 4. Special Report 5B. Washington, D.C.: U.S. Government Printing Office.
1963a   *U.S. Census of Population: 1960. Educational Attainment.* Subject Report PC(2)-5B. Washington, D.C.: U.S. Government Printing Office.
1963b   *U.S. Census of Population: 1960. Occupation by Earnings and Education.* Subject Report PC(2)-7B. Washington, D.C.: U.S. Government Printing Office.
1973a   *U.S. Census of Population: 1970. Occupational Characteristics.* Subject Report PC(2)-7A. Washington, D.C.: U.S. Government Printing Office.
1973b   *U.S. Census of Population: 1970. Earnings by Occupation and Education.* Subject Report PC(2)-8B. Washington, D.C.: U.S. Government Printing Office.

# FOUR

## PATTERNS OF DISCRIMINATION AGAINST WOMEN

*The purpose in this section on women, as it was in Part Three, is to aid the understanding of patterned discrimination. How does systematic discrimination against women operate, and what are its consequences? How and when did American women become restricted to the roles of housewife and mother, and how did the ideology arise that has supported such relatively complete accommodation to this subordinate status throughout the social organization? The paper on sex-role stereotyping of women and occupations in Part Two, and the two on the women's movement in Part Six, also help provide answers to such questions.*

*The social class position of the married woman has long been determined mainly by her husband's occupation. However, in the first selection in this section, Nilson reports that her interviewees in Milwaukee took the occupations of husband and wife into account about equally in hypothetical determinations of a wife's social standing, with some variations. In identifying their personal class standing, according to a study based on data from four election surveys from 1960 to 1970, married women gave about as much weight to their own occupational attainments as to those of their husbands (Ritter and Hargens, 1975).*

*If Nilson's findings are representative of the society, it appears that new measures of class rank are overdue. The majority of married women are now in the labor force, and the percentage is rising. Sociologists have used data on the occupation, income, and education of the "male head of household" to measure the class standing of the entire household. Students of stratification usually have defined social classes as rankings of families. Evidently it is time for sociologists (and the United States Bureau of the Census) to consider the person to be the basic unit in the class system rather than the family (Acker, 1973). If a measure of the class standing of the household is desired, Nilson's findings suggest a status-sharing index, combining the statuses of its members.*

*The origin of the traditional status of women in American society is not lost in the mists of time. The selection by Easton documents the great changes in relationships between males and females attending industrial development during the nineteenth century. She emphasizes the ways males used their power to prevent alternative developments and to enforce the domestic positions of housewife and mother, and the shaping of sexist beliefs into an ideology of femininity to justify the rightness of the subordinate status of women. Another study documents parallel developments in France during the same century (Silver, 1973).*

*In her contribution, Huber deals with the impact of the technological revolution, stressing especially male control of the distribution of resources outside the home. She analyzes the ways in which public education, governmental policies, unionization, and other institutional developments became enmeshed in the pattern of female subordination. She notes factors responsible for the reentry of women into the labor force, and the way women were channeled into certain kinds of work and restricted to a limited set of rewards in the male-dominated world of occupations (see also, Epstein, 1973; 1976). While stressing these effects of industrialization, Huber rejects the view that the subordinate status of women is a peculiarly capitalistic product.*

*Census data for 1970 are used in the selection by Long to investigate relationships between family mobility and the wife's employment outside the home. It appears that the migration of husbands takes priority over that of wives, and that this helps maintain patterns of sex discrimination in pay. An analysis based on the 1960 census showed a direct relationship between the economic attainment of women and remaining unmarried (Havens, 1973). It appears that marriage has hampered the career success of women, and Long's results suggest that a major factor in this is family moving to forward the career of the husband. It may also be that some successful women have avoided marriage partly because of expectations about the husband's mobility.*

*Hong's analysis indicates major changes in the status of women in today's China, but the survival of some of the traditional differentiation in sex roles in the family, and considerable economic and political inequality between the sexes. While attributing some of the resistance to change to the difficulty of eliminating the ancestral cult, and the traditional kinship system, he emphasizes the central role of the concepts of yin and yang. Ideological forces, both old and new, are apparently at the center of Chinese developments in the status of women (Record and Record, 1976).*

## REFERENCES

*Acker, Joan*
1973  "Women and Social Stratification: The case of Intellectual Sexism." American Journal of Sociology 78 (January): 936–45.
*Epstein, Cynthia*
1973  "Positive Effects of the Multiple Negative: Explaining the Success of Black Professional Women." American Journal of Sociology 78, 4 (January): 912–35.
1976  "Sex Roles," Chapter 9 in Robert K. Merton and Robert Nisbet, Contemporary Social Problems. New York: Harcourt Brace Jovanovich.
*Hacker, Helen Mayer*
1951  "Women as a Minority Group." Social Forces 30 (October): 60–69.
*Havens, Elizabeth M.*
1973  "Women, Work, and Wedlock: A Note on Female Marital Patterns in the United States." American Journal of Sociology 78, 4 (January): 975–81.
*Record, Jane Cassels, and Wilson Record*
1976  "Totalist and Pluralist Views of Women's Liberation: Some Reflections on the Chinese and American Settings." Social Problems 23, 4 (April): 402–14.
*Ritter, Kathleen V., and Lowell L. Hargens*
1975  "Occupational Positions and Class Identifications of Married Working Women: A Test of the Asymmetry Hypothesis." American Journal of Sociology 80, 4 (January): 934–48.
*Silver, Catherine Bodard*
1973.  "Salon, Foyer, Bureau: Women and the Professions in France." American Journal of Sociology 78, 4 (January): 836–51.

# The Social Standing of a Married Woman[*]

## Linda Burzotta Nilson

*Department of Sociology*
*University of California, Los Angeles*

*The traditional manner of designating a married woman's social status by her husband's occupational attainment is questioned, and a framework is proposed for reconceptualizing a married woman's social standing in terms of both her own and her husband's occupational attainments. The results of a Milwaukee area survey of a random sample of adults reveal that persons take both a wife's and a husband's occupational attainments into approximately equal account in an additive way in evaluating her social standing. However, as the husband's status declines, when she is a housewife, and when the wife's occupational level equals or exceeds her husband's, she has slightly less status self-determination. Variations in the accordance of status determination between husband and wife by respondents' sex are also examined.*

Source: Linda Burzotta Nilson, "The Social Standing of a Married Woman," Social Problems 23, 5 (June 1976): 581–92. Copyright © 1976 by the Society for the Study of Social Problems. Reprinted by permission of the Society and the author.
*This research was partially funded by The Small Grants Committee of the Department of Sociology, University of Wisconsin-Madison. The author wishes to thank William H. Sewell, Archibald O. Haller, and Warren O. Hagstrom for their helpful suggestions and advice. Responsibility for any error is her own. A similar version of this paper was presented at the annual meetings of the Pacific Sociological Association in Victoria, B. C., April, 1975.

# INTRODUCTION

Sociologists have traditionally treated a woman's social standing, i.e., the community's evaluation of her status, within the context of the family as the unit of social stratification. Family socioeconomic status is typically measured by head-of-household's occupation, income and/or education, which are usually those of the father or the husband. A woman's status is assumed to be determined originally by her father and later by her husband (Parsons, 1953; Davis, 1949; Williams, 1951; Barber, 1957; Turner, 1964; Wallace, 1966). Recent empirical research reveals at least two major problems with the traditional family-centered framework. First, this approach masks the independent effects of the mother on children's status attainments. Under many conditions her effects are considerable (Cohen, 1958; Krauss, 1964; Sewell and Shah, 1968). The wife is gainfully employed in 37 percent of all intact American families (U.S. Department of Labor, 1969:10–23), and she brings extra economic and experiential resources for the socioeconomic attainment of her children.

Second, the assumption that the mother has no independent effect on her children's mobility is based on the erroneous and circular argument that like-marries-like and thereby transmits consistent status socialization to offspring (Davis, 1949; Parsons, 1953). But like does not always marry like. While most married couples have similar status backgrounds, 25 percent of all wives have a higher educational level than their husbands, especially in older age groups. In about one-third of all dual working families, especially in the working class, the wife has a social class level, measured by education and occupation, higher than her husband (Haug, 1973:91–92). If occupational roles are grouped into eight census categories that rank roughly according to prestige, then employed spouses rank equally in only 22 percent of the cases. The wife outranks her husband in 42 percent, and he outranks her in 36 percent. In over one-fourth of the cases the difference between spouses is three levels or more (Barth and Watson, 1964). Thus the family once may have been a practical and meaningful unit of stratification before married women poured into the labor force during this century. But it no longer can serve this purpose adequately. The increasing acceptability of the working wife and her greater accessibility to jobs confer on the woman a greater responsibility and a clearer basis for her own status evaluation in the society.

The recent approach of Rossi et al. (1974) to measure household social standing uses the family as the unit of stratification while circumventing the major problems involved in past studies. The Rossi study presented raters with a series of vignettes describing households in terms of both the husband's and the wife's educational levels and occupations. Respondents rated the social standing of each hypothetical household on a nine-point scale. In this study, husband's occupation was found to count about one-and-a-half times the wife's occupation and his education twice as much as hers in determining household social standing. These results raise considerable doubt about the traditional assumption that the social evaluation of the family members is determined by that of the husband. The Rossi et al. results indicate that the wife's contribution is also important.

What then are the determinants of a woman's social standing, specifically that of a married woman? The issue has been raised (Duncan, 1961; Acker, 1973; DeJong et al., 1971), but thus far only Felson and Knoke (1974) have researched the social status of a married woman. They defined the issue in terms of the weight a married woman gives to her own educational and occupational achievements vis-à-vis those of her husband and her father in her subjective class placement. Their partitioning of the variance procedure revealed that their sample of married women attached little importance to their own status accomplishments in their class identification, whether or not they worked. Male head-of-household characteristics and combined family income had the strongest direct effects. Their findings tend to favor the status-borrowing model of female status attainment which proposes that a woman borrows her status from her father or husband, over the status-sharing model, which hypothesizes that a married woman's status is a combined product of her own and her husband's status accomplishments.

Felson and Knoke's study does not address itself to social standing of women as evaluated by members of the community. And given their alternatives for subjective class placement—lower-class, working-class, middle-class, and upper-class—the major distinction to be made by respondents was between working-class and middle-class. Housewives presumably judge their status on the basis of their husband's. Dual working families in which both spouses have either blue-collar or white-collar employment, about 62 percent of such families (Barth and Watson, 1964), do not allow the separate effects of the husband and the wife on her subjective class placement to be clearly distinguished. So the choices of the greatest research interest are those of wives in dual working families in which one marital partner is employed in a blue-collar occupation and the other in a white-collar job. Probably these cases were also a minority in Felson and Knoke's sample and provided much of the basis for their findings.

Whether the issue is the social standing of individuals or of households, occupation seems to be the most effective single indicator of status evaluation; its effect outweighs or encapsulates the effects of income and education (Reiss, 1961; Rossi et al., 1974). In the present study, community evaluations are made of the social standing of a married woman in fifty-six hypothetical marital-occupational situations. Our intention is to separate out the independent effects of the husband's occupation and the wife's occupation in determining the wife's social standing. We expect that social standing will be accorded to a married woman as a basically additive function of both her husband's and her own occupations, with each given comparable but not necessarily the same weight. The increasing employment of married women in an ever wider variety of occupations and the clear effect that the wife has on household social standing provide some support for this hypothesis.

## THE DESIGN OF THE STUDY

The telephone survey on which this study is based was conducted on a random sample of 479 adults in the Milwaukee area during the summer of 1974 by the Wisconsin Survey Research Laboratory. Milwaukee was the nineteenth largest standard metropolitan area in the U.S. in 1970 (U.S. Bureau of the Census, 1972:189). Thus, a sample of the Milwaukee area has the advantage of assuring a wide distribution of respondents on age educational attainment, income, and type of employment. A computer program randomly generated 1700 possible Milwaukee area telephone numbers. Only residential numbers that were in service and were answered when called six or fewer times were used for the 15-minute telephone interviews. Given that about 95 percent of the Milwaukee area residents have telephones, and given our response rate of 67.5 percent, the final sample of responses effectively represents .95 × 67.5 of the Milwaukee area population, or 62.22 percent.[1]

The occupations in the husband-wife combinations to be evaluated were selected on the basis of their wide distribution across the prestige spectrum. Refer to Table 1. Respondents were asked to evaluate the wife's social standing as "Excellent," "Above average," "Average," "Below average," or "Less." The fifty-six marital-occupational combinations were grouped according to the wife's occupation, an arrangement which reduced respondent fatigue. In addition, this procedure may have helped to prevent the results from being an artifact of the form of the survey questions. Husband's occupation changed randomly, after the wife's occupation was specified. Thus attention was called to his attainment.[2] Social standing scores for each marital-occupational combination are computed as a weighted frequency average of all ratings in the same way that NORC prestige scores were obtained for occupations (Reiss, 1961).

In order to discern the independent effects of a husband's and wife's occupational attainments on community evaluations of her social standing, we will regress the wife's social standing scores across marital-occupational situations $(Y)$ on the husband's occupational standing scores $(X_H)$, i.e., the social standing scores accorded a man in the occupations, and on the wife's occupational standing scores $(X_W)$, i.e., the social standing scores accorded a woman in the occupations. (See Table 1.) The additive model is expressed in equation 1.

$$Y = B_{X_H}X_H + B_{X_W}X_W$$

We use standardized regression coefficients because we want to assess the relative strength of the effects of husband's occupation and wife's occupation on her social standing. The standardized coefficients will not distort our results because (1) the correlations between $X_H$ and $X_W$ are zero across all respondent subgroups and (2) their means and standard deviations are very much the same across all subgroups. However, since their means and variances are partially a product of the design, attention will also be given to the unstandardized regression coefficients. Coefficients in equation 1 will be obtained for all marital-occupational situations, for those in which the husband has higher occupational standing than his wife (husband-higher), and for those in which the wife's occupational standing equals or exceeds her husband's (wife-higher). The term status determination will be used to indicate the effect of the husband's or the wife's occupational standing on the wife's social standing.

Unstandardized regression coefficients will be used to discern how the wife's relative amount of status determination varies with her husband's occupational standing. The direction and degree of this dependency can be found by obtaining the slope of the wife's effect, with interaction, as the first-order derivative of Y with respect to $X_W$ in the equation below.

TABLE 1

Prestige Scores for the Selected Occupations and Social Standing Scores
for a Man and a Woman in the Selected Occupations

| | NORC PRESTIGE SCORE[a] | SIEGEL'S METRIC SCORE[b] | SOCIAL STANDING FOR MAN[c] | SOCIAL STANDING FOR WOMAN[c] |
|---|---|---|---|---|
| Physician | 93 | 82 | 91 | 90 |
| Civil Engineer | 86 | 67 | 81 | 79 |
| Public Grade School Teacher | — | 60 | 73 | 79 |
| Bookkeeper | 70 | 47 | 68 | 73 |
| Plumber | 65 | 40 | 74 | 66 |
| Assembly Line Worker | — | 27 | 58 | 56 |
| Janitor/Janitress | 48 | 16 | 54 | 51 |
| Housewife | — | — | — | 69 |

[a] Hodge, Siegel, and Rossi (1964). The NORC studies asked respondents to give their "idea of the general social standing" of ninety occupations. No information about the sex of the incumbent was given.

[b] Siegel's (1971) scores are metric transformations of scores from several prestige studies, including NORC. Some of the scores given are the average of the metric scores from more than one study. Siegel calculated that at least four point differences are significant at the .05 level. Occupations selected here differ in prestige by even greater distance.

[c] Respondents were also asked to give their evaluation of the "general social standing" of a man or a woman in the selected occupations. None of the other prestige studies above specified sex of incumbent. The details of this social standing study and score differences by sex of incumbent in other occupations may be found in Nilson (1976). This study generally supports the hypothesis that scores for women are higher than for men in female-stereotyped occupations and scores for men are slightly higher in male-typed occupations. These social standing scores are used here as occupational standing scores for the hypothetical husbands and wives in marital-occupational situations.

$$Y = a + b_{X_H}X_H + b_{X_W}X_W + b_{X_HX_W}X_HX_W$$

$$\frac{\partial Y}{\partial X_W} = b_{X_W} + b_{X_HX_W}X_H$$

Two interpretations of the coefficients in equation 2 are possible. First, if $b_{X_HX_W}$ is positive, then the higher the $X_H$, the husband's occupational standing, the higher the slope, i.e., the stronger the effect of the wife on her social standing. So as the husband's occupational standing rises, the wife's degree status determination does also. If $b_{X_HX_W}$ is negative, then the higher the $X_H$, the lower the slope. In other words, as the husband's standing rises, the wife's status determination drops.

Since $b_{X_HX_W}$ measures the effect of the multiplicative combination of the spouses' occupational standings on the wife's social standing, another interpretation of the values in equation 2 is possible. If husband's occupational level, $X_H$, is held constant, $b_{X_HX_W}$ indicates the effect of a change in the wife's occupational standing on the change in her social standing relative to her occupational level. Thus if $b_{X_HX_W}$ is positive, a change in her occupational standing has a greater effect on her social standing as her occupational standing rises. But if the coefficient is negative, a change in the wife's occupational standing loses effect on her social standing as her occupational standing rises.

Values in equation 2 will be obtained for all marital-occupational situations, for husband-higher situations, and for wife-higher situations, although since the latter two sets have fewer cases in the regression, the coefficients will have lower reliability.

It will also be important to repeat the above data analysis separately for male and female respondents, after doing it for all respondents. It is possible that men and women accord social standing to a married woman in somewhat different ways.

Great care must be taken in assessing these data, however, as the degree of multicollinearity present appreciably increases the standard errors of the regression coefficients. Correlations between the interaction term and $X_H$ or $X_W$ run .687 and over and are higher in the husband-higher and wife-higher situations than over all marital-occupational situations. We may be confident in our interpretation of them only when it is consonant with the initial regression analysis in equation 1.

## RESULTS

Table 2 displays the regression coefficients which indicate the effects of the husband's occupational standing $(X_H)$ and the wife's occupational standing $(X_W)$ on respondents' assessments of the wife's social standing.[3] Let us first consider the results from all respondents. It is first apparent that both the standardized and unstandardized regression coefficients are of comparable value for the husband's and the wife's effect, no matter which spouse has the higher occupational standing. In fact, the coefficients for the wife's effect are usually slightly higher than those for the husband's effect. *If there is one conclusion to be drawn, it is that the husband's occupational status alone does not determine the social standing evaluations given to the wife by this sample of adults.* These results make the assertion that a woman is simply accorded the status of her husband quite untenable.

The men and women in the sample apparently use similar criteria in making their evaluations of the social standing of a married woman. Over all marital-occupational situations, both sexes give about equal weight to the occupational standings of husband and wife, as indicated by the comparable values of the standardized and unstandardized regression coefficients in Table 2. However, in the husband-higher situations, the men give about twice as much status determination to the wife as to her husband; the size of the wife's coefficient, whether standardized or unstandardized, is approximately twice the size of the husband's. The women, on the other hand, take both the husband's and the wife's occupational attainments into about equal account in assessing her social standing. In the wife-higher situations, the wife's occupational standing has a slightly greater effect on her social standing than does her husband's when men make the evaluations, while the reverse is true when women make the status assessments. With the exception of the social status ratings given by the men in the husband-higher situations, it is evident that

TABLE 2

Regression of Wife's Social Standing (Y) on Husband's ($X_H$) and Wife's ($X_W$)
Occupational Standing, by All Respondents, by Men and by Women[b]

| | ALL RESPONDENTS | | | | | |
|---|---|---|---|---|---|---|
| | *ALL H-W COMB.* | | *H > W* | | *W ⩾ H* | |
| Variable | b | B | b | B | b | B |
| $X_H$ | .487[a] | .635[a] | .426[a] | .459[a] | .495[a] | .510[a] |
| $X_W$ | .541[a] | .713[a] | .574[a] | .640[a] | .580[a] | .610[a] |
| | Constant −4.118 | | Constant −1.250 | | Constant −7.917 | |
| | F-value 270.33[a] | | F-value 161.83[a] | | F-value 103.81[a] | |
| | $N = 56$ | | $N = 30$ | | $N = 26$ | |
| | $R^2 = .907$ | | $R^2 = .917$ | | $R^2 = .892$ | |
| | MEN | | | | | |
| Variable | b | B | b | B | b | B |
| $X_H$ | .440[a] | .583[a] | .341[a] | .347[a] | .413[a] | .468[a] |
| $X_W$ | .535[a] | .722[a] | .644[a] | .719[a] | .535[a] | .587[a] |
| | Constant .004 | | Constant 1.284 | | Constant 1.276 | |
| | F-value 161.05[a] | | F-value 135.25[a] | | F-value 55.82[a] | |
| | $N = 56$ | | $N = 25$ | | $N = 31$ | |
| | $R^2 = .853$ | | $R^2 = .918$ | | $R^2 = .785$ | |
| | WOMEN | | | | | |
| Variable | b | B | b | B | b | B |
| $X_H$ | .513[a] | .661[a] | .457[a] | .572[a] | .582[a] | .597[a] |
| $X_W$ | .489[a] | .685[a] | .440[a] | .529[a] | .531[a] | .517[a] |
| | Constant −2.713 | | Constant 4.650 | | Constant −10.657 | |
| | F-value 257.91[a] | | F-value 101.52[a] | | F-value 183.69[a] | |
| | $N = 56$ | | $N = 29$ | | $N = 27$ | |
| | $R^2 = .903$ | | $R^2 = .878$ | | $R^2 = .934$ | |

[a] *Statistically significant at the .01 level.*
[b] *The reader is cautioned not to regard the results of the tests of significance too seriously because of the systematic attrition of the sample.*

both men and women base their status evaluations of a married woman on both her husband's and her own occupational positions.

In Table 3, we see the wife's social standing scores computed from the ratings of all respondents, to observe the variations in scores across husband-wife occupational combinations more closely. These scores are not new data but merely the components of the regression analysis in Table 2 for all respondents. First, we can see that, with the elimination of the housewife column at the far right, scores descend from the top left corner to the bottom right, as prestige studies would lead us to predict. The score tables of male and female respondents follow the same pattern. The scores tend to decline down the columns and across the rows from left to right at comparable rates. If the husband were primary in determining the wife's social standing, there would be little variation across the rows, and almost all the variation would take place down the columns. If the wife were clearly dominant, there would be little variation down the columns, and almost all the variation would occur across the rows.

We can see the validity of the status-sharing hypothesis of female status attainment in the large degree of variation both across rows and down columns.

Housewife, we have noted, is a relatively respected position for a married woman, comparable in status to a good white-collar occupation. As the husband's occupational standing varies, two important findings come to light. First, the scores of a housewife are more dependent on the husband's standing than the scores of a gainfully employed married woman. The social standing of the housewife drops in point value at a faster rate than the social standing of an employed wife as her husband's occupational standing declines. From the situation in which she is married to a physician to the situation in which she is married to a janitor, the social standing of the housewife drops 29 points. For a wife who is employed, the point drop between the situation in which the husband is a physician to the situation in which he is a janitor averages 16 points in Table 3. Second, the higher the occupational standing of the husband, the higher the social standing of the housewife relative to the social standing of women employed in gainful occupations, that is, the higher the prestige of the occupation she must have in order to gain social standing via employment. Having an occupation outside the home is certainly no guarantee of enhanced status for a woman. Felson and Knoke (1974) found, more extremely, that employment adds nothing to the subjective status of a married woman and may even detract from it.

Changes in the housewife's social standing may reflect people's evaluations of the home production functions she performs according to her husband's income. As his income rises, the housewife presumably purchases more of the services and mechanical conveniences which increase her productivity of time-usage, particularly in the highly regarded area of child-rearing. She thus obtains increasing social standing for mechanizing and contracting housework functions while developing the more creative roles of hostess, home decorator, and mother.

The way a wife's status determination is dependent upon her husband's occupational standing is evident by the values of $b_{X_H X_W}$ in Table 4. We must be careful to draw only tentative conclusions here because of multicollinearity problems. None of the values are statistically significant at even the .05 level, but our interest is only in the signs, not in the size of the interaction, which is small (see note 3). The value of the coefficient is positive in the regression of the scores of all respondents, the men, and the women over all of the marital-occupational situations. So to a small degree a wife's status self-determination seems to increase as her husband's occupational standing rises. In the husband-higher situations, the men and women diverge, however. The unstandardized interaction coefficient is again positive with respect to the social standing evaluations of the women, but it is negative to those of the men. In the evaluations of the men, then, the higher the occupational standing of the man a woman marries, the smaller her contribution to her own social standing. While the respondents as a whole seem to accord a wife a slightly greater role in her own status determination as her husband's occupational attainments rise in the wife-higher situations, as indicated by the positive $b_{X_H X_W}$, the men do so to a greater degree than do the women.

The unstandardized interaction coefficient tells how varying the wife's occupational level affects her social standing. A reexamination of Table 4 shows that, with the exception of the men's ratings of the husband-higher situations,

**TABLE 3**

**Social Standing Scores Accorded to a Married Woman in Designated Marital-Occupational Situations by All Respondents**

| HUSBAND'S OCCUPATION | WIFE'S OCCUPATION | | | | | | | |
|---|---|---|---|---|---|---|---|---|
| | PHYSICIAN | CIVIL ENGINEER | PUBLIC GS TEACHER | BOOKKEEPER | PLUMBER | ASSEMBLY LINE WORKER | JANITRESS | HOUSEWIFE |
| Physician | 91 | 85 | 79 | 78 | 73 | 69 | 67 | 83 |
| Civil engineer | 88 | 82 | 80 | 74 | 71 | 66 | 64 | 75 |
| Public gs teacher | 84 | 78 | 74 | 69 | 67 | 62 | 60 | 71 |
| Bookkeeper | 79 | 72 | 73 | 70 | 66 | 63 | 54 | 66 |
| Plumber | 76 | 71 | 69 | 67 | 68 | 60 | 58 | 62 |
| Assembly line worker | 75 | 66 | 66 | 62 | 60 | 58 | 53 | 59 |
| Janitor | 69 | 67 | 65 | 60 | 60 | 54 | 53 | 54 |

TABLE 4

Unstandardized Regression Coefficient ($b_{X_HX_W}$) in the Regression of
Wife's Social Standing (Y) on Husband's ($X_H$) and Wife's ($X_W$)
Occupational Standings and Their Interaction ($X_HX_W$) by
All Respondents, by Men, and by Women

|  | ALL H-W COMB. | H>W | W>H |
|---|---|---|---|
| All Respondents | .004 | .006 | .008 |
| Men | .005 | −.006 | .022 |
| Women | .003 | .004 | .003 |

a change in her occupational standing has a slightly greater effect on her social standing as her occupational level rises. In the exceptional case, where $b_{X_HX_W}$ is negative, a change in her occupational standing has less effect as her attainment level rises. This finding is not an artifact of the selection of occupations, since the prestige point difference between occupations is relatively uniform and is always significant at the .05 level. However, it does not indicate that her status determination, relative to her husband, is actually increasing with her occupational standing in all the respondent evaluations except for the men's under husband-higher conditions. What it does show is that the social standing scores obtained tend to exhibit slightly greater variance as the wife's occupational standing rises, holding the husband's constant. The men's scores in the husband-higher situations, however, are more variant as the wife's occupational level drops.[4] We may have more confidence in this finding because it is consonant with the previous result from a different analysis of the data that, uniquely, the men give a wife of lower attainment than her husband twice as much status determination as they gave him.[5]

## SUMMARY AND CONCLUSIONS

The sample as a whole, men and women, tend to subscribe to the status-sharing model of female attainment more closely than to competing models. That is, people take the occupational attainments of both a husband and a wife into roughly equal account in an additive way when assessing her social-standing. This finding holds true whether the husband or the wife has the higher occupational level. In fact, the male respondents attach somewhat more weight to the wife's occupational accomplishments than to her husband's, especially when she has the lower standing. This extra margin of status determination given the wife in this situation involves a trade-off, however. Her social standing would be higher, in terms of points, if the husband had greater determination over her status, since he has the higher occupational standing. However, to her social standing advantage, the men take her lower attainment somewhat less into account as her husband's occupational level rises.

Where status self-determination operates most in a wife's favor is in the wife-higher situations, and here she has no significant margin over her lower status husband. In fact, the effect of her occupational standing on her social standing increases very slightly as her husband's occupational position rises. In other words, she tends to lose status self-determination as her husband's status drops, when she most needs the effect of her own accomplishments to overcome the depreciating effect of her husband's status.

Thus, when status self-determination is least helpful to a woman in enchancing her social standing, i.e., in those situations where her husband's status is higher than hers, she generally has more status determination. But when status self-determination is most valuable to her, i.e., when her occupational standing is equal to or higher than her husband's, she usually has less status determination. Of course, where both husband and wife are in very prestigious occupations, this phenomenon may only be due to a ceiling effect.[6]

The social standing of a housewife is more dependent on her husband's occupational attainment than is the social standing of a gainfully employed woman. However, the higher the occupational status of the husband, the more prestigious the occupation of the wife must be for her to gain social standing through her own employment. A husband of moderate to high occupational status makes the marginal status gains of even prestigious employment preciously small for a woman, considering the effort.

These results clearly contradict the sociological truism that a married woman simply takes her social standing from her husband, particularly when she is employed. They are consistent with the findings of Rossi et al. (1974) that her attainments make a considerable contribution to family social standing. Felson and Knoke's (1974) study suggests that when wives are unemployed or have jobs that are very different in prestige from their husband's, the wives themselves weigh their husband's occupational and educational attainments considerably more than they do their own in assessing their class placement. According to the results here, many people seem to allow such women more status determination than they give themselves. Both this respondent sample and the wives agree, however, that gainful employment, especially lower status employment, is less enhancing to a married woman's social standing than is the position of housewife.

The difference in the proportion of variance explained by the wife's attainment between this study and Rossi's suggests that social standing is allocated on somewhat different criteria depending on the social unit in question. When people consider a household as a unit, then the male head-of-household's attainments are definitely more important than his wife's. On the other hand, when the wife is evaluated as an individual unit, her occupational accomplishments seem to be given much greater weight, about as much as her husband's. How much a married man claims social standing independent of his wife is a question still yet to be answered. Whether a sociologist chooses to measure social standing in terms of the household unit or the individual makes a difference in the sources and actual evaluation of a person's social standing.

## NOTES

1   The total sample is predominantly married, young, high school educated, and employed in middle prestige occupations with moderate family income. Although efforts were made to equalize the sex distribution, there is a higher proportion of

females (59.5 per cent) slightly over one-third of whom are full-time housewives. Missing data are minimal and present no likelihood of serious respondent bias from this source. Predictably, the respondents somewhat overrepresent the well-educated, the affluent, the young, and the females of the Milwaukee area sampling frame.

2  This final form of response elicitation was arrived at after three pretests:

"Now I will read a list of husband and wife occupational situations. Some of the combinations are unusual and some are common. I'd like you to think in terms of only the wife's social standing. That is, when I give you her occupation and her husband's occupation, tell me your idea of the *general social standing* of the *wife* in that situation. In making your choice, try to think of the occupations in general and not about any individuals you might know in these jobs."

An item score is a weighted frequency average of all respondent ratings of that item. The percentage frequency of an "Excellent" social standing response is weighted by five, that of an "Above average" response by four, and so on. The sum of these products is then divided by five. In Rossi's (1974) study, respondents were given cards on which husbands' and wives' education and occupation varied randomly. While this personal interview technique is preferable to the one used here in general, it was necessary in the Rossi study because respondents were asked to consider more than just two factors.

3  When an interaction term, $B_{X_H X_W} X_H X_W$, was added to the basic additive equation 1, no significant amount of additional variance was explained. The increment in the $R^2$ ranges from −.003 to .006, with the exception of .035 in the men's wife-higher evaluations. The status accordance process for a married woman seems not to be multiplicative.

4  While, strictly speaking, parametric statistics should not be applied to ordinal level data, such as prestige or social standing scales, it has become the safe convention to do so to permit simpler and more powerful data manipulation techniques.

5  The social standing scores accorded to a married woman show the same variance for men and for women in the sample.

6  Additional analyses show that, at least under wife-higher conditions, the amount of status determination of the wife increases slightly with the educational level and occupational prestige level of respondents and decreases with their age level. No relationships are discernible in the husband-higher situations.


## REFERENCES

*Acker, J.*
1973  "Women and social stratification: The case of intellectual sexism." American Journal of Sociology 78 (January): 935–945.
*Barber, Bernard*
1957  Social Stratification, New York: Harcourt, Brace.
*Barth, E., and W. Watson*
1964  "Questionable assumptions in the theory of social stratification." Pacific Sociological Review 7 (Spring): 11–16.
*Blau, Peter M., and Otis D. Duncan*
1967  The American Occupational Structure, New York: Wiley.
*Cohen, E.*
1958  "Parental factors in educational mobility." Unpublished Ph.D. dissertation. Harvard University, Cambridge, Massachusetts.

*Davis, Kingsley*
1949 Human Society. New York: Macmillan.
*De Jong, P., M. J. Brawer, and S. S. Robin*
1971 "Patterns of female intergenerational occupational mobility: A comparison with male patterns of intergenerational occupational mobility." American Sociological Review 36 (December): 1035–1042.
*Duncan, O. D.*
1961 "A socioeconomic index for all occupations." Pp. 109–138 in Albert J. Reiss, Jr., et al., Occupations and Social Status. New York: Free Press.
*Felson, M., and D. Knoke*
1974 "Social status and the married woman." Journal of Marriage and the Family 36 (August): 516–521.
*Haug, M.*
1973 "Social class measurement and women's occupational roles." Social Forces 52 (September): 86–98.
*Hodge, R. W., P. Siegel, and P. Rossi*
1964 "Occupational prestige in the United States." American Journal of Sociology 70 (November): 286–302.
*Krauss, I.*
1964 "Sources of educational aspirations among working class youth." American Sociological Review 29 (December): 867–879.
*Nilson, L. B.*
1976 "The occupational and sex related components of social standing." Sociology and Social Research.
*Parsons, T.*
1953 "A revised analytical approach to the theory of social stratification." Pp. 92–128 in Reinhard Bendix and Seymour Martin Lipset (eds.), Class, Status and Power. Free Press.
*Reiss, Albert J., Jr.*
1961 Occupations and Social Status, New York: Free Press.
*Rossi, P. et al.*
1974 "Measuring household social standing." Social Science Research 3 (September): 169–190.
*Sewell, W. H., and V. Shah*
1968 "Parents' education and children's educational aspirations and achievements." American Sociological Review 33 (April): 191–201.
*Siegel, P.*
1971 "Prestige in the American occupational structure." Unpublished Ph.D. dissertation, University of Chicago, Chicago, Illinois.
*Turner, R.*
1964 "Some aspects of women's ambitions." American Journal of Sociology 70 (November): 271–285.
*United States Bureau of the Census*
1972 Census of the Population: 1970. Vol. 1, Characteristics of the Population. Part A. Number of Inhabitants. Section 1: United States, Alabama-Mississippi. Washington, D.C., Government Printing Office.
*Wallace, Walter L.*
1966 "The perspective of college women." In Wallace (ed.) Student Culture, Chicago: Aldine.
*Williams, Robin M., Jr.*
1951 American Society. New York: Knopf.

# Industrialization and Femininity: A Case Study of Nineteenth Century New England*

## Barbara Easton

*University of California, Santa Cruz*

*Femininity as we now know it was developed in the United States in the nineteenth century. Books for women, mainly published in New England, proclaimed that woman's place was in the home, that her primary task was child-raising, and that she must accept subordination to her husband's authority. These ideas reflected real changes in women's lives as their families moved from farming villages to industrializing towns. As they lost their functions in the family economy, their dependence on men was heightened and the basis for what little power they held eroded. But women's domesticity was not a necessary result of industrial capitalism. Women could have worked outside the home while children were cared for communally or by their fathers. It was*

*Source:* Barbara Easton, "Industrialization and Femininity: A Case Study of Nineteenth Century New England," Social Problems 23, 4 (April 1976): 389–401. Copyright © 1976 by the Society for the Study of Social Problems. Reprinted by permission of the Society and the author.
*I would like to thank Lillian Rubin for the help she has given me in the development of this article.

*men who benefitted from women's domesticity, male power that enforced it,*
*and the ideology of femininity that induced women to accept it.*

From the earliest days of American history men's and women's roles in work,
family, and society have been ordered according to ideas of what is appropriate
for each sex. In the seventeenth century, white settlers brought ideas about
masculinity and femininity with them from Europe, and structured their families and communities in accordance with these ideas. During that century, and
for most of the eighteenth century as well, most people took these sex roles
largely for granted. It was not until the beginning of the nineteenth century
especially in New England, that the role of women became the subject of
widespread concern and discussion. Out of that concern a changed concept of
femininity emerged. In this paper, I will describe that concept of femininity,
show how it was related to the emergence of an industrial economy, and
suggest that the ideas about women that were established during that period
were influenced by the development of capitalism and to some degree shaped
its further development.

The change in women's roles from the seventeenth and eighteenth centuries to the nineteenth was dramatic. In the seventeenth and eighteenth centuries, the vast majority of New Englanders lived on family farms that were part
of farming villages. Each family owned a plot of land that was large enough
to produce a large variety of crops and to support some livestock or poultry;
families used the common grazing and wood-gathering lands. There was a
rough division between men's and women's work: the men were responsible
for most of the work in the fields; the women, for looking after the infants who
arrived in rapid succession, and for work that could be done in and around the
home. Boys learned to plant, cultivate, and harvest crops; girls learned the skills
involved in turning raw agricultural materials into usable goods. Women spun,
wove, finished cloth, and made it into clothes; they knitted; made candles,
soaps, and brooms; they made liquors, cheese, and preserves; they made medicine, and tended the sick. They also cooked, cleaned their houses, and took care
of babies and small children. The division of labor between the house and the
fields was practical rather than rigid. There was no taboo against women
raising crops as long as they were close enough to the house to hear a baby's
cry, and women often tended vegetable gardens, and cared for poultry. Similarly, men worked in the house during the winter when there was little work
in the fields, doing the work that was considered too heavy for women, such
as tanning leather or making furniture.

A farm could not operate without at least a husband and wife, and it helped
to have a large number of sons and daughters. Sometimes, if a couple did not
have enough children of one sex or the other, children from other families were
brought in as servants, and treated very much like the couple's children. The
role of women on the New England farm was extremely important. They bore,
and largely raised, the children who provided labor for the farm. Their work
of turning raw materials into goods was essential to the family economy and
to survival, no less so than the work of the men (Demos, 1970: chapter five;
Morgan, 1944: chapter two: Ryan, 1975: chapter one).

In a limited way, Puritan law reflected the importance of women's role in
the New England settlements. A Massachusetts law, taken over from English

common law, required that a man leave a third of his estate to his wife as long as she had done a normal amount of work. The courts rectified wills that did not meet this standard. While Puritan law was biased against women as, for example, in the denial of property rights in a woman's first marriage, it was nevertheless more favorable to women than it would be in the nineteenth century in New England or anywhere else in the United States. Puritan women had some limited property rights: any property held by a woman became her husband's when she married, but if her husband died (or if the couple divorced, a rare event) and she remarried, she could retain ownership of any property she held (Morgan, 1944: chapter two: Flexner, 1968:63 ff.). Beyond the relatively favorable position of women in Puritan law, the Puritan view that anything that transpired within Puritan society was the concern of that society often worked to women's benefit. If a husband's mistreatment of his wife came to the attention of the court, the court was obliged to interfere regardless of whether the wife complained about her husband's behavior. The husband's crime was against Puritan society and God himself, not only against his wife (Morgan, 1944:39ff.).

It is true that very little of the land held by the Puritans was owned by women. But in a society in which land was relatively easy to acquire but could not be utilized without family labor, men and women were in important ways economically dependent upon one another, giving women a certain leverage within the family. Just as the economic position of Puritan women seems to have been stronger than was indicated by their property-hold, the status of women in Puritan society seems to have been higher than would be indicated by the official, or Biblical, view of women. Every Puritan child knew that "in Adam's fall, we sinned all," and that it was Eve and the snake who were responsible for that fall. Puritan ministers, on the relatively rare occasions when they preached or wrote about family relations, reminded their audiences that men held authority over women. As one minister wrote, "the Husband is called the Head of the Woman [1 Corinthians 11:3]. It belongs to the Head, to rule and govern" (Wadsworth, 1712:34). And at least some ministers showed great uneasiness about female sexuality. In reprimanding women for what he considered immodest dress, Cotton Mather, a prominent seventeenth century minister and Puritan intellectual, spoke of sexuality as if it were a matter of women enticing men—as in Adam's fall. "For the nakedness of the Back and Breasts," he wrote, "no reason can be given: unless it be that a Woman by showing a fair skin enkindle a *foul Fire* in the Male Spectators" (Mather, 1692:59).

Although, on the one hand, Puritan ministers quoted the Bible as authority for this harsh view of women, on the other hand, they tended to moderate these pronouncements in their own discussions of women and family relations. One minister wrote in a tract on family relations. "Though the Wife is the Weaker Vessel, yet honour is to be put on her in her inferior Station ... Though the husband governs her, he must not treat her as a Servant, but as his *own Flesh;* he must love her as himself [Eph. 5:33]. He should make his Government of her, as easie and gentle as possible; and strive more to be loved than fear'd: though neither is to be excluded." (Wadsworth, 1712:34–35). And even Cotton Mather, who was probably more troubled by female sexuality than were most Puritans, noted with some surprise that the role of women in the Holy Commonwealth was not what one would have expected from the daughters of Eve. In trying to account for women's high standing in Puritan society, he recalled the burdens that they had to bear (1692:48–49):

*I have seen it without going a Mile from Home, that in a Church of between three or four hundred Communicants, there are but few more than one hundred Men, all the rest are Women, of whom Charity will think no Evil. Possibly, one reason for it is, there are more Women in the World than Men, but this is not all the Reason. It seems that the curse in the Difficulties both of Subjection and of Childbearing, which the Female Sex is doomed unto, has been turned into a blessing, . . .*

Just as Puritan women were more upstanding than Cotton Mather's reading of the Bible led him to expect, there seems to have been more equality between husbands and wives than the Biblical model of the family suggested. In the cooperative farm household, men's and women's roles often overlapped. In Puritan tracts on family life, men and women were as likely to be referred to as "heads of the household" or "parents," as they were to be spoken of as "husbands and wives" or "mothers and fathers." In these tracts, there was little discussion of "motherhood" or, for that matter, "fatherhood." Even in tracts that were specifically directed towards women, such as Benjamin Colman's *The Honour and Happiness of the Vertuous Woman* (1716), the woman's relations with her children were generally discussed under the heading of "parenthood," and the mother herself was as likely to be referred to as a parent as she was to be described as a mother. Except for childbirth, the nursing of babies, and a special responsibility to be models to their daughters (as were fathers to be models to their sons), Puritan ministers did not speak of responsibilities of mothers that were peculiar to them as women. This lack of attention to motherhood as a special category probably reflected the fact that on these family farms, childcare was not solely a maternal responsibility; boys often began to do some work with their fathers by the time they were six or seven, and in the winter months, when everyone in the family worked or played in the big room in the house, the father's authority over the children was as immediate as was the mother's.

Another indication that men and women had more actual equality in Puritan New England than ministers' pronouncements about male authority and female subjection would lead us to believe lies in the frequency with which women were brought to court for abusing their husbands or other men, verbally or physically. John Demos (1970:95) has found that in Plymouth Colony, women were as likely to be charged with "abusive carryage" towards their husbands or other men, as were men to be charged with such behavior towards women. New England women seem to have been self-respecting and assertive. It seems likely that it was the role of women on the family farm and their security in the knowledge of their central role in family survival that made this possible.

Femininity as we understand it played little part in the Puritan understanding of women's role in the family or in society. Puritan women were told to obey their husbands, but the social graces, childlike innocence, and role of moral authority that later came to be associated with womanhood had little place on the New England farm. In Boston, however, and the other port towns,

life was different, especially for the merchants, who began to form a community of their own in the seventeenth century. By the eighteenth century, the
merchant class was a wealthy and powerful section of society, with strong ties
to the English upper class and a life style that was increasingly influenced by
English fashions. The men of this class were often able to support their wives
through the profits they made in trade. These men could require less of their
wives in the way of productive skills—clothes and other goods were imported
from England and could be bought in the Boston stores—and more in the way
of decorative qualities and social graces. Their homes were becoming centers
of social life and their wives were expected to develop those social graces which
would allow them to be good hostesses (Ryan, 1975:98 ff.). By the end of the
eighteenth century, literature was being imported from England, and to some
extent published in the United States, that urged women of this class to develop
the graces of the lady. In these books we can see the development of distinct
models for masculine and feminine personalities. One author (Gisborne,
1797:23) described the difference between the two:

*Women's brows were not intended to be ploughed with wrinkles, nor their*
*innocent gaiety damped by abstraction. They were perpetually to please, and*
*perpetually to enliven. If we were to plan the* edifice, *they were to furnish the*
*embellishments. If we were to lay out and cultivate the garden, they were to*
*beautifully* fringe *its borders with flowers. If we were to superintend the*
*management of kingdoms, they were to be the fairest ornaments of those*
*kingdoms, the embellishers of society, and the sweeteners of life.*

This concept of womanhood retained, even accentuated, female inferiority.
Like farm women, these upper-class women were urged to develop a range of
abilities; motherhood had not yet become the primary focus of women's lives.
But the abilities that upper-class urban women were to cultivate were very
different from those of rural women. One author (Bennett, 1795:94) wrote:

*To be obedient Daughters, faithful Wives, and prudent Mothers; to be useful*
*in the affairs of a House; to be sensible Companions, and affectionate friends,*
*are, without doubt, the principle objects of female duty. The accomplishments,*
*therefore, which you should acquire, are those that will contribute to render*
*you serviceable in domestic, and agreeable in social life.*

This concept of womanhood was shaped by the experience of the English
upper classes and formulated in such a way that it was attainable by at least
some women of the merchant class, especially its upper levels. Such women
could be supported by their husbands, had a fair amount of time for social life,
and could send their daughters to academies where their education included
decorative arts, and their social graces could become polished. While this style
of femininity had no relevance for farm women, it came to the United States
at a time when, at least in New England, an increasing number of families were
congregating in town centers, ceasing to farm, and in other ways cutting themselves off from rural life; the men of these town families earned a living by the
crafts and trades, such as tanning, cabinet-making, forging iron, or milling flour
—often the skills that had occupied them part-time when they were farmers.

During the late eighteenth and early nineteenth centuries, a number of inventions were brought to the United States that made it possible to produce cloth more cheaply in factories than at home. In 1813 the first New England factory was established that produced cloth from start to finish; from 1815 to 1830 the price of cotton declined from 42¢ a yard to 7½¢ a yard (Tryon, 1917:276). For women who lived in or near towns, where they could buy cloth from the factories or from stores, there remained little incentive to work all day at the loom to weave four or five yards of such cloth. Some of this freed female labor was absorbed by the factories which employed almost entirely women, especially young, unmarried women. And some women did piece-work at home for factory owners or merchants. But the number of women who worked in or for the mills was small in relation to the female population of New England. In 1832 only 2.2% of Massachusetts women worked in the mills (Abbott, 1906:482). Most town women (and increasingly, farm women as well), found that they were spending less time making things for their families and more time cooking, cleaning their houses, and tending to the needs of their children and husbands. Their men were increasingly likely to spend their days away from home, working in shops, stores, or mills. Responsibility for childcare and care of the home had devolved more and more upon the women.

At the same time that these changes were taking place in the commercial and industrial world, books began to appear in the northeast, especially in New England, that described to women their duties as mothers and wives and instructed them in how to fulfill them. The men and women who wrote these books were often teachers, doctors, or ministers. Some of them wrote that their books were intended for women of the "middling classes"; most of the authors themselves could have been included in the upper level of this class.

These books reflected a sharp shift in the socially sanctioned roles women were expected to play in their families. Where for the Puritans, and for the authors of late eighteenth century ladies' books, motherhood had been only one of a woman's tasks, these nineteenth century writers saw childcare as the most important of a woman's responsibilities. One author announced that "the best pleasures of a woman's life are to be found in the faithful discharge of her maternal duties" (An American Matron, 1836:174). Others recognized that some women might find motherhood more of a burden than a pleasure and urged them to accept its restrictions. *The Young Lady's Own Handbook* (anon., 1836:174), for example exhorted:

*The most anxious ... if not the most important duty of married life, is that which is due to children ... To accomplish ... these duties, a woman must be domestic. Her heart must be at home. She must not be on the look-out for excitement of any kind, but must find her pleasure as well as her occupation in the sphere which is assigned to her. St. Paul knew what was best for woman, when he advised her to be domestic.*

Women were urged to subordinate their own needs and desires to those of their husbands: the muted inequality of Puritan women had been replaced by a demand for outright subservience. The wife was to provide her husband with a refuge from the harsh outside world: she was to avoid disagreements with him and make sure that family life went smoothly. "The balance of concession devolves upon the wife," proclaimed one domestic guidebook.

"Whether the husband concede or not, she must. . . ." The same author saw domesticity, a willingness to stay at home, as central to a woman's subjugation of herself to her children and husband. Some women, he wrote, resented confinement in the home; but in this her desires were at odds with the happiness and well-being of her family, and must be restrained. "She cannot discharge the duties of a wife, much less those of a mother, unless she prefers home to all other places and is only led abroad from a sense of duty, and not from choice" (Alcott, 1837:83).

This increased emphasis on motherhood, and on the subservience of the wife to her husband, reflected the economic realities of the age and the concommitant loss of women's productive functions. These women were spending more time with their children because they had fewer other things to do, and because, with their husbands working outside the home, they had more responsibility for childcare than had their mothers and grandmothers. The loss of productive work also brought with it a greatly increased dependence upon men, a deterioration in women's power in relation to that of their husbands and fathers. In the agrarian society of Puritan New England, men and women had been interdependent, and family life and economic interest had merged. Husbands and wives needed each other's labor for survival, and needed each other for emotional support and for the raising of a family. In the towns of the nineteenth century these relationships were undergoing profound changes. Women who no longer did productive work were economically entirely dependent upon either their husbands or their fathers. Men needed wives to bear and raise children, to take care of their social and emotional needs, but not to participate in the family economy.

The corollary to women's dependence was heightened male dominance, a dominance reinforced by the law. Puritan law had been biased against women but had still allowed them some rights. They could appear in court in their own defense; in some cases, the courts intervened unasked on their behalf. With the weakening of the Puritan church, Puritan law concerning the family had gradually been replaced by English common law. According to this tradition, once women were married they were represented legally by their husbands; they were "dead in the law." A married woman could not sue or be sued; she could not sign contracts; and any money that she inherited, earned, or brought to the marriage through a dowry was the property of her husband. Such laws had been gradually incorporated into state legal codes through the 18th century, but they affected fewer women in the Colonial economy, since few people earned money and the market was rudimentary. By the nineteenth century, with the development of towns and a growing market economy, laws excluding women from the courts and forbidding them to hold property put them at a serious disadvantage to men.

Furthermore, the supervision of family life that Puritan courts had engaged in was no longer possible. The individualist philosophy that was coming to pervade the towns and cities of nineteenth century New England allowed for no such intrusions into the family, now seen as the private domain of the husband and father. One minister wrote, in a nineteenth century guidebook to family life (Humphrey, 1840:16):

*Every family is a little state, an empire within itself, bound together by the most endearing emotions, and governed by its patriarchal head, with whose prerogative no power on earth has a right to interfere. Every father is the constituted head of his household. God has made him the supreme earthly legislator over his children, accountable, of course, to Himself, for the manner in which he executes his trust; but amenable to no other power, except in the most extreme cases of neglect, or abuse.*

The loss of economic functions eroded the basis of women's power in the family, the loss of legal rights deprived them of weapons that they might have used to fight male domination. Industrialization made this weakening of women's position possible but it did not make it necessary. As women's productive work was moved from the home to the factory, married women as well as single could have gone to work in the factories. Women could have gone to work in the towns as storekeepers, artisans, and professionals. Children could have been cared for in nurseries and kindergartens, by grandparents, or by their fathers. It was not industrialization that kept women in their homes in the early nineteenth century, but the deeply engrained tradition of women's primary responsibility for home and childcare. Once machines took production from the home, the political and economic power of men, together with the absence of much demand for female labor outside the home, combined to keep women in their domestic role.

It was women's dependence that laid the basis for the nineteenth century ideology of female submission. If women were to accept that subservience, it was necessary that they internalize male dominance, rather than simply obeying men out of fear of the law or of withdrawal of economic support. The tasks that women retained when they ceased to produce goods were primarily emotional and psychological: raising children, helping them to develop personalities that would allow them to fit into the increasingly difficult roles of town life, and giving their husbands the emotional support that made it easier for them to function in society. Mere brandishment of male power was not enough to make women accept this limited role. They needed also to be convinced of its importance.

Making domesticity and subservience to men acceptable to women was the task of the guidebooks to wifehood and motherhood, and, more generally, of the ideology of femininity. The elements of this ideology that were central to this task were, first, that children required fulltime, undivided adult attention; second, that women were specially endowed to provide this care (and to create the homes that their husbands needed as well); and finally, that domesticity would shield women from the evil of the outside world and bring them status and power mediated through their families.

The Puritans had believed that children were born in sin, that it was the responsibility of parents to try to chastise them out of it, but that all, even adults who had evidence of salvation, were doomed to struggle against sinful impulses all their lives. Where Puritan parents were told that their children were fundamentally and irrepressibly sinful, nineteenth century authors of women's books told mothers that their babies were innocent and pure and must be shielded from the corrupting influences of the outside world. One author wrote (Child, 1831:9).

*The mind of a child is not like that of a grown person, too full and too busy to observe everything; it is a vessel empty and pure—always ready to receive, and always receiving. Every look, every movement, every expression, does something toward forming the character of the little heir to immortal life ... [If a child comes into contact with] evil passions such as anger or other wrong feelings, evil enters into his soul, as the imperceptible atmosphere he breathes into his lungs: and the beautiful little image of God is removed farther and farther from his home in heaven.*

While children had to be protected from the corrupting influence of society, at the same time, at least if they were male, they had to be equipped to take part in that society. Thus child raising was a difficult and important task; the child's plasticity meant that every aspect of it required careful thought. Mothers were given detailed instructions: a typical book contained chapters on how to inculcate religion in children, how to train them to be obedient, how a mother might achieve the firmness and self-control necessary to develop her children's characters (Abbott, 1833). Another book included such chapters as "Means of Developing the Bodily Sensations of Earliest Infancy," "Early Cultivation of the Intellect," "Management in Childhood," "Proper Amusements and Employments," and "A List of Good Books for Various Ages" (Child, 1831).

Raising children, then, was difficult, but fortunately, women were assured, they had special abilities for it largely due to their innate warmth and morality. "The female breast is the natural soil of Christianity," wrote one author *(The American Lady's Preceptor,* Anon., 1813:71). It was through their role as mothers that women could attain power, most importantly over their sons *(The Lady's Companion,* Anon., 1856:10):

*The earliest days of our statesmen, of poets, of our men of profound thought and original mind, are passed in the nursery, under the constant care and superintendance of females ... How many a fair child has been nipped in the bud by improper treatment in early days; and how many have been brought to full perfection and beauty by the judicious care and attention of a mother ...*

Through their sons, women could exert a powerful influence over society without leaving their homes. Abbott (1833:159) reminded them:

*Thus far the history of the world has been composed of the narrations of oppression and blood ... Where shall we look for the influence which shall change this scene, and fill the earth with the fruits of peace and benevolence? It is to the power of divine truth, to Christianity as taught from a mother's lips ... She who was first in transgression, must be yet the principal earthly agent in the restoration.*

In arguing that children's innocence placed them in need of undivided attention, that women's nature equipped them for this role, and that through this role, women could reform society, the authors of women's books assumed a review of human nature that differed fundamentally from the Puritan conception. These changed ideas about human nature were in part a product of the erosion of Calvinism in New England and the increasing dominance of New England's religious and intellectual life by liberal forms of Protestantism, especially Universalism and Unitarianism. Calvinism had preached the doctrine of original sin, the utter depravity of human beings, and their total reliance upon God for salvation. The liberals who began to challenge Calvinism in the second half of the eighteenth century rejected the idea of human depravity and replaced it with that of human ability, human potential for good and for an active role in salvation. Such ideas gained much ground among the churches of early nineteenth century New England and in the academies and colleges; most of the authors of women's guidebooks espoused this new liberalism.

In the conflict of these ideologies and the victory of liberalism, one can see the decline of an agrarian society, in which people felt little control over their world, and emergence of a capitalist system in which, in its early stages, some people sensed that they could affect their conditions and destiny and felt a new optimism and self-confidence. But the new concept of human nature also derived from changes in role requirements within the family, especially in the role of women; the idea that children were innocent and malleable helped to explain and justify women's confinement in the home. Probably child rearing had in fact become somewhat more difficult; fathers were not around much to help, and the life of an industrializing town, for which these children were being prepared, was more difficult and complex than life in a farming village had been. But childcare could have been arranged in other ways. The main beneficiaries of women's domesticity were not the children but the men. It was they who were freed to participate fulltime in the industrializing, market economy, to accrue the money and power that participation in that society could bring, and to gain the authority in their families that came with this division of labor.

This male power was not openly questioned, or even discussed, by early nineteenth century New England women. Self-conscious feminism did not appear until the mid-nineteenth century, and then it was strongest among women of professional families, often relatively well educated. But there is evidence that the town women of the "middling classes" felt and resented the increased power of their husbands and fathers. In a larger study (Easton, 1975) I have shown that there was a striking change in the content of New England women's religious conversion experiences from the mid-eighteenth to the mid-nineteenth century. Eighteenth century women's conversion experiences had, like men's, centered around remorse over a diffuse sense of sin, of distance from God and religion. In the nineteenth century, men tended to move away from orthodox religion, while women began to discover that their central sin was a desire to rebel: against God, the Bible, the minister. Women reported that they found themselves hating God's power, and wanting to overthrow it. But they knew that such rebellion was both hopeless and damnable. They considered their conversions accomplished when they suppressed their fury, accepted God's omnipotence, and could regard him as a loving father rather than an enemy.

The center of conversion for these women was accommodation to the inevitable—male dominance. Rebellion itself was defined and defeated by the assumption that male power was unshakable: if to challenge God was hopeless and inevitable, acquiescence must follow. Some women, after conversion, carried rebellion into their families by going to religious meetings against the order of their husbands or fathers, or by denouncing their men for irreligion. Here again, male authority was challenged, but only in the name of obedience to higher male authority: that of God and Christ.

One reason that women tended to accept domesticity, with the male dominance that it involved, was that the other side of female subservience and economic dependence was male economic support. The grandmothers, and even the mothers, of these women had worked at demanding tasks for long hours. Most colonial farm women, especially in the early stages of settlement, worked from before dawn through the evening almost every day of the week at a series of complex tasks that left them with little freedom to enjoy a moment with their children or men.

Women were impelled to accept domesticity not only because of its material benefits but because it was surrounded by a seductive ideology. Women were told that in devoting themselves to their husbands and children, their position would be enhanced: that even though their work seemed trivial, in fact it held families together, and was the basis of society itself. They were told that they were secluded from the outside society because they might otherwise be tainted by it, and that they were superior to it and to the men who inhabited it. And they were told that the seclusion that preserved their purity would also bring them power. These promises must have been very appealing to women whose mothers and grandmothers had worked so hard in frontier settlements, who had carried half the burden of running the farm without corresponding status or power. The prospect of being relieved of productive work and of only having to mind the children, clean the house, and cook must have been very enticing. Unfortunately for these women, however, by the middle of the nineteenth century, the psychological strains brought on by powerlessness and dependency were already taking their toll; vague, often undiagnosable illnesses became widespread among women in the New England towns (Wood, 1973).

Finally, married women accepted domesticity because in early nineteenth century New England towns most women didn't have much choice. Some women could get jobs in the textile mills, but except in Rhode Island these mills employed only single women. Some women did continue to work instead of marrying, but this brought with it social isolation; there was no place for unmarried women in the towns. Thus they were pressed into domesticity by the constraints of the society in which they lived.

These women probably did acquire a certain dubious power through their acceptance of domesticity. To the extent that they did hold sway over family and personal life, men must have felt that women had the power to exclude them from or allow them into the realm of emotional ties and warmth. But the price of this nebulous influence was submission to male authority and adhesion to a rigid and anti-sexual moral code. Women were told to hold their own sexuality suspect (Alcott; 1837:85):

*There is a species of love, if it deserves the name, which declines soon after marriage, and it is no matter if it does . . . There can be no objection to external love, where it is a mere accompaniment to that which is internal. What I object to, is making too much of it; or giving it a place in our hearts which is disproportioned to its real value. Our affections should rather be based chiefly on sweetness of temper, intelligence, and moral excellency.*

The idea that women must put aside sexuality in order to be moral was a product of the Victorian view that sexuality was evil, but it also probably rested on a sense that concern with one's own satisfaction was incompatible with the selflessness required of the mother and the submission required of the wife. The price of domestic comfort, therefore, was a loss of self-assertion in sexual as well as in economic and social life.

Probably the great majority of married women in early New England towns stayed home with their children and were supported by their husbands. At this time only the beginnings of what would become a working class existed in New England. Most men were farmers; those who left the farms became craftsmen, tradesmen, or professionals. There was a large group of servants, but these were usually young people who could expect to move up in society. Most factory jobs, especially in textiles, were filled by young women from rural or "middle class" town families who would leave the factories when they married. This was a temporary labor force, not a working class. If industry had developed earlier than it did, or on a larger scale, women might have been drawn into work outside the home as they lost their productive role within it. But as it was, women's agrarian productive functions were destroyed without being replaced by industrial ones. It was in this vacuum that women's domestic role took shape, and in this situation that the new concept of femininity was formulated.

As long as there was no working class in New England and its population was almost entirely native-born, English-speaking, and Protestant, domesticity was accessible to most town women. But after 1840 a working class, composed in large part of immigrants, began to develop in these towns. These immigrants were forced to take the work that brought lowest status and pay, especially factory work, the conditions of which declined as immigrant labor became available. By the late nineteenth century, the influx of immigrants had become a flood; by this time most immigrants were neither English-speaking nor Protestant, but Catholics and Jews from southern and eastern Europe. The differences between the immigrants and the more established population made it easier to force worse conditions of life and work on the arrivals even though they had come in response to the promise of American prosperity. Most of the women in these groups could not attain the American domestic ideal. Many of them, especially when they first entered the United States, worked in factories, as domestics, or at other low-paid jobs; others worked at home for merchants or industrialists. As new immigrant groups, and then blacks, entered the working class, the longer established immigrants could move up in the occupational structure; it became possible for many women to stay at home, supported by their husbands. But the poverty of working class life still precluded any real attainment of the domestic ideal. A woman who lived in a tenement could not give undivided attention to developing her children's personalities.

Through the nineteenth century and into the twentieth, most white Protestant urban women continued to stay at home, supported by their husbands, often in surroundings that made it possible for them to come somewhere near the domestic ideal. This role was a luxury made possible by immigrant labor. Without it, the process of industrialization would have pulled native-born Americans, both men and women, into industrial work. The ideal of domesticity, formed in an earlier period of capitalism, was kept alive not only because domesticity continued to be possible for native-born women but because many of the immigrant groups brought with them ideas about women's place that meshed with the American ideal. As in the pre-industrial United States, in these peasant cultures women had worked in the home and cared for children.

Some immigrants tried to maintain this tradition by working as family units in industry, or continuing to work at home, but for pay.[1] They maintained the hope that as they rose in society, their women would be able to withdraw from industry and devote themselves fulltime to the families. For many, this became possible.

The great wealth of the United States made possible the massive immigration of the late nineteenth and early twentieth centuries, which in turn made possible the maintenance of the domestic role for so many American women. The domestic ideal, established before the development of large-scale industry, limited the options open to American capitalism by making it more difficult to draw women into industry, adding to the pressures to look outside the Northern states to Europe and the American South for new sources of labor. But the domestic ideal also divided and weakened the working class by providing an index of upward mobility, by holding forth the elusive goal of a private life protected from the pressures of the industrial world, and making the housewife the symbol of that goal.

## NOTES

1 Jews were the only major immigrant group who had a tradition of women working outside the home; it was partly for this reason that Jewish women entered industry and the labor movement in such large numbers in the early twentieth century. Other immigrant groups resisted the incorporation of women into industrial work, and the consequent disruption of traditional family patterns. Italians, for instance, often sought situations in which they could work as family units; where this was not possible the men might forbid the women to work (McLaughlin: 1971).

## REFERENCES

*Primary sources:*
*Abbott, John C.*
1833   The Mother at Home: Or, the Principles of Maternal Duty. Boston.
*Alcott, William A.*
1837   The Young Wife, or Duties of Woman in the Married Relation. Boston.
*Anonymous*
1811   The Maternal Physician: A Treatise on the Nurture and Management of Infants. By an American Matron. New York
1813   The American Lady's Preceptor: A Compilation of Observations, Essays, and Poetical Effusions Designed to Direct the Female Mind in a Course of Pleasing and Instructive Reading. Baltimore.
1836   The Young Lady's Own Book: A Manual of Intellectual Improvement and Moral Deportment. Philadelphia.
1856   The Lady's Companion. Edited by a Lady. Philadelphia.
*Bennett, John*
1795   Strictures on Female Education. Worcester.

*Child, Mrs. Lydia*
1831   The Mother's Book. Boston.
*Colman, Benjamin*
1716   The Honour and Happiness of the Vertuous Woman. Boston
*Gisborne, Thomas*
1797   An Enquiry into the Duties of the Female Sex. London.
*Humphrey, Heman*
1840   Domestic Education. Amherst.
*Mather, Cotton*
1692   Ornaments for the Daughters of Zion. Boston.
*Wadsworth, Benjamin*
1712   The Well-Ordered Family. Boston.


*Secondary sources:*
*Abbott, Edith*
1906   "The history of industrial employment of women in the United States: An intro-
       ductory study." Journal of Political Economy 8 (October): 461–501.
*Demos, John*
1970   A Little Commonwealth: Family Life in Plymouth Colony, New York: Oxford
       University Press.
*Easton, Barbara*
1975   Women, Religion and the Family: Revivalism as an Indicator of Social Change in
       Early New England. Unpublished Ph.D. Dissertation. Berkeley: University of Cali-
       fornia.
*Flexner, Eleanor*
1968   Century of Struggle: the Woman's Rights Movement in the United States. New
       York: Atheneum.
*McLaughlin, Virginia Yans*
1971   "Patterns of work and family organization: Buffalo's Italians." Journal of Interdisci-
       plinary History 2 (Autumn): 229–314.
*Morgan, Edmund S.*
1944   The Puritan Family: Religion and Domestic Relations in Seventeenth Century
       New England. New York: Harper and Row.
*Ryan, Mary P.*
1975   Womanhood in America: from Colonial Times to the Present. New York: Franklin
       Watts.
*Tryon, Rolla May*
1917   Household Manufactures in the United States, 1640–1860. Chicago: University of
       Chicago Press.
*Wood, Ann Douglas*
1973   " 'The fashionable diseases': women's complaints and their treatment in nine-
       teenth century America." Journal of Interdisciplinary History 1 (Summer): 25–52.

# Toward a Sociotechnological Theory of the Women's Movement*

## Joan Huber

*University of Illinois*
*Urbana-Champaign*

*The degree of sex stratification in a society is based on the extent to which males dominate the distribution of resources outside the reproductive unit. The industrial revolution increasingly transferred productive functions outside the family while it reduced women's reproductive functions. These trends reduced women's functions to custodial childcare and domestic service. While industrial demands for labor drew women first into the factory and later into the office, their supply and pay were regulated by male-dominated institutions, such as labor unions and schools. Only after married women entered the labor force on a long-term basis did the Women's Movement develop into a force which could not be reversed.*

Source: Joan Huber, "Toward a Sociotechnological Theory of the Women's Movement," Social Problems 23, 4 (April 1976): pp. 371–88. Copyright © 1976 by the Society for the Study of Social Problems. Reprinted by permission of the Society and the author.
*I am indebted to Rae Lesser Blumberg, Marcus Felson, Myra Marx Ferree, Kenneth Land, David Lewis, Karen Oppenheim Mason, Barbara Reskin, Robert Schoen, and Joe Spaeth for comments on an early draft of this paper. I am grateful to Lillian Rubin for penetrating criticm of the last two drafts and to William Form for vigorous criticism of every draft of this paper.

The most recent women's movement, which I shall refer to in capitals as the Women's Movement to distinguish it from earlier forms, emerged in the political turmoil of the late sixties. In the early sixties, many college students had been idealistically attracted to the Black Movement, but when blacks took over their own movement, white youth were ejected. They soon found another cause. The escalating Viet Nam War—and the rising draft calls on the campus —stimulated many college students to join loosely with New Left radicals and other groups in a vigorous egalitarian movement. When young radical women found that the total transformation of society was to stop short at the kitchen door, they began to meet in small groups to engage in consciousness-raising, collectively identifying the social mechanisms that kept women down. At the same time older professional women, aware of their continuing second class status, attempted to remove legal restrictions on women's work (Freeman, 1975). In time, the two streams tended to coalesce.

One basic theme pervades feminist literature: Women are kept in their place by their responsibility for childcare and domestic work. This proposition implies that the problem is not only women's invisibility in market and political institutions but also men's invisibility in the home. Many men still see only one side of the problem: desegregating the world of work, hard as that may be. The other side may be even harder: bringing men back in—to the kitchen, to the bathroom when it is time to scour the kiddies, and to the utility room which contains a fancy many-dialed machine that many men have not mastered. The most intractable issue is childcare—a problem of equality in parental responsibility that has hardly been addressed (Lorber, 1975). Institutions that would support shared childcare are almost non-existent; hence even those couples who favor equality for women find it almost impossible to incorporate their convictions into their lifestyles.

The purpose of this paper is to analyze the factors responsible for the emergence of the Women's Movement in order to assess its prospects for the future. The task is difficult for researchers in any one discipline because the data must come from all of the social sciences; furthermore, until recently women's work was almost ignored.[1] This paper argues that the decline in fertility and the shift of productive work from home to factory in the past two centuries has upset the equilibrium of sex stratification in industrial societies. The basic theoretical premise is that the right to distribute and exchange valued goods and services to those not in a person's domestic unit confers power and prestige in all societies. This leads to the hypothesis that male dominance results from the frequency with which men control extra-domestic distribution (Friedl, 1975:8). With industrialization, fertility rates dropped, women were less often pregnant, and—whether because of fewer pregnancies or because of a technology that separated feeding from lactation—time spent in lactation was reduced dramatically. Production of household goods was transferred to the factory, but women's work there was controlled in response to the ebb and flow of demand for male labor. Women's entry into white collar work was regulated differently but the result was similar: they were crowded into occupational ghettos. The situation seemed more equitable before 1940 when the typical woman worker who was young and unmarried entered the labor force only briefly until she married and returned to tend to home and children. After 1940, when the female work force was increasingly composed of married women with children, women workers were more likely to be aware of their permanent second class status and their double burden of domestic work. In the egalitarian climate of the sixties, women's awareness that the ideology of equal opportunity did not apply to them helped to precipitate the Women's Movement.

## TECHNOLOGY AND BIOLOGY

Although a substantial literature supports the belief that the basic cause of sex stratification is biological, examination of the biological differences relevant to the division of labor shows that all but one are of degree rather than kind. Physiologically, men tend to be larger and stronger; women tend to be more durable (Madigan, 1957; Bayo and Glanz, 1955). The extent to which psychological differences result from biology or socialization is open to question; recent research emphasizes socialization (Whiting and Edwards, 1973; Maccoby and Jacklin, 1974). Whatever the cause, the overlap is too great to assign such factors much, if any, importance.

Only one biological difference categorically separates women and men: No man can bear a child. Yet technology permits humans to transcend biological characteristics. This common sense observation—people can fly although no one is born with wings—is made only because it is so often forgotten in discussions of women's place. That women can bear children is, to date, a fact of nature, but that women are assigned the responsibility of rearing children is a man-made fact subject to change. Even though no man has a womb, it is now technologically possible for men to share equally in the important and delicate task of socializing the next generation. How did this come about?

### The Decline in Fertility

Two quantum changes have given men equal opportunity for childrearing. The first is the long-term fall in fertility rates. I speak of this decline as long-term to stress that it has been going on for more than 200 years and is now apparently a permanent characteristic of industrial societies.

The primary reason for the decline apparently was the perception that children were no longer economic assets; by the second half of the nineteenth century this perception became increasingly common in Western Europe (United Nations, 1973:89). The primary demographic source of the fall in fertility was the decline in mean completed parity of married women from about seven children to less than three, achieved by cessation of childbearing at progressively earlier marital durations (United Nations, 1973:68). The principal method by which the decline was achieved was coitus interruptus—historically the principal male contraceptive technique; the female method was abortion (Tietze, 1968:383). These are still the chief methods of birth control world-wide, increasingly replaced by newer methods only since 1960 (Kirk, 1968:344).[2]

However much the fertility decline might have been desired by the individuals who brought it about, it made governments nervous when they finally perceived what was happening. The emergence, in the 1930s, of demography as a science reflected those governmental concerns about decreasing fertility.

Governments feared that low or negative growth rates would yield too few military personnel. Also they thought that population increase was necessary for economic growth—a view supported by some demographers today (Sauvy, 1968:355). It was those concerns that, at least partly, motivated efforts to make motherhood more attractive and underlaid governmental support of restrictive and protective legislation for women in the work force.

While such movements had little or no effect on the declining birth rate before World War II (for when the majority of a population wants to control family size, it apparently acts without regard for official policy or law [Eldridge, 1968:387]), the feminists of that era were caught in a difficult bind. The reality of the industrial work world was a horror for *all* who worked in its factories —men as well as women and children. Under those conditions, to argue against protective legislation or to oppose any movement that showed hope of getting women and children out of the factories was difficult indeed. A long term perspective was necessary to make that argument comprehensible, as well as an understanding of the connection between women's social status and their relationship to the distributive and productive forces of the society. Feminists in the 1920s, as I will show later, split on the issue of whether motherhood was the essence of womanhood, and its corollary—the demand that women be removed and/or protected from full participation in the public, productive sphere—was an issue on which the movement of that era eventually foundered.

By the 1950s, however, owing to rapid progress in controlling deaths without a compensating decrease in the birth rate after World War II, scholarly worry about decreasing fertility reversed. Public opinion paralleled scholarly views. Since then, approval for measures to restrict fertility has increased sharply—birth control services for teenage females who request them, birth control education in public high schools (Blake, 1973a), and abortion (Jones and Westoff, 1973 but see Blake, 1973b). Concern with the environment also rose sharply from 1965 to 1970 (Erskine, 1972:120) with some scholars now arguing that high fertility rates positively affect the rate of environmental degradation (Preston, 1971).

It is important that governments as well as individuals now apparently view low fertility rates as desirable because it implies less support for policies to improve women's maternal status at the expense of their social status. It is reasonable to speculate that low fertility rates will continue (barring atomic holocaust and the re-emergence of hunting and gathering societies, if we are lucky) on a wide scale. Meanwhile, this question emerges with increasing clarity: If the average woman is only briefly incapacitated for paid work, and if she is expected to work for an increasing portion of her adult life, on what grounds can we rationally assign the major burden of parenthood to women?

## Lactation

The second change that makes it possible for men to rear children as effectively as women is the improvement in methods of infant feeding that became widespread after the early years of the twentieth century. The fact that a baby's survival in its first years no longer depends on the ability of its mother to breastfeed it cannot be overemphasized. Techniques of food sterilization have shattered the ancient dependency of a baby on a lactating woman. The lack of such techniques in the nineteenth century, coupled with higher birth-rates, was doubtless a reason why, even to feminists, the woman issue seemed so intractable. Early feminist issues focused mainly on activities like voting, owning property, and access to higher education—issues that were less affected by pregnancy and lactation than was the household division of labor. The separation of childbearing and childrearing, like the separation of ownership and management, was a possibility only dimly seen at the time.

While industrialization was tranforming children from economic assets to economic liabilities, it also was creating the modern labor market. Landless peasants became urban industrial workers. Women became a low-wage labor reserve. In a broad sense, the labor force participation of working class women was regulated in the nineteenth century; that of middle-class women, in the twentieth century. The results are visible today.

## REGULATING WOMEN BLUE COLLAR WORKERS

During industrialization, populations were urbanized and a modern labor market emerged—a literate workforce, geographically and occupationally mobile. Non-monetized work performed on the basis of status became paid employment performed (more or less) on the basis of contract. Everywhere the ideology of equal opportunity emerged and came to justify inequality of reward. The most efficient way to motivate workers to perform industrial jobs is, after all, to make individuals feel responsible for their own fates (Ossowski, 1963). While the importance of this pervasive ideology cannot be overemphasized, it is not foolproof. For whenever sizable groups with some political clout discover that despite their best efforts they are not getting a fair share, social movements emerge. In the nineteenth century, male industrial workers, struggling for better wages and more control over their work, persistently threatened the stability of governments. Until recently no one noticed that all the great worker movements of the nineteenth century were men's movements.

Women were almost invisible in labor movements in the nineteenth century although their labor force participation never was and is not now in doubt. The question has always been how to regulate the quantity and locus of their participation. Regulating the employment of working class women was not difficult because those who might have been their natural sex allies—middle-class women—and their class allies—working-class men—saw such regulation as a primary goal. Under the guise of humanitarian concerns for women and children, and resting the movement on the primacy of maternal duties for women, they joined together to limit women's participation in the world of work.

The industrial revolution affected working and middle-class women differently. Early in industrialization women were excluded from learning skills, leaving working-class women unfit for anything but household work and low-wage jobs (Abbott, 1913: 254; Clark, 1919:300; Holcombe, 1973:174), a situation with parallels in the industrializing world today (Boserup, 1970). In contrast, wives of prosperous bourgeoisie were idled and assumed mainly ornamental and childbearing functions while their productive activities were assigned to male employees (Stern, 1932:444). The children of middle-class women are reared by working-class women. Nineteenth century feminists, economically unproductive and dependent on men, attacked women's exclusion from the perquisites of upper and middle-class men: education for the professions and civil service, control of property, extension of the vote, and supported measures to reduce the hours women could work in factories.

Working-class men and their leaders were primarily concerned with reducing women's hours of work for four reasons. First, although they depended on their wives' earnings, they wanted to be masters in their own homes (Rowbotham, 1974). A complaint early in industrialization was that women could find work when men could not, undermining the authority of the family (Smelser, 1959:ch. 9).

Second, many radicals and reformers were ambivalent about birth control. Factory owners had used Malthusian analysis to justify lower wages; higher wages were thought to inspire higher fertility which would, in turn, only reduce the level of subsistence. Because of the conservative implication of Malthusian theory, radicals rejected the idea that poverty was caused by overpopulation. Socialists tended to identify contraceptives as an upper-class device foisted on the lower classes to avoid basic social change. In the 1820s, this belief surfaced in Britain—a belief that troubled English radicals then and that still troubles socialists a century later (Rowbotham, 1974).

Third, socialists assumed that capitalism was the root cause of the woman issue. Engles, Bebel, and Lenin understood what domestic drudgery did to women but they expected that under socialism the state would assume women's domestic functions; the family would wither away. Radical and reform feminists in the United States at the turn of the century also thought that capitalism caused women's problems (Rossi, 1973:474). The fact that working women bear a double burden in both socialist and nonsocialist countries casts doubt on this assumption. By 1964, for example, only five percent of household work was performed by state employees in the Soviet Union (Geiger, 1968:184). But the tendency of radicals and laborites to attribute women's position to capitalism persists.

Fourth, and most important, was the fact that women were used as a reserve labor force which, ultimately, served to drive male wages down. As soon as they could organize to drive out these low-wage competitors, male workers did so. Early in industrialization, there was little opposition to women and child workers because working-class families had little choice. As male wages were reduced again and again, only the earnings of the entire family enabled it to subsist (Fuller, 1944:415)—a situation similar to that of migrant agricultural workers today. But such a situation becomes a self-perpetuating vicious circle. Since women and child workers were typically supplementary earners, they could be induced to work for ever lower wages, thus aiding in the further depression of the wages of their husbands and fathers.

Thus, the wage threat was real. In the United States in mid-nineteenth century, women's wages were about half of men's (Wood, 1929:494). Children in the cotton factories performed many kinds of work "better than adults" and cost only one-third as much (Adams, 1875:124). The first Annual Report of the United States Commissioner for Labor for 1885 and the Dewey Report for 1890 noted that the wages of adult women were somewhat less than three-fifths and those of children and youth somewhat more than one-third the wages of adult males (Long, 1960:104).

Under such circumstances those workers who can, organize to bargain collectively with management for rules that exclude their low-wage competitors. Whenever unemployment was high—which was fairly often in the nineteenth century—working men agitated to eliminate women's and children's competition. By the turn of the century, women, blacks, Orientals, other ethnics, and children had been largely removed from competition for high-wage jobs (Aronowitz, 1973; Hill, 1967, 1973). But we are getting ahead of the story. Before we examine women's experience with labor unions later in the nineteenth century, let us briefly discuss how children were eliminated from the labor market and what effect that had on women.

## Compulsory Education

The employment of children in mills and mines was a horror of industrialization. Humanitarian agitation to control or eliminate child labor began early in the nineteenth century and increased through time. Agitation for public education began a little later. It is difficult to assess the impact of humanitarian reformers. But the fact is that as industries became more capital-intensive, children were not hired because they could no longer be profitably employed and because male workers in those industries could organize to keep them out. In the twentieth century children were employed only in low-wage, non-unionized industries.

The children extruded from the mills, the mines, the farms, and the streets were embraced by the public schools. By the 1880s public education was compulsory in almost all industrial countries. Why? The received view in the United States is that it was motivated by the belief that republican ideals and democratic equality could be promoted only by general education at the public expense (Kandel, 1944). But the received view is based on faulty historiography, and the story is yet to be told (Cremin, 1965:45). Dobbs (1969:152) suggests that unoccupied youth in growing cities posed sufficient threat to social order to alarm the taxpayers. Katz (1971) suggests that the middle class wanted to educate its children at public expense.

Whatever the reasons for its success, public education stimulated the idea, paradoxically, that mothers belonged at home to give the children a hearty breakfast and see that they looked respectable when they went off to learn how to be upwardly mobile. Over time the birth rate fell, the school year lengthened, and the required years of attendance increased. But the mother's free time did not increase because a rapidly rising standard of living meant that the children had to be better dressed and odor-free in order to keep up with other children. Instead of producing goods, mothers spent more time chasing dirt. Mothers with very high aspirations for the children had to haul them to the right museums and expose them to symphony concerts, lest they be flummoxed by a question on Renoir or Beethoven when they took their college entrance examinations. By the middle of the twentieth century, women's investment in their children's human capital seemed so natural that most people forgot it was a comparatively recent development (Rossi, 1964). Forgotten, too, was the fact that this particular brand of motherhood was, first, a product of womens' exclusion from the productive work force; and, second, an ideal that could be only very imperfectly realized by most women in most families. For most working class families of America—in the present era or in the recent past —have had to rely on the wife's working outside the home for at least some period during the marriage.

### Labor Unions

The history of women's exclusion from high-wage industrial jobs goes back almost a century and deals with unions' refusal to admit women to membership or to organize them, and with the development of labor legislation designed to protect their maternal status. By the 1880s the frontier had closed, recurrent depressions made agriculture risky, and factory jobs were, therefore, more attractive to men than earlier in the century. European immigration was heavy. Massive unemployment plagued urban areas. Skilled workers had ample reason to eliminate low-wage competitors. Women were just one of a number of groups that unions excluded from high-wage jobs.

The idea that women were *excluded* from high-wage jobs does not represent the dominant view of labor leaders or students of the labor movement. Most labor history is written from the vantage point of workmen's interests, a legacy of nineteenth century class politics. Since women were viewed as auxiliary earners whose problems stemmed from an exploitive industrial system, their interests vis-à-vis those of men are underplayed to the point of invisibility. In 1903, John Mitchell (1973:131) stated the mainstream view succinctly: "If trade unionism had rendered no other service to humanity, it would have justified its existence by its efforts on behalf of working women and children." Because it represents a minority view, the literature dealing with unions' exclusion of women is slender indeed. For example, in an annotated bibliography on women in American labor history from 1825 to 1935 (Soltow, Forché, and Massre, 1972:22–49), only 12 of the 112 items listed under "Trade Unions" depart from the mainstream view.

Chafe (1972:ch. 3), whose account I follow, states that to some extent women's low participation in the labor movement reflected the work they did: low-wage jobs in candy factories, textile mills, and laundries. But fundamentally, women failed to become part of the trade union movement because they were not invited in until the late 1930s. The American Federation of Labor (AFL) treated women workers with open hostility and did almost nothing to organize them. Both Gompers and his successor, William Green, attacked the presence of married women in the work force and asserted that women should marry and care for families. When a group accused the Executive Council of the AFL of prejudice, Gompers replied that the AFL discriminated against any non-assimilable race. Even when women organized themselves, they were denied recognition.

Because it organized workers by industry rather than skill, the formation of the Congress of Industrial Organizations (CIO) improved the situation of workers excluded by the skill-apprenticeship system of the AFL. Yet sex inequality continued to pervade organized labor even in the most "progressive" unions.[3] For example, half the members of the Amalgamated Clothing Workers were women but the union sanctioned lower wages for women than for men and granted women only token recognition as officers (Chafe, 1972:87).

In addition to union exclusion, women were also restricted by labor legislation designed to protect their maternal status. Let us examine this legislation.

### Protective Labor Legislation

The movement for labor legislation stemmed from workers' desire to exact higher wages and better working conditions from management. The movement for *protective* labor legislation stemmed from the desire of male workers to restrict the competition of women and children and from the humanitarian impulses of middle and working-class reformers to protect women and children from the worst features of the industrial system.

Protective legislation appeared much earlier in Britain than in the United States. Beginning in 1802, statutes progressively limited the working hours first of children, then of women till by 1847 the 10 hour day was standard in British factories. Because factories needed uniform work schedules, the hours of men were also reduced (Tolles, 1968:419).

In the United States, because the employee's right to bargain with the employer was held unconstitutional, protective legislation arrived much later but the British pattern was repeated: women and children first. Until 1932, liberals tried to protect women; conservatives, to keep them free. By 1896, only 13 states restricted women's working hours (the easiest way to exclude women from high-wage jobs) and the constitutionality of these was doubtful (Brandeis, 1935). In 1908, however, the Supreme Court unanimously established the constitutionality of legislation on women's health, exempting women from the freedom-of-contract doctrine because they needed special protection. A "liberal" court thus exempted women from a doctrine detested by everyone sympathetic to labor. Feminists who objected to women's being singled out were accused of anti-labor sentiments. The result of the 1908 decision was a spate of legislation between 1909 and 1917, a peak year when the court passed almost all the labor legislation that came before it. A conservative trend followed, peaking in 1923 when Justice Sutherland held that the 19th (voting) Amendment established sex equality, hence special legislation for women was unconstitutional. Labor leaders deplored the decision.

The issue of protective legislation split the women's movement in the 1920s. In 1923, the National Women's Party (NWP) proposed an Equal Rights Amendment to eliminate special legislation for women. It was opposed by the League of Women Voters (LWV), descendant of the National American Women's Suffrage Association. What separated the two groups was the issue whether women's maternal functions preceded all others, since the argument for protection stemmed from employed women's double burden. The NWP claimed that protective legislation merely excluded women from high-wage jobs; the LWV, that it eased the burden of women workers. Both the NWP and the LWV were composed primarily of middle-class women, many of them strong supporters of the labor movement. The issue was whether women were to be primarily productive workers or primarily child caretakers. Unlike many nineteenth century feminists, the NWP clearly saw the implications of this issue.

The issue of special women's legislation tended to disappear in the Roosevelt era which brought legislation giving American workers benefits long taken for granted elsewhere. Whether New Deal legislation discriminated by sex has never been systematically investigated. Certainly some of it was discriminatory. In four NIRA codes women were permitted to receive lower wages than men; the industries affected were those that employed the largest proportions of women (Chafe, 1972:85).

How effective was protective legislation, either in easing women's burdens or excluding them from high-wage jobs? The evidence is unclear because most of the literature is deductive argument, devoid of evidence. Persons associated with unions or the Department of Labor tended to think such legislation improved women's lot.[3] A rare empirical study held that it did not. Baker (1925) investigated protective legislation's effects in New York State. Examination of specific jobs in specific industries showed that within a few years after it took effect, women were virtually excluded from high-wage jobs. Laws would restrict women's working hours; then unions would require workers to take the night shift for a specified period of time to acquire seniority. Since women were prohibited to do night work, they were excluded from the seniority system. The law penalized skilled women most but the result was felt by all women workers because it automatically threw them back into already overcrowded occupations, into competition with less skilled women (Baker, 1925:427, 433).

Whatever protective legislation's actual effects, labor unions have supported it. The AFL-CIO failed to support the ERA (which would nullify such legislation) till October 1973, and it still shows ambivalence, apparent in the California ERA fight (Miller and Linker, 1974).[5] A rare opinion study on measures to restrict women's work found working women most opposed and men employed in manufacturing least opposed to such restrictions (Duncan and Evers, 1975).

Thus women's opportunities for skilled work respond to the ebb and flow of demand for male workers.[6] Women became skilled manual workers before, during, and immediately after World War I but were driven out during the Depression. Again in World War II, women became skilled workers but only today do they form as high a proportion of skilled workers in the United States as in 1920. Currently, women blue collar workers are crowded into the underclass of dirty service workers and into non-durable goods manufacturing (Bibb and Form 1975). White collar workers, to whom we now turn, were crowded too but their ghetto was cleaner and brighter.

## REGULATING WOMEN WHITE COLLAR WORKERS

In the twentieth century, the blue collar proportion of the workforce changed little but the white collar proportion mushroomed. Despite the enormous growth of that sector of the work force, women were crowded into the low-salary white collar occupations. The mechanisms were less formal than those that were applied to blue collar women because white collar males, typically unorganized, lacked a handy organizational weapon. White collar women like their blue collar counterparts, were indirectly controlled through their socialization. If that failed, more direct mechanisms were called into play.

Socialization for childcare responsibility affected women in three ways. First, it made them ambivalent about the relation of work and family roles— whether in the United States (Mason and Bumpass, 1975), the Soviet Union

(Wilensky, 1968:243), or Eastern Europe (Matejko, 1974:215). Public opinion, including women's, generally holds that a woman's first duty is to her family. In 1900, dissapproval of unmarried women's working was confined to the upper classes (Smuts, 1959:137) but disapproval of married women's working was apparently widespread (Oppenheimer, 1970:42). As late as 1968, only 47 percent of United States women thought that married women should contribute to family income (Erskine, 1971). A recent analysis based on a "patch-work quilt of sample surveys" shows, however, that the proportion of women supporting the traditional division of labor has declined from 1964 to 1974 and the proportion supporting women's rights in the labor market has increased (Mason, Czajka, and Arber, 1975).

Second, socialization predisposes women to train for and seek non-ladder jobs. Little girls—when their aspirations are high—want to be school teachers. Little boys want to be business executives.[7]

Third, socialization encourages women to adopt behavior patterns poorly suited for the world (Chafetz, 1974; Henshel, 1974; Weitzman, 1975). Adolescent boys want to master a subject; girls are concerned with the impression they make (Rosenberg and Simmons, 1975).

More directly, women have been excluded from high level white collar training and employment by refusal to admit or hire them;[8] often their numbers in colleges and professional schools are restricted by quota systems and requirements of higher performance scores for women than for men. Women are still underrepresented in colleges and professional schools all over the world (Zimmer, 1975). Whether this is the result of prior socialization or direct exclusion is unknown, but both work powerfully to reinforce one another. The informal practices which isolate women from major communication networks and, consequently, exclude them from high-salary occupations has recently been well-documented (Epstein, 1970a, 1970b; Rossi and Calderwood, 1973).

Women have reason to be discontented with current patterns of sex stratification. Because they can bear children and are expected to rear them, they occupy second class status in the job world—the main arena for status and prestige in industrial societies (Tsuchigane and Dodge, 1974:105). But why did the most broad-based women's movement to date emerge in the late sixties rather than earlier? Persistent discrimination against any group is not sufficient to provoke a collective response. What is needed is the perception of an "unfair" situation coupled with the conviction that something can be done about it. The answer lies in the rapid increase in women's labor force participation after 1940.

## WOMEN'S EMPLOYMENT SINCE 1940

From 1870 to 1950, women's labor force participation increased gradually. In 1900, 20 percent of women between the ages of 18 and 64 worked; mostly young and unmarried, they would work for a few years, marry, and leave the labor force never to return. By 1940 their participation increased only to 30 percent and the lifecycle pattern was about the same. After 1940, however, married women formed an increasingly large proportion of women workers owing to a number of factors such as the expansion of clerical occupations, a decrease in the supply of young unmarried women, and the increase in college attendance which gave rise to the need for added family income when children approached college age (Oppenheimer, 1970, 1973, 1974).

Furthermore, women apparently perceive the connection between fertility and employment. It was long known that women's labor force participation is inversely related to their fertility (Preston and Richards, 1975); new evidence shows that women's *plans* for employment substantially affect the number of children they plan to bear (Waite and Stolzenberg, in press).

Working is apparently becoming normative for married women, even for those with children. The working woman is no longer a deviant, obliged to explain why she works. Plausibly, if women are no longer defensive about working, they may turn to question whether the ideology of equal opportunity applies to them. The answers increase their discontent.

First, the earnings differential by sex persists. All over the industrialized world women earn half to two-thirds the earnings of men (Lydall, 1968:55). Wage differentials in the United States, well documented (Featherman and Hauser, 1975), are increasing (Blau, forthcoming).

Yet women need their earnings as much as men do. The divorce rate continues to rise—1973 data show that four of nine marriages may end in divorce (Preston, 1975). Poor compliance records characterize court-ordered child-support payments (Eckhardt, 1968)—still the only empirical study of this important topic. Finally, three-fifths of all women workers are single, widowed, divorced, or separated, or have husbands whose earnings are less than $7,000 a year (U.S. Department of Labor, 1974).

Whether they work or not, women still bear the brunt of domestic work and are expected to deal with internal family issues and disruptions (Coser and Rokoff, 1971). Employed women work longer hours than employed men in the United States (Hedges and Barnett, 1972:10), British Columbia (Meissner et al., 1975), the Soviet Union (Dodge, 1966:94; Brown, 1968:45; Geiger, 1968:60; Lipset and Dobson, 1973:174), and Eastern Europe (Matejko, 1974:215; Scott, 1974). A comparison of time budgets of urban Soviet workers showed little change in the allocation of domestic work by sex between 1920 and 1960 (Sacks, 1975). Childcare facilities are inadequate world wide, the shortage is increasing in the United States (Roby, 1973:6), and little is known about basic needs and costs (Rowe and Husby, 1973; Waldman and Whitmore, 1974:56). An added handicap for working mothers is the fact that schools are located in residential districts while the jobs are in the downtown business district, making it difficult to mix jobs with childcare responsibilities (Friedl, 1975:137).

## WILL THE WOMEN'S MOVEMENT FADE?

This paper argued that the secular decline in fertility and the shift of productive work from home to factory resulted in men's monopolizing the exchange of valued goods and services while, owing to their childrearing responsibility, women monopolize increasingly trivialized domestic work and second class jobs. Current sex stratification patterns are better adapted to an age when fertility could not easily be controlled. On the assumption that stratification systems adapt to the range of possibilities determined by the level of technology (Lenski and Lenski, 1973), it seems likely that women will continue to press for equality in childrearing responsibility, since such equality is now technologically feasible. Historically, fertility levels fell when individual families defined children as economic liabilities. Will fertility rates drop still further if women define children as a personal liability? What kind of support patterns would make childbearing sufficiently attractive (but not too attractive) to maintain "desired" fertility rates? The thrust of the Women's Movement poses this basic question.

Unlike earlier women's movements which focused on a narrower range of rights, the current movement includes all human activity in its scope. The problem is dual: bringing women into the world of work and bringing men into the "world" of the home. In the absence of children this is no problem. Any adult can easily learn to clean up its own daily mess. But what if, as seems probable, men do not want an equal share of childrearing? Then pressure for extra-familial agencies will increase. Whether this will improve matters for children is also unknown. Perhaps the results are mixed.

Techological change brings many unanticipated consequences. The Women's Movement is the unplanned result of the change in what traditionally has been defined as women's work—childcare and domestic chores. But unless these changes be undone, the Women's Movement is here to stay.

## NOTES

1   The history of the U.S. family has been neglected (Bailyn, 1960:76), and changes affecting women's work and family lives in the nineteenth and twentieth centuries are unexplored (Scott and Tilly, 1975:640); a comprehensive history of the U.S. colonial economy has yet to be written (Cremin, 1970:638). Women have been invisible in anthropology (Friedl, 1975:6), economics (Bell, 1974), history (Stern, 1944:443; Tilly, 1975), and sociology (Millman and Kanter, 1975).

2   Considering the importance of the problem, the bibliography on the way humans give life or refuse to give it is astonishingly meagre (Sauvy, 1961:55). Himes's (1970) medical history of contraception, first published in 1936, is the only large-scale effort to document the attempt to control fertility from prehistory to modern times (Tietze, 1970:vii).

3   The situation is much the same. Women's proportion of union membership rose from 18 percent in 1952 to 22 percent in 1972. Women are still almost absent from high national offices (Bergquist, 1974:5, 7).

4   A Woman's Bureau study (U.S. Department of Labor, 1928) and a later government report (Pidgeon, 1937) concluded that restrictions on women's hours had not increased the substitution of men for women nor prevented women's promotion to supervisory positions. The National Manpower Council also (1957:333) concluded that the restrictive consequences were slight; but this conclusion is based on a misinterpretation of Baker's (1925) research. A small minority of women laborites held that restrictions ensured that women's low wages would be even lower (Breckinridge, 1906), but others claimed that the arguments favoring restriction of men's hours applied a hundred-fold to women's (Goldmark, 1905).

5   Most unions and the Department of Labor continue to show little interest in women workers. The Department of Labor has seen little need for affirmative action for women (Hedges and Bemis, 1974). The coalition of Labor Union Women formed in 1974 received no financial aid from the AFL-CIO nor is it formally recognized by them, in contrast to the UAW which funds a director for its women's department (Raphael, 1974:32).

6   Blumberg (1976a, 1976b) notes the importance of fluctuations in the supply of male labor in accounting for occupational segregation. Her suggestive analysis (Blumberg, 1976a) shows that, despite a formally egalitarian ideology, women were gradually excluded from the more productive jobs in the kibbutz. Although the kibbutz collectivized childcare and domestic service to free women for more productive work, no men were assigned to childcare and no mechanisms insured equal participation of the sexes in domestic services. An important factor was the arrival of young male immigrants that the kibbutz was committed to absorb; they gradually replaced women in agricultural work. Eventually, service work absorbed 90 percent of kibbutz women.

7   Women college graduates are less able than men graduates to capitalize on their education investment (Spaeth, 1975). Czech women university graduates receive the same wages as working men who completed the ninth grade (Scott, 1974:6). U.S. women college graduates working fulltime year round receive the same wages as men who have not completed high school (U.S. Bureau of the Census, 1973:1, 242).

8   The study of economic discrimination dates only from 1957; economists had been reluctant to interpret systematic group differentials as exploitation (Becker, 1968:208). Most theories fail to show how economic variables in the model interact with the central event to be explained (Marshall, 1974:861). For a good sociological analysis of discrimination, see O'Conner (1975).

## REFERENCES

*Abbott, Edith*
1913   Women in Industry. New York: Appleton.
*Adams, Francis*
1875   The Free School System of the United States. London: Chapman and Hall.
*Armytage, W. H. G.*
1970   Four Hundred Years of English Education. Cambridge: Cambridge University Press.
*Aronowitz, Stanley*
1973   False Promises: The Shaping of American Working Class Consciousness. New York: McGraw-Hill.
*Bailyn, Bernard*
1960   Education in the Forming of American Society. Chapel Hill: University of North Carolina Press.
*Baker, Elizabeth Faulkner*
1925   Protective Labor Legislation. New York: Columbia University Press.
*Bayo, Francisco, and Milton P. Glanz*
1965   "Mortality experiences of workers entitled to old-age benefits under OASDI 1941–1961." Social Security Administration, Actuarial Study 60. Washington, D.C.: U.S. Government Printing Office.
*Becker, Gary S.*
1968   "Discrimination, economic." Pp. 208–210 in David Sills (ed.), International Encyclopedia of the Social Sciences 4. New York: Macmillan and The Free Press.

*Bell, Carolyn Shaw*
1974   "Working women's contributions to family income." Eastern Economic Journal 1 (April/July): 3–9.

*Bernard, Jessie*
1974   The Future of Motherhood. New York: Dial Press.

*Bibb, Robert, and William H. Form*
1974   "Sexually segments blue collar labor markets and inequality of earnings." Working paper 75–10. Department of Sociology. University of Illinois, Urbana-Champaign.

*Blake, Judith*
1973a   "The teenage birth control dilemma and public opinion." Science 180 (May): 708–712.
1973b   "Elective opinion and our reluctant citizenry." Pp. 447–467 in Howard J. Osofsky and Joy D. Osofsky (eds.), The Abortion Experience. New York: Harper and Row.

*Blau, Francine*
in press   "Women in the labor force." In Ann Yates and Shirley Harkness (eds.), Women and Their Work, Palo Alto: Mayfield.

*Blumberg, Rae Lesser*
1976a   "The erosion of sexual equality in the kibbutz." In Joan Roberts (ed.), Women Scholars on Women. New York: McKay.
1976b   "Women and work around the world." In Alice Sargent (ed.), Beyond Sex Roles. St. Paul: West.

*Boserup, Ester*
1970   Women's Role in Economic Development. London: George Allen & Unwin.

*Boyd, Monica*
1974   "Equality between the sexes: results of Canadian Gallup polls." Paper presented at the meetings of the Canadian Sociology and Anthropology Association.

*Brandeis, Elizabeth*
1935   "Labor legislation." Pp. 339–697 in Don Lescohier and Elizabeth Brandeis, Volume III of John R. Commons, History of Labor in the United States, 1896–1932. New York: Macmillan.

*Breckinridge, Sophonisba B.*
1906   "Legislative control of women's work." Journal of Political Economy 14 (February): 107–109.

*Brown, Donald R. (ed.)*
1968   The Role and Status of Women in the Soviet Union. New York: Teachers College Press of Columbia University.

*Carden, Maren Lockwood*
1974   The New Feminist Movement. New York: Russell Sage Foundation.

*Chafetz, Janet*
1919   Working Life of Women in the Seventeenth Century. London: George Routledge.

*Coser, Rose Laub, and Gerald Rokoff*
1971   "Women in the occupational world: Social disruption and conflict." Social Problems 18 (Spring): 535–554.

*Cremin, Lawrence A.*
1965   The Wonderful World of Elwood Patterson Cubberley: An Essay on the Historiography of American Education. New York: Teachers College Press of Columbia University.
1970   American Education: The Colonial Experience, 1607–1783. New York: Harper and Row.

*Dobbs, A. E.*
1969   Education and Social Movements 1700–1850. [1919] Reprints of Economic Classics. New York: August M. Kelley.

*Dodge, Norton T.*
1966   Women in the Soviet Economy. Baltimore: The Johns Hopkins Press.

*Duncan, Beverly, and Mark Evers*
1975   "Measuring change in attitudes toward women's work." Pp. 129–156 in Kenneth

C. Land and Seymour Spilerman (eds.), Social Indicator Models. New York: Russell Sage Foundation.

*Eckhardt, Kenneth W.*
1968   "Deviance, visibility and legal action: The duty to support." Social Problems 15 (Spring): 470–477.

*Eldridge, Hope T.*
1968   "Population: Population policies," Pp. 380–388 in David Sills (ed.), The International Encyclopedia of the Social Sciences 12. New York: Macmillan and The Free Press.

*Epstein, Cynthia*
1970a   "Encountering the male establishment: Sex-status limits on women's careers in the professions." American Journal of Sociology 75 (May): 965–982.
1970b   Woman's Place: Options and Limits in Professional Careers. Berkeley: University of California Press.

*Erskine, Hazel Gaudet*
1971   "The polls: Women's role." Public Opinion Quarterly 34 (Summer): 275–290.
1972   "The polls: Pollution and its costs." Public Opinion Quarterly 36 (Spring): 120–135.

*Featherman, David, and Robert Hauser*
1975   "Sexual inequalities and socioeconomic achievement in the U.S., 1962–1973." Working Paper 75–10. Madison: Center for Demography and Ecology, University of Wisconsin.

*Ferree, Myra Marx*
1974   "A woman for president? Changing responses, 1958–72." Public Opinion Quarterly 38 (Fall): 390–99.

*Form, William*
1973   "The internal stratification of the working class." American Sociological Review 38 (December): 697–711.

*Freeman, Jo*
1975   The Politics of Women's Liberation. New York: David McKay.

*Friedl, Ernestine*
1975   Women and Men: An Anthropologist's View. New York: Holt, Rinehart and Winston.

*Geiger, Kent*
1968   The Family in Soviet Russia. Cambridge: Harvard University Press.

*Goldmark, Josephine*
1905   "The necessary sequel of child-labor laws." American Journal of Sociology 11 (November): 312–325.

*Hedges, J. N., and S. E. Bemis*
1974   "Sex stereotyping: Its decline in the skilled trades." Monthly Labor Review 97 (May): 14–22.

*Henshel, Anne-Marie*
1973   Sex Structure. Don Mills, Ont.: Longman Canada.

*Hill, Herbert*
1967   "The racial practices of organized labor," Pp. 365–402 in A. M. Ross and Herbert Hill, Employment, Race, and Poverty. New York: Harcourt, Brace & World.
1973   "Anti-oriental agitation and the rise of working-class racism." Society 10 (Jan.–Feb.): 43–54.

*Himes, Norman E.*
1970   Medical History of Contraception. [1936] New York: Schocken.

*Holcombe, Lee*
1973   Victorian Ladies at Work. Hamden, Conn.: Shoe String.

*Jones, Elise and Charles Westoff*
1973   "Change in attitudes toward abortion." Pp. 468–481 in Howard J. Osofsky and Joy D. Osofsky, The Abortion Experience. New York: Harper and Row.

*Katz, Michael B. (ed.)*
1971   School Reform: Past and Present. Boston: Little Brown.

*Kirk, Dudley*
1968   "Population: The field of demography." Pp. 342–349 in David L. Sills (ed.), International Encyclopedia of the Social Sciences 12. New York: Macmillan and The Free Press.

*Lemons, J. Stanley*
1973   The Woman Citizen: Social Feminism in the 1920s. Urbana: University of Illinois Press.

*Lenski, Gerhard and Jean Lenski*
1973   Human Societies. New York: McGraw-Hill.

*Lipset, Seymour Martin, and Richard Dobson*
1973   "Social stratification and sociology in the Soviet Union." Survey 88 (Summer): 114–185.

*Long, Clarence D.*
1960   Wages and Earnings in the United States, 1860–1890. Princeton: Princeton University Press.

*Lopata, Helena Znaniecki*
1971   Occupation: Housewife. New York: Oxford University Press.

*Lorber, Judith*
1975   "Beyond equality of the sexes: The question of the children." The Family Coordinator 24 (October): 465–472.

*Lydall, Harold*
1968   The Structure of Earnings. London: Oxford at the Clarendon Press.

*Madigan, Francis S. J.*
1957   "Are sex mortality differentials biologically caused?" Milbank Memorial Fund Quarterly 35:203–223.

*Marshall, Ray*
1974   "The economics of racial discrimination: A survey." Journal of Economic Literature 12 (September): 849–871.

*Mason, Karen Oppenheim, and Larry L. Bumpass*
1975   "U.S. women's sex-role ideology, 1970." American Journal of Sociology 80 (March): 1212–1219.

*Mason, Karen Oppenheim, John Czajka, and Sara Arber*
1975   "Change in U.S. women's sex-role attitudes, 1964–74." Mimeographed paper.

*Matejko, Alexander*
1974   Social Change and Stratification in Eastern Europe. New York: Praeger.

*Meissner, Martin, Elizabeth Humphreys, Scott Meis, and Jack Scheu*
1975   "No exit for wives: Sexual division of labour and the cumulation of household demands." Mimeographed paper.

*Miller, Margaret, and Helene Linker*
1974   "Equal rights amendment campaigns." Society 11 (May/June): 40–53.

*Millman, Marcia, and Rosabeth Moss Kanter (eds.)*
1975   Another Voice: Feminist Perspectives on Social Life and Social Science. Garden City: Anchor Press.

*Mitchell, John*
1973   Organized Labor. [1903] Clifton, N.J.: Kelley.

*National Manpower Council*
1957   Womanpower. New York: Columbia University Press.

*O'Connor, James F.*
1975   "Discrimination against married women in the public schools, 1940–41." Working Paper 75-09. Urbana-Champaign: Department of Sociology, University of Illinois.

*Oppenheimer, Valerie Kincade*
1970   The Female Labor Force in the United States. Berkeley: University of California Press.
1973   "Demographic influence on female employment and the status of women." American Journal of Sociology 78 (January): 184–199.

1974 "The life-cycle squeeze: the interaction of men's occupational and family life cycles." Demography 11 (May): 227–245.

*Pidgeon, Mary Elizabeth*
1937 Women in the Economy of the United States of America: A Summary Report. Washington, D.C.: U.S. Government Printing Office.

*Preston, Samuel H.*
1975 "Estimating the proportion of American marriages that end in divorce." Sociological Methods and Research 3 (May): 453–459.

*Preston, Samuel H., and Alan Thomas Richards*
1975 "The influence of women's work opportunities on marriage rates." Demography 12 (May): 209–222.

*Raphael, Edna*
1974 "Working women and their membership in labor unions." Monthly Labor Review 97 (May): 27–33.

*Roby, Pamela (ed.)*
1973 Child Care—Who Cares? New York: Basic Books.

*Rossi, Alice S.*
1964 "Equality between the sexes: a modest proposal." Daedalus 93 (Spring): 607–652.

*Rossi, Alice S. (ed.)*
1973 The Feminist Papers. New York: Columbia University Press.

*Rossi, Alice S., and Ann Calderwood (eds.)*
1973 Academic Women on the Move. New York: Russell Sage Foundation.

*Rosenberg, Florence R., and Roberta G. Simmons*
1975 "Sex differences in the self-concept in adolescence." Sex Roles 1 (June): 147–160.

*Rowbotham, Sheila*
1974 Hidden from History. New York: Random House.

*Rowe, Mary Potter, and Ralph Husby*
1973 "Economics of child care: Costs, needs, and issues." Pp. 98–122 in Pamela Roby (ed.). Child Care—Who Cares? New York: Basic Books.

*Sacks, Michael Paul*
1975 "Unchanging times: A comparison of the everyday life of Soviet working men and women between 1923 and 1966." Paper presented at annual meetings of the American Sociological Association.

*Safilios-Rothschild, Constantina*
1974 Women and Social Policy. Englewood Cliffs: Prentice-Hall.

*Sauvy, Alfred*
1961 Fertility and Survival. London: Chatto and Windus.

*Scott, Hilda*
1974 Does Socialism Liberate Women? Boston: Beacon.

*Scott, Joan, and Louise Tilly*
1975 " Women's work and the family in nineteenth century Europe." Comparative Studies in Society and History 17 (January): 36–64.

*Smelser, Neil*
1959 Social Change in the Industrial Revolution. Chicago: University of Chicago Press.

*Smuts, Robert W.*
1959 Women and Work in America. New York: Columbia University Press.

*Soltow, Martha Jane, Carolyn Forché, and Murray Massre*
1972 Women in American Labor History, 1825–1935: An Annotated Bibliography. East Lansing: Michigan State School of Labor and Industrial Relations and Libraries.

*Spaeth, Joe L.*
1975 "Differences in the occupational achievement process between male and female college graduates." Paper presented at the annual meetings of the American Sociological Association.

*Stern, Bernhard J.*
1944 "Woman, position in society: Historical." Pp. 442–451 in E. R. A. Seligman (ed.), Encyclopedia of the Social Sciences 15. New York: Macmillan.

*Suter, Larry and Linda Waite*
1976    "Worker, housewife, mother: Role decisions of young women." Mimeographed paper.

*Tietze, Christopher*
1968    "Fertility control." Pp. 382–388 in David Sills (ed.). International Encyclopedia of the Social Sciences 5. New York: Macmillan and the Free Press.

*Tilly, Charles (ed.)*
in press    "Questions and conclusions." Historical Studies of Changing Fertility. Princeton: Princeton University Press.

*Tilly, Louise*
1975    "Industrialization, the position of women, and women's history." CRSO Working Paper 118. Ann Arbor: Department of Sociology, University of Michigan.

*Tilly, Louise, Joan W. Scott, and Miriam Cohen*
in press    "Women's work and European fertility patterns." Journal of Interdisciplinary History.

*Tolles, Arnold*
1968    "Wages: Wage and hour legislation." Pp. 418–424 in David Sills (ed.), International Encyclopedia of the Social Sciences 16. New York: Macmillan and The Free Press.

*Tsuchigane, Robert, and Norton Dodge*
1974    Economic Discrimination Against Women in the United States. Lexington: Lexington Books.

*United Nations*
1973    The Determinants and Consequences of Population Trends 1. Population Studies No. 50. New York: Department of Economic and Social Affairs.

*U.S. Bureau of the Census*
1973    "Earnings by occupation and education." Census of Population: 1970. Subject Reports, Final Reports PC(2)-8B. Washington, D.C.: U.S. Government Printing Office.

*U.S. Department of Labor*
1928    Summary: The Effects of Labor Legislation on the Employment Opportunities of Women. Women's Bureau Bulletin No. 68. Washington, D.C.: U.S. Government Printing Office.
1974    "Twenty facts on women workers."

*Waite, Linda J, and Ross M. Stolzenberg*
in press    "Intended childbearing and labor force participation of young women" American Sociological Review.

*Waldman, Elizabeth, and Robert Whitmore*
1974    "Children of working mothers, March 1973." Monthly Labor Review 97 (May): 50–58.

*Weitzman, Lenore*
1975    "Socialization." Pp. 105–144 in Jo Freeman (ed.), Women: A Feminist Perspective. Palo Alto: Mayfield.

*Whiting, Beatrice, and Carolyn Pope Edwards*
1973    "A cross-cultural analysis of sex differences in the behavior of children aged three through eleven." Journal of Social Psychology 97 (December): 171–188.

*Wilensky, Harold*
1968    "Women's work: Economic growth, ideology, structure." Industrial Relations 7 (May): 235–248.

*Wood, Thomas*
1929    A History of Women's Education in the United States 1. New York: Science Press.

*Zimmer, Troy*
1975    "Sexism in higher education: A cross-national analysis." Pacific Sociological Review 18 (January): 55–67.

# Women's Labor Force Participation and the Residential Mobility of Families*

## Larry H. Long

*Population Division*
*Bureau of the Census*

*Families in which the wife works are more likely to undertake short-distance moving and slightly less likely to undertake long-distance migration than families in which the wife does not work. The effect of the wife's employment is greater in raising the family's local mobility rates than in lowering migration rates. The reasons behind these findings are explored along with the implied consequences. It is concluded that the migration of husbands interferes substantially with career development among wives and in this way contributes to explaining why women earn less than men at the same age, occupation, and education level.*

*Many young households give the impression of being on the basis of perfect equality. But as long as the man retains economic responsibility for the couple this is only an illusion. It is he who decides where they will live according to the demands of his work; she follows him from city to country or vice versa*

*Source:* Reprinted from Social Forces 52, 3 (March 1974): 342–48. "Women's Labor Force Participation and the Residential Mobility of Families," by Larry H. Long. Copyright © 1974. The University of North Carolina Press.

*This article is from a larger study supported in part by the Center for Population Research of the National Institute of Child Health and Human Development.

*to distant possessions to foreign countries; their standard of living is set according to his income; the daily, weekly, annual rhythms are set by his occupation. . . .*

This article attempts an empirical test of this statement by de Beauvoir (1949) as to place of residence—and changes in place of residence—on the part of married couples. The question is this: to what extent does the wife's work influence the residential mobility of families? If the wife's job is invariably subordinated to that of the husband then there should be no difference in the likelihood and frequency of migration between families in which the wife works and those in which she does not work.

The most reasonable alternative hypothesis is that families in which the wife works are less migratory than those in which she does not work. The basic reasoning behind this hypothesis is that an opportunity for the husband to move is seldom accompanied by one for the wife and that under such circumstances husbands make sacrifices by not moving out of deference to the wife's career. But finding only small differences in migration propensity between families in which the wife works and those in which she does not work could probably be taken as evidence that the employment of wives exercises only a small influence on the migration patterns of their husbands.

Also to be investigated is the effect of the wife's employment on short-distance moving. Little has been written about the subject and in the absence of previous empirical investigation we test the hypothesis that there are no differences in the likelihood of short-distance mobility between families in which the wife works and those in which she does not work.

The hypotheses to be tested are part of a larger question as to the family contexts in which decisions are made about residential mobility. Researchers often point out that most analyses of migration are in terms of persons as units, although most moves are made by entire families (see Beshers, 1967; Glick, 1965). Furthermore, most migration analyses consider only men. The purpose of this article is to investigate the effect of one aspect of family structure—the wife's employment status—on the family's residential mobility and to encourage other research into the way family structure influences migration and how migration influences family structure.

## HYPOTHESES AND DATA

The first hypothesis to be tested is that there are no migration differences between families in which the wife works and those in which she does not work. The alternative hypothesis is that families in which the wife works are less migratory than families in which she does not work. These hypotheses were tested with data from special tabulations of the March *Current Population Surveys* and with data from the 1970 Census.

Each month's *Current Population Survey* consists of about *50,000* households and is a representative sample of the United States population. The March questionnaire contains questions for each member of the household asking whether current (March) residence is the same as in the preceding

March. If the answer is no, additional questions ascertain whether the move was across county or state boundaries. Movement between counties is often accepted as an operational definition of migration (Bureau of the Census, 1972). In order to produce the detailed tabulations needed for this study, the March samples from 1966 through 1971 were combined and treated as one large sample.

Table 1 shows rates of moving within counties, between counties (including moves between states), and between states for men at different age groups and with nonfarm occupations according to whether married and if married whether at the survey date the wife was in the paid labor force. "Other marital status" in the table includes men who are single (never married) as well as men who are divorced, widowed, or separated from their spouse.

Table 1 shows that at each age group except 20–24 married men have lower migration rates (rates of moving between counties) than men in other marital statuses. Furthermore beyond age *30* married men also have lower rates of local moving (within counties) than men in other marital statuses. It appears, therefore, that there is a good deal of both short- and long-distance moving associated with getting married and setting up a household, but thereafter married men are more residentially stable than unmarried men.

These findings are pointed out because it is frequently observed that family life sometimes entails residential movement. For example, Peterson (1969:266) states that

*In the United States today not only do married couples move about as well as single persons, but they are often motivated to do so precisely because of their family life—in order to have a larger house for an increasing number of children, in order to live in a "nicer" neighborhood or close to a better school, and so on.*

While it is true that families often move for these reasons, it should be emphasized that married couples make significantly fewer residential changes over the course of a lifetime than persons who never marry or who experience marital disruption.

The original question was: Are married men with working wives as migratory as married men whose wives do not work? Based on the evidence in Table 1, the answer appears to be no. Except at ages *20–24,* men whose wives were working at the survey date were consistently less likely to have moved between counties during the preceding year than men whose wives were not working at the survey date. For moves of longer distance (between states) there were no exceptions, for at every age men with working wives were less likely to have undertaken interstate migration during the preceding year than men whose wives were not working at the survey date.

The alternative hypothesis, therefore, receives some support, but there is a possible bias because the above evidence relates only to the wife's employment at the end of the migration interval. A more definitive test will be given in the next section, where the wife's employment status at the beginning and end of a five-year migration interval will be considered. For the moment, we simply note that men whose wives were working at the survey date were less migratory during the preceding year than men whose wives were not working at the survey date.

## TABLE 1

Men 20 to 64 Years Old with Nonfarm Occupations—
Percent Geographically Mobile During Preceding Twelve Months,
According to Type of Mobility, Age, Marital Status, and (if Married)
Whether Wife Was in the Paid Labor Force at the Survey Date

| | NUMBER (000) | PERCENT MOVING WITHIN COUNTIES | PERCENT MOVING BETWEEN COUNTIES | PERCENT MOVING BETWEEN STATES |
|---|---|---|---|---|
| *20 to 24 years old* | | | | |
| Married, wife present | 14,099 | 39.8 | 19.2 | 8.8 |
| Wife in paid labor force | 6,405 | 42.0 | 19.7 | 8.5 |
| Wife not in paid labor force | 7,694 | 38.0 | 18.8 | 9.0 |
| Other marital status | 13,561 | 14.9 | 13.5 | 8.5 |
| *25 to 29 years old* | | | | |
| Married, wife present | 24,994 | 23.5 | 12.4 | 5.8 |
| Wife in paid labor force | 9,653 | 27.1 | 10.8 | 5.1 |
| Wife not in paid labor force | 15,341 | 21.3 | 13.3 | 6.3 |
| Other marital status | 31,635 | 20.4 | 13.1 | 7.4 |
| *30 to 34 years old* | | | | |
| Married, wife present | 24,230 | 14.7 | 7.8 | 3.6 |
| Wife in paid labor force | 8,429 | 17.0 | 6.3 | 2.7 |
| Wife not in paid labor force | 15,801 | 13.5 | 8.5 | 4.1 |
| Other marital status | 4,256 | 20.9 | 10.0 | 4.8 |
| *35 to 44 years old* | | | | |
| Married, wife present | 52,817 | 8.9 | 4.9 | 2.5 |
| Wife in paid labor force | 21,398 | 9.5 | 3.8 | 1.8 |
| Wife not in paid labor force | 31,419 | 8.5 | 5.7 | 3.0 |
| Other marital status | 7,295 | 17.0 | 7.2 | 3.5 |
| *49 to 54 years old* | | | | |
| Married, wife present | 49,931 | 6.2 | 2.7 | 1.3 |
| Wife in paid labor force | 22,623 | 6.5 | 3.0 | 0.8 |
| Wife not in paid labor force | 27,308 | 5.9 | 3.3 | 1.7 |
| Other marital status | 7,021 | 14.4 | 4.9 | 2.4 |
| *55 to 64 years old* | | | | |
| Married, wife present | 32,571 | 4.6 | 1.9 | 0.7 |
| Wife in paid labor force | 13,119 | 4.6 | 1.4 | 0.3 |
| Wife not in paid labor force | 19,452 | 4.5 | 2.2 | 1.0 |
| Other marital status | 4,771 | 10.7 | 3.9 | 0.8 |

*Source: March* Current Population Surveys, *summed from 1966-71.*

On an a priori basis there seemed little reason to think that the employment of wives would have any effect whatsoever on short-distance moving. But Table 1 shows that at every age group men whose wives were working at the survey date were *more* likely to have moved within counties during the preceding year than men whose wives were not working. Thus, having a wife who works may inhibit long-distance movement but appears to promote short-distance movement.

Additional tabulations were prepared (but are not shown) controlling for occupation. These tabulations supported the same conclusions as those emerging from Table 1. Controlling for occupation (ten nonfarm groups) revealed that: (1) beyond age *25* or *30* married men had lower rates of moving within or between counties than men who were not married, and (2) married men whose wives were working at the survey date were more likely to have moved within counties but less likely to have moved between counties or states during the preceding year than men whose wives were not working at the survey date.

Tabulations of mobility status according to age, occupation, and marital status were also prepared for women but are not shown. These revealed the expected pattern, namely, that beyond age *25* and for each occupation, married women were appreciably less likely to be mobile (either within counties or between counties) than unmarried women.

Thus there is a clear demonstration that marriage ties people to a given locality. To return to the initial quotation, there is reason to believe that wives who share in the economic responsibility of the household by holding a job influence both the short-distance mobility of their families (increasing it) and the long-distance mobility (decreasing it). But up to now the evidence has been limited to characteristics after moving.

## EMPLOYMENT STATUS AT THE BEGINNING OF THE MIGRATION INTERVAL

With the above information, it is impossible to differentiate clearly the effects of employment status on migration and the effects of migration on employment status (see Goldscheider, 1971; Masnick, 1968; Miller, 1969). During the years in question, the *Current Population Survey* did not include questions on characteristics of persons before moving, but the 1970 Census obtained information on residence in 1965 and activity in 1965 (working, going to college, or being in the Armed Forces).

These data are not ideal for our purposes because the five-year migration interval (in contrast to a one-year interval) may mask several changes of residence and entries to and withdrawals from the labor force, and considerable time may elapse between the time of a move and the time of enumeration. Nevertheless, the census data can be used to test the hypotheses previously offered. Table 2 shows rates of moving within counties and between states for the 1965–70 period according to the husband's age and the wife's employment status in 1965.

These data reinforce earlier conclusions about a wife's employment raising local mobility rates. Column 1 shows that at each of the five age groups men

## TABLE 2
### Married Men 20 to 59 Years Old in 1965 with Nonfarm Occupations in 1970—
Percent Moving Within Counties and Between States Between 1965 and 1970, According to Wife's Employment Status in 1965

| | PERCENT MOVING WITHIN COUNTIES 1965–70* | PERCENT MOVING BETWEEN STATES 1965–70* | PERCENT OF WIVES EMPLOYED IN 1970 | | | |
|---|---|---|---|---|---|---|
| | | | NON-MOVERS† | MOVERS WITHIN COUNTIES | MOVERS BETWEEN COUNTIES WITHIN A STATE | MOVERS BETWEEN STATES |
| *Husbands 20 to 24 in 1965* | | | | | | |
| Wife employed in 1965 | 46.6 | 18.8 | 54.0 | 48.2 | 42.0 | 41.0 |
| Wife not employed in 1965 | 42.6 | 18.8 | 25.7 | 31.7 | 34.0 | 35.4 |
| *Husbands 25 to 29 in 1965* | | | | | | |
| Wife employed in 1965 | 41.6 | 13.9 | 63.6 | 55.3 | 46.3 | 41.7 |
| Wife not employed in 1965 | 34.9 | 13.1 | 23.6 | 25.4 | 23.7 | 23.4 |
| *Husbands 30 to 39 in 1965* | | | | | | |
| Wife employed in 1965 | 29.4 | 7.7 | 78.9 | 70.8 | 60.8 | 54.7 |
| Wife not employed in 1965 | 23.8 | 9.0 | 25.4 | 26.3 | 25.4 | 23.9 |
| *Husbands 40 to 49 in 1965* | | | | | | |
| Wife employed in 1965 | 19.7 | 4.1 | 83.7 | 78.5 | 69.6 | 61.7 |
| Wife not employed in 1965 | 16.6 | 5.4 | 21.9 | 23.6 | 24.2 | 22.8 |
| *Husbands 50 to 59 in 1965* | | | | | | |
| Wife employed in 1965 | 16.1 | 2.5 | 80.9 | 76.6 | 67.9 | 57.4 |
| Wife not employed in 1965 | 14.3 | 3.1 | 12.9 | 15.9 | 16.7 | 16.8 |

*Source: Bureau of the Census (1973: Table 11).*
*Percent based on total reporting residence in 1965.
†Persons living in the same house in 1965 and 1970.

whose wives were working in 1965 were more likely to move within counties during the subsequent five years than men whose wives were not working in 1965. Thus it is quite clear that at all ages a working wife raises her family's local mobility rate.

How might a working wife promote short-distance moving? Part of the answer may be that most short-distance moves are undertaken for reasons connected with housing (Bureau of the Census, 1966; Lansing and Mueller, 1967). In the Census Bureau study about two-thirds of married men *18–64* years old who had moved within counties during the preceding twelve months said that the desire for a better house or a house located in a better neighborhood or in a more convenient location (to work, schools, shopping, etc.) was the reason for their having moved. Thus housing considerations can be said to account for about two-thirds of within-county moving on the part of families.

Finding that families with a working wife are more likely to undertake within-county moving than other families may suggest that an important motivation for married women working is the desire for a better house, a better neighborhood, or a more convenient location. The income earned by working wives appears to enable the family to upgrade its housing and the fact that at each age men with working wives were more mobile within counties suggests repeated moving over the family life cycle to successively more desirable housing.

The general effect, therefore, of the wife's employment on short-distance movement appears about the same whether one considers employment only at the end of the migration interval (Table 1) or at the beginning of the migration interval (Table 2). But the effect of her employment on long-distance migration appears somewhat less when one considers employment at the beginning rather than at the end of the migration interval.

Column 2 of Table 2 shows that for men *20–24* years old there were no differences in 1965–70 interstate migration rates between families in which the wife was and was not working in 1965. At ages *25–29* men whose wives were working in 1965 were actually slightly more likely to move between states during the subsequent five years than men whose wives were not working. Only after her husband is past 30 does a working wife decrease the likelihood of her husband's interstate migration.

A working wife thus appears to have little effect on her husband's long-distance migration in the early years of his career—the years when long-distance migration is most likely to occur. Only after her husband has become established in his career does a wife's employment reduce the readiness with which he relocates to a new job in a different state. Of course, this conclusion applies only to the general case. It is possible that a professionally employed wife has greater effect on her husband's long-distance migration than do other working wives.

Columns 3, 4, 5, and 6 of Table 2 show the conditional probability of the wife's being employed in 1970 given her employment status in 1965. These columns were included to show the probability of the wife's continuing her employment when moves of increasing distance are made. For example, among women employed in 1965 and married to men who were *20–24* in 1965, *54.0* percent of those who did not move were still employed in 1970. With increasing distance of move this percent is steadily reduced to *41.0*. The same pattern holds true for all later ages shown.

It would appear therefore that any geographical movement is unfavorable to the wife's continued participation in the labor force. And the greater the distance moved (at least up to a point) the greater the likelihood of her dropping out of the labor force.

## ENTERING AND LEAVING THE LABOR FORCE

Table 3 shows rates of moving within counties and between states for married men according to age and wife's employment status in 1965 and 1970. For the wife's employment status, there are four possible combinations: (1) employed in 1965 but not 1970, (2) employed in 1970 but not in 1965, (3) employed at both dates and (4) employed at neither date.

TABLE 3

Married Men 20 to 59 Years Old in 1965 with Nonfarm Occupations in 1970—
Percent Moving Within Counties and Between States Between 1965 and 1970,
According to Age and Wife's Employment Status in 1965 and 1970

| | *AGE OF HUSBAND IN 1965* | | | | |
|---|---|---|---|---|---|
| | *20 TO 24* | *25 TO 29* | *30 TO 39* | *40 TO 49* | *50 TO 59* |
| *PERCENT MOVING WITHIN COUNTIES, 1965–70\** | | | | | |
| Wife employed in 1965 only | 45.0 | 40.6 | 31.6 | 22.3 | 18.0 |
| Wife employed in 1970 only | 42.1 | 36.4 | 24.5 | 17.4 | 16.6 |
| Wife employed at both dates | 48.4 | 42.4 | 28.6 | 19.1 | 15.6 |
| Wife employed at neither dates | 42.9 | 35.4 | 23.6 | 16.4 | 14.0 |
| *PERCENT MOVING BETWEEN STATES, 1965–70\** | | | | | |
| Wife employed in 1965 only | 20.7 | 17.7 | 12.9 | 8.2 | 5.0 |
| Wife employed in 1970 only | 20.7 | 12.6 | 8.4 | 5.4 | 3.7 |
| Wife employed at both dates | 16.6 | 10.7 | 5.8 | 3.1 | 1.8 |
| Wife employed at neither date | 17.8 | 13.2 | 9.2 | 5.3 | 2.9 |

*Source: Bureau of the Census (1973: Table 11).*
*\*Percent based on total reporting residence in 1965.*

Of course, such data do not reveal all entries to and withdrawals from the labor force. Some women could have entered and left the labor force many times during the five-year period, but only the difference between activity in 1965, and activity in 1970 would have been counted. Similarly, not all geographical moves are counted; some persons may have moved several times, but only the difference between place of residence in 1965 and place of residence in 1970 would have been counted. Furthermore, a good deal of time may have elapsed since migrating, allowing some wives to have reentered the labor force after dropping out when the move took place. Nevertheless, these data provide to date the best test of the sort of questions addressed in this article.

Note first the migration patterns of men whose wives were employed at both dates and those whose wives were employed at neither date. Men whose wives were employed at both dates invariably had higher within-county rates of moving and lower interstate migration rates than men whose wives were employed at neither date. Continued participation of wives in the labor force, therefore, produces high (but not always the highest) rates of within-county moving and low rates of interstate migration (the lowest shown in Table 3). Non-participation of wives in the labor force is associated with low (usually the lowest) rates of within-county moving and high (but not the highest) rates of interstate migration.

Wives who were employed in 1965 but not 1970 indicate a withdrawal (at least temporarily) from the labor force. By dropping out of the labor force wives increase both the short-distance mobility and long-distance migration of their husbands. Men whose wives were employed in 1965 but not 1970 had high rates of within-county moving (the highest beyond age 30) as well as the highest rates of interstate migration.

Finding that a wife who drops out of the labor force increases her husband's mobility is in accord with interpretations offered by other studies. Miller (1966) offered the tentative conclusion that interstate migration generally raised labor force participation rates among men but often lowered labor force participation rates for women. She suggested that this was because many wives gave up their jobs when their husbands moved over long distances and were unable to find new jobs by the survey date. Her study has been criticized (Goldscheider, 1971; Masnick, 1968) because the data referred only to labor force participation at the end of a five-year migration interval and did not control for marital status. The data in Table 3, however, do have the necessary controls and support her interpretation.

Miller's chief interest was in the possible effects of the husband's migration on the wife's labor force participation whereas the present article has been more interested in considering the effect of the wife's labor force participation on the husband's migration. Quite obviously either variable can and should be considered dependent as well as independent. In fact, we may say that occurrence of either event lowers the likelihood of occurrence of the other: participation of wives in the labor force decreases the likelihood of the family's migration (at least when the husband is over *30*), but migration when it occurs, lowers the likelihood of the wife's continued participation in the labor force.

The effect of wives entering the labor force during the mobility interval is difficult to account for. Men whose wives were employed in 1970 but not 1965 generally had low rates of within-county moving but fairly high rates of interstate migration. The high migration rates may reflect some moves specifically undertaken to aid the wife's entry into the labor force, as when the move is from places with few job opportunities for women (e.g., rural areas) to places with greater job opportunities (e.g., metropolitan areas).

## DISCUSSION

The evidence presented above shows that a working wife gives a couple more freedom of choice as to which neighborhood to live in but less freedom of choice as to whether to move to a different city. But because a working wife reduces her husband's long-distance migration by a rather small amount we conclude that the migration of husbands interferes substantially with the formulation and achievement of clear occupational goals among women—a point that is frequently acknowledged (Holmstrom, 1972; Poloma and Garland, 1971: Rapoport and Rapoport, 1971; Weissman and Paykel, 1972; Wolfle, 1971).

Such disruptions in women's careers brought about by the migration of their husbands seem certain to lower women's earnings. It has been adequately demonstrated that women earn less than men at the same age and with the same educational level, occupation, and years in the labor force (Suter and Miller, 1973). At least some of the income differences between men and women arise from the interruptions of women's careers caused by the migration of their husbands and the inability of many (if not most) wives to use migration to further their careers in the same ways that most men do. Any effort at quantifying the degree of economic discrimination against women should consider this as one component of income differences between men and women.

Good evidence that the husband's migration may not only result in the wife's dropping out of the labor force (at least temporarily) but often lowers earnings among wives who are able to continue working is given by Gallaway (1969a: 1969b). Gallaway found that for men interregional migration was, on the average, accompanied by an increase in earnings. But for women interregional migration was associated with no change, or a decrease in earnings. His study did not control for marital status, but the most likely explanation of his findings is that interregional migration is most often purposive among men but resultant among women.

It might even be argued that the husband's migration influences not only the career development of the wife but also the initial choice of career. Such occupations as elementary school teaching, nursing, and secretarial work are traditional occupations of women. They are also fairly readily transferred from one area to another and can be practiced in almost any part of the country. It may be that the geographical transferability of these occupations has played a part in their perpetuation as favorite career choices of women.

## REFERENCES

*Beshers, James.*
1967    *Population Processes in Social Systems.* New York: Free Press.
*Bureau of the Census.*
1966    "Reasons for Moving: March 1962 to March 1963." *Current Population Reports.* Series P-20, No. 154. Washington, D.C.: U.S. Government Printing Office.
1972    "Mobility of the Population of the United States: March 1970 to March 1971." *Current Population Reports.* Series P-20, No. 235. Washington, D.C.: U.S. Government Printing Office.
1973    "Census of Population: 1970." *Mobility for States and the Nation.* Final Report PC(2)-2B. Washington, D.C.: U.S. Government Printing Office.
*de Beauvoir, Simone.*
1949    *The Second Sex.* New York: Bantam Books, 1970.

*Gallaway, Lowell E.*
1969a   "The Effect of Geographic Labor Mobility on Income: A Brief Comment." *Journal of Human Resources* 4 (Winter): 103–9.
1969b   *Geographic Labor Mobility in the United States: 1957 to Labor Mobility in the United States: 1957 to 1960.* Washington, D.C.: U.S. Government Printing Office.
*Glick, Paul C.*
1965   "Census Data as a Source for Theses and Dissertations in the Field of Sociology." *Milbank Memorial Fund Quarterly* 63 (January): 17–30.
*Goldscheider, Calvin.*
1971   *Population, Moderization, and Social Structure.* Boston: Little, Brown.
*Holmstrom, Lynda Lyle.*
1972   *The Two-Career Family.* Cambridge: Schenkman.
*Lansing, John B., and Eva Mueller.*
1967   *The Geographic Mobility of Labor.* Ann Arbor: Institute for Social Research. University of Michigan.
*Masnick, George.*
1968   "Employment Status and Retrospective and Prospective Migration in the United States." *Demography* 5: 79–85.
*Miller, Ann R.*
1966   "Migration Differentials in Labor Force Participation: United States, 1960." *Demography* 3: 58–67.
1969   "Note on Some Problems in Interpreting Migration Data from the 1960 Census of Population." *Demography* 6(February): 13–16.
*Peterson, William.*
1969   *Population.* New York: Macmillan.
*Poloma, Margaret M., and T. Neal Garland.*
1971   "The Married Professional Woman: A Study in the Tolerance of Domestication." *Journal of Marriage and the Family* 33(August): 531–40.
*Rapoport, Rhona, and Robert Rapoport.*
1971   *Dual-Career Families.* Middlesex, England: Penguin Books.
*Suter, Larry E., and Herman P. Miller.*
1973   "Components of Differences between the Incomes of Men and Career Women." *American Journal of Sociology* 78(January): 962–74.
*Weissman, Myrna, and Eugene S. Payke.*
1972   "Moving and Depression in Women." *Society* 9(July/August): 24–8.
*Wolfle, Dael.*
1971   *The Uses of Talent.* Princeton: Princeton University Press.

# The Role of Women in the People's Republic of China: Legacy and Change*

## Lawrence K. Hong, Ph.D.

*Associate Professor*
*Department of Sociology*
*California State University, Los Angeles*

*After 25 years of communist rule, women in China have made significant progress toward emancipation. However, some aspects of traditional sex role differentiation still persist in the family. Furthermore, in work outside the home, women still experience discrimination in pay and important jobs. In the political area, women are still discriminated against on the national level. Most of the important government positions are held by men. Although the magnitude of sex inequality in the past can explain some of these legacies, a more complete explanation must take into account the survival of the concept of Yin-Yang, the patrilineal kinship system; the Ancestral Cult in China; and the inadequacy of the socialist revolution.*

*Source:* Lawrence K. Hong, "The Role of Women in the People's Republic of China: Legacy and Change," Social Problems 23, 5 (June 1976): 545–57. Copyright © 1976 by the Society for the Study of Social Problems. Reprinted by permission of the Society and the author.
*The author wishes to thank Professors Marion Dearman and William Darrough for their comments and suggestions. I am especially indebted to Professor Lillian Rubin for sharing many of her ideas with me. Without her generosity, encouragement, and patience, this paper would not have been possible.

*The misery that Chinese Women have suffered for thousands of years has now reached a limit. The trammels of a patriarchal social system and oppression by imperialism and its tools—the warlords, compradors, gangster politicians, corrupt officials, local tyrants and evil gentry—have kept women from achieving political and economic independence and have literally made them into commodities, playthings, parasites (Institute of the People's Movement, 1902?:2).*

The foregoing declaration appeared in the opening chapter of a Communist publication in the 20s. It gives evidence to the Chinese Communist Party's long interest in the emancipation of women (China Reconstruct, 1975:40–41). In 1950, one year after the party's triumph over the Nationalists, the new government immediately kept its promise by issuing a new Marriage Law, designed to eradicate all social inequalities between the sexes. However, in spite of the government's earnest effort in the last twenty-five years, some important aspects of social inequality between the sexes still persist in China today, albeit some significant progress has been made. The present paper is an attempt to describe some of the legacies and changes, and to offer an explanation for the stamina of male supremacy in China.

Since outsiders are not able to conduct scientific social surveys in China at this time, the present study must rely on other approaches. The material presented here comes from published articles and reports, and from interviews with a number of emigrants and Chinese who have recently visited their relatives in China. The author has interviewed ten female emigrants who have spent at least their entire childhood and adolescence in Communist China, and eight Hong Kong Chinese who recently visited their relatives on the mainland. The interviews were informally conducted over a period of time. The data obtained from the interviews were compared with published reports to identify common themes.

The composite picture that has emerged from the comparison suggests that women in China today have made significant progress toward emancipation, but they are still far from achieving full equality in their family, work, and political roles.

**FAMILY ROLE**

One of the first major reforms initiated by the Communist Party after its ascendance to power in China was the complete overhauling of the marriage and family laws. In 1950, the government promulgated a new marriage law. Some of its articles that have a direct bearing on the role of women in the family are (C. K. Yang, 1950a:221–226):

Article 7. Husband and wife are companions living together and shall enjoy equal status at home.

Article 9. Both husband and wife shall have the right to free choice of occupations and free participation in work or in social activities.

Article 10. Both husband and wife shall have equal rights in the possession and management of family property.

Article 11. Both husband and wife shall have the right to use his or her own family name.

Article 12. Both husband and wife shall have the right to inherit each other's property.

Apparently, the Chinese have succeeded in attaining most of these ideals. All the emigrants and visitors interviewed assert that both husband and wife are free to engage in work and social activities outside the home and are equal in the management of family property and income. They also report that it is a common practice in China today for the wife to use her own family name.[1] Furthermore, according to the emigrants, Chinese women have also gained equal rights in divorce: divorce by mutual consent or upon insistence of either spouse is now acceptable practice. However, it seems that the Chinese are only partially successful in creating a truly equalitarian family. While all the interviewees agree that the old patriarchal system of husbands having more authority does not exist anymore, they are also quick to note that wives still have to do all the household chores, such as taking care of the children, cleaning, cooking, and doing the laundry. This tradition of sex role differentiation reported by emigrants and Chinese visitors has also been observed by a group of sixteen American students and teachers who visited China in 1971. The following is an excerpt from their report:

*The old patriarchal division of labor which relegated all the household tasks to women has not been very much modified in the People's Republic of China. Everywhere we went we asked whether men share in the duties of the home. Occasionally we were assured that men pitch in and do a little something around the house. The women in one household at the Hong-qiao Commune proudly told us that all the men in the home know how to cook and do cook sometimes. But almost everywhere when we asked who washes the clothes by hand, who takes care of the children after they come home from school, who buys the food, who cooks the meals, who cleans the house, who does the sewing, the answer was, "The wife, of course." (Committee of Concerned Asian Scholars, 1972:282)*

A sociologist at the University of Notre Dame made a similar observation. After visiting China in 1973, he reports: "(The) division of labor in the family remains the same. Women do the cooking, laundry, and sewing while men engage in employment outside the home" (Liu, 1973:19).

Besides adhering to the traditional division of labor in the family, the Chinese also appear to retain the traditional attitude toward children of different sexes: girls are protected but boys are preferred. For example, a number of interviewees claim that when a family has a choice to send a boy or a girl to the rural area for "rustication," the family usually sends the boy because the family does not want the daughter to be too far away from home.[2] Also, two emigrants report that special middle schools for girls were operating in Shanghai at least until 1965. The general policy of having women retired from work at age 50 and men at 60 (Topping, 1971:190; Liu, 1973:19) is also consistent with the protective attitude toward females.

The protective attitude toward girls is complemented by the traditional preference for boys. Most of the interviewees assert that the desire to have at least a son to continue the family line is still evident in China, especially in the rural area (where 80 percent of the people live). This observation is supported by a recent comment by Chairman Mao. In his 1970 interview with Edgar Snow, Chairman Mao made the following remark in disputing Snow's commendation on the success of China's birth control program:

*No, . . . I had been taken in! In the countryside a woman still wanted to have boy children. If the first and second were girls, she would make another try. If the third one came and was still a girl, the mother would try again. Pretty soon there would be nine of them, the mother was already 45 or so, and she would finally decide to leave it at that. (Snow, 1971:27)*

In sum, traditional sex-role attitudes still exist in China, in spite of the successful removal of the formal status and the authority of the husband as the head of the household.

### WORK ROLE

As mentioned earlier, Chinese women today are free to participate in work outside the home. As early as the mid-50s, the government launched a campaign to encourage married women to seek outside employment. Those who do not work outside the home are called "family women" and have to justify their "nonproductive" position (Huang, 1961). Apparently, the Chinese have been successful in removing the traditional stigma attached to working mothers. All the interviewees found no unfavorable attitude toward mothers working outside the home in China, and thought mothers satisfied with the day-care facilities provided by the government near their work place.

Statistics released by the government also show that the number of women in the labor force has been increasing rapidly. For example, in 1957, there were only three million women workers, but by the end of 1959 the number had increased to eight million. Although no official statistics were released after 1959, a reliable source has estimated that as many as 100 million women are now working in state-run factories and that about 50 percent of the farm workers are women (Hai, 1973:431–32).

However, in spite of their gain in the right to work outside the home, Chinese women are still discriminated against in pay and in holding important jobs. Flagrant violations of the principle of equal pay for equal work are most conspicuous in the rural area. One of the Hong Kong Chinese, who recently visited her relatives on the mainland, reports that mothers in the countryside sometimes refer to their daughters as "my little 7½-pointer" because for doing the same work, a man would usually get 10 workpoints a day, while a woman received 7½ points. A similar incident is mentioned in a recent issue of the *China Reconstruct* (1975).

Any reference to social inequality in contemporary China by the *China Reconstruct* is noteworthy because the magazine has a reputation for publishing articles showing only the favorable aspects of life under communism. The following is an excerpt from a recent article. "How Our Village Got Equal Pay for Equal Work," written by the head of the Hsiaochinchuang Brigade Women's Association.

*Our base rate is determined at meetings held once a year. Each brigade member says what he thinks his work is worth and the others discuss it. At a meeting not long ago, while two-thirds of the men confidently stated 10 points, only one strong woman had the courage to bid even 9½. None of the other strong women dared bid over eight. This was when the brigade Communist Party branch asked that the evaluation be stopped and organized a series of meetings to criticize male supremacy.*

*When we began the evaluation, some men had said, "All a man has to do is stick out his fist and he does as much as a woman does in six months. If women want the same base rate, they have to do just as we do in plowing, planting, digging ditches and carrying sacks of grain." We pointed out that women had never had the chance to learn some of these jobs. If you only make the strength and skill the basis of your comparison you'll be pitting men's strong points, physiologically and historically, against women's weak points. First and foremost, the comparison should be on attitude toward, on patriotic and collectivist thinking and contribution to the collective. . . .*

*This kind of evaluation made a dent in the thinking of many of the men. Some of the men team leaders pointed out that in many ways the women showed greater concern for the collective than the men. . . .*

*After comparison on these various aspects, two-thirds of the men still got 10 points. Out of 136 women, 16 got 10 points and 40 others got 9 or over. A total of 116 women got a higher rating than before (Chou, 1975:8–9).*

The above narrative shows that pay discrimination is a tenacious problem in China; women in this commune still receive less workpoints even after a series of meetings to "reeducate" the men. Furthermore, the narrative also reveals that both Chinese men and women today still believe that physically men are more capable in certain jobs. The examples cited here are not isolated incidents. Many examples have been reported and severely criticized by recent government publications such as *Red Flag* and the *People's Daily* (see Hai, 1973).

Besides discrimination in pay, Chinese women also face discrimination in obtaining important jobs. One of the emigrants who has lived fifteen years in Communist China told the author:

*When I was attending middle school in Shanghai, the teacher took us to visit the factories all the time. Both men and women worked in the factories, but the "responsible persons" in the factories were always men. In the universities, almost all the professors were men. Women usually taught primary schools. In the hospitals, most of the doctors were men, and all the nurses were women.*

Similar observations have been made by recent western visitors. The group of American students and teachers who have visited China in 1971 report:

*We found that even in factories where the workers are mostly female, the leadership is heavily male. For example, at the Soochow Embroidery Factory, where 80 percent of the workers are women, the revolutionary committee has seven women, twelve men, and the elected head of the committee is a man, as usual. In the primary school we visited in Nanking, the leading committee is proportionately representative with six women and one man in a school whose teachers are almost all women, but even there the head of the revolutionary committee is its one male member (Committee of Concerned Asian Scholars, 1972:274).*

## POLITICAL ROLE

Of the three areas pertaining to the status of women in China, the political area appears to have made the least progress—in spite of the high level of political participation by the women at the grassroot level. According to the interviewees and the published reports, many young women were members of the Red Guard during the Cultural Revolution in the 60s and many are also very active in the local political committees and associations today. However, their high level of political activity at the lower level is not matched at the higher level; women are conspicuously underrepresented on the national political organizations. Evidence of this type of discrimination is clearly revealed in the membership of the various government organs appointed or elected by the Fourth National People's Congress recently held in Peking (January, 1975), and in the composition of the congress itself. From Table 1, we can see that males dominated the State Council, the Standing Committee, the Presidium, and the Congress to an extreme degree; not only are males the heads of the government organs, but they also outnumber the females by an enormous margin as members.

The State Council is the central government of the People's Republic of China. Although it is accountable to the National People's Congress and the Standing Committee, the State Council, in practice, is the most powerful organ in China. As Table 1 shows, there are only 3 women in this important council: of the 12 Vice-Premiers, only 1 is a woman, and of the 29 ministers, only 2 are women (Minister of Water Conservancy and Power, and Minister of Public Health). The former Premier—Chou En-lai—was male.[3]

The Standing Committee, which is the permanent organ of the National People's Congress, also has substantial power. According to the new Constitution (1975), the committee is responsible for interpreting laws, enacting decrees, ratifying and renouncing foreign treaties, and making diplomatic appointments. The membership of this committee is again heavily dominated by men: of the 22 Vice-Chairmen, only 3 are women, and of the 144 members, only 39 are women. The committee chairman, as usual, is male.

Similarly, men outnumber women by a substantial margin in the Presidium and in the National People's Congress. In the Presidium (whose function is not specified in the Constitution), the Secretary General is male, and only 44 of the 218 members are female. The National People's Congress is composed of deputies elected from the whole country. As prescribed by the Constitution, the National People's Congress is the legislative body of the

TABLE 1

Frequency Distributions of Male and Female Holding Constitutional Offices
in the People's Republic of China (1975)

| CONSTITUTIONAL OFFICES | MALE | FEMALE |
|---|---|---|
| The State Council | | |
| Premier | 1 | |
| Vice-Premiers | 11 | 1 |
| Ministers | 27 | 2 |
| Standing Committee | | |
| Chairman | 1 | |
| Vice-Chairmen | 19 | 3 |
| Members | 105 | 39 |
| The Presidium | | |
| Secretary General | 1 | |
| Members | 174 | 44 |
| Fourth National People's Congress Deputies[a] | 2250 | 635 |

*Source:* China Reconstruct, *Supplement (1975:6–9).*

[a]*Frequencies of male and female deputies are not exact counts. The publication states that there were 2,885 deputies of which over 22 percent were female.*

republic; its functions include making laws, amending the Constitution, approving the state budget, and appointing the Premier and the members of the State Council. In theory, the congress should reflect the social, economic, and sex compositions of the country. However, as Table 1 reveals, of the 2,885 deputies elected to serve in the congress, only 635 are women.

## PUZZLES AND EXPLANATIONS

The persistence of sex inequality in contemporary Chinese social and political life is perplexing, in view of the long history of association of the communist's and the women's liberation movements in China, and the enormous amount of energy that the regime has spent in promoting equality in the past twenty-five years (see Huang, 1961, 1972). It would be convenient, but not sufficient, to attribute the legacy solely to the magnitude of inequality in the past. Other equally deep-rooted traditions, such as the stigma attached to working mothers, extended families, political apathy, and private ownership of property, have been successfully eradicated with less time and effort. Furthermore, Chinese women in other parts of the world, such as Hong Kong, appear to have made about the same amount of progress without too much fanfare (Hong, 1973).

Hence, in order to explain the slow rate of change in the status of Chinese women, one must take into consideration other factors: among them, the stamina of the ancient concept of Yin-Yang, the tenacity of the patrilineal kinship system, the survival of the ancestral cult, and the inadequacy of the socialist revolution.

First, the concept of Yin-Yang that has dominated the Chinese view of life for thousands of years is still deeply entrenched in the contemporary Chinese psyche. This outlook recognizes two primal modalities, Yin and Yang, which permeate all things, living and non-living, material and non-material. Yin, the feminine element, is a conglomeration of qualities that are soft, weak, dark, cool, calm, inner-directed, and downward. Yang, the masculine element, is the exact opposite of all these traits. Furthermore, this theory holds that everything in the universe is the product of the interaction of Yin and Yang (Lee, 1971). In accord with this theory man and woman are regarded as the best examples illustrating the elements of Yin and Yang: the two sexes are opposite modalities and their interaction (sexual union) gives rise to new phenomena (offspring). One of the natural progressions of this cosmic view is that man and woman should play their roles according to their natural scripts, since they are different in their Yin-Yang propensities. Thus, since women are conceived as weak, passive, and inner-directed, they should work near their homes and should not engage in activities that require strenuous physical exertion. Since there is a tendency for the prestige and the perceived importance of a job to be positively correlated with the distance between the locations of the job and the home and the amount of physical strength required to perform the task (especially in non-industrialized societies), women are not likely to hold high status jobs.

It must be noted that the Yin-Yang conceptualization, in its abstract form, is not a sexist attitude but the *basis* of all the Chinese sexist attitudes; almost everything in the universe can be given the attribute of Yin or Yang (female or male)—e.g., valley is Yin and mountain is Yang, water is Yin and fire is Yang.

It is a world view or a psychic structure allowing the Chinese to fit all the seemingly unrelated phenomena into a meaningful whole. Man and woman are only two of the dichotomies in the universe of opposites. Therefore, the Yin-Yang concept is more subtle, more global, and more powerful in influencing male and female relationships than discrete attitudes toward the sexes (as those in the West).

For at least two reasons, the Chinese government has never taken any official position on the concept of Yin-Yang, despite its various campaigns against other traditions. One of the reasons is the close correspondence between the Yin-Yang outlook on reality and the Marxist Dialectic. Both theories hold that all phenomena in the world are composed of polarities and that change is produced by the interaction of opposite modalities. The striking similarity of the two theories is vividly revealed in the following two passages; one, taken from Lee Jung Young's interpretation of the I Ching, the ancient classic which constitutes the major source of the Yin-Yang formulation, and the other, from Mao Tse-tung's interpretation of Marxist Dialectics. With respect to Yin-Yang as expressed in the I Ching, Lee wrote:

*There is nothing in the world that does not have its opposite. This is the way of nature. Everything comes in opposites ... There polarities are the basis for all things which exist in the world. However, this polarity is not possible without unity. As Chang Tsai said, duality is impossible without unity and the unity cannot exist without duality. Duality is necessary for the unity of all polarities and unity is essential for the polarities of interrelationship ... The movement of duality toward union and that of separation from the union create changes ... The principle of changes is nothing other than the relationship between the counterpoles, which came to be known in China as Yin and Yang. (1971:66–67)*

Mao Tse-tung offered an almost identical cosmic view. In an essay "on Contradiction:" he wrote:

*The universality or absoluteness of contradiction has a twofold meaning. One is that contradiction exists in the process of development of all things, and the other is that in the process of development of each thing a movement of opposites exists from beginning to end.*

*Engels said, "Motion itself is a contradiction." Lenin defined the law of the unity of opposites as "the recognition (discovery) of the contradictory, mutually exclusive, opposite tendencies in all phenomena and process of nature (including mind and society)." Are these ideas correct? Yes, they are. The interdependence of the contradictory aspects present in all things and the struggle between these aspects determine the life of all things and push their development forward. There is nothing that does not contain contradiction; without contradiction nothing would exist. (1968:30–31)*

Apparently, Mao Tse-tung was aware of the similarity between the Yin-Yang formulation and the Marxist Dialectics because in the same essay, he claimed that a dialectical world outlook has existed in China since ancient times (1968:29).[4] Other Chinese communist intellectuals also found these parallels. At a meeting in Peking University during which the relative merits of various traditional Chinese thoughts were discussed, two early philosophers with a Yin-Yang inclination, Lao Tsu and Chuang Tsu, were able to escape repudiation because of the presence of dialectical ideas in their works (Bush, 1970:403–404).[5]

Another factor underlying the survival of the Yin-Yang outlook in contemporary China is its practical implication. In China today, one of the criteria for determining the acceptability of any philosophical idea or theory is that it must be able to apply to real life; a pure theory is regarded as "idealistic" and is not acceptable (see Mao, 1968:23; Bush, 1970:348–361). An indication that Yin-Yang is a practical concept is derived from its alleged relationship to the highly publicized medical technique, acupuncture.

The theory of acupuncture is based on the assumption that organs in the body are connected to specific locations on the surface of the skin through a network of meridians (or channels of energy), divided into two groups through which Yin or Yang flows. Furthermore, the heart, lung, spleen, kidney, and liver are designated Yin organs, while the stomach, intestines, and gall bladder are designated Yang. The theory of acupuncture argues that when the balance of Yin and Yang is upset or when their normal distribution in the body is disrupted, the person becomes ill. According to Wu Wei-p'ing, a professor of acupuncture, "the profound understanding of the existence of meridians lies within this concept of Yin-Yang" (1962:24).

There are strong indications that acupuncture and theories of medical etiology in China today are still strongly influenced by the Yin-Yang conceptualization. For example, in a 1970 interview with Maria Antonietta Macciocchi, a journalist of the Italian Communist Party newspaper, *Unita,* a doctor in Huashan Hospital commented:

*As we examine the human body, we consider that it is always a unity of opposites. Its various parts are united, one to the others: they are in opposition and at the same time depend on each other; they are linked and act upon each other. A pathological change in one part of the body can affect the organs of the other parts, or the whole body. . . . (Macciocchi, 1972:279)*

Apparently, the doctor can combine the Yin-Yang concept of etiology with the rhetoric of Marxist Dialectics. The clearest indication that Yin-Yang is still part of the medical concept in China, however, comes from two recent publications from Peking. Both publications, *A Complete Book of Acupuncture* (Yang, 1973) and *Acupuncture* (Hopei New Medical College, 1975) refer to Yin-Yang directly in their descriptions of acupuncture.[6]

Further evidence suggesting that the Yin-Yang ideology still prevails among the Chinese people in general may be seen in the popularity of Tai Chi Chuan (Shadow Boxing), a system of physical exercises derived directly from the Yin-Yang theory (see Feng and Wilkerson, 1970). This form of exercise is openly practiced by men and women in China today.

In view of the dialectical and practical characters of Yin-Yang, it is understandable why the concept still prevails in modern China. It is also evident that as long as the Chinese mind remains shackled by Yin-Yang, Chinese women will never be truly freed from their bondage.

The second obstacle that appears to hinder the full emancipation of women in China is the patrilineal kinship system (not to be confused with the defunct patriarchal authority system). This form of descent traces the family line of an individual through the male members of the family only and thus provides men with a special role in the society. Even though it has successfully eliminated the patriarchal authority in the family, for unclear reasons, the Chinese government has never attempted to change the kinship system to a bilateral form, a change that would have facilitated equality between the sexes. In fact, the new marriage law promulgated after the revolution has the effect of preserving the patrilineal descent system by stipulating that: "The question of prohibiting marriage between collateral relatives by blood (up to the fifth degree of relationship) is determined by custom" (Foreign Language Press, 1973:2). This law, first promulgated in 1950, is still in effect as indicated by the 1973 publication. By allowing the traditional custom that regulates marriage between collateral relatives to remain in existence, the patrilineal principle is reaffirmed because the custom is based on the conception that "family blood" is passed on from father to son.

Furthermore, emigrants and recent visitors have also reported that Ancestral Worship is still practiced in China, especially in the countryside (also see Time, 1975:22). Letters from the readers published in the Chinese newspapers also confirm the persistence of this practice (China News Analysis, 1970; MacInnis, 1972:328).[7] The significance of this religious conviction is that it and the patrilineal system interlock, supporting one another. The Ancestral Cult subscribes to the belief that forebearers on the father's side have an important influence on the fortunes and misfortunes of their descendants and, therefore, they have to be venerated (M. C. Yang, 1966; Hsu, 1967; Hong, 1972). The survival of this religious behavior in contemporary China—despite repeated efforts by the government to discourage it—not only gives further evidence of the persistence of the patrilineal system but also helps to explain why the system has survived; for the believers, it is of utmost importance that the male line in the family be perpetuated so that the "burning of incense" (ancestral worship) can be continued from generation to generation (see Hsu, 1967). While the patrilineal kinship system and the Ancestral Cult still persist in China, one can understand why sons are still valued over daughters, and men still have a special role in society.

Finally, all these—the legacy of sex inequality and its remnant perpetuators, such as the concept of Yin-Yang, the patrilineal kinship system, and the Ancestral Cult—raise a larger question: the question of the adequacy of the socialist revolution to affect the liberation of women. In fact, one of the contentions of many Western feminists is that women's liberation cannot depend on the socialist revolution because male supremacy is independent of the type of economic system (see Firestone, 1970). In view of the lingering sex inequality in the People's Republic of China and other socialist countries (see Serkoff, 1975; Hendrix, 1975), one must agree that the evidence so far favors the feminist contention.

As elsewhere, one of the basic problems in socialist countries is that the issue of women has always been secondary in their political priority. Consequently, women's liberation in socialist (and other) countries has not received sufficient support to reach its final goal. For example, in Communist China, issues pertaining to women, such as marriage, family planning, and maternal employment, are evaluated in terms of the welfare of the collective rather than in terms of the rights of the women as individuals.[8] As a result, the intensity of state support for these issues tends to fluctuate according to national economic and political needs as perceived by the leadership. Consequently, the women's movement in China has not been able to maintain a sustained momentum, despite the strong impetus it received more than 25 years ago.

Recently (1974), another campaign has been launched to push for sex equality. However, the fate of this new effort is difficult to predict because, like many of the previous ones, it is subsumed under a larger political issue—this time in the context of attacking Lin Piao (the late Defense Minister and the designated heir to Mao) and the ideas of Confucius (see Southern University, 1974; China Reconstruct, 1975; Goldman, 1975).

## SUMMARY AND CONCLUSION

After twenty-five years of communist rule, Chinese women have made some progress toward full equality. The old patriarchal authority pattern no longer exists; the traditional attitude toward employed mothers has changed; and many married and unmarried women work outside the home. Women are also very active in local political groups. However, recent reports from emigrants, visitors, and other sources indicate that inequality still exists. In the area of family life, women still have a major responsibility for housework, and sons are still valued over daughters. The traditional protective attitude toward girls also seems to survive. In the area of employment, women still experience job and pay discrimination. Most of the important jobs in politics, the educational system, agriculture, factories, and hospitals are held by men.

Although some of these legacies can be attributed to the magnitude of sex inequality in the past, a more satisfactory explanation must take into consideration the persistence of the concept of Yin-Yang, the patrilineal kinship system the Ancestral Cult in China, and the inadequacy of the socialist revolution.

Finally, the persistence of sex-role inequality and its perpetuators in Chinese society raises questions about the inadequacy of the socialist revolution as a vehicle for women's liberation. Sex inequality is more basic and deeper than economic inequality, and therefore it may not be eliminated by changing the economic order and treating it as a secondary issue. Clearly, if China (as well as other socialist and non-socialist countries) desire to eradicate sex inequality completely, it must view the issue as a separate entity independent of other political concerns. Moreover, it must deal with the issues with full intensity until the problem is resolved, regardless of political ramifications and repercussions.

## NOTES

1 Before the Communist revolution, Article 1000 of the 1930–31 Civil Code of the Republic of China stipulates that the wife has to assume the husband's surname (Lang, 1946:115). In formal practice, there are two variations in the use of surname by married women during the pre-revolution period: (a) use the husband's surname only, (b) add husband's surname to wife's surname, as in Spanish tradition. In everyday usage, married women are usually referred to as "so-and-so's wife" (e.g., Wong's Wife) or "Mrs. so-and-so" (in Chinese equivalence). However, married women from the upper classes frequently use two names: her own family name and her husband's. For example, Mme. Chiang Kai-shek (wife of the late President of Republic of China in Taiwan) is frequently referred to as Mme. Chiang as well as Sung mei-ling, her own family name. All the conventions mentioned above are still in use in Hong Kong and Taiwan.

2 Rustication is the program of sending millions of middle-school and university graduates from the cities to the countryside. Before the Cultural Revolution in the late 60s, the object of the program was to help agricultural production in the rural areas. During the Cultural Revolution, the rusticated youth surged back to the cities as Red Guards. After the Cultural Revolution, they and other youth were sent back to the countryside again to be re-educated by the peasants.

3 Chou died in January, 1976. At the time of writing, Hua kuo-feng has been appointed acting premier (Los Angeles Times, 1976). Earlier, it was reported that Teng hsiao-ping would become premier. Both of them are male.

4 Mao has explicitly rejected the concept of Tao, a component of the Yin-Yang formulation, it should be noted. Tao is the Absolute or the Alpha and the Omega in the Yin-Yang theory. Mao found the concept unacceptable because of its static nature (Mao, 1968:26). Significantly, he made no reference to Yin-Yang in his rejection of Tao.

5 See Wieger (1969:147). Kaltenmark (1969:37–43), Day (1962:18–19), and other major commentaries on Chinese philosophy for the Yin-Yang elements in the works of Lao Tsu and Chuang Tsu.

6   The influence of Yin-Yang concept in the application of acupuncture in China today has also been mentioned in a U.S. Department of Health, Education and Welfare publication (1973:67–68).

7   Paper money (square pieces of paper with gold or silver colors printed on them) were still produced and sold in China at least until 1966 for ancestral and other religious ceremonies. A letter to the editor of *Chinese Youth,* No. 8, 1966 states: "... my mother went downtown and bought back several catties of paper money to burn for her dead ancestors." (See MacInnis, 1972:328 for full letter). Similarly, the August 12, 1970, issue of the *Fukien Daily* published a letter from a reader complaining that "superstitious practices" and "ancient sacrifices to the gods" are organized by the peasants (China News Analysis, 1970). Further evidence suggesting that traditional religious practices still persist in China may be inferred from the reactivation of the Religious Affairs Bureau in 1971 (MacInnis, 1972:375) and the reaffirmation of religious freedom in the 1975 Constitution.

8   This problem is not confined to socialist countries. In the United States the welfare of the big business frequently has a higher priority than the requirements of individual citizens in the governmental allocation of resources.

## REFERENCES

*Bush, Richard C.*
1970   Religion in Communist China, Nashville: Abingdon Press.
*China News Analysis*
1970   23(October):3.
*China Reconstruct*
1975   March.
*Chou, Keh-Chou*
1975   "How our village got equal pay for equal work." China Reconstruct (March): 6–9.
*Committee of Concerned Asian Scholars*
1972   China! Inside the People's Republic. New York: Bantam Books.
*Day, Clarence Burton*
1962   The Philosophers of China. New York: Philosophical Library.
*Feng, Gia-fu, and Hugh L. Wilkerson*
1970   Tai Chi-A Way of Centering and I Ching. Toronto: Macmillan.
*Firestone, Shulamith*
1970   The Dialectic of Sex. New York: William Morrow.
*Foreign Language Press*
1973   The Marriage Law of the People's Republic of China. Peking.
*Goldman, Merle*
1975   "China's anti-Confucian campaign. 1973–74." The China Quarterly 63 (September): 435–462.
*Hai, Fong*
1973   "Women's movement in Communist China." Communist China in 1971. Hong Kong: Union Research Institute.
*Hendrix, Kathleen*
1975   "Liberation, Soviet style." Los Angeles Times, (June 10).
*Hopei New Medical College*
1975   Acupuncture. Peking: People's Health Press.
*Hong, Lawrence K.*
1972   "The association of religion and family structure: the case of the Hong Kong family." Sociological Analysis 33 (Spring): 50–57.

1973    "A profile analysis of the Chinese family in an urban industrialized setting." International Journal of Sociology of the Family 3 (March): 1–9.

*Hsu, Francis L. K.*
1967    Under the Ancestor's Shadow. Garden City, N.Y.: Doubleday.

*Huang, Lucy Jen*
1961    "Some changing patterns in the Communist Chinese family." Marriage and Family Living 23 (May): 137–146.
1972    "Mate selection and marital happiness in the mainland Chinese family." International Journal of Sociology of the Family 2 (September): 121–138.

*Institute of the People's Movement*
1920?   Problems of Women in China. Hunan, China.

*Kaltenmark, Max*
1969    Lao Tsu and Taoism. Stanford: Stanford University Press.

*Lang, Olga*
1946    Chinese Family and Society. New Haven: Yale University Press.

*Lee, Jung Young*
1971    The Principle of Changes: Understanding the I Ching. New Hyde Park, N.Y.: University Books.

*Liu, William T.*
1973    "Journey to Nan-chang." Notre Dame Magazine 2 (August): 10–27.

*Los Angeles Times*
1976    February 7.

*Macciocchi, Maria Antonietta*
1972    Daily Life in Revolutionary China. New York: Monthly Review Press.

*MacInnis, Donald E.*
1972    Religious Policy and Practice in Communist China. New York: Macmillan.

*Mao, Tse-Tung*
1968    Four Essays on Philosophy. Peking: Foreign Language Press.

*Serkoff, Jack*
1975    "Chauvinism alive in socialistic countries." Los Angeles Times (June 6).

*Snow, Edgar*
1971    "A conversation with Mao Tse-tung." Life (April 30): 46–48.

*Southern University*
1974    Proletariat's Anti-Confucius Struggle in the History of Our Country. Department of Philosophy, Peking: People's Press.

*Time*
1975    (February, 3): 22–32.

*Topping, Seymour*
1971    "Welfare plan assures minimum living standard." Pp. 187–190 in Tillman Durdin, James Reston, and Seymour Topping (eds.), The New York Times Report from China, New York: Quadrangle Books.

*U.S. Department of Health, Education and Welfare*
1973    Public Health in the People's Republic of China. No. (NIH) 73–76. Washington, D.C.

*Wiegar, Leo*
1969    A History of the Religious Beliefs and Philosophical Opinions in China. New York: Paragon Book Reprint Corp.

*Wu, Wie-p'ing*
1962    Chinese Acupuncture. Rustington, Sussex: Health Science Press.

*Yang, C. K.*
1959a   The Chinese Family in Communist Revolution. Cambridge, Mass.: M.I.T. Press.
1959b   A Chinese Village in Early Communist Transition. Cambridge, Mass.: M.I.T. Press.

*Yang, Ji-Chou*
1973    A Complete Book on Acupuncture. Peking: People's Health Press.

*Yang, Martin C.*
1966    A Chinese Village. New York: Columbia University Press.

# FIVE

## ETHNICITY, PLURALISM, AND ASSIMILATION

*Perhaps ethnic identification is more important in American life since the mid-1960s, or perhaps sociologists have just rediscovered it and emphasized it more. The continued existence of ethnic identities among European immigrant groups has been well demonstrated, and racial minorities seem to have a stronger sense of cultural identity since the rise of the black power movement. In the third generation or later immigrant groups have been found to differ from other Americans in political behavior, occupational patterns, family life, choice of friends, leisure-time activities, and attitudes about many matters (Laumann, 1972; Greeley and McCready, 1974). Several studies have demonstrated that religious and ethnic identities have persisted in the suburbs as well as in the central cities (Newman, 1973:77–78).*

*The selection by Yancey, Ericksen, and Juliani reviews information and commentary about ethnicity, and emphasizes the importance of adaptations to conditions faced by the group, rather than the ancestral culture. This is consistent with the view taken by Glazer and Moynihan in their monograph on the ethnic groups of New York City (1963:13–23). They rejected the view that ethnic differences had merged in the presumed melting pot, and held that a group keeps adapting and developing a changing identity as it is being assimilated. During the first and second generations an immigrant group loses many of its traditional ways, usually including language. But, say Glazer and Moynihan, common political and economic interests remain, along with ties of family, religion, friendship, and fraternal and protective organizations. Continuing discrimination, as well as competition and conflict with new groups over jobs, housing, and schools, can unite groups that have already experienced considerable assimilation (Newman, 1973: 182–83).*

*Some definitions of aspects of the opposite processes of pluralism and assimilation will help. The general meaning of pluralism is the coexistence and mutual toleration of groups that retain their separate identities, and it has three dimensions: (1) cultural pluralism—group maintenance of their own cultures, without pressure to be assimilated; (2) structural pluralism—participation by different groups in different social institutions and informal social arrangements; and (3) political, or power, pluralism—the distribution of political power among many interest groups, not equally, but with equal rights to organize and gain political influence. These are empirical dimensions—aspects of pluralism as social reality. Pluralism as an ideological position is the view that the cultures and identities of different groups ought to be preserved (Schermerhorn, 1970:122–28). When it is said that a particular group has a pluralistic orientation, it wants to retain at least its own identity.*

*Assimilation of a group means the loss of its separate identity as it merges with the dominant community, and it has three phases: (1) cultural assimilation—acculturation, or replacement of the group's cultural traits with those of the dominant community; (2) structural assimilation—integration into patterns of participation in institutions and informal social structures; and (3) disappearance of a sense of identity as a separate group. The term integration is often used to refer especially to the institutional side of structural assimilation. In his influential treatment of assimilation, Gordon maintains that inclusion of the group in patterns of participation in the primary groups of the dominant community rapidly accelerates the loss of the group's identity. Cultural assimilation may proceed a long way before this aspect of structural assimilation occurs (Gordon, 1964:70–81). Glazer and Moynihan (above) saw*

*New York's ethnic groups as largely assimilated culturally, but structurally and politically quite pluralistic.*

*Ethnic relations in Canada are discussed in the selection by Burnet, and the Glazer-Moynihan view of ethnicity is related to the government's program of multiculturalism within a bilingual framework. Before reading this it would be helpful to review the selection in Part One by Clairmont and Wien, in which it is stressed that the Canadian approach to its ethnic and race relations has always been pluralistic. The issues now are what the nature of the pluralistic mosaic is to be in the future, and what means to use to attain it.*

*Studies have been made in a number of cities of minority participation in voluntary associations, apparently a good predictor of participation in voting and other political activities. The one reported here by Williams, Babchuk, and Johnson was made in Austin, Texas, and included comparisons of blacks, whites, and Mexican Americans. The isolation and cultural inhibition explanations have not fared any better in most other studies than in this one, and problems of interpretation are now centered on the compensation and ethnic community theories. These theories are clearly summarized in the selection. Comment is in order about two statements in the conclusion: (1) Greeks and Italians are evidently not so thoroughly assimilated as was thought for a time, and (2) the Southern Christian Leadership Conference was a product of the Montgomery Bus Boycott, not its organizer.*

*Other studies support the Williams-Babchuk-Johnson finding that blacks participate more in voluntary organizations than whites with similar education, and one interpretation is that compensation accounts for some of the black activity while ethnic community pressures account for some (Olsen, 1970). The finding that the low rates of Mexican American participation increase when education is controlled for has been reported in some studies, but not in others, and one suggestion is that public and private kinds of social participation ought to be distinguished (Antunes and Gaitz, 1975). It would also be useful to take into account the extent to which participation is in the ethnic group's own organizations and primary groups rather than in those of the community at large. Better understanding of social participation may help unravel the complexities of pluralism and assimilation.*

*The selection by Alba reports the use of data on intermarriage to determine the amount of assimilation of national groups, all of them Catholic. Finding the rate to be high, he concludes that the ethnic ties of these groups have become weak, and that both cultural and primary group assimilation have proceeded quite far. Researchers who have found ethnic identities to be alive and well in the third and fourth generations have generally relied on data on other matters, often acknowledging the large amount of intermarriage. For instance, in a study in Catholic parishes in Providence, Rhode Island, in 1966, third-generation people expressed considerably more ethnic identification than did those in the first and second generations. Yet the third generation was largely removed from the ethnic neighborhood, two-thirds of them were intermarried, and few belonged to an ethnic organization. These third-generation people expressed resentment of discrimination, and anxiety about black demands for equality—suggesting a strengthening of their ethnic identity by competition with newer arrivals in the ghetto for jobs, housing, and educational opportunities (Goering, 1971).*

*We have noted Gordon's emphasis on the role of assimilation into primary groups in the dominant community. Unfortunately, his restriction of the concept of structural assimilation to this level has apparently led to some neglect of the role of integration into economic, political, and other institutional structures, in discussions of pluralism and assimilation. Shannon's contribution on the economic absorption of blacks and Mexican Americans is interpreted, in part, in terms of institutional discrimination. It suggests many hurdles on the way to economic security, much less equality, despite the civil rights laws and programs of federal assistance. Prior generations of ghetto occupants also developed their own organizations and friendships to help them survive and get over the hurdles. Many of today's urban migrants have apparently concluded that the dominant community will not permit their assimilation, especially into its primary group networks. Therefore they emphasize pride in their continuing identity and the development of more political and economic power with which to defend and help the group.*

*Studies of the overall pattern of integration in racially mixed urban areas are rare. The report by Molotch of an imaginative observational study on Chicago's South Shore indicates that thoroughgoing integration does not necessarily follow demographic integration (the occupancy by two race groups of the same or adjacent areas). Molotch observed rather few equal-status contacts. He found many ways in which the groups limited their interaction, especially in private, informal situations, and he found little "transracial solidarity."*

# REFERENCES

*Antunes, George, and Charles M. Gaitz*
1975    "Ethnicity and Participation: A Study of Mexican-Americans, Blacks and Whites." American Journal of Sociology 80, 5 (March): 1192–1211.
*Glazer, Nathan, and Daniel Patrick Moynihan*
1963    Beyond the Melting Pot: The Negroes, Puerto Ricans, Jews, Italians, and Irish of New York City. Cambridge, Massachusetts: The M.I.T. Press.
*Goering, John M.*
1971    "The Emergence of Ethnic Interests." Social Forces 49, 3 (March): 379–84.
*Gordon, Milton M.*
1964    Assimilation in American Life: The Role of Religion and National Origins. New York: Oxford University Press.
*Greeley, Andrew M.*
1974    Ethnicity in the United States: A Preliminary Reconnaisance. New York: John Wiley and Sons.
*Laumann, Edward O.*
1972    Bonds of Pluralism: The Form and Substance of Urban Social Networks. New York: Wiley-Interscience.
*Newman, William M.*
1973    American Pluralism: A Study of Minority Groups and Social Theory. New York: Harper and Row.
*Olsen, Marvin E.*
1970    "Social and Political Participation of Blacks." American Sociological Review 35, 4 (August): 682–97.
*Schermerhorn, Richard A.*
1970    Comparative Ethnic Relations: A Framework for Theory and Research. New York: Random House.

# Emergent Ethnicity: A Review and Reformulation*

## William L. Yancey

## Eugene P. Ericksen

## Richard N. Juliani

*Temple University*

*This paper is a review and partial reformulation of the sociological literature on the persistence of ethnicity in American society. In contrast to the traditional emphasis on the transplanted cultural heritage as the principal antecedent and defining characteristic of ethnic groups, we suggest that the development and persistence of ethnicity is dependent upon structural conditions characterizing American cities and position of groups in American social structure. Attention is focused on the question: under what conditions does ethnic culture emerge? Specifically, what social forces promote the crystallization and development of ethnic solidarity and identification? As an emergent phenomenon, ethnicity continues to develop with the changing positions of*

*Source:* William L. Yancey, Eugene P. Ericksen, and Richard N. Juliani, "Emergent Ethnicity: A Review and Reformulation," American Sociological Review 41, 3 (June 1976): 391—403. Copyright © 1976 by the American Sociological Association. Reprinted by permission of the Association and the authors.
*Support for this research was received from Temple University, the Center for Studies of Metropolitan Problems, National Institute of Mental Health (Grant # RO1MH25244) and the Institute for Survey Research, Temple University.

*groups and individuals within society. As society changes, old forms of ethnic culture may die out but new forms may be generated.*


The analysis of ethnicity in American sociology has been dominated by an argument between the assimilationist and pluralist perspectives. Both positions have emphasized the cultural origins of ethnic groups. This underlying assumption has never been tested, nor has the structural context of the argument been specified. The assimilationist position is that cultural differences between national origin groups pass through later generations in progressively diluted forms and ultimately disappear in modern society. This position rests on the assumption that the importance of ascribed status and ascriptively oriented relations wane with increasing modernization and the accompanying emphasis on universalism and achievement. As Blau and Duncan (1967:429) write: "... a fundamental trend toward expanding universalism characterizes industrial society. Objective criteria of evaluation that are universally accepted increasingly pervade all spheres of life and displace particularistic standards of diverse ingroups, intuitive judgement, and humanistic values not susceptible to empirical verification." In spite of the popularity of this view, we feel there are important theoretical reasons (e.g., Cohen, 1974; Mayhew, 1968) and empirical evidence (e.g., Laumann, 1973, Granovetter, 1974) indicating that it may be false.

The pluralist position, on the other hand, emphasizes the persistence of cultural heritage as the basis of the continued importance of ascriptive groups (Abramson, 1973; Greeley, 1974). Yet these writers have failed to explore the possibility that such differences could be due to structural conditions which each immigrant group and their descendants have encountered. Lieberson notes in criticizing the cultural explanation for the propensity of immigrants from northern and western Europe to engage in agriculture:

*Since the new immigrants, using a geographical distinction, came predominantly after the great development and settlement of the national agricultural regions, they were not in a position comparable to that of the old immigrants coming during the mid-nineteenth century. (1963:63)*

Lieberson's position leads to the hypothesis that the behavior of immigrants and their descendants would vary significantly depending on whether they have lived under conditions which generated and/or reinforced an "ethnic community" in the United States. As Kosa (1956) has demonstrated for Hungarians in New York and Toronto, when group members have different American experiences, their attitudes, behavior, and valuation of group membership are different.

The monolithic treatment of ethnicity, used in much contemporary empirical research, has not paid attention to differences within an ethnic group. One example of this failure is Duncan and Duncan's (1968) research on occupational mobility by national origin groups. For some groups, differences in the pattern of occupational mobility were found and were described as being characteristic of the entire group. The same differences could have been found if a significant minority within any national origin group had a unique experience in the United States while the remainder of the group shared a more general pattern. The distinctive situation of the subgroup, rather than cultural heritage or possible discrimination as implied by the Duncans, would explain group differences. In short, we suggest that it is not only necessary to test for differences between groups, but also to identify those conditions which produce ethnicity and ethnically related behavior.

The contrasting view of ethnicity developed here is that rather than an ascribed constant or a temporarily persistent variable, ethnicity and ethnically based ascription are emergent phenomena. Rather than viewing ethnicity or ascribed status generally as being inevitably doomed by the processes of modernization, we suggest that ethnic groups have been produced by structural conditions which are intimately linked to the changing technology of industrial production and transportation. More specifically, ethnicity, defined in terms of frequent patterns of association and identification with common origins (Haller, 1973; Greeley, 1974), is crystallized under conditions which reinforce the maintenance of kinship and friendship networks. These are common occupational positions, residential stability and concentration, and dependence on common institutions and services. These conditions are directly dependent on the ecological structure of cities, which is in turn directly affected by the processes of industrialization.

We do not wish to suggest that this is a complete model. Our focus is on the American immigrant experience and is limited to the situation which Lieberson (1961) has characterized as superordinate indigenous group and subordinate migrants. The factor of racial and biological distinctiveness has been fully explored in previous statements of ethnic relations. Similarly, we have not examined either the antecedents or consequences of intergroup conflict as a facilitator of intergroup solidarity. There are some cases where ideologically oriented immigrant groups have come to the United States and self-consciously tried to maintain their heritages and, as Glazer observed (1954), ideological groups frequently develop after arrival in the United States. These groups have found a unique, often autonomous place in the American social structure (Hostetler, 1968), and even then there is modification in their ideology and heritage (Handlin, 1961).

This paper is in two sections. The first is a discussion of the historical and ecological conditions leading to the formation and persistence of ethnic communities in cities. The second section focuses on contemporary patterns of urban ethnic groups. Here we discuss the implication of changing ecological conditions for the maintenance and development of ascriptive associations and identification in contemporary American cities.

## OCCUPATIONAL CONCENTRATION
## OF IMMIGRANTS

Systematic evidence (Lieberson, 1963; Hutchinson, 1956) indicates that immigrant cohorts are differentially located in the American occupational structure. Unlike the widely held model of each immigrant cohort moving into the stratification system at its lowest point, pushing up those who had come before them, and then being pushed themselves by later arrivals, all groups did not enter at the lowest occupational levels. Lieberson (1963:173) reports that for some ". . . there was a decline in occupational position from first to the second generation." He points out that to understand the occupational concentrations of immigrants it is necessary to consider both the diverse educational and occupational skills which immigrants brought, as well as the specific working opportunities which were available at the time of their arrival.

Ward (1971) described the American economy between 1850 and 1920 as becoming more diversified and industrial, with substantial concentration of expansion in midwestern cities. Duncan and Lieberson (1970) have shown that in the first part of this period economic expansion occurred in older port cities of Boston, Philadelphia, New York, and Baltimore; as well as in midwestern cities located along water transport routes, such as Cincinnati, St. Louis, Chicago, and Pittsburgh. In the second part of this period, characterized by Duncan and Lieberson as the age of steam and steel technology, opportunities continued to expand in the older cities, but the most rapid expansion occurred in the midwestern cities convenient for the development of the iron and steel industries. Some of these were new cities, such as Detroit, Buffalo, Cleveland, and Milwaukee. Some were older cities such as Chicago and Pittsburgh. New York as the port of entry remained the destination of many immigrants. As shown by Ward (1971), the Germans and Irish, who were earlier immigrants, concentrated in the older cities such as Philadelphia and St. Louis. By contrast, the newer immigrants from Poland, Italy, and Russia concentrated in Buffalo, Cleveland, Detroit, and Milwaukee, as well as in some of the older cities with expanding opportunities. Different migration patterns occurred for immigrants with and without skills. Davie (1947) has shown that Jewish immigrants with higher skills were more likely than the unskilled to obtain "matching" occupations in America. Rewards for skilled occupations were greater, and the skilled immigrant went to the cities where there were opportunities to practice his trade. Less highly skilled workers went to the cities with expanding opportunities. Thus, the Italian concentration in construction and the Polish in steel were related to the expansion of these industries as these groups arrived (Golab, 1973). The Jewish concentration in the garment industry may have been a function of their previous experience as tailors, but it is also dependent upon the emergence of the mass-production of clothing in the late nineteenth century.

Similarly, the Irish propensity to participate in the urban political bureaucracy may be understood best in terms of the expansion of city governments in the mid-19th century, rather than as an Irish cultural aptitude for coping with bureaucracy as suggested by Glazer and Moynihan (1963).

The choice of residence and occupation was also influenced by the presence of friends and relatives. Their influence can be seen in the connections made between origins and destinations in the process of international migration. Park and Miller (1921) first described the process of "migration chains." In recent years, they have been documented by studies of immigration to New Zealand (Lochore, 1951), to Australia (Borrie, 1954; Price, 1963), and to the United States (MacDonald and MacDonald, 1964), as well as migration within the United States (Goldstein, 1958). In the case of Italians, recent research has suggested that the *padrone* system, which imported contract laborers for industrial agents, was less important than networks of friends and relatives as the mechanism by which migration was structured (Nelli, 1971; Vecoli, 1964).

The occupational concentration of an immigrant cohort provided at least four potential sources for maintaining group solidarity. Given similarity of occupational status, it is likely that a cohort was characterized by similar economic status. To the degree that behavior is associated with economic status, we should expect some similarity of life styles (Kriesberg, 1963). Second, similarity in occupation provided common social and economic interests (Hannerz, 1974). To the degree that occupational position is related to class consciousness, one expects some degree of group solidarity among cohorts (Centers, 1949; Leggett, 1968). Third, immigrants who were concentrated in a single factory or industry should have had a relatively high degree of interpersonal association stemming from their work relationships (Reiss, 1959). Finally, and perhaps most important, during a time when transportation was not available, industrial workers were forced to live near their employment (Pratt, 1911). Each of these factors—life style, class interests, work relationships and common residential areas—facilitated the development of group consciousness.

## RESIDENTIAL CONCENTRATIONS

The expansion of the industrial economy not only provided specific occupational opportunities to cohorts of immigrants destined for different cities, but also altered urban ecology. Industrialization, coupled with the introduction of the electric streetcar in the late 19th century and the automobile and truck in the early 20th century, had major effects upon the internal ecology of urban residence and institutions (Hawley, 1971; Ward, 1971). These changes in urban ecology, in turn, had a direct effect on the relative concentration and autonomy of ethnic settlements as well as upon the formation of ethnic communities and subcultures.

The establishment of immigrant "ghettoes" in cities must be viewed in relation to the stages of development of American cities. Pre-industrial cities have been described by Pirenne (1925) and Sjoberg (1955) where the affluent lived in central locations, the poor on the periphery and tradesmen and craftsmen between the rich and the poor. Manufacturing typically occurred in small establishments which were not particularly concentrated. The journey to work was short. The central location of the affluent gave them maximum access to commercial activities.

The concentric zone model, described by Burgess (1922), referred to a period in which commerce was centralized. In this period the scale of industrial production grew. This was due to the growth of the market and access to raw materials, encouraged by the railroads and technological innovations which made it possible to have large-scale manufacturing. Industries also became more concentrated. It was difficult to transport coal and heavy raw materials except by railroad. The cost of transporting other goods encouraged centralization where access to other industries and markets was maximized. Limited and costly transportation made it necessary for industrial workers to live near where they worked. The advent of the omnibus and streetcar made it possible, however, for higher status workers to live in successive concentric rings of more expensive and new housing (Warner, 1962).

In contrast, the mid-twentieth century city is characterized by the dispersal of commercial and industrial activities made possible by the expanded use of the motor truck, petroleum and electricity as energy sources, and electronic communication. In addition, industrial workers make considerable use of the automobile to get to work, thus loosening the relationship between work and residence.

The popular belief has been that assimilation of immigrant groups began after the establishment of ghettoes in the center of cities. These concentrations supposedly dispersed as immigrants and their descendants became more directly involved in the mainstream of American life. Warner and Burke (1969), however, point out that this process occurred only for a limited time span in American urban history and then only in some cities. Their position is that "... most foreign immigrants to American cities never lived in ghettoes and most immigrant ghettoes that did exist were the product of the largest cities and the eastern and southern European immigrants of 1880–1940." Statistical evidence is admittedly fragmentary, but it does suggest that prior to 1880, immigrant groups, mainly Irish, Canadian, British, and German, were dispersed throughout the city with concentration only in a few points. Warner and Burke attribute this dispersal to two conditions: (1) the distribution of the limited stock of available housing and (2) the small scale of most urban economic activity. The latter discouraged the formation of purely residential or purely commercial districts.

Ward (1971), in basic agreement with Warner and Burke, argues that residential patterns in American cities of the mid-nineteenth century were transitional between pre-industrial and modern. Because the first major influx of immigrants occurred before either urban employment became centralized or local transportation improved, the residential patterns of the earlier immigrants were not concentrated. However, after about 1850 "the central concentration of urban employment ... strongly influenced the location and characteristics of the residential areas of new immigrants, most of whom sought low cost housing close to their places of employment" (Ward, 1971:105).

At least one study of the journey to work, in New York City in 1907, documented the fact that low-paid industrial workers were forced by economic pressures to live close to their places of work (Pratt, 1911). Pratt concluded his important, but little-known study of ethnic congestion with the statement:

*In view of the fact that our foreign population is the most unskilled, and therefore, the lowest paid, and that it is employed in industries working the longest hours, the tendency to live in congested districts near the workplace cannot occasion very great surprise. This tendency—and the fact that the aliens form the largest part of our most congested population is admitted—has been frequently seized upon as the explanation of congestion, and hence these theorists have logically enough demanded restriction of immigration as a remedy for congestion. However, if congestion were due to the desire ... of our alien population to live in congested districts, we should expect those employed within a reasonable distance of Manhattan to make every effort to live there. But this is exactly contrary to the facts ... the Italians, Jews and Slavic peoples, who have oftenest been indicted for congestion, have proved themselves innocent and their positive unwillingness to live in Manhattan, when escape is offered, is evidenced by every group of workers in the factories outside of Lower Manhattan. (1911:187)*

Before the concentration of large scale employment, work opportunities for immigrants were scattered and their residential locations were correspondingly scattered. In the later period, to the extent that work opportunities were concentrated, the immigrant "ghettoes" were also concentrated.

Some evidence for this interpretation is found in data compiled by Lieberson (1963). In Boston, the indices of segregation for the Irish from native whites for the years 1850, 1855, and 1880 were 20.7, 26.0, and 14.7. The corresponding indices for Germans were 31.0, 38.6, and 30.7. Trends toward residential assimilation were small and did not continue through to 1950 when the corresponding indices of segregation *increased* to 25.5 and 34.8. In contrast to these groups, the Poles, Russians, and Italians who arrived later were more segregated in 1880 and 1930. Their indices were 61.5, 53.8, and 73.8, respectively, in 1880 and in 1930 were 50.4 for the Poles, 64.9 for the Russians, and 53.5 for the Italians. Similar patterns were found in other cities—although with more limited historical data. Lieberson (1963:14) found that ". . . length of residence in the United States of the immigrant groups and their differences in socioeconomic level were both found to be independently influencing the magnitude of the immigrant groups segregation." While this can be viewed as evidence for the process of assimilation, we suggest that it can best be interpreted in terms of the ecology of occupations and residence characterizing the city when immigrant residential patterns were established.

The "old" immigrants were never segregated to the same extent as the "new" immigrants. There appears to be somewhat of a principle of what might be called "ecological inertia"; i.e., once a pattern becomes established, its effects can be seen in later years. Or, conversely, interpretation of urban social structure at one point in time requires knowledge of the patterns that came before, as well as the contemporary forces which continue to operate.

## THE DEVELOPMENT OF ETHNIC COMMUNITIES

The influence of residential patterns on the development and maintenance of ethnic communities varied with the particular historical period. There is evidence that the institutional character of neighborhoods is related to the nature of informal networks (Foley, 1950). The earliest urban neighborhoods contained the major institutions of work, religion, family, leisure, and, to a considerable degree, government and social control (Pirenne, 1925; Sjoberg, 1955). By the middle of the 19th century, American cities were in a transition from the pre-industrial and industrial. While urban neighborhoods may have been institutionally complete, in general the early immigrants dispersed rather than settled in concentrated ghettoes. Thus, few residential areas contained large concentrations of groups, economic or ethnic, which could establish clearly bounded identities (Warner, 1968; Laurie, 1973).

A very different situation occurred when large waves of immigrants were arriving around the turn of the century. The advances in transportation technology and increased specialization of land use had direct consequences for the relative completeness of urban residential areas. Urban neighborhoods were progressively deprived of their total social system characteristics as particular activities were transferred to more specialized areas. The separation of work and residence for upper income workers, and further development of separate industrial, commercial, leisure, and residential areas, resulted in the decline of the multiple institutional and functional character of some earlier urban neighborhoods (Warren, 1963).

These trends were particularly characteristic of the newer, outlying areas, the streetcar and automobile suburbs, but not of older, center city neighborhoods. As the journey to work was problematic for the poor, so, presumably, was the journey to other services. Contemporary research indicates that lower status urban residents are more dependent on institutions and services in the immediate neighborhood (Foley, 1950). Similarly, higher attachment to local neighborhoods, institutions, and informal networks appears to be associated with lower status (Fried, 1963) as well as length of residence (Kasarda and Janowitz, 1974) and stage in the life cycle (Bell and Boat, 1957). We expect that similar relationships existed in early twentieth century cities.

It is in the older, centrally located neighborhoods where one expects the development and use of a wide range of local institutions such as food stores, bars, schools, churches, mutual aid societies, fraternal associations, and newspapers. And it is in these neighborhoods with their local institutions where interpersonal networks develop and are maintained (Fitzpatrick, 1966; Dahya, 1974; Charsley, 1974). A recent investigation of ethnicity in Montreal is indicative of the role of common institutions for the development and maintenance of an ethnic community. Breton found relationships between the size of the immigrant cohort, their ability to speak the native language, the percentage of the group who were manual workers and the institutional completeness of the ethnic community. The latter in turn was found to be closely related to the character of the interpersonal networks. Breton (1964:197) writes: "The institutions of an ethnic community are the origin of much social life in which the people of that community get involved and as a consequence become tied together in a cohesive interpersonal network."

Although usually interpreted in terms of assimilation, Lieberson's (1963) research on ethnic residential patterns can also be seen as strong evidence of the impact of residential concentrations for the maintenance of ethnic solidarity. He found that those groups which were residentially segregated were more sharply differentiated in their occupational composition, more deviant in patterns of occupational mobility, less likely to become American citizens, less likely to speak English, and more likely to be endogamous. This argument suggests that within a national origin group those members who live outside of areas of concentration are more assimilated than those living within areas of concentration.

The effect of the residential community on ethnic membership is directly relevant to the current controversy regarding ethnic endogamy. The classic studies of Kennedy (1944; 1952) and Herberg (1955) suggested that increasing patterns of religious endogamy and ethnic exogamy had resulted in a triple melting pot of Catholic, Protestant, and Jew. In contrast to these earlier studies, Abramson (1973) has reported that, among Catholics, patterns of national endogamy have been maintained. Endogamy was found to be highest among the Spanish-speaking and Italians and lowest among the Germans and Irish. Because residential propinquity has been shown to influence the selection of marriage partners (Katz and Hill, 1958; Warren, 1966), Kennedy's findings can be interpreted in terms of the lessened residential concentration of national groups. Abramson's apparently contradictory findings are similarly interpretable. Although the evidence is not direct, those groups which Abramson finds to be the most endogamous are also those Lieberson (1963) found to be the most segregated.

The argument that ethnic communities became crystallized in American cities in response to the American urban conditions is not new. Glazer (1954), Handlin (1961), and Vecoli (1964) have pointed out that some ethnic groups evolved from smaller, more regional bases of organization and identification to larger nationalistic ones after they arrived in America. Nelli (1970:5) concludes his study of Italians in Chicago saying that "... community and group consciousness among 'Southerners' in the United States did not cross the Atlantic, but developed in the new homeland." Killian (1970) has pointed out that white southern migrants, although of diverse origins, formed a relatively cohesive hillbilly community in Chicago. Finally, recent research on urban blacks, both historical (Hershberg, 1973) and contemporary (Long, 1974), has refuted the traditional emphasis on black southern culture as the root cause of urban ghetto life. Thus, mounting evidence suggests that the examination of ethnic experience should use the urban American-ethnic community, rather than the place of origin as the principal criterion of ethnic group membership. Integration into the mainstream of American life should refer to the American ghetto rather than the European rural village as the point of departure (Handlin, 1951).

This general view also suggests that much of the substance of ethnic cultures may be the result of a selective process which consists of a constantly evolving interaction between the nature of the local community, the available economic opportunities, and the national or religious heritage of a particular group. As Gans (1962a) has shown for the Italian community of the Boston West End, those aspects of a group's original heritage which are appropriate adaptations to the American conditions, as well as those which may have been irrelevant, may remain intact. In contrast, those which are inappropriate or lead to unnecessary negative consequences may be expected to die out. Those that come into conflict with existing American institutions may become issues around which ethnic institutions, consciousness, and identities are formed. The apparently persisting influence of the Old World traits appears different for different groups. In some cases such as Jewish values (Fuchs, 1968), Italian mutual aid societies (Vecoli, 1964), and Polish and Italian family structures (McLaughlin, 1971), the effect of cultural heritage appears strong; in other instances such as Jewish mutual aid societies (Glanz, 1970) or Italian community cohesion (Nelli, 1971), the new setting appears more important. What is necessary is the identification of the conditions associated with the demise and/or retention of cultural traits.

## ETHNICITY AND COMMUNITY IN CONTEMPORARY SOCIETY

Large scale immigration from Europe to the United States essentially was cut off in 1924. Since that time the largest distinctive groups of migrants to northern cities have been southern blacks and Puerto Ricans. Two important questions arise. What factors have contributed to the continued salience of ethnicity for descendants of European immigrants? And, what are the differences in ethnicity and community between blacks and Puerto Ricans and European ethnics?

The ecological bases of urban institutions and communities are different today from what they were three-quarters of a century ago. The influence of the concentration of occupation opportunities on the development of working-class neighborhoods has been altered. With the continued development of transportation, the truck and the high-speed expressway in particular, industries are no longer forced to locate in centralized areas or near railroads or rivers. This new flexibility also enables industry to search for relatively low-cost sites away from urban centers. Consequently, industrial firms increasingly have moved from the centralized core of the city to differentiated areas of commercial and industrial activity near the fringes of metropolitan regions. The remaining occupational opportunities, while diminishing, are concentrated in low-wage, less technically advanced and economically more vulnerable industries (Fusfeld, 1969) and in the unskilled service occupations associated with governmental or commercial activities remaining in central locations.

Since the end of World War II, with the advent of widespread automobile use, the close relationship between the location of employment and that of residence has also been greatly loosened. In particular, this is true for the more affluent workers (Hoover and Vernon, 1959). Therefore, while earlier ethnic communities were formed around expanding industrial opportunities recent ghettoes have been developed at a time when opportunities were leaving central locations.

These changes in the ecology of urban areas removed the structural conditions which supported ethnicity in the past. These changes have produced at least three rather different types of residential communities. The interpersonal networks, their relationship to the urban economy, and the salience and importance of the ethnicity manifested are different in each.

First, there has been the development of what Gans (1962b) has called "quasi-communities." These are upper and middle income suburbs that do not have the institutional, industrial, and associational cohesion of earlier residential areas. Second, there are the more recently formed ghettoes of blacks and Puerto Ricans. Finally, there are residual forms of residential communities formed in the earlier part of this century. These are the urban villages studied by Gans (1962a), Whyte (1943), and Young and Willmott (1957). They appear to have some of the characteristics of the older ethnic communities and newer ghettoes.

The urban village, characterized by concentrated networks and organizations among residents of a similar ethnicity, confounds the effects of ethnicity and the effects of community. The classic study of Bethnal Green (Young and Willmott, 1957) illustrates this point. Young and Willmott found that there was a high rate of local interaction, that newly married couples tended to move only a short distance from their parents, that kinship ties were maintained, that there was primary dependence on local institutions, and that personal connections were used to obtain jobs. These behavior patterns are commonly associated with contemporary ethnic communities in the United States. In these neighborhoods, what is commonly viewed as "ethnic behavior" may be a manifestation of community, a reflection of the exigencies of working-class life, and is ethnic only by coincidence. The close correspondence between working-class communities and ethnicity is suggested by Berger's (1960:95) note that: "Our image of working class life is dominated by ethnic motifs." Two detailed investigations of the Boston West End (Gans, 1962a; Fried, 1974) have concluded that even though that area was widely recognized as an Italian community, the effect of the ethnicity was secondary to that of community and class. In the follow-up study of former Bethnal Green residents who had moved to the suburbs, Willmott and Young (1957) found that patterns of interaction had dropped and that the sense of community was not redeveloped. In an American study of visiting patterns with relatives, Klatsky (1974) found that distance was the principal predictor of frequency of contact with relatives. Once distance was controlled, the effects of ethnicity and religion were minor.

The ethnicity found in black and Puerto Rican ghettoes is clearly different from that of the urban village. We have already observed that these communities are removed from the best economic opportunities. Ethnographic research demonstrates that these communities are also characterized by a social organization containing relatively strong informal networks (Liebow, 1967; Valentine, 1968). These networks are not tied to economic opportunities. Sheppard and Striner (1965) have noted:

*Job information is a critical need among Negroes. While labor economists and other social scientists may be the first to know—after employers, perhaps,— that unemployment rates are going down and job opportunities (in certain occupations and industries) are going up, unskilled Negro workers may be the last to know or may never know.*

In short, the segregation of these new ethnics from the best economic opportunities is social as well as geographic.

The situation of the contemporary urban white ethnic may be only marginally better. He would have an advantage over the urban black by virtue of his longevity in the urban economy and thus would have access to knowledge and influence which is crucial in obtaining jobs (Granovetter, 1974). But to the extent that the urban villages are located near older, less productive and declining industries, this information is less useful. The research of Gans (1962a) and Granovetter (1974) has demonstrated the negative effect of membership in local networks at the exclusion of ties outside of the neighborhood. With the continued movement of industries from central locations, the provincialism of these neighborhoods and associations can be expected to be increasingly disadvantageous. Thus, the strength of community identification and the quality of life manifested there are, in part, responses to residues of earlier historical periods and, in part, responses to the increasingly more marginal social and economic positions of the white working-class neighborhoods (Howard, 1971).

All of this is not to imply that ethnic behavior can only be maintained in localized communities. Ethnic salience and identification, as transmitted through the family and friends, can be maintained, whether they are in the same neighborhood or not. Moreover, the establishment of ethnic organizations on a cosmopolitan level can reinforce the salience of ethnicity. Etzioni (1959) has examined ethnicity as a factor operating in a variety of contexts from the extreme of a geographically based "totalistic" community with predominantly local patterns of interaction and primary dependence on local institutions to the other extreme of a residentially dispersed group "maintained by communication and active in limited social situations." Examples of the latter are church and synagogue attendance, marching in a Saint Patrick's or Columbus Day parade, voting for a political candidate of a similar ethnicity, or supporting a political cause associated with the country of origin, such as the emigration of Russian Jews to Israel or the reunification of Ireland. This "situational ethnicity" is likely to be found in the more cosmopolitan networks of residents of the "quasi-communities"—such as the post–World War II suburbs. It is clearly different from the ethnicity found in the white urban village or the colonized ghetto.

These observations suggest that ethnicity should not be regarded as an ascribed attribute with only two discrete categories, but as a continuous variable. The effect of ethnic or national heritage will vary depending upon the situation of a group. Indeed, the small amount of explained variance contributed by one's specific ethnic category, observed by Duncan and Duncan (1968) on occupational attainment, could partly be due to the fact that ethnicity was treated as an ascribed trait. Immigrants and sons of immigrants who never lived in an ethnic neighborhood and who have not attended parochial schools were placed in the same category as others for whom the salience of national origin may have been much greater.

## CONCLUSION

Much that has been written about race, ethnicity, social class, and community has centered around the issue of the importance of culture in determining life styles. Our review of this literature suggests that much of it is based on empirically untested assumptions about the importance of the portable heritage which a group brings from one generation and place to another. We suggest that a more parsimonious explanation of ethnic and community behavior will be found in the relationship of the ethnic community to the larger macroscopic structure of the society—particularly in the constraints of occupation, residence and institutional affiliation.

Something of a paradox is found in the position that has been developed here. On the one hand, we have suggested that much of the behavior that is commonly associated with ethnicity is largely a function of the structural situations in which groups have found themselves. On the other hand, we have also argued that ethnicity defined in terms of frequent patterns of association and identification with common origins (Haller, 1973) is generated and becomes crystallized under conditions of residential stability and segregation, common occupational positions, and dependence on local institutions and services. More specifically, we are suggesting that, within the structural parameters characterizing urban working-class life generally, ethnic culture—as heritage—is most likely to become crystallized and persist.

In order to resolve these arguments, it is necessary not only to test for the effects of ethnic heritage (Duncan and Duncan, 1968; Greeley, 1971; Laumann, 1973; Abramson, 1973), but also to identify the conditions under which ethnicity is particularly salient. We expect to find ethnic sub-cultures under conditions giving rise to communities in general. Communities are usually viewed as being geographically based, but what is most important appears to be face-to-face interaction (Hillery, 1955; Homans, 1950). It is possible, as Kosa (1956) has shown, for ethnic networks to exist in geographically dispersed groups, yet the effect of ethnicity may be strongest among members who are geographically clustered. In either case, such ethnic networks may depend on the availability of significant others, such as grandmothers who value ethnic culture, and other community members with feelings of obligation and responsibility. People are more or less dependent on their community at various stages of the life cycle; for example, when looking for a job, when a child is born, when a wife goes to work and needs babysitters, when a person becomes old and needs care. These and other day-to-day needs may be served by neighbors, friends, or institutions. When these are of the same ethnicity, the likelihood of ethnic behavior and identification with ethnic origins should be greater.

While the appropriate research is yet to be done, several things seem to be relatively clear. First, being a descendant of an immigrant does not necessarily make an individual an ethnic in America. Certain conditions are also necessary. We echo Cohen's (1974:xv) recent statement that "unless we recognize differences in degree of manifestation we shall fail to make much progress in the analysis of ethnicity. To put it in the idiom of research, ethnicity is a variable." Second, the conditions which generate ethnicity are not created only for immigrants or others with unique origins. They also exist for native-born Americans without a particular foreign heritage. In such cases, communities are likely to be generated that are similar to ethnic communities. Furthermore, we see no reason why such communities as South Boston, Bethnal Green, Harlem, or Harlan do not develop some sense of common origin and pride. Finally, it is clear that ethnicity is not dead but much alive today, although it is something very different than the way it has usually been presented. Rather than a constant ascribed trait that is inherited from the past, ethnicity is the result of a process which continues to unfold. It is basically a manifestation of the way populations are organized in terms of interaction patterns, institutions, personal values, attitudes, life styles, and presumed consciousness of kind. The assumption of a common heritage as the essential aspect of ethnicity is erroneous. Ethnicity may have relatively little to do with Europe, Asia, or Africa, but much more to do with the exigencies of survival and the structure of opportunity in this country. In short, the so-called foreign heritage of ethnic groups is taking shape in this country.

## REFERENCES

*Abramson, Harold J.*
1973   Ethnic Diversity in Catholic America. New York: Wiley.
*Bell, Wendel, and M. Boat*
1957   "Urban neighborhoods and informal social relations." American Journal of Sociology 62:391–8.

*Berger, Bennett M.*
1960   Working Class Suburb. Berkeley: University of California Press.
*Blau, Peter M., and Otis Dudley Duncan*
1967   The American Occupational Structure. New York: Wiley.
*Borrie, W. D.*
1954   Italians and Germans in Australia. Melbourne: Chesire.
*Breton, Raymond*
1964   "Institutional completeness of ethnic communities and the personal relations of immigrants." American Journal of Sociology 70:193–205.
*Burgess, Ernest W.*
1922   "The determination of gradients in the growth of the city." Proceedings of the American Sociological Society 18:85–97.
*Centers, Richard*
1949   Psychology of Social Classes. Princeton, N.J.: Princeton University Press.
*Charsley, S. R.*
1974   "The formation of ethnic groups." Pp. 337–68 in Abner Cohen (ed.), Urban Ethnicity. London: Tavistock.
*Cohen, Abner*
1974   "Introduction." Pp. ix–xxv in Abner Cohen (ed.), Urban Ethnicity. London: Tavistock.
*Dahya, Badr*
1974   "Pakistani ethnicity in industrial cities in Britain." Pp. 77–118 in Abner Cohen (ed.), Urban Ethnicity. London: Tavistock.
*Davie, Maurice*
1947   Refugees in America. New York: Harper.
*Duncan, Beverly, and Otis D. Duncan*
1968   "Minorities and the process of stratification." American Sociological Review 33:356–64.
*Duncan, Beverly, and Stanley Lieberson*
1970   Metropolis and Region in Transition. Beverly Hills, Calif.: Sage.
*Etzioni, Amitai*
1959   "The ghetto—A re-evaluation." Social Forces 39:225–62.
*Fitzpatrick, Joseph P.*
1966   "The importance of community in the process of immigrant assimilation." International Migration Review 1:6–16.
*Foley, Donald L.*
1950   "The use of local facilities in a metropolis." American Journal of Sociology 56:238–46.
*Fried, Marc*
1963   "Grieving for a lost home." Pp. 151–71 in Leonard S. Duhl (ed.), The Urban Condition. New York: Basic Books.
1974   The World of the Urban Working Class. Cambridge: Harvard University Press.
*Fuchs, Lawrence H.*
1968   American Ethnic Politics. New York: Harper and Row.
*Fusfeld, Daniel R.*
1969   "The basic economics of the urban and racial crisis." Research Seminar on the Economics of the Urban and Racial Crisis, University of Michigan.
*Gans, Herbert*
1962a   The Urban Villagers. New York: Free Press.
1962b   The Urbanism and suburbanism and ways of life: a reevaluation of definitions." Pp. 625–48 in Arnold Rose (ed), Human Behavior and Social Processes. Boston: Houghton Mifflin.
*Glanz, Rudolf*
1970   Jew and Italian: Historic Group Relations and the New Immigration (1881–1924). New York: Klau.

*Glazer, Nathan M.*
1954  "Ethnic groups in America: from national culture to ideology." Pp. 158–72 Morroe
       Berger, Theodore Abel, and Charles Page (eds.), Freedom and Control in Modern
       Society. New York: Van Nostrand.
*Glazer, Nathan, and Daniel P. Moynihan*
1963  Beyond the Melting Pot. Cambridge, Mass.: M.I.T. Press.
*Golab, Caroline*
1973  "The immigrant and the city: Poles, Italians, and Jews in Philadelphia, 1870–1920."
       Pp. 203–30 in Allen F. Davis and Mark H. Haller (eds.), The Peoples of Philadelphia.
       Philadelphia: Temple University.
*Goldstein, Sidney*
1958  Patterns of Mobility, 1910–1950. Philadelphia: University of Pennsylvania Press.
*Granovetter, Mark S.*
1974  Getting a Job: A Study of Contacts and Careers. Cambridge, Mass.: Harvard Univer-
       sity Press.
*Greeley, Andrew M.*
1971  Why Can't They Be Like Us? New York: Dutton.
1974  Ethnicity in the United States. New York: Wiley.
*Haller, Mark H.*
1973  "Recurring themes." Pp. 277–91 in Allen F. Davis and Mark Haller (eds.), The
       Peoples of Philadelphia. Philadelphia: Temple University Press.
*Hannerz, Ulf*
1974  "Ethnicity and opportunity in urban America." Pp. 37–76 in Abner Cohen (ed.),
       Urban Ethnicity. London: Tavistock.
*Handlin, Oscar*
1951  The Uprooted. Boston: Little, Brown.
1961  "Historical perspectives on the American ethnic group." Daedalus 90: 220–32.
*Hawley, Amos*
1971  Urban Society: An Ecological Approach. New York: Ronald Press.
*Herberg, Will*
1955  Protestant-Catholic-Jew. New York: Doubleday.
*Hershberg, Theodore, John Modell, and Frank Furstenberg*
1973  Family Structure and Ethnicity: A Historical and Comparative Analysis. Philadel-
       phia Social History Project, University of Pennsylvania.
*Hillery, G. A.*
1955  "Definitions of community: areas of agreement." Rural Sociology 20:111–23.
*Homans, George*
1950  The Human Group. New York: Harcourt, Brace.
*Hoover, Edgar M., and Raymond Vernon*
1959  Anatomy of a Metropolis. Cambridge, Mass.: Harvard University Press.
*Hostetler, John*
1968  Amish Society. Baltimore: Johns Hopkins Press.
*Howard, John*
1971  "Public policy and the white working class." Pp. 52–70 in Irving Horowitz
       (ed.), The Use and Abuse of Social Science. New Brunswick, N.J.: Transaction
       Books.
*Hutchinson, Edward P.*
1956  Immigrants and Their Children. New York: Wiley.
*Kasarda, John D., and Morris Janowitz*
1974  "Community attachment in mass society." American Sociological Review 39: 328–
       40.
*Katz, Alvin M., and Reuben Hill*
1958  "Residential propinquity and marital selection: A review of theory, method and
       fact." Marriage and Family Living 20:27–35.

*Kennedy, Ruby J. Reeves*
1944   "Single or triple melting pot? Intermarriage trends in New Haven, 1870–1940." American Journal of Sociology 49:331–39.
1952   "Single or triple melting pot? Intermarriage trends in New Haven, 1870–1950." American Journal of Sociology 58:56–9.
*Killian, Lewis*
1970   White Southerners. New York: Random House.
*Klatsky, Sheila R.*
1974   Patterns of Contact with Relatives. Rose Monograph Series. Washington, D.C.: American Sociological Association.
*Kosa, John*
1956   "Hungarian immigrants in North America: Their residential mobility and ecology." Canadian Journal of Economics and Political Science 22:358–70.
*Kriesberg, Louis*
1963   "Socio-economic rank and behavior." Social Problems 10:334–52.
*Laumann, E. O.*
1973   Bonds of Pluralism. New York: Wiley.
*Laurie, Bruce G.*
1973   "Fire companies and gangs in Southwark: The 1840s." Pp. 71–88 in Allen F. Davis and Mark Haller (eds.), Peoples of Philadelphia: Temple University Press.
*Leggett, John C.*
1968   Class, Race, and Labor. New York: Oxford University Press.
*Lieberson, Stanley*
1961   "The impact of residential segregation on ethnic assimilation." Social Forces 40:52–7.
1963   Ethnic Patterns in American Cities. New York: Free Press.
*Liebow, Elliot*
1967   Tally's Corner. Boston: Little, Brown.
*Lochore, R. A.*
1951   From Europe to New Zealand. Wellington: A. A. and A. W. Reed.
*Long, Larry H.*
1974   "Poverty status and receipt of welfare among migrants and non-migrants in large cities." American Sociological Review 39:46–56.
*MacDonald, John S., and Leatrice MacDonald*
1964   "Chain migration, ethnic neighborhood formation and social networks." Milbank Memorial Fund Quarterly 42:82–97.
*Mayhew, Leon*
1968   "Ascription in modern societies." Sociological Inquiry 38:105–20.
*McLaughlin, Virginia Yans*
1971   "Patterns of work and family organization among Buffalo's Italians." Journal of Interdisciplinary History 2:299–314.
*Nelli, Humbert S.*
1970   The Italians in Chicago: 1880–1930. New York: Oxford University Press.
*Park, Robert E., and Herbert A. Miller*
1921   Old World Traits Transplanted. New York: Harper.
*Pirenne, Henri*
1925   Medieval Cities: Their Origins and the Revival of Trade. Princeton, N.J.: Princeton University Press.
*Pratt, E. E.*
1911   Industrial Causes of Congestion of Population in New York City. New York: Columbia University Press.
*Price, Charles A.*
1963   Southern Europeans in Australia. Melbourne: Oxford University Press.
*Reiss, Albert*
1959   "Rural-urban and status differences in interpersonal contacts." American Journal of Sociology 65:182–95.

*Sheppard, Harold, and Herbert E. Striner*
1966  Civil Rights, Employment and Social Status of American Negroes. Kalamazoo, Michigan: Upjohn Institute.

*Sjoberg, Gideon*
1955  "The preindustrial city." American Journal of Sociology 60:438–45.

*Valentine, Charles*
1968  Culture and Poverty. Chicago: University of Chicago Press.

*Vecoli, Rudolph J.*
1964  "Contadini in Chicago: A critique of the uprooted." Journal of American History 51:404–17.

*Ward, David*
1971  Cities and Immigrants. New York: Oxford University Press.

*Warner, Sam Bass*
1962  Street Car Suburbs: The Process of Growth in Boston. 1870–1900. Cambridge, Mass.: Harvard University Press.
1968  The Private City. Philadelphia: University of Pennsylvania Press.

*Warner, Sam Bass, and Colin Burke*
1969  "Cultural change and the ghetto." Journal of Contemporary History 4:173–88.

*Warren, Bruce L.*
1966  "A multiple variable approach to the assortative mating phenomenon." Eugenics Quarterly 13:285–90.

*Warren, Ronald L.*
1963  The Community in America. Chicago: Rand McNally.

*Whyte, William Foote*
1943  Street Corner Society. Chicago: University of Chicago Press.

*Young, Michael, and Peter Willmott*
1957  Family and Kinship in East London. London: Routledge and Kegan Paul.

# Ethnicity: Canadian Experience and Policy

## Jean Burnet

*Glendon College, York University*

A provocative recent book on ethnic relations is *Ethnicity: Theory and Experience,* edited by Nathan Glazer and Daniel P. Moynihan (1975). The essays brought together in the book are concerned not with documenting the fact that, since the melting pot did not melt, ethnic groups exist and will in all probability continue to exist in the United States—this is now taken for granted—but with consolidating a new and more dynamic view of ethnicity and applying it to the United States and a number of other societies. That view stresses ethnic groups as forms of social life rather than survivals from the past, as mobilizers of interests rather than bearers of cultures or traditions, and as collectivities with which people choose to identify rather than as groups into which they are born and from which they sometimes struggle to escape. In the realm of ethnic relations what is true of the United States is by no means necessarily true of Canada. Nonetheless it seems worthwhile to examine the Canadian situation in the light of Glazer and Moynihan's volume, particularly since the essay on Canada (Porter, 1975) is the only one in the volume that is based on the old view of ethnicity.

In the introduction, Glazer and Moynihan quote an unnamed U.S. Army colonel, director of Army Equal Opportunity Programs, who proposed that

*Source:* Jean Burnet, "Ethnicity: Canadian Experience and Policy," Sociological Focus 9, 2 (April 1976): 199–207. Copyright © 1976 by the North Central Sociological Association. Reprinted by permission of the Association, the editors of Sociological Focus, and the author.

racial discrimination was "the relationship between two groups of people, wherein one group has defined the rules by which the other group must act" (Glazer and Moynihan, 1975:14). However apt this characterization is of racial discrimination, it describes neatly the relationship between colonizers—first French, then British—and colonized Native Indians and Inuit (and later perhaps French Canadians) in Canada. It is true that the Native Indians and the Inuit, and to a considerable degree many of the French Canadians also, were until recently so isolated as to be hardly part of Canadian society, but what Edgar Dosman (1972:13) says of the Indians was true also *mutatis mutandis* of the others:

*The life of an Indian was never isolated from all contacts with white society, only from most. He was numbered and rationed, and closely watched. He could do almost nothing without the permission of the Indian agent: buy or sell; slaughter cattle; be educated; drink or travel. . . . The outside world . . . not only determined the Indian's income, living conditions, education and mobility; it also made every attempt to shape his culture and personality.*

The Army colonel's characterization describes also the relationship of Canadians of British origin to Canadians of other origins for most of the country's history. For a long time the dominance of the British was unquestioned. At first this was because the numbers of those of other origins was small, and included at least two kinds of people incapable or undesirous of issuing a challenge. These were on the one hand individuals who though of other than British origin had before their arrival spent some time in Great Britain, the West Indies, or the United States and had already acquired a knowledge of the English language and some variety of British culture, whatever their sense of identity;[1] and on the other hand groups, notably religious sects, whose separatist tendencies led them to acquiesce in the structures of the larger community as long as they had freedom in the areas of life they deemed most important. Later, British dominance was still unchallenged because of the "liberal expectancy" (Glazer and Moynihan, 1975; Gordon, 1975) that most immigrant ethnic groups would lose their distinctive characteristics and merge in a modern, urban, industrial society, envisaged as English-speaking and dominated by a science and technology that was largely made in the U.S.A. That is—and here I am reading between Milton Gordon's (1964) lines—Anglo-conformity would triumph. The ethnic groups that had physical badges of identity, the Asians and the blacks, could not merge, or at any rate could not merge easily; hence efforts were made through immigration regulations to exclude them as far as possible.

During a relatively recent part of the period in which Canadians of British origin have defined the rules by which other groups had to act, the ideology concerning ethnic relations in Canada was summed up in the term mosaic, and its floral and gustatory analogues—bouquet, flower garden, salad, vegetable soup, stew. The mosaic was proudly contrasted with the American melting pot. However, less effort was expended by Canadian governments to maintain the mosaic than was spent by governments in the United States to keep the melting pot bubbling: in the public school systems and in broadcasting, to take only one example from provincial and one from federal jurisdiction, no tangible aid was given to ethnic groups in preserving their old-world heritages, and, on the contrary, considerable pressure was exerted in the direction of "integration" or "assimilation." The mosaic was lent support chiefly in speeches by governors general and by politicians.

Meanwhile, changes affecting the ethnic composition of the Canadian population and ethnic relations within Canada were occurring constantly. There was a steady increase in the heterogeneity of the population in terms of ethnic origin, which is the statistic concerning ethnicity that the Canadian census provides. In 1871, the first census year after Confederation, 60.5 per cent of the population was of British origin, 31.1 percent of French origin, 0.7 percent of Indian and Eskimo origin, and 7.7 percent of other origins;[2] a hundred years later, the percentage of British origin had dropped to 44.6, 28.7 per cent were of French origin, 1.4 per cent of Native Indian origin, and 23.4 per cent of other origins. Further, whereas in 1871 the 7.7 per cent of the population that was not British, French, or Native Indian or Eskimo was chiefly of two Northern European origins closely akin to the British, the Germans and the Dutch, in 1971 the corresponding 23.4 per cent was drawn from virtually every people of the world, with the West Indians, Portuguese, Chinese, and Indians among the newest and most rapidly expanding origin categories (Palmer, 1975:206–7).

There was also a steady increase in the numbers of those of other than British, French, and Native Indian and Inuit origins who were Canadians by birth and breeding. In 1971, in spite of the massive postwar immigration, 85 per cent of the population was Canadian born, and of those of Ukrainian ethnic origin, 82 per cent were Canadian born; of those of Scandinavian origin, 78 per cent; of those of German origin, 75 per cent; and of those of Polish origin, 67 per cent (Census of Canada, 1971). The presence of people of non-British, French, or Native Indian or Inuit origin who were second, third, fourth, or fifth generation Canadians was shaking the vertical mosaic.

So was the presence among immigrants of increasing numbers of the urbanized, educated, skilled, and politically sophisticated. Even in the 1920s, when immigration regulations still favoured agricultural labourers, the trend could be seen. After World War II, it became stronger: in the late 1940s people displaced from highly developed parts of Europe immigrated; in the 1950s the skilled and educated were sought out to fill positions in the expanding economy to which Canadian educational and training facilities were not geared (Porter, 1965:40–8); and in the late 1960s racially discriminatory selection procedures were replaced by a stress on education and training. The result can be seen in such facts as that in 1961 whereas 6.6 per cent of native-born Canadians had some university education or a university degree, 10.3 per cent of post-war immigrants had some university education or a university degree, including 20.8 per cent of those of Russian ethnic origin, 17.4 per cent of those of Hungarian ethnic origin, 15.1 per cent of those of Jewish ethnic origin and 14.3 per cent of those of Asian ethnic origins (Kalbach, 1970:190, 192–3), and that there has certainly been a recent trend, and probably a long-standing one, for increasing proportions of immigrants to be able to speak one or both of the official languages on their arrival in the country (Manpower and Immigration, 1974:91).

Finally, economic developments were drawing formerly isolated peoples into the industrial system. A few of the sects, notably the Hutterites, managed to take from it what they required without surrendering their total way of life, but the Native Peoples were more vulnerable. Whether they remained on reservations or in the North or joined the drift towards the city,[3] they were increasingly confronted with rules they had had no share in making and often found difficult to comprehend.

The changes became dramatically evident in the 1960s. In that decade, against a background of ethnic movements in virtually every part of the world, with the decline of Great Britain in power and prestige and that of the United States in prestige, and with the Black Revolution in the United States, the relations between English-Canadians and French-Canadians, never easy but heretofore hardly desperate, entered a critical stage. The death of Premier Duplessis, the Quiet Revolution, the terrorist acts of the FLQ, the setting up in 1963 of the Royal Commission on Bilingualism and Biculturalism, Expo 67, General de Gaulle's cry of "Vive le Quebec libre," and the founding of the Parti Quebecois were some of the events of the tumultuous period.

As the crisis progressed, the relations of the Native Peoples and the immigrant ethnic groups also began to be examined critically. Governmental concern with the Native Peoples resulted, among other things, in the voluminous *Survey of the Contemporary Indians of Canada,* directed by H. B. Hawthorn and M. A. Tremblay (1967, 1968). Although "the other ethnic groups" received offhanded recognition in the terms of reference of the Royal Commission on Bilingualism and Biculturalism, and somewhat greater recognition in the inclusion among the ten Commissioners of two Canadians (one of Polish background and the other of Ukrainian background) who had immigrated to Canada after World War II,[4] it was not the original intention of the government to have the Commission probe deeply into their place in Canadian society. The extensive research programme of the Commission included little about them: two studies of Italian immigrants, one done in Montreal and one in Edmonton; a small study of attitudes of Montreal Jews towards French-Canadian nationalism and separatism; about a dozen essays on the contribution of particular ethnic groups to the cultural enrichment of Canada; some brief investigations carried out almost surreptitiously by members of the other ethnic groups who had obtained jobs on the research staff, and comparative data gathered incidentally by people focusing on ... English-French relations.

However, the immediate and vehement response of some members of "the other ethnic groups" to the phrase "two founding races" *("deux peuples fondateurs")* in the terms of reference, the briefs submitted at public and private hearings of the Commission, and the discussion sparked by the publication of John Porter's *The Vertical Mosaic* in 1965 all contributed to a realization that the issue of the role of the immigrant ethnic groups in Canadian society had to be faced. Consequently, the Commission devoted Book IV of its report to the other ethnic groups.

The Commissioners assumed that many, perhaps most, Canadians of other origins would participate fully or partially in English-Canadian or French-Canadian society. They urged both societies to make it easy for others to enter. But they still accepted what has lately begun to be questioned, that Canada needed immigrants, and they recognized that a Canada made up of two societies, one English-speaking and the other French-speaking, had a stake in variety. Thus, they stated that, far from requiring that members of the ethnic groups other than the British and French surrender the cherished symbols of their identity, the governments should assist those who wanted to do so to maintain such symbols. They stressed that in the past the contributions of the other ethnic groups to Canada had been invaluable:

*In the broadest sense of the term "culture," the sheer fact that men came from elsewhere to take part in building the country has contributed to our cultural enrichment. When they arrived, their essential concern was to continue the work of carrying civilization into the thinly populated areas. By settling the country they helped to lay the basis for Canada's cultural growth.*

*In a narrower sense Canadian culture has been the richer for the knowledge, skills, and traditions which all the immigrant groups brought with them. Their many distinctive styles of life have gradually increased the range of experience, outlook, ideas and talents which characterize the country. Cultural diversity has widened out horizons: it has also given opportunities—not always seized upon—for varied approaches to the solution of our problems.*

*Finally, the coming together of diverse peoples in Canada also benefited our culture in the humanistic sense of the term. For a long time the frontier was not a rich soil for the arts and letters. Many of the frontiersmen had taken little part in the artistic life of their homeland, or if they had, they were forced to forgo such pursuits in the new country. As it matured, however, Canadian society turned to the search for grace and leisure, and the folk traditions preserved by the sons and daughters of the early settlers combined with the artistic sense, the talents, and the skills of later immigrants to add new dimensions to literature, music, and the plastic arts in Canada. (Royal Commission on Bilingualism and Biculturalism, 1967, paras. 16–18.)*

By implication they recognized that the contributions of such groups would continue to be necessary for social, economic, political and artistic growth and creativity. They made sixteen recommendations, as well as numerous suggestions, concerning the reception of immigrants, the support of the languages and cultural symbols of the other ethnic groups, and the dissemination of information about those groups (Royal Commission on Bilingualism and Biculturalism, 1970).

The response of the federal government to Book IV was presented by the Prime Minister to the House of Commons on October 8, 1971, in the form of a policy of multiculturalism within a bilingual framework, whereby the government would assist "the various cultures and ethnic groups that give structure and vitality to our society," encouraging them "to share their cultural expression and values with other Canadians and so contribute to a richer life for us all." Governmental support was to take four forms:

*First, resources permitting, the government will seek to assist all Canadian cultural groups that have demonstrated a desire and effort to continue to develop a capacity to grow and contribute to Canada, and a clear need for assistance, the small and weak groups no less than the strong and highly organized.*

*Second, the government will assist members of all cultural groups to overcome cultural barriers to full participation in Canadian society.*

*Third, the government will promote creative encounters and interchange among all Canadian cultural groups in the interest of national unity.*

*Fourth, the government will continue to assist immigrants to acquire at least one of Canada's official languages in order to become full participants in Canadian society. (House of Commons Debates, 1971.)*

In order to carry out the policy, programmes for grants and for research were developed, a member of the cabinet was made responsible for multiculturalism,[5] the Canadian Consultative Council on Multiculturalism was set up to advise the Minister, and the Canadian Ethnic Studies Advisory Committee on Multiculturalism was established to advise the Department of the Secretary of State. Several provinces, the earliest among them Alberta, Manitoba, and Ontario, also proclaimed policies of multiculturalism and made provision for the implementing of the policies.

It may seem that the policy of multiculturalism within a bilingual framework was intended, as its designation suggests, to treat ethnic groups as bearers of cultures, and to enable them to maintain those cultures, and the languages that were their armatures, in Canada. Such was the interpretation of the Canadian Consultative Council on Multiculturalism, which in its First Annual Report (1975) pressed for greater support for the cultures and especially the languages of the various ethnic groups composing the population. It was also the interpretation of some of the most distinguished opponents of multiculturalism, including John Porter and prominent French Canadian intellectuals such as Claude Ryan and Guy Rocher (1969, 1972).

The French Canadians considered that the policy of multiculturalism put in jeopardy the more equal partnership for which their people had been striving and towards which the major recommendations of the Royal Commission on Bilingualism and Biculturalism were directed. They felt that it put all cultures save the British on an equal footing, and found small comfort in the statement that multiculturalism was to be within a bilingual framework. They shared the view of the Royal Commissioners and spokesmen for the Canadian Consultative Council on Multiculturalism that cultures were dependent on languages: hence, they reasoned, multiculturalism—if it were to be meaningful at all—would give rights to the unofficial languages at the expense of French.

John Porter's stand was that multiculturalism was detrimental to progress and to equality of opportunity, two of his highest values. Cultures were disappearing with the advance of science and technology; multiculturalism, in shoring up dying cultures, prevented those who cherished them from participating fully in the benefits of a universalistic post-industrial way of life. Unexpectedly, Porter in his essay in *Ethnicity: Theory and Experience* stated that bilingualism could survive (1975:303).

That multiculturalism, if it is interpreted as the full and vital maintenance of distinctive ways of life by all of Canada's peoples within a single society, is impossible hardly rules it out as an objective of governmental policy. However, in the statements made in presenting the policy, there is evidence that multiculturalism in that sense was not intended. Rather, the aim was the recognition and encouragement of ethnicity as understood by Glazer and Moynihan and most of their collaborators. Evidence lies in the very announcement of the policy. First of all, multiculturalism was to be within a bilingual framework; thus, to the extent that cultures require the support of distinctive languages fully employed in all domains, those related to other tongues than English and French could not flourish (cf. Lupul, 1973). In addition, culture has to do with the preservation of the recurrent, of tradition, of heritage, and some degree of segregation or isolation seems conducive to, if not essential for, such preservation; yet the announcement stresses freedom, growth, and creativity, and also sharing, interchange, and participation.

It may be countered that during the first four years the programmes instituted under the rubric of multiculturalism have stressed folk culture and linguistic maintenance. They have stressed the former more, and the latter less, than spokesmen for some ethnic organizations have wished. Both emphases can be related at least as logically to a policy of invigoration of ethnic groups as to a policy of cultural maintenance. Folk culture was a part of the experience of some early immigrants to Canada, but of few since World War I. Even the early immigrants—peasants rather than folk (cf. Redfield, 1962)—had scarcely participated in a vital and complete folk culture. Folk dancing and singing, folk costumes and festivals, then, are often not being retained in present-day Canada, or even revived: rather, they are being learned. The prominence that they receive in the activities of contemporary groups and the fund-giving of governmental agencies is not simply a result of outside stereotypes of the various ethnic groups as quaint folk, however. It is a result of the search of ethnic groups whose members in Canada are highly differentiated according to ways of life in the old land, and time of arrival, region of settlement, educational and occupational achievement, political persuasion, and the like in the new land, for symbols of their ethnic identity that are acceptable to all. The search leads back into a legendary past, when life was simpler and the people unified (Hughes, 1955:186).

Similarly, the language of one's fathers, particularly as taught in the public school systems, is in many instances something to be learned anew rather than retained. For many of the immigrants to Canada, past and present, have known a variety of their language remote from the standard or the literary variety; some have, of course, had only oral knowledge of their regional or temporal dialect. Supplementary or part time schools may at times have given instruction in dialects, but all schools emphasizing literacy have imparted the standard or the literary variety of various tongues. This has given Canadians of different origins access to the literary treasures of their forebears, but not to the full culture of those groups at home, usually somewhat privileged groups, whose means of communication is the standard language. The dissemination of the standard or the literary language in Canada, then, again seems intended to unify a highly differentiated group rather than to maintain or preserve a culture brought to Canada from elsewhere.

It may also be countered that if the government had meant polyethnicity instead of multiculturalism it would have said so. However, both the Royal Commission on Bilingualism and Biculturalism and the framers of the policy of multiculturalism within a bilingual framework had a number of reasons, some of which are no longer valid, for avoiding the term *ethnic,* except in the phrase ethnic origin category: the word was considered to be less well known than the word culture. Since the early 1970s, however, the term has gained greater currency and has lost its opprobrium.

It has also lost its ascriptive character. "If it is easy to resign from the group," said Everett Hughes in 1948 (15), "it is not truly an ethnic group." But many people have some choice of ethnic allegiance, because of changes in the suzerainty or the political boundaries of their homelands, or because of interethnic marriages; even blacks may sometimes resign from their ethnic group, or "pass" as whites. In Canada during or after the world wars thousands changed the ethnic origin they claimed from German to Dutch or Austrian or Russian (Ryder, 1955); recently Rudolf Kogler and Benedykt Heydenkorn (1974) have accounted for the decrease in the number of Canadians of Polish origin between the 1961 and 1971 censuses by changes from Polish to Jewish, Ukrainian, Anglo-Saxon, and other groups; and the increase of more than 100,000 in the number of Canadians of Ukrainian origin between 1961 and 1971, in the virtual absence of immigration of people of Ukrainian origin, is explicable only by changes of ethnic origin.[6]

Thus the policy of multiculturalism within a bilingual framework is entirely consonant with the conception of ethnicity being formulated by the scholars represented in the Glazer and Moynihan volume. It is intended to recognize and foster ethnicity as a modern and Canadian phenomenon whereby those who choose to identify with an ethnic group may derive satisfaction from that identification. It does not imply, as Pierre van den Berghe (1975) has recently suggested, legal or constitutional entrenchment of ethnic groups as has occurred in some other countries, if only for the reason that the ethnic composition of Canada is still in flux, even as the concept ethnicity is "a term still on the move" (Glazer and Moynihan, 1975:1).

The public servants who devised the policy and the politicians who adopted it were of course not concerned simply with acknowledging a sociological phenomenon. Some were English Canadians who wanted to play off the other ethnic groups against the separatists in Quebec; some were members of the other ethnic groups who felt that their turn at the pork-barrel had come; some were politicians whose dominating interest was remaining in office. But some were idealists, who envisaged a Canada in which peoples of all ethnic origins and all ethnic identities would be much more equal than at present, and who felt that there was greater likelihood of achieving this through acceptance and even celebration of ethnic differences than through denial of them, and through collective action than through individual social mobility.

It is too early yet to tell to what extent the hopes of the idealists will be realized. There are still many unsolved problems in the policy of multiculturalism within a bilingual framework. These include how to persuade French Canadians that multiculturalism does not threaten, and indeed may be used to enhance, the position of the French language in Canada; how to ensure that governmental support does not strengthen the more conservative factions and the older generation within particular ethnic groups at the expense of the more venturesome and the younger, and large and well-organized ethnic groups at the expense of small and weak ones; how to provide opportunities for teaching the official languages and for providing other services to immigrants without appearing to alienate them from their ethnic groups; and how to make the policy serve the interests of the "visible minorities," whose numbers are increasing, as well as the interests of the white ethnic groups.[7] If solutions are found to such problems, multiculturalism within a bilingual framework may well contribute to equality among Canadians, and thus to Canadian unity.

## NOTES

1  For example, Philip de Grassi, who was one of the first Italians to settle in what is now Toronto and for whom a street in the city is named, had been captured while an officer in Napoleon's army and transferred to England. There he had received a commission in the British army, married an English woman, and taught languages in Chichester for sixteen years before immigrating to Canada in 1831. The renowned

Casimir Gzowski, whose many accomplishments included building the International Bridge at Niagara, took part in the Polish insurrection of 1830–31, after which he was interned and eventually shipped to America. There he learned English, worked in a law office and as an engineer in canal and railway construction, and married an American girl, before moving to Canada in 1842.

2    The percentage given for those of other origins includes a small number whose origin was not stated.

3    The twelve cities that in 1971 had the largest number of Indian residents had a total of almost 30,000, according to the census; ten years before, the total for those cities of Indians and Inuit was 7,700, and in 1951, it was 3,300. The census figures are probably underestimates because of the mobility of some of the Indians and the nature of their lodgings.

4    Professors Paul Wyczynski and J. B. Rudnyckyj.

5    Dr. Stanley Haidasz was the first to have the charge; he was succeeded by the Hon. John Munro.

6    Archie Belaney, the Englishman who chose to be the Indian Grey Owl, is a well-known and intriguing case of change of identity; at least, there is considerable evidence that something other than mere imposture was involved.

7    This article was completed before the Hon. John Munro's announcement, in late November, 1975, of a change in emphasis in the policy of multiculturalism from cultural maintenance to group understanding. The change seems designed to meet some of these problems.

# REFERENCES

*Canadian Consultative Council on Multiculturalism*
1975    First Annual Report. Ottawa: Information Canada.
*Census of Canada*
1974    Census of Canada, 1971, catalogue 92–738, Vol. 1, Part 4.
*Dosman, Edgar J.*
1972    Indians: The Urban Dilemma. Toronto: McClelland and Stewart.
*Gordon, Milton M.*
1964    Assimilation in American Life. New York: Oxford University Press.
*Glazer, Nathan, and Daniel P. Moynihan*
1975    "Introduction." Pp. 1–26 in Nathan Glazer and Daniel P. Moynihan (eds.), Ethnicity: Theory and Experience. Cambridge, Mass.: Harvard University Press.
*Hawthorn, H. B. (ed.)*
1967    A Survey of the Contemporary Indians of Canada, volume 1. Ottawa: Queen's Printer.
1968    A Survey of the Contemporary Indians of Canada, volume 2. Ottawa: Queen's Printer.
*House of Commons Debates*
1971    "Statement of P. E. Trudeau." October 8.
*Hughes, E. C.*
1948    "The study of ethnic relations." Cited from reprint, pp. 153–158 in E. C. Hughes (ed.), The Sociological Eye. Chicago: Aldine-Atherton, 1971.
1955    "New peoples." Cited from reprint, pp. 174–190 in E. C. Hughes (ed.), The Sociological Eye. Chicago: Aldine-Atherton, 1971.
*Kahlbach, Warren E.*
1970    The Impact of Immigration on Canada's Population. Ottawa: Queen's Printer.
*Kogler, Rudolf, and Benedykt Heydenkorn*
1974    "Poles in Canada, 1971." Pp. 27–36 in Benedykt Heydenkorn (ed.), Past and Present. Toronto: Canadian Polish Research Institute.

*Lupul, Manoly*
1973   "Multiculturalism within a lingual framework: An essay in definition." Paper presented to the Conference of the Western Association of Sociology, Banff, December 30.

*Manpower and Immigration*
1974   A Report of the Canadian Immigration and Population Study. 2: The Immigration Program. Ottawa: Information Canada.

*Palmer, Howard*
1975   Immigration and the Rise of Multiculturalism. Toronto: Copp Clark.

*Porter, John*
1965   The Vertical Mosaic. Toronto: University of Toronto Press.
1975   "Ethnic pluralism in Canadian perspective." Pp. 267–304 in Nathan Glazer and Daniel Patrick Moynihan (eds.), Ethnicity: Theory and Experience. Cambridge, Mass.: Harvard University Press.

*Redfield, Robert*
1962   "Tribe, peasant, and city." Pp. 282–294 in Margaret Park Redfield, Human Nature and the Study of Society: The Papers of Robert Redfield, Vol. 1. Chicago: University of Chicago Press.

*Royal Commission on Bilingualism and Biculturalism*
1967   Report: Book 1, General Introduction. Ottawa: Queen's Printer.
1970   Report: Book 4, The Cultural Contribution of the Other Ethnic Groups. Ottawa: Queen's Printer.

*Ryder, Norman B.*
1955   "The interpretation of origin statistics." Canadian Journal of Economics and Political Science 21:466–479.

*Rocher, Guy*
1969   "Le Canada: Un pays a rebatir?" Cited from reprint, pp. 109–116 in Le Quebec en Mutation. Montreal: Hutubise HMH, 1973.
1972   "Les ambiguites d'un Canada bilingue et multiculturel." Cited from reprint, pp. 117–126 in Le Quebec en Mutation. Montreal: Hutubise HMH, 1973.

*van den Berghe, Pierre L.*
1975   "Ethnic pluralism in industrial societies: A special case?" Paper presented at Conference on Multiculturalism and Third World Immigrants in Canada, Edmonton, September 3–5.

# Voluntary Associations and Minority Status: A Comparative Analysis of Anglo, Black, and Mexican Americans[*]

## J. Allen Williams, Jr.
*The University of Nebraska-Lincoln*

## Nicholas Babchuk
*The University of Nebraska-Lincoln*

## David R. Johnson
*The University of Nebraska-Lincoln*

*The study focused on the voluntary associations of Anglo, Black, and Mexican Americans in Austin, Texas. A Sample of 380 respondents provide the data. An information interview was used; trained interviewers coming from the same*

*Source:* J. Allen Williams, Jr., Nicholas Babchuk, and David R. Johnson, "Voluntary Associations and Minority Status: A Comparative Analysis of Anglo, Black, and Mexican Americans," American Sociological Review 38, 5 (October 1973): 637–46. Copyright © 1973 by the American Sociological Association. Reprinted by permission of the Association and the authors.

*This study is part of a larger study supported by the U.S. Department of Housing and Urban Development (H-1037 LIHD). We wish to thank J. Neils Thompson, principal investigator of the larger study, and our colleague John Lane, coinvestigator for the Sociological Studies Section. This paper is a revision of a paper read at the annual meeting of the American Sociological Association, New Orleans, 1972.

*ethnic background as the respondent were employed. Ethnicity proved to be an important variable in predicting social participation, with Blacks having the highest and Mexican Americans having the lowest participation rate. Using multiple classification analysis, a number of structural variables were introduced as controls; and these variables, particularly education, were found to be responsible for the difference between Anglo and Mexican Americans. Blacks continued to have significantly higher rates of participation in voluntary associations after controlling on other variables. Both isolation and cultural inhibition theories can be found in previous literature to account for low participation rates among people having a subordinate status, and compensatory and ethnic community theories have been used to account for high rates of affiliation among these same groups. The findings from this study tend to cast doubt on isolation and cultural inhibition theories and to support compensatory and ethnic community theories.*

There is mounting evidence that participation in voluntary associations enhances the likelihood of voting and actively participating in the polity (cf. Lipset et al., 1956; Almond and Verba, 1963; Rose, 1967; Sallach et al., 1972). Membership is typically seen as bringing individuals into contact with those who are already active, especially persons who join instrumental groups. Association with others is a catalyst for involvement. Furthermore, it is generally recognized that groups can be more effective in bringing about social change than can individuals working alone. In a related vein, several studies have pointed out that members of the working and lower classes who become involved with voluntary associations, e.g., Community Action Programs, and who remain affiliated, acquire social skills highly useful in bringing about needed reforms (cf. Vanecko, 1969; Lyden and Thomas, 1969). For example, such persons learn how to present grievances to appointive bodies, acquire knowledge of how governmental agencies operate and which strategies will be most effective in bringing about a particular goal. Also, there is support for the proposition that social participation in associations produces a more favorable self-image and decreases feelings of powerlessness and isolation (cf. Erbe, 1964; Aberback, 1969; Zurcher, 1970).

Given these and other important consequences of participation in voluntary associations, it's important to know who participates and why. Some of the answers to these questions are already known. Indeed, as can be seen from the reviews of the literature presented in Babchuk and Booth (1969) and Curtis (1971), a substantial and essentially consistent list of findings has emerged from studies undertaken in this area. However, despite an impressive literature, some aspects of participation are not clear. The literature related to the extent of participation among minorities is one of the most confusing. One often cited set of studies, Hyman and Wright's (1958, 1971), indicates that Black Americans are less likely to belong to voluntary groups than whites. On the other hand, several studies have reported that Black people are more likely to participate than whites (cf. Mayo, 1950; Babchuk and Thompson, 1962; Orum, 1966; Olsen, 1970). As for the nation's second largest ethnic minority, the Mexican American, many investigators claim that they seldom belong to voluntary associations (cf. Heller, 1966; Rubel, 1966; Briegel, 1970). Others have strongly disputed this proposition (cf. Romano, 1968; Montiel, 1970; Alvarez, 1971).

Reasons often given for the limited participation of minority groups fall within what might be called "isolation" theory. Essentially, the argument is that these persons do not participate because they are not integrated into the society. They lack the social skills necessary for participation and are not aware of the possible benefits of affiliating. In addition, minority persons may be barred from groups because of their ethnicity. While these reasons apply equally to Black and Mexican Americans, an additional argument maintains that Mexican American culture inhibits joining voluntary groups because the culture emphasizes loyalty to the home and family. Men are said to confine activities outside the family to informal relations with male friends. Women are said to be restricted to working in the home, visiting relatives, and attending church services.

Suggestions given for active participation by minorities can generally be subsumed under the heading of "compensatory" theory.

*It has been noted that he (a Black person) may become an inveterate joiner in clubs or cliques with high-sounding names and much ritualism . . . these are attempted compensations for a lack of capacity for relatedness.* [1]

While this theory has been applied mainly to Blacks, its propositions are relevant to any segment of society which is subordinate socially. The contention is that those in lower status positions affiliate and participate in voluntary associations for prestige, ego enhancement, and achievement restricted or denied them in the larger society. In a recent paper, Olsen (1970) suggested an alternative thesis to account for active participation which he calls " ethnic community" theory.[2] In this theory, those in a given ethnic community develop a consciousness of each other and hence cohesiveness because of pressures exerted against them by outsiders. For example, the Polish Americans organized such groups as the Polish Roman Catholic Union and Polish Falcons (Lopata, 1964) and Italian Americans formed the Mazzini Society not only to maintain ethnic identity and help immigrants assimilate, but as pressure groups. In other words, through a sense of ethnic community, minority members form groups to deal with an alien environment and problems forced on them by the majority.

Isolation and cultural inhibition theories posit that minorities rarely participate in voluntary associations, while compensatory and ethnic community theories suggest that these characteristics generate much participation. The purpose of this paper is to provide data related to these seemingly contradictory theories. Despite the large literature on voluntary associations, no studies have compared participation rates of Mexican Americans with those of Blacks and Anglos. The present study includes all three groups and thus allows for a clearer test of the possible role played by minority status in relation to participation than is afforded by comparing a single minority group to the dominant group. Furthermore, though some studies have measured the effect of ethnicity while controlling for education, occupational prestige, and age, several other factors have been found to limit or enhance participation which have not been introduced systematically as controls. These variables are sex, presence of young children in the household, length of residence in the community, home ownership, and whether the individual is head of the household. Failure to control for these factors, or to seek their possible interaction with ethnicity, suggests potentially spurious associations between ethnicity and social participation. The present study includes all the aforementioned variables and uses a method which estimates the ethnic effect on participation, controlling for these other variables simultaneously.

## SAMPLING AND DATA COLLECTION

The data for this study were collected in late 1969 and early 1970 in Austin, Texas. Primarily due to housing discrimination, the vast majority of Austin's Black and Mexican Americans are confined to certain clearly defined sections of the city. These ghettos and barrios are low-income areas. A sampling problem was efficiently locating Anglos comparable to the minority persons who would be drawn into the sample. After some preliminary testing, the procedure used was to randomly select households from all city blocks having an average rent of less than $50 or the equivalent in housing value. This method provided sufficient variation within ethnic categories on the control variables while at the same time producing enough minority group members for data analysis.[3]

An information interview was used as the data-collecting instrument. The schedule was pretested on households chosen by the same method used for selecting the study sample. To minimize interviewer bias, trained interviewers were used who were familiar with the city's low-income areas and whose ethnic descent matched those they interviewed (cf. Williams, 1964, 1968). Many interviews with Mexican Americans were conducted in Spanish, and Black interviewers were given freedom to "translate" the wording of interview questions into the language of the ghetto whenever they deemed it necessary. Using this procedure more than compensated for the possible lack of comparability in phrasing that might have ensued from a totally structured interview; it enhanced the likelihood of communication between the interviewer and the respondent on the meaning of the questions.

Respondents were interviewed in their homes. Both the household head and spouse (among married couples) were interviewed. The sample included 147 married household heads, their wives, sixteen unmarried male heads, and seventy unmarried female household heads, yielding a total of 233 households and 380 respondents. To the extent that there was a sampling error in the sample of household heads, there could be a correlated bias in the sample of their spouses. However, as we discuss below, precautions were taken in the data analysis which controlled for this possibility.

Aided recall was used to measure membership and participation in voluntary associations. To illustrate, respondents were asked, "Now I would like to ask you about possible kinds of memberships in different organizations (right now, not years ago). Do you presently belong to any church-related organizations?" This questioning procedure was repeated for each category of association; moreover, types of associations were mentioned to assist the respondent to recall and identify memberships. Under veteran's groups, for example, the American Legion, the American G.I. Forum, the Veterans of Foreign Wars (or their auxiliaries) were mentioned to insure that respondents would include all groups they were currently affiliated with.


## METHOD OF DATA ANALYSIS

The first step in analysis was developing categories for the research variables. The dependent variable, membership in voluntary associations, was computed as a mean score, i.e., the average number of organizations belonged to by a particular population.[4] The primary independent or treatment variable is ethnicity, Anglo, Black, and Mexican American. Home ownership, sex, and whether the respondent is a household head are obvious dichotomies. Presence of children under six in the household was divided into 0, 1, and 2 or more. Length of residence in the city was divided into 0 to 3 years, 4 to 9 years, 10 to 19 years, and 20 or more years. Occupational prestige and level of education were categorized in the manner suggested by Hollingshead (1957) except that those with no education were placed in a separate category.

The ethnic groups were compared by the mean number of voluntary associations belonged to by each group. Multiple classification analysis (cf. Andrews et al., 1967) was used to examine the remaining differences in social participation among ethnic groups after statistically controlling for all other independent variables. This procedure treats each category of each independent variable as a dummy variable. Using additive multiple least-squares regression, it adjusts the mean of the dependent variable for each category of the independent variables by the amount of deviation from the total sample (grand) mean that is due to intercorrelation with other independent variables in the analysis. This method is equivalent to adjusting the means of the treatment group for intercorrelations with covariates in the analysis of covariance (cf. Cohen, 1968). In this instance, ethnicity is the treatment variable; and the other independent variables are the covariates.

During a preliminary examination of the data a statistically significant interaction (P <.05) between ethnicity and sex was discovered after covariance adjustment. Black and Mexican American women were found to have higher participation rates than males in their groups; whereas, Anglo men have a higher participation rate than Anglo women. Consequently, the final analysis was conducted keeping the sex groups separate within the ethnic categories.

After controlling on the independent variables, an examination was made of the mean participation rates; and statistical tests of significance were made between ethnic groups within sex categories, e.g., Anglo males compared to Black males. The statistical significance of the difference in the adjusted means of the ethnic groups were estimated from F tests computed using the differences in explained variance of full and restricted forms of the multiple classification analysis (Bottenberg and Ward, 1965). The full model included all six ethnic-sex categories and all controls. In the restricted models, one ethnic contrast (e.g., Anglo males compared to Black males) was dropped from the equation and replaced by a single category designating both groups (e.g., one category including Anglo and Black males). The difference in the explained variance in the full model (which, for example, assumes that Black and Anglo males have different population means) and the restricted model (which, for example, assumes that Black and Anglo males have the same population mean) were tested with F ratios with 1 and 347 degrees of freedom.

## FINDINGS

The mean participation rate in voluntary associations for all respondents is .897 with a standard deviation of 1.504. As can be seen from the class means (the actual rates of participation) presented in Table 1, Black men and women have higher rates of participation than their Anglo counterparts. Mexican Americans, regardless of sex, have lower rates than either Anglos or Blacks.

TABLE 1

**Mean Participation Rates in Voluntary Associations by Ethnicity and Sex before and after Covariance Adjustment[a]**

| ETHNICITY AND SEX | NUMBER | CLASS MEAN | ADJUSTED MEAN |
|---|---|---|---|
| Black American: | | | |
| Male | 44 | 1.364 | 1.158 |
| Female | 75 | 2.013 | 1.955 |
| Anglo American: | | | |
| Male | 39 | 1.077 | .547 |
| Female | 50 | .560 | .427 |
| Mexican American: | | | |
| Male | 80 | .325 | .441 |
| Female | 92 | .370 | .712 |

[a]*Control variables are age, education, occupational prestige, presence of young children in the household, length of residence in the community, home ownership, and whether the respondent is a household head.*

Presence of young children in the home, advanced age, short-term residence in the city, tenant status, limited education, and low occupational prestige are all factors which could inhibit social participation. These variables are somewhat differently distributed within the three ethnic samples and thus could have produced spurious associations between ethnicity and participation in voluntary associations. Furthermore, the Black sample was found to contain a somewhat larger proportion of female-headed households than the other two groups. If being the head of a household is associated with active participation in organizations, then it was possible that the participation rate for Black females was enhanced by having a larger proportion of heads than the other two groups of women. Given these possibilities, the participation rates were adjusted by holding these variables constant. As can be seen from the adjusted means presented in Table 1, the participation rates for Blacks and Anglos are decreased slightly after controlling on the other variables; whereas, the Mexican American rates are increased. This indicates that the lower rates of participation among the Mexican Americans can be accounted for by the differential distribution of the other independent variables among the samples.

As mentioned, tests of significance were made between the mean participation rates among ethnic groups within sex categories. These tests were made after controlling on all other independent variables. As shown in Table 2, Black men and women have significantly higher rates of participation than the other two ethnic groups; whereas, there is no significant difference at the .05 level between Anglo and Mexican American men and between Anglo and Mexican American women.

Table 3 shows the relative contribution of each independent variable to variation in the mean participation rates both before and after controlling on all other independent variables. The square of eta for the ethnicity variable is

TABLE 2

Results of Tests of Significance between Mean Participation Rates in Voluntary Associations after Covariance Adjustment[a] among Ethnic Groups within Sex Categories[b]

| TEST CATEGORIES | LEVEL OF SIGNIFICANCE[c] |
|---|---|
| Males: | |
| Anglo by Mexican American rates | n.s. |
| Anglo by Black American rates | .01 |
| Black by Mexican American rates | .01 |
| Females: | |
| Anglo by Mexican American rates | n.s. |
| Anglo by Black American rates | .01 |
| Black by Mexican American rates | .01 |

[a] Control variables are age, education, occupational prestige, presence of young children in the household, length of residence in the community, home ownership, and whether the respondent is a household head.

[b] The regression model used, assumes values of the dependent variable are sampled independently of one another. As 147 of the households have both a husband and wife in the sample, this assumption is violated. Since there are only 233 independently sampled households, the degrees of freedom in the sample would be 233 rather than 380 if there were perfect congruence of husband-wife participation scores, and the efficiency of the significance tests would be reduced. While perfect congruence of husband-wife scores was not found in the sample, all F ratios were recomputed using the reduced degrees of freedom to yield a "conservative" test of the effect of violating the assumption of independence of dependent variable observations. All differences using 380 degrees of freedom significant beyond the .05 level were significant beyond the .05 level with 233 degrees of freedom, and all differences not significant at the .05 level using the full degrees of freedom also were not significant at the .05 level using the reduced degrees of freedom. The reduction in the efficiency introduced by this violation of a regression analysis assumption, therefore, does not affect the conclusions summarized in the table.

[c] n.s. means not statistically significant beyond the .05 level and .01 means statistically significant beyond the .01 level.

.189 and beta-squared is .143. In other words, before introducing the controls, ethnicity appeared to explain 18.9 percent of the variation; whereas, after controlling on these variables, ethnicity accounts for an estimated 14.3 percent of the variation in the dependent variable.[5] Nevertheless, although beta-squared is slightly smaller than the square of eta, this introduction of controls provides greater assurance that ethnicity is an important variable in accounting for participation in voluntary associations. Inspection of the table's other findings shows that education is the only variable among those examined which equals ethnicity in importance. Taken together, the variables account for 38.3 percent of the variation in rates of participation.

TABLE 3

Relative Contribution to Variation in Mean Participation Rates
by Eight Independent Variables before and after Covariance Adjustment[a]

| VARIABLES | ETA-SQUARE | BETA-SQUARE |
|---|---|---|
| Ethnicity-sex[b] | .189 | .143 |
| Occupation | .045 | .007 |
| Education | .161 | .177 |
| Age | .024 | .037 |
| Home ownership | .035 | .010 |
| Length of residence in the city | .009 | .005 |
| Children under six in the household | .017 | .004 |
| Head of household | .003 | .007 |

[a]*Covariance adjustment refers to controlling for all of the other variables listed in the table.*

[b]*As mentioned, due to the statistically significant interaction between ethnicity and sex, sex categories within the ethnic groups were kept separate.*

## INTERPRETATION AND FURTHER
## THEORETICAL CONSIDERATIONS

The above findings do not support isolation theory which suggests that minority peoples rarely participate in voluntary associations because they are set off from society. On the contrary, the findings show that Black people have a significantly higher rate of participation in associations than Anglos; this difference clearly is not due to education, occupation, length of residence in the city, presence of young children in the home, home ownership, age, or being head of a household.

Cultural inhibition theory, which for the most part has been applied to Mexican Americans, posits that minority-group culture contains values, norms, and beliefs which differ from the Anglo American majority and which tend to prevent social participation in voluntary organizations. The findings from this study indicate that Mexican Americans are not significantly different from Anglos in social participation once certain structural (not cultural) variables are taken into account.

Compensatory or ethnic community theory or both are supported by the findings. It is not clear whether compensatory theory is more salient than ethnic community theory in explaining participation or whether the two theories complement each other; a research design different from the one used would be needed to disentangle these two theories. For example, information is needed on such things as the specific goals (formal and informal) of various organizations, the motivations of members for joining, the degree of ethnic identification among minority-group members. In other words, a useful study in this regard would focus on organizations and their members. The present study focused on the population at large and asked who belongs to associations and who does not. Nevertheless, it does offer leads for future research.

It is quite possible that a particular voluntary association can fulfill both compensatory and ethnic community needs. For example, an individual can gain a sense of importance or ego enhancement from participating in an association designed to combat racial discrimination. However, some organizations may be more clearly directed toward fulfilling compensatory needs (e.g., a social club); whereas others appear almost entirely directed toward changing aspects of the larger society (e.g., a pro-ethnic organization). With this in mind, participation by type of association was computed for each ethnic-sex category. The findings are presented in Table 4.[6]

The percentages of Black Americans belonging to different associations show no clear pattern of belonging primarily to "compensatory" or to "ethnic community" organizations. Social clubs, fraternal organizations, and recreation groups which might be thought of as emphasizing compensatory needs have about the same percentages belonging as do such possibly ethnic-community-oriented associations as pro-ethnic groups, neighborhood improvement organizations, and job-related associations. Church-related groups might be considered compensatory in nature; and it is true that such organizations can serve as a source of self-esteem, emotional expression, and respectability. However, numerous Black churches, especially those in urban areas, have operated as focal points for social action. Belonging to the P.T.A. (and in the present sample this includes 88.9 percent of Black women with school-age children!) supports the compensatory explanation to the extent that education is perceived as a means toward upward mobility. It is plausible, however, that the observed interest in education also indicates a strong concern for the welfare of the ethnic community.

In the Southwest, Mexican Americans appear to be subject to discrimination similar to that which characterizes Blacks in all parts of the United States. On this basis, it seemed possible that Mexican Americans might react to discrimination similarly to Blacks and that the pattern of affiliating with groups might be parallel for the two groups. As shown, however, Blacks have a significantly higher rate of participation in associations; and, Table 4 shows that the pattern of affiliation differs as well. Unlike Black Americans, respondents of Mexican descent tend to concentrate in two types of organizations, church-related groups and the P.T.A. And, these two organizations are difficult to

**TABLE 4**

**Ethnicity and Sex by Type of Organizational Membership**

| | ETHNICITY AND SEX | | | | | |
| --- | --- | --- | --- | --- | --- | --- |
| | BLACK AMERICAN | | ANGLO AMERICAN | | MEXICAN AMERICAN | |
| TYPE OF ASSOCIATION | % MALE (N = 44) | % FEMALE (N = 75) | % MALE (N = 39) | % FEMALE (N = 50) | % MALE (N = 80) | % FEMALE (N = 92) |
| Church-related | 25.0 | 48.0 | 7.7 | 10.0 | 7.5 | 10.9 |
| P.T.A. | 6.8 | 26.7 | 12.8 | 12.0 | 12.5 | 18.5 |
| Fraternal organizations | 16.9 | 13.3 | 10.3 | 2.0 | 0.0 | 0.0 |
| Social clubs | 4.5 | 5.3 | 2.6 | 0.0 | 2.5 | 1.1 |
| Recreational groups | 9.1 | 2.7 | 10.3 | 2.0 | 1.3 | 1.1 |
| Pro-ethnic organizations | 11.4 | 4.0 | 0.0 | 0.0 | 0.0 | 0.0 |
| Neighborhood improvement organizations | 4.5 | 10.7 | 0.0 | 0.0 | 1.3 | 1.1 |
| Job-related associations | 6.8 | 10.7 | 20.5 | 2.0 | 3.8 | 0.0 |
| Alumni organizations | 6.8 | 8.0 | 7.7 | 2.0 | 0.0 | 0.0 |
| Civic clubs | 2.3 | 2.7 | 2.6 | 4.0 | 0.0 | 0.0 |
| Veterans groups | 4.5 | 1.3 | 2.6 | 0.0 | 0.0 | 1.1 |
| Other | 9.1 | 10.7 | 17.9 | 12.0 | 2.5 | 1.1 |

characterize as emphasizing either compensation or ethnic community to the exclusion of the other. Some scholars might argue that participation in church-related groups associated with the Catholic Church in the Southwest is almost exclusively compensatory. However, even if subsequent research bears them out, Mexican American membership in the P.T.A. could express concern for the welfare of the Mexican American community as a whole.

## CONCLUSIONS

From the present findings, it is reasonable to conclude that removing the socioeconomic disparity between Anglo and Mexican Americans would result in a Mexican American participation rate in voluntary associations equal to that of Anglos. Black Americans, on the other hand, have a significantly higher rate of social participation than Anglos. A major problem for future research will be to explain the different rates and patterns of affiliation between Black and Mexican American minorities. A possible key to this difference may be a difference in awareness of minority status, i.e., a difference in the extent to which minority individuals perceive themselves and their group as objects of collective discrimination. In a manner similar to the development of class consciousness as a requisite for class action, some Black Americans seem to have gained a sense of ethnic community, Black consciousness, which has led to action-oriented social participation.

It may be too late within the purview of the theories outlined above to study most European-linked minorities. For example, Greek and Italian Americans, apart from name identity, have already become largely assimilated and acculturated into the larger society. We can only speculate that at one time compensatory and ethnic community needs played a major role in hastening this process. However, compensatory and ethnic community theories lend themselves to test in the case of several visible minorities, apart from Blacks, existing in society today.

From an historical perspective and given our present state of knowledge of intergroup relations, it seems plausible that compensatory rather than ethnic community theory, until recently, provided a better explanation for Black participation. Although acculturated, Blacks were probably led by such factors as high visibility, subordinate status, and overt discrimination to fall back on each other and organize into groups to maintain their dignity and achieve personal fulfillment. Social integration, though viewed by many as an important goal, was not believed possible.

Black consciousness, surfaced with greater force through such successes as the Montgomery bus boycott organized by the S.C.L.C., lunch counter sit-ins by Black students, the development of CORE and the somewhat more recent emergence of militant groups like the Black Panthers. Together these have given greater force to ethnic identity and feelings of Black pride. If this process is occurring, and the evidence suggests that it is, then ethnic community theory should play an increasingly important role in helping us understand the participation of Black Americans in voluntary associations. We should expect a sense of ethnic community to become increasingly salient in fostering participation by other visible minorities, particularly American Indians, Mexican Americans, and United States residents from Puerto Rico and Cuba. These minorities are subject to practices of discrimination and prejudice comparable in some ways to those leveled against Blacks. All have begun to organize militant associations to express their identity and consciousness, e.g., the American Indian Movement, the La Raza Unida Party, the Young Lords. At present, these and similar organizations do not appear to have the broad base of support of such groups as the N.A.A.C.P., but these ethnic minorities appear to be on the threshold of changing their patterns of participation. The present study provides empirical evidence within a theoretical framework which might guide research on patterns of participation of such visible minorities and offers cues about what such research endeavors are likely to uncover.

## NOTES

1  Myrdal et al. (1944:952–55) suggested that Blacks were prone to join associations, particularly expressive ones, to compensate for discrimination. This view was reiterated some years later by Kardiner (1959:418) who observed that: Whereas these writers tended to view this behavior as "pathological," Orum (1966:34) was the first to label the exaggerated tendency for Blacks to affiliate as "compensatory" in the more general sense of fulfilling needs not readily available in the larger society. He did so to describe Babchuk and Thompson's (1962) rationale for the high rate of Black participation found in their research.

2  In earlier works, Blacks were not seen as creating pressure groups to change the condition of caste life, even though such groups existed. Yet many writers were aware that pressure groups might be effective were Blacks to develop an ethnic consciousness and press for change; indeed, a chapter in Myrdal (1944: 810–57) entitled "Negro Improvement and Protest Organizations" was devoted to the subject, and Lane (1959) suggested this idea in relation to political participation. However, the specific idea of ethnic community as an explanation for participation in voluntary associations was not articulated until Olsen did so in 1970.

3  It is possible that middle-class people living in low-rent areas differ in social participation from middle-class people living in medium- or high-rent areas. However, the participation rates of the higher status persons in the present sample are similar to rates reported in other studies using sampling procedures which included medium- and high-rent areas.

4  The data were analyzed also using "belonging to one or more associations" and "not belonging to any associations." The findings are essentially the same.

5  Andrews et al. (1969:117–19) point out that the square of beta is not exactly interpretable as the percent of explained variation in the dependent variable. This is why we have referred to beta-squared as an estimate. The important point for the present study is that this coefficient provides us with measures of the *relative* importance of the various predictors.

6  Table 4 gives the actual percentages belonging to each type of association. Since no controls are introduced for socioeconomic status or situation, comparison between ethnic groups should be made with caution.

## REFERENCES

*Aberback, Joe D.*
1969    "Alienation and political behavior." American Political Science Review 63 (March): 86–99.

*Almond, Gabriel, and Sidney Verba*
1963    The Civic Culture. Princeton, N.J.: Princeton University Press.

*Alvarez, Salvador*
1971    "Mexican American community organizations." El Grito 4 (Spring): 91–100.

*Andrews, Frank, James N. Morgan and John A. Sonquist*
1967    Multiple Classification Analysis: A Report on a Computer Program for Multiple Regression Using Categorical Predictors. Ann Arbor, Michigan: Institute for Social Research, The University of Michigan.

*Babchuk, Nicholas, and Alan Booth*
1969    "Voluntary association membership: A longitudinal analysis." American Sociological Review 34 (February): 31–45.

*Babchuk, Nicholas, and Ralph V. Thompson*
1962    "Voluntary associations of Negroes." American Sociological Review 27 (October): 647–55.

*Bottenberg, Robert A., and Joe H. Ward, Jr.*
1963    Applied Multiple Linear Regression. Lackland Air Force Base, Texas: 6570th Personnel Research Laboratory, Aerospace Laboratory, Aerospace Medical Division, Air Force Systems Command.

*Briegel, Kaye*
1970    "The development of Mexican-American organizations." Pp. 160–78 in Manual P. Servin (ed.), The Mexican-Americans: An Awakening Minority. Beverly Hills, California: Glencoe Press.

*Cogen, Jacob*
1968    "Multiple regression as a general data-analytic system." Psychological Bulletin 70 (December): 426–43.

*Curtis, James*
1971    "Voluntary association joining: A cross-national comparative note." American Sociological Review 36 (October): 872–80.

*Erbe, William*
1964    "Social involvement and political activity: A replication and elaboration." American Sociological Review 29 (April): 198–215.

*Heller, Celia S.*
1966    Mexican-American Youth: Forgotten Youth at the Crossroads. Cambridge, Mass.: Schenkman Publishing Company.

*Hollingshead, August B.*
1957    Two Factor Index of Social Position. New Haven: Mimeographed. Hyman, Herbert H. and Charles R. Wright.
1971    "Trends in voluntary association membership of American adults: Replication based on secondary analysis of national sample surveys." American Sociological Review 36 (April): 191–206.

*Kardiner, Abram*
1959    "Explorations in Negro personality." Pp. 413–23 in Marvin K. Opler (ed.), Culture and Mental Health. New York: Macmillan.

*Lane, Robert E.*
1959    Political Life: Why and How People Get Involved in Politics. New York: The Free Press.

*Lipset, Seymour M., Martin Trow, and James Coleman*
1956    Union Democracy, New York: The Free Press.

*Lopata, Helena Z.*
1964    "The function of voluntary associations in an ethnic community: 'Polonia.' " Pp.

203–23 in Ernest W. Burgess and Donald J. Bogue (eds.), Contributions to Urban Sociology. Chicago: University of Chicago Press.

*Lyden, Fremont James, and Jerry V. Thomas*
1969    "Citizen participation in policy-making: A study of a community action program." Social Science Quarterly 50 (December): 631–42.

*Mayo, Selz C.*
1950    "Age profiles of social participation in rural areas of Wake County, North Carolina." Rural Sociology 15 (December): 242–51.

*Montiel, Miguel*
1970    "The social science myth of the Mexican-American family." El Grito 3 (Summer): 56–63.

*Myrdal, Gunner, Richard Sterner, and Arnold Rose*
1944    An American Dilemma. New York: Harper and Brothers.

*Olsen, Marvin E.*
1970    "Social and political participation of Blacks." American Sociological Review 35 (August): 682–97.

*Orum, Anthony M.*
1966    "A reappraisal of the social and political participation of Negroes." American Journal of Sociology 72 (July): 32–46.

*Romano, Octavio Ignacio*
1968    "The anthropology and sociology of the Mexican-Americans: The distortion of Mexican-American history." El Grito 2 (Fall): 13–25.

*Rose, Arnold*
1967    The Power Structure. New York: Oxford University Press.

*Rubel, Arthur J.*
1966    Across the tracks: Mexican-Americans in a Texas City. Austin: The University of Texas Press.

*Sallach, David L., Nicholas Babchuk, and Alan Booth*
1972    "Social involvement and political activity: Another view." Social Science Quarterly 52 (March): 879–92.

*Vanecko, James J.*
1969    "Community mobilization and institutional change: The influence of the community action program in large cities." Social Science Quarterly 50 (December): 609–30.

*Williams, J. Allen, Jr.*
1964    "Interviewer-respondent interaction: A study of bias in the information interview. Sociometry 27 (September): 338–52.

*Williams, J. Allen, Jr.*
1968    Interviewer role performance: A further note on bias in the information interview." Public Opinion Quarterly 32 (Summer): 287–94.

*Wright, Charles, and Herbert H. Hyman*
1958    "Voluntary association memberships of American adults: Evidence from national sample surveys." American Sociological Review 23 (June): 284–94.

*Zurcher, Louis A.*
1970    Poverty Warriors. Austin: The University of Texas Press.

# Social Assimilation Among American Catholic National-Origin Groups[*]

## Richard D. Alba

*Herbert H. Lehman College, CUNY*

*The current resurgence of interest in white ethnicity largely has taken the form of asserting the continued vitality of ethnic communities. Current scholars, following Gordon's (1964) well-known distinction between acculturation and social or structural assimilation, acknowledge the great extent of acculturation but maintain that, nonetheless, social assimilation has not taken place. They claim, in other words, that primary relationships are generally between individuals of like ethnicity. This paper, using data about Catholic national-origin groups in the early 1960s, finds little support for these present assertions of ethnic vitality.*

It has become almost a cliche to open any paper about white ethnicity[1] with an acknowledgment of how little we know. Despite that initial diffidence, most

*Source:* Richard D. Alba, "Social Assimilation Among American Catholic National-Origin Groups," American Sociological Review 41, 6 (December 1976): 1030–1046. Copyright © 1976 by the American Sociological Association. Reprinted by permission of the Association and the author.
*The work reported in this paper was supported by a Russell Sage Graduate Student Fellowship and an NIMH grant. Number 1 RO1 MH23806-01 SSR, to Donald Treiman, principal investigator, at the Center for Policy Research. I am very grateful for the help of many people, especially Harold Abramson, Allen Barton, Pat Bova, Steven Cohen, Jonathan Cole, Herbert Gans, John Hammond, Charles Kadushin, Gwen Moore, Stephen Steinberg, Donald Treiman and two anonymous reviewers.

then proceed on the assumption that we do, after all, know something: namely, that ethnicity survives in some form among the descendants of 19th and 20th century immigrants and it especially survives at the level of primary attachments, which remain largely ethnically homogeneous.

That the Americanization of immigrants and their descendants is far advanced has long been recognized and for almost as long discounted as proof of their ultimate assimilation (Gordon, 1964; Parenti, 1967; Glazer and Moynihan, 1970; Greeley, 1971). But as a result of this recognition, the search for viable elements of ethnicity has moved away from culture and toward what might be called "community." That is, following Gordon's (1964) enormously influential exposition of ethnicity and assimilation, a distinction usually is made between two different kinds of assimilation: acculturation, the acquisition of the culture of the natives; and social or structural assimilation, the integration with them at the primary level, including marriage. It is assumed that acculturation can occur without social assimilation. Individuals can participate in ethnically heterogeneous secondary relationships—for example, on the job—by virtue of their sharing a common culture and return home to the ethnically segregated worlds of neighborhood, friendship, and family. Thus, ethnicity survives as long as there are ethnic communities—concentration of ethnically homogeneous individuals whose primary attachments are to each other—whatever the extent of acculturation.

Much of the recent writing on white ethnicity has assumed that social assimilation is very limited in extent or, equivalently, that ethnic segregation remains strong. Thus, recent writers should be called "social pluralists" (Newman, 1973) rather than "cultural pluralists," despite the current fashionability of the latter phrase. Greeley (1972:275), for example, asserts:

*when it comes to choosing relationships where either intimacy or trust are involved, there is still a strong tendency to choose people of whom we can say, in effect, if not in fact, "Your mother knew my mother."*

Parenti (1967:724), after summarizing a wide range of studies of ethnicity, reaches the strong conclusion:

*... the vast pluralistic parallel systems of ethnic and institutional life show impressive viability; structural assimilation seems neither inevitable nor imminent.*

Indeed, the assumption of "social pluralism" pervades the recent literature on white ethnicity, appearing in various guises in Glazer and Moynihan (1970), Greeley (1971), Novak (1972), Abramson (1973), and numerous others. Many of these writers propose a view of American society as a mosaic of distinct ethnic blocs, with strong social barriers to widespread contact between the members of different blocs. This view is reflected in the current resurgence in the use of hyphenated nationality terms like "Italian-American" and "Polish-American." And, in circular fashion, the popularity of these terms appears to attest to the truth of the underlying view.

In addition, the assumption of "social pluralism" has an important theoretical relationship to other assertions of ethnic vitality. In the light of Gordon's work, that assumption appears necessary if *any* claims about ethnic distinctiveness are to be made. As Gordon (1946:81) states in one of his widely quoted passages, "once structural assimilation has occurred ... all other types of assimilation will naturally follow." Recent authors generally have accepted Gordon's view. Thus, for example, those who would like to celebrate ethnic cultural distinctiveness (Novak, 1972; Gambino, 1974) ultimately fall back on the assumption that families, peer groups, and neighborhoods are ethnically homogeneous and, hence, are efficient transmitters of ethnic cultures.

In important ways, then, the assumption of "social pluralism" is the keystone of the current description of white ethnicity. Nevertheless, it has not been the subject of careful and systematic empirical examination. As I will argue below, many of the studies cited in its support are of individual ethnic communities and, consequently, have serious deficiencies when used to measure trends in the population at large. Also, much of what little quantitative evidence there is, derived from national and regional surveys, suffers from serious conceptual deficiencies, especially in the flawed use of the "network" as an organizing concept.

This paper addresses a basic question: is the social assimilation of national-origin groups in the United States as limited as is generally assumed? In answering this, I hope to overcome the inherent theoretical difficulties of much previous research by conceptualizing ethnic communities as ethnically homogeneous primary networks. With appropriate concepts in hand, I will then analyze the extent of social assimilation among Catholic national-origin groups by a reanalysis of an important and much-used body of data, the Catholic Americans study, already analyzed by Greeley and Rossi (1966), Greeley (1971), and Abramson (1973).

## SOME DEFICIENCIES

Parenti (1967) provides a major summary of available data about ethnic groups. In arguing for the continued vitality of the ethnic community, he cites a number of studies of such communities—for example, those by Whyte (1955) and Gans (1962) of Italian-American communities in Boston:

*Similar findings were made by Whyte and Gans in their respective studies— done twenty years apart—of Italian-American communities in Boston. American styles, language, sports, and consumption patterns predominated, but interpersonal relations and social group structures were almost exclusively Italian-American in both the North End of the 1940's and the West End of the 1960's. (Parenti, 1967:719)*

These two well-known studies are typical of the community studies which have been used to speak to the question of social assimilation, but they have serious deficiencies for that purpose. A typical study is carried out by an observer who lives for a time in a predominantly ethnic neighborhood and immerses himself in the subworld of the group. The choice of a research site makes it difficult for the researcher to make statements about social assimilation, since the most assimilated usually have left the neighborhood, and the focus of his study makes it likely that he will be most interested in the least assimilated members of the group.

Generalization about the extent of assimilation from such data is extremely hazardous. It is easy to see how Parenti's summary of the findings of Whyte and Gans could apply to those living in the neighborhoods they studied, but is difficult to gauge its accuracy for those of Italian ancestry generally. In short, it must be recognized that the mere persistence of ethnic neighborhoods does not indicate that most members of a given ancestry group live in such neighborhoods, nor does it disprove that social assimilation is widespread among those outside of ethnic neighborhoods.[2]

For the same reason, caution must be exercised in interpreting the results of studies based on samples located by devices intended to be efficient in locating the members of a particular ethnic group. The logic of such devices usually is to look for concentrations of group members, i.e., ethnic communities, and thus they inherently favor the socially less assimilated members of the group. For example, Gallo (1974), in a recent study of Italian-Americans asserts that his respondents show little social assimilation. However, his sample was selected from lists of potential respondents supplied by community contacts (Gallo, 1974:25), and his finding of little social assimilation is therefore not surprising.

The most useful data for measuring the extent of social assimilation within various ethnic groups are drawn from random national or regional samples, since these permit analysis of a representative sample of all individuals of a given ancestry—the most as well as the least socially assimilated. While there are data of these kind—the already-mentioned Catholic Americans study, for example—findings about social assimilation drawn from them usually are flawed by a failure to present a consistent conception of the ethnic community.

The measures of social assimilation most often found in survey data concern ancestry and marriage, although there are some concerning friendship—for example, the Detroit Area Study analyzed by Laumann (1973). A universal problem in analyzing ancestry and marriage data stems from the presence of individuals with ethnically mixed ancestry. It is usual to ignore their presence in analyzing marriage patterns and to employ some rule to assign each respondent to a unique ethnic group. The usual rule is that a respondent is assigned to the main nationality group in his father's ancestry, a practice justified by the assumption that ethnic identity is transmitted through the surname (Abramson, 1973:67). Thus, Abramson and Greeley, following this rule, define an endogamous marriage as one where the nationalities of the spouses' fathers are the same, regardless of what other nationalities are involved. That an endogamous marriage by this rule is not necessarily one within an ethnic community is obvious when it is realized that this rule can classify as endogamous a marriage where both spouses are of mixed ancestry and the nationalities of their mothers are different.

Thus, a basic problem of the studies mentioned so far is their failure to cope theoretically with mixed ancestry as part of the process of social assimilation (and, in fact, these and other studies deal only cursorily with mixed ancestry, if they deal with it at all). But the well-known portraits of ethnic communities (Whyte, 1955; Gans, 1962; Suttles, 1968) feature overwhelming ethnic homogeneity in primary relationships. Consequently, in order to examine the "social pluralist" position, it is necessary to distinguish, at least initially, between those with pure ancestry and those with mixed ancestry.

The question of how individuals with mixed ancestry ethnically identify themselves, raised in justifying the classification rule mentioned above, is a substantial one, but its use to resolve ambiguities in the definition of social assimilation confuses crucial theoretical issues. It is quite possible that an individual with mixed ancestry has an ethnic identification, as Greeley (1971:93) argues, in the sense that he prefers one of the nationalities in his background, but the mere possession of an ethnic identity does not guarantee that he exists within an ethnically homogeneous primary milieu. Thus, while the question of identity is important, it is given the wrong theoretical priority when used to define endogamy. If we are willing to assume that a basic theoretical dimension of ethnicity is ethnic segregation at the primary level, then the extent to which segregation is maintained must be measured directly. Whether the characteristics of individuals with ethnically homogeneous relationships are different from those with ethnically heterogeneous ones—whether, for example, ethnic identity is more salient for the former than for the latter—is theoretically subsequent and can be addressed once we have satisfactorily categorized individuals by their levels of social assimilation.

## ANCESTRY AND MARRIAGE AS MEASURES OF SOCIAL ASSIMILATION

Any community can be described as a collection of primary networks in which individuals are linked through the relationships of kinship or friendship or by virtue of being neighbors. The networks of this description are abstractions of the quotidian interactions between people, as represented, for example, by the social event of a visit. This view of a community is well summarized by Bott (1957:216):

*The immediate social environment of an urban family consists of a network rather than an organized group. A network is a social configuration in which some, but not all, of the component external units maintain relationships with one another. The external units do not make up a larger whole. They are not surrounded by a common boundary.*

The ethnic communities, which have been studied by Whyte (1955), Gans (1962), Suttles (1968) and others, are usually defined as territorial units which possess a high concentration of individuals of like ethnicity; in other words, they are defined as ethnic neighborhoods. They also can be defined as ethically homogeneous primary networks, as these and other studies show. For example, Gans (1962:35) asserts:

*[S]ocial relationships are almost entirely limited to other Italians, because much sociability is based on kinship, and because most friendships are made in childhood, and are thus influenced by residential propinquity.*

In terms of primary relationships, ethnic communities are largely self-contained (see also Breton, 1964).

With the network view of an ethnic community in mind, the social assimilation of any individual can be defined as a function of the ethnic composition of his primary network, the network whose nodes include those with whom he shares close and intimate relationships and perhaps even those who are "one remove" from him in the sense that they share primary relationships with his primary partners but not with him (Barnes, 1969; Granovetter, 1973). An individual is socially assimilated to the extent that the members of his primary network differ from him in national ancestry or are of mixed ancestry.

It should be noted that social assimilation by this definition is separation from an ethnic community, not integration with a majority group. The primary network of the socially assimilated individual need not include members of any majority group—usually defined as Anglo-American Protestants in American society—but only others who are different from himself. Also, by this definition, the network of a socially assimilated individual need not include others from many different backgrounds; they may all be from one so long as it is different from that of the individual. We will return later to this point.

Information about ancestry and marriage can be used to ascertain the composition of one part of this network, that formed by the respondent's and spouse's blood kin. Implicit in conventional discussion of intermarriage are two levels of distinction based on marriage and ancestry. In the first, those with mixed ancestry are distinguished from those with pure ancestry. In the second, those with pure ancestry are divided between the exogamously and the endogamously married.[3] In conformity to conventional usage, it appears sensible to distinguish three categories of social assimilation based on ancestry and marriage: endogamous marriage, exogamous marriage, and mixed ancestry. These three categories form a neat temporal sequence, since mixed ancestry follows from exogamous marriage but not from endogamous marriage.

Although there is a clear distinction in terms of social assimilation between the first category and the remaining two, there is no clear distinction between these last two. That is, it is not clear that mixed ancestry represents a stage of greater social assimilation than intermarriage (or vice versa); it might therefore be argued that the two categories should be merged. Nevertheless, maintaining this tripartite distinction offers some important advantages; chiefly, it allows a careful examination of the ultimate impact of intermarriage. In support of the "social pluralist" position, some (Greeley, 1971:82–94; Newman, 1973:162–4) argue that even intermarriage will not weaken ethnic segregation because the intermarried or, in the usual form of the argument, their children "reaffiliate" themselves with one of the ethnic communities in their backgrounds. Maintaining the tripartite distinction allows us to examine this argument, with careful attention to the possibility that one category is more likely than the other to be ethnically reabsorbed.

Despite the initial clarity of the tripartite distinction, there are a few ambiguities in a full operationalization of exogamy and endogamy. Classification is clear when both the individual and his spouse have the same pure ancestry or their backgrounds are completely distinct, but not when an individual of pure ancestry is married to one of partially overlapping mixed ancestry (for example, an individual of Irish ancestry married to one of Irish and German ancestry). Following the logic above, it seems reasonable to classify such marriages as exogamous, since the resulting kinship network is ethnically diverse. While not all the spouse's relatives differ in nationality from the individual, some do. The problem can be resolved in another way if we require consistency with the temporal sequence of the categories. Since the children of the marriages in question are of mixed ancestry, the marriages are exogamous.

Since the data from which rates of endogamy are computed are usually survey data, other problems arise when the respondent lacks knowledge about his or his spouse's ancestry. It may seem strange to attempt to retain such cases for analysis, but confession of ignorance is, of course, a possible response to a question; such cases normally are dropped from analysis only because their interpretation is elusive. However, it seems plausible that for many socially assimilated individuals ethnicity is not a salient social characteristic and, consequently, they do not know their own ancestry and, even more, the ancestries of important members of their primary network. Conversely, there is little reason to assume that an individual member of an ethnic community does not recognize the ethnic homogeneity of his network or the presence of an exception, should there be any.[4] Thus, to classify unknown ancestry as missing information is, in all probability, to understate the true extent of social assimilation. Individuals who do not know their own ancestry must be omitted from the analysis of any ancestry group, but those who know their own ancestry but not that of their spouse can be included and, in accordance with the argument above, are classified as exogamously married. In summary, for the purposes of this paper, only those marriages where an individual and his spouse are known to have the same pure ancestry are classified as endogamous.

## DATA

The data I will use to measure the social assimilation of national-origin groups are taken from the Catholic Americans study (Greeley and Rossi, 1966). These data represent a random sample of the total noninstitutionalized Catholic population between the ages of 23 and 57 in 1963. The size of the sample is 2071, reflecting an interview completion rate of 77%.

This data set has some outstanding virtues for the study of ethnicity. It contains excellent questions about ethnic background, and they allow for complexity in response. The interview schedule asks separately for the main ethnic backgrounds of the respondent's mother and father.[5] In either case, two or more categories may be indicated as appropriate. Identical information is requested for the respondent's spouse's parents.

Thus, one rare feature of this data set is that it allows for a precise accounting of respondents with ethnically mixed or hybrid ancestry. A respondent will be defined as having mixed ancestry when he reports two or more nationality categories for either parent or the nationality categories of his mother and father are different. By this definition, people with mixed ancestry comprise almost 30% of the sample. A second rare feature of this data set is that it carefully records the ethnic background of the respondent's spouse, thereby allowing clear identification of interethnic or exogamous marriages.[6]

The categories used to record ethnicity in the interview schedule are: English; Irish; German; Scandinavian; French (largely French-Canadian); Italian; Polish; Lithuanian; all other eastern European; Spanish (including Puerto Rican), labeled "Hispanic" in the text which follows; Other; and Don't Know. Three categories will be ignored in the statistical presentation of data: the Scandinavian category because it is so small and the Other and Don't Know categories because they are small and their ethnic composition is unclear. The Lithuanian category will be merged into the other eastern European category, based on a rough geographic and ethnic similarity.

Two different tabulations will be used to report information about ancestry and marriage for each group. In one, the percentage formed by those with mixed ancestry among all those with at least some ancestry from the group will be reported. In the other, the percentage formed by the intermarried among the currently married with pure ancestry from the group will be reported.

The remainder of this paper will be divided into three parts. The first will examine the rates of mixed ancestry and interethnic marriage for the groups in these data, comparing them to a previous examination by Abramson (1973). The second will examine the trends of these rates from their variation by generations and age for each group. The third will examine the relationship of ancestry and marriage to social assimilation generally, bringing to bear the remaining information in these data about the ethnic composition of the respondent's primary network.

## RATES OF MIXED ANCESTRY AND INTERMARRIAGE

In examining rates of mixed ancestry and intermarriage, special attention should be paid to the old/new distinction among ethnic origins. Briefly, the old groups are those from northern and western Europe and they generally arrived before the new groups, those from southern and eastern Europe. The old groups in these data are the English, Irish, Germans, and, arguably, the French.[7] The new groups are the Italians, Poles, and other eastern Europeans. The Hispanic group is mainly Latin American in origin and is even more recently arrived than the new groups. The old groups are generally considered to be more assimilated than the new groups or Hispanics, a fact usually explained by their greater physical and cultural similarity to the earliest European settlers and their greater length of residence.

Abramson's analysis of these data reaffirms the meaningfulness of the old/new distinction. He finds the rates of mixed ancestry and intermarriage to be higher among the old groups than among the new groups or Hispanics, although some new groups, the Poles and other eastern Europeans, show changes in the direction of greater social assimilation. Nonetheless, Abramson (1973:66) finds that, overall, these data testify to the continued power of national origins in the limited amount of social assimilation to be found in them.

*The Mexicans, the Puerto Ricans, the French-Canadians, and the Italians are not disappearing into the greater body of American Catholicism. They are marrying into their own groups, at a rate of better than six out of every ten. But even more surprisingly, the present-day Irish and German Catholics, whose families have been in the United States for three or more generations, maintain endogamous marriages by proportions of more than 40 per cent. . . .*

A natural question is whether the same conclusions about the limited extent of social assimilation would be reached if the definitions of mixed ancestry and intermarriage outlined earlier were used. As I argued there, these definitions are more suitable for identifying the possible constituency of ethnic communities than those used by Abramson. Table 1 shows the rates of mixed ancestry and intermarriage computed by Abramson[8] and those computed using the operational definitions of previous sections. The column "Diff." reports the differences between these two rates for each group and is positive when the Abramson rate is lower than the rate computed here.

TABLE 1

Rates of Mixed Ancestry and Intermarriage for Catholic National-Origin Groups, as Computed by Abramson and under the Definitions Here[a]

|  | MIXED ANCESTRY | | |
| --- | --- | --- | --- |
|  | *DEFINITIONS HERE* | *ABRAMSON[b]* | *DIFF.[c]* |
| English | 79.8 (263) | 73 (45) | 6.8 |
| Irish | 61.4 (497) | 35 (269) | 26.4 |
| German | 54.7 (503) | 27 (234) | 27.7 |
| French | 51.5 (260) | 21 (153) | 30.5 |
| Other Eastern European[d] | 27.8 (223) | 12 (166) | 15.8 |
| Polish | 33.8 (237) | 11 (170) | 22.8 |
| Italian | 10.3 (379) | 7 (336) | 3.3 |
| Hispanic | 8.8 (148) | 4 (119) | 4.8 |
|  | INTERMARRIAGE | | |
| English | 93.2 (44) | 88 (27) | 5.2 |
| Irish | 69.3 (163) | 57 (179) | 12.3 |
| German | 67.5 (197) | 55 (165) | 12.5 |
| French | 43.2 (111) | 32 (112) | 11.2 |
| Other Eastern European[d] | 57.1 (140) | 58 (128) | −.9 |
| Polish | 58.7 (138) | 50 (135) | 8.7 |
| Italian | 41.1 (304) | 34 (256) | 7.1 |
| Hispanic | 19.7 (117) | 12 (88) | 7.7 |

[a] *The base for each rate is reported in parentheses.*
[b] *These rates are taken from Abramson's Table 9 (1973:53).*
[c] *This column reports the differences between Abramson's rates and those calculated here.*
[d] *This category combines the categories "Lithuanian" and "Other Eastern European" reported by Abramson.*

The most obvious finding is that of greater social assimilation under the definitions used here.[9] With one exception, all differences in Table 1 are positive. Looking at their magnitudes, there are some large differences, found predominantly in the rates of mixed ancestry. Four of the differences there are over 20%, while no difference between intermarriage rates is that great.

In terms of groups, the differences are greatest for the groups of the old immigration—the Irish, Germans, and French (social assimilation is so extensive among the English by any definition that neither makes much difference). For two of these groups, the Irish and Germans, the rates computed here present a picture of their social assimilation substantially different from that presented by Abramson. For the Irish, six out of ten, and for the Germans, over five out of ten with some ancestry from the group have mixed ancestry. And nearly seven out of every ten individuals with pure Irish or German ancestry intermarry. The extent of their social assimilation can only be judged as appreciable.

Excluding the English, Irish, and Germans, the groups in these data have rates of mixed ancestry and intermarriage, by the present definitions, compatible with a view that their social assimilation is limited. For example, over four out of every ten Poles and other eastern Europeans are endogamously married, as are nearly six out of ten Italians and French and over eight of ten Hispanics (see also Cohen, 1975). Thus, the present definitions modify but do not completely overturn Abramson's conclusions about social assimilation, at least insofar as it can be assessed from aggregate group rates.

Nonetheless, even while acknowledging the importance of endogamy among these groups, it is appropriate to ask whether there are apparent changes in the extent of their social assimilation. These groups are recently arrived and thus many of their members are from early generations, and many of the marriages in these data were contracted a long time before they were collected. It is quite possible, then, that members of later generations or those recently marrying are intermarrying more frequently than the rates in Table 1 indicate. In either case, a change in the direction of greater social assimilation would indicate that the aggregate rates of Table 1 are not stable and can be expected to change in the future.

## TRENDS AS INDICATED BY GENERATIONS AND AGE

There are two basic ways of identifying the trend of any characteristic of ethnic groups: through its variation by generations of residence and through its variation by age (Alba, 1976). Each has its own inherent rationale. The generational variation, the more common way (Lieberson, 1973), is useful in this respect because it usually can be assumed that the generational composition of a group will change in the future and, more precisely, that the proportion formed by its later generations will increase. Thus, the future characteristics of the group increasingly will become the characteristics of its later generations in the present.

The age variation of a measure can be used in certain situations to forecast its future level in a group because the group's present older cohorts increasingly will be replaced by its present younger cohorts. The interpretation of age is often subject to some ambiguity because effects of aging are confounded with those of historical change in a single age variation (Riley et al., 1972; Mason et al., 1973; Foner, 1974). Insofar as a measure is affected by the process of aging, the predictive use of its variation by age is vitiated because its average level in any age cohort will change as the cohort ages. I have argued at length elsewhere (Alba, 1976) that ancestry and marriage are reasonably free of this difficulty. The age variation of a measure like these is predictive because the future level of the measure in the group as a whole increasingly will become its present level in the group's younger cohorts.

The generational[10] and age variations of ancestry for each group are presented in Table 2 and the equivalent variations of marriage[11] are presented in Table 3.[12] The age and generational changes for each measure are reported group by group in the columns labeled "Diff." Each column reports the difference between the latest generation or youngest age cohort and the earliest generation or oldest age cohort (formulas: latest-earliest; youngest-oldest). Its sign is such that when positive it indicates a trend in the direction of greater social assimilation.

The most obvious finding from these two tables is the virtual universality of a trend toward increasing social assimilation, evident in the patterns of change of both ancestry and marriage. Except for two groups—the English and Hispanics, the most and least socially assimilated, respectively, in these data —the direction of change for each measure, in both its age and generational variation, is toward greater social assimilation. A detailed examination of these tables, proceeding group by group, strongly contradicts the common assumption that ethnic segregation at the primary level is persisting. I exempt the

TABLE 2

Rate of Mixed Ancestry by Generations and Age for Each Ethnic Group[a]

| | FIRST GENER-ATION | SECOND GENER-ATION | THIRD GENER-ATION | FOURTH GENER-ATION | DIFF.[b] |
|---|---|---|---|---|---|
| English | 36.4 (11) | 86.0 (50) | 88.8 (98) | 72.5 (102) | 36.1 |
| Irish | 27.8 (18) | 47.5 (101) | 65.8 (222) | 67.3 (150) | 39.5 |
| German | 23.1 (26) | 40.6 (128) | 60.3 (232) | 65.8 (114) | 42.7 |
| French | 14.3 (21) | 32.5 (83) | 69.8 (96) | 64.3 (56) | 50.0 |
| Polish | — (5) | 18.4 (125) | 51.7 (89) | 68.8 (16) | 50.4 |
| Eastern European | 16.7 (24) | 14.1 (135) | 62.7 (51) | — (10) | 46.0 |
| Italian | 3.6 (28) | 2.5 (275) | 38.8 (67) | — (8) | 35.2 |
| Hispanic | 4.7 (64) | 6.7 (60) | 28.6 (14) | — (9) | 23.9 |
| | 30 OR UNDER | 31–40 | 41–50 | 51 OR OVER | DIFF.[b] |
| English | 83.0 (53) | 74.4 (78) | 81.1 (90) | 81.6 (38) | 1.4 |
| Irish | 71.7 (106) | 58.7 (167) | 60.8 (153) | 52.2 (67) | 19.5 |
| German | 67.0 (100) | 55.9 (152) | 54.0 (174) | 36.0 (75) | 31.0 |
| French | 54.9 (71) | 51.8 (85) | 51.6 (64) | 46.2 (39) | 8.7 |
| Polish | 50.0 (54) | 36.2 (69) | 24.7 (77) | 20.6 (34) | 29.4 |
| Eastern European | 53.2 (47) | 29.7 (64) | 18.5 (81) | 10.0 (30) | 43.2 |
| Italian | 30.0 (70) | 11.7 (120) | 3.0 (134) | 0.0 (54) | 30.0 |
| Hispanic | 17.1 (35) | 7.8 (64) | 3.0 (33) | 6.3 (16) | 10.8 |

[a] The base for each rate is reported in parentheses.

[b] This column reports the difference between the latest generation or youngest age cohort and the earliest generation or oldest age cohort (formulas: latest-earliest; youngest-oldest).

TABLE 3

Rate of Intermarriage by Generations and Age for Each Ethnic Group[a]

|  | FIRST GENER-ATION | SECOND GENER-ATION | THIRD GENER-ATION | FOURTH GENER-ATION | DIFF.[b] |
|---|---|---|---|---|---|
| English | —   (6) | —   (4) | 100.0  (11) | 87.0 (23) | −13.0 |
| Irish | 33.3 (12) | 57.5  (40) | 79.1  (67) | 74.4 (43) | 41.1 |
| German | 55.6 (18) | 77.4  (62) | 59.5  (84) | 75.0 (32) | 19.4 |
| French | 46.7 (15) | 27.1  (48) | 60.7  (28) | 58.8 (17) | 12.1 |
| Polish | —   (5) | 57.8  (90) | 64.9  (37) | —   (4) | 7.1 |
| Eastern European | 29.4 (17) | 58.3 (103) | 73.3  (15) | —   (4) | 43.9 |
| Italian | 29.2 (24) | 38.9 (239) | 59.5  (37) | —   (3) | 30.3 |
| Hispanic | 13.2 (53) | 24.0  (50) | —   (6) | —   (8) | 14.8 |

|  | 30 OR UNDER | 31–40 | 41–50 | 51 OR OVER | DIFF.[b] |
|---|---|---|---|---|---|
| English | —   (8) | 93.8  (16) | 93.8  (16) | —   (4) | 0.0 |
| Irish | 82.1 (28) | 59.4  (64) | 74.5  (47) | 73.9 (23) | 8.2 |
| German | 74.1 (27) | 72.4  (58) | 71.6  (74) | 47.4 (38) | 26.7 |
| French | 53.8 (26) | 36.1  (36) | 40.0  (30) | 44.4 (18) | 9.4 |
| Polish | 65.2 (23) | 63.2  (38) | 57.4  (54) | 45.5 (22) | 19.7 |
| Eastern European | 72.2 (18) | 70.7  (41) | 50.8  (61) | 36.8 (19) | 35.4 |
| Italian | 69.0 (42) | 38.3  (94) | 39.8 (118) | 26.5 (49) | 42.5 |
| Hispanic | 13.0 (23) | 21.4  (56) | 16.7  (24) | 28.6 (14) | −15.6 |

[a] The base for each rate is reported in parentheses.

[b] This column reports the difference between the latest generation or youngest age cohort and the earliest generation or oldest age cohort (formulas: latest-earliest; youngest-oldest).

English from this examination because their level of social assimilation was already so high in Table 1 that no further increases could reasonably be expected.

The Irish and Germans can be discussed together since their patterns of change in social assimilation are quite similar. While the extent of their social assimilation was great in Table 1, the trends in Table 2 and 3 point to even greater levels in the future. In these two groups, about two-thirds of those in later generations, the third and fourth, and over two-thirds of their youngest members, those 30 or under, have mixed ancestry. Except for third-generation Germans, over three-quarters of those from later generations and about three-quarters of their youngest members intermarry.

Turning to the new groups, it is evident from Tables 2 and 3 that their social assimilation is sharply increasing. Their later generations and younger members have large proportions of individuals with mixed ancestry, although the Italians lag behind the other groups in this respect. Their later generations and younger members also have large proportions of intermarried individuals. While third-generation Italians are somewhat below the third-generation members of other new groups in this respect as well, nearly seven out of every ten of the youngest Italians intermarry. Since the youngest age cohort shows the intermarriage rate current at the time the data were collected, it is clear that Italians were intermarrying then at a high rate.

The two remaining groups, the French and Hispanics, differ from the groups described above in that their social assimilation is neither extensive nor strongly increasing. There are not sufficient numbers of Hispanics in the third and fourth generations to make an accurate assessment of how their social assimilation varies by generations, but it appears that the French of later generations are substantially more socially assimilated than those of earlier generations. When we turn to age, however, we find weak and inconsistent patterns of change in social assimilation. If we again use the rate of intermarriage in the youngest age category as a measure of the current rate for each group, then these two groups show the weakest current rates among the groups in these data; only one-half of the youngest French and one of eight of the youngest Hispanics intermarry.

The observed persistence of the French and Hispanics in these data is corroborated by the findings of other researchers. In particular, Fishman and his colleagues (1966) found French-Canadians, Hispanics, and pre-War Germans to be distinctive in the extent to which their later generations retained use of the mother tongue. The distinctiveness of the first two is probably explained by their New World origins and their resulting proximity to a homeland (Abramson, 1973; Lieberson et al., 1975).

Despite the limited social assimilation of the French and Hispanics, these data show extensive and increasing social assimilation, as measured by ancestry and marriage, among American Catholic national-origin groups—groups whose membership is overwhelmingly composed of the descendants of 19th and 20th century immigrants (Jones, 1960). Contrary to Abramson's conclusions from these data, rates of mixed ancestry and intermarriage appear very high among the old groups, except for the French. They also appear to be increasing sharply among all the new groups. The Italians—whom Abramson (1973), Gallo (1974), and others have found to be socially unassimilated—were already intermarrying a decade ago, when these data were collected, at a rate near those of the socially assimilated groups.

Arguments could still be made to limit the conclusions drawn from the data presented so far. As noted earlier, it has been argued that ancestry and marriage are not measures of social assimilation because the intermarried or their children are absorbed by one of the ethnic communities in their backgrounds. In this argument, intermarriage is viewed as a "trade" between ethnic blocs and not as a breakdown of the boundaries between them. If it is correct, then the primary networks of the intermarried or those with mixed ancestry (or both) must be ethnically homogeneous beyond the diversity introduced by ancestry and marriage. While the Catholic Americans study does not contain detailed questions about the national backgrounds of others in the respondent's primary network, it does contain some limited questions which can be used to address this argument.

## ANCESTRY AND MARRIAGE IN RELATION TO
## SOCIAL ASSIMILATION GENERALLY

The relationship of ancestry and marriage to an individual's closeness to others of diverse backgrounds can be examined from a part of the questionnaire containing questions about the respondent's perceived social distance from a number of racial, religious, and nationality groups. The respondent was asked to check the closest relationship he has had to any member of each of a list of groups.[13] This list of possible relationships is (in order from most to least intimate): relative; best friend; close friend; friend; neighbor; coworker; knew in school; acquaintance; stranger or never met one. The list of racial and religious groups includes (in order and designated as on the questionnaire): Irish-American; Protestant; Italian-American; German-American; Jew; Scandinavian [sic]; Polish-American; Negro.

In tabulating the responses to these items, I have collapsed the original nine possible relationships into three: relative; close friend, corresponding to the questionnaire categories "best friend" and "close friend"; not close, containing all remaining questionnaire categories. In constructing these three new categories, I have, of course, emphasized relationships which are close and intimate.

Some respondents in these data are related to members of particular racial, religious and nationality categories by virtue of ancestry or marriage. Thus, a respondent of German ancestry or one married to someone of German ancestry is likely to respond that his closest relationship to a German-American is that of relative. This response is not related to ethnic diversity beyond the diversity created by the immediate facts of ancestry and marriage. Such responses have been removed from the table which follows.[14]

The likelihood that an individual is close to some member of any category is also affected by the factor of propinquity, by whether or not he lives near some concentration of that category's members. Clearly, an individual is unlikely to encounter a member of a group which is only sparsely represented in the area where he resides. Thus, to be certain that any relationship of ancestry and marriage to closeness to a member of some category does not merely reflect the vagaries of the regional and size-of-place distributions of that category's members, the tabulations for each category will be restricted to respondents who reside in a region and size-of-place where its members are concentrated. For example, the tabulation of closeness to Jews excludes any respondent who resides outside the largest metropolitan areas of the Middle Atlantic States, where Jews are heavily concentrated.[15]

Table 4 tabulates the respondent's closeness to each racial, religious, and nationality category by a variable which combines information about his ancestry and marriage. The three categories of this latter variable contain the in-married, intermarried, and the currently-married with hybrid ancestry, respectively; the third category is restricted to the currently-married to maintain consistency with the definitions of the first two. The column labeled "Diff." reports two differences for each tabulation. The upper differences compares the in-married and the intermarried in terms of the percentage who are not close to some member of the appropriate category. The lower difference makes the equivalent comparison for the in-married and the hybrid and married. In each case, a positive difference indicates that greater social assimilation in ancestry and marriage is linked to greater likelihood of closeness to a member of the category in question.

In an initial assessment, Table 4 suggests that ethnic diversity in ancestry and marriage is related to other kinds of ethnic diversity in the primary network. Generally, the in-married provide a clear contrast to the intermarried

TABLE 4

Respondent's Closeness to Others of Diverse Backgrounds
by His Ancestry and Marriage[a]

| RESPONDENT'S CLOSENESS TO: | IN- MARRIED | INTER- MARRIED | HYBRID AND MARRIED | DIFF.[b] | SIGNIF.[c] |
|---|---|---|---|---|---|
| **Negro:** | | | | | |
| Relative | 0.0 | 0.2 | 0.2 | | |
| Close friend | 4.3 | 4.3 | 3.9 | | |
| Not close | 95.7 | 95.5 | 95.9 | 0.2 | |
| | 100.0 | 100.0 | 100.0 | −0.2 | |
| | (563) | (625) | (458) | | |
| **Jew:** | | | | | |
| Relative | 4.8 | 7.0 | 2.9 | | |
| Close friend | 23.8 | 23.9 | 26.5 | | |
| Not close | 71.4 | 69.0 | 70.6 | 2.4 | |
| | 100.0 | 100.0 | 100.0 | 0.8 | |
| | (105) | (71) | (68) | | |
| **Protestant:** | | | | | |
| Relative | 12.6 | 20.2 | 27.8 | | |
| Close friend | 29.9 | 42.8 | 41.9 | | |
| Not close | 57.5 | 37.0 | 30.3 | 20.5 | p<.005 |
| | 100.0 | 100.0 | 100.0 | 27.2 | |
| | (525) | (484) | (284) | | |
| **Irish-American:** | | | | | |
| Relative | 22.2 | 22.2 | 31.7 | | |
| Close friend | 21.3 | 29.9 | 24.4 | | |
| Not close | 56.5 | 47.9 | 43.9 | 8.6 | |
| | 100.0 | 100.0 | 100.0 | 12.6 | |
| | (207) | (117) | (41) | | |
| **German-American:** | | | | | |
| Relative | 15.8 | 15.1 | 21.3 | | |
| Close friend | 11.8 | 20.0 | 17.2 | | |
| Not close | 72.4 | 64.9 | 61.5 | 7.5 | p<.05 |
| | 100.0 | 100.0 | 100.0 | 10.9 | |
| | (304) | (225) | (122) | | |
| **Scandinavian:** | | | | | |
| Relative | 11.1 | 26.7 | 9.5 | | |
| Close friend | 5.6 | 30.0 | 38.1 | | |
| Not close | 83.3 | 43.3 | 52.4 | 40.0 | p<.05 |
| | 100.0 | 100.0 | 100.0 | 30.9 | |
| | (18) | (30) | (21) | | |
| **Polish-American:** | | | | | |
| Relative | 13.1 | 19.9 | 17.2 | | |
| Close friend | 17.5 | 21.3 | 21.3 | | |
| Not close | 69.4 | 58.8 | 61.5 | 10.6 | |
| | 100.0 | 100.0 | 100.0 | 7.9 | |
| | (206) | (221) | (174) | | |

**TABLE 4**  (*Continued*)

| RESPONDENT'S CLOSENESS TO: | IN-MARRIED | INTER-MARRIED | HYBRID AND MARRIED | DIFF.[b] | SIGNIF.[c] |
|---|---|---|---|---|---|
| Italian-American: | | | | | |
| Relative | 11.8 | 18.6 | 25.0 | | |
| Close friend | 19.7 | 30.2 | 33.3 | | |
| Not close | 68.4 | 51.2 | 41.7 | 17.2 | p<.05 |
| | 100.0 | 100.0 | 100.0 | 26.7 | |
| | (76) | (86) | (96) | | |

[a] *Ns (given in parentheses) vary from subtable to subtable as a result of exclusions. Each subtable excludes those related to a member of the category in question by ancestry or marriage. Also excluded are those respondents who reside outside the regions and places of concentration of the members of that category.*

[b] *This column reports the differences in the percentages not close between the in-married and others. The upper number is the difference between the in-married and intermarried: (in-married)–(intermarried). The lower number is the difference between the in-married and the hybrid and married: (in-married)–(hybrid and married).*

[c] *This column reports the statistical significance of the entire subtable.*

and those with hybrid ancestry. Except in relation to two categories—blacks and Jews—the in-married are less likely to report a close relationship than are the intermarried and those with mixed ancestry. There is, however, little difference between the latter two. The greater distance of the in-married from each category is consistent with their likely membership in an ethnic community and their resulting immersion in ethnically homogeneous primary groups. Conversely, of course, the greater closeness of the intermarried and those with hybrid ancestry is consistent with their likely separation from ethnic communities and their greater exposure to a diversity of individuals.

The two categories which are exceptions to the general pattern are blacks and Jews. Greater closeness to these two categories is not linked to greater social assimilation in ancestry and marriage. Their distinctiveness is probably attributable to their general social distance from white American Catholics. The exclusion of blacks is more striking and less surprising. Virtually no one claims to have a black relative, and only about 5% of the sample claim any close relationship to a black; but very few sample members claim a Jewish relative either. For the remainder of this section, I will ignore these two categories and confine myself to the remaining ones, composed, of course, of white Christians.

For the remaining categories, the link between greater closeness to their members and greater social assimilation in ancestry and marriage possibly is attributable to two different kinds of exposure. The first is recorded in the line of each tabulation which reports the percentage who claim a relative from the category in question. These claimed kinships cannot be attributed to the ancestries of the respondents and their spouses, since those with such links have been eliminated from each tabulation. Hence, they can be attributed only to the actions of their other kin, who themselves marry individuals of different ethnic backgrounds, thereby further diversifying the respondents' primary groups. Despite this apparent passivity, these claimed kinships do indicate to some extent the diversity of an individual's milieu. If an individual is situated in an ethnically intermixed subsociety—for example, if he grew up in an ethnically integrated neighborhood and attended integrated schools—then it is likely that his other kin have the same background and that their marriages reflect the surrounding ethnic diversity. Nonetheless, this kind of exposure does not appear to explain much of the difference between the in-married and others in closeness to diverse groups. The differences in the percentages who claim a relative are generally small, and the intermarried and hybrid and married are not always more likely than the in-married to make such a claim.

The second kind of exposure is the obvious one. The individual encounters others of different ethnic backgrounds, and bonds of warm friendship grow with some. This kind of exposure, recorded in the percentages who claim close friendships, does explain part of the link betweeen greater social assimilation in ancestry and marriage and greater closeness to different groups. The in-married are less likely to report a close friendship to some member of each category than are the intermarried or the hybrid and married. Moreover, the true differences between the in-married and others are somewhat understated by the differences in Table 4. By the requirements of the questionnaire, anyone claiming a relative from some category cannot also claim a close friend from that category, since the relationship of "relative" is closer than that of "best friend" or "close friend." If we eliminate from each subtable all respondents who report a relative from the category in question, on the grounds that we cannot determine whether they also have a close friend from that group, the differences between the in-married and others generally would be enhanced.

Thus, those who are not in-married form more ethnically diverse friendships than do the in-married, but the exact causes of this greater diversity cannot be determined from these data. In all probability, those who are not in-married encounter by chance a greater variety of people from which to choose their friends. However, equally probable is that the in-married, like the West Enders who sought companionship among those who were "relatively compatible in terms of background, interests, and attitudes" (Gans, 1962:76), have a greater preference for those of similar ethnic backgrounds.

Before summarizing the relationship of Table 4 to the question which prompted this section, some difficulties of interpretation should be noted. Any inferences about the comparative diversity of the primary networks of individuals with different characteristics are indirect—from differences in their closeness to individuals from specific groups. Outside of ancestry and marriage, these data do not offer a direct measurement of the composition of the individual's primary network, collectable by questions such as: "What are the ethnic backgrounds of your best friends?" And indirect inferences from differences in closeness to specific groups are complicated by the varied nature of the groups involved. The magnitudes of the differences in Table 4, for example, appear to vary in accordance with the characteristics of each group: especially, its relative size in its region and place of concentration and thus the likelihood of a chance encounter with one of its members; and the salience of membership in the group and thus the likelihood that an encounter will be recognized. To the extent that the group is small or membership in it is not salient, differences in exposure or claimed exposure are reduced (Alba, 1974).

Nonetheless, the *consistency* of the differences in Table 4 between the in-married and others strongly supports the interpretation of ancestry and marriage as measures of social assimilation generally. For whatever reason, the intermarried and those with hybrid ancestry appear to have more ethnically diverse primary networks, in ways that cannot be explained by ancestry and marriage, than do the in-married. As an aside, it should be noted that this is true even in relation to Protestants, despite the oft-presumed impermeability of religious boundaries (Kennedy, 1944; 1952; Herberg, 1960; cf. Cohen, 1975). In conjunction with the findings of this section, the trends of ancestry and marriage in Tables 2 and 3 appear to herald great changes in the extent of ethnic integration at the primary level.

In conclusion, the intermarried and those with hybrid ancestry do not appear to be reabsorbed by ethnic communities. They do not participate in ethnically homogeneous networks, even when the diversity introduced by marriage and ancestry is discounted. The differences in Table 4 can be understood only by assuming that, whether by opportunity or choice, ethnicity is generally less important as a determinant of primary relationships for those who are socially assimilated in ancestry and marriage.

## CONCLUSION

Recent scholars of ethnicity correctly have objected to the vision of American society as a melting pot which quickly dissolves distinctive ethnic traits, pointing to the ethnic differentiation which remains a visible feature of the American social landscape. In so doing, they have posited an alternative model of ethnicity, "social pluralism," which proclaims the continued segregation of national-origin groups at the primary level.

The Catholic national-origin groups examined here are ones to which their alternative model should apply. These groups are overwhelmingly composed of the descendants of 19th and 20th century immigrants as well as members of a religious minority. Indeed, scholars such as Parenti (1967), Greeley (1971), Abramson (1973), and Gallo (1974) have claimed the applicability of the model to specific Catholic groups, if not most or all of them. Nonetheless, the picture conveyed by these data is one of extensive and increasing social assimilation, even as long ago as 1963 when they were collected, contradicting any assumption of universal ethnic vitality. The age of these data should not be used to vitiate findings from them. The trends of ancestry and marriage by age and generations guarantee a sustained period of increasing social assimilation, as the older cohorts in these data are replaced by their younger cohorts and early generations die off. Additionally, the increasing rates of intermarriage visible here guarantee long-term increases in the numbers of those with mixed ancestry.

This paper does not present an alternative theory of ethnicity and assimilation. It speaks only to common assumptions about the factual extent of social assimilation and the persistence of ethnic communities. I have already noted two exceptions—Hispanics and French-Canadians—to the general pattern among the groups here. Even looking at those groups where social assimilation is extensive or strongly increasing, there are differences in its rate which require explanation. The existence of these and other discrepancies testifies to our need for a general theory of ethnicity and assimilation. Such a theory will require two levels of analysis. At the group level, it must specify those group traits which explain differing group fates in American society. At the individual level, it must identify those characteristics of individuals which explain why in any group some assimilate more than others.

Moreover, the increasing social assimilation of the groups in these data does not mean that they are blending into an ethnically homogeneous mass, that ethnic differentiation will completely disappear. For one thing, social assimilation is not complete, even among those groups where it is extensive and increasing. For another, there are two exceptions to the general pattern here and, undoubtedly, there are others not represented in these data.

Finally, and very importantly, the analysis here does not indicate that even socially assimilated individuals should be considered as part of an ethnically homogeneous mass. The ethnic composition of one individual's primary network cannot be assumed as equal to that of every other, reflecting the mixture of ethnicities in a single integrated subsociety. At the least, this composition varies from place to place, reflecting the varying regional concentration of groups. It probably varies by the social characteristics of the individual as well, especially his social status (see Alba, 1974:107–18) and ethnicity, reflecting the probabilities that individuals with given characteristics will encounter each other, as well as share those traits which promote friendship (Lazarsfeld and Merton, 1954). Thus, ethnic differentiation may continue at the primary level in the sense that integration is greater within clusters of similarly situated groups than between them (see Gurak and Kritz, 1975).

Nevertheless, despite qualifications and additional questions, one conclusion stands firm: social assimilation has proceeded much further than many acknowledge. While reports of the death of ethnic communities were premature, contrary reports of their continued vitality are greatly exaggerated.

## NOTES

1  In this paper, as implied by its title, the term "ethnicity" refers only to national origins, not to religion or race.
2  It might be objected that Lieberson's study (1963) shows ethnic groups to be very segregated residentially and thus implies that a study of ethnic neighborhoods would be adequate to measure the characteristics of groups as a whole. However, the data from which he infers residential segregation have important limitations. Most important is that they are census data, in which nationality is not recorded for the native born of native-born parents, making identification of third and later generations impossible. In addition, the last year of his analysis is 1950, and it is reasonable to think that important changes have taken place since then.
3  I will use the terms "in-marriage" and "endogamous marriage" interchangeably as well as the terms "intermarriage" and "exogamous marriage."
4  Members of ethnic communities typically show great sensitivity to ethnicity as a social characteristic. Suttles (1968:10) gives the following revealing accounts:

As I acquired friends and informants, my own ethnicity became a serious problem. A few people worked over my genealogy trying to find some trace that would allot me to a known ethnic group. After close inquiry, one old Italian lady announced with peals of laughter, "Geraldo, you're just an American." She did not mean it as a compliment and afterwards I remember being depressed.

Child (1943) and Whyte (1955) give similar accounts.

5   The questions used to elicit information about the respondent's ethnicity are, "What is your main national background-on your father's side? On your mother's side?" Similar questions were used to elicit information about the ethnicity of the respondent's spouse.

6   However well I may have justified the classification of a respondent who does not know his spouse's ancestry as exogamously married, I have violated a usual convention of analysis and some assessment of the impact of this decision therefore is needed. Thirty marriages, or less than 2.5% of the total of endogamous and exogamous marriages, are affected by this decision. The analysis here therefore is not strongly affected by it.

7   The French in this sample are mostly French-Canadian. While their ultimate origins are in Western Europe, they are more recent in their arrival than other old groups and, in addition, suffer the burdens of minority status in another English-speaking society.

8   Abramson's rates are taken from his Table 9 (Abramson, 1973:53).

9   In attempting to understand the differences in Table 1, it should be noted that Abramson has made some sizable exclusions in calculating his rates. As noted earlier, the general effect of exclusions is to bias results in the direction of lower observed rates of mixed ancestry and intermarriage because those cases whose classification is questionable, even in the slightest, are generally found among the socially assimilated.

In defining the bases for his rates, Abramson chose to consider only respondents who were born Catholic, had only Catholic parents, and are presently married to a Catholic. When respondents married to non-Catholic spouses are excluded, for example, more interethnic marriages—i.e., marriages between individuals of different national backgrounds—than not are excluded. When the children of one or more non-Catholic parents are excluded, more individuals with mixed ancestry than not are excluded. The effect of these exclusions, then, is to limit the concepts of intermarriage and mixed ancestry and to lower their observed rates.

10   I have followed the usual conventions in defining generational groupings. The first generation contains the foreign born; the second contains those who are native born but have at least one foreign-born parent; the third contains the native born of native-born parents but one or more foreign-born grandparents (or who do not know how many of their grandparents were foreign born); the fourth contains the native born of native-born parents and grandparents.

11   Abramson also presents the age and generational variations of marriage, but not ancestry. His analysis, however, does not lead to an assessment of the trends of social assimilation.

12   Percentages based on ten or fewer cases are not reported.

13   More precisely, the interviewer says:

Here is a list of ways we might know different people. Which kind of person on that card is the *closest relationship* you have had with each of the following groups? (Hand respondent card G.) First, an Irish-American—what is the closest association you have had with an Irish-American?

The interviewer then reads the remainder of the list of ethnic groups.

14   In tabulating responses to any nationality category, I have eliminated any respondent who reports that his or his spouse's ancestry includes that nationality. In tabulating responses to any religious category, I have eliminated any respondent

who reports that his mother, father, or spouse belongs to that religion. Finally, in tabulating the responses to the one racial category (Negro), I have eliminated any respondent who reports that his or his spouse's ancestry includes some Other nationality (a category which I assume includes blacks; the questionnaire does not have a specific question about race).

15    The region and size-of-place concentrations were defined only for groups which represent small proportions of the whole population: the nationality groups and Jews. Any census region or size-of-place with more than 20% of a group was defined as part of its region and place of concentration. For Catholic groups, the regional and place distributions were taken from these data; for non-Catholic and partly-Catholic groups, some tabulations by Greeley (1974) were used. For a complete specification of the region and place of concentration of each group, see Alba (1974:304–6).

## REFERENCES

*Abramson, Harold J.*
1973   Ethnic Diversity in Catholic America. New York: Wiley
*Alba, Richard D.*
1974   Assimilation among American Catholics. Unpublished PhD. dissertation. Sociology Department, Columbia University.
1976   "Age and generations in the analysis of ethnic change." Paper presented at the meetings of the Eastern Sociological Society.
*Barnes, J. A.*
1969   "Networks and political process." Pp. 51–76 in J. Clyde Mitchell (ed.), Social Networks in Urban Situations. Manchester: Manchester University Press.
*Bott, Elizabeth*
1957   Family and Social Network. London: Tavistock.
*Breton, Raymond*
1964   "Institutional completeness of ethnic communities and the personal relations of immigrants." American Journal of Sociology 70:193–205.
*Child, Irwin L.*
1943   Italian or American? Second Generation in Conflict. New Haven: Yale University Press.
*Cohen, Steven M.*
1975   "Ethnic assimilation in the United States: Intergroup marriage and friendship." Unpublished paper. Queens College, City University of New York.
*Fishman, Joshua, Vladimir C. Nahirny, John E. Hofman, and Robert G. Hayden*
1966   Language Loyalty in the United States. The Hague: Mouton.
*Foner, Anne*
1974   "Age stratification and age conflict in political life." American Sociological Review 39:187–96.
*Gallo, Patrick J.*
1974   Ethnic Alienation: The Italian-Americans. Cranbury, N.J.: Fairleigh Dickinson University Press.
*Gambino, Richard*
1974   Blood of My Blood: The Dilemma of the Italian-Americans. New York: Doubleday.
*Gans, Herbert*
1962   The Urban Villagers. New York: Free Press.
*Glazer, Nathan, and Daniel P. Moynihan*
1970   Beyond the Melting Pot. 2nd ed. Cambridge, Mass.: M.I.T. Press

*Gordon, Milton M.*
1964   Assimilation in American Life. New York: Oxford University Press.
*Granovetter, Mark*
1973   "The strength of weak ties." American Journal of Sociology 78:1360–80.
*Greeley, Andrew M.*
1971   Why Can't They Be Like Us? New York: Dutton.
1972   "The new ethnicity & blue collars." Dissent. 19:270–7.
1974   Ethnicity in the United States: A Preliminary Reconnaissance. New York: Wiley.
*Greeley, Andrew M., and Peter Rossi*
1966   The Education of Catholic Americans. Chicago: Aldine.
*Gurak, Douglas, and Mary Kritz*
1975   "Ethnic intermarriage in the United States: Patterns of pluralism." Paper presented
       at the meetings of the American Sociological Association.
*Herberg, Will*
1960   Protestant-Catholic-Jew. Rev. ed. Garden City: Anchor.
*Jones, Maldwyn Allen*
1960   American Immigration. Chicago: University of Chicago Press.
*Kennedy, Ruby Jo Reeves*
1944   "Single or triple melting pot? Intermarriage trends in New Haven, 1870–1940."
       American Journal of Sociology 49:331–9.
1952   "Single or triple melting pot? Intermarriage in New Haven, 1870–1950." American
       Journal of Sociology 58:56–9.
*Laumann, Edward O.*
1973   Bonds of Pluralism. New York: Wiley.
*Lazarsfeld, Paul F., and Robert K. Merton*
1954   "Friendship as a social process." Pp. 18–66 in M. Berger, T. Abel, and C. H. Page
       (eds.), Freedom and Control in Modern Society. Princeton: Van Nostrand.
*Lieberson, Stanley*
1963   Ethnic Patterns in American Cities. New York: Free Press.
1973   "Generational differences among blacks in the North." American Journal of Sociol-
       ogy 79:550–65.
*Lieberson, Stanley, Guy Dalto and Mary Ellen Johnston*
1975   "The course of mother-tongue diversity in nations." American Journal of Sociology
       81:34–61.
*Mason, Karen Oppenheim, William M. Mason, H. H. Winsborough, and W. Kenneth
Poole*
1973   "Some methodological issues in cohort analysis of archival data." American Socio-
       logical Review 38:242–57.
*Newman, William M.*
1973   American Pluralism: A Study of Minority Groups and Social Theory. New York:
       Harper and Row.
*Novak, Michael*
1972   The Rise of the Unmeltable Ethnics. New York: Macmillan.
*Parenti, Michael*
1967   "Ethnic politics and the persistence of ethnic identification." American Political
       Science Review 61:717–26.
*Riley, Matilda White, Marilyn Johnson, and Anne Foner*
1972   Aging and Society. Vol. 3. New York: Russell Sage.
*Suttles, Gerald D.*
1968   The Social Order of the Slum. Chicago: University of Chicago Press.
*Whyte, William F.*
1955   Street Corner Society. Chicago: University of Chicago Press.

# False Assumptions About the Determinants of Mexican-American and Negro Economic Absorption*

## Lyle W. Shannon

Iowa Urban Community Research Center
and University of Iowa

*It generally is believed that with age and time in the urban industrial community, differences between rural-reared and urban-reared persons decline or disappear. This longitudinal study of 973 families (280 Mexican-Americans, 280 Negroes, and 413 Anglos) in Racine, Wisconsin, finds little significant change (1960–1971) in the relative position of Mexican-Americans and Negroes on occupational level, income, and level of living, even though controls for age, education, urban work experience, time in the community, and other pertinent variables are introduced. These findings suggest that the community is organized in such a way as to facilitate better the economic absorption of its Anglo in-migrants than Negroes from the South or Mexican-Americans from the Southwest, in spite of the fact that numerous programs were introduced in the United States during the 1960s, with the purpose of aiding the less fortunate in our society. Race/ethnicity remains the most powerful determinant of a family's position in the community.*

*Source:* Lyle W. Shannon, "False Assumptions About the Determinants of Mexican-American and Negro Economic Absorption," Sociological Quarterly 16, 1 (Winter 1975): pp. 3–15. Copyright © 1975 by the Midwest Sociological Society. Reprinted by permission of the Society, the editors of Sociological Quarterly, and the author.

## INTRODUCTION AND BACKGROUND

It generally is believed that with age and time in the urban industrial community, differences between rural-reared and urban-reared persons decline or disappear. That differences between immigrant Mexican-Americans and Negroes and their hosts (a not too receptive majority of Whites or Anglos) should as readily decline presupposes that the community is organized to welcome these immigrants into its bosom as willingly and as understandingly as it did the Anglo rural migrants.[1]

We shall examine a set of longitudinal data on Mexican-Americans and Negroes in Racine, Wisconsin,[2] in order to determine if they have become more like their Anglo hosts in terms of occupations, income, and level of living over a period of 11 years, and we shall utilize appropriate controls for age, urban work experience, education, and so on.

While the initial findings in this study of economic absorption and cultural integration (1959–1961)[3] were based on interviews with 280 Mexican-Americans, 280 Negroes, and 413 Anglos circa 1960, we now have interview data obtained in 1971 with 75 percent of the original respondents.[4] In addition to that, we have data on another 20 percent of the original respondents obtained from surviving spouses, children, or other sources.[5]

The comparisons presented have been made in two ways. First, the interrelationships obtained from the 973 respondents circa 1960 have been compared with the interrelationships obtained with those who were alive and from whom we secured data in 1971 (text leading up to and including Tables 1, 2, and 3). Second, various comparisons were made with a number of controls (Tables 4, 5, and 6) so that the relationships obtained in 1971 are compared with the relationships based only on those same persons from 1960.

## AGE AND TIME IN THE COMMUNITY
## AS DETERMINANTS OF ECONOMIC ABSORPTION

We have hypothesized that if the Mexican-American and Negro experience (the process of economic absorption) is similar to that of the White or Anglo, then differences between Mexican-Americans, Negroes, and Anglos should decline with continuing time in the community (Racine). Table 1 presents the data in its simplest form, first without controls for age of male head of household, and then with controls for his age. The variables included in this table were selected from an array of measures, with occupational level of male head of household,[6] total family income,[7] and the seven-item possessions scale[8] considered to be most representative.

Change was measured by determining what proportion of each race/ethnic group was at or above a given occupational, income, or possessions level. The proportion of Anglos at this level was considered to be parity or 100 percent. The proportion of Mexican-Americans or Negroes at or above a given level was divided by the proportion of Anglos at or above that level in order to determine at what percent of Anglo parity each of the other groups would be found each year.

TABLE 1

Tau Coefficients of Correlation for Race/Ethnicity and Occupational Level,
Family Income, and Possessions Scale, 1960 and 1971, With and Without
Controls for Age of Male Head of Household[a]

| | 1960* | 1971** | 1960***<br>−35 YEARS 35+ | | 1971<br>−45 YEARS 45+ | |
|---|---|---|---|---|---|---|
| Occupational level | .493 | .408 | .453 | .462 | .351 | .431 |
| Family income | .265 | .343 | .259 | .297 | .354 | .380 |
| Possessions scale | .300 | .140 | .190 | .227 | .040ns | .099 |

[a] *Race/ethnic variation was significant at the .001 level for all variables both years with the exception of the instance indicated by ns.*

*Mexican-Americans were lowest on occupational level and income, followed by Negroes, with Anglos highest in 1960. Negroes were lowest on the seven-item possessions scale followed by Mexican-Americans.*

**Negroes were lowest on income and possessions in 1971 and Anglos highest, while the occupational level ranking remained the same as in 1960.*

***Mexican-Americans were lowest on each measure, followed by Negroes, with Anglos highest with the exception of the possessions scale in 1960 and income and possessions for persons less than 45 years of age in 1971, where Negroes and Mexican-Americans reversed their order.*

The occupational level of Mexican-Americans rose (a percent of parity increase of 17 points from 55 to 72 percent of the proportion of Anglos at the operatives and above level, and 22 to 29 at the craftsmen, foremen, and above level) between 1960 and 1971, while Negroes remained in the same relative position (78–79 at the operatives and above level, 41 at the craftsmen, foremen, and above level). This convergence of percentages resulted in less occupational level difference between the three ethnic groups in 1971 than in 1960, as indicated by a decline in Kendall's Tau from .493 to .408. It should be noted that if all three race/ethnic occupational distributions were the same with a given cutting point, such as percentage at or above craftsmen and foremen, then Tau would be zero. As the occupational distribution of Anglos, Negroes, and Mexican-Americans becomes distinctly separated with little or no overlap, Tau approaches 1.00. With the dichotomized occupational data to which we have just referred, Tau cannot exceed .889 since some overlap is necessary unless every Anglo, for example, is at a higher occupational level than every Mexican-American or Negro, and in this case Tau still remains .889.

While the median income of Mexican-American families rose (a parity increase of 4 points from 75 to 79), the Negro median declined (from 88 to 78), thus resulting in more overall differences in 1971 than in 1960 and an increase in Tau from .265 to .343. Mexican-Americans had a median possessions score of 5.09 in 1960 and 5.40 in 1971 while Negroes had scores of 4.72 in 1960 and 5.39 in 1971. Anglos had a median of 5.54 in 1960 and 5.77 in 1971. The consequence was a decline in differences in level of living as measured by the possessions scale, represented by a decrease in Tau from .300 to .140. The overall results are mixed, two declines and one increase in Tau.

Migrants differ, on the average, in a variety of respects from their non-migrant counterparts and from those persons who comprise the majority of the host community. Age is a variable that has frequently been cited, with migrants being younger. Differences in the ages of males did exist, with the

Anglos some seven to eight years older than Negroes and Mexican-Americans in 1960 and among those surviving and interviewed in 1971 some five to six years older. The question of age differences between race/ethnic groups must therefore be dealt with if we are to eliminate it as an explanation of the differences in economic absorption that appear to be related to race/ethnicity.

In 1960 there was practically no within-group relationship between the measures of economic absorption and age, the highest correlation being only .143, and that not statistically significant. In 1971 there was a significant but not large age-related difference for total family income among Mexican-Americans (Tau—.221), with older Mexican-American male headed families having somewhat lower incomes. Although some decline in Taus may be expected, we would not expect the race/ethnic differences in economic absorption already noted in Table 1 to change markedly when age of male head of household is controlled. In the case of occupational level we note that the slight effect of age does result in a decline in the Taus for 1960 and in a decline in the Tau for those less than 45 years of age in 1971. The Taus for family income declined for the younger age category in 1960 but increased for the older age category in 1960 and for both age categories in 1971. Only in the case of possessions was the decline in Tau with controls for age sufficient to say that differences in the age distribution of Mexican-Americans and Negroes vs. Anglos had any sizeable effect on the findings. While some effect of age differences between race/ethnic categories remains within each age group, the fact that the age-controlled Taus remain fairly close to the magnitude of the uncontrolled Taus in 9 or 10 out of 12 cases markedly reduces any claim that might be made for age difference as a powerful determinant in our findings on the relationship of measures of economic absorption to race/ethnicity.

The fact that age-controlled Taus declined very little or increased for occupational level and income between 1960 and 1971 reduces any claim that economic absorption takes place with a mere 10 or 12 years of time in the community. Perhaps the 1960–1971 time period (12 years) for samples of persons who were already adults when the study began in 1959 measured a period too late in life for much change to have taken place in their positions in the world of work. We shall, therefore, select another control variable, one which encompasses a larger segment of the male's experience, and that is number of years of urban work experience, including those in Racine. Theoretically, race/ethnic correlations with measures of economic absorption should decline with increasing time in the community (1960–1971), particularly among younger males who were in the lowest years of the urban work experience category in 1960.

## AGE, TIME IN THE COMMUNITY, AND URBAN WORK EXPERIENCE AS DETERMINANTS OF ECONOMIC ABSORPTION

In 1960, years of urban work experience[9] had a Tau coefficient of correlation with race/ethnicity of .320. Those surviving from the 1960 sample on whom we obtained data in 1971 had a Tau coefficient of .313. Thus, race/ethnicity is more highly correlated with occupational level (.493 in 1960 and .408

in 1971) and income (.343 in 1971) than are years of urban work experience. While we cannot reject the hypothesis that differences in economic absorption are, in part, a function of years of urban work experience, the durability of race/ethnic variation is even more readily seen if we control for length of urban work experience by dichotomizing each group on a basis of whether or not male heads of household had less than 10 or more than 10 years of urban work experience in 1960, and less than 20 or more than 20 in 1971 (see Table 2). We continue to find substantial variation in each measure of economic absorption by race/ethnicity within either years of urban work experience category; all vary significantly at the .001 level with one exception. Although this simple control for years of urban work experience reduces the variation in measures of economic absorption by race/ethnicity in most categories, the race/ethnic relationship does not disappear. It becomes even more apparent that race/ethnic variation is persistent or increases with years of urban work experience and usually remains significant with continuing time in the community (1960 to 1971).

TABLE 2

Tau Coefficients of Correlation for Race/Ethnicity and Occupational Level,
Family Income, and Possessions Scale, 1960 and 1971, With and Without
Controls for Years of Urban Work Experience[a]

|  | *1960\** | *1971\*\** | *1960\*\*\**<br>*−10 YEARS 10+* | | *1971*<br>*−20 YEARS 20+* | |
|---|---|---|---|---|---|---|
| Occupational level | .493 | .408 | .395 | .401 | .328 | .386 |
| Family income | .265 | .343 | .231 | .336 | .350 | .349 |
| Possessions scale | .300 | .140 | .167 | .254 | .088ns | .113 |

[a] *Race/ethnic variation was significant at the .001 level for all variables both years with the exception of the instance indicated by ns.*
*\*Same race/ethnic rankings as in Table 1.*
*\*\*Same race/ethnic rankings as in Table 1.*
*\*\*\*Mexican-Americans were lowest on each measure, followed by Negroes, with Anglos highest with the exception of the possessions scale in 1960. Those Negroes and Mexican-Americans with less than 20 years of urban work experience in 1971 for occupational level and income reversed their order.*

This leads us to wonder to what extent (if we are to assess methodologically the importance of work experience) years of urban work experience were related to measures of economic absorption within each group, and whether the importance of this measure has changed between 1960 and 1971. In 1960, each of the measures of economic absorption was correlated with years of urban work experience for Mexican-Americans and Negroes ranging from .134 to .253 (Negro urban work experience and total family income), but never higher than .117 for Anglos (see Table 3). In 1971, none of the correlations exceeded .128, and in every case they were lower than the corresponding correlation for 1960 (now shown in Table 3). Although there is not much within-group variation in economic absorption based on differences in years of urban work experience, Mexican-Americans and Negroes did have consistently higher correlations between absorption measures and urban work experience than did Anglos, regardless of age.

When age of male head of household is controlled by dichotomizing each group at less than 35 or more than 35 years of age, the within-group correlations change, indicating, as would be expected, that there are age-influenced differences in the relationship of economic absorption to years of urban work experience within groups. What one immediately discerns, however, as shown in Table 3, is that the relationship between measures of economic absorption and years of urban work experience, with age of male head of household controlled, changes, but not in a simple and easily interpretable fashion.

Let us, therefore, examine the data, group by group. Older Mexican-Americans are in the high urban work experience category by a ratio of 2 to 1, while younger Mexican-Americans are in the low urban work experience category by a ratio of 3 to 2. In each case, the correlation between job level and work experience weighs heavily on the fact that those with less experience have low level jobs. Among older Mexican-Americans, those with the highest level jobs were in the longer urban work experience category by a ratio of 8 to 1. In the younger age category, however, where there is a statistically significant relationship, the important factor is that those with low level jobs had less urban work experience by a ratio of 2.5 to 1. Although neither correlation is high, the data do show clearly that while neither age nor urban work experience guarantees high level jobs for Mexican-American males, those older persons with higher level jobs are also persons with longer years of urban work experience. Among the younger persons, those with low level jobs are more likely to have had less urban work experience. Among older Negro males, those who have the best jobs are also more likely to be those with the most urban work experience, while among younger Negro males there is relatively little relationship between job level and experience.

Although there is no relationship between urban work experience and job level for older Anglos (older Anglos were in the highest experience category by a ratio of more than 10 to 1), it must be remembered that in both experience categories Anglos were skewed upward more than were Mexican-Americans and Negroes. While the correlations shown in Table 3 suggest that urban

TABLE 3

Tau Coefficients of Correlation for Years of Urban Work Experience (1960)
and Measures of Economic Absorption With and Without
Controls for Age of Male Head of Household

| | MEXICAN-AMERICAN | | | NEGRO | | | ANGLO | | |
|---|---|---|---|---|---|---|---|---|---|
| | TOTAL | −35 | 35+ | TOTAL | −35 | 35+ | TOTAL | −35 | 35+ |
| Occupational level | .201 | .265† | .188 | .143 | .126 | .247† | .028 | .181 | −.034 |
| Family income | .145 | .152 | .182 | .253† | .283° | .332° | .117 | .144 | −.019 |
| Possessions scale | .146 | .247† | .043 | .134 | .121 | .196 | .090* | .293° | .042 |

*Chi Square significant at .001 level.*
° *Chi Square significant at .01 level.*
† *Chi Square significant at .05 level.*

experience has more pay-off for Mexican-Americans and Negroes (within their limited range of occupations) than it has for Anglos, this supposedly greater pay-off is an artifact of the Anglo occupational distribution. Furthermore, and this must not be forgotten, the correlation of occupational level and race/ethnicity (Tau .493; males 35+, Tau .472; males –35, Tau .453) far exceeds that of any of the occupational level correlations that we have mentioned in this discussion, i.e., one's race/ethnicity is a more powerful determinant of job level than are age or urban industrial work experience.

Let us now turn to a discussion of total family income. In the case of Mexican-Americans, the relationship of income to years of urban work experience is lower than that obtained for occupational level, with older, high income males having more urban work experience, and younger, low income males having less urban work experience. Similarly, older, high income Negro males had more urban work experience, and younger, low income males had less urban work experience. Income was more highly correlated with work experience than was occupation for each Negro age group. And again, while there was no relationship between income and years of urban work experience for older Anglos (they were skewed toward high income, of course), it was clear that the younger Anglos' incomes tended to be more skewed toward higher levels than those of Mexican-Americans and Negroes, regardless of the amount of urban work experience.

We must continue to point out that only in the case of Negroes do the correlations just presented compare with the correlation of income and race/ethnicity (Tau .265; age 35+, Tau .297; age –35, Tau .259). Basically, race/ethnicity has had more influence on income than have other variables, but among Negroes, years of urban industrial work experience, particularly when controlled for age, seem to influence income considerably.

In the case of the seven-item possessions scale, it should be noted that Tau was .300 when this variable was correlated with race/ethnicity, was .277 for those 35 years of age or older, and was .190 for those less than 35 years of age. Among young Mexican-Americans and Anglos, the correlation of the possessions scale with years of urban work experience exceeded the appropriate age and race/ethnic correlations with which they were compared.

While there was practically no relationship between the possessions scale score and urban work experience for older Mexican-Americans, younger males with urban experience were more skewed toward the high end of the scale than were males without this experience. This was the case for older but not for younger Negroes. While older Anglos had high possessions scores, these were unrelated to urban work experience, in contrast to young Anglos for whom those urban work experience tend to have higher possessions scores than do their less experienced counterparts.

Be all of this as it may, we cannot yet conclude that years of urban industrial work experience have this limited influence on measures of economic absorption, and here we return to the original statement that differences between race/ethnic groups are expected to decline with continued time in the community.

## THE JOINT EFFECTS OF AGE, URBAN
## WORK EXPERIENCE, AND EDUCATION
## ON MALES' OCCUPATIONAL LEVEL
## RACE/ETHNIC DIFFERENCES

This suggests that the relationship of each of the measures of economic absorption to race/ethnicity should be examined with simultaneous controls for years of urban work experience and age of male head of household, and then with at least one further control that might be considered a determinant of level of economic absorption. The following three tables become, then, the most precise test of the hypothesis that differences in levels of economic absorption decline with time in the community.

The data on males' present occupational level are presented in Table 4. In order to make the comparison of relationships in 1960 and 1971 even more precise, we have included in the 1960 correlations only those males on whom we also obtained data in 1971.[10] Table 4 very clearly shows that while most age, education, and years of urban work experience categories do show a decline in race/ethnic variation in occupational level between 1960 and 1971, differences do persist, and in some categories more than in others.

The largest decline, and perhaps the only change of sufficient magnitude to mention, is that for younger workers who, by 1971, had been in the community at least 11 years but less than 20. In both 1960 and 1971 it should be noted, the smallest race/ethnic differences were among the younger workers, those

TABLE 4

Tau Coefficients of Correlation for Occupational Level
of Same Male Heads of Household in 1960 and 1971 and Race/Ethnicity
With Controls for Years of Urban Work Experience, Age, and Education[a]

| | | 1960 | | | | 1971 | |
|---|---|---|---|---|---|---|---|
| | | −10 YEARS | 10 YEARS OR + | | | −20 YEARS | 20 YEARS OR + |
| Age { | 35+ | .427* | .433* | Age { | 45+ | .455*‡ | .393* |
| | 35− | .385* | .340* | | 45− | .250°‡ | .312* |
| | | LESS THAN 9 YEARS OF EDUCATION | | | | | |
| Age { | 35+ | .200 | .325* | Age { | 45+ | .416†‡ | .266† |
| | 35− | .392° | .271† | | 45− | .081 | .155 |
| | | 9 YEARS OR MORE OF EDUCATION | | | | | |
| Age { | 35+ | .624° | .410*‡ | Age { | 45+ | .716° | .238° |
| | 35− | .246†‡ | .402* | | 45− | .363†‡ | .292°‡ |

[a] *In computing Tau all race/ethnic groups were ranked by occupational level with Mexican-Americans lowest and Anglos highest except in those marked with ‡.*

*Chi Square significant at .001 level.

° Chi Square significant at .01 level.

† Chi Square significant at .05 level.

‡ Rank Negro, Mexican-American, Anglo.

who entered the industrial order at a period when there were fewer barriers to equality and at a time when there was less demand for strictly unskilled labor.

When we examine the effect of age on the relationship of race/ethnicity to job level by 1971 within the same years of urban work experience category, we find that race/ethnic differences are definitely greatest for the older age category in comparison with the younger among those with the least urban work experience, and that these differences are least with age among those with the most urban work experience. In other words, although race/ethnic occupational level differences tend to decline with time, they definitely persist for older immigrant Mexican-Americans and Negroes who have had the least urban work experience and who, therefore, remain at the lowest occupational levels as the years go by. Both time dimensions have been against this older group while both time dimensions favored catching up for younger Mexican-Americans and Negroes.

Since education has been considered an important determinant of occupational level, we now examine its effect on these findings by running the same set of correlations with the samples divided into those with nine years of education or more, and those with less than nine years of education. Race/ethnic differences occurred in every group.[11] While race/ethnic occupational level differences declined in five out of eight categories by 1971, the fact remains that even with age, years of urban work experience, and education controlled, there were significant race/ethnic variations in occupational levels in every category in 1960 and in most categories by 1971.[12]

## THE JOINT EFFECT OF AGE, URBAN WORK EXPERIENCE, AND WIFE'S EMPLOYMENT ON FAMILY INCOME RACE/ETHNIC DIFFERENCES

The next set of correlations (Table 5) deals with total family income, a variable which should not be quite as clearly related to age of husband and years of urban work experience. Before wife's work status was introduced as a control, differences among older persons tended to be greatest for those with 10 or more years of urban work experience: among the more experienced, those who were 35 years of age or more differed the most; among younger persons, those with the least experience differed the most. When wife's employment status is utilized as a control, and those with working wives were considered, the correlations that were present in 1960 between race/ethnicity and total family income declined in three out of four age and urban work experience categories, but did remain significant in two categories. In families where the wife was not employed, race/ethnic differences in total family income remained, and were significant in three out of four categories.

**TABLE 5**

Tau Coefficients of Correlation for Total Family Income
of Same Male Heads of Household in 1960 and 1971 and Race/Ethnicity With
Controls For Years of Urban Work Experience, Age, and Employment Status of Wife[a]

| | | 1960 | | | | 1971 | |
| --- | --- | --- | --- | --- | --- | --- | --- |
| | | *–10 YEARS* | *10 YEARS OR +* | | | *–20 YEARS* | *20 YEARS OR +* |
| Age { | 35+ | .256† | .418* | Age { | 45+ | .170 | .372* |
| | 35– | .251† | .149 | | 45– | .410* | .296° |
| | | *WIFE EMPLOYED* | | | | | |
| Age { | 35+ | .387‡ | .490* | Age { | 45+ | .089‡ | .337° |
| | 35– | .186 | –.324 | | 45– | .368†‡ | .074 |
| | | *WIFE NOT EMPLOYED* | | | | | |
| Age { | 35+ | .435† | .429* | Age { | 45+ | .287 | .398* |
| | 35– | .285° | .324° | | 45– | .441°‡ | .429* |

[a] *In computing Tau all race/ethnic groups were ranked by occupational level with Mexican-Americans lowest and Anglos highest except in those marked with ‡.*

*\* Chi Square significant at .001 level.*

° *Chi Square significant at .01 level.*

† *Chi Square significant at .05 level.*

‡ *Rank Negro, Mexican-American, Anglo.*

## THE JOINT EFFECT OF AGE, URBAN WORK EXPERIENCE, AND CREDIT BUYING ON POSSESSIONS SCALE RACE/ETHNIC DIFFERENCES

The third set of correlations relates possessions to race/ethnicity with controls for age of male head of household and years of urban work experience (see Table 6). Race/ethnic differences are found in almost every age and years of urban work experience category, but when the samples are divided according to whether or not the family is purchasing household possessions or a car on credit, differences among those purchasing on credit in 1971 (except for older persons with 20 or more years of urban work experience) all but disappear. In other words, differences in all but one category disappear with time in the community. By contrast, among those not purchasing on credit, race/ethnic differences are greater in 1971 for both urban work experience categories among older persons, and continue for both categories of younger persons. Time in the community has increased differences among older persons, while it has decreased differences among younger persons. The essence of this set of correlations is that credit purchasing and continuing time in the community between 1960 and 1971 has tended to eliminate race/ethnic differences in level of living measured by our seven-item possessions scale (except for older persons with 20 or more years of urban work experience), while continuing time in the community (1960–1971) has not eliminated differences for those who are not purchasing on credit, and has even increased differences for older persons. To be even more explicit, the average correlation of possessions scale scores and race/ethnicity in 1960 of those purchasing on credit exceeds their average correlation in 1971, while the average correlation in 1960 of those not purchasing on credit is not much different from the average for 1971. Credit purchasing by Mexican-Americans and Negroes has reduced race/ethnic differences in level of living while similar differences have not been reduced among those who are not purchasing on credit.

## SUMMARY AND CONCLUSIONS

We have not discussed the nature of life in Racine for Mexican-Americans and Negroes because, from what we have seen, it is similar to that for race/ethnic minorities in other industrial communities in the North. While there may be differences for city size, Mueller's (1973) work indicates that one need not worry about the general applicability of mobility research to only the city in which it has been conducted. Grebler et al. (1970) have dealt with life in the barrio and countless others have described life in the ghetto. Most of this research, however, has been in communities of either the Southwest with sizeable barrios, or in Northern industrial communities with more distinctly demarcated ghettos, where communication and interaction with the larger community is decidedly more limited than in Racine. Whatever we have observed is probably generalizable to other Northern communities in which there is some concentration of Negroes and Mexican-Americans in two or three areas, but where there is no single large, almost completely self-sufficient ghetto or barrio from which the residents seldom depart.

TABLE 6

Tau Coefficients of Correlation for Possessions of
Same Male Heads of Household in 1960 and 1971 and Race/Ethnicity With
Controls for Years of Urban Work Experience, Age, and
Whether or Not Purchasing on Credit

| | | 1960 | | | | 1971 | |
|---|---|---|---|---|---|---|---|
| | | *–10 YEARS* | *10 YEARS OR +* | | | *–20 YEARS* | *20 YEARS OR +* |
| Age | 35+ | .211† | .215* | Age | 45+ | .289‡ | .128* |
| | 35– | .149‡ | .234* | | 45– | .141‡ | .042 |
| | | | *PURCHASING ON CREDIT* | | | | |
| Age | 35+ | .337 | .313*‡ | Age | 45+ | .033 | .333* |
| | 35– | .129 | .197‡ | | 45– | .049 | .038 |
| | | | *NOT PURCHASING ON CREDIT* | | | | |
| Age | 35+ | .263‡ | .153* | Age | 45+ | .525†‡ | .168* |
| | 35– | .190‡ | .368°‡ | | 45– | .136 | .255‡ |

*Chi Square significant at .001 level.*
° *Chi Square significant at .01 level.*
† *Chi Square significant at .05 level.*
‡ *Rank Negro, Mexican-American, Anglo.*

Controlling for age of male head of household, continuing time in the community, and years of urban work experience did not eliminate or systematically reduce race/ethnic variation in the three measures of economic absorption that we have considered. No within race/ethnic group correlations between age of male head of household or years of urban work experience and occupational level, family income, or the possessions scale exceeded race/ethnic variation in these measures, with the exception of years of urban work experience for Negroes and family income.

By controlling for age of male head of household and for education, we found that in 1971, males 45 years of age or over, with at least nine years of education and with less than 20 years of urban work experience, were more differentiated occupationally than were those in any other age and education category, indicating that Mexican-Americans and Negroes in this category were faring least well of all in comparison with their Anglo counterparts. But most interesting is the extent to which race/ethnic occupational variation persisted with continuing time in the community for persons with nine or more years of education, regardless of their age and urban work experience.

Race/ethnic family income differences decreased between 1960 and 1971 when only those male-headed households with working wives were considered (except for younger males with less than 20 years of urban work experience), but significant race/ethnic differences remained in two of the four categories. For those who did not have working wives, race/ethnic variation remained essentially the same, and was significant in three out of four categories.

Three of the four race/ethnic differences in possessions scores found in 1960 remained in 1971, but was reduced and significant in only one category (older residents with more than 20 years of urban work experience). On the other hand, it was found that race/ethnic differences in possessions scores declined with credit buying (except for older persons in the community 20 years or more), but that differences remained, particularly among older persons not buying on credit.

Since the question of completed vs. incomplete careers may be raised, a word should be said about this in conclusion. When we selected out all male heads of household who were 50 years of age or more in 1960—and on whom we obtained occupational data in 1971 for that year, at the time of their death, or until such time as we lost them—and dichotomized by years of urban work experience, we found that race/ethnic differences remained essentially the same. For those less than 50 years of age in 1960, differences declined, from a Tau of .427 to one of .252 for those who had less than 10 years of urban work experience in 1960, and from a Tau of .424 to one of .388 for those who had 10 or more years of urban work experience. These changes suggest that while the die was cast for older Mexican-American and Negro males, younger males have experienced the mobility that has taken place, particularly the Mexican-Americans. Our next step will be to select out these occupationally mobile Mexican-Americans in order to determine if they are differentiated from others with the same age, education, and urban work experience characteristics in any way that might serve to explain their mobility. On the other hand, they may, as I suspect, simply be the lucky ones who just happened along at the right time.

## NOTES

1    There has been an extensive literature on this subject but it should be noted that most studies have dealt with White or Anglo inmigrants in comparison with other Whites or Anglos who have always lived in the city. See Shannon (1961a and 1961b). The major research findings by sociologists and anthropologists on the assimilation and acculturation of migrants to cities have more recently been summarized by Shannon and Shannon (1967).

2    The Racine, Wisconsin, study of inmigrant labor was conducted from 1958 to 1965 with grants from the National Institutes of Health (Projects RG 5342, RG 9980, GM 10919, and CH 00042) and from the National Science Foundation. Since 1962 the project has been located at the University of Iowa. Our current restudy has been supported by NIH grants (MH 18196 and MH 18321) since 1970. The project has also been supported by the College of Liberal Arts, the Graduate College, and the Division of Extension and University Services at the University of Iowa.

3    These have been described in a variety of papers but are summarized in Shannon and Shannon (1973).

4    We have conceptualized the process of economic absorption and cultural integration in much the same manner as has Samuel N. Eisenstadt (1954). We realize, of course, that much of the literature has dealt with the processes of acculturation and assimilation, perhaps because that is what social scientists and others believe should happen to minority groups. For a review of this literature, see Broom et al. (1954), Spiro (1955), and Peterson and Scheff (1965). For an analysis of the literature on the problem with emphasis on 12 European countries see Beiner (1963).

5    Findings on economic absorption are reported in Shannon and McKim (1974).

6    The occupational level code categories, from high to low, are as follows: (1) professional, technical, managerial, proprietor; (2) clerical and sales; (3) craftsmen, foremen; (4) operatives; (5) maintenance and service; (6) private household labor; (7) industrial labor; and (8) farmer and agricultural labor. When age, education, and other controls were utilized, it was necessary to collapse these eight categories so as to have a fairly even distribution of the marginals and few low expected values for the cells in each table and subtable. In order to collapse the eight categories into three and to have a distribution of Mexican-Americans and Negroes that satisfied us, it was necessary to select cutting points which tended to result in concentration of the Anglos in the highest categories. The highest occupational level category consists of craftsmen, foremen, and above; the middle category is composed of operatives; and the lowest category is maintenance and service and below.

7    This is a figure for total family income computed from all sources of income mentioned in the interview. As with the occupational level codes, collapsing problems were encountered. Again, in order to best deal with the Mexican-Americans and Negroes, the three categories selected were: $0 to $4,999; $5,000 to $6,999; and $7,000 and above.

8    Data were collected on a variety of possessions indicative of level of living. The items contained in the seven-item scale include: refrigerator, television, washing machine, newspaper subscription, telephone, sewing machine, and 1957 or newer car (1968 or newer car in 1971). Adjacent scale scores were collapsed so that four instead of eight categories were utilized when several controls were involved. This scale had a coefficient of reproducibility in 1960 of .905 and in 1971 of .937.

9    Years of urban work experience includes years in Racine as well as those prior to Racine. The eight categories—(1) 0–5 years, (2) 6–9 years, (3) 10–14 years, (4) 15–19 years, and (5) 20 years or more—were collapsed to 10 years or more and less than 10 years when multiple controls were utilized in hypothesis testing.

10   When the correlations described in the following paragraphs were run on all 1960 male heads of household, essentially the same results were obtained.

11   While the highest correlation was for that group whose members had less than 10 years of urban work experience, were age 35 or more, and had nine years or more of education, there was only one Mexican-American in that category. Older and more educated immigrant Anglos were doing comparatively better than were their Negro peers.

12   It would seem that the greatest race/ethnic variation remained, and in fact increased, for those older workers with nine or more years of education who had the fewest years of urban work experience, but there was only one Mexican-American in this category. All of the Anglos were at the highest occupational level. Race/ethnic variation also increased for older workers with less than nine years of education in the fewest years of urban work experience category.

## REFERENCES

*Beiner, G.*
1963   Rural Migrants in Urban Setting. Netherlands Ministry of Social Work and the European Society for Rural Sociology. The Hague: Martinus Nijhoff.
*Broom, L., B. J. Siegel, E. Z. Vogt, and J. B. Watson*
1955   "Acculturation: An exploratory formulation." American Anthropologist 56 (December): 963–1002.
*Eisenstadt, Samuel N.*
1954   The Absorption of Migrants. London: Rutledge and Kegan Paul.
*Grebler, Leo, Joan W. Moore, and Ralph G. Guzman*
1970   The Mexican-American People. New York: The Free Press.
*Mueller, Charles W.*
1973   "City effects on socioeconomic achievements: The case of larger cities." The University of Wisconsin-Madison: Working Paper 73-17. Center for Demography and Ecology.
*Peterson, C. L., and T. J. Scheff*
1965   "Theory, method, and findings in the study of acculturation: A review." International Review of Community Development 13–14:155–176.
*Shannon, Lyle W.*
1961a   "Goals and values in agricultural policy and acceptable rates of change." Chapter 12 in Goals and Values in Agricultural Policy. Ames: Iowa State University Press.
1961b   "Occupational and residential adjustment of rural migrants." Chapter 11 in Labor Mobility and Population in Agriculture. Ames: Iowa State University Press.
*Shannon, Lyle W., and Magdaline W. Shannon*
1973   Minority Migrants in the Urban Community: Mexican-American and Negro Adjustment to Industrial Society. Beverly Hills: Sage Publications.
1967   "The assimilation of migrants to cities: Anthropological and sociological contributions." Chapter 12 in Leo Schnore and Joe Feagin (eds.), Urban Research and Policy Planning. Beverly Hills: Sage Publications.
*Shannon, L. W., and J. L. McKim*
1974   "Mexican-American, Negro, and Anglo improvement in labor force status between 1960 and 1970 in a midwestern community." Social Science Quarterly (June).
*Spiro, M.*
1955   "The acculturation of American ethnic groups." American Anthropologist 57 (December): 1240–1252.

# Racial Integration in a Transition Community [1]

## Harvey Molotch

*University of California, Santa Barbara*

*An attempt is made to record conditions under which various forms of racial integration occur in a changing community and the relationship between those conditions and the means by which members of the two races attempt to cope with the challenges of sharing biracial social environments. Racial headcounts are reported for various kinds of social settings and impressions are provided of the nature and differential consequences on blacks and whites of biracial interaction in such environments. Racial integration is found to be very limited in frequency and intensity, despite biracial propinquity. It is especially limited in those circumstances where interpersonal behavior is ordinarily informal, spontaneous, or intense. Transracial solidarity occurs only in circumstances in which cross-racial cues of similarity, reliability, and trust are strong relative to other opportunities for social solidarity.*

Although the in-migration of blacks into previously white areas generally leads to eventual all-black occupancy, thus continuing the pattern of residential racial segregation in U.S. cities (cf. Taeuber and Taeuber, 1965), it is possible that at least during the transition period, geographical propinquity may lead to some degree of racial integration. Three possible forms of integration may conceivably realize themselves during the transition process: (1) *demographic* integration, whereby a given setting contains both blacks and whites in some specified proportions; (2) *Biracial interaction,* whereby non-antagonistic social interaction is occurring between blacks and whites to some specifiable extent;

*Source:* Harvey Molotch, "Racial Integration in a Transition Community," American Sociological Review 34, 6 (December 1969): 878–93. Copyright © 1969 by the American Sociological Association. Reprinted by permission of the Association and the author.

(3) *Transracial solidarity,* defined as conditions in which whites and blacks interact freely and without constraint, and in a manner such that race ceases to function as an important source of social cleavage or as a criterion for friendship and primary group selection. This report describes the extent, form, and most common contexts of these various sorts of integration in one changing area on the South Shore. Utilizing the data gathered, an attempt will be made to explicate the more general processes at work which, in the context of black-white propinquity, inhibit or promote the cross-racial sharing of social life. (In another publication, the author has described the speed and ecological patterns of South Shore's transition. cf. Molotch, 1969).

## GENERAL STRATEGY

There have been many descriptions of communities striving for integra-tion, yet seldom do data on the subject of actual interracial contact go beyond the anecdotal level. Many community studies (cf. Johnson, 1965; Biddle and Biddle, 1965) cheerfully recount instances when whites and blacks serve on the same committee or come together in a constructive joint enterprise. Precise information is lacking which would indicate the frequency of such contacts, the contexts in which they most often appear, or the dynamics of their develop-ment. The absence of such information inhibits the development of a sound theory of cross-racial interaction and, at a more practical level, precludes rigor-ous comparative analysis or evaluation of various forms of intervention which have integration as their goal.

An attempt is thus made in the present study to depict objectively the extent and forms of integration in South Shore. Basic to the more mechanical means utilized to carry out this task was a two-year (July 1965–July 1967) participant observation study in the community—particularly of the area's major community organizations and its subsidiary committees and groups (cf. Molotch, 1967, 1968, 1969). Data of a more precise sort were gathered by taking simple head counts of the racial composition of various local settings—includ-ing schools, churches, recreation facilities, retail shops, and voluntary orga-nizations. In some instances, reports of organizational officers were utilized; in others, organizational group-photographs appearing in the local community newspaper or on bulletin boards were inspected. In most instances, however, actual visits were made to the setting and the numbers of whites and blacks present were recorded. The racial mix of such settings is taken as an important clue to the possible existence of other forms of integration as well.

## THE STUDY AREA

"South Shore" commonly denotes not only a specific aerial unit of the city of Chicago, but also a certain "community." That is, the phrase brings to the mind of Chicagoans, and especially those living in the South Side, an image of certain geographical boundaries, certain landscapes and landmarks and a certain life style. Both residents and non-residents utilize the concept "South Shore" as a means of identifying those living within its boundaries. The imagery has traditionally been one of middle-class living, lakeside recreation and well-kept lawns, homes, and buildings. South Shore has long been administratively utilized by local politicans, religious denominations, public and private civic agencies, and businesses in distributing services and in naming stores and branch offices. Persons indigenous to the area have used the term "South Shore" to name their own shops and organizations and to adopt as constituencies for such institutions those persons living within its boundaries.

That South Shore is an entity which continues to have an existence in the minds of local residents was documented by a series of informal interviews carried out by the writer on the major business arteries of the area (cf. Molotch, 1966, 1968, Chap. 2). Passersby were stopped and asked such questions as: "What area is this?" "What part of town is this?" The answer would almost always be South Shore, although additional probing would often reveal additional place names corresponding to the smaller scale elementary school districts which serve the region. Community boundaries were established by utilizing the answers to such questions as "How far does South Shore go?" or "Where does this area end?" Under varying conditions of context and an individual's purposes in reporting such information, the relevant unit of "community" might be smaller than South Shore (e.g. an elementary school district) or considerably larger (e.g. the South Side, or Chicago). For present purposes it is asserted that South Shore is one important source of community identification utilized by both local and non-local residents and that, in this sense, it is a meaningful unit of analysis. Further, the common recognition of the area and widespread tendency to self-identify oneself as a resident of "South Shore" is indicative of a common stake in the area, and thus a basis for the commonalty of interests and the "we feeling" which McKenzie (1923:344) held to be the defining attribute of community.

Approximately 80% of South Shore's 70,000 residents have come to live in basically sound apartment structures—generally of the walk-up variety, mostly constructed in the early 1930s.[2] In terms of the characteristics of its population, housing and geographic location, it is generally prototypical of racially changing communities in the United States (cf. Taeuber and Taeuber, 1965; Fishbein, 1962). Its residents were, at least when racial change began in 1960, Protestant, Catholic, and Jew in approximately equal proportions.[3] By the time the data for this study was gathered, South Shore's population was approximately one-third black, with blacks preponderant in the Northwestern portion of the area (contiguous to the previously existing ghetto), whites predominant in the southeastern region (adjoining the Chicago lake shore) and mixed occupancy in more central areas.

A strong community organization, the South Shore Commission was formed in anticipation of racial change and eventually came to subscribe explicitly to the goal of "stable racial integration" for the area. By the close of the study period, the Commission was widely cited for its success—success at organizational growth (a $90,000 annual budget and a paid staff of six), and success in the near-achievement of "stable racial integration" in the area. The city government, school authorities, and private welfare groups were all enthusiastic Commission supporters; both local and national media touted it for its "grass roots success" at "preserving" racial integration in the community.[4]

## ORDERED SEGMENTATION IN SOUTH SHORE

It needs to be noted that the inhibitions to integration in an area such as South Shore can not be properly understood by reliance upon such concepts as "prejudiced attitudes," "bigotry," or white "status anxiety," as these terms are ordinarily employed to "explain" interracial avoidance behavior. It is reasonable to anticipate that what Suttles (1968) refers to as "ordered segmentation" is natural to any community; thus, the fact that South Shore blacks differed from South Shore whites in terms of religion (few black Catholics, no Jews), ethnicity, economic status (blacks lower),[5] stage of life cycle (blacks younger with more children), and length of residency in the area would all act to deter many sorts of biracial contact. That is, racial distinctions coincided with other commonly utilized bases for social differentiation.

Urban settings have as their critical social characteristic the fact that intimate relationships between all parties are precluded by the sheer vastness of the numbers involved (cf. Wirth, 1938). Selection is thus necessary. In South Shore, as everywhere else in American society, people are "up tight" in the presence of people who are unknown, unproven, and thus, to them, undependable. The genuine psychic (and occasionally, physical) risks, which accompany encounters with strangers, lead local residents to develop certain techniques for "gaining associates, avoiding enemies and establishing each other's intentions" (Suttles, 1968:234). These techniques evolve in the search for cues which bespeak similarity, or existence of some other form of personal tie (e.g. mutual friendship, blood relationship) which would imply dependability and trustworthiness. Where such cues are not forthcoming, mutual avoidance behavior (or outright hostility) results.

In the case at hand not only authentic social and demographic differences exist between the black and white populations, taken as a whole, but there are also differences of a more subtle sort in virtually all black-white confrontations. A few examples may be cited. Whites and blacks in South Shore *sound* different; among whites, speech varies with length of residence in Chicago, family status background, and ethnicity. Blacks have an analogous internal pattern of speech differentiation—in addition to a common touch of Southern Negro dialect, not quite absent even among the most "middle-class" of Chicago-born blacks. Young blacks *walk* differently from young whites; many of the boys, especially, utilize a swagger which sets them apart from their white school mates (cf. Suttles, 1968; Finestone, 1957). Without carrying out a complete inventory of black and white habits and folkways, we know these differences exist, and that, whether they speak of them or not, both blacks and whites in South Shore were sensitive to them.

## PUBLIC PLACES AND PRIVATE BEHAVIOR

All of these distinctions, some obvious and some subtle, are more or less problematic for the persons involved, depending upon the public place in which whites and blacks happen to come together. "Public" places are defined, for the present discussion, as settings in which no *explicit* criteria exist for the exclusion of any person or group. Yet public places vary in the degree to which they tend to actually exclude certain types of persons or social groups. Given the inhibitions to random intimacy which exist in urban settings, public places can be viewed as exclusive in the degree to which they serve as arenas for the kinds of informal, intimate, and uninhibited sorts of behaviors ordinarily associated with informal peer group activity. In contrast, public places are inclusive in so far as they act as settings in which formalized roles are routinely attended to carefully by participants—places in which participants expect that they, as well as others, will guardedly attend to the performance of prescribed activity and behavior. Thus, public places may be differentiated according to the degree to which they serve as arenas for public as opposed to more "private" behavior.

## RETAIL STORES

An example of a relatively *public* place for *public* behavior is the local retail store. Such settings in South Shore are rather formal in that patrons arrive to purchase merchandise and then exit. Although various forms of informal activity occur, including chats between owners and customers, the usual undirected patter and diffuse banter evident in lower-class business settings (cf. Suttles, 1968) tend to be absent.

Yet despite the relatively formal nature of shopping in South Shore (relative both to shopping in other kinds of areas and to other South Shore public settings), it is indeed a social activity as well as a utilitarian one. Shopping is the social activity which most frequently takes adult residents out of their homes and into the community. An examination of racial compositions of shopping settings may, in addition to providing bench-mark data on the status of "demographic" integration in this important social setting, also indicate something of the extent to which a significant "opportunity context" exists for the promotion of other kinds of integration.

South Shore has two major internal shopping strips (71st and 79th Streets) both of which run east-west traversing black, mixed, and white residential areas. These streets are depicted in Figure 1 along with a portrayal of the approximate racial composition of the surrounding neighborhoods. Each of the shopping strips was visited during business hours of shopping days, and racial head counts were made for all street-level retail establishments (including restaurants and taverns) on both streets.[6]

Racial retail shopping patterns were found to generally coincide with racial residential patterns. That is, individual stores and business blocks surrounded by predominately black residents were patronized almost exclusively by blacks; those in white areas by whites; those in mixed areas by members of both races. Table 1 presents the results of headcounts taken of shopping blocks; Table 2 presents results of the same operation in terms of composition of individual stores.

If a setting is arbitrarily considered to be demographically integrated if at least 10% of its population consists of members of each race, then it can be said that the 71st Street area is integrated for its entire length and that 70% of its shops are integrated. However, 79th Street is generally segregated in its entire

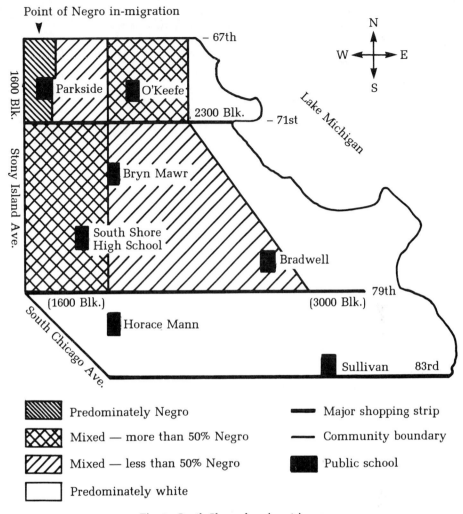

Point of Negro in-migration

— 67th

2300 Blk.    — 71st

1600 Blk.

Stony Island Ave.

Parkside

O'Keefe

Lake Michigan

N

W ← → E

S

Bryn Mawr

South Shore High School

Bradwell

79th

(1600 Blk.)    (3000 Blk.)

South Chicago Ave.

Horace Mann

Sullivan    83rd

▨ Predominately Negro

▧ Mixed — more than 50% Negro

▨ Mixed — less than 50% Negro

☐ Predominately white

▬ Major shopping strip

— Community boundary

■ Public school

Fig. 1  **South Shore shopping strips.**

length with only 22% of its shops integrated. The congruence of this pattern with the nature of the surrounding residential areas would indicate that the factor of distance outweighs other possible considerations (e.g. the desire for psychically "safe" shopping territory) in determining shopping patterns.

Certain interesting exceptions to this pattern are provided by those establishments which by their nature or traditional neighborhood usage render personal services and/or which serve as settings for informal, more intimate interaction. All barber and beauty shops, regardless of location, were segregated. Establishments catering to recreational and social needs were often segregated; three of seven restaurants on otherwise integrated 71st Street were serving only whites, whereas all six super markets on the same street were integrated. Perhaps consistent not only with its attraction for customers of a

TABLE 1

Racial Composition of South Shore Shopping Areas[a]

| STREET AND HUNDRED BLOCK[b] | NUMBER OF BLACK PATRONS IN SHOPS | NUMBER OF WHITE PATRONS IN SHOPS | TOTAL BOTH RACES | PERCENT OF ALL PATRONS WHITE |
|---|---|---|---|---|
| 71st Street | | | | |
| 1600, 1700 | 35 | 6 | 41 | 15 |
| 1800, 1900 | 67 | 36 | 103 | 35 |
| 2000, 2100 | 74 | 142 | 216 | 66 |
| 2200, 2300 | 19 | 148 | 167 | 89 |
| 79th Street | | | | |
| 1600, 1700 | 49 | 3 | 52 | 6 |
| 1800, 1900 | 33 | 40 | 73 | 55 |
| 2000, 2100 | 2 | 29 | 31 | 94 |
| 2200, 2300 | 5 | 36 | 41 | 88 |
| 2400, 2500 | 0 | 41 | 41 | 100 |
| 2600, 2700 | 8 | 211 | 219 | 96 |
| 2800, 2900 | 5 | 92 | 97 | 95 |
| 3000, . . . . | 1 | 93 | 94 | 99 |

[a] Based on a single visit, daytime weekday count, April, 1967.
[b] Each row represents two sides of two shopping blocks.

particular ethnicity, but also with its function as a social setting, the kosher butcher shop was the only food store which was not serving a biracial clientele.

## SATURDAY NIGHT RACIAL PATTERNS

This tendency toward greater segregation of social and recreational settings is confirmed by analogous data collected on a Saturday night during the same time period. Not only is it the case that Americans typically reserve Saturday night as a social, festive occasion, but that almost all activities which occur during those hours partake of a heightened air of sociability.[7] With many of the retail stores closed, but with bars and restaurants open and catering to large numbers of persons, both 71st and 79th Streets were more segregated at night than during the day.[8] Table 3 presents the results of a "head-count" made of business establishments open on a Saturday night.

The integrated types of settings on Saturday night included motion picture theaters (a leisure setting, ordinarily with minimal interaction), several restaurants, and those grocery stores and supermarkets keeping late hours. Yet even in the case of restaurants and groceries, there was a tendency toward increased segregation on Saturday night, compared to weekdays. South Shore's two bowling alleys, integrated by day, become all-black at night.

This tendency toward Saturday night segregation (including a significant increase in the numbers of blacks relative to whites on the streets) may be

**TABLE 2**
Racial Composition
of Individual Stores on Two
Shopping Strips. Daytime South Shore[a]

| SHOPPING STREET | NUMBER OF "WHITE" STORES[b] | NUMBER OF PERSONS IN "WHITE" STORES | NUMBER OF "BLACK" STORES[b] | NUMBER OF PERSONS IN "BLACK" STORES | NUMBER OF INTEGRATED STORES[b] | NUMBER OF PERSONS IN INTEGRATED STORES | PERCENT OF ALL STORES INTEGRATED | PERCENT OF ALL PERSONS INTEGRATED |
|---|---|---|---|---|---|---|---|---|
| 71st Street | 4 | 85 | 2 | 16 | 14 | 235 | 70 | 70 |
| 79th Street | 12 | 212 | 2 | 21 | 4 | 67 | 22 | 22 |

[a] Consideration was given only to shops serving 8 or more persons.
[b] Stores classified as "White" or "Black" were those in which at least 90% of persons on the premises were of the same race. "Integrated" stores were those in which fewer than 90% of persons on the premises were of the same race.

TABLE 3

Racial Composition of
South Shore Shopping Areas, Saturday Night[a]

| SHOPPING STREET | NUMBER OF "WHITE" STORES[b] | NUMBER OF PERSONS IN "WHITE" STORES | NUMBER OF "BLACK" STORES[b] | NUMBER OF PERSONS IN "BLACK" STORES | NUMBER OF INTEGRATED STORES[b] | NUMBER OF PERSONS IN INTEGRATED STORES | PERCENT OF ALL STORES INTEGRATED | PERCENT OF ALL PERSONS INTEGRATED |
|---|---|---|---|---|---|---|---|---|
| 71st Street | 4 | 120 | 10 | 300 | 10 | 141 | 42 | 34 |
| 79th Street | 14 | 359 | 7 | 272 | 2 | 19 | 9 | 3 |

[a]Consideration was given only to establishments observed to be serving 8 or more persons.

[b]Stores classified as "White" or "Black" were those in which at least 90% of persons on the premises were of the same race. "Integrated" stores were those in which fewer than 90% of persons on the premises were of the same race.

explained in various ways. It may be due to a white fear of being in a black setting at night when "crime in the streets" is a more salient concern. Or, whites may be simply experiencing different forms of recreation than blacks —forms which are only available outside of South Shore (e.g. in the Loop area). The increased segregation of non-recreation settings may simply reflect that these are the hours in which black housewives, more likely to be working during the day, are shopping for household goods. Such factors notwithstanding, the fact that South Shore's business district, integrated by day but segregated (and heavily black) at night, is consistent with the observation that intimate contexts tend to inhibit integration. It is reasonable to find that during the hours reserved for intimacy, segregation increases.

Special scrutiny of one sort of segregated leisure setting, the neighborhood tavern, can provide some insight into explaining the metamorphasis of places from white to black status. There was almost total racial segregation in taverns with, in certain places, *alternating* black and white establishments along a given block.[9] Tavern owners can themselves influence racial patterns by, in the words of one bartender-owner, "give them (blacks) the big hello." But the several tavern owners who were interviewed felt that although the owner can influence the racial process, he cannot determine it. A bar "just becomes colored" as blacks patronize it with increasing frequency. For white tavern patrons, it is simply a matter of "the colored took the place over" or "the colored forced everybody out." Such were the phrases used to explain again and again "what happened" to a particular establishment which once was frequented by whites but eventually became a black setting.

To make sense of this "explanation" of tavern change, it must be noted that of all public settings in South Shore, probably none was more private than the neighborhood tavern. That is, although the tavern is officially open to the public, it is in fact (at least in South Shore) an intimate setting frequented by a small and stable group of "regulars" who use the establishment as the very focal point of their social lives.[10] For the few middle-class taverns in South Shore (which also were segregated) this characterization is likely less accurate than for working class establishments. But even here, the tavern is a place where people "let their hair down," where back-stage and on-stage behavioral routines (cf. Goffman, 1959) tend to merge and thus where increased social vulnerability makes for anxiety in the presence of persons who fail to emit satisfactory signals of trustworthiness and forgiving acceptance of what may be transgressions of various normative codes. Thus blacks, who share mannerisms, clothing tastes, musical preferences, and other tavern-specific behavior habits at variance with white cultural counterparts are "outsiders" in the white environment. Their very presence can thus serve to inhibit the very kind of interactions for which the tavern is sought out by neighborhood whites; they can thus "take-over" an establishment by simply being in it.[11]

## OUTDOOR RECREATION

Parks are a day-time setting in which informal social activity is routine.[12] A headcount was made at South Shore's largest park ("Rainbow Beach"), which provides facilities (e.g. tennis, beach bathing, formal gardens, field houses) available nowhere else in South Shore. On a sunny Sunday in May 1967, only two of the several thousand persons at the park were black, and these were small children in the company of white adults. It should be noted that Rainbow Beach Park in 1962 was the scene of a nonviolent civil rights "wade-in," protesting the racial segregation of some of the city's beaches (including Rainbow). Ironically, this much publicized event and the accompanying acrimonious remarks by whites, may have served to dramatize Rainbow Beach's *de facto* status as a white public place, thus deterring blacks from risking the cost of a subsequent spontaneous visit. That Rainbow Beach was also a place where individuals routinely appear in abbreviated costume (bathing suits, tennis clothes, etc.), and thus routinely expose body areas ordinarily considered private, would act to increase anxieties stemming from interpersonal vulnerability.

Yet the special circumstances of Rainbow Beach was actually not significant since almost all of South Shore's parks were racially segregated—including those completely internal to the community and without any known history of "incidents." Seven smaller parks and playlots were inspected on the same warm Sunday; almost all were catering exclusively to small children with a few parents supervising. The only park catering to adult "passive recreation" (located on South Shore Drive at 68th Street) was occupied by 13 white adults and three white children, all of whom sat on benches, and one black child who sat with his dog on the grass at an opposite end of the small greensward.

South Shore's six remaining parks were all scenes of active recreation. In those parks located in segregated areas (either all black or all white), participation was limited to persons of the same race as the surrounding area. Thus at a soccer field at Phillips and 82nd, all game participants and spectators (approximately 200) were white; only black children were present at two playlots (one at Parkside School, 69th at East End, and one at O'Keeffe School, 69th at Merrill) located in predominately (although not exclusively) black areas.

One park located in a racially mixed residential area (69th at Oglesby) served only black children. The playlot at Bryn Mawr School (74th at Chappel), also located in a biracial residential area, was being utilized by approximately 50 black children and 40 white children. One ball game was in progress; all players were white. Of the various playgroups, only one—a dyad—was racially mixed, although the two playlots were serving equal numbers of white and black children.

Rosenblum Park, at 76th Street and Bennett, stands contiguous to both black and white residential areas. Seven ball games were in simultaneous progress at the time observations were made, all consisting of adolescent boys. Four games were all-black; two were all white; one was racially mixed. The two tot lots in the park are situated in diagonally opposite corners of the recreation area, with clear visibility from one to the other. The tot lot in the Northwest corner was being utilized by approximately 35 black children, one white child, and seven supervising black adult women. The tot lot in the Southwest corner of the park showed an opposite racial pattern; it was being utilized by 20 white children, one black child and four white supervisors. It is noteworthy that two such playlots in the same park situated at a distance of no more than 200 feet from one another should be almost completely racially segregated.

The lack of evidence of demographic integration leads to the suspicion that South Shore residents, when taking outdoor recreation as well as public indoor recreation, do not lead integrated social lives. Members of different races do not mingle once they arrive in parks. For children, some limited cross-racial contact seems to occur; for adults, there seems to be none whatsoever.

## SCHOOLS

Schools in a community are a crucial determinant of the social lives of children; they provide settings for intimate interaction and their attendance boundaries tend to circumscribe a child's opportunities for friendship formation (Roper, 1934). For some parents, schools are also a social setting (e.g., PTA, volunteer work), but because of parents' more numerous alternative sources of social interaction, and because of the relatively small proportion of their time spent in school contexts, the school is of much less social significance.

The racial composition of South Shore's public schools for 1963 through 1966 are presented in Table 4. As is common in transition areas in which attendance is based on the "neighborhood" principle, schools closest to the original point of Negro in-migration (the area's northwest corner) are most heavily black, with an increasing number of schools becoming predominately black over time. In 1966, two of the community's six elementary schools were demographically integrated (again, using the 10% convention). The South Shore High School and one of the three Catholic schools were also demographically integrated.[13]

TABLE 4

Racial Composition of South Shore Public Schools

1963, 1964, 1965, 1966

| | PROPORTION OF STUDENT BODY BLACK | | | |
| --- | --- | --- | --- | --- |
| SCHOOL | 1963 | 1964 | 1965 | 1966 |
| Parkside | 90.3 | 96.6 | 97.8 | 99.1 |
| O'Keeffe | 39.8 | 67.3 | 85.4 | 93.9 |
| Bryn Mawr | 16.3 | 37.2 | 55.2 | 66.1 |
| Mann | 7.0 | 26.6 | 43.0 | 55.1 |
| Bradwell | 0.1 | 0.2 | 0.7 | 3.7 |
| Sullivan | 0.0 | 0.0 | 0.0 | 2.3 |
| South Shore High[a] | 1.5 | 7.0 | 24.8 | 41.8 |

*Sources: 1963 data:* Chicago Sun-Times, *October 24, 1963; 1964, 1965 data:* Southeast Economist *(Chicago) October 17, 1965; 1966 data:* Southeast Economist *(Chicago) October 23, 1966.*

[a]*High school boundary zone was modified between 1964 and 1965 with the inclusion of Parkside and O'Keeffe and the exclusion of a larger all-black elementary school as "feeder" schools in the fall, 1965. The net effect of this change on the high school's racial composition was negligible.*

PTA meetings held in 1966 at the three integrated public schools (Mann, Bryn Mawr, and the high school) were attended by members of both races— as were PTA meetings at the predominately black O'Keeffe school, which drew an approximately equal number of whites and blacks to its meetings, although its student body was 74% black. In general, whites participated most in South Shore's school affairs, including in its biracial schools. In all schools in which any appreciable number of white children were enrolled, whites dominated the adult organizations. Thus all newly elected officers of the high school PTA were white despite the fact that over 42% of the school's student body were black at the time of the 1967 PTA Spring elections. In other biracial schools, as in almost all of South Shore's biracial settings, blacks were always under-represented in top leadership positions.

## RELIGIOUS INSTITUTIONS

South Shore's religious organizations provide settings which are a mix of formality and informality. During worship services individuals find them-selves in a situation whereby virtually every move of every participant, includ-ing gestures and signs of affect, is determined either by explicit ritual, tradition or local habit. It other types of church activity, such as funerals, weddings, bowling games, club meetings, etc., social interaction is more spontaneous, intense, and intimate.

It is thus not surprising to find that whatever integration existed in church organizations, existed primarily in terms of worship activity and not in terms of church para-religious social life. Four of South Shore's 16 Protestant churches hold integrated (again, by the 10% criterion) church services, one had an integrated *membership* list. Table 5 presents a detailed summary of the racial composition of South Shore's churches and church-related schools.[14]

Church life, outside of worship services, was virtually completely segre-gated and completely white. Two church membership screening committees had a black member (to help find the "good element," according to the white chairman); several churches had black Sunday school teachers and one church had two black women helping to establish a youth program. Of these "active" blacks (as was true of most black church members in South Shore), all were women.

In part, the near-total absence of blacks from church social life was a result of deliberate white exclusion. In one case, revealed with dismay by the pastor of the church involved (and subsequently confirmed by an interview with the "victim"), a black woman, upon invitation of the pastor's wife, joined a church bowling team which previously had only white members. The other bowlers' resultant demand that the woman be excluded were resisted by the clergyman. In consequence, the bowling team severed formal ties with the church. Rather than force such issues, thereby risking damage to church programs, most South Shore clergymen seemed to handle the inevitable role strain by insisting upon "welcoming" blacks to church services (thus fulfilling official denominational dictates as well as their own stated positions of "conscience") while permitting social activities to continue in a segregated fashion. This "compromise" can be

**TABLE 5**

**Racial Composition of South Shore's Christian Churches and Church-Related Schools**

| DENOMINATION OF CHURCH | NUMBER OF CHURCH MEMBERS (PARISHIONERS) | NUMBER OF BLACKS IN MEMBERSHIP | PERCENT OF MEMBERSHIP BLACK | NUMBER SUNDAY ATTENDERS | NUMBER BLACK SUNDAY ATTENDERS | PERCENT SUNDAY ATTENDERS BLACK | NUMBER ENROLLED IN SUNDAY SCHOOL | NUMBER OF BLACKS IN SUNDAY SCHOOL | PERCENT OF SUNDAY SCHOOL BLACK |
|---|---|---|---|---|---|---|---|---|---|
| Protestant: | | | | | | | | | |
| Community | 1,775 | 14 | 0.8% | 625 | 27 | 4.3% | 350 | 160 | 45.0% |
| Episcopal | 450 | 30 | 6.6% | 250 | 25 | 10.0% | 87 | 20 | 23.0% |
| Lutheran | 305 | 25 | 8.0% | 113 | 10 | 8.8% | 45 | 25 | 55.0% |
| Methodist | 650 | 25 | 3.8% | 200 | 30 | 15.0% | 390 | 250 | 64.0% |
| Methodist | 210 | 21 | 10.0% | 90 | 9 | 10.0% | 159 | 157 | 99.0% |
| Christian Science | 250 | 1 | 0.4% | 250 | 7 | 2.8% | 160 | 12 | 7.5% |
| Bible Church | 75 | 5 | 6.6% | 65 | 35 | 53.0% | 150 | 100 | 66.0% |
| Sub-Totals | 3,715 | 121 | 3.3% | 1,593 | 143 | 8.9% | 1,360 | 724 | 53.0% |
| Nine other Prot. churches | 2,285 | 0 | – | 994 | 0 | – | 140 | 0 | – |
| Prot. totals | 6,000 | 121 | 2.0% | 2,587 | 143 | 5.5% | 1,500 | 724 | 48.0% |
| Catholic:[a] | | | | | | | | | |
| (1) Catholic | 1,200[b] | 70[b] | 5.0% | 4,000 | 100 | 2.5% | 485 | 110 | 23.0% |
| (2) Catholic | 1,900[b] | 1[b] | 0.5% | 3,000 | 0 | – | 200 | 10 | 5.0% |
| (3) Catholic | 2,700[b] | 325[b] | 12.0% | 9,000 | 477 | 53.0% | 732 | 40 | 5.5% |
| Catholic totals | 5,800[b] | 396[b] | 6.8% | 16,000 | 577 | 3.6% | 1,417 | 160 | 11.0% |

[a]Catholic school data refer to day school enrollments, not Sunday school. Except for Church No. 3, attendance data based on actual head counts on a Sunday, Spring 1966.

[b]Refers to number of families, rather than individuals.

Other sources: Reports of clergymen to the writer and to E. Maynard Moore, III. (cf. Moore, 1966).

said to have "worked," given the formality and constrained behavior characteristic of the church service, in contrast to the very different nature of other
church-related activity.

Another important variation in church racial patterns, one strikingly revealed in Table 5, was the difference in the degree to which black children,
compared to black adults, were being served by South Shore churches. Eight
church Sunday schools were at least 10% black; in one case a church with only
10% black membership had a Sunday school which was 98% black. Fully 48%
of Protestant Sunday school attenders were black; 11% of those enrolled in
Catholic day schools were black.

This contrast between adult and child integration in church settings is
again suggestive of the significance of interpersonal vulnerability as a determinant of racial patterns. Parents (of both races) were willing to place their
children in racially mixed settings because such settings provided no psychic
difficulties for *them* (the parents). Children, perhaps having different criteria
for mutual identification and for establishing boundaries of community (e.g.,
sex, age, territory, athletic standing), were possibly less likely to find such
settings painful, although the segregation patterns at play, as well as evidence
presented by Suttles (1968, Chapters 9, 10), would suggest otherwise. In any
event, children are not as free as their parents to pick and choose their social
settings, regardless of the inconvenience or personal discomfort they might
experience.

An Exception: The Baptist Church. A fundamentalist Baptist church,
located in a predominately Negro area, stood apart from all other religious
institutions in South Shore in that equal numbers of whites and blacks attended
services; it was, in other respects as well, the most completely integrated of all
South Shore religious institutions.[15] It was also distinct in that worship services were a more basic part of the life of the church than in other denominations. Worship was a time of spontaneity and much animated social interaction.
Church members were working class and lower-middle class; it was the poorest
church in South Shore—poor in terms of the income of its worshippers,
and almost the poorest in terms of annual church budget. Among South
Shore clergy, its minister had the least familiarity with the "liberal" conventional wisdom concerning the role of the urban ministry, the "crisis in
the city," etc.—utterances which permeated interview responses from
most other area clergy. This fundamentalist minister was the only South
Shore clergyman to ever indicate a past history of "prejudice" toward
blacks.

That such conditions gave rise to the only case of trans-racial solidarity in a church context is perhaps surprising; for this reason the Baptist
church and several other such "deviant" cases will be discussed at length in
a later discussion. For the present, however, it should be noted that the
conditions of spontaneity and intimacy characteristic of fundamentalist
religion could lead *only* to one of two states: either complete racial exclusion
*or* complete racial integration with concomitant total acceptance. If blacks
were to be present at all, their presence would have to be unreservedly
accepted; otherwise, the resultant inhibitions would have destroyed the
nature of the religious experience and thus the very reason for the coming
together.

## VOLUNTARY ASSOCIATIONS

Many national charity and service organizations (e.g. Lions, American Legion, Veterans of Foreign Wars, B'nai B'rith) had chapters serving the South Shore area and all were exclusively white.[16] Of over 50 organizational group photographs published in the *Southeast Economist*[17] (the community newspaper serving the area), none which involved South Shore residents included blacks. The South Shore Country Club, the boards and officer corps of two local hospitals and of the Chamber of Commerce were also without black participants.

That charity and service groups, organizations which are generally based in friendship cliques, were not integrated is not surprising. That the governing bodies of major local institutions were also exclusively white can be taken to simply reflect a combination of similar social patterning of organizational participation linked with the positions of the two races in the American stratification system.

## THE SOUTH SHORE COMMISSION

The most prominent exception to the general pattern of black exclusion (or omission) from the ranks of important community groups was the South Shore Commission which, at least after 1964, was biracial in its leadership as well as in membership. Although blacks remained greatly under-represented in Commission leadership positions during the study period, several on the Board of Directors and one of six officers were black. Many of the Commission's subgroups were also biracial, including several committees and various block club organizations. But it is quite safe to say that since only a small proportion of South Shore's residents involved themselves in any block club or other Commission activity,[18] its effectiveness in creating biracial contacts was probably limited to a small leadership group in the community.

From its very inception, the Commission was not an informal social organization; as an association of Protestants, Catholics, and Jews, it had from the beginning brought together persons who were less than at complete ease in each other's presence. It continued to function primarily as an instrumental organization, and not as a setting for intimate socializing as blacks were brought into membership. Thus, the Commission provided a series of public meetings, outings, and fund-raising entertainments wherein public behavior was the accepted norm.

In the context of Commission activity, as in the case of other biracial voluntary organizations in South Shore, cross-racial interaction was more formal and guarded than were interactions (also quite formal) between members of the same race. Because of the uniqueness of biracial interaction in American society, blacks and whites were in the difficult situation of having to create *de novo* a formal mode for social interaction, giving the obvious and subtle differences between blacks and whites and the lack of mutual knowledge of what the other party might consider "appropriate" talking behavior. Thus there was a need to avoid the unknown transgressions which might occur if spontaneous behavior were to run its course. This was accomplished by both blacks and whites by resort to a zealous interpersonal courtesy (to ward off any conceivable slight or "misunderstanding"), unrelenting pleasantness, and a well-understood, tacit, mutual agreement to limit the subject of all conversation to small talk. Behavior was carefully guarded; words and expressions were selected with extraordinary care.

For blacks, this heightened self-consciousness generally resulted in deferential postures toward their white colleagues, and an ongoing monitoring of behavior to avoid any possible controversy which might set them in opposition to policies favored by any significant number of whites. Several substantive examples may be cited. The Commission was known by black members to be cooperating through its tenant referal service with landlords who refused to rent housing to non-whites. The actions entailed in such cooperation were probably illegal under the Chicago Fair Housing Ordinance and were a source of distress to black Commission members. Yet they preferred, in the words of one, not to "make a fuss" against a policy which they indicated (to the writer) they found obnoxious. Similarly, black Commission members assented to quota systems for maintaining whites in buildings and blocks which otherwise would have become predominately black. Again, there was public acquiescence in spite of privately held feelings that such policies were improper and also in violation of the Housing Ordinance.

That this effect of biracial interaction was most pronounced in the case of blacks, and not whites, is perhaps explicable in terms of another important feature of biracial interaction in South Shore: blacks and whites seldom come together as equals. This fact thus adds an additional dimension to the vulnerability of the "alien" persons who were not only in a numerical minority but, because of such status differences, were especially vulnerable to the sanctions of those who possessed so disproportionate an amount of wealth, power, and expertise.

These status differences were pervasive. In general, blacks moving into South Shore were of lower socioeconomic status than the whites they replaced.[19] The same status differentiation was reflected within organizational contexts such as the Commission. Thus, white males of the Commission's governing board were almost all proprietors, lawyers, physicians, and stock brokers, and black members were salesmen, school teachers, and low-level supervisors.

Furthermore, unlike white leaders, blacks did not find their way to the Board because of their state of personal wealth, power, or expertise, but instead because of their race and an acceptance of Commission goals. The Commission originally "took in" blacks in order to be more "representative" and to avoid being labeled "racist" or "bigoted," and blacks were thus largely interchangeable with any number of other blacks, with the consequence that their status vis-à-vis their white "colleagues" could only suffer. Several black members were viewed approvingly by whites as "real work horses" who made a "fine contribution," but none had the contacts with the political, religious, and business leaders of Chicago which were seen to be the really important determinants of South Shore's future. A good "work horse" may be hard to find, but a member of the Chicago School Board or the editor of a Chicago daily newspaper is impossible to replace. Such differences in the degree to which people are important to an organization's goals do not bode well for parity in interpersonal relationships.

The case of biracial interaction in the Commission would seem to provide an explanation for the findings generated by tests of the "contact hypothesis." A large body of literature suggests that more "favorable" white attitudes toward blacks results from biracial interaction in which whites and blacks share the same status, are in mutually dependent roles, and where contact is "intimate" rather than superficial.[20] These are precisely the conditions in which social vulnerability to alien and unknown individuals is minimized for members of both races. Where such conditions are not present, the contact hypothesis suggests that biracial interaction is expected to yield either no effects or an increased amount of "negative" white evaluation of blacks.

Indeed, these latter results were the consequences in such groups as the Commission. For whites, participation with blacks led to the observation that they (blacks) "aren't real leaders," or, in the words of one of the area's most liberal clergymen, they aren't "take charge people." The middle-class analogue of the "lazy colored boy" remained the dominant white stereotype. For blacks, interaction in such settings would seem to debilitate energies as whites come to be seen as the real makers of decisions and holders of power (cf. Piven and Cloward, 1967). The really crucial organizational skills which blacks observed were those involving the utilization of contacts (e.g. friends in high places) and resources (e.g., personal fortunes) which they neither possessed nor stood a very good chance of ever possessing.

## "MARGINAL GROUPS": INSTANCES OF TRANSRACIAL SOLIDARITY

In addition to the case of the Baptist church, of which mention has been previously made, there were three other contexts in South Shore which seemed to have provided settings in which transracial solidarity could be said to have been extant. These were "marginal" organizations—marginal in that meetings were held only on an irregular basis and in that they were organizations founded on premises of dissent and protest which limited their appeal to only a small number of participants. One such group was a local branch of Veterans for Peace in Vietnam, an organization with leftist political orientations (including several persons of militant Marxist ideology) which held occasional meetings above a South Shore store during the study period. Another group was the O'Keeffe Area Council—technically a part of the South Shore Commission but with an active leadership which, because of its rather "pro-Negro," anti-"establishment" orientation, was often independent of the Commission in spirit and in action.

Finally, there was the South Shore Organization for Human Rights, a group active in fostering open occupancy and other civil rights goals in South Shore and metropolitan Chicago. This group was indigenous to South Shore, having been stimulated by a young clergyman during his rather brief association with a South Shore Protestant church. Like Veterans for Peace and the O'Keeffe Area Council, its active membership consisted of only a handful of persons, but, unlike the other groups, it carried out independent programs such as "testing" the racial practices of local real estate firms, as well as the racial policies of a tenant referral service managed by the South Shore Commission.

These three organizations differed from other South Shore institutions not only in terms of their militancy and marginality, but also in terms of the "tone" of biracial interactions shared by members. In all of these contexts, as in the case of the Baptist Church, interaction across racial lines seemed to come easily; interaction was unstilted, informal, and direct. Except possibly for the Veterans for Peace, these were all informal social organizations, with blacks and whites living out shared social as well as shared institutional lives. Race ceased to operate as a source of cleavage or determinant of institutional roles.

In other respects, these groups were quite diverse. The Baptist Church was largely working-class with many recent migrants from the South and Appalachia. The O'Keeffe Council consisted of young well-educated professionals; to a lesser extent, the same was true of the Organization for Human Rights. Veterans for Peace was an extremely diverse group of blue collar workers, small businessmen, and a few professionals. Congregators of the Bible Church were apolitical, religious fundamentalists; members of the other groups were identified with secular, left-leaning ideologies.[21]

Yet there were certain important similarities. Within each of these groups, race and status differences were not correlated; businessmen or professionals within each were as likely to be black as white.[22] In addition, these groups were alike in that members were in an alien environment. The church was surrounded by more solid, richer congregations: Veterans for Peace, the Organization for Human Rights, and the O'Keeffe Council existed in the shadow of the powerful South Shore Commission and other "moderate" or conservative institutions which supported Chicago's and the nation's on-going political arrangements. The various deviant traits of these groups' members thus created a situation in which organizational alternatives within the South Shore area were lacking. The result may have been an organizational commitment of sufficient strength to overcome any inhibitions which racial differences might have created. Finally, members of these groups were similar in that most were either new to the South Shore area, or, because of their youth, new to South Shore organizational life. A lack of previous ties to existing structures may thus similarly facilitate commitments to organizations which, in that they are biracial, operate with new kinds of *modus vivendi*.

## SUMMARY

Although South Shore's total racial composition provided initial evidence of some forms of racial integration in the area, social life is essentially segregated. The nature of the contexts in which varying forms of integration are found suggests that fear of exposure and mutual suspiciousness between members of the two races inhibit biracial sharing of public places which serve as loci of private behavior. Thus some degree of demographic integration and a slight amount of biracial interaction can occur in public places in which public behavior traditionally ensues. That is, extensive integration (primarily by demographic indices) occurs in places such as retail shops, church chapels, and formal organizations oriented toward the accomplishment of instrumental goals. In such settings, social interaction across racial lines is not reflective of transracial solidarity. Nor can the results of such interaction be assumed to promote eventual solidarity, given the problematic power disparities which are general concomitants of such black-white interaction. Presumably because of the greater psychic and practical dilemmas it would create, integration of any sort is absent from informal settings such as church socials, service clubs, taverns, Saturday night bowling and parks.

Women, because they are more local in their activity and interests, are more likely than men to find themselves in biracial circumstances. Protestants are more likely than are Catholics or Jews, and children—perhaps because they are less free to vary their milieu according to preference—to have the most experience of biracial contact.

Although there are some communalities in the problems which both blacks and whites face under conditions of biracial propinquity and contact, the consequences on the two groups are not identical. In South Shore, as in the rest of the society, the integration "experiment" opens with the most important and useful institutions, organizations, and settings as white, and the "challengers" or "invaders" as black. *The circumstances are thus not parallel.* The widely shared community conceptions so generated of "intruders" versus "preservers," applied to blacks and whites respectively, provide still another distinction consistent with the status and power disparities widely observed to exist between blacks and whites. Not only is the development of transracial solidarity made more difficult as a result, but, in addition, the psychic difficulties which blacks must face when entering the alien white context is further intensified.[23] That is, biracial interaction challenges members of both races to overcome certain fears of the dissimilar, the unproven, and the threatening. But for blacks, there is the added problem of knowing that in presenting oneself in a biracial setting, one is challenging and "pushing" to gain something otherwise unavailable. The modal black response would seem to be either a show of hostility (as in some manifestations of the current phase of the civil rights movement) or, as was common in South Shore, a show of deference and total capitulation to white preferences.

Integration of a thoroughgoing type, what has been termed "transracial solidarity," occurred in South Shore in only a few settings. These were instances in which there were cross-racial communalities of a shared and deviant ideology (mutual recognition of which provided bases for the development of needed social alternatives); an equality in occupational status and organizational usefulness (thus providing cross-racial parity in interpersonal vulnerability); and, among both blacks and whites, a lack of previously constituted local organizational ties (thus precluding habit and/or social pressures from inhibiting affiliation with groups which have integration as one of their innovative features).

All settings observed in South Shore (an attempt was made to be exhaustive) which share these characteristics were found to approximate the circumstances of transracial solidarity; no other instances of this form of integration was found. If other possible contingencies to racial integration are to be uncovered, or if those observed in South Shore are to be confirmed as determinant (either singly, or in some "value-added," combination), additional case studies and eventual comparative analysis will be necessary. But for the present; it is well to note that the conditions cited as concomitants of transracial solidarity in South Shore are precisely those which are likely to provide the overarching cues of similarity, reliability, and trust which would seem requisite for the building and maintenance of racially integrated associations, institutions, and community.

## NOTES

1   The author wishes to thank Tamotsu Shibutani and J. Michael Ross for helpful comments on an earlier draft of this manuscript and John Dyckman for his assistance in carrying out observations. Financial support was provided by a grant from the Bowman C. Lingle Foundation to the Center for Urban Studies, University of Chicago, and by a Faculty Research Fellowship, University of California, Santa Barbara.

2   Data are based on 1960 census reports as contained in Kitagawa and Taeuber (1963). (South Shore is taken to constitute census tracts 635 through 644 and the northerly portion [above 83rd Street] of tracts 662 through 665).

3   Impressionistic estimates based on reports of local clergymen.

4   See, for example: "Self-Help Pays Off in South Chicago," *Christian Science Monitor,* (Boston), July 21, 1967; "The South Shore Plan," *Chicago Sun Times,* April 14, 1967.

5   Changes in South Shore's welfare case loads, crime rates, etc. provide some evidence documenting this point (see Molotch, 1968). Although differences in net income between black and white family units is generally small (or nonexistent) in changing areas, the fact that black households are more likely to have multiple breadwinners and that black males are more likely to hold blue-collar jobs, are differences indicative of real status differences. (See Taeuber and Taeuber, 1965, Chaps. 7, 8).

6   For some types of establishments, such as beauty shops, there was no way to make a complete count unobtrusively; in such instances, only those patrons visible through plate glass windows were counted. Employees, detectable by uniforms, positions behind counters, or general demeanor, were excluded from the counts.

7   It is for this reason that for persons excluded from social activity on Saturday night, these hours are, as the lyrics of the popular song imply, "the loneliest night of the week."

8   For example, the 71st Street daytime count included only one segregated bar whereas the night count included six segregated bars. Given the fact that many retail shops are closed at night, the prevalence of open bars has the consequence of dramatically increasing the *proportion* of establishments which are segregated as well as the absolute number of segregated establishments.

9   Except for one bar which was observed as having one black patron and nine white patrons, all 21 South Shore taverns were completely segregated on Saturday night.

10   Gans (1962) has confirmed that this pattern is also the case for Italian-American working class males.

11   The same phenomenon can be observed in the case of houseguests' "taking over" a home by simply being in it for a period longer than that desired by the hosts. Guests, who often can not "understand" if confronted with such an accusation, can avoid the problem by either "becoming just like a member of the family" (i.e. host accepts guest as an intimate) or by devising schemes whereby extensive absences from the scene can be gracefully arranged.

12   The situation is not strictly comparable to taverns, however, in that the relative expansiveness of space may permit a greater degree of insularity to an intimate gathering.

13   Unfortunately, no intensive observations were made of student life within schools.

14   Interviews with local clergy were carried out during the Summer of 1965 and Spring of 1966. The author personally interviewed 12 clergymen; additional interview material was provided by E. Maynard Moore III, who based part of his interview schedule upon that of the author's, thus generating a total of 23 comparable cases. Respondents interviewed by both investigators generally gave identical responses to the two researchers. (Cf. Moore, 1966).

15   The divergence in this church between the number of Negro *attenders* and number of black *members* (as indicated by data in Table 5) was due to the fact that a "personal revelation" was a requisite for formal membership; many blacks were thus in the situation of having formal induction pending such a revelation.

16   The author has been advised that a tutoring center at the South Shore YMCA was being operated during the study period on a racially integrated basis. Pressures of time did not permit a first-hand investigation of this program.

17   *The Southeast Economist* serves South Shore as well as a much larger region of the South Side as a "community newspaper." An organization was considered to be located in South Shore if at least half of all addresses of those photographed were within the study area.

18   The Commission's "grass roots" were actually rather shallow. It is likely that there were no more than 12 block clubs operating during the study period, although statements printed about South Shore in national and local media implied there were many more. (Cf. Molotch, 1968:71).

19   See note 5.

20   Various studies have yielded somewhat conflicting evidence on the validity of the "contact hypothesis." Three classic studies which indicate a positive relationship between "improvement" in white attitudes toward blacks with increasing contact are Deutsch and Collins (1951); Starr *et al.* (1949); and Merton *et al.* (1949). Three reports providing evidence for the opposite conclusion are Allport and Kramer (1946); Kramer (1950); and Winder (1952). A synthesis of these mixed findings, one which is consistent with the criteria for effective positive attitude change is specified in the above test, appears in Wilner *et al.* (1955).

21   These findings are consistent with other studies which have uncovered the extremely diverse conditions under which racial integration occurs and the seeming irrelevance of "prejudice" or racial "attitude" in determing when and where integration exists. Grier and Grier (1960) found integrated housing developments to be heterogeneous in terms of the income, education, ethnicity, stage of life cycle, and geographical origin of residents. Supporting findings are also reported in Rapkin and Grigsby, 1960, and Mayer, 1960.

22   Membership status of the Baptist church was relatively homogenous. Veterans for Peace was led by a well-to-do black funeral director and several of his black business colleagues, whereas whites included in their ranks (along with a few professionals) a TV repairman and a sign painter. The O'Keeffe Council included in its top leadership cadre a black businessman and a black lawyer along with a white businessman and a white engineer. The Organization for Human Rights was dominated by a white clergyman and a group of black and white women who were either white collar workers or had middle-class husbands.

23   Levy (1968) provides a description of an instance (whites in the southern civil rights movement) in which the tables are turned, that is, where biracial interaction occurs in a black dominated context (with analogous intensification of difficulties for *whites*).

## REFERENCES

*Allport, Gordon, and Bernard Kramer*
1946   "Some roots of prejudice." Journal of Psychology 21 (Fall): 9–39.
*Biddle, William, and Loureide Biddle*
1965   The Community Development Process: The Rediscovery of Local Initiative. New York: Holt, Rinehart and Winston.
*Deutsch, Morton and Mary Collins*
1951   Interracial Housing: A Psychological Evaluation of a Social Experiment. Minneapolis: University of Minnesota Press.
*Finestone, Harold*
1957   "Cats, kicks and color." Social Problems 5 (July): 3–13.
*Fishbein, Annette*
1962   The Expansion of Negro Residential Areas in Chicago. Unpublished Master's dissertation, Department of Sociology, University of Chicago.
*Gans, Herbert*
1962   The Urban Villagers. New York: The Free Press.
*Goffman, Erving*
1959   The Presentation of Self in Everyday Life. New York: Doubleday.
*Grier, George, and Eunice Grier*
1960   Privately Developed Interracial Housing. An Analysis of Experience. Berkeley: University of California Press.
*Johnson, Philip A.*
1965   Call me Neighbor, Call me Friend. New York: Doubleday.
*Kitagawa: Evelyn and Karl Taeuber (eds.)*
1963   Local Community Fact Book: Chicago Metropolitan Area, 1960. Chicago: Chicago Community Inventory, University of Chicago.
*Kramer, Bernard M.*
1950   Residential Contact as a Determinant of Attitudes Toward Negroes. Unpublished Ph.D. dissertation. Department of Social Relations, Harvard University.
*Levy, Charles J.*
1968   Voluntary Servitude: Whites in the Negro Movement. New York: Appleton-Century-Crofts.
*McKenzie, Roderick O.*
1923   The Neighborhood: A Study of Local Life in the City of Columbus, Ohio. Chicago: University of Chicago Press.
*Mayer, Albert J.*
1960   "Russel Woods: Change without conflict: A case study of neighborhood racial transition in Detroit." In Nathan Glazer and Davis McEntire (eds.), Studies in Housing and Minority Groups. Berkeley: University of California Press.
*Merton, Robert, et al.*
1949   "Social facts and social fictions: The dynamics of race relations in Milltown" New York: Columbia University Bureau of Applied Social Research.
*Molotch, Harvey*
1966   "Urban community boundaries: A case study" Working Paper No. 60, Center for Social Organization Studies, University of Chicago, multilith.
1967   "Toward a more human human ecology: An urban research strategy" *Land Economics* 43:3 (August): 336–341.
1968   Community Action to Control Racial Change. Unpublished Ph.D. dissertation, Department of Sociology, University of Chicago.
1969   "Racial change in a stable community." American Journal of Sociology 75 (forthcoming).

*Moore, E. Maynard, III*
1966   The Church and Racial Change in South Shore. Unpublished paper, The Divinity School, University of Chicago.
*Piven, Francis Fox, and Richard Cloward*
1967   "The case against racial integration." Social Work 12 (January): 12–21.
*Rapkin, Chester, and William Grigsby*
1960   The Demand for Housing in Racially Mixed Areas. Berkeley: University of California Press.
*Roper, Marion*
1934   The City and the Primary Group. Unpublished Ph.D. dissertation, Department of Sociology, University of Chicago.
*Star, Shirley, Robin M. Williams, Jr., and Samuel A. Stouffer*
1949   "Negro Soldiers" in Samuel Stouffer et al., The American Soldier: Adjustment During Army Life. Vol. I. Princeton: Princeton University Press.
*Suttles, Gerald*
1968   The Social Order of the Slum. Chicago: University of Chicago Press.
*Taeuber, Karl, and Alma Taeuber*
1965   Negroes in Cities. Chicago: Aldine.
*Wilner, Daniel, Rosabelle Walkley, and Stuart Cook*
1955   Human Relations in Interracial Housing: A Study of the Contact Hypothesis. Minneapolis: University of Minnesota Press.
*Winder, Alvin*
1952   White Attitudes Towards Negro-White Interaction in an Area of Changing Racial Composition. Unpublished Ph.D. dissertation. Committee on Human Development, University of Chicago.
*Wirth, Louis*
1938   "Urbanism as a way of life" American Journal of Sociology 44 (July).

# SIX

## MINORITY PROTEST
## AND CHANGE

*Only to the extent that members of a minority share the belief that they can improve their group status do they support collective actions toward change. Programs of action seem futile to those who feel totally powerless. The kind of action supported by members of a group depends on what values and beliefs are shared. A given approach may gain little support under some conditions but a great deal under others. Apparently each strategy has advantages and limitations, and particular conditions under which it can contribute to change in intergroup relations. The emphasis in the first four selections in this section is on public protest and direct confrontation. The focus in the two selections on the women's movement is more on political action.*

*Programs of change through public education, economic improvement of the group, lawsuits in which discriminatory practices are challenged, legislation, or political participation (voting, influencing appointments, or holding office) are all supported by people who believe these regular channels of influence are open to them, and have the potential to change group statuses. When people believe the usual institutional means for affecting their status are ineffective or unavailable, they may resort to public protest and tactics of direct confrontation of those who hold power over them. Protesters also believe that effective channels for expressing their protest are available to them, a belief encouraged by governmental commitment to freedom of speech and assembly.*

*Overreaction to minority protest frequently occurs, especially when the society has not been used to such actions. Even people who do not feel directly threatened by minority competition for jobs, housing, or educational opportunity may become anxious about peace and order, and about their own security. The dominant community may mistake the more militant forms of protest and confrontation for total rebellion against the system, and the police and other agents of social control may respond in strongly repressive ways. Determined but nonviolent protests have often been misunderstood, and violent ones are even more likely to be defined as all-out rebellion rather than protest for reforms.*

*The role of the black church in protest and change has been little studied, but frequently has been held to be accommodating rather than militant, an assertion often buttressed by reference to the study by Gary Marx. In the selection by Nelsen, Madron, and Yokley, a reanalysis of the Marx data, which came from a national sample of black adults, is reported. After reaching a different conclusion, the researchers then report on their own data from Bowling Green, Kentucky. They found black sectarianism to be associated with accommodation, but more orthodox beliefs and participation in established black churches to be associated with support for protest.*

*What has been the role of white churches in the civil rights developments? During the crises over desegregation in the South, some white clergymen did not support integration (Campbell and Pettigrew, 1959), while others actively favored it. Studies had often shown prejudice against minorities to be associated with the degree of orthodoxy of religious beliefs, but a causal connection was rejected in a questionnaire study of Episcopalians in North Carolina. Prejudice appeared to be due to a localistic or provincial outlook rather than to orthodoxy (Roof, 1974).*

*Challenges to dominance often result in protests against change, and other collective responses on the part of members of the dominant community. The contribution by Levesque shows the great collective effort evidently made by whites in the six states of the Deep South, and North Carolina, to maintain political power after the passage of the Voting Rights Act of 1965. This is interpreted in the framework of Smelser's theory of collective behavior (Smelser, 1963). There had been violent incidents and other strong opposition to efforts to register black voters in the South, but only after the 1965 Act was passed did the collective action occur to get all whites to register and vote.*

*Most of the studies of the feelings of relative powerlessness of blacks and other racial minorities made during and since the 1960s have been studies of attitudes and beliefs. A rare attempt to demonstrate the actual absence of blacks from important decision-making positions in the community is reported in the article by Flaming, Palen, Ringlien, and Taylor. The data for 1968, a time when feelings of relative (but not total) powerlessness among urban blacks were generally high, are compared with similar evidence from a study in Chicago.*

*Like the selection by Levesque on voting, the Ransford study of blue collar reactions to protest by blacks and students focuses on reactions in the dominant community to increased competition, and on anxieties about losing some of their gains to blacks. These concerns reflect shifts in power, and in the structure of intergroup relationships generally. Ransford cautions that the associations are only moderately large, and we should add that this is only one study in one city. These findings are a reminder that the dominant community is not all of one mind, and that position in the class system may affect the outlooks and actions of racial and ethnic groups. It would be intersting to know if ethnic identity affected the attitudes of these blue collar workers toward black protest. In a study of third-generation Italians and Irish in Providence, Rhode Island, the strength of ethnic identity was associated with opposition to the black protest for equal rights (Goering, 1971).*

*The selection by Freeman shows how the black power movement influenced the rise of the women's movement, especially of its younger, more informal side. Three propositions are used in an attempt to explain why and how the movement emerged when it did. Strong legal and ideological foundations were established from 1963 to 1966, and women had been experiencing economic deprivation in relation to comparably qualified men (Knudsen, 1969); but not until several years later did the movement accelerate rapidly. Perhaps more emphasis ought to be given to the court victories in the late 1960s, over discrimination in employment and promotions. These cases, and especially the award of large amounts of back pay in the AT&T case, aroused expectations for equal treatment to new levels.*

*The selection by Welch demonstrates that women's support on particular issues cannot be predicted from their support for the liberation movement as a whole. The movement is diverse and not highly coordinated. On the whole, women who support the movement have apparently acted on the belief that they can achieve equal treatment through existing political, legal, and educational means. Use has also been made of direct confrontation and negotiation with decision-makers, and of an occasional, orderly demonstration.*

## REFERENCES

*Campbell, Ernest Q., and Thomas F. Pettigrew*
1959    Christians in Racial Crisis: A Study of Little Rock's Ministry. Washington, D.C.: Public Affairs Press.

*Goering, John M.*
1971    "The Emergence of Ethnic Interests." Social Forces 49, 3 (March): 379–84.

*Knudsen, Dean D.*
1969    "The Declining Status of Women: Popular Myths and the Failure of Functionalist Thought." Social Forces 48, 2 (December): 183–93.

*Marx, Gary*
1979    "Religion: Opiate or Inspiration of Civil Rights Militancy among Negroes?" American Sociological Review 32 (February): 64–72.

*Roof, Wade Clark*
1974    "Religious Orthodoxy and Minority Prejudice: Causal Relationship or Reflection of Localistic World View." American Journal of Sociology 80, 3 (November): 643–64.

*Smelser, Neil J.*
1963    Theory of Collective Behavior. New York: The Free Press.

# Black Religion's Promethean Motif: Orthodoxy and Militancy[1]

## Hart M. Nelsen

*Catholic University of America*

## Thomas W. Madron

## Raytha L. Yokley

*Western Kentucky University*

*Black religion as inspiration of and opiate for militancy is explored on the basis of data collected in an urban community in the upper South. Orthodoxy is shown to be positively related to militancy, while sectarianism is inversely related. Orthodoxy, viewed as churchlike ideology, is shown to be significantly related to church participation. Sectarianism, interpreted as part of the general culture of less educated blacks, is tangential to the religious system per se. Sectarianism is unrelated to participation in a religious organization. The results of a secondary analysis of the Gary Marx data are also reported.*

The traditional view of black religiosity has been that it is otherworldly and thus draws attention away from problems of this world, including denials and abrogations of civil rights. Kramer (1970, p. 232) summarized the literature written in this vein: "The church does not function to change the social facts,

*Source:* Hart M. Nelsen, Thomas W. Madron, and Raytha L. Yokley, "Black Religion's Promethean Motif: Orthodoxy and Militancy," American Journal of Sociology 81, 1 (July 1975): 139–46. Copyright © 1975 by the University of Chicago. Reprinted by permission.

but to make them more bearable; it is in that sense a conservative institution that channels discontents."

The seminal analysis on this topic was completed by Powdermaker (1943), who compared from a functional viewpoint the dependency situations of child and slave with regard to the problem of masochism and the meek, free black. For both situations she asked whether the black accepted his position or, if not, how culture channeled the aggression that was aroused. She located the concealment of aggression response among black Christians who turn the tables on the oppressor ("the last shall be first") and have a feeling of moral superiority.[2] She noted that this cultural process, by which blacks learned the functional role of acquiescence, was breaking down. Young blacks, even in rural areas, were using the church as a social center, and an otherworldly religious orientation was disappearing.

At present the most widely quoted work on the relation between black religion and militancy is that by Gary Marx (1967, p. 69), who combined subjective importance assigned to religion, frequency of attendance at worship services, and orthodoxy into an overall measure of religiosity and then showed an inverse relationship between religiosity and militancy among black metropolitan respondents interviewed in 1964. After introducing as single controls such variables as education, age, region, sex, and denomination, he concluded that the relationship continued to exist even with their introduction.

Yet Marx noted that "even for the militants, a majority were scored either 'very religious' or 'somewhat religious,' " and consequently, "for many, a religious orientation and a concern with racial protest are not mutually exclusive" (1967, p. 70). There is, as he realized, a dual orientation of religion: as both opiate and inspiration of civil rights militancy. His conclusion was that otherworldly religiosity tends to inhibit civil rights militancy, while religiosity with temporal concern tends to inspire it (1967, pp. 71–72). Concerning the present state of black religion (especially of an otherworldly ilk), he wrote (1967, p. 72): "Until such time as religion loosens its hold over these people or comes to embody to a greater extent the belief that man as well as God can bring about secular change, and focuses more on the here and now, religious involvement may be seen as an important factor working against the widespread radicalization of the Negro public."

## REANALYSIS OF THE MARX DATA

Marx's general finding that religiosity acts as an opiate of civil rights militancy could be due in part to an inverse relationship between sectarianism and militancy instead of one between religiosity in general and militancy. It could be more markedly due to his not having controlled simultaneously for education, sex, and other correlates of militancy and religiosity. From his own reanalysis of the data, Marx (1969, pp. 94–105) reported five variables concerned with religiosity: denomination, number of memberships in church organization, attendance at worship services, subjective importance of religion, and orthodoxy of belief. He found all of these variables to be inversely correlated with militancy. We subjected the Marx data to secondary analysis by means of multiple classification analysis (MCA) (Andrews, Morgan, and Sonquist 1967), using these variables in addition to age, education, religion, and sex.

Our findings appear in Table 1, where it can be seen that all $\eta$ (or zero-order) coefficients are significant at the .01 level.[3] The $\beta$ coefficients for the background predictors (those used by Marx as single controls in his 1967 analysis) remain significant at this level, but all of the $\beta$ coefficients for the religious variables lack significance at the .05 level. Our interpretation of the findings is not that black religiosity is unrelated to militancy, but that the direction of effect depends on the kind of religiosity. That is, there is indeed a dual orientation of black religion. While Marx's review of the literature indicates the validity of this perspective, the possibility is not fleshed out by his data.

**TABLE 1**
**Effects of Selected Predictors on Militancy (Marx Data)**

| PREDICTORS[a] | $\eta$ | $\beta$ |
|---|---|---|
| Education | .28 | .20 |
| Sex | −.16 | −.14 |
| Age | −.21 | −.10 |
| Region | .19 | .10 |
| Orthodoxy | −.21 | −.08* |
| Importance of religion | −.21 | −.08* |
| Denomination | −.18 | −.06* |
| Attendance | −.12 | −.04* |
| Church organizational memberships | −.09 | −.00* |

*Note:* R = 36.

[a] *The predictors were coded as follows: education—grade 8 or less, grades 9–11, grade 12, some college or more; sex—male, female; age—29 and younger, 30–44, 45–59, 60 and older; region—South, North; orthodoxy—seven categories from low to high; importance of religion —five categories from not important at all to extremely important; denomination—Episcopal-Presbyterian-Congregational, Catholic-none (following Marx), Methodist, American Baptist, Southern Baptist, other Baptist, sects and cults; attendance—five categories from less than once a year to more than once a week; number of church organizational memberships —none, one or more.*

*P>.05.

## THE FINDINGS FROM AN ANALYSIS
## OF NEW DATA

We now turn to the results of an analysis of data collected in an urban community (1970 population of 36,253) in the upper South in 1970–71. Included were variables for religiosity and civil rights militancy. Race relations in the community had undergone considerable change in recent years: thus our data provided a good test of the religiosity-militancy relationship, in view of the stereotype of southern, black religion as otherworldly and inversely related to militancy. Yet the writings by Powdermaker gave promise of considerable change in the role of religion in the black person's struggle for self-affirmation or freedom.

We employed a disproportionately stratified, systematic random sample drawn from a list of housing units in Bowling Green, Kentucky. Individual respondents were selected through a randomizing procedure for each household. Those interviewed were individuals 18 years of age or older who considered themselves permanent residents of the city. We had black interviewers attempt to interview in 418 black households; a total of 405 black adults were interviewed, giving a completion rate of 96%.[4]

Seven measures were employed in our analysis: civil rights militancy as the dependent variable[5] and education, sex, age, orthodoxy, sectarianism, and religious associational involvement as predictors. Education and age were measured in number of years. Sex was coded male (0) and female (1). Missing data were very infrequent. Let us now turn to how we constructed our indices.

In general, item scores were transformed into Z-scores for respondents for whom the data were complete. If a respondent gave answers for at least half of the items, the mean of the known items was assigned to each missing one. If fewer than half of the items were answered, no allocation was made until the end of the procedure. The scale score was simply the sum of the item Z-scores for the respondent. Any respondent not assigned a scale score by this method was given the total-score mean. Because the scale score was essentially at the ordinal level of measurement, the data were ranked within each race, and the ranks were transformed to standard scores with a mean of 50 and standard deviation of 10. These scores are, in essence, normalized T-scores. In developing indices we followed the criteria suggested by Guilford (1965, p. 481)—that interitem correlation coefficients should fall between .10 and .60 and that item–total-score correlation coefficients should be in the .30–.80 range. In addition, we determined Cronbach's $a$. All reliability tests were run on the unweighted data for all respondents.

The index of associational involvement was constructed to focus on two related activities: involvement in a religious organization, as expressed by church attendance, and involvement in the organizational life of a congregation. For each of these we utilized two items—regularity of attendance during the past year and attendance during the past seven days for the former and, for the latter, involvement in activities or organizations of the church, other than attending services, and self-reporting on both keeping informed about the church attended and having some influence on its decisions. For the four items $a = .63$.

Separate measures were constructed for orthodoxy and sectarianism in order to differentiate between individuals holding churchlike and those holding sectlike beliefs. A churchlike ideology, unlike a sectlike one, would not entail rejection of worldly interests, including the desire for an improved position for blacks in society. From a Durkheimian position, Hoge (1974, p. 185) linked the strength of traditional groups, or social solidarity, and a high level of orthodoxy. For our data, orthodoxy, or churchlike belief, should be linked with black community cohesion. Considering the importance of the black church to the black community over time and the saliency of militancy, a prediction of a positive relationship between orthodoxy and militancy follows. For orthodoxy we used a belief in heaven and hell and the beliefs that it is more important to go to church than to be active in politics, that the Bible is God's Word and all it says is true, and that the Ten Commandments and other scriptural statements about behavior should be followed because they are rules

God has provided for the leading of Christian lives (not rules to be interpreted to fit the situation). For sectarianism also four items were employed—beliefs that testifying about one's religious experience should be part of regular services, that God sends misfortune and illness as punishment for sins, that ministers should feel a call to the ministry (rather than have training), and that the world will soon come to an end. Two clearly demarcated factors resulted from a principal-components factor analysis with varimax rotation: orthodoxy and sectarianism (the items for each were appropriately loaded on the two factors). Factor scores were then computed, using the weighted data.

The intercorrelations among the independent variables are shown in Table 2. For the analyses reported in the remainder of the paper, we used multiple linear regression.

**TABLE 2**

**Product-Moment Correlations Among the Predictors**

|  | SEX | AGE | ORTHO-DOXY | SECTAR-IANISM | ASSOCIATIONAL INVOLVEMENT |
|---|---|---|---|---|---|
| Education | .13 | −.47 | −.05 | −.29 | .24 |
| Sex | — | −.06 | .06 | .00 | .19 |
| Age | — | — | .20 | .10 | .00 |
| Orthodoxy | — | — | — | .10 | .26 |
| Sectarianism | — | — | — | — | −.04 |
| Associational involvement | — | — | — | — | — |

*Note: Any correlation equal to or greater than ± .12 is significant at the .01 level.*

Table 3 presents the $\beta$ weights for the three religious variables we used, with militancy as the dependent variable. Sectlike religious ideology was inversely related to militancy, while churchlike religious ideology (or orthodoxy) was positively related. Associational involvement was not significantly (.05 level) related to militancy.

In Table 4 we present the relationships between the three background variables (education, sex, and age) and orthodoxy and sectarianism. Age is positively related to orthodoxy, and since it is inversely related to militancy, it might tend to suppress the relationship between orthodoxy and militancy. Education is inversely related to sectarianism, and since it is positively related to militancy, the sectarianism-militancy relationship could be spurious.

**TABLE 3**

**Religious Variables as Predictors of Militancy**

| PREDICTORS | $\beta$ |
|---|---|
| Sectarianism | −.20** |
| Orthodoxy | .17** |
| Associational involvement | −.02* |

*Note: R = .24.*
*\*P>.05.*
*\*\*P<.01.*

Table 5 presents the effects of all predictors (background and religious) on militancy. Education is the most important variable, followed by orthodoxy, in predicting militancy. While sectarianism is negatively related to militancy ($P$ < .05), clearly their relationship was reduced by introducing the other predictors (especially education) into the analysis.[6] Associational involvement was not significantly related to militancy.

## DISCUSSION

Beginning with Powdermaker's observation that the cultural process by which blacks learned acquiescence was breaking down and knowing that the trends to which she pointed, including rising educational levels, have continued to the present day, making for the acculturation of blacks in terms of the larger value system (for a more complete discussion of this, see Nelsen and Nelsen [1975]), we concluded that black religion should not simply be inversely coupled with militancy. Rather, we argued for a positive role on the part of orthodoxy. From the second table it can be seen that orthodoxy was positively related to associational involvement ($r = .26$); indeed, in our own research, we are assessing politicization effects of the black church and ministry on parishioners and children of parishioners. On the other hand, the absence of a relationship between sectarianism and associational involvement ($r = -.04$)

TABLE 4

Education, Sex, and Age as Predictors of Orthodoxy and Sectarianism

| PREDICTORS | $\beta$ WEIGHTS FOR | |
| | ORTHODOXY[a] | SECTARIANISM[b] |
| --- | --- | --- |
| Education | .04* | −.31** |
| Sex | .07* | .04* |
| Age | .22** | −.05* |

[a] R = .21.
[b] R = .29.
*P>.05.
**P<.01.

TABLE 5

Effects of Background and Religious Variables on Militancy

| PREDICTORS | ZERO-ORDER | |
| | $r$ | $\beta$ |
| --- | --- | --- |
| Education | .28*** | .25*** |
| Orthodoxy | .14*** | .21*** |
| Sex | −.10*** | −.14*** |
| Sectarianism | −.18*** | −.12** |
| Age | −.16*** | −.08* |
| Associational involvement | .03* | −.06* |

Note: R = 38.
*P>.05.
**P<.02.
***P<.01.

suggests that researchers are in error when they tag the black church with encouraging otherworldly religion. We interpret sectarianism as part of the general culture shared by less educated blacks; it is only tangential to the religious system per se. With rising educational levels, sectarianism should greatly diminish (the relationship between age and education was −.47). With higher levels of education, religiosity in general should be coupled with greater feelings of militancy on the part of blacks.

Since the black church is, in part, an expression of the black community, it may be expected to develop and elaborate an ideology (and theology) of black power not only as a defense against white racism but also as an appeal to disaffected black youth feeling "the dehumanizing effects of a spurious white Christian culture" (Wilmore, 1968). We expect that the black church will expand its prophetic role as critic and moral judge of the larger society, because this role is part of its tradition and because at this time its members and other blacks in the community are especially receptive to this stance. This is not to identify religious ideology as a major force in causing militancy. Indeed, our own findings indicate that religious belief is not especially potent in either fostering militancy or muting it, despite the avowals of writers to the contrary. To the extent that beliefs affect militancy, the direction of effect depends on the character of the beliefs held. In the main, we do not find that religiosity and especially the black church represent a conservative force that channels discontent. It is not an agency of social control in the service of white. Rather, within black religion can be located a Promethean motif, namely, that blacks find in a churchlike orientation a stimulus for militancy and protest.

## NOTES

1   This study was completed under the support of a grant from NIMH of the National Institutes of Health (no. 1 RO1 MH 16573). The authors wish to thank Samuel Blizzard and Ernest Q. Campbell, who served as consultants at critical points. The Marx data were furnished to us by the Inter-University Consortium for Political Research of the University of Michigan.

2   A misleading gloss of the Powdermaker analysis would provide a characterization of the black church and black religiosity as inducing feelings of guilt, passivity, and low self-esteem. For such a view, see Grier and Cobbs (1968, 1971). A complement to this thesis of lowered self-esteem and self-denial is the view of the black church as an agency of social control; this view is present to a small degree in Cone (1969, pp. 91–115) and Glenn (1964, pp. 629–30).

3   Although we have taken the liberty of reporting tests of significance, the reader should be cautioned that the $F$-tests of significance from the sums of squares given by the MCA program are based on the assumption of simple random sampling. The sampling design used by Marx did not meet this assumption; thus the reader should place more importance on the size of the $\eta$ and $\beta$ coefficients.

4   Our design also included the interviewing of whites (we do not report data for them here). Because the white sample was disproportionate, we used a weighting system in order to obtain a sample reflecting the entire community. The weighting was minimal for the black sample. Because we intend to report at a later time the results

of a similar analysis including the white data, we utilize the weighted black data here. Findings from an analysis using unweighted data are not divergent from those we present here.

5   The militancy variable contained eight items, including attitude toward such diverse matters as civil rights generally, black power, and support of integration by the government. For the wording of the eight items, see Nelsen and Nelsen (1975).

6   A check indicated that there was no significant interaction between orthodoxy and sectarianism in their joint relation to militancy.

## REFERENCES

*Andrews, Frank, James Morgan, and John Sonquist*
1967   *Multiple Classification Analysis.* Ann Arbor: Institute for Social Research, University of Michigan.
*Cone, James*
1969   *Black Theology and Black Power.* New York: Seabury.
*Glenn, Norval D.*
1964   "Negro Religion and Negro Status in the United States." Pp. 623–39 in *Religion, Culture, and Society.* edited by Louis Schneider. New York: Wiley.
*Grier, William H., and Price M. Cobbs*
1968   *Black Rage.* New York: Basic Books.
1971   *The Jesus Bag.* New York: McGraw-Hill.
*Guilford, J. P.*
1965   *Fundamental Statistics in Psychology and Education.* 4th ed. New York: McGraw-Hill.
*Hoge, Dean R.*
1974   *Commitment on Campus.* Philadelphia: Westminster.
*Kramer, Judith R.*
1970   *The American Minority Community.* New York: Crowell.
*Marx, Gary T.*
1967   "Religion: Opiate or Inspiration of Civil Rights Militancy among Negroes?" *American Sociological Review* 32 (February): 64–72.
1969   *Protest and Prejudice.* Rev. ed. New York: Harper & Row.
*Nelsen, Hart M., and Anne K. Nelsen*
1975   *Black Church in the Sixties.* Lexington: University Press of Kentucky.
*Powdermaker, Hortense*
1943   "The Channeling of Negro Aggression by the Cultural Process." *American Journal of Sociology* 48 (May): 750–58.
*Wilmore, Gayraud S., Jr.*
1968   "The Case for a New Black Church Style." *Church in Metropolis* 18 (Fall): 18–22.

# White Response to Nonwhite Voter Registration in Southern States [*]

## Russell J. Levesque

*University of Arizona*

The purpose of this paper is to consider changes in white and nonwhite[1] voter registration in certain Southern states as a means of describing the relationship between in-group cohesion and out-group threat (Sumner, 1906). The examination will be in terms of the changes that occurred in Southern voting registration as a result of the passage of the Voting Rights Act of 1965, Public Law 85–315 (U.S. Commission on Civil Rights, 1968). This legislative act appears to have created a situation of voter registration competition between the whites (dominant in-group) and nonwhites (out-group) in the South which had not previously existed.

Theoretically, there are several reasons (Berelson and Steiner, 1964) for expecting a relationship between in-group cohesion and out-group threat. These reasons are: (1) communication between majority and minority group tends to be restricted in nature, superficial, or subject to considerable misunderstanding (Suchman et al., 1958); (2) the ethnic identification becomes centrally important, especially for the minority (Radue et al., 1949); (3) the minority group develops hostile, stereotyped attitudes toward other groups in society, including the majority (MacCrone, 1947).

*Source:* Russell J. Levesque, "White Response to Nonwhite Voter Registration in Southern States," Pacific Sociological Review 15, 2 (April 1972): 245–55. Copyright © 1972 by the Publisher, Sage Publications, Inc. Reprinted by permission.

*This paper is a revised version of that which won the student paper award at the annual meeting of the Pacific Sociological Association, Honolulu, Hawaii, April, 1971. We are pleased to present it to our readers.

Theory concerning potential secondary groups, such as the type that indulges in collective behavior, resolves itself with Smelser (1968), who lists the requirements for collective behavior to occur. These are: (1) appropriate structural conditions, (2) strain, (3) spread of generalized belief, (4) precipitating factors, and (5) mobilization for action. The appropriate structural condition was the Voting Rights Act of 1965, Public Law 85–315, which made it possible for nonwhites to register to vote without imposed sanctions. Strain was the resulting competition to get the eligible voting population registered. Spread of generalized belief was the threat of a nonwhite takeover of the South, if the nonwhites obtained control of the vote. Precipitating factors were: (a) publicity; (b) involvement of outside agencies, organizations, and individuals; (c) conflict; and (d) other factors. Mobilization for action was the campaign by both groups to get their members registered to vote. These requirements for collective behavior to occur are based on short-term response, even though the elements of collective behavior may have been present in other forms over a long period of time. The central elements in collective behavior are: (1) an awareness of the group, and (2) a power object for focus. Historically, the nonwhites in the United States have tended to be ineffective since they apparently did not have a power object upon which to focus. The Voting Rights Act of 1965 seems to have provided the nonwhites such a power object. It seems to have generated a competition situation centering on voter registration. It gave the white population an awareness of a voting group, the nonwhites, with whom they were going to have to compete; and gave the nonwhites an awareness of their potential political strength as a group.

It is our intention to demonstrate that the out-group threat posed by mass nonwhite voter registration in Southern states resulted in an increased white voter registration which attempted to achieve 100% white voter registration. This demonstration of in-group cohesion, resulting from awareness and the spread of a generalized belief, could only be achieved by the whites forming a voter coalition in response to the perceived out-group threat. Coalition (Coser, 1956) permits the coming together of elements that because of mutual antagonisms would resist other forms of unification. Thus, if several parties face a common opponent, a unifying bond is created between them and a coalition is formed. These defensive alignments contain only the minimum of unifying elements necessary to conduct a struggle, because the participants in such coalitions frequently have only one interest in common: a concern for their survival as independent units. Participants in a coalition area are free to pursue their separate aims in all areas except in that common purpose for which the coalition has been formed.

Internal cohesion is likely to be increased in the group which engages in outside competition. This outside competition mobilizes the group's defenses, among which is the group's reaffirmation of its value system against that of the outside competition. The competition then consists of a test of power between antagonistic parties. As a result, exclusion is attained, and maintenance of this exclusive standing requires the group to be an internally cohesive competitive group.

The principal manifestation of threat and competition leading to coalition and cohesion, with which this study deals, is that of nonwhite voter registration leading to a response by white voter registrants. The hypothesis for this study is that:

*A perceived threat to a dominant in-group (whites) in terms of increased voter registration by an out-group (nonwhites) will result in a response by the in-group which will attempt to achieve maximum (100%) voter registration.*

## CONCEPTS AND OPERATIONAL DEFINITIONS

Developing the hypothesis leads to the following scheme and operational definitions, presented in Table 1. In this paper, competition is defined in terms of voter registration in which one side gains and the other side loses by having numerical superiority in voters registered within their ethnic group. White difference (WDIFF) is the response of the percentage of the white population previously unregistered (1964) as voters, who are currently registered (1967), representing a gain (or loss) over previous white voter registration. Nonwhite difference (NDIFF) is the percentage increase (or decrease) in nonwhite voters currently registered (1967), representing a gain or loss over previous (1964) nonwhite voter registration. White registration (WREG) is the percentage of the white voters who were registered in 1964.

In this attempt to evaluate the impact of nonwhite voter registration on white voter registration, the problem is to investigate the relationships between the independent variables (1) threat (a) potential (POTEN), (b) salience (SALEN), and (c) intensity (TENSE); (2) nonwhite difference (NDIFF) in voter registration; and (3) white voter registration (WREG), and the dependent vari-

TABLE 1

Indicators of Threat

| ASPECTS OF THREAT | LATENT[a] | MANIFEST[b] |
|---|---|---|
| Potential (POTEN) | | |
| Strength | Percentage of nonwhite voting age population available for registration | Percentage of total voter registration that is nonwhite |
| Mobilization | Nonexistent or low in the initial stage | Percentage of nonwhite voting age population registered to vote |
| Salience (SALEN) | Ratio of the present white registered voters to the nonwhite voters registered (e.g., 4 to 1) | |
| Intensity (TENSE) | Percentage of nonwhites not registered as voters | Percentage of nonwhite voters registered who were not previously registered |

[a] *Latent threat is the perceived threat before Voting Rights Act of 1965 in terms of voter registration.*

[b] *Manifest threat is the perceived threat (actualized) after Voting Rights Act of 1965 in terms of voter registration (a form of latent threat for voting).*

able white difference (WDIFF) in voter registration. While it is understood that most social change such as voter registration may be affected by multiple causes, the interest in this study is primarily in the independent variables that influence change in white voter registration (white difference in voter registration). Threat is viewed in terms of the perception of the threat by the dominant white in-group. The indicators of threat are perceived by the dominant in-group to be: (a) the aspects of threat, and (b) whether threat is latent or manifest. The aspects of threat are (a) potential threat, which has strength in terms of the eligible nonwhite voting population that could be mobilized to vote against the dominant white in-group; (b) salience of the threat, which is perceived as the percentage of unregistered nonwhite voters. As the nonwhites register to vote, the threat becomes actualized. The threat is transformed from latent to manifest. However, once actualized, the perceived threat becomes a form of latent threat for voting supremacy.

For clarification, it should be noted that recent work on nonwhite voting (Keech, 1968; Feagin and Hahn, 1970; Holloway, 1969; Matthews and Prothro, 1966) and its impact have pointed to increased nonwhite voter registration and nonwhite voter cohesion. A search of the literature leads to references on nonwhite voter registration in specific areas involving limited data (Bergman, 1968; Davis, 1966; and Ebony, 1966). Traditional volumes (Peterson, 1963; and Scammon, 1968) treat party affiliations and voting outcomes without regard to ethnicity. Apparently, the only current empirical data of magnitude on white and nonwhite voter registration is in the U.S. Commission on Civil Rights report (1968). Therefore, while the emphasis of current work in sociology and political science has centered on nonwhite voting, the area of white response to nonwhite voter registration appears to have received only cursory examination.

## DATA AND RESULTS

In this study, the data are taken from 1968 federal voter registration statistics[2] for 440 counties in seven Southern states: Alabama, Florida, Georgia, Louisiana, Mississippi, North Carolina, and South Carolina. The data are divided into two groups: white, and nonwhite, for five factors: (a) 1960 voting age population, (b) number of individuals involved in pre-act (1964) registration, (c) the percentage of individuals involved in pre-act (1964) registration, (d) the number of individuals involved in post-act (1967) registration, (e) the percentage of individuals involved in post-act (1967) registration.

Voter registration data for 440 Southern counties provided the first indication of response and probable competition for voter registration supremacy; 124 of the 440 counties surveyed had achieved a 100% to 100+%[3] white voter registration in 1967.

In examining the same data (Table 2) to determine how many of the 440 counties approached the 100% mark (90.0% to 99.9%) from a 50.0% level or more, it was found that 70 counties showed an increase in white voter registration.

In addition, there is the category of the counties that were in the 100% to 100+% range of white voters registered both in 1964 and in 1967. This factor

## TABLE 2
### White Voter Registration Response
$n = 440$ Counties

| INCREASE IN VOTER REGISTRATION | | | ALABAMA (67) | FLORIDA (67) | GEORGIA (159) | LOUISIANA (64) | MISSISSIPPI (29) | NORTH CAROLINA (126) | SOUTH CAROLINA (46) |
|---|---|---|---|---|---|---|---|---|---|
| 1964 | 1967 | | | | | | | | |
| Range | To | | | | | | | | |
| 50.0 to 59.9 | 100% to 100+% | | 2 | 0 | 1 | 0 | 0 | 0 | 0 |
| 60.0 to 69.9 | | | 1 | 0 | 1 | 1 | 2 | 0 | 0 |
| 70.0 to 79.9 | | | 3 | 0 | 8 | 1 | 2 | 0 | 0 |
| 80.0 to 89.9 | | | 4 | 4 | 10 | 15 | 3 | 0 | 0 |
| 90.0 to 99.9 | | | 10 | 4 | 21 | 19 | 2 | 0 | 11 |
| Counties total | | | 20 | 8 | 41 | 36 | 9 | 0 | 11 |
| % of counties | | | 29.9 | 11.9 | 25.8 | 56.2 | 31.0 | 0.0 | 23.8 |
| 50.0 to 59.9 | 90.0% to 99.9+% | | 1 | 0 | 0 | 1 | 0 | 1 | 0 |
| 60.0 to 69.9 | | | 4 | 0 | 1 | 1 | 0 | 2 | 0 |
| 70.0 to 79.9 | | | 2 | 1 | 5 | 3 | 4 | 0 | 3 |
| 80.0 to 89.9 | | | 2 | 3 | 11 | 3 | 4 | 0 | 2 |
| 90.0 to 99.9 | | | 4 | 1 | 5 | 2 | 2 | 0 | 2 |
| Counties total | | | 13 | 5 | 22 | 10 | 10 | 3 | 7 |
| % of counties | | | 19.3 | 7.4 | 13.8 | 15.6 | 34.4 | 37.5 | 15.2 |
| 100% to 100+% | 100% to 100+% | | 17 | 18 | 30 | 9 | 9 | 0 | 7 |
| Counties total | | | 17 | 18 | 30 | 9 | 9 | 0 | 7 |
| % of counties | | | 29.8 | 26.8 | 18.8 | 14.0 | 13.7 | 0.0 | 15.2 |
| Total percentage of counties indicating increase, or maintenance of the 100% to 100+% level, in registration | | | 79.0 | 46.1 | 58.4 | 85.8 | 79.1 | 37.5 | 54.2 |

may also be indicative of a form of white voter registration response in main-taining a perfect level (100%) of white voter registration, since it requires an effort to maintain 100% voter registration. The data indicates that 90 of the 440 counties were able to maintain a 100% or 100+% white voter registration.

Since the seven states surveyed showed a significant increase in white voter registration (284 out of 440 counties) in 1967, this suggested that there had been a strong response by the whites, in terms of registering to vote, to the Voting Rights Act of 1965.

In order to further analyze the data, it was decided to use path analysis (Duncan, 1966; Land, 1969; Li, 1956). Path analysis offers a method of determin-ing the direct and indirect effects of the variables on each other. In this study of 440 Southern counties, it was found that only 359 of the counties had data suitable for computer programming.[4]

Using Figure 1 to explain white voter registration (WREG) in terms of the direct effects, which are in the same direction but of greater magnitude than the correlations suggest, for example: 0.33 versus 0.17, 0.14 versus 0.06, and –0.27 versus –0.10, indicates that there are strong indirect effects between potential threat (POTEN) and intensity of threat (TENSE), and between intensity of threat (TENSE) and white registration (WREG), with the indirect effects going in both directions. This indicates that there are indirect effects which may be confounding the direct effects. With regard to the nonwhite difference (NDIFF) in registration, the effects are all in the same direction. However, one of the direct effects is greater than the correlations, while the other direct effects are smaller. This may have occurred because of interrelated effects. The total effects of the three threat variables, potential (POTEN), salience (SALEN), and inten-sity (TENSE), on white difference (WDIFF) in voter registration is small. Only one is significant, and that is intensity (TENSE), at 0.18. The direct effects are all negative and small (–0.03, –0.04, and –0.05).

The indirect effects of all three threat variables and white difference are significant. For example, white voter registration and nonwhite difference in voter registration explain about one-half (48%) of white difference in voter registration. This is an indication that the indirect effects are quite strong.

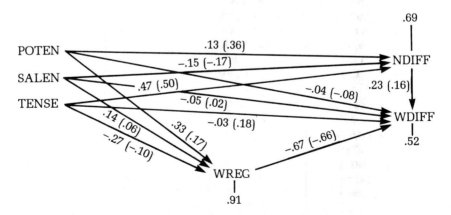

**Fig. 1   Total direct and indirect effects of (a) the aspects of threat, (b) white voter registration in 1964, and (c) the effect of nonwhite voter registration in 1967, on (d) the white voter registration in 1967.**

However, the direct effect (.23) and the indirect effect (.16) of nonwhite difference in voter registration on white difference are also large enough to be significant.

## DISCUSSION

It appears that prior to the Voting Rights Act of 1965 the Southern whites did not perceive the nonwhites as a threat in the area of voting. With the advent of the Voting Rights Act of 1965, the Southern whites then perceived a nonwhite threat to their voting supremacy and an awareness of the situation resulted in white collective behavior in the form of a voting registration coalition. It is concluded that the hypothesis is substantiated, and it is inferred that as a result of a perceived threat to a dominant in-group (eligible Southern white voters), in terms of increased voter registration by an out-group (eligible Southern nonwhite voters), the ensuing voter registration competition situation resulted in a strong increase in nonwhite voter registration, which caused the white voter registration to approach or exceed the 100% mark in many Southern counties.

## NOTES

1  Nonwhite is the term used in U.S. Commission on Civil Rights (1968: 12). Nonwhite will be used in this paper, rather than Negroes or Black Americans, since over 95% of the nonwhites in the South are Black Americans.
2  See U.S. Commission on Civil Rights (1968:222–256). Countywide data, pre-act and post-act, is not available for the four Southern states of Arkansas, Tennessee, Texas, and Virginia. In addition, only certain counties provided data in the states of Mississippi and North Carolina (hence the 440 counties in the seven Southern states).
3  A percentage of 100+ voters registered indicates a higher amount of voters registered than the official population count for the county. The apparent overregistration may be attributable to population changes through natural increases and migration. Rectification usually occurs with later census counts and during periodic reregistration of all eligible voters.
4  Path analysis was conducted utilizing computer programs BMD-02R (Multiple Regression) and BMDP (Beta Weights), on file at the University Computer Center, and in the Department of Sociology, University of Arizona, Tucson. Eighty-one of the counties had a zero non-white voter registration in 1964. The computer will not divide by zero, consequently the N was reduced to 359. Recent adjustments in the program and a rerun of the data, indicate increased significance as we go to press.

## REFERENCES

Berelson, Bernard, and Gary A. Steiner
1964  Human Behavior: An Inventory of Scientific Findings. New York: Harcourt, Brace & World.

*Bergman, Peter M.*
1968    The Negro in America. New York: Harper & Row.
*Coser, Lewis A.*
1956    The Functions of Social Conflict. New York: Free Press.
*Davis, John P.*
1966    The American Negro Reference Book. Englewood Cliffs, N.J.: Prentice-Hall.
*Duncan, Otis Dudley*
1966    "Path analysis: sociological examples." Amer. J. of Sociology 72 (July): 1–16.
*Ebony*
1966    The Negro Handbook. Chicago: Johnson.
*Feagin, Joe R., and Harlan Hahn*
1970    "The second reconstruction: Black political strength in the South." Social Sci. Q. 51
        (June): 42–56.
*Holloway, Harry*
1969    The Politics of the Southern Negro: From Exclusion to Big City Organization. New
        York: Random House.
*Keech, William R.*
1968    The Impact of Negro Voting: The Role of the Vote in the Quest for Equality.
        Chicago: Rand McNally.
*Land, Kenneth C.*
1969    "Principals of path analysis." In E. F. Borgatta (ed.), Sociological Methodology 1969.
        San Francisco: Jossey-Bass.
*Li, C. C.*
1956    "The concept of path coefficient and its impact on population genetics." Biometrics
        (June): 190–199.
*Matthews, Donald R., and James W. Prothro*
1966    Negroes and the New Southern Politics. New York: Harcourt, Brace & World.
*Peterson, Svend*
1963    A Statistical History of the American Presidential Elections. New York: Ungar.
*MacCrone, I. D.*
1947    "Reaction to domination in a color-caste society: A preliminary study of the race
        attitudes of a dominated group." J. of Social Psychology 26:86.
*Radue, Marion, Helen Thager, and Haduseah Davis*
1949    "Social perception and attitudes of children." Genetics Psych. Monographs 40:417.
*Scammon, Richard M.*
1968    America At The Polls. Pittsburgh: Governmental Affairs Institution.
*Smelser, Neil J.*
1968    Essays in Sociological Explanation. Englewood Cliffs, N.J.: Prentice-Hall.
*Suchman, Edward A., et al.*
1958    Desegregation: Some Propositions and Research Suggestions. New York: Anti-
        Defamation League of B'nai Brith.
*Sumner, William G.*
1906    Folkways. Boston: Ginn.
*United States Commission on Civil Rights*
1968    Political Participation. Washington, D.C.: U.S. Government Printing Office.

# Black Powerlessness in Policy-Making Positions*

## Karl H. Flaming
*University of Wisconsin-Milwaukee*

## J. John Palen
*University of Wisconsin-Milwaukee*

## Grant Ringlien
*Milwaukee Social Development Commission*

## Corneff Taylor
*Milwaukee Urban League*

Studies of ghetto violence, most notably the Report of the National Advisory Commission of Civil Disorders (1968), have documented Black exclusion from the opportunity structure in terms of high unemployment among Black ghetto youth, inadequate housing, and failing educational opportunities for low income Black ghetto residents. While riot studies have focused attention on the exclusion of Blacks from entry level jobs, only limited notice has been given

*Source:* Karl H. Flaming, J. John Palen, Grant Ringlien, and Corneff Taylor, "Black Powerlessness in Policy-Making Positions," Sociological Quarterly 13, 1 (Winter 1972): 126–33. Copyright © 1972 by the Midwest Sociological Society. Reprinted by permission of the Society, the editors of Sociological Quarterly, and the authors.
*This paper is a revised and corrected version of the report, "Black Powerlessness in Milwaukee Institutions and Decision-Making" Milwaukee: Community Relations Social Development Commission and Milwaukee Urban League, 1970.

to the extent of Black exclusion from positions of power in major institutional sectors. Community power studies also have provided relatively limited information on Black participation in community decision-making. It is the thesis of the present paper that Blacks are effectively excluded from the decision-making process at the community level.

A recent study of black powerlessness in Chicago examined the extent to which Blacks were excluded from positions of influence in major institutional sectors (Baron et al., 1968). Their findings indicated that Negroes occupied only 2.6 percent or 285 of the 19,997 top policy-making positions in the Chicago area (Baron, 1968:28). Black representation in Chicago was greatest in the elected public sector, welfare and religious voluntary organizations and industrial unions. In the words of the Chicago study:

*The sectors and individual groups in the Chicago area with the highest Negro representation were those with a Negro constituency-elective offices, supervisory boards, labor unions, and religious and welfare organizations (Baron, 1968:29).*

There was a virtual absence of Black representation in the policy-making positions of the private institutions such as business corporations, banks, insurance companies, universities, and professional business organizations.

How representative are these findings of Black powerlessness in other metropolitan areas? The authors of the Chicago study suggest that their city is atypical in that it "... has proportionately more Negro-controlled businesses, larger than neighborhood operations, than any other major city in the North" (Baron, 1968:28). They then hypothesized that "... similar surveys in other Northern metropolitan areas would turn up an even smaller percentage of Negro policy-makers in the business world" (Baron, 1968:28).

Our research tests this hypothesis by examining the degree to which Blacks are found in key policy-making positions in the Milwaukee, Wisconsin, metropolitan area. In this study a total of 4,930 policy-making positions in the business, public governmental, academic, and voluntary sectors were identified and the number of Blacks holding such policy-making positions were identified.

## METHODOLOGY

At the time of this study, the city of Milwaukee had a population of approximately 750,000 of which 90,000, or 12 percent, were Black. The county was 9 percent Black while the total SMSA population was over 1,400,000, of which 6.9 percent was classified as non-white.

This study, as in the earlier Chicago report, assumes that men who hold power are those who have been elevated to policy-making positions in powerful institutions such as insurance firms, city boards and commissions, universities, and labor unions. Policy-making positions were defined as those which the major goals and orientation of the organization are set. As in the Chicago study, every effort was made to include the total universe of policy-making positions.

Within Milwaukee County four major institutional areas were identified. These were the private sector (business, industry, law, etc.); the public-governmental sector (city county, and federal elective, appointive, civil service, etc.); academic (school boards, principals, administrators, etc.); and the voluntary sector (labor unions, civic service organizations, etc.). The following are the criteria used to identify policy-making positions:

**A.** Public Governmental Sector

1) *Elected Officials.* Milwaukee County elected officials, elected city officials, state senators and assemblymen from Milwaukee County, United States congressmen from Milwaukee County, judges of the Milwaukee County and circuit courts.

2) *Appointive Supervisory Boards.* Policy-making positions in this area include both city and county supervisory boards and commissions.

Milwaukee County: Included is the entire range of boards and commissions. The majority of the positions on these boards are filled by appointment of the county executive, and confirmation of the county board. The governor, circuit court judges, county court, and judges of civil jurisidiction are also responsible for appointment. A complete list of these boards and commissions is available. Milwaukee County also has a number of standing committees composed mainly of county board supervisors.

City of Milwaukee: Included are boards and commissions appointed by the mayor, or appointed by the mayor with approval of the common council.

3) *Local Administration.* These positions include posts filled by appointment and civil service.

4) *Regional Administration, U.S. Government.* These positions include those filled by federal civil service, and by Presidential appointment. U.S. district judges, U.S. attorney, clerk U.S. district court, U.S. marshal, referee in bankruptcy, director of internal revenue, (regional representative), public relations advisor, collector of customs, and postmaster.

**B.** Private Sector

1) *Banks.* The research figures include all banks in Milwaukee with admitted assets in 1968 of at least $10 million. For these enterprises, the statistics will cover all directors, officers, and executive posts in the areas of responsibility of trusts and cashiers.

2) *Insurance.* The data on this area includes all insurance writing firms which are based in Milwaukee County and have admitted assets in 1968 of at least $8 million. For these firms, the statistics include all directors and officers with Wisconsin residence.

3) *Business and Industrial Concerns.* The figures include all enterprises, manufacturing, wholesale and retail trade, construction, public utilities, and service industries based in Milwaukee County with 1,000 or more employees (nation-wide) or annual sales of more than 12 million dollars. The figures for these firms include directors and corporate officers whose permanent residences are in Wisconsin. Also included are the executives responsible for the following policy areas: sales, general management, advertising, production, finance, traffic, personnel, and purchasing. The figures also include firms not based in Mil-

waukee County but employing more than 700 persons in Milwaukee. The figures also include all Milwaukee-based enterprises; buses and trucks, with operating revenues of more than 3 million annually.

4) *Hospitals.* All hospitals in the Milwaukee area were polled for their board of directors. Because of federal requirements in order to become certified, certain decisions are already made. But any further decisions that affect the patients or general policy comes from the board of directors. Also all hospitals in Milwaukee County were surveyed since most of the hospitals that directly serve the geographical area of the Inner City North are small private establishments. Thus, if a set of criteria like those below were constructed many of the servicing hospitals would not be surveyed.

5) *Legal Profession.* In this area the figures include all law firms in the City of Milwaukee with six or more partners and/or those Milwaukee law firms which represent at least two public-owned corporations in the Milwaukee area. For law firms included, the statistics include partners and associates of those firms.

C.  Academic Community

This area includes policy-making positions in public primary and secondary schools. Included are school board members, heads of various divisions in school administration, principals, and vice-principals. Public and private institutions of higher education (colleges, universities, technical schools, etc.) are also included. In this area, the study is limited to degree-granting institutions. Policy-making positions are considered to include the following positions: regents, board of trustees, administration (president, vice president, registrar, etc.), and deans, assistant deans, and or directors of colleges or schools of instruction within the universities.

D.  Voluntary Sector

All major voluntary organizations are included, exploring [sic] both directors and top staff positions. These include commercial associations, major social service and planning agencies, and other major associations.

*Labor Unions.* The figures include all international unions based in Milwaukee County with 10,000 or more members; all labor district councils in Milwaukee County with membership of 5,000 or more; and all local unions in Milwaukee with 3,000 members or more. The statistics include all full-time staff and officers. In addition, the department and district directors are included for all district councils. The business representatives or business manager are also included.

The criteria for inclusion of organizations differed from the Chicago study in that (1) the size criteria for inclusion was lowered to allow for the difference in city size, (2) the Milwaukee Labor Council helped formulate more representative parameters for this sub-sector and, (3) a hospital sub-sector, not included in the Chicago study, was added to cover the area of health care.

The collection of data varied somewhat in each of the organizational areas. Data for the public administrative area was already available for the most part. In the area of corporations, a complete list of all Milwaukee corporations was obtained from *Poor's Register of Corporations, Directors, and Executives, 1968,* and *Geographical Index.* Listings of directors, presidents, vice-presidents, and managers were found in *Poor's Register of Corporations, Directors, and Executives, 1968.* Policy-making positions in voluntary associations, labor unions, and universities were obtained from the organizations themselves or from knowledgeable sources. Letters, telephone conversations, and interviews were used to obtain information on the size of the organization. If the organization met the criteria for inclusion in the study taken then the names of those persons occupying policy-making positions were obtained.

Of the 4,930 positions surveyed, there were 1,867 policy-making positions in the business sector, 856 policy positions in the public governmental sector, 553 positions in the academic sector, and 655 positions in the voluntary sector. As in the Chicago study, all policy-making positions were ranked equally. The data thus reflect the presence or possible potential for Negro influence rather than actual exercised power or influence.

## FINDINGS

A total of 1,867 policy-making positions in the private sector were surveyed. Included were business and industrial concerns, law firms, banks, stock brokerage firms, insurance companies, and hospitals. Qualifying for the study were 44 Milwaukee-based business and industrial concerns with a thousand or more employees or annual sales of over twelve million dollars and non-locally based firms employing at least 700 persons; sixteen banks with announced assets of at least ten million dollars; seven major insurance companies; 26 law firms with six or more partners or with at least two public-owned corporations as clients; and 24 private hospitals.

As Table 1 documents, only *one* Black occupied any of the 1,867 key positions in the business sector. The all-but-total absence of Negroes in these critical positions is a major handicap to expanding Black entrepreneurship. At the time of the study, the Milwaukee Negro community did not have representation in major business firms. Only one Black held a major policy position.

As Table 2 indicates, Blacks fared somewhat better in the public-governmental sector. There, twenty Blacks held 42 of the 856 (4.9%) policy-making

TABLE 1

The Percentage of Blacks in Policy-Making Positions in the Private Sector

| SELECTED AREAS | NUMBER OF POSITIONS | NUMBER OF BLACKS | PERCENT OF BLACKS |
|---|---|---|---|
| Business and industrial concerns | 622 | 0 | 0.0 |
| Law firms | 399 | 0 | 0.0 |
| Banks | 413 | 0 | 0.0 |
| Stock brokerage | 68 | 0 | 0.0 |
| Insurance firms | 145 | 0 | 0.0 |
| Hospitals | 220 | 1 | 0.5 |
| Total | 1,867 | 1 | 0.5 |

positions in the city and county. Of the 121 elected positions only five were held by Negroes. Thirty-six of the 588 appointive positions (6.1%) were held by Blacks. Only two Blacks (1.4%) were found in any city or county administrative post with policy-making potential. Negro representation was strongest in the city, where Blacks were twelve percent of the population. Here they held 8.3 percent of the elective and 7.2 percent of the appointive positions.

TABLE 2

The Percentage of Blacks in Policy-Making Positions
in the Public Government Sector

| SELECTED AREAS | NUMBER OF POSITIONS | NUMBER OF BLACKS IN POSITIONS | PERCENT OF BLACKS IN POSITIONS |
|---|---|---|---|
| Officials elected at large | 66 | 1 | 1.5 |
| City of Milwaukee elected positions | 24 | 2 | 8.3 |
| City of Milwaukee administration | 81 | 1 | 1.2 |
| City of Milwaukee appointed Bds. & Com. | 387 | 28 | 7.2 |
| Milwaukee County elected positions | 31 | 2 | 6.5 |
| Milwaukee County administration | 66 | 0 | 0.0 |
| County appointed Boards and Commissions | 201 | 8 | 4.0 |
| Total | 856 | 42 | 4.9 |

The picture of limited Black participation was similar in the academic sector. Table 3 shows that of a total of 553 policy-making positions, Blacks held 21 or 3.8 percent. However, in the highest policy-making positions (public school board, Board of Vocational and Adult Education, and University Regents) there was no Black representation. Some Black representation was found in the next lower level, positions concerned with the administration of public education (principals, vice-principals, assistants, and central administrators). Blacks were also absent from the 118 administrative positions surveyed in the private academic sector.

Highest Negro representation was found in the voluntary sector. Table 4 indicates that Blacks were highly visible in programs and organizations primarily concerned with minority groups and poverty problems. Of the 472 policy-making posts in the voluntary service organizations, 125 or 26.5 percent were held by Blacks. However, the majority of these voluntary organizations, such as the Urban League, or the O.E.O.-funded Social Development Commission, possessed only limited community influence. Blacks were most visible in organizations dealing directly with minority group problems. On the other hand, it is noteworthy that in civic (Association of Commerce, Bar Association, Board of Realtors) as opposed to service organizations, only two of the 121 posts were held by Blacks. Finally, within organized labor, there were no Blacks in the 26 policy-making posts and only two Blacks were found in the 36 regional decision-making positions surveyed.

## DISCUSSION

The study supports the hypothesis that Blacks in northern metropolitan areas would constitute an even smaller percentage of potential policy-makers than they did in the Chicago study. Milwaukee Blacks are clearly absent from policy-making positions with the exclusion being most pronounced in the business sector, where only one Black was found in the 1,867 policy positions. This suggests that Blacks in medium to large size northern cities may be even more poorly represented than Blacks in the largest cities.

In reality, Milwaukee Blacks are even *more poorly* represented than the above data indicate. There are two major reasons for this. First, according to Negro decision-makers, Blacks who are appointed to decision-making positions are those who are best known to, and have the widest acceptance in, the White community. More militant Blacks, while they may be known, tend to be distrusted. A second related factor is that those few Blacks who are known and acceptable to White decision-makers tend to be appointed to a much larger number of positions than their white peers. Thus, a limited number of Blacks tend to be repeatedly used and reused as representatives of the Black community. For example, 605 Whites held 814 policy-making positions in the public government sector while at the same time only 20 Blacks held 42 positions in the same sector. The same pattern of Black duplication was found in the other sectors where a significant number of Blacks were present. Given the level of specialization and professionalism required in our society, this duplication of Black leaders further weakens actual Black participation in decision-making.

### TABLE 3
**The Percentage of Blacks in Policy-Making Positions in the Academic Sector**

| *SELECTED AREAS* | *NUMBER OF POSITIONS* | *NUMBER OF BLACKS* | *PERCENT OF BLACKS* |
|---|---|---|---|
| Elementary—Secondary | | | |
| Public | | | |
| School Board | 14 | 0 | 0.0 |
| Administration | 68 | 4 | 5.9 |
| Bd. or Vocational & Adult Education | 7 | 0 | 0.0 |
| Principals | 157 | 5 | 3.2 |
| Vice-Principals | 80 | 5 | 6.3 |
| Assistants | 31 | 2 | 6.5 |
| Colleges and Universities | | | |
| Public | | | |
| Regents | 17 | 0 | 0.0 |
| Administration | 23 | 2 | 8.7 |
| Deans & Directors | 38 | 3 | 7.9 |
| Private | | | |
| Regents | 64 | 0 | 0.0 |
| Administration | 24 | 0 | 0.0 |
| U. Officials, Deans & Assistant Deans | 30 | 0 | 0.0 |
| Total | 553 | 21 | 3.8 |

TABLE 4

The Percentage of Blacks in Policy-Making Positions in the Voluntary Sector

| SELECTED AREAS | NUMBER OF POSITIONS | NUMBER OF POSITION HOLDERS | PERCENT OF BLACKS |
|---|---|---|---|
| Voluntary Organizations | | | |
| Service | 472 | 125 | 26.5 |
| Civic | 121 | 2 | 1.7 |
| Labor Organizations | | | |
| Regions | 36 | 2 | 5.6 |
| Local | 26 | 0 | 0.0 |
| Total | 655 | 129 | 19.7 |

Black decision-makers are more likely to be found in civil rights and welfare oriented positions. This pattern dilutes the degree of Black influence even in those areas where Black representation is most frequent. Further limiting Black influence in these sectors is the discovery that a small number of Black representatives "acceptable" to White decision-makers were repeatedly used in "Black slots." These same Blacks were present on numerous committees and boards. As a result, they simply do not have the same amount of time to devote to each issue as do their White counterparts.

A related question raised by this research is whether Blacks must necessarily be represented by Blacks. We can think of a number of reasons why such representation is necessary. In the short run, Whites can possibly obtain more for Blacks than Black representatives can for themselves. However, such paternalism is debilitating at best and devastating at worst. A paternalistic approach prevents the emergence of viable Black leadership. Black leaders can also bring different insights and perspectives to problems. For example, the Milwaukee case provides evidence that Blacks in positions of power have raised issues which Whites in similar positions could not, or would not raise. In the case of open housing legislation, the only Black member of the Milwaukee Common Council in the mid-sixties introduced an open housing ordinance. It was defeated 19–1.

The symbolic influence of visibly signifying to both the Black and White communities that Blacks can legitimately achieve power should also be emphasized. Black attitudes concerning the causes of riots during the sixties emphasize Black alienation from local decision-makers. In Milwaukee, as in other cities which experienced civil disturbances, Blacks felt that decision-makers did not care about the problems of the inner city (Slesinger, 1968).

## RECOMMENDATIONS FOR FURTHER STUDY

The findings of this study and the earlier Chicago work suggest that additional research is needed regarding the implications of the exclusion of Blacks from positions of power in major institutional sectors. In particular, additional information is needed in the areas of: (1) avenues of access for Blacks to positions of power, (2) the implications of the kind of credentials required of a Black to be acceptable, (3) the relatively greater difficulty of Black movement into areas involving economic power, and (4) the relatively greater difficulty of Blacks moving into positions having high symbolic importance and prestige.

The four areas of avenues of access, acceptability to established decision-makers, economic power vested in the position, and prestige vested in the position suggest a number of hypotheses. We, for example, would hypothesize that:

a   Blacks have a greater probability of occupying high appointive positions than high elective positions on civil service positions.

b   The probability of a Black being appointed to a position having a potential for power is directly related to the similarity of his political and economic philosophy to that of Whites already occupying positions of power.

c   Significant Black participation in the making of decisions is inversely related to the amount of resources involved.

d   Black representation is inversely related to the relative prestige of the formal position held.

The research reported in this paper clearly documents the extent to which Blacks are excluded from the decision-making process in one large midwestern city. We have also described the highly structured pattern of token representation of Negroes in positions that clearly affect the welfare of the Black community, and the exclusion of Blacks from positions controlling economic power. Finally, we have suggested several theoretical directions for examining in greater detail the full implication of black powerlessness in decision-making positions.

## REFERENCES

*Baron, H. M.*
1968   "Black powerlessness in Chicago," *Trans*action (November): 27–33.
*National Advisory Commission on Civil Disorders*
1968   Report of the National Advisory Commission on Civil Disorders. Washington, D.C.: U.S. Government Printing Office; also New York: Bantam Books.
*Slesinger, Jonathan A.*
1968   Community Opinions Regarding the Summer, 1967, Disturbances in Milwaukee. Unpublished.

# Blue Collar Anger: Reactions to Student and Black Protest[*]

## H. Edward Ransford

*University of Southern California*

*The hypothesis that working class respondents are especially antagonistic toward the black and student movements is tested with a sample of white Los Angeles residents (n = 477). In support of the hypothesis, working class persons and those with less than a high school education (in contrast to those higher in the occupational and educational hierarchies) are more likely to:*

*(a) express punitive attitudes toward student demonstrators,*

*(b) oppose granting students more power, and*

*(c) feel blacks are pushing too hard for things they don't deserve.*

*To locate rationales that would explain these relationships, intervening and specification variables were introduced in the analysis. These variables are: respect for authority, belief in the American Dream, belief that the needs of the working man are neglected, and perceived powerlessness. Substantial support for these explanations of blue collar anger is found.*

*Source:* H. Edward Ransford, "Blue Collar Anger: Reactions to Student and Black Protest," American Sociological Review 37, 3 (June 1972): 333–46. Copyright © 1972 by the American Sociological Association. Reprinted by permission of the Association and the author.
*An earlier version of this paper (In which Vincent Jeffries was junior author) was presented at the 1971 meeting of the American Sociological Association in Denver, Colorado, September, 1971. Professor Jeffries participated as co-investigator in all phases of a larger research project from which these data were taken. I am especially indebted to Vincent Jeffries for helpful suggestions and criticisms of earlier drafts of this paper. I also gratefully acknowledge the comments of Joseph Gusfield and Thomas Lasswell. This investigation was supported by Biomedical Sciences Support grant FR-07012-03 from the General Research Support Branch, Division of Research Resources, Bureau of Health Professions Education and Manpower Training, National Institutes of Health.

Little is known about the reactions of the white majority to campus protest and black demands. It seems obvious that a great many majority-group Americans are angry, even outraged, by such incidents as student takeovers of buildings or by black power demands for reparations or preferential hiring in industry. The major question of this paper is whether this anger is randomly distributed in the socioeconomic structure, or is far more likely to be found in the working class environment. Are blue collar people uniquely antagonistic toward the goals and methods of student and black demonstrators?

A number of recent themes in the race and stratification literature suggest that working class people should be more antagonistic toward black protestors than those higher in the socioeconomic structure. Van den Berghe observes that race relations in the United States have shifted from total subordination of blacks in power, privilege, and prestige ("paternalistic" race relations) to a kind of competitive relationship found in advanced industrial societies.

*In such a dynamic industrial society with its great geographical mobility and its stress on impersonal market mechanisms and universalistic and achieved criteria of occupational selection, race relations are quite different from what they are under agrarian conditions. The master-servant model with its elaborate caste etiquette and its mechanisms of subservience and social distance breaks down to be replaced by acute competition between the subordinate caste and the working class within the dominant group. (van den Berghe, 1967:29, 30)*

In industrialized, multiracial societies when the caste-paternalistic lid is lifted, the white working class is most likely to feel threatened by black upward mobility. Working class people have small, but hard earned, amounts of power, privilege, and prestige that they are anxious to protect (Skolnick, 1969:210–240).

In addition to van den Berghe's description of the macro processes, a number of more specific rationales link blue collar position with anger toward protest activity. It is these more middle range and measurable rationales that form the core of this paper.

## THEORETICAL EXPLANATIONS
## AND HYPOTHESES

At least three somewhat distinct (though partly overlapping) explanations can be advanced for the hypothesis that working class people will be more antagonistic toward student and black demands than people higher in the class structure. All three indicate that the protest methods and demands of students and blacks grate especially hard on the values, outlooks, and economic fears of the working class person.

### 1. The Conformity-Idealization
### of Authority Explanation

A number of studies indicate that the blue collar environment stresses the value of respect for authority. In the socialization of children, for example, a recent study (Kohn, 1969) shows that blue collar parents are more likely to emphasize obedience and neatness in contrast to middle class parents who emphasize internal dynamics such as curiosity and self realization. The stress on conformity and obedience is due in part to occupational environments. Blue collar persons typically are in occupations which demand repetition, conformity, and adherence to rules. Thus Kohn and Schooler (1969) find that men's opportunities to exercise occupational self direction—that is, to use initiative, thought, and independent judgment in work—interpret much of the relationship between class and authoritarian orientations. Other studies indicate that working class persons are less sophisticated in cognitive thinking. Being less well read and educated, as well as isolated from people with different views from their own, their thinking is concrete, simple, and stereotyped (Lipset, 1960:87–126). Lane and Lerner (1970:105) make the same point when they note that blue collar men emphasize attributes of individuals rather than attributes of abstract systems. They hold to simple moral and ethical perceptions of the world rather than perceptions involving relativity of judgment or competing values. The lesser degree of cognitive or abstract thinking feeds into the same point, that working class people are more likely to conform to basic institutions than to question the existing system.

From this perspective, it follows that working class persons will be more outraged by campus protest and black demands than those higher in the class structure. Student protest and black protest symbolize a classic flaunting of authority and downgrading of institutions. The four letter words, the styles of dress, and the direct confrontation methods all suggest disrespect for authority.

## 2. Belief in the American Dream—Neglect of Workingman's Needs

This revised class conflict model, as opposed to a Marxian model in which the white working class is a revolutionary force for change, sees the blue collar worker as reaffirming traditional beliefs in the openness of the American system. Hostility is directed toward the black lower class as undeserving of special opportunity as well as toward white liberal persons in power who seek to remake traditional America at the workingman's expense. Working class people have made modest economic gains through union victories and through their own hard work and sacrifice. They are far from economically secure, however. They believe poor people and black people are at the bottom of the class structure because of their own laziness, not because of racism or other institutional barriers (Lane and Lerner, 1970). Given their beliefs in hard work and the openness of the American structure, working class persons are hostile toward ghetto rioters and black demands for quotas and preferential job treatment. It is not simply that they feel blacks do not deserve special opportunity. They are angry because it seems to them that they are being asked to pay the biggest price for "social justice" (See Schneider, 1970). If they yield to demands for special opportunities and super-seniority for black workers, they, not the secure upper-middle-class people, face the greatest threat of being laid off.

From the workingman's point of view, far too much attention is being paid to the poor, and especially the black poor. In a recent survey (Newsweek, 1969), 65 percent of white middle Americans felt that blacks have a better chance than whites to get financial help from the government when they're out of work. Increasingly, white workers perceive that it is easier for an unemployed black to get aid and sympathy than a hard working white. Further, working class people are angry because they perceive that they are taxed heavily to support welfare budgets for the poor, and they have fewer mechanisms like business expense accounts, to escape taxation. In short, they feel they are paying for the special opportunities given minority persons—compensations they believe to be unnecessary in a free and open society.

Although this second explanation for blue collar anger (the American Dream and neglect of the working man's needs) is more clearly related to antagonism toward black militance, it also ties in with antagonism toward campus activism. A perception of the American system as open and just is antithetical to the student activist view that the American system is racist, elitist, exploitative, and excessively authoritarian. Further, the quintessence of the American Dream is sending one's children to college so they can advance in the social structure and have a better life. It is only with great sacrifice, however, that the working class family can send their children to college. The shouting of affluent youth, "On Strike—Shut It Down!" is a multiple outrage to blue collar people. Activist students are not only attacking American values, but threatening to close an only recently opened channel of mobility for working class children.

## 3. The Powerlessness Explanation

From this point of view, a critical dimension of the disaffection of white working class people is their sense of powerlessness over "radical" changes occuring in the country, and over political decisions directly affecting their lives. Working class people may perceive that they have few means to affect political change. Their occupational roles do not evoke respect and power in the larger society. Even in their own union the rank and file often have no real voice in making policy.

Recent student and black protest has, no doubt, heightened these feelings of political powerlessness. The worker may perceive that black and student militants have reached power centers and are forcing institutional changes that seem to him a distributive injustice or direct threat (for example, preferential hiring for blacks, relaxed extrance requirements and special aid for minority college students, and plans for increased school and residential integration that may affect him especially as an inner city resident living close to the ghetto). Of the "power structure's" various components, blue collar workers may view the government as especially hard to move and preoccupied with the problems of blacks.

The powerlessness explanation would predict that white working class people who feel politically powerless, i.e., who expect public officials to be unresponsive to their needs, will be especially antagonistic toward student and black activists. Each gain in power for militant students or blacks may be perceived as a reciprocal loss in power, status, or a way of life for the working class person.

Note that the concept of powerlessness used in this study denotes a perception of the social system and does not necessarily refer to personal apathy or fatalism. Indeed, the more militant white action responses to black and student protest (such as "hard hat" demonstrations or the Tony Imperiale Armed Citizens Committee) suggest a high degree of personal confidence and efficacy combined with a low expectancy of being able to move a large impersonal system through normative action.[1]

There is a distinct difference in the logic of the first two explanations and this third powerless explanation. The first two view class position as the source of certain outlooks and values (respect for authority, belief in the American Dream, and belief that needs of working class persons are neglected); and these in turn prompt antagonism toward student and black rebels. That is, we are dealing with "interpretation" logic or variables that intervene between X and Y.[2] In the powerlessness explanation we are specifying which segments of the white working class will be most antagonistic toward student and black activists, i.e., using a "specification" logic. Stated differently, powerlessness per se does not clearly lead to antagonism toward student and black activists (many supporters of student and black demands may feel alienated from establishment politics); but rather, it is the combination of the blue collar perception of distributive injustice and feelings of powerlessness that should prompt antagonism toward students and blacks.

## HYPOTHESES

From the above discussion, we hypothesize that working class respondents compared to those higher in the socioeconomic structure will be more likely to report: (a) hostility toward student demonstrators, (b) opposition to the student demand for increased power in running the university, and (c) a feeling that blacks are pushing too hard and too fast for things they don't deserve. In each hypothesis we predict a negative linear relationship between socioeconomic status and antagonism toward student and black militants.

Using a partial correlation technique, we develop refinements of these basic hypotheses to test for the importance of the three above theoretical explanations.

In addition to the test of main hypotheses, two supplementary questions will be explored: will class position continue to predict hostility toward student and black demonstrators with (1) age held constant and (2) sex held constant? For example, have recent developments in generation consciousness and youth culture become so important that young adults will be more sympathetic to student and black protest regardless of socioeconomic position?

## SAMPLE AND MEASUREMENT
## OF VARIABLES

Data for this study consist of the responses of a probability sample of 477 Caucasian adults (twenty-one years or older) to a personal interview schedule.

The sample was drawn from white areas of Los Angeles, primarily in the San Fernando Valley during the latter part of 1969 and the first few months in 1970. Not only was this a period of extreme campus unrest nationally, but on two campuses in or near the sample area, student demonstrators took control briefly of campus offices. The valley section of the Los Angeles Metropolitan Area contains a population of approximately one million. Although the sample is undoubtedly typical of some suburban areas across the country, a somewhat special characteristic of this territory should be noted. The San Fernando Valley is a large sprawling suburban region without the white, ethnic communities one finds in Newark, Chicago, Wisconsin, or New York. For example, there is no Italian or Polish neighborhood in the valley. Some evidence suggests that blue collar hostility toward demonstrators is apt to be especially acute when working class position is mixed with ethnic identification (Greeley, 1969). In such working class ethnic communities, common frustrations and interpretations of a demonstration may be easily shared and developed. Accordingly, any relationship that we find between socioeconomic position and hostility may exist even more so in working class ethnic communities elsewhere in the country.[3]

Though subjects were selected by a probability model (involving random areas, blocks, and block corners as interviewer starting points) the sample should be classified as "disproportional stratified" since blue collar areas were oversampled to provide sufficient cases for testing the hypotheses.[4] We controlled carefully for the respondent's sex. Approximately equal numbers of males and females (one respondent per household) were interviewed.[5] Finally, it should be emphasized that the working class respondents in our sample are employed and in predominantly semi-skilled or highly skilled positions. That is, we are testing hypotheses dealing with the "organized" working class vs. strata above this group. There were too few lower blue collar respondents in our sample to view separately (80% craftsmen, foremen, and operatives vs. 20% unskilled).

**Independent Variable**

Socioeconomic status, the study's independent variable, is indexed by occupation and education taken as separate measures. Though occupation and education are commonly combined into an index of SES, it seemed important in this paper to view their effects separately since they tap slightly different aspects of the working class anger thesis. For example, education seems more likely to be associated with intellectual flexibility and breadth of perspective. Occupation, at least in Marxian theory, would seem more likely to be associated with work-related hostilities and peer group communication. For example, blue collar workers may develop common interpretations of radical demonstrations because of their occupations, quite apart from their educational experiences.

The occupations were coded into an ordinal scale with blue collar lowest, business white collar (clerical, sales, and managerial) intermediate, and professional white collar high. Professionals were ranked above "business white collar" because so few high ranking executives and major business owners are in the sample compared to the more uniformly high status for the professionals.

For example, using the Bogue scale (Bogue, 1963) which ranks occupations in status from 44 to 180, the mean score for the blue collar group was 92.5, for business white collar 116.1, and for professionals 137.1

### Dependent Variables

Hostility toward student demonstrators is measured by the following three items (marginal percentages in parenthesis):

1. *Even if they don't break the law, college students who are involved in demonstrations should be expelled (Agree 36% Disagree 64%).*
2. *College students who break the law during campus demonstrations should be given the strongest punishment possible by law (Agree 70% Disagree 30%).*
3. *College students who engage in illegal demonstrations deserve to be beaten by the police (Agree 13% Disagree 81% DK 6%).*

On finding a fairly high association among the items (Gammas ranging from .60 to .93) a trichotomized index was constructed. Those agreeing with two or three of the items were called "high" in hostility toward student demonstrators; those agreeing with one were called "medium" and those disagreeing with all were called "low."

The following single item was used to measure feelings toward the issue of student power:

*Students should be given more say in running the colleges (Agree 47% Disagree 53%).*

Antagonism toward black protest was measured by the following items:

1. *Negroes deserve the things they are asking for (Agree 60% Disagree 40%).*
2. *Negroes are asking for special treatment from whites to which they are not entitled (Agree 67% Disagree 33%).*
3. *Negroes are pushing harder and faster than they have a right to (Agree 48% Disagree 52%).*

With high association among the items (Gammas ranging from .51 to .79) a trichotomized index was formed with the same cutting points as the student hostility score.

### Intervening and Specification Variables

Respect for authority was measured by four F scale items that seemed most directly related to obedience to authority and conformity. An example is the item: "The most important thing to teach children is absolute obedience to their parents" (Agree 63% Disagree 37%).

Belief in the American Dream and neglect of working man's needs required two separate measures. "Belief in the American Dream" was measured by a two-item index[6] (example: "If anyone is poor in this country today he has only himself to blame." Agree 32% Disagree 68%); while "neglect of workingman's needs" was captured by a single item ("There's more concern today for the 'welfare bum' who doesn't want to work than for the hard working person struggling to make a living." Agree 74% Disagree 26%).

Political powerlessness was measured by a score consisting of three forced choice items.[7] Two of the items were taken from a scale developed by Neal and Seeman (1964), the third from a scale developed by Olsen (1969). Two examples are: "I don't think public officials care much what people like me think." (25%) versus "People like me can have an influence on what the government does." (75%); and "The average citizen can have an influence on government decisions." (69%) versus "This world is run by the few people in power and there's not much the little guy can do about it." (31%).

Note that these are somewhat rough indices of attitude variables with few items per index and a minimum demonstration of unidimensionality. As a result, the findings must be regarded as less than conclusive.

## FINDINGS

Is the working class person more hostile toward student and black demands than those higher in the socioeconomic structure?

Table 1 shows that this is indeed the case, with occupation moderately correlated with each dependent variable and education showing a stronger relationship. For example, 50% of the blue collar workers score high on student hostility, compared to only 25% of professionals. Education is an even more powerful independent variable, ranging from 50 to 18%. About half the blue collar workers and persons with a high school education or less agree with at least two of the very punitive student hostility items. The most striking relationship in Table 1 is the association between education and the belief that black demands are unjustified. Seventy-seven percent of those with less than high school feel blacks are pushing too hard as opposed to 31% of the college graduates.

Though it was considered essential to differentiate between occupational and educational status in this analysis, it also seemed important to assess the impact of each with the other held constant. Overall, partial correlation analysis (linearity is assumed in each relationship) reveals that education more strongly determines antagonism toward student and black militants than does occupation.[8] However, these general correlations may be masking important subgroup comparisons. Accordingly, Table 2 presents the joint effects of occupation and education on antagonism in cross-tabular form. For ease of presentation, only the "high antagonism" end of the dependent variables are shown (the total linear relationships are captured by the gammas). Unfortunately, it was not possible to have the entire educational range for each occupation. Under-

## TABLE 1

**Independent Variables (Occupation and Education) by Student Demonstrator Hostility, Student Power, and Black Demands Unjustified**

| | STUDENT DEMONSTRATOR HOSTILITY % | | | | OPPOSITION TO STUDENT POWER % | | | BLACK DEMANDS UNJUSTIFIED | | | |
|---|---|---|---|---|---|---|---|---|---|---|---|
| | LOW | MEDIUM | HIGH | N | LOW | HIGH | N | LOW | MEDIUM | HIGH | N |
| **Occupation:** | | | | | | | | | | | |
| Blue collar | 12 | 37 | 50 | (163) | 34 | 66 | (164) | 12 | 18 | 70 | (164) |
| Business white collar* | 26 | 44 | 30 | (159) | 52 | 48 | (162) | 21 | 33 | 46 | (155) |
| Professional white collar | 34 | 41 | 25 | (137) | 50 | 50 | (139) | 29 | 31 | 40 | (131) |
| | | Gamma = -.32 p<.001 | | | | Gamma = -.21 p<.01 | | | Gamma = -.34 p<.001 | | |
| **Education:** | | | | | | | | | | | |
| Less than high school | 3 | 47 | 50 | (60) | 27 | 73 | (63) | 8 | 15 | 77 | (60) |
| High school graduate | 15 | 40 | 45 | (149) | 42 | 58 | (149) | 17 | 24 | 59 | (150) |
| Some college | 35 | 36 | 29 | (152) | 49 | 51 | (153) | 22 | 31 | 47 | (146) |
| College graduate | 36 | 46 | 18 | (104) | 60 | 40 | (106) | 37 | 32 | 31 | (99) |
| | | Gamma = -.37 p<.001 | | | | Gamma = -.30 p<.001 | | | Gamma = -.37 p<.001 | | |

*Refers to clerical, managerial and sales.

Note: Statistical significance determined by chi square.

standably, there were too few blue-collar-college graduates and white-collar less than-high-school persons to compute percentages for these subgroups. Nevertheless, within each occupational group are three meaningful education levels that allow for important comparisons. On the issue of "student demonstrator hostility," Table 2 shows that about half the blue collar persons are highly antagonistic regardless of educational achievement. However, for the white collar groups (business, professional) education has much more impact on hostility toward student demonstrators. One possible interpretation is that the "blue collar situation," explicated in the three theoretical statements, overrides any effects of education. Conversely, many white collar workers are somewhat more removed from this situation (of perceived powerlessness, distributive injustice, neglect of workingman etc.) so that an individual's education may have far greater effects. A less pronounced but similar pattern—homogeneity of outlook in the blue collar category versus large differences in the white collar group—can be seen with "opposition to student power" and "black demands unjustified." The one exception is the uniquely antagonistic response toward black demands of blue-collar less-than-high-school persons. Table 2 also reveals that hostile attitudes toward students and blacks are not unique to the blue collar group. They are shared by less well educated business and professional persons, in particular high school graduates. For example, professional persons with a high school degree show approximately the same proportion opposed to student power as blue collar workers. Similarly business white collar persons with a high school degree have the same proportion antagonistic toward student demonstrators as blue collar persons.

Our next task is to find if these relationships between socioeconomic status and antagonism operate for both the males and the females in the sample. The three theories for working class anger (conformity, American Dream–worker neglect, powerlessness) seem to apply most direcly to the blue collar male. However, as co-managers of the household, blue collar wives would probably share some of the same frustrations as their husbands. Though the overwhelming percentage of women sampled were not employed outside the home, it seems logical to expect that they would resemble their husbands in outlook toward students and blacks. Table 3's data suggest that the association between occupation and student-black antagonism operates for both males and females, but is consistently stronger for males. This is especially true for the correlation between occupation and "black demands unjustified." The relationship is twice as strong for males as for females, with blue collar males being the most antagonistic toward black demands. We can speculate that blue collar males are unusually hostile because they are hit most directly by the work world frustrations defined in the three theories. However, when education is the independent variable, the relationships are more nearly equal in strength for males and females. Education probably reflects slightly different personal characteristics than does occupation, such as intellectual breadth and flexibility. Perhaps this dimension is more uniform for males and females regardless of employment status.

People in blue collar jobs and those with less than high school graduation are clearly more antagonistic. But are the theoretical reasons we have advanced for blue collar anger correct? To what extent do respect for authority, belief in the American Dream, and belief that worker needs are neglected, interpret the relationship between SES and student-black antagonism? One may first note

TABLE 2

Percent Scoring "High" on Student Demonstrator Hostility,
Opposition to Student Power, and Black Demands Unjustified,
by Education with Occupation Controlled

| EDUCATION | % HIGH STUDENT HOSTILITY | N | % HIGH OPPOSITION TO STUDENT POWER | N | % HIGH BLACK DEMANDS UNJUSTIFIED | N |
|---|---|---|---|---|---|---|
| BLUE COLLAR | | | | | | |
| Less than high school | 54 | (48) | 74 | (50) | 81 | (48) |
| High school graduate | 48 | (62) | 61 | (61) | 66 | (65) |
| Some college | 51 | (37) | 62 | (37) | 61 | (36) |
| College graduate | — | — | — | — | — | — |
| | Gamma = −.15 N.S. | | −.17 N.S. | | −.25 p<.20 | |
| BUSINESS WHITE COLLAR | | | | | | |
| Less than high school | — | — | — | — | — | — |
| High school graduate | 48 | (56) | 51 | (57) | 54 | (56) |
| Some college | 19 | (62) | 50 | (62) | 46 | (59) |
| College graduate | 16 | (32) | 33 | (33) | 29 | (31) |
| | Gamma = −.38 p<.02 | | −.23 p<.15 | | −.20 p<.15 | |
| PROFESSIONAL WHITE COLLAR | | | | | | |
| Less than high school | — | — | — | — | — | — |
| High school graduate | 35 | (31) | 65 | (29) | 59 | (27) |
| Some college | 27 | (41) | 50 | (42) | 40 | (40) |
| College graduate | 18 | (65) | 41 | (66) | 31 | (62) |
| | Gamma = −.30 p<.06 | | −.33 p<.05 | | −.38 p<.02 | |

Note: Statistical significance determined by chi square.

(Table 4) that occupation and education correlate with each of the three intervening variables, and they in turn, correlate with antagonism toward students and blacks.[9] However, our theory states that blue collar anger results from the combination of respect for authority, worker neglect and belief in the American Dream. Accordingly, we need a statistical design that will handle the combined effect of all three intervening variables. Table 5 presents partial correlations (Pearsonian) between socioeconomic status and the student-black antagonism variables with the intervening variables held constant singly and in combination.[10] Our expectation is that the strength of the relationship between SES and antagonism will diminish considerably with these intervening variables held constant. In all instances the original zero order relationship drops appreciably with all three variables controlled. For example, the original r between education and student demonstrator hostility is a moderate −.31, but drops to −.12 with the three intervening variables simultaneously controlled. Table 5 also reveals that the control for respect for authority reduces the zero order correlation slightly more than the other intervening variables. However,

TABLE 3

Percent Scoring "High" on Student Demonstrator Hostility,
Opposition to Student Power, and Black Demands Unjustified, by the
Independent Variables (Occupation, Education), with Sex Controlled

| | *% HIGH STUDENT HOSTILITY* | *N* | *% HIGH OPPOSITION TO STUDENT POWER* | *N* | *% HIGH BLACK DEMANDS UNJUSTIFIED* | *N* |
|---|---|---|---|---|---|---|
| | | | *MALES* | | | |
| Occupation | | | | | | |
| Blue collar | 57 | (70) | 67 | (70) | 81 | (70) |
| Business white collar | 30 | (79) | 54 | (81) | 52 | (79) |
| Professional white collar | 23 | (61) | 48 | (62) | 37 | (59) |
| | Gamma = −.40 p<.001 | | Gamma = −.24 p<.20 | | Gamma = −.49 p<.001 | |
| Education | | | | | | |
| Less than high school | 57 | (28) | 79 | (29) | 82 | (27) |
| High school graduate | 50 | (52) | 52 | (50) | 69 | (52) |
| Some college | 34 | (70) | 57 | (70) | 56 | (69) |
| College graduate | 19 | (69) | 45 | (71) | 35 | (68) |
| | Gamma = −.39 p<.001 | | Gamma = −.25 p<.02 | | Gamma = −.44 p<.001 | |
| | | | *FEMALES* | | | |
| Occupation | | | | | | |
| Blue collar | 43.5 | (85) | 64 | (88) | 61 | (87) |
| Business white collar | 29 | (80) | 42 | (81) | 40 | (76) |
| Professional white collar | 20 | (76) | 51 | (77) | 42 | (72) |
| | Gamma = −.25 p<.05 | | Gamma = −.18 p<.02 | | Gamma = −.23 p<.05 | |
| Education | | | | | | |
| Less than high school | 44 | (32) | 67 | (34) | 73 | (33) |
| High school graduate | 42 | (97) | 61 | (99) | 54 | (98) |
| Some college | 24 | (82) | 46 | (83) | 39 | (77) |
| College graduate | 17 | (35) | 29 | (35) | 23 | (31) |
| | Gamma = −.35 p<.001 | | Gamma = −.37 p<.001 | | Gamma = −.38 p<.001 | |

*Note: Statistical significance determined by chi square.*

since the intervening variable indices did not have the same number of items one cannot conclude that respect for authority is a more important intervening link than the belief in the openness of the American system or the belief that workingman's needs are neglected. The only surviving relationships are those between education and black antagonism (partial R = −.16 p < .01) and occupation and black antagonism (partial r = −.16 p < .01). Apparently, there are other reasons for hostility that we have not fully measured, for example, a perceived threat from black economic progress.

TABLE 4

Correlation Coefficients (Pearsonian) Between Independent Variables and Intervening Variables and Between Intervening Variables and Dependent Variables

|  | *INTERVENING VARIABLES* | | |
|---|---|---|---|
| *A. INDEPENDENT VARIABLES* | *RESPECT FOR AUTHORITY* | *BELIEF IN AMERICAN DREAM* | *NEGLECT WORKINGMAN'S NEEDS* |
| Occupation | –.26* | –.18* | –.21* |
| Education | –.37* | –.23* | –.22* |
|  | *DEPENDENT VARIABLES* | | |
| *B. INTERVENING VARIABLES* | *STUDENT DEMONSTRATOR HOSTILITY* | *OPPOSED TO STUDENT POWER* | *BLACK DEMANDS UNJUSTIFIED* |
| Respect for authority | .48* | .35* | .36* |
| Belief in American dream | .36* | .28* | .37* |
| Neglect workingman's needs | .44* | .33* | .47* |

*\* = p < .01.*

*Note: Statistical significance determined by student's T (one-tailed) test.*

## Specification: Control for Powerlessness

Table 6 largely supports the hypothesis that working class persons who feel politically powerless will be especially antagonistic toward the student and black movements. Consistently, SES is more strongly associated with antagonism toward rebels for the "highs" in powerlessness than for the "lows" in powerlessness (though some differences are small). Further, the blue collar group and the less-than-high-school group scoring high in powerlessness are more antagonistic toward students and blacks than anyone else in the sample. The relationship least affected by this control is one between education and black demands unjustified. Perhaps the least skilled perceive themselves threatened directly by black economic advancement, and this holds whatever their feelings of political powerlessness.

## Control for Age

Are younger working class respondents more sympathetic with black and student demands? Has the youth movement invaded the socioeconomic structure to the extent that the outlooks of younger "working class" respondents will be similar to the outlooks of younger "middle class" respondents? For brevity, the data will be described rather than shown in table form. Occupation and education persist in predicting student power and black demands unjustified with three age groups held constant (21–30, 31–45, and over 45). But among the young (21–30) occupation is only weakly associated with student hostility (Gamma = –.23 p = N.S.) and education washes out completely as a predictor

TABLE 5

**Partial Correlations Between Independent Variables (Occupation and Education) and the Dependent Variables with Respect for Authority, Belief in American Dream, and Neglect of Workingman, Controlled Singly and Jointly**

| | ZERO ORDER | (1) RESPECT FOR AUTHORITY CONTROLLED | (2) AMERICAN DREAM CONTROLLED | (3) WORKER NEGLECTED CONTROLLED | SIMULTANEOUS CONTROL 1, 2, AND 3 |
|---|---|---|---|---|---|
| **Correlation Between Occupation and:** | | | | | |
| Student demonstrator hostility | -.20* | -.09 | -.17* | -.14* | -.07 |
| Opposed to student power | -.14* | -.06 | -.12* | -.09 | -.04 |
| Black demands unjustified | -.25* | -.18* | -.23* | -.19* | -.16* |
| **Correlation Between Education and:** | | | | | |
| Student demonstrator hostility | -.31* | -.16* | -.25* | -.24* | -.12* |
| Opposed to student power | -.24* | -.12* | -.18* | -.18* | -.09 |
| Black demands unjustified | -.32* | -.20* | -.24* | -.23* | -.16* |

* = p < .01.
Note: Statistical significance determined by student's T (one-tailed test).

of student hostility (Gamma = −.05, p = N.S.). In other words, younger "working class" respondents feel much the same as younger "middle class" respondents on the question of punitive treatment toward student protestors: both groups tend to be non-punitive. But on the question of student power and black demands, the younger blue collar workers are just as antagonistic as older blue collar workers. In fact, the greatest polarization by class occurs within the young group. For example, 76% of young blue collar workers feel black demands are unjustified vs. only 29% of young white collar professionals (Gamma = 50, p < .02). On the issues of student power and black demands, young blue collar workers and young well-educated professionals are worlds apart in outlook.

## DISCUSSION AND CONCLUSIONS

The thesis that white working class people are highly antagonistic toward students and blacks demanding massive changes receives moderate support from this analysis. We stress the term, "moderate support." Though there is a definite socioeconomic differential (especially for males and those scoring high in political powerlessness), fairly sizeable segments of all educational and occupation strata have reacted with anger to protest of the 1960s. Still, blue collar workers are found to be more uniformly high in antagonism toward student and black protest regardless of educational level; whereas, white collar workers display more heterogeneity of outlook according to educational achievement. This suggests that merely acquiring education will not substantially reduce the blue collar worker's level of hostility toward militants.

Not only are the major relationships between SES and antagonism supported but, given the limitations of indices with only a few items, we find some confirmation for each of the three theoretical explanations (respect for authority, American Dream-worker needs neglected, and political powerlessness.) However, the partial correlation table indicates that the explanations do not fully interpret the correlations between SES and "black demands unjustified." Further research is needed to locate other rationales for blue collar anger and to test for their relative effects.

An especially interesting finding is that for two dependent variables (student power and black demands unjustified) the greatest class polarization was found among young adults. This finding supports Lipset's contention that the generation gap is grossly overstated and that the greatest differences in political outlook and behavior are within the youth group rather than between age cohorts (Lipset, 1970:370–372).

The mass media have probably tended to overstereotype the white working man as a narrow-minded, intolerant bigot. His angry responses to students and blacks are often viewed as the effect of a prejudiced personality. In contrast, our model shows blue collar anger to be rooted in the actual or perceived social situation. From this perspective, much of the workingman's anger is a rational response to tangible strains, independent of personal bigotry. A lack of decision-making power on the job, the fact of hard earned dollars going for tax programs to aid blacks with no comparable programs for working class whites, a power

structure unresponsive to the needs of the workingman—these stresses probably affect working class anger as much as personal prejudice.

In addition, white working class people who feel politically powerless are
especially antagonistic toward student and black protestors. Research in the
black community conducted shortly after the Watts riot (Ransford 1968) suggests a parallel finding: blacks who scored high in social powerlessness (low
expectancy of gaining redress through institutional channels) were more willing to use violence to get their rights. Similarly, a violence commission report

**TABLE 6**

Percent Scoring "High" on Student Demonstrator Hostility,
Opposition to Student Power, and Black Demands Unjustified, by the
Independent Variables (Occupation, Education), with Powerlessness Controlled

| | *% HIGH STUDENT HOSTILITY* | *N* | *% HIGH OPPOSITION TO STUDENT POWER* | *N* | *% HIGH BLACK DEMANDS UNJUSTIFIED* | *N* |
|---|---|---|---|---|---|---|
| | *LOW POWERLESSNESS* | | | | | |
| Occupation | | | | | | |
| Blue collar | 43 | (79) | 60 | (80) | 65 | (79) |
| Business white collar | 30 | (101) | 44 | (104) | 42 | (100) |
| Professional white collar | 23 | (101) | 53 | (102) | 36 | (94) |
| | Gamma = −.29 | | Gamma = −.07 | | Gamma = −.29 | |
| | p<.01 | | N.S. | | p<.01 | |
| Education | | | | | | |
| Less than high school | 36 | (25) | 67 | (27) | 75 | (24) |
| High school graduate | 41 | (92) | 55 | (94) | 56 | (93) |
| Some college | 30 | (98) | 50 | (99) | 43 | (94) |
| College graduate | 18 | (77) | 43 | (77) | 32 | (72) |
| | Gamma = −.32 | | Gamma = −.20 | | Gamma = −.32 | |
| | p<.001 | | N.S. | | p<.01 | |
| | *HIGH POWERLESSNESS* | | | | | |
| Occupation | | | | | | |
| Blue collar | 60 | (71) | 72 | (71) | 75 | (73) |
| Business white collar | 28 | (57) | 54 | (57) | 54 | (54) |
| Professional white collar | 30 | (36) | 40 | (37) | 43 | (37) |
| | Gamma = −.36 | | Gamma = −.41 | | Gamma = −.38 | |
| | p<.01 | | p<.01 | | p<.01 | |
| Education | | | | | | |
| Less than high school | 59 | (34) | 77 | (35) | 77 | (35) |
| High school graduate | 50 | (56) | 61 | (54) | 66 | (56) |
| Some college | 28 | (53) | 55 | (53) | 57 | (51) |
| College graduate | 19 | (26) | 32 | (28) | 30 | (27) |
| | Gamma = −.42 | | Gamma = −.40 | | Gamma = −.40 | |
| | p<.001 | | p<.01 | | p<.01 | |

*Note: Statistical significance determined by chi square.*

(Skolnick, 1969) notes that militant white reactions to protest (armed citizens groups) are found especially among those who are angered by excessive concern for minorities and who feel ignored by the polity. Apparently the potential exists for black as well as white militant action when individuals perceive a distributive injustice and, in addition, feel blocked in gaining redress through institutional channels.

This situation is clearly described by what Lipset (1970:510) has termed the "New American Dilemma," viz., how to square the American promise with lower class ghetto life for blacks, and at the same time not withdraw the promise from the white working class. A recent statement by Pete Hamill summarizes this dilemma well:

*The working class white man is actually in revolt against taxes, joyless work, the double standards and short memories of professional politicians, hypocrisy, and what he considers the debasement of the American Dream.... Any politician who leaves the white man out of his political equation does so at very large risk. The next round of race riots might not be between people and property but between people and people. And that could be the end of us. (Hamill, 1969)*

## NOTES

1    The several definitions and measures used for the concept powerlessness have caused confusion in recent studies. For example, the consistently used interpretation for the correlation between powerlessness and violence in my Watts research (Ransford, 1968) was powerlessness *as a low expectancy of gaining redress through institutional channels* (voting, the courts, civil rights movement etc.). However, a few recent reports on riot participation and riot attitudes have cast my findings into the category of apathy and fatalism (Forward and Williams, 1970; Paige, 1971). For a comment and rejoinder on the relationship between powerlessness and black militancy, see Ransford (1971) and Forward and Williams (1971).

Another conceptual distinction relevant to this study distinguishes political efficacy from political trust (Paige, 1971). The study suggests that self reported rioters in the Newark disorder were high on political efficacy but low on political trust. Paige notes that most measures of political efficacy blur these two dimensions. Applied to this study, it is possible that working class whites scoring high on political powerlessness feel equally a distrust of government as well as an inability to influence it. Although the distinction between efficacy and trust is important, the problem is to develop a measure of efficacy/powerlessness that is not contaminated by distrust. Thus in Paige's study, to avoid the distrust element, political efficacy was operationally defined as "political information" and finally measured by the (black) respondent's ability to identify the race of nine black and white officials. Obviously, there is a great gap between the nominal definition of efficacy and the final measure of racial information. The problems of developing a measure of system powerlessness free of system distrust are so great that one seems required to choose between a certain amount of distrust "mixed in" or an index with a serious problem in internal validity. Although some distrust may be built into our measure of powerlessness, the items seem most directly concerned with a low expectancy of affecting government through normative action.

2    When one treats a psychological variable (e.g., "respect for authority") as intervening between a social structural variable (e.g., occupational status) and another psychological variable (e.g., attitudes toward black demands), it is possible that the intervening variable is not historically or even logically prior but merely part of the same psychological outlook—in this case, a specific example of a more general orientation. However, in this analysis a more plausible interpretation is that the intervening attitudes result logically from the working class situation, have developed over a period of time, and logically precede current attitudes toward student and black protest. Note in addition, there is no direct contamination between the intervening and dependent variables, that is, no mention of students, blacks, or protest in the intervening variable items.

3    Another possible sample bias is that only those who voted in the 1969 Yorty-Bradley mayoral election were included. This selection procedure could have produced a bias toward the best informed and most politically active residents. However, due to the extremely emotional issues in this election, (a take-over of city hall by black power extremists and a drastic decline in law and order) in my judgment the sample is not highly biased toward either the best informed or the most politically active. Unusually high voter turnout indicated that many normally politically apathetic persons did vote in this election.

4    The decision to sample primarily from the San Fernando Valley was based on the need for a predominantly white area with widely differing socioeconomic levels within the Los Angeles city limits (city residents were needed to study the Yorty-Bradley mayoral election, another aspect of the project). As a result, integrated racial areas such as Crenshaw-Baldwin Hills district as well as areas of white concentration outside the city limits were excluded from the sample design. The San Fernando Valley was divided into 115 units of equal geographical size. Twenty areas from the Eagle Rock section of Los Angeles (not a part of the Valley) were also included. Random areas were selected as well as random blocks within these areas. Approximately eleven interviews were conducted in each selected area (fifteen to twenty interviews in blue collar areas).

5    Since ninety percent of the females did not have full-time occupations outside the home, most were classified by their husband's occupation. Their education level, however, is their own.

6    Gamma = .63 for the two items.

7    Gamma intercorrelation = .76, .71, and .52.

8    The Pearsonian r between occupation and education is .49 in these data. The r between occupation and "student demonstrator hostility" is $-.20$ $p < .01$; with education controlled $r = -.08$ N.S. In contrast, the r between education and "student demonstrator hostility" is $-.31$ $p < .01$; with occupation controlled $r = -.24$ $p < .01$. The r between occupation and "opposition to student power" is $-.14$ $p < .01$; with education controlled $r = -.04$ N.S. In contrast, the r between education and "opposition to student power" is $-.24$ $p < .01$. The r between occupation and "black demands unjustified" is $-.25$ $p < .01$; with education controlled $r = -.12$ $p < .05$. In comparison, the r between education and "black demands unjustified" is $-.30$ $p < 01$; with occupation controlled $r = -.19$ $p < .01$. This analysis (showing education to be the more powerful independent variable) must be viewed as suggestive rather than conclusive. For a discussion of the problems in assessing the independent effects of correlated variables, see Blalock (1964).

9    In the relationships between occupation and the intervening variables there is, again, a definite sex pattern with occupation having a stronger effect for males than females. For example, the r between occupation and authoritarianism is $-.35$ $p < .001$ for the males and $-.18$ $p < .01$ for the females. For "Belief in the American

Dream" the comparable r's are –.27 p < .001 vs. –.10 p < .06. For "Neglect working-man's needs" the r for males is –.35 p < .001 vs. –.09 p < .10 for females.

10    For the correlation and partial correlation analysis (Tables 4 and 5) all attitude variables were "opened" to include four ranks. For example, the one item measure of "worker needs neglected" contained all four Likert levels (strongly agree, agree, disagree, strongly disagree) instead of the two rank (agree, disagree) version used in the cross-tabulation tables. For a discussion of the use of the product moment correlation coefficient with ordinal data, see Labovitz (1967).

# REFERENCES

*Blalock, H. M.*
1963    "Correlated independent variables: The problem of multicollinearity." Social Forces 42 (December): 233–237.

*Bogue, Donald*
1963    Skid Row in American Cities. Chicago: University of Chicago Press.

*Forward, John R, and Jay R. Williams*
1970    "Internal-external control and black militancy." Journal of Social Issues 26 (Winter): 75–92.

*Forward, John R., and Jay R. Williams*
1971    "Rejoinder" Journal of Social Issues 27:233–236.

*Greely, A. M.*
1969    "America's not so silent minority." Los Angeles Times, Opinion. (Dec. 7): 1–2.

*Hamill, Pete*
1969    "The revolt of the white lower middle class." New York Times (April 14).

*Kohn, Melvin*
1969    Class and Conformity. Illinois: Dorsey.

*Kohn, Melvin, and C. Schooler*
1969    "Class, occupation and orientation." American Sociological Review 34 (October): 659–678.

Labovitz, Sanford
1967    "Some observations on measurement and statistics." Social Forces 46 (December): 151–160.

*Lane, Robert E., and Michael Lerner*
1970    "Why hard-hats hate hairs." Psychology Today 4 (November): 45.

*Lipset, Seymour M.*
1960    Political Man. New York: Doubleday: 87–126.

*Lipset, Seymour M., and E. Raab*
1970    The Politics of Unreason. New York: Harper.

*Neal, Arthur G., and Melvin Seeman*
1964    "Organizations and powerlessness: A test of the mediation hypothesis." American Sociological Review 29 (April): 216–226.

*Newsweek*
1960    "The troubled American: A special report on the white majority." 71 (October 6): 28–73.

*Olsen, M.*
1969    "Two categories of political alienation." Social Forces 47:228–299.

*Paige, Jeffery M.*
1971    "Political orientation and riot participation." American Sociological Review 36 (October): 810–820.

*Ransford, H. Edward*
1968    "Isolation, powerlessness and violence: A study of attitudes and participation in the Watts riot." American Journal of Sociology 73 (March): 581–591.
*Ransford, H. Edward*
1971    "Comment on: Internal-external control and black militancy." Journal of Social Issues 27:227–232.
*Schneider, Michael M.*
1970    "Middle America." The Center Magazine (Nov./Dec.): 2–9.
*Skolkick, Jerome H.*
1969    The Politics of Protest: Report to the National Commission on the Causes and Prevention of Violence. New York: Ballantine Books.
*van den Berghe, Pierre L.*
1967    Race and Racism. New York: John Wiley and Sons.

# The Origins of the Women's Liberation Movement[1]

## Jo Freeman
*University of Chicago*

The emergence in the last few years of a feminist movement caught most thoughful observers by surprise. Women had "come a long way," had they not? What could they want to be liberated from? The new movement generated much speculation about the sources of female discontent and why it was articulated at this particular time. But these speculators usually asked the wrong questions. Most attempts to analyze the sources of social strain have had to conclude with Ferriss (1971, p. 1) that, "from the close perspective of 1970, events of the past decade provide evidence of no compelling cause of the rise of the new feminist movement." His examination of time-series data over the previous 20 years did not reveal any significant changes in socioeconomic variables which could account for the emergence of a women's movement at the time it was created. From such strain indicators, one could surmise that any time in the last two decades was as conducive as any other to movement formation.

I

The sociological literature is not of much help: the study of social movements "has been a neglected area of sociology" (Killian 1964, p. 426), and, within that field, virtually no theorists have dealt with movement origins. The *causes* of social movements have been analyzed (Gurr 1970; Davies 1962), and the *motivations* of participants have been investigated (Toch 1965; Cantril 1941; Hoffer 1951; Adorno et al. 1950), but the mechanisms of "how" a movement is constructed have received scant attention.[2] As Dahrendorf (1959, p. 64) commented, "The sociologist is generally interested not so much in the origin of social phenomena as in their spread and rise to wider significance." This interest is derived from an emphasis on cultural processes rather than on people as the major dynamic of social change (Killian 1964, p. 426). Consequently, even the "natural history" theorists have delineated the stages of development in a way that is too vague to tell us much about how movements actually start (Dawson and Gettys 1929, pp. 787–803; Lowi 1971, p. 39; Blumer 1951; King 1956), and a theory as comprehensive as Smelser's (1963) is postulated on too abstract a level to be of microsociological value (for a good critique, see Currie and Skolnick [1970]).

Part of the problem results from extreme confusion about what a social movement really is. Movements are rarely studied as distinct social phenomena but are usually subsumed under one of two theoretical traditions: that of "collective behavior" (see, especially, Smelser 1963; Lang and Lang 1961; Turner and Killian 1957) and that of interest-group and party formation (Heberle 1951; King 1956; Lowi 1971). The former emphasizes the spontaneous aspects of a movement; and the latter, the structured ones. Yet movements are neither fully collective behavior nor incipient interest groups except in the broadest sense of these terms. Rather, they contain essential elements of both. It is "the dual imperative of spontaneity and organization [that] ... sets them apart from pressure groups and other types of voluntary associations, which lack their spontaneity, and from mass behavior, which is altogether devoid of even the rudiments of organization" (Lang and Lang 1961, p. 497).

Recognizing with Heberle (1951, p. 8) that "movements *as such* are not organized groups," it is still the structured aspects which are more amenable to study, if not always the most salient. Turner and Killian (1957, p. 307) have argued that it is when "members of a public who share a common position concerning the issue at hand supplement their informal person-to-person discussion with some organization to promote their convictions more effectively and insure more sustained activity, a social movement is incipient" (see also Killian 1964, p. 426). Such organization(s) and other core groups of a movement not only determine much of its conscious policy but serve as foci for its values and activities. Just as it has been argued that society as a whole has a cultural and structural "center" about which most members of the society are more or less "peripheral" (Shils 1970), so, too, can a social movement be conceived of as having a center and a periphery. An investigation into a movement's origins must be concerned with the microstructural preconditions for the emergence of such a movement center. From where do the people come who make up the initial, organizing cadre of a movement? How do they come together, and how do they come to share a similar view of the world in circumstances which compel them to political action? In what ways does the nature of the original center affect the future development of the movement?

## II

Most movements have very inconspicuous beginnings. The significant elements of their origins are usually forgotten or distorted by the time a trained observer seeks to trace them out, making retroactive analyses difficult. Thus, a detailed investigation of a single movement at the time it is forming can add much to what little is known about movement origins. Such an examination cannot uncover all of the conditions and ingredients of movement formation, but it can aptly illustrate both weaknesses in the theoretical literature and new directions for research. During the formative period of the women's liberation movement, I had many opportunities to observe, log, and interview most of the principals involved in the early movement.[3] The descriptive material in Section III is based on that data. This analysis, supplemented by five other origin studies made by me, would support the following three propositions:

*Proposition 1:* The need for a preexisting communications network or infrastructure within the social base of a movement is a primary prerequisite for "spontaneous" activity. Masses alone don't form movements, however discontented they may be. Groups of previously unorganized individuals may spontaneously form into small local associations—usually along the lines of informal social networks—in response to a specific strain or crisis, but, if they are not linked in some manner, the protest does not become generalized; it remains a local irritant or dissolves completely. If a movement is to spread rapidly, the communications network must already exist. If only the rudiments of one exist, movement formation requires a high input of "organizing" activity.

*Proposition 2:* Not just any communications network will do. It must be a network that is *co-optable* to the new ideas of the incipient movement.[4] To be co-optable, it must be composed of like-minded people whose background, experiences, or location in the social structure make them receptive to the ideas of a specific new movement.

*Proposition 3:* Given the existence of a co-optable communications network, or at least the rudimentary development of a potential one, and a situation of strain, one or more precipitants are required. Here, two distinct patterns emerge that often overlap. In one, a crisis galvanizes the network into spontaneous action in a new direction. In the other, one or more persons begin organizing a new organization or disseminating a new idea. For spontaneous action to occur, the communications network must be well formed or the initial protest will not survive the incipient stage. If it is not well formed, organizing efforts must occur; that is, one or more persons must specifically attempt to construct a movement. To be successful, organizers must be skilled and must have a fertile field in which to work. If no communications network already exists, there must at least be emerging spontaneous groups which are acutely atuned to the issue, albeit uncoordinated. To sum up, if a co-optable communications network is already established, a crisis is all that is necessary to galvanize it.

If it is rudimentary, an organizing cadre of one or more persons is necessary. Such a cadre is superfluous if the former conditions fully exist, but it is essential if they do not.

Before examining these propositions in detail, let us look at the structure and origins of the women's liberation movement.

## III

The women's liberation movement manifests itself in an almost infinite variety of groups, styles, and organizations. Yet, this diversity has sprung from only two distinct origins whose numerous offspring remain clustered largely around these two sources. The two branches are often called "reform" and "radical," or, as the sole authoritative book on the movement describes them, "women's rights" and "women's liberation" (Hole and Levine 1971). Unfortunately, these terms actually tell us very little, since feminists do not fit into the traditional Left/Right spectrum. In fact, if an ideological typography were possible, it would show minimal consistency with any other characteristic. Structure and style rather than ideology more accurately differentiate the two branches, and, even here, there has been much borrowing on both sides.

I prefer simpler designations: the first of the branches will be referred to as the older branch of the movement, partly because it began first and partly because the median age of its activists is higher. It contains numerous organizations, including the lobbyist group (Women's Equity Action League), a legal foundation (Human Rights for Women), over 20 caucuses in professional organizations, and separate organizations of women in the professions and other occupations. Its most prominent "core group" is the National Organization for Women (NOW), which was also the first to be formed.

While the written programs and aims of the older branch span a wide spectrum, their activities tend to be concentrated on legal and ecomonic problems. These groups are primarily made up of women—and men—who work, and they are substantially concerned with the problems of working women. The style of organization of the older branch tends to be traditionally formal, with elected officers, boards of directors, bylaws, and the other trappings of democratic procedure. All started as top-down national organizations, lacking in a mass base. Some have subsequently developed a mass base, some have not yet done so, and others do not want to.

Conversely, the younger branch consists of innumerable small groups—engaged in a variety of activities—whose contact with each other is, at best, tenuous. Contrary to popular myth, it did not begin on the campus nor was it started by the Students for a Democratic Society (SDS). However, its activators were, to be trite, on the other side of the generation gap. While few were students, all were "under 30" and had received their political education as participants or concerned observers of the social action projects of the last decade. Many came direct from New Left and civil rights organizations. Others had attended various courses on women in the multitude of free universities springing up around the country during those years.

The expansion of these groups has appeared more amoebic than organized, because the younger branch of the movement prides itself on its lack of organization. From its radical roots, it inherited the idea that structures were always conservative and confining, and leaders, isolated and elitist. Thus, eschewing structure and damning the idea of leadership, it has carried the concept of "everyone doing her own thing" to the point where communication is haphazard and coordination is almost nonexistent. The thousands of sister chapters around the country are virtually independent of each other, linked only by numerous underground papers, journals, newsletters, and cross-country travelers. A national conference was held over Thanksgiving in 1968 but, although considered successful, has not yet been repeated. Before the 1968 conference, the movement did not have the sense of national unity which emerged after the conference. Since then, young feminists have made no attempt to call another national conference. There have been a few regional conferences, but no permanent consequences resulted. At most, some cities have a coordinating committee which attempts to maintain communication among local groups and to channel newcomers into appropriate ones, but these committees have no power over any group's activities, let alone its ideas. Even local activists do not know how big the movement is in their own city. While it cannot be said to have no organization at all, this branch of the movement has informally adopted a general policy of "structurelessness."

Despite a lack of a formal policy encouraging it, there is a great deal of homogeneity within the younger branch of the movement. Like the older branch, it tends to be predominantly white, middle class, and college educated. But it is much more homogenous and, unlike the older branch, has been unable to diversify. This is largely because most small groups tend to form among friendship networks. Most groups have no requirements for membership (other than female sex), no dues, no written and agreed-upon structure, and no elected leaders. Because of this lack of structure, it is often easier for an individual to form a new group than to find and join an older one. This encourages group formation but discourages individual diversification. Even contacts among groups tend to be along friendship lines.

In general, the different style and organization of the two branches was largely derived from the different kind of political education and experiences of each group of women. Women of the older branch were trained in and had used the traditional forms of political action, while the younger branch has inherited the loose, flexible, person-oriented attitude of the youth and student movements. The different structures that have evolved from these two distinctly different kinds of experience have, in turn, largely determined the strategy of the two branches, irrespective of any conscious intentions of their participants. These different structures and strategies have each posed different problems and possibilities. Intramovement differences are often perceived by the participants as conflicting, but it is their essential complementarity which has been one of the strengths of the movement.

Despite the multitude of differences, there are very strong similarities in the way the two branches came into being. These similarities serve to illuminate some of the microsociological factors involved in movement formation. The forces which led to NOW's formation were first set in motion in 1961 when President Kennedy established the President's Commission on the Status of Women at the behest of Esther Petersen,[5] to be chaired by Eleanor Roosevelt.

Operation under a broad mandate, its 1963 report (*American Women*) and subsequent committee publications documented just how thoroughly women are still denied many rights and opportunities. The most concrete response to the activity of the president's commission was the eventual establishment of 50 state commissions to do similar research on a state level. These commissions were often urged by politically active women and were composed primarily of women. Nonetheless, many believe the main stimulus behind their formation was the alleged view of the governors that the commissions were excellent opportunities to pay political debts without giving women more influential positions.

The activity of the federal and state commissions laid the groundwork for the future movement in three significant ways: (1) it brought together many knowledgeable, politically active women who otherwise would not have worked together around matters of direct concern to women; (2) the investigations unearthed ample evidence of women's unequal status, especially their legal and economic difficulties, in the process convincing many previously uninterested women that something should be done; (3) the reports created a climate of expectations that something would be done. The women of the federal and state commissions who were exposed to these influences exchanged visits, correspondence, and staff and met with each other at an annual commission convention. Thus, they were in a position to share and mutually reinforce their growing awareness and concern over women's issues. These commissions thus created an embryonic communications network among people with similar concerns.

During this time, two other events of significance occurred. The first was the publication of Betty Friedan's (1963) book, *The Feminine Mystique*. An immediate best seller, it stimulated many women to question the status quo and some to suggest to Friedan that a new organization be formed to attack their problems. The second event was the addition of "sex" to Title VII of the 1964 Civil Rights Act. Many men thought the "sex" provision was a joke (Bird 1968, chap. 1). The Equal Employment Opportunity Commission (EEOC) certainly treated it as one and refused to adequately enforce it. The first EEOC executive director even stated publicly that the provision was a "fluke" that was "conceived out of wedlock" (Edelsberg 1965). But, within the EEOC, there was a "pro-woman" coterie which argued that "sex" would be taken more seriously if there were "some sort of NAACP for women" to put pressure on the government. As government employees, they couldn't organize such a group, but they spoke privately with those who they thought might be able to do so. One who shared their views was Rep. Martha Griffiths of Michigan. She blasted the EEOC's attitude in a June 20, 1966, speech on the House floor (Griffiths 1966) declaring that the agency had "started out by casting disrespect and ridicule on the law" but that their "wholly negative attitude had changed—for the worse."

On June 30, 1966, these three strands of incipient feminism were knotted together to form NOW. The occasion was the last day of the Third National Conference of Commissions on the Status of Women, ironically titled "Targets for Action." The participants had all received copies of Rep. Griffith's remarks. The opportunity came with a refusal by conference officials to bring to the floor a proposed resolution that urged the EEOC to give equal enforcement to the sex provision of Title VII as was given to the race provision. Despite the fact that these state commissions were not federal agencies, officials replied that one government agency could not be allowed to pressure another. The small group of women who had desired the resolution had met the night before in Friedan's hotel room to discuss the possibility of a civil rights organization for women. Not convinced of its need, they chose instead to propose the resolution. When the resolution was vetoed, the women held a whispered conversation over lunch and agreed to form an action organization "to bring women into full participation in the mainstream of American society now, assuming all the privileges and responsibilities thereof in truly equal partnership with men." The name NOW was coined by Friedan, who was at the conference researching her second book. Before the day was over, 28 women paid $5.00 each to join (Friedan 1967).

By the time the organizing conference was held the following October 29–30, over 300 men and women had become charter members. It is impossible to do a breakdown on the composition of the charter membership, but one of the first officers and board is possible. Such a breakdown accurately reflected NOW's origins. Friedan was president, two former EEOC commissioners were vice-presidents, a representative of the United Auto Workers Women's Committee was secretary-treasurer, and there were seven past and present members of the State Commissions on the Status of Women on the 20-member board. Of the charter members, 126 were Wisconsin residents—and Wisconsin had the most active state commission. Occupationally, the board and officers were primarily from the professions, labor, government, and the communications industry. Of these, only those from labor had any experience in organizing, and they resigned a year later in a dispute over support of the Equal Rights Amendment. Instead of organizational expertise, what the early NOW members had was media experience, and it was here that their early efforts were aimed.

As a result, NOW often gave the impression of being larger than it was. It was highly successful in getting publicity, much less so in bringing about concrete changes or organizing itself. Thus, it was not until 1969, when several national news media simultaneously decided to do major stories on the women's liberation movement, that NOW's membership increased significantly. Even today, [1972] there are only 8,000 members, and the chapters are still in an incipient stage of development.

In the meantime, unaware of and unknown to NOW, the EEOC, or to the state commissions, younger women began forming their own movement. Here, too, the groundwork had been laid some years before. Social action projects of recent years had attracted many women, who were quickly shunted into traditional roles and faced with the self-evident contradiction of working in a "freedom movement" without being very free. No single "youth movement" activity or organization is responsible for the younger branch of the women's liberation movement; together they created a "radical community" in which like-minded people continually interacted with each other. This community consisted largely of those who had participated in one or more of the many protest activities of the sixties and had established its own ethos and its own institutions. Thus, the women in it thought of themselves as "movement people" and had incorporated the adjective "radical" into their personal identities. The values of their radical identity and the style to which they had been trained by their movement participation directed them to approach most problems as political ones which could be solved by organizing. What remained was to translate their individual feelings of "unfreedom" into a collective consciousness. Thus, the radical community provided not only the necessary network of communication; its radical ideas formed the framework of analysis which "explained" the dismal situation in which radical women found themselves.

Papers had been circulated on women,[6] and temporary women's caucuses had been held as early as 1964, when Stokely Carmichael made his infamous remark that "the only position for women in SNCC is prone." But it was not until late 1967 and 1968 that the groups developed a determined, if cautious, continuity and began to consciously expand themselves. At least five groups in five different cities (Chicago, Toronto, Detroit, Seattle, and Gainesville, Florida) formed spontaneously, independent of each other. They came at a very auspicious movement. The year 1967 was the one in which the blacks kicked the whites out of the civil rights movement, student power had been discredited by SDS, and the organized New Left was on the wane. Only draft-resistance activities were on the increase, and this movement more than any other exemplified the social inequities of the sexes. Men could resist the draft; women could only counsel resistance.

What was significant about this point in time was that there was a lack of available opportunities for political work. Some women fit well into the "secondary role" of draft counseling. Many did not. For years, their complaints of unfair treatment had been ignored by movement men with the dictum that those things could wait until after the revolution. Now these movement women found time on their hands, but the men would still not listen.

A typical example was the event which precipitated the formation of the Chicago group, the first independent group in this country. At the August 1967 National Conference for New Politics convention, a women's caucus met for days but was told its resolution wasn't significant enough to merit a floor discussion. By threatening to tie up the convention with procedural motions, the women succeeded in having their statement tacked to the end of the agenda. It was never discussed. The chair refused to recognize any of the many women standing by the microphone, their hands straining upward. When he instead called on someone to speak on "the forgotten American, the American Indian," five women rushed the podium to demand an explanation. But the chairman just patted one of them on the head (literally) and told her, "Cool down little girl. We have more important things to talk about than women's problems."

The "little girl" was Shulamith Firestone, future author of *The Dialectic of Sex* (1971), and she didn't cool down. Instead, she joined with another Chicago woman, who had been trying to organize a women's group that summer, to call a meeting of those women who had half-heartedly attended the summer meetings. Telling their stories to those women, they stimulated sufficient rage to carry the group for three months, and by that time it was a permanent institution.

Another somewhat similar event occurred in Seattle the following winter. At the University of Washington, an SDS organizer was explaining to a large meeting how white college youth established rapport with the poor whites with whom they were working. "He noted that sometimes after analyzing societal ills, the men shared leisure time by 'balling a chick together.' He pointed out that such activities did much to enhance the political consciousness of the poor white youth. A woman in the audience asked, 'And what did it do for the consciousness of the chick?' " (Hole and Levine 1971, p. 120). After the meeting, a handful of enraged women formed Seattle's first group.

Groups subsequent to the initial five were largely organized rather than emerging spontaneously out of recent events. In particular, the Chicago group was responsible for the creation of many new groups in that city and elsewhere and started the first national newsletter. The 1968 conference was organized by the Washington, D.C., group from resources provided by the Center for Policy Studies (CPS), a radical research organization. Using CPS facilities, this group subsequently became a main literature-distribution center. Although New York groups organized early and were featured in the 1969–70 media blitz, New York was not a source of early organizers.[7]

Unlike NOW, the women in the first groups had had years of experience as local-level organizers. They did not have the resources, or the desire, to form a national organization, but they knew how to utilize the infrastructure of the radical community, the underground press, and the free universities to disseminate ideas on women's liberation. Chicago, as a center of New Left activity, had the largest number of politically conscious organizers. Many traveled widely to Left conferences and demonstrations, and most used the opportunity to talk with other women about the new movement. In spite of public derision by radical men, or perhaps because of it, young women steadily formed new groups around the country.

Initially, the new movement found it hard to organize on the campus, but, as a major congregating area of women and, in particular, of women with political awareness, campus women's liberation groups eventually became ubiquitous. While the younger branch of the movement never formed any organization larger or more extensive than a city-wide coordinating committee, it would be fair to say that it has a larger "participationship" than NOW and the other older branch organizations. While the members of the older branch knew how to use the media and how to form national structures, the women of the younger branch were skilled in local community organizing.

## IV

From this description, there appear to be four essential elements contributing to the emergence of the women's liberation movement in the mid-sixties: (1) the growth of a preexisting communications network which was (2) co-optable to the ideas of the new movement; (3) a series of crises that galvanized into action people involved in this network, and/or (4) subsequent organizing effort to weld the spontaneous groups together into a movement. To further understand these factors, let us examine them in detail with reference to other relevant studies.

1. Both the Commissions on the Status of Women and the "radical community" created a communications network through which those women initially interested in creating an organization could easily reach others. Such a network had not previously existed among women. Historically tied to the family and isolated from their own kind, women are perhaps the most organizationally underdeveloped social category in Western civilization. By 1950, the 19th-

century organizations which had been the basis of the suffrage movement—
the Women's Trade Union League, the General Federation of Women's Clubs,
the Women's Christian Temperance Union, the National American Women's
Suffrage Association—were all either dead or a pale shadow of their former
selves. The closest exception was the National Women's Party (NWP), which
has remained dedicated to feminist concerns since its inception in 1916. However, since 1923, it has been essentially a lobbying group for the Equal Rights
Amendment. The NWP, having always believed that a small group of women
concentrating their efforts in the right places was more effective than a mass
appeal, was not appalled that, as late as 1969, even the majority of avowed
feminists in this country had never heard of the NWP or the ERA.

References to the salience of a preexisting communications network appear
frequently in the case studies of social movements, but it has been given little
attention in the theoretical literature. It is essentially contrary to the mass-
society theory which "for many . . . is . . . the most pertinent and comprehensive
statement of the genesis of modern mass movements" (Pinard 1968, p. 682). This
theory hypothesizes that those most likely to join a mass movement are those
who are atomized and isolated from "a structure of groups intermediate between the family and the nation" (Kornhauser 1959, p. 93). However, the lack
of such intermediate structures among women has proved more of a hindrance
than a help in movement formation. Even today, it is those women who are
most atomized, the housewives, who are least likely to join a feminist group.

The most serious attack on mass-society theory was made by Pinard (1971)
in his study of the Social Credit Party of Quebec. He concluded that intermediate structures exerted *mobilizing* as well as restraining effects on individuals'
participation in social movements because they formed communications networks that assisted in the rapid spread of new ideas. "When strains are severe
and widespread," he contended, "a new movement is more likely to meet its
early success among the more strongly integrated citizens" (Pinard 1971, p. 192).

Other evidence also attests to the role of previously organized networks in
the rise and spread of a social movement. According to Buck (1920, pp. 43–44),
the Grange established a degree of organization among American farmers in
the 19th century which greatly facilitated the spread of future farmers' protests.
In Saskatchewan, Lipset (1959) has asserted: "The rapid acceptance of new ideas
and movements . . . can be attributed mainly to the high degree of organization. . . . The role of the social structure of the western wheat belt in facilitating
the rise of new movements has never been sufficiently appreciated by historians and sociologists. Repeated challenges and crises forced the western farmers
to create many more community institutions . . . than are necessary in a more
stable area. These groups in turn provided a structural basis for immediate
action in critical situations. [Therefore] though it was a new radical party, the
C.C.F. did not have to build up an organization from scratch." More recently,
the civil rights movement was built upon the infrastructure of the Southern
black church (King 1958), and early SDS organizers made ready use of the
National Student Association (Kissinger and Ross 1968, p. 16).

Indirect evidence of the essential role of formal and informal communications networks is found in diffusion theory, which emphasizes the importance
of personal interaction rather than impersonal media communication in the
spread of ideas (Rogers 1962; Lionberger 1960), and in Coleman's (1957) investigations of prior organizations in the initial development of conflict.

Such preexisting communications networks appear to be not merely valuable but prerequisites, as one study on "The Failure of an Incipient Social Movement" (Jackson, Peterson, Bull, Monsen, and Richmond 1960) made quite clear. In 1957, a potential tax-protest movement in Los Angeles generated considerable interest and public notice for a little over a month but was dead within a year. According to the authors, its failure to sustain itself beyond initial spontaneous protest was largely due to "the lack of a pre-existing network of communications linking those groups of citizens most likly to support the movement" (Jackson et al. 1960, p. 40). They said (p. 37) that "if a movement is to grow rapidly, it cannot rely upon its own network of communication, but must capitalize on networks already in existence."

The development of the women's liberation movement highlights the salience of such a network precisely because the conditions for a movement existed *before* a network came into being, but the movement didn't exist until afterward. Socioeconomic strain did not change for women significantly during a 20-year period. It was as great in 1955 as in 1965. What changed was the organizational situation. It was not until a communications network developed among like-minded people beyond local boundaries that the movement could emerge and develop past the point of occasional, spontaneous uprising.

2. However, not just any network would do; it had to be one which was co-optable by the incipient movement because it linked like-minded people likely to be predisposed to the new ideas of the movement. The 180,000-member Federation of Business and Professional Women's (BPW) Clubs would appear to be a likely base for a new feminist movement but in fact was unable to assume this role. It had steadily lobbied for legislation of importance to women, yet as late as "1966 BPW rejected a number of suggestions that it redefine . . . goals and tactics and become a kind of 'NAACP for women' . . . out of fear of being labeled 'feminist' " (Hole and Levine 1971, p. 81). While its membership has become a recruiting ground for feminism, it could not initially overcome the ideological barrier to a new type of political action.

On the other hand, the women of the President's and State Commissions on the Status of Women and the feminist coterie of the EEOC were co-optable, largely because their immersion into the facts of female status and the details of sex-discrimination cases made them very conscious of the need for change. Likewise, the young women of the "radical community" lived in an atmosphere of questioning, confrontation, and change. They absorbed an ideology of "freedom" and "liberation" far more potent than any latent "antifeminism" might have been. The repeated contradictions between these ideas and the actions of their male colleagues created a compulsion for action which only required an opportunity to erupt. This was provided by the "vacuum of political activity" of 1967–68.

The nature of co-optability is much more difficult to elucidate. Heretofore, it has been dealt with only tangentially. Pinard (1971, p. 186) noted the necessity for groups to "*possess* or *develop* an ideology or simply subjective interests congruent with that of a new movement" for them to "act as mobilizing rather than restraining agents toward that movement" but did not further explore what affected the "primary group climate." More illumination is provided by the diffusion of innovation studies which point out the necessity for new ideas to fit in with already-established norms for changes to happen easily. Furthermore, a social system which has a value "innovativeness" itself (as the radical community did) will more rapidly adopt ideas than one which looks upon the habitual performance of traditional practices as the ideal (as most organized women's groups did in the fifties). Usually, as Lionberger (1960, p. 91) points out, "people act in terms of past experience and knowledge." People who have had similar experiences are likely to share similar perceptions of a situation and to mutually reinforce those perceptions as well as their subsequent interpretation.

A co-optable network, therefore, is one whose members have had common experiences which predispose them to be receptive to the particular new ideas of the incipient movement and who are not faced with structural or ideological barriers to action. If the new movement as an "innovation" can interpret these experiences and perceptions in ways that point out channels for social action, then participation in social movement becomes the logical thing to do.

3. As our examples have illustrated, these similar perceptions must be translated into action. This is the role of the "crisis." For women of the older branch of the movement, the impetus to organize was the refusal of the EEOC to enforce the sex provision of Title VII, precipitated by the concomitant refusal of federal officials at the conference to allow a supportive resolution. For younger women, there were a series of minor crises. Such precipitating events are common to most movements. They serve to crystallize and focus discontent. From their own experiences, directly and concretely, people feel the need for change in a situation that allows for an exchange of feelings with others, mutual validation, and a subsequent reinforcement of innovative interpretation. Perception of an immediate need for change is a major factor in predisposing people to accept new ideas (Rogers 1962, p. 280). Nothing makes desire for change more acute than a crisis. If the strain is great enough, such a crisis need not be a major one; it need only embody symbolically collective discontent.

4. However, a crisis will only catalyze a well-formed communications network. If such networks are only embryonically developed or only partially co-optable, the potentially active individuals in them must be linked together by someone. As Jackson et al. (1960, p. 37) stated: "Some protest may persist where the source of trouble is constantly present. But interest ordinarily cannot be maintained unless there is a welding of spontaneous groups into some stable organization." In other words, people must be organized. Social movements do not simply occur.

The role of the organizer in movement formation is another neglected aspect of the theoretical literature. There has been great concern with leadership, but the two roles are distinct and not always performed by the same individual. In the early stages of a movement, it is the organizer much more than any "leader" who is important, and such an individual or cadre must often operate behind the scenes.[8] Certainly, the "organizing cadre" that young women in the radical community came to be was key to the growth of that branch of the women's liberation movement, despite the fact that no "leaders" were produced (and were actively discouraged). The existence of many leaders but no organizers in the older branch of the women's liberation movement and its subsequent slow development would tend to substantiate this hypothesis.

The crucial function of the organizer has been explored indirectly in other areas of sociology. Rogers (1962) devotes many pages to the "change agent" who, while he does not necessarily weld a group together or "construct" a movement, does do many of the same things for agricultural innovation that an organizer does for political change. Mass-society theory makes reference to the "agitator" but fails to do so in any kind of truly informative way. A study of farmer's movements indicates that many core organizations were organized by a single individual before the spontaneous aspects of the movement predominated. Further, many other core groups were subsidized by older organizations, federal and state governments, and even by local businessmen (Salisbury 1969, p. 13). These organizations often served as training centers for organizers and sources of material support to aid in the formation of new interest groups and movements.

Similarly, the civil rights movement provided the training for many another movement's organizers, including the young women of the women's liberation movement. It would appear that the art of "constructing" a social movement is something that requires considerable skill and experience. Even in the supposedly spontaneous social movement, the professional is more valuable than the amateur.

## V

The ultimate results of such "construction" are not independent of their origins. In fact, the attitudes and styles of a movement's initiators often have an effect which lasts longer than they do. Those women and men who formed NOW, and its subsequent sister organizations, created a national structure prepared to use the legal, political, and media institutions of our country. This it has done. The EEOC has changed many of its prejudicial attitudes toward women in its recent rulings. Numerous lawsuits have been filed under the sex provision of Title VII of the Civil Rights Act. The Equal Rights Amendment has passed Congress. Complaints have been filed against over 400 colleges and universities, as well as many businesses, charging violation of Executive Order 11246 amended by 11375, which prohibits sex discrimination by all holders of federal contracts. Articles on feminism have appeared in virtually every national news medium, and women's liberation has become a household word.

These groups have and continue to function primarily as pressure groups within the limits of traditional political activity. Consequently, their actual membership remains small. Diversification of the older branch of the movement has been largely along occupational lines and primarily within the professions. Activity has stressed using the tools for change provided by the system, however limited these may be. Short-range goals are emphasized, and no attempt has been made to place them within a broader ideological framework.

Initially, this structure hampered the development of older branch organizations. NOW suffered three splits between 1967 and 1968. As the only action organization concerned with women's rights, it had attracted many different kinds of people with many different views on what and how to proceed. With only a national structure and, at that point, no local base, it was difficult for individuals to pursue their particular concern on a local level; they had to persuade the whole organization to support them. Given NOW's top-down structure and limited resources, this placed severe limits on diversity and, in turn, severe strains on the organization. Additional difficulties for local chapters were created by a lack of organizers to develop new chapters and the lack of a program into which they could fit. NOW's initiators were very high-powered women who lacked the time or patience for the slow, unglamorous, and tedious work of putting together a mass organization. Chapter development had to wait for the national media to attract women to the organization or the considerable physical mobility of contemporary women to bring proponents into new territory. Locally, women had to find some common concern around which to organize. Unlike that of New York, which had easy access to the national media and many people skilled at using it, the other chapters had difficulty developing programs not dependent on the media. Since the national program consisted almost exclusively of support of legal cases or federal lobby-ing, the regional chapters could not easily fit into that either. Eventually, connections were made; and, in the last year, national task forces have begun to correlate with local efforts so that individual projects can combine a national thrust with instrumentation on the local level. After initial difficulties, NOW and the other older branch organizations are thriving at this point because they are able to effectively use the institutional tools which our society provides for social and political change. Yet, these groups are also limited by these tools to the rather narrow arenas within which they are designed to operate. The nature of these arenas and the particular skills they require for participation already limit both the kind of women who can effectively work in older branch groups and the activities they can undertake. When their scope is exhausted, it remains to be seen whether organizations such as NOW will wither, institu-tionalize themselves as traditional pressure groups, or show the imagination to develop new lines for action.

The younger branch has had an entirely different history and faces differ-ent prospects. It was able to expand rapidly in the beginning because it could capitalize on the infrastructure of organizations and media of the New Left and because its initiators were skilled in local community organizing. Since the prime unit was the small group and no need for national cooperation was perceived, multitudinous splits increased its strength rather than drained its resources. Such fission was often "friendly" in nature and, even when not, served to bring ever-increasing numbers of women under the movement's umbrella.

Unfortunately, these masses of new women lacked the organizing skills of the initiators, and, because the idea of "leadership" and "organization" were in disrepute, they made no attempt to acquire them. They did not want to deal with traditional political institutions and abjured all traditional political skills. Consequently, the growth of the movement institutions did not go beyond the local level, and they were often inadequate to handle the accelerating influx of new people into the movement. Although these small groups were diverse in kind and responsible to no one for their focus, their nature determined both the structure and the strategy of the movement. One result has been a very broad-based creative movement to which individuals can relate pretty much as they desire with no concern for orthodoxy or doctrine. This branch has been the major source of new feminist ideas and activities. It has developed several ideological perspectives, much of the terminology of the movement, an amaz-ing number of publications and "counter-institutions," numerous new issues, and even new techniques for social change. the emphasis of this branch has been on personal change as a means to understand the kind of political change desired. The primary instrument has been the consciousness-raising rap group which has sought to change women's very identities as well as their attitudes.

Nonetheless, this loose structure is flexible only within certain limits, and the movement has not yet shown the propensity to transcend them. While rap groups have been excellent techniques for changing individual attitudes, they have not been very successful in dealing with social institutions. Their loose, informal structure encourages participation in discussion, and their supportive atmosphere elicits personal insight; but neither is very efficient in handling specific tasks. While they have been of fundamental value to the development of the movement, they also lead to a certain kind of political impotency. It is virtually impossible to coordinate a national action, or even a local one, assuming there could be any agreement on issues around which to coordinate one.

Individual rap groups tend to flounder when their numbers have exhausted the virtues of consciousness raising and decide they want to do something more concrete. The problem is that most groups are unwilling to change their structure when they change their tasks. They have accepted the ideology of "structurelessness" without realizing its limitations.

The resurgence of feminism tapped a major source of female energy, but the younger branch has not yet been able to channel it. Some women are able to create their own local-action projects, such as study groups, abortion counseling centers, bookstores, etc. Most are not, and the movement provides no coordinated or structured means of fitting into existing projects. Instead, such women either are recruited into NOW and other national organizations or drop out. New groups form and dissolve at an accelerating rate, creating a good deal of consciousness and very little action. The result is that most of the movement is proliferating underground. It often seems mired in introspection, but it is in fact creating a vast reservoir of conscious feminist sentiment which only awaits an appropriate opportunity for action.

In sum, the current status of the women's movement can be said to be structurally very much like it was in its incipient stages. That section which I have called the older branch remains attached to using the tools the system provides, while the younger branch simply proliferates horizontally, without creating new structures to handle new tasks.

## NOTES

1 I would like to thank Richard Albares and Florence Levinsohn for having read and criticized earlier versions of this paper.

2 "A consciously directed and organized movement cannot be explained merely in terms of the psychological disposition or motivation of people, or in terms of a diffusion of an ideology. Explanations of this sort have a deceptive plausibility, but overlook the fact that *a movement has to be constructed* and has to carve out a career in what is practically always an opposed, resistant or at least indifferent world" (Blumer 1957, p. 147; italics mine).

3 As a founder and participant in the younger branch of the Chicago women's liberation movement from 1967 through 1969 and editor of the first (at that time, only) national newsletter, I was able, through extensive correspondence and interviews,

to keep a record of how each group around the country first started, where the organizers got the idea from, who they had talked to, what conferences were held and who attended, the political affiliations (or lack of them) of the first members, etc. Although I was a member of Chicago NOW, information on the origins of it and the other older branch organizations comes entirely through ex post facto interviews of the principals and examination of early papers in preparation for my dissertation on the women's liberation movement. Most of my informants requested that their contribution remain confidential.

4   The only use of this significant word appears rather incidentally in Turner (1964, p. 123).

5   Then director of the Women's Bureau.

6   "A Kind of Memo," by Hayden and King (1966, p. 35) circulated in the fall of 1965 (and eventually published), was the first such paper.

7   The movement in New York has been more diverse than other cities and has made many major ideological contributions, but, contrary to popular belief, it did not begin in New York. In putting together their stories, the news media, concentrated as they are in New York, rarely looked past the Hudson for their information. This eastern bias is exemplified by the fact that, although the younger branch of the movement has no national organization and abjures leadership, all but one of those women designated by the press as movement leaders live in New York.

8   The nature and function of these two roles was most clearly evident in the Townsend old-age movement of the thirties. Townsend was the "charismatic" leader, but the movement was organized by his partner, real estate promoter Robert Clements. Townsend himself acknowledges that, without Clement's help, the movement would never have gone beyond the idea stage (see Holzman 1963).

## REFERENCES

Adorno, T. W., et al
1950    The Authoritarian Personality. New York: Harper.
Bird, Caroline.
1968    Born Female: The High Cost of Keeping Women Down. New York: David McKay.
Blumer, Herbert
1951    "Social Movements." In New Outline of the Principles of Sociology, edited by A. M. Lee. New York: Barnes & Noble.
1957    "Collective Behavior." Review of Sociology: Analysis of a Decade, edited by Joseph B. Gittler. New York: Wiley.
Buck, Solon J.
1920    The Agrarian Crusade, New Haven, Conn.: Yale University Press.
Cantril, Hadley
1941    The Psychology of Social Movements. New York: Wiley.
Coleman, James
1957    Community Conflict. New York: Free Press.
Currie, Elliott, and Jerome H. Skolnick
1970    "Critical Note on Conceptions of Collective Behavior." Annals of the American Academy of Political and Social Science 391 (September): 34–45.
Dahrendorf, Ralf
1959    Class and Class Conflict in Industrial Society. Palo Alto, Calif.: Stanford University Press.
Davies, James C.
1962    "Toward A Theory of Revolution." American Sociological Review 27 (1): 5–19.

*Dawson, C. A., and W. E. Gettys*
1929   *An Introduction to Sociology.* New York: Ronald.
*Edelsberg, Herman*
1965   N.Y.U. 18th Conference on Labor." *Labor Relations Reporter* 61 (August): 253–55.
*Ferriss, Abbott L.*
1971   *Indicators of Trends in the Status of American Women.* New York: Russell Sage.
*Firestone, Shulamith*
1971   *Dialectics of Sex.* New York: Morrow.
*Friedan, Betty*
1963   *The Feminine Mystique.* New York: Dell.
1967   "N.O.W.: How It Began." *Women Speaking* (April).
*Griffiths, Martha*
1966   Speech of June 20, *Congressional Record.*
*Gurr, Ted*
1970   *Why Men Rebel.* Princeton, N.J.: Princeton University Press.
*Hayden, Casey, and Mary King*
1966   "A Kind of Memo." *Liberation* (April).
*Heberle, Rudolph*
1951   *Social Movements.* New York: Appleton-Century-Crofts.
*Hoffer, Eric*
1951   *The True Believer.* New York: Harper.
*Hole, Judith, and Ellen Levine*
1971   *Rebirth of Feminism.* New York: Quadrangle.
*Holzman, Abraham*
1963   *The Townsend Movement: A Political Study.* New York: Bookman.
*Jackson, Maurice, Eleanora Petersen, James Bull, Sverre Monsen, and Patricia Richmond*
1960   "The Failure of an Incipient Social Movement." *Pacific Sociological Review* 3, no.
       1 (Spring): 35–40.
*Killian, Lewis M.*
1964   "Social Movements." In *Handbook of Modern Sociology,* edited by R. E. L. Faris.
       Chicago: Rand McNally.
*King, C. Wendell*
1956   *Social Movements in the United States.* New York: Random House.
King, Martin Luther, Jr.
1958   *Stride toward Freedom.* New York: Harper.
*Kissinger, C. Clark, and Bob Ross.*
1968   "Starting in '60: Or From SLID to Resistance." *New Left Notes,* June 10.
*Kornhauser, William*
1959   *The Politics of Mass Society.* New York: Free Press.
*Lang, Kurt, and Gladys Engle Lang*
1961   *Collective Dynamics.* New York: Cromwell.
*Lionberger, Herbert F.*
1960   *Adoption of New Ideas and Practices.* Ames: Iowa State University Press.
*Lipset, Seymour M.*
1959   *Agrarian Socialism.* Berkeley: University of California Press.
*Lowi, Theodore J.*
1971   *The Politics of Disorder.* New York: Basic.
*Pinard, Maurice*
1968   "Mass Society and Political Movements: A New Formulation." *American Journal
       of Sociology* 73, no. 6 (May): 682–90.
1971   *The Rise of a Third Party: A Study in Crisis Politics.* Englewood Cliffs, N.J.:
       Prentice-Hall.
*Rogers, Everett M.*
1962   *Diffusion of Innovations.* New York: Free Press.

*Salisbury, Robert H.*
1969   "An Exchange Theory of Interest Groups." *Midwest Journal of Political Science,*
      vol. 13, no. 1 (February).
*Shils, Edward*
1970   "Center and Periphery." In *Selected Essays.* Center for Social Organization Studies.
      Department of Sociology, University of Chicago.
*Smelser, Neil J.*
1963   *Theory of Collective Behavior.* New York: Free Press.
*Toch, Hans*
1965   *The Social Psychology of Social Movements.* Indianapolis: Bobbs-Merrill.
*Turner, Ralph H.*
1964   "Collective Behavior and Conflict: New Theoretical Frameworks." *Sociological*
      *Quarterly.*
*Turner, Ralph H., and Lewis M. Killian*
1957   *Collective Behavior.* Englewood Cliffs. N.J.: Prentice-Hall.

# Support Among Women for the Issues of the Women's Movement*

## Susan Welch

*University of Nebraska, Lincoln*

*Using both data from a national and community sample, this paper explores support among women for issues relevant to the women's rights movement and the extent to which the issues of the movement are perceived as a coherent whole by women. Five distinct issue dimensions emerged. Support for or agreement with each of the issue areas was only slightly correlated with support for the others. Thus, some types of women are supportive of the variety of issues and in agreement with the basic assumptions of the movement while others are more selective in their support. In general, support for any particular issue area is greater than support for women's liberation, yet even those opposing women's liberation agree with the position of the women's movement on a majority of issues examined.*

The women's liberation movement is composed of a wide variety of groups, spokesmen, and goals. Its members have evidenced a growing sense of injustice, group self-consciousness and pride, and the external support that charac-

*Source:* Susan Welch, "Support Among Women for the Issues of the Women's Movement," Sociological Quarterly 16, 2 (Spring 1975): 216–27. Copyright © 1975 by the Midwest Sociological Society. Reprinted by permission of the Society, the editors of Sociological Quarterly, and the author.
*The author would like to express thanks to Celeste Wiseblood and Peg Hornbeck for their assistance in collecting and analyzing the data presented herein, and to Alan Booth for his useful comments on an earlier version of the paper.

terize a developing social movement (Turner and Killian, 1957:259–264). As a movement, it has been influential in focusing attention on the status of women in American society and in bringing about some changes in the legal structure and, perhaps, even in public attitudes. Much has been written about the leaders of the movement, their goals and ideas, and the genesis of the various components of the women's movement. (A few recent works include Hole and Levine, 1971; Epstein, 1971; see also Huber, 1973.) Little analysis of the attitudes of women themselves toward the movement and the various issue orientations of the movement has been done. Little empirical evidence exists concerning sources of support for the women's movement, nor is it known whether the wide variety of positions taken by several women's organizations—changing abortion laws and ending discrimination against women in employment, increasing the number of women political officeholders and reforming divorce laws, providing day care centers and promoting job opportunities for women in large corporations—are perceived by women as issues relating to the general theme of women's rights, or as discrete issues with no common strand.

Heterogeneity in support for the women's movement may be expected given its diversity of structure and appeals (Freeman, 1973). An older branch, often called the reform or the women's rights branch, focuses on legal and economic problems while a second part of the movement, consisting of small local groups, is more concerned with consciousness raising and/or with action devoted to promoting more radical change within the system (Freeman, 1973; Firestone, 1971). Still other parts of the women's movement are concerned with the welfare of particular kinds of women: Chicanos, domestic workers, women in academia, lesbians, and so forth.[1] Thus the women's movement is a coalition of widely diverse groups, each with its own specific goals and areas of concern. The elements of the coalition, therefore, shift from issue to issue, so at one time or another under the women's rights umbrella are found groups as diverse as the Witches, Redstockings, National Organization for Women, and the Business and Professional Women of America. The very nature of such a coalition means that specific goals sought by one segment of the movement may be opposed by others. Leaders of the various Women's Liberation organizations have been content to maintain a loose confederation, partially out of lack of choice, but also because of the potential of such a large diverse group in creating mass support for these goals that can be agreed upon.

The women's movement, in essence, offers a "cafeteria" of appeals (Toch, 1965). Women can support the movement for a variety of reasons including economic self-interest, promotion of self-esteem, or strictly social and companionship needs. Substantial differences can be expected, then, even among those who in general support women's rights, to say nothing of the differences which include those who do not even support the notion of women's rights.

This paper will analyze women's opinions on women's rights issues in terms of sources of support for a heterogeneous movement. In doing so, several hypotheses will be tested:

1   There are distinct components of women's issues; for example, those who support abortion reform do not necessarily support women political candidates.

2   Sources of support among women for each set of issues will be different, although each issue will find greatest support among the liberal and young.

3   Support for the women's liberation movement will be less than support for the specific proposals made by women's groups. That is, some may support the issues but have negative connotations about the term "women's liberation" and thus evince no support for the movement *per se.* Conversely, support for women's liberation will not automatically indicate support for the discrete issues and proposals of the movement, due to the "cafeteria" style appeal.

## DATA AND METHODS

These hypotheses are tested using data from two sources. The most extensive analysis focuses on interview data from 304 women in a middle western city of about 160,000. This data is referred to as the "local" data.[2] However, since one might legitimately question whether women from that particular setting are representative of any other group of women, comparisons to data from a nationwide survey conducted by NORC in the spring of 1972 are made, where possible. Not only are the simple frequency distributions of the national and local samples quite similar on those issues covered in the national survey, but the intercorrelations between demographic variables and positions of the women's issues are nearly identical in most cases.[3]

General levels of support for these issues in the national and local samples are compared in Table 1. Those differences of more than a few percentage points seem to be on those two questions where a wording or response choice differed.[4] Not only are the frequency distributions in the two groups similar, but analysis of the correlations indicates that both the local and national sample display similar relationships with standard social, economic, and other demographic variables.[5] Religion and age, however, are more strongly related to attitudes on the abortion reform issue in the local sample than in the national one. With this exception, the patterns of response found in the national and local samples, both in terms of patterns of distribution and correlates of attitudes, are so similar as to give us confidence that the women sampled in the "local" sample are not an unorthodox group with respect to the national population of women, at least with regard to this particular set of issues. Thus, because the local data is much richer with regard to information gleaned about women's issues, the findings from this sample are examined in more detail below.

## DIMENSIONS OF WOMEN'S ISSUES

Given the variety of foci of the mainstream women's organizations, we would expect to find considerable heterogeneity in support among women for various issues. To test this heterogeneity, 18 items were factor analyzed. These

**TABLE 1**

Local and National Support for Some Selected Issues
and Attitudes Pertaining to Women's Rights

| | LOCAL | | NATIONAL | |
|---|---|---|---|---|
| *Political* | | | | |
| Would vote for a woman for: | | | | |
| President[1] | 63% | (298) | 74% | (771) |
| Congress | 90 | (298) | * | |
| Senate | 90 | (300) | * | |
| State Legislature | 92 | (293) | * | |
| County Sheriff | 41 | (298) | * | |
| Women understand politics as well as men | 83 | | * | |
| *Abortion Reform* | | | | |
| In favor of legalized abortion if: | | | | |
| Rape (or incest)[1] | 86 | (293) | 79 | (761) |
| Birth defects possible | 77 | (302) | 78 | (758) |
| Danger to mother's health | 81 | (295) | 86 | (767) |
| Child is unwanted[1] | 49 | (301) | 37 | (760) |
| Anytime in first three months | 55 | (303) | * | |
| *Business Opportunities* | | | | |
| Approve of woman earning money in business or indus- | | | | |
| try even if she has husband to support her | 81 | (297) | 68 | (784) |
| Believe women can run businesses as well as men | 62 | (301) | * | |
| If women have the same ability as men, they will have as | | | | |
| good a chance to become a business executive | 13 | (291) | | |
| *Other* | | | | |
| Women get as good a break as men | 18 | (300) | * | |
| Government should provide day-care center | 79 | (300) | * | |
| End alimony under any condition | 10 | (297) | * | |
| *Women's Liberation* | | | | |
| Favorable | 39 | (300) | 41[2] | |
| Unfavorable | 27 | (300) | 44 | |

*Not asked in national poll.

[1]*President: local respondents were offered an "unsure" category, chosen by 18 percent, while national respondents were offered only a dichotomous choice. Abortion if rape: local survey added "or incest." Abortion if child unwanted: national survey question was "if she (woman wanting abortion) is married and doesn't want more children," while local survey was phrased "if child is unwanted."*

[2]*This data is from a Starch Poll reported in Parade, April 15, 1973. No sample size was given, only that it was from a "national cross section." In the national polls, the question was worded: "While I might not agree with all their tactics, in general I agree with the goals of the Women's Liberation Movement." In the local survey the question was worded: "In general, what is your attitude toward the Women's Liberation Movement?"*

items include the range of issues presented in Table 1. A primary axis factor analysis was performed and the six factors with communalities over 1.0 were subjected to an oblique rotation.[6] Table 2 presents the results of the rotation.

The first, and by far the strongest, factor is one that might be labeled an "anti-women's rights" factor. Those items loading high on it (and negatively) are the items that have some symbolic as well as substantive importance to

TABLE 2

Factor Analysis* of Attitudes Relating to Women's Rights

|  | I** | II | III | IV | V | VI |
|---|---|---|---|---|---|---|
| 1. Abortion if child is unwanted | −69 | 26 | 48 | −18 | 12 | 26 |
| 2. Abortion anytime in first three months | −75 | 21 | 32 | −09 | 20 | 18 |
| 3. Support for Women's Liberation Movement | −54 | 27 | 14 | −33 | 29 | 09 |
| 4. Would vote for: woman for President | −50 | 40 | −07 | −29 | 32 | 07 |
| 5. Would vote for: woman for Congress | −27 | 66 | 09 | −16 | 22 | 08 |
| 6. Would vote for: woman for Senator | −24 | 59 | 21 | −07 | 09 | 10 |
| 7. Would vote for: woman for state legslr. | −23 | 93 | 17 | −12 | 56 | 27 |
| 8. Abortion if rape or incest | −36 | 29 | 75 | −27 | 09 | 14 |
| 9. Abortion if possibility of birth defect | −39 | 30 | 81 | −24 | 13 | 15 |
| 10. Abortion if danger to health of mother | −25 | 19 | 71 | −18 | 15 | 01 |
| 11. Women can run businesses as well as men | −36 | 28 | 17 | −32 | 72 | 09 |
| 12. Women understand politics as well as men | −33 | 29 | 24 | −12 | 56 | 09 |
| 13. Would vote for: woman for sheriff | −43 | 24 | 05 | −20 | 43 | 17 |
| 14. Women get as good a break as men | 19 | −19 | −13 | 71 | −28 | −14 |
| 15. Women have as good a chance as men to be an executive | 11 | −02 | −16 | 50 | −04 | −04 |
| 16. Ever wanted to be member of opposite sex | −06 | −03 | 08 | −26 | 26 | 36 |
| 17. Approve of alimony | 17 | −14 | −01 | 02 | −07 | −61 |
| 18. Approve of women earning money in business | 22 | 27 | 21 | −16 | −04 | 06 |
| Eigenvalue in unrotated matrix | 4.2 | 1.8 | 1.6 | 1.3 | 1.1 | 1.1 |

*The matrix presented is the factor structure matrix of a principal axis factor analysis subjected to oblique rotation. Data used here and in the following tables are the local data.

**I, Women's rights; II, women's politics; III, abortion reform; IV, perception of unequal treatment of women; V, perception of women's equal abilities; and VI, women's independence.

women's rights advocates. They are some of the issues that have received a substantial degree of publicity and are identified with women's liberation: support for what is essentially abortion on demand, support for the women's liberation movement, and support for a woman President. The latter two items, however, do not load quite as highly as the two abortion items. Support for a woman as county sheriff, the office most women apparently view other women as being unfit for, loads moderately on this dimension. Table 1 indicates that these are issues on which opinion among women is rather evenly divided in both samples.

A second factor, labeled "Women in politics," is composed of issues relating to women as political candidates for legislative bodies. Women who score high on this dimension are ready to support women for public offices at the Congressional and state legislative level. The questions dealing with voting for President and, at the opposite extreme, for county sheriff do not load high here. These offices are apparently viewed in a somewhat different light than the legislative offices. Apparently women as members of legislative bodies are accepted by almost all women (Table 1). The other two offices are not yet seen by many as appropriate for women, perhaps because of their executive leadership nature.

The third factor clearly deals with abortion reform and is so labeled. Overall, as Table 1 shows, strong support is provided in both samples for abortion reform, but not to the point of supporting abortion if the parents simply don't want another child. Those who favor this much freedom are only 39 percent to 55 percent of the sample. Thus, it is not surprising that the questions essentially permitting "abortion on demand" do not load strongly on the abortion reform dimension, although the "abortion if child is unwanted" does load moderately (.48).

A fourth dimension consists of items measuring perceptions of how equally women are treated in American society: do women get as good a break as men, do women have as good a chance as men to be a business executive? Loading moderately in the reverse direction on this factor is the belief that women are as competent as men in business matters. Table 1 indicates that only a very small minority of women in fact do believe women have as good a chance to be an executive (13 percent), or in general get as good a break as men do in society (18 percent). Most women perceive inequality in treatment then, whether or not they feel that something should be done to remedy it.

A fifth dimension deals with perception of women's equal abilities. High scorers on this dimension believe that women understand politics as well as men (83 percent believe so) and could run businesses as well as men (62 percent believe so), and would vote for women as state legislators (92 percent). Belief that women are competent is negatively related to belief that women are treated equally: those who believe women have as good a chance as men to be executives also believe that women are not as competent, thus providing themselves with an explanation of why large numbers of women are not executives. The reverse is also true: those who believe women are as competent tend to believe they do not receive an equal chance.

A final dimension is somewhat unclear, and will not be dealt with in further analyses. The item loading most highly here is agreement with the practice of awarding alimony. A second item loading moderately is a positive response to the question "Have you ever wanted to be a member of the opposite sex?"

Table 3 presents a matrix of intercorrelations among the five factors. It, along with the factor analysis, indicates that the various issues associated with the women's movement are not perceived as a single cluster; furthermore, the groupings of dimensions that do not occur are not highly related among themselves. At best, the correlations are moderate, many are negligible. As predicted, support for abortion reform, for example, is not related by and large to support for women as political candidates. Perceptions of inequalities in the treatment of women is not necessarily related to perceptions of competence or to support for women's liberation. Support for women as political candidates is itself not a homogeneous area in that support for women as legislative candidates is unrelated to support for women as candidates for other offices. Approval of women's rights seems to load highly with abortion on demand and approval of a woman President, but it is only moderately related to the other abortion and legislative candidate issues and to perceptions of women as being competent or being treated equally.

Thus, while there is substantial consensus by women on some issues and perceptions (legislative candidates, equality of treatment, for example), other issue and perceptual areas are not yet seen by women as having a common link. Instead, they are viewed as separate kinds of issues: issues with little or no relationship to one another. In fact, support for the general issues of women's

TABLE 3

Relationship among Factors of Women's Issues

|                            | I          | II        | III       | I         |
|----------------------------|------------|-----------|-----------|-----------|
| 1. Women's rights          |            |           |           |           |
| 2. Legislative candidates  | .37* (28)  |           |           |           |
| 3. Abortion reform         | .30  (39)  | .19 (25)  |           |           |
| 4. Equality of treatment   | .24  (19)  | .16 (07)  | .18 (21)  |           |
| 5. Competence              | .29  (41)  | .20 (38)  | .05 (30)  | .25 (18)  |

*In this table, the signs for dimension I have been reversed so that a positive correlation with other dimensions indicates support for women's rights and support for legislative candidates, abortion reform, and belief that women are equal in competence to men and that women are not treated equally in society. Correlations in parentheses are those based on the computed scores—see below. All correlations are Pearson's r.*

rights is not even strongly correlated with the other dimensions, so that a generalized support for women's liberation does not necessarily carry over to support for specific issues.

A further confirmation of this last point can be seen by comparing those groups favoring, opposing, and undecided about the Women's Liberation Movement. If we look at their support for the range of issues and their agreement with certain attitudes favorable to Women's Liberation, we do find differences among the groups. Out of a total possible score of 17 agreements (Table 1), those who favor women's liberation score 14.1 (SD 2.7), those who are undecided score 12.1 (SD 2.9), and those who oppose the idea score only 10.3 (SD 3.7). Yet a range less than 4 points separating the opposing groups indicates a substantial amount of common ground between those women who have not found favor with the idea of women's liberation and those who have.

## DEMOGRAPHIC AND ATTITUDINAL CHARACTERISTICS OF SUPPORTERS OF WOMEN'S ISSUES

### Women's Rights

The women's rights issues (abortion on demand and support for a woman for President) display the greatest differences among women of any of the issue areas. Table 4 indicates that age is the strongest correlate of support for women's rights. This relationship between youth and support for women's rights is in accord with the popular image; young women have been more exposed to ideas that do not conform with the traditional view of what the woman's role is since their mean educational level is slightly higher.[7]

Education is also strongly related to support for women's rights, but these differences are not as striking as those age-related differences. Those with more education are more supportive of women's rights than those with less education. In addition to the greater exposure an education gives to views different from the traditional one of "woman's place is in the home," an education also

## TABLE 4
### Demographic and Attitudinal Correlates of Sources of Support for Women's Issues

| | WOMEN'S RIGHTS[1] | WOMEN'S LIBERATION MOVEMENT | WOMEN IN POLITICS | ABORTION REFORM | PERCEPTION OF INEQUALITY OF TREATMENT | PERCEPTION OF COMPETENCE OF WOMAN |
|---|---|---|---|---|---|---|
| Age | -.41*** | -.36*** | -.11 | -.26*** | -.19** | -.21** |
| Education | .22*** | .27*** | .15 | .15 | .20** | .28*** |
| Housewife | -.19** | -.15 | -.14 | -.21** | -.10 | -.21 |
| Occupational Status | .14 | .20* | .10 | .13 | .08 | -.17 |
| Religious Practice | .31*** | .18** | .13 | .35*** | .05 | .19** |
| Ever Married | -.16* | -.20*** | -.08 | -.04 | .02 | -.09 |
| Political Party Identification | .13* | .19*** | .01 | .06 | .08 | .14* |
| Liberalism | .37*** | .42*** | .20** | .19* | .21** | .38** |
| Attitude toward Women's Liberation | .38*** | — | .19** | .21*** | .24*** | .36*** |

[1] Signs have been adjusted so that a positive correlation indicates high support with high age, education, occupational status, and so forth. Other codes:

Housewife: (1) yes; (0) no.

Occupation: (1) Blue collar; (2) Clerical and sales; (3) Professional and white collar.

Religious Practice: (1) Catholic—attends church weekly; (2) Catholic—attends church less than once per week; (3) Protestant—attends church weekly; (4) Protestant—attends church less than once per week.

Ever married: (1) yes; (0) no.

Party Identification: Seven point scale ranging from (1) strong Republican through (7) strong Democrat. Independents coded at (4).

Liberalism: Five point scale (1) most conservative through (5) most liberal.

*Significant at .05; **at .01; ***at .001. All correlations are Pearson's r.

lends itself to more accurate perceptions of treatment accorded and opportunities available to women.

One's religious practice is moderately related to support for women's rights. Those who attend church regularly, whether Protestant or Catholic, are less likely to be supportive of women's rights than those who do not attend church regularly. The differences between regular and non-regular church attenders is constant at each age level. A reason for this relationship is not clear; it may be that regularity of church attendance is another aspect of a traditional frame of mind, that many denominations stress the traditional role of woman as wife and mother, or that in most denominations the church structure is controlled by males.

Those women who have never been married are slightly more supportive of women's rights than those who have been or are currently married. Whether a woman is currently married, however, makes no difference in her attitude toward women's rights. This seems to imply that the attitudinal differences are not caused by the status of being married, but perhaps again are caused by the age or educational differential between the never and ever married groups. We do find that the never married are a younger group (80 percent are less than 25 years old, compared with only 20 percent of the ever married groups who are less than 25 years old). Among the under-25 age group, support for women's rights is stronger in the never married group, but at the other age levels the differences are inconsistent and small. What the differences between the ever married and never married then reflect is largely the differences between young married women and young unmarried working women or students, the latter being more supportive of the movement.

Being a housewife seems to affect attitudes toward the women's movement more than simply being married; the housewife is less supportive of women's rights than the non-housewife. If we examine the relationship controlling for age and for education (on the possibility that more older women are housewives than younger women, or that more poorly educated women are housewives than ones with higher education), we find that the differences between the housewife and non-housewife group increase as age increases and as education decreases. That is, status as a housewife makes less difference among young women and highly educated women than it does among older and less well-educated women. Presumably, young and well-educated women, whether housewives or not, have been exposed more to media publicity about women's issues and status in society or, particularly in the case of young women, may have peers supportive of the women's movement. Overall, however, the condition of being a housewife would seem to play a large role in shaping women's attitudes toward the movement.[8] Aside from the differences between housewifes and non-housewives occupational differences seem to affect these attitudes very little.

Among attitudinal characteristics, we find that self-categorization as a "liberal" corresponds strongly to support for women's rights. Those who see themselves as "very liberal" are strongly supportive of women's rights, with the most conservative group being quite opposed. Not surprisingly, support for women's liberation also is moderately associated with support for women's rights. The party identification of the respondent was weakly linked with support for women's rights; weak and independent Democrats and independent Republicans were more supportive than strong Democrats or weak or strong Republicans.

## Women's Liberation

Support for women's liberation displays a pattern similar to support for women's rights. Support for women's liberation is found among the young more than the old, the educated more than the less educated, the liberal more than the conservative, the never married more than the married (though again this is a function of age). Housewives are slightly more opposed to women's liberation than working women. Here we see other occupational differences. Professional and white collar women are more supportive of women's liberation than any of the other classifications: clerical and sales personnel, blue collar workers, or other types of workers. Religious practice, however, makes less difference in support for women's liberation than it did for support for women's rights. The differences among the four groups are irregular and not large. Party identification shows some association in that strong and weak Republicans tend to be less supportive of women's liberation than any of the other groups.

## Women in Politics

Support for women in politics is little related to any of the demographic variables under consideration. The only statistically significant differences are between those who are housewives and those who are not, with the latter being slightly more supportive. Support for women as legislators is very mildly related to being liberal and supporting women's liberation, but these relationships are not large. The lack of significant differences among groups of women can be explained by the near unanimity of the sample on these questions (Table 1).

## Abortion Reform

As expected, we find that abortion reform support is moderately linked to religious practice in that Catholics who attend church regularly are the least supportive of abortion reform. Catholics who do not attend church regularly are more supportive of abortion reform than Protestants who are regular attenders, but less favorable to reform than Protestants who are infrequent church attenders. Support for abortion reform is almost equally strongly related to age, with those in the youngest age groups being more supportive. Being a housewife is slightly related to a lower level of support for abortion reform. Abortion reform displays a relatively slight link to liberal sentiment and to support for women's liberation.

## Perception of Unequal Treatment of Women

Perception of unequal treatment of women is not strongly linked to any demographic characteristic.[9] While younger women, more highly educated women, never married women, and non-housewives are likely to perceive more inequality in the treatment women are given, these differences are not at all large. On the whole, whatever their social, economic, or other demographic characteristics are, most women do perceive that women in society are treated unequally. The highest linkage on this variable is found with support for women's liberation, although the association is not strong. The causal relationship here is not clear; probably the perception of unequal treatment generates support for the women's liberation movement, although supporting the movement may, in its turn, lead to increased awareness of discrimination against women. Perception of inequality is also slightly related to liberalism; those who are very liberal are most apt to see discrimination and unequal treatment.

## PERCEPTION OF THE COMPETENCE OF WOMEN

Perception that women are equally as competent as men in politics and business is moderately related to education; the most educated are most likely to believe that women are equally competent. It is slightly less related to age, where the youngest women speak in terms of women's equal competence. Non-housewives are also more likely to agree that women are equal in competence, as are those who are infrequent church attenders, regardless of denomination. The perception of the equal ability of women is strongly related to liberalism; self-designated liberals are much more likely to agree that women are equally competent than are conservatives. Almost as strongly related is attitude toward women's liberation; those who support women's liberation believe that women have equal competence.

## SUMMARY

We find, in summary, that our hypotheses are in large part borne out.

1. There are distinct dimensions of women's issues. While some common support (and opposition) persists over all the dimensions, generally the women in our sample did not see the set of women's issues as a coherent whole. Support for or agreement with each of the issue areas was only slightly correlated with support for the others (Table 3).

2. Following from this, while there were some common sources of support for each of the dimensions among the women, by and large different attributes were relevant to different issues. Young people and those who considered themselves liberals were supportive on all dimensions (although sometimes the associations were not large). However, on the women in politics and the perception of unequal treatment dimensions, there were few differences among the women. The abortion dimension found religious and age distinctions important, but only slight differences among those with varying levels of education, occupational status, or housewife condition. The women's rights, women's liberation, and perceptions of women as equally competent were most closely tied with differences in the demographic and attitudinal characteristics of liberalism, education, and age. Surprisingly, while housewives were consistently less supportive of the various dimensions than those who were not housewives, these differences were not large; no correlation involving the housewife status was over .21. Whether one had ever been married or not was even less related to support for the various women's issues, thus casting some

doubt on the claim that supporters of women's liberation were largely to be found among those women who "could not find a man." The differences between the never and ever married are, in part, explainable by the different age levels of the two groups, since the never married are a younger group. Differences among blue collar and white collar women are not large except in the case of support for the women's liberation movement, where professional and white collar women were more supportive. The party affiliation of the women did not appear to be associated with attitudes toward these issues except on the women's liberation issue where strong and weak Republicans were less supportive.

3. As Table 1 shows, support for women's liberation is less than support for any particular issue, even the sticky abortion issue. Yet, those who oppose women's liberation have a mean agreement with over 10 of the 17 specific issues or statements representing a variety of women's issues.[10] Those who are against "women's liberation" are not necessarily opposed to any given issue that the movement has raised; in fact, they probably are supportive of most of them. It would appear that many women have been frightened by the notion of "women's liberation" and will profess not to believe in it, yet are supportive of what the movement stands for, in a large part. On the other hand, those who support women's liberation seem generally supportive of most of the other issues (mean score 14.1).

In sum, while some types of women are supportive of the variety of women's issues and agree with basic assumptions of the movement, others are more selective in their support. On a few issues there is near unanimity among the women while on others there are substantial cleavages. These empirical findings lend support to the notion of women's movement as a hetereogeneous one offering a "cafeteria" of appeals.

Finally, support for the women's movement cannot be evaluated solely by measuring support for the liberation movement *per se.* Rather, support is more accurately evaluated by an examination of the issues of concern to the movement. The differences in support among various groups for various issues reflect in some part the differences in needs and goals of the women themselves. It does appear that there is a large potential women's constituency for politicians or others willing to move on some of the issues discussed here. Support for these issues is much more widespread than support for the symbol of "women's liberation."

## NOTES

1 See also Firestone's (1971:32–37) categorization of women's groups as conservative feminists, politics, and radical feminists.

2 The respondents were chosen in a random sample of names from a phone book. When listings that were not private households fell into the sample, the next listing was chosen. The interviews were done in April, 1972.

3 The NORC Center, University of Chicago, provided the national data through its National Data Program for the Social Sciences. The Center, of course, assumes no responsibility for the analysis and interpretations here.

4 For example, the local survey asked whether or not the respondent approved of abortions "if the child is unwanted," while the national survey asked "if the

parents don't want more children." The latter wording perhaps casts the parents in a selfish light while the former wording would seem to induce pity for a child born unwanted, and thus perhaps raise support for abortion in that instance. The largest difference in the two samples was found in the question of approval for wives working if they have husbands capable of supporting them; nevertheless, both groups strongly approve.

5    Correlates of Attitudes: A Comparison of Local and National Responses[*]

| | WOMEN'S OPPORTUNITIES | | ABORTION REFORM | |
|---|---|---|---|---|
| | NATIONAL | LOCAL | NATIONAL | LOCAL |
| Age | −.29 | −.31 | −.16 | −.34 |
| Religion[*] | .00 | .02 | −.08 | −.24 |
| Religious Service Attendance | .05 | .11 | .23 | .29 |
| Education | .24 | .21 | .25 | .17 |
| Race | .10 | −.01 | −.10 | −.05 |
| Marital Status | −.18 | −.13 | −.07 | −.05 |
| Party Identification | −.03 | −.03 | .09 | .10 |
| Ideal Number of Children Wanted | −.05 | −.10 | −.29 | −.28 |

*Coded: 1, Catholic; 0, Not Catholic.*

In the national sample, correlations of .13 are significant at the .001 level; in the local sample, correlations of .15 and above are significant at that level.

In order to simplify comparison between the two samples, the six items common to both surveys were grouped into two indices—one containing two items, the other containing the four abortion reform items common to the two surveys.

6    Unlike orthogonal rotation, oblique rotation does not require the usually invalid assumption that the dimensions are unrelated.

7    In this and the analysis reported below, cross-tabular controls were introduced to investigate relationships more thoroughly. They are not presented here for reasons of space but more detail will gladly be supplied on request.

8    Unfortunately, no data on how long women have been housewives is available; thus we do not know if the women have ever worked, have recently become housewives, have future work plans, and the like. Such data would be very useful in further examining the impact of the role of being a housewife on attitudes toward women's issues.

9    For a recent report on a variety of legal and business discrimination see Shannahan. Bird (1968) provides an extended review of the treatment of women in the business world. See also Epstein (1971); and the June, 1973, issue of *MS.* for a report of the status of women in the business and financial world.

10    It should be emphasized here that the issues under investigation in this paper are rather moderate ones; we would not expect high agreement among anti-women's liberation individuals if we asked about more radical proposals such as abolition of the nuclear family. However, the kinds of issues discussed here are those that the mainstream of the movement has focused upon: discrimination, both economic and political; socialization to feelings of inferiority and incompetence; lack of freedom to control one's own body; and so forth.

## REFERENCES

*Bird, Caroline*
1968    Born Female: The High Cost of Keeping Women Down. New York: David McKay.
*Dixon, Marlene*
1969    "The rise of women's liberation." Pp. 186–200 in Masculine/Feminine. Betty Roszak and Theodore Roszak (eds.). New York: Harper and Row.
*Epstein, C. F.*
1971    Women's Place. Berkeley: University of California Press.
*Freeman, J.*
1973    "The origins of the women's liberation movement." American Journal of Sociology 78 (January): 792–811.
*Friedan, Betty*
1963    The Feminine Mystique. New York: Dell.
*Firestone, Shulamith*
1971    The Dialectic of Sex. New York: Bantam.
*Hole, Judith, and E. Levine*
1971    The Rebirth of Feminism. New York: Quadrangle.
*Huber, Joan (ed.)*
1973    Changing Women in a Changing Society. Chicago: University of Chicago Press.
*Shannahan, E.*
1973    "All the pigs are more equal." New York Times, Section 4, July 29, p. 5.
*Toch, Hans*
1965    The Social Psychology of Social Movements. Indianapolis: Bobbs-Merrill.
*Turner, Ralph, and Lewis Killian*
1957    Collective Behavior. Englewood Cliffs, New Jersey: Prentice-Hall.

# Name Index

# Subject Index